John Townshend

A treatise on the wrongs called slander and libel

And on the remedy by civil action for those wrongs

John Townshend

A treatise on the wrongs called slander and libel
And on the remedy by civil action for those wrongs

ISBN/EAN: 9783742866929

Manufactured in Europe, USA, Canada, Australia, Japa

Cover: Foto ©Thomas Meinert / pixelio.de

Manufactured and distributed by brebook publishing software (www.brebook.com)

John Townshend

A treatise on the wrongs called slander and libel

A TREATISE

ON THE WRONGS CALLED

SLANDER AND LIBEL,

AND ON

THE REMEDY BY CIVIL ACTION FOR THOSE WRONGS.

By JOHN TOWNSHEND.

NEW YORK:

BAKER, VOORHIS & CO., PUBLISHERS,

66 NASSAU STREET.

LONDON: STEVENS & HAYNES.

1868.

BAKER & GODWIN, PRINTERS,
PRINTING-HOUSE SQUARE, N. Y.

PREFACE.

Over thirty years' practice in my profession, with no inconsiderable experience in libel suits, taught me the difficulties in the law regarding defamation; difficulties, which will be readily understood by all those who have endeavored to master the subject. I undertook to prepare the following essay, supposing that by rendering, in some measure, my experience available to the student and the practitioner, I could mitigate—to remove would be impossible— the obstacles to an understanding of the Law of Libel. I may have fallen far short of accomplishing the end I contemplated, but I cannot believe that my labor has been wholly in vain.

In prosecuting my work I have availed myself freely, but not unfairly, of the labors of my precursors in the same field of thought, and I acknowledge my indebtedness for much assistance thus derived. To ELBRIDGE T. GERRY, Esq., of

the New York Bar, my thanks are especially due
for his politely giving me the benefit of his extensive
library; nor should I omit to record my obligations to my wife for much valuable and intelligent
aid in the prosecution of my work.

Conscious of its many imperfections, and be-
speaking for it an indulgent reception, I nevertheless experience much satisfaction in publishing the
following essay. I know that in so doing I ter-
minate what has been no trifling task, and I hope
and believe I thereby discharge

My debt to my profession.

JOHN TOWNSHEND.

New York, August, 1868.

CONTENTS.

CHAPTER I.

INTRODUCTORY.

CHAPTER II.

HOW ONE MAY AFFECT ANOTHER BY LANGUAGE.

CHAPTER III.

RIGHTS ; DUTIES ; WRONGS; REMEDIES.

CHAPTER IV.

WHAT IS THE GIST OF THE ACTION FOR SLANDER OR LIBEL.

CHAPTER V.

WRONGFUL ACTS.   ELEMENTS OF A WRONG.

CHAPTER VI.

PUBLICATION.   PUBLISHER.

CHAPTER VII.

CONSTRUCTION OF LANGUAGE.

CHAPTER VIII.

WHAT LANGUAGE IS ACTIONABLE.

CHAPTER IX.

DEFENCES.

CHAPTER X.

CORPORATIONS.

CHAPTER XI.

PROCEEDINGS IN AN ACTION.

CHAPTER XII.

PARTIES.

CHAPTER XIII.

PLEADING. THE COMPLAINT.

CHAPTER XIV.

PLEADING. ANSWER. DEMURRER.

CHAPTER XV.

VARIANCE. AMENDMENT.

CHAPTER XVI.

EVIDENCE FOR PLAINTIFF.

CHAPTER XVII.

EVIDENCE FOR DEFENDANT.

TABLE OF CASES.

B

c

D

TABLE

TABLE

WORKS OF REFERENCE.

— •◆• —

[For the convenience of those who may desire further information on the subject of Slander and Libel, we subjoin the following list of publications, to which
reference may be made.]

TREATISE ON LIBEL. By Sir Thomas Mallett, Judge of the Queen's Bench,
England. (Referred to by Finnerty when brought up for Judgment.)

AN ESSAY ON THE LIBERTY OF THE PRESS, chiefly as it respects personal
slander. By Bishop Hayter.

"ANOTHER LETTER TO MR. ALMON ON MATTERS OF LIBEL."—"The position that it is not material whether the libel be true or false, or whether
the person that made it be of good or ill fame, is a proposition of truth
and the provision of a sanctuary for weak and wicked men, who may
be employed as ministers or judges."

THE PEOPLE. Dedicated to Sir Francis Burdett, Bart. By an unlettered
man. Printed for the Author, and sold by M. Jones, 5 Newgate Street,
London. 1811.
[This work professes to contain an analysis of Pitt's system, and to
show the great danger of the theory, and with regard to libels.
To trace that theory to its origin, and that it is directly contrary
to the reformed religion and the New Testament.]

LAW OF LIBEL (ON THE), with strictures on the self-styled Constitutional
Society. By John Hunt. 8vo. London, 1823.

ERSKINE'S SPEECH in the case of the King v. Williams, for publishing
Paine's Age of Reason; with Mr. Kyd's reply and Lord Kenyon's
charge to the Jury.—*Trials, col. xviii., N. Y. State Library.*

THE ENGLISHMAN'S RIGHT; or, a Dialogue between a Barrister at Law and
a Juryman, concerning the antiquity, use, power, and duty of Jurors,
by the Law of England. Extract in appendix to trial of John Lambert for libel.—*Trials, vol. xv., N. Y. State Library.*

JURYMAN TOUCHSTONE (THE); or, A full refutation of Lord Mansfield's
opinion in Crown Libels. 8vo. London, 1784.

A LETTER ON LIBELS AND WARRANTS. (Referred to, 1 Biographical Anec-
dotes, by Almon, p. 226.)

MASSEY'S HISTORY OF ENGLAND. Vol. 2. As to Dowdeswell's Bill to make juries judges of the Law in libel cases.

SPEECH OF SIR ROBERT PEEL, in vindication of the House of Commons claim to publish its proceedings. London, 1837.

A LETTER TO LORD LANGDALE on the recent proceedings of the House of Commons on the subject of privilege. By Thomas Pemberton, M. P. 2d edit. London, 1837.

OBSERVATIONS ON THE RIGHTS AND DUTIES OF JURIES in trials for Libels, with remarks on the origin and nature of the Law of Libels. By J. Towers. 8vo. Dublin, 1785.

FREE SPEECH. An oration by Daniel Webster, A. D. 1814.

LECTURE ON THE LAW OF LIBEL. By James T. Brady, Esq.

AN APOLOGY FOR THE FREEDOM OF THE PRESS. By the Rev. Mr. Robert Hall. London, 1821.

BOLLAN ON THE RIGHT OF EVERY MAN TO THINK AND SPEAK FREELY. (Referred to Quincy's Massachusetts Reports, p. 270.)

OF SLANDER AND FLATTERY. A sermon by Jeremy Taylor.

ERSKINE'S SPEECHES on subjects connected with the Liberty of the Press.

"DISCUSSION OF THE LAW OF LIBEL as at present received, in which its authenticity is examined; with incidental observations on the Legal effect of Precedent and Authority." Pamphlet. London, 1785. Ascribed to J. W. Adair.

SKENE ON CRIMES. 25th chapter of title 2—Of famous Libels and Seditious Speeches.

TRACT ON LIBEL. By Lord Bacon. Mentioned in the memoirs of T. Hollis, p. 169.
   [It is referred to in a note to T. Holt White's edition of Milton's Areopagitica, and the annotater adds: "My inquiries after this pos-posthumous publication have been fruitless." Query. If the same tract as one entitled "Certain observations upon a Libel. By Lord Bacon, A. D. 1592," to be found in several editions of Bacon's works.]

LORD SIDMOUTH'S CIRCULAR respecting libels.

EARL GRAY'S SPEECH on the above circular. House of Lords, 1817.

TINDAL'S CONTINUATION of Rapin's History of England as to Pulteney's Bill to prohibit the circulation of unlicensed newspapers.

DOMESTIC ANNALS OF SCOTLAND. By Chambers. Vol. 1, p. 126.

DODSLEY'S ANNUAL REGISTER. A. D. 1792.
E

MR STAMMER's PAMPHLET on the case of Rex v. D'Israeli.
> [I have been unable to find a copy. It is referred to 1 Townsend's Modern State Trials, 260.]

BACON's ABRIDGEMENT, tit. Slander, Courts Ecclesiastical.

SHEPPARD's ABRIDGEMENT, tit. Libel.

BLUE LAWS OF CONNECTICUT.

OTTO THESAURUS. Vols. 8, 4.

COOTE's ECCLESIASTICAL COURTS, tit. Defamation.
BURN's ECCLESIASTICAL LAW, tit. Defamation.

QUINCY's MASSACHUSETTS REPORTS, A. D. 1761 to A. D. 1777. See pages 260, 267, 270, 278, 309—Charge as to law of libel.
Page 245—As to right of the court to commit for libel.
Page 561—Discussion on the right of juries to judge of law and fact.

ESSAI HISTORIQUE SUR LA LIBERTÉ d'ecrere chez les ancienes et au moyen age, sur la liberté de la press, &c , &c. Par G. Peignot.

ENCYCLOPEDIA BRITTANICA, supplement; art. Liberty of the Press.

JACOB's LAW DICTIONARY, titles Justification, Court of Piepowders, Copia Libelli Deliberanda, Scandall.

VINER's ABRIDGEMENT, tit. Good Behaviour.

McDOUGALL's CASE, 3 Documentary History of New York, 534; cited 10 Abbott's Practice Reports, 170; and see id. p. 169.

FREEDOM OF WIT AND HUMOR. By Lord Shaftesbury. A. D. 1709.

CONSIDERATIONS ON THE LAW OF LIBEL as relating to publications on the subject of religion. By John Search. Ridgway, 1833.
> [This pamphlet is referred to 11 London Law Magazine, 444. John Search is a fictitious name.]

THE CRAFTSMAN, No. 281, vol. viii., p. 213.
> [Contains the reasons why the Commons would not agree to the clause which revived the old printing act, delivered at a conference with the Lords, 1695.]

A DIGEST OF THE LAW CONCERNING LIBELS containing all the resolutions in the books on the subject, and many MS. cases, &c., by a gentleman of the Inner Temple. 4to. London, 1765.

REASONS AGAINST THE INTENDED BILL for laying restraint on the Liberty of the Press. London, 1792.

ESSAY ON THE LIBERTY OF THE PRESS. Richmond, 1803.

LONDON QUARTERLY REVIEW. April, 1865. Libel and freedom of the Press.

EDINBURG REVIEW. Review of George on Libel. Abuses of the Press, vol. 22. Review of Holt on Libel, 2d edition, vol. 27. French Law of Libel, vol. 82. Libels on Christianity, vol. 58.

WESTMINISTER REVIEW.   Review of Mence on Libel, vol. 3.

LONDON LAW MAGAZINE.   Application of Libel, vol. 2.   The Law of Libel,
vol. 11.   Communicating slanderous words in answer to inquiries, vol.
84.   Presumptions of Law and presumptive evidence, vol. 6   The province of the Judge distinguished from the province of the jury, vol. 12.

SOLICITORS' JOURNAL.   The Law of Libel, vol. 8.   Libels on Professional
Men, vol. 9.   Law of Libel, vol. 10.

CITY HALL REPORTER.   Slander, p. 160.

CORNHILL MAGAZINE, January, 1867.

ECLECTIC REVIEW, March, 1867.

KNICKERBOCKER MAGAZINE.   Scandal and Envy, vol. 38.

CHRISTIAN EXAMINER, vols. 16, 17.
    "   DISCIPLINE, vol. 3.

WESTERN LAW JOURNAL, vol. 2.   N. 8.

AMERICAN ENCYCLOPEDIA, art. Libel.

AMERICAN LAW JOURNAL.   (Hall, Baltimore), vol. 1.   Commonwealth v.
Duane, Commonwealth r. Cobbett, State of Maryland r. Irvine, Carr v.
Hood, Van Vechten v. Hopkins. Vol. 3.   The People v. Frothingham,
Libel on General Hamilton.   Vol. 4.   Rex v. Creavy.

AMERICAN QUARTERLY REVIEW, vol. 5, (A. D. 1829), contains a Review of
Holt's Law of Libel.

AMERICAN LANCET.   Report of Libel Trial in New York, A. D. 1831.

TRIAL OF JOHN STOCKDALE for a libel on the House of Commons, in the
Court of King's Bench in 1789—with an argument in support of the
Rights of Juries—London, 1790.

THE TRIAL OF THEOPHILUS SWIFT for a Libel on the Fellows of the Dublin University, and the Trial of the Rev. DR BURROWS for a libel on
Theophilus Swift, published together with notes by Theophilus Swift.

REPORT OF THE MAHARAJ Libel case, Bombay, 1862, as to which see
Westminister Review, January, 1864.

PAMPHLET TRIALS, of Joseph T. Buckingham for Libel on John N. Maffit;
of David Lee Childs for Libel on John Keys; of Daniel Isaac Eaton for
Libel entitled "Politics for the People, or Hogs-wash;" of Dr. Newman; of Aston Williams; of Francis S. Beattie; of William Hone.

AMONG THE PAPYRI unearthed from the ruins of Herculaneum is an
essay on Freedom of Speech, by Philodemus.   It forms part of a
work entitled "PHILODEMI Περὶ 'Ρητορικῆς, ex Herculanensi Papyro
restitutuit, Latinè vertit, et Dissertationibus auxit. [E. GROS, Parisiis:
1840.   Publisher.]

SLANDER AND LIBEL.

CHAPTER I.

INTRODUCTORY.

Language as a means of effecting injury. Slander—Libel—Defamation. Redress. The Law of Libel. Object in view. Division of subject. Attempts to define Libel.

§ 1. Among the means which one individual may employ to affect another or to affect society in general are sounds and signs.[1] Language, in so far as it is the medium for communicating or exciting ideas, consists of a system of sounds and signs, and is the chief among the sounds and signs which affect individuals or society in general.[2] Language expressed in sound is oral language or speech. Language expressed in signs is writ-

---

[1] As ringing bells, firing guns, beating drums, clapping hands, hooting, &c., see *Martin* v. *Nutkin,* 2 P. Wms. 266; *Soltan* v. *De Held,* 2 Sim. N. S. 133; 21 Law Journ. Rep. N. S. Ch. 153; 16 Jur. 326; 9 Eng. Law and Eq. Rep. 104; *Moshier* v. *Utica & Sch. R. R. Co.,* 8 Barb. 427; *Cole* v. *Fisher,* 11 Mass. 137; *Loubz* v. *Hafner,* 1 Dev. 185; *Gregory* v. *Brunswick,* 6 M. and G. 953; *Trustees, &c.,* v. *Utica, &c.,* 6 Barb. 313; *Davidson* v. *Isham,* 1 Stock. 186; *Fish* v. *Dodge,* 4 Denio, 311.

[2] There is nothing in nature but may be an instrument of mischief (L'd Chief J. Pratt in *Chapman* v. *Pickersgill,* 2 Wils. 145).

"A very great part of the mischiefs which vex the world arise from words." (*Burke in a letter to his Son.*)

Words are contained under the general expression of a human act, as also signs which have the same effect with words. (*Wood's Civil Law,* 28.)

2

ten language, or writing and effigy. By writing[2] is intended to be understood every means of symbolizing language by alphabetic characters, with every kind of implement, as pen, pencil, graver, type; with every kind of pigment, as ink, lead, chalk; on

Language is not the only mode by which reputation may be injured. "Scandal signifies a report or rumor or an *action* whereby one is affronted in public." (*Jacobs' Law Dict.*) Thus, in *Brewer* v. *Day*, 11 M. and W. 625, one cause of special damage was that defendants, by causing plaintiff's goods to be seized on an unfounded claim for debt, occasioned his customers to think him insolvent; and in trespass for breaking and entering plaintiff's dwelling, upon false charge of having stolen property concealed therein, *per quod* she was injured in her credit, it was held that the jury might give damages as aggravated by the false charge (2 *Maule and Selw.* 77). As to injury to reputation by act see *Beaumont* v. *Reeve*, 8 Adol. and Ell. 483; and 1 Siderfin, 375, where one Cooper brought an action upon the case against Witham and his wife, for that the wife maliciously intending to marry him, did often affirm that she was sole and unmarried, and importuned *et strenue inquisivit* the plaintiff to marry her; to which affirmation he gave credit, and married her, when *in acto* she was wife of the defendant; so that the plaintiff was much troubled in mind, and put to great charges, and damnified in his reputation. He had a verdict, but no judgment; for by Twisden, J., the action lies not, because the thing here done is felony; no more than if a servant be killed, the master cannot have an action *per quod servitium amisit, quod curia concessit ;* see also Vidian's Entries, where is a form of declaration for saying: Regard brothers went to a house which was a brothel and ought to be torn down, special damage that the house was torn down.

Language, however licentious and abusive, is not a trespass (*Adams* v. *Rivers*, 11 Barb. 397), but may constitute an imprisonment (*Homer* v. *Battyn*, Buller's N. P. 62; *Pike* v. *Hanson*, 9 N. H. Rep. 491); and cruelty (*Durant* v. *Durant*, 1 Hagg. Ecc. R. 769; *Lockwood* v. *Lockwood*, 2 Curteis Ecc. R. 281, cited and approved *Bihin* v. *Bihin*, 17 Abbott's Rep. 26). A recognizance to keep the peace is not forfeited by reproachful words (4 Bl. Com. ch. xviii). As to speech being the foundation of a criminal prosecution, see 2 Bishop on Crim. Law, § 813.

If a man menaces my tenants at will of life and member, *per quod* they depart from their tenures, an action upon the case will lie against him, but the threatening without their departure is no cause of action. 9 H. 7, 8, Vin. Ab. Actions Case, N. c. 21.

Action lies for threatening workmen to maim and prosecute them, whereby the master lost the selling of his goods, the men not daring to go on with their work (*Garret* v. *Taylor*, Cro. J. 567 pl. 4, A. D. 1621; see, however, *Ashley* v. *Harrison*, 1 Esp. 48 and *post*).

[2] Writing includes printing (*Saunderson* v. *Jackson*, 2 Bos. and Pul. 288; *Henshaw* v. *Foster*, Pick. 318) and marks with a lead pencil (*Geary* v. *Physic*, 5 B. and C. 238; *Classon* v. *Bailey*, 14 Johns. 484). See Bouvier's Law Dict. tit. Effigy.

any kind of substance, as paper, parchment, linen, wood, copper, steel, stone. And by effigy being intended to be understood every other means of communicating or exciting ideas other than by speech or by writing. Effigy, therefore, includes pictures, statues, gestures.

§ 2. The effect of language may be beneficial or injurious. If injurious, the injury *may* amount to a wrong, entitling the party wronged to redress by law. The designations of the wrong and of its remedy and of the wrong doer differ according to the means employed to effect the wrong.

§ 3. One may be so injuriously affected by speech as to be what is termed slandered; and, in that event, the speech so affecting him is called slander[4] or a slander, and the speaker is denominated a slanderer.

---

[4] Slander is defaming a man in his reputation by speaking or writing words which affect his life, office or trade; or which tend to his loss of preferment in marriage or service, or to his disinheritance, or which occasion any particular damage. (*Introduction to the Law relative to trials at Nisi Prius. By a Learned Judge* [*Lord Bathurst*]. Vol 1. p. 3.)

Slander is the imputation: 1. Of some *temporal* offence for which the party might be indicted and punished in the temporal courts. 2. Of an existing contagious disorder, tending to exclude the party from society. 3. An unfitness to perform an office or employment of profit, or want of integrity in an office of honor. 4. Words prejudicing a person in his lucrative—possession [qy. profession], or trade. 5. Any untrue words occasioning actual damage. (1 *Hilliard on torts*, ch. vii. § 3.)

Slander is defined to be " the publishing of words in *writing, or by speaking*, by reason of which the person to whom they relate becomes liable to suffer some corporeal punishment, or to sustain some damage." (*Bac. Abr.*)

" Slander being an unwritten or unprinted libel, and libel a written or printed slander." (1 *Hilliard on torts*, ch. vii. § 2.)

The word slander, as used in former times, seems to have had a meaning different to that in which it is now used. Thus : " But because some are wrongfully slandered (*accused*), King Henry I. ordained that none should be arrested or imprisoned for a slander (*accusation*) of mortal offence, before he was thereof indicted by the oaths of honest men before those who had authority to take such indictments." (*Mirrour of Justices*, ch. 11, § 22.) " In this same year the mysseles (lepers) thorow-oute Cristendom were *slaundered* that they had made covenaunt with Saraaenes for to poison all Christen men." (*Capgrave, Chronicle of England*, p. 186.)

§ 4. One may be so injuriously affected by writing or effigy as to be what is termed libeled ; and, in that event, the writing or effigy so affecting him is called libel or a libel, and he who puts forth such writing or effigy (the publisher or venter) is denominated a libeler.[5]

In a document addressed by the Dean and Chapter of Aberdeen to Bishop Gordon, dated January 5, 1558, is the following:

"*Imprimis*, that my Lord Bishop cause the kirkmen within his diocie to reform themselves in all their *slanderous* manner of living, and to remove their open concubines, as well great as small. *Secundo*, that his Lordship will be so good as to show edificative example—in special in removing and discharging himself of the company of the gentlewoman by whom he is greatly *slandered ;* without the which be done, diverse that are partners say they cannot accept counsel and correction of him which will not correct himself," &c., &c.—*Reg. Aberd.*, lxi.

If any *slanderously* charge another with any false crime (*Ridley's Civil Law*, 31); and in the *Statute*, 3 Edw. 1 ch. 34, none are to publish false news whereby *slander* may grow between the king and his people.

Mis-say, to slander, to speak ill. (*Spencer.*)

"I would not, * *
Have you so *slander* any moment's leisure
As to give words or talk with the Lord Hamlet." (*Shakespeare.*)

[5] "Libeller—he who shall, to the infamy of another, write, compose, or publish a book, song, or fable, or maliciously procure any of those acts to be done, is guilty of a *libel.*" (*Just. Inst.*)

"The distinction between the satirist and the libeller is, that the one speaks of the species, the other of the individual ; the one holds the glass to thousands in their closets, that they may contemplate the deformity, and thereby endeavor to reduce it, and thus by private mortification avoid public shame. Thus the satirist privately corrects the fault, like a parent, while the libeller mangles the individual like an executioner." (*Joseph Andrews*, vol. 2, p. 5.)

"And indeed there is not in the world a greater error than that which fools are apt to fall into, and knaves with good reason to encourage the mistaking a satirist for a libeller." (*Pope, Anon. Satires and Epistles—Advertisement.*)

"The early English satirists were mighty in their vocation against the lawyers, the regular and secular clergy, and the more eminent professors. The political ballad-mongers aimed higher. They stoutly supported Simon de Montfort against Henry the Third. This support was probably the occasion for the statute of 1275, 'against slanderous reports or tales to cause discord betwixt king and people.'" (See *The Barons' War, &c.*, by W. II. Blaauw, M. A.; *The Miracles of Simon de Montfort*, Camden, Soc. Pub.)

A Barrator is a mover of suits and quarrels in courts * * * * * by spreading false rumors and reports to raise discord among neighbors. (1 Coke Ins. 368.) Lampooner (see 3 Lev. 248.)

§ 5. So, too, at least in England, one may be so injuriously affected by language, whether in the form of speech, writing, or effigy, as to be what is termed defamed ;[5] in which event the language so affecting him is called defamation, and he from whom the language proceeds is denominated a defamer.

§ 6. Again, by means of language may be effected a wrong termed " a malicious prosecution," as also the wrong termed " slander of title." Neither to the authors of these wrongs nor to the parties affected has any descriptive appellation been assigned.

§ 7. Besides slander, libel, defamation, malicious prosecution and slander of title, language is the means by which may be effected, at least in England, the offences called treason,[7] heresy, sedition, blasphemy, profanity, scandalum magnatum, calumny, scolding, brawling, menaces, deceit, perjury, and many more.[8]

---

[5] *Defamed* seems formerly to have been used in the sense of charged, thus in the forms of indictment referred to in " The Mirrour of Justices," we find it so used ; as thus : " I say, Sebourge there is *defamed* by good people of the sin of heresy," &c., and in Lord Somers' Tract on Grand Juries, " the constitution intrusts such inquisitions in the hands of persons of understanding * * * that might suffer no man to be falsely accused or *defamed*." " Thieves openly defamed and known." (4 Bl. Com. ch. xxii.) " There is a *fame* against Mr. Spencer for not burying Edward Merrick as a christian ought to be." (*Calender of State Papers, Domestic Series, of the reign of Charles I.*, 1633–1634. Edited by John Bruce.)

" To diffame is, as Bartol saith, to utter reproachful speeches of another with an intent to raise up an ill fame of him and therefore himself expresseth the act itself in these words : *Diffamare est in mala fama ponere*. Albeit diffamations properly consist in words, yet may they also be done by writing, as by diffamatory libels, and also by deeds as by signs and gestures of reproach, for these no less show the malicious mind of the diffamer than words do." (*Ridley Civil Law*, 839.)

[7] In the United States there must be some overt act to constitute the act of treason. (*Bouvier's Law Dict. tit. Treason.*)

[8] Scolding often repeated to the disturbance of the neighborhood makes it a nuisance, always punishable at the leet and therefore indictable. (*The Queen v. Foxby*, 6 Mod. 145.) As to Brawling see *Stephen's Ecclesiastical Statutes*, p. 336, and copious notes ; and see *Jacob's Law Dict.*, tit. Cuckinstool. In Denmark there was a species of libel called Bersöglisvisur or free-speaking song. When King Mag-

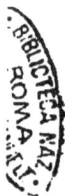

§ 8. Slander is a private wrong or tort, cognizable by the common law, the remedy for which is a civil action formerly known as an " action on the case for words," and now as an action or the action of or for slander.[8]

§ 9. Libel is both a public wrong or crime and a private wrong or tort, cognizable by the common law. The remedy for the public wrong is by indictment or criminal information. The remedy for the private wrong is a civil action, now known as an action or the action of or for libel.

§ 10. Defamation is an ecclesiastical offence, cognizable only in the ecclesiastical courts, by a proceeding in such courts.

§ 11. The redress sought in the actions of slander and libel is a pecuniary compensation called damages for the injury sustained by the party complaining, to be recovered against the party complained against, and is intended solely for the benefit of the complainant ;[10] on the other hand, the proceeding in the ecclesiastical court is, in theory at least, one solely for the benefit of the party complained against. It is to awaken him to a

---

nus (say about A. D. 1040) gave dissatisfaction to his subjects, a meeting was held at which lots were drawn as to which one of those assembled should address one of these songs to the King. See *Det Norske Folkes Historie*, 3 vols., Christiania, 1852–5; also *Den Danske Erobring af England og Normandiet*, Copenhagen, 1863. See *North British Review*, Nov., 1863.

[8] Slander is not like libel an indictable offence. (*Bailey* v. *Dean*, 5 Barb. 297.) Nor is a single precedent of any criminal proceeding for unwritten imputations upon the characters of individuals to be found, except in cases of high treason, * * and it must have been as constituting rather an offence against the government, than an injury to the individual, and being therefore seditious that words reflecting on a magistrate in the immediate execution of his office were for the first time in the reign of Queen Anne held to be indictable. (*Reg.* v. *Langley*, 2 Ld. Raym. 1060; Holt R. 654.) But I am not aware that Mr. Starkie has adverted to this case, or to the doctrine which is laid down in it. (1 *Mence on Libel*, 90.)

[10] " Action for slander is to recover damages for *words spoken* of a person who is thereby injured in his reputation, and for *words spoken* of a person which affect his life, office, profession, or trade, or which tend to his loss, or occasion any particular or special damage to him.", (*Onslow* v. *Horne*, 3 Wilson, 177.)

sense of the sin he has committed, and cause him to do penance therefor *pro salute animœ.* In a proceeding for defamation no damages are nor can be awarded to the party defamed. The defamer may be censured, compelled to recant the defamation, to perform penance and pay costs, and for disobedience to the court's decree be excommunicated. Beyond this the ecclesiastical court has no power.[11]

§ 12. The law applicable to the wrongs here termed slander and libel is sometimes designated the law of libel; sometimes the law of defamation; and sometimes the law of slander and libel. For no better reason than that it is the one most in use we shall adopt the term law of libel.

§ 13. The term law of libel, as generally understood, comprises the law as applicable to nearly all of the wrongs which may be effected by means of language. Our purpose, however, is not to consider the whole of the law of libel so understood, but so much of it only as applies to slander and to libel as a private wrong.

§ 14. As it is *sometimes* only that words which affect another amount to a wrong, we purpose to ascertain, if we can, what are the rules by which to test in any particular instance of words affecting another, whether they do or do not

---

[11] The ecclesiastical law is part of the English common law. (*Reg.* v. *Millis,* 10 Cl. and F. 534, 671; and see *Catterall* v. *Catterall,* 1 Robertson, 580; *Bishop on Marriage and Divorce,* § 9.) But has no status in the State of New York. (31 Barb. 49, 60.)

The power of the ecclesiastical court is the infliction of penance *pro salute animœ* and awarding costs, but not damages. (4 Co. 20, 2 Inst. 492.) The sentence of an ecclesiastical court in a proceeding for defamation has its counterpart in the Scotch Law under the name of Palinode.

As to suits in spiritual or ecclesiastical courts they are for the reformation of manners or for punishing of heresy; *defamation,* laying violent hands on a clerk and the like. * * * Things that properly belong to these jurisdictions are matrimonial and testamentary and defamatory words for which no action lies at law, as for calling one adulterer, fornicator, usurer or the like. (*Jacob's Law Dict.,* tit. Courts Ecclesiastical.) The courts of Piepowder had jurisdiction of certain actions for slander. (*Jacob's Law Dict.,* tit. Court of Piepowders.)

constitute a wrong, what kind of wrong, and what is its appropriate remedy.   In the execution of this purpose we desire not merely to collect, epitomize and classify under appropriate titles the reported adjudications, but to probe the subject to its core and unfold the principles which it involves ; to show not only what has been decided, but the principles of those decisions ; to lay down, if we can, such rules as will enable one under any given state of circumstances to determine when a wrong, as slander or libel, has occurred, when a remedy may properly be sought and how it may be pursued and obtained.   To accomplish this aim we shall advert to some elementary principles, the relevancy of which may not at once be apparent, but the reason for which will be observed as we proceed, and without a reference to which we should in vain attempt to make ourselves or our subject understood.

§ 15. A thorough investigation into elementary principles seems peculiarly necessary in treating on the law of libel, because it is a branch of the law in which, perhaps, more than any other, principles have, from various causes, been most subject to perversion by undue influences, have been less scientifically treated and more superficially considered.   The law of libel has been denounced as vague, fluctuating and incomprehensible.   Of the decisions on the subject many are conflicting, more are scarcely reconcilable, and the reasoning in support of all is, with very few exceptions, more or less weak, obscure, and unsatisfactory.   It has almost been claimed or conceded that there is something so subtle in the principles of the law of libel as to elude detection, and the law of libel has come to be regarded as a parasitical growth on the main body of the law, presenting features so exceptional as to render inapplicable those general principles which govern other branches of legal science.[12]   It will be our endeavor to show that properly under-

---

[12] A noted peculiarity of the law of libel is its vagueness and uncertainty. (*Encyc. Brit.*, voce libel.)   Holt, writing in 1816, says : " It is indeed in the very nature of the subject (*The Law of Libel*) that it is extremely difficult to clear it of those popular conceits and of that vagueness of generality which adhere to it as a question of political discussion. (*Holt on Libel*, Preface.)

stood there is nothing exceptional in the wrongs called slander and libel, nor in the legal principles applicable to those wrongs, that these wrongs are governed by the same principles which apply to all other wrongs, and that there is nothing in the law of libel itself which should render it less easy to comprehend than any other division of jurisprudence.

§ 16. While profoundly sensible of the difficulty properly to execute this, our self-imposed task, and of our comparative inability to do justice to the subject, we nevertheless flatter ourselves that we shall be able to lay before our readers a more systematic outline of the principles of the law of libel than any which has hitherto been offered or attempted.[18]

§ 17. Chief among the difficulties to be encountered is the combatting many of the existing theories and ideas on the subject, most of them coming down to us with the prestige of high authority, hallowed by time and all of them received for law. We esteem it an error and a misfortune that among text writers on legal subjects there has been such a reverence for precedent, such an unquestioned following the one of the other, so little attempt at enlarged and connected views of their subjects in their principles untrammeled by precedent, rendering text books collections of materials for essays rather than essays. For ourselves, we brave being deemed presumptuous, in the hope that we may be useful, and where, after the many years of patient reflection we have bestowed upon our subject, we have

---

[18] "Though I could not be ignorant either of the difficulty of the matter which he that taketh in hand shall soon find, or much less of my own inability, which I had continual sense and feeling of, yet because I had more means of absolution than the younger sort, and more leisure than the greater sort, I did think it not impossible to work some profitable effect, the rather because where an inferior wit is bent and conversant upon one subject, he shall many times, with patience and meditation, dissolve and undo many knots, which a greater wit, distracted with many matters, would rather cut in two than unknit; and at the least, if my invention or judgment be too barren or too weak, yet, by the benefit of other arts, I did hope to dispose or digest the authorities and opinions * * in such order and method, as they should take light one from another, though they took no light from me." (*Bacon's introduction to his Pleading on the Statute of Uses.*)

arrived at any conclusions which conflict with existing ideas or decisions, we shall be deterred neither by the antiquity of the precedent, nor the high position of its author, nor its indorsers, from expressing our dissent. Besides a general and connected view of the subject, we shall study to present a faithful record of all the adjudged decisions and dicta, and as we really have no pet theory to maintain, and are influenced solely by the desire to elicit the true principles on which the law concerning our subject is based, we shall be especially careful throughout to distinguish from received authorities what are merely our inferences or suggestions; and we promise our readers most religiously to abstain from any intentional garbling of authority, or the willful withholding of any decision or dicta, in order to support any particular view or theory. The meagre attempts heretofore made to reduce the subject into any systematic form will oblige us, to a considerable extent, to treat the subject as *res nova.*

§ 18. We have divided our subject into two principal divisions—slander and libel. Slander and libel have this in common, that each may be, and usually is, effected by means of language. As we have described them, their distinguishing feature of difference is that the one is effected by oral language, the other by written language. To language in writing is attributed in *most* cases a greater capacity for injury than is attributed to language spoken or speech, so that language which, if spoken, gives no right to redress, may, if reduced to writing, give a cause of action.[14] It is proper to say that the broad dis-

---

[14] A distinction was very early taken in the Roman law between slander spoken and written, and the *injuria verbalis* was deemed to constitute a much lower degree of injury than the *malum carmen* and *famosus libellus.* (Holt on Libel, N. Y. Ed. 21.) Holt wrote in 1816. He says, p. 225: "It has *lately* become a question whether there be any difference between written and unwritten slander;" and then he refers to *Bradley* v. *Methuen*, 2 Ford's MS. 78, in which Lord Hardwicke is reported to have said that courts do make a distinction "between words written and bare words." In Thorley's case, 4 Taunt. 355, the question was, Whether an action would lie for words *written*, when such action would not lie for them if *spoken?* "For myself," said Chief Justice Mansfield, "I cannot, upon principle, make any difference between words written (as to the right which

tinction we have drawn between slander and libel is not one universally adopted;[15] indeed it is not the one, in our judgment, the most logically correct; but we adopt it partly in deference

---

arises out of them to bring an action) and words spoken; but the difference has been recognized by the courts for at least a century backwards, and has been established by Lords Hardwicke, Hale, Holt, and others."

This species of defamation [libel] is usually called *written scandal*, and hereby receives an aggravation in that it is presumed to have been entered upon with coolness and deliberation, and to continue longer, and to propagate wider and further than any other *scandal*. (*Bac. Abr.*)

The distinction between *verbal* and *written slander* proceeds upon the principle that words are often spoken in heat upon sudden provocations, and are fleeting and soon forgotten, and therefore less likely to be permanently injurious; while written slander is more deliberate and malicious, more capable of circulation in distant places, and consequently more likely to be permanently injurious. (1 *Chit. Gen. Pr.* 45.)

The *great distinction* between libel and slander is, "that from a libel damage is always implied by law, whereas some kinds of slander only are actionable without proof of special damage." (*Broom's Comm.* p. 513 [762].)

Words written and published may be actionable which, if spoken, would not be so without special damage. But they must be such as, in the common estimation of mankind, are calculated to reflect shame and disgrace upon the person concerning whom they are written, or hold him up as an object of hatred, ridicule and contempt. (*Fonville* v. *Nease*, Dudley, S. C. 303.) As to what is libelous, and as to the distinction between libel and slander. (*Rice* v. *Simmons*, 2 Harring. 417; *Layton* v. *Harris*, 3 Harring. 406.) Vox emissa volet, litera scripta manet. (*Beebe* v. *Bank of N. Y.*, 1 Johns. 529, 571.) Scribere est agere. (*The People* v. *Rathbun*, 21 Wend. 509–540.)

There was something superstitious in the horror with which the Icelanders regarded a libel, and no offence among them was more surely or bloodily avenged than the publication of satirical verses, or the setting up of a *Nid*—that is, an insulting or indecent figure, or a horse's head on a pole on the lands of another. (See "The Story of Burnt Njal; or, Life in Iceland at the End of the Tenth Century." By George W. Dasent, D. C. S.) It is a marked trait in the character of the Russian people to "feel corporeal punishment less sensibly than a verbal insult. This idea has a religious foundation; a good Christian cannot admit that the punishment of fustigation which has been inflicted on the Saviour of humanity can be for a man a stain of infamy; he believes that a verbal insult affects the immortal part of man, whereas a blow only produces suffering to the least noble part of his being." (Essai sur l'Histoire de la Civilization en Russie. Par Nicolas de Gerebtzoff. Paris, 1858, vol. 2, p. 575. Westminster Review, January, 1864—Art. Russia.)

[15] It does not apply to the wrong called slander of title, nor to language affecting one in his calling or office, nor to proceedings in the ecclesiastical courts. As

to a very prevalent use of the terms slander and libel, to distinguish between an injury by speech and an injury by writing,
and partly because by this arrangement one word suffices to denote to which particular branch of the subject we refer. In
our opinion, the more logical arrangement would be to take
slander or defamation as the generic term, and then indicate
the division by the epithets oral and written. There are, however, objections to this division—among others, that it omits
effigy. Another mode of dividing the subject is to take libel
for the generic term, and then distinguish the kind by the epithets defamatory, seditious, &c.[16] This is objectionable on

<hr />

to this last see *Ware* v, *Johnson*, 2 Sir Geo. Lees Cases in Eccles. Courts, 103.
Holt says, p. 211 N. Y. Edit.: " It is evident, moreover, from the authorities that
words written of a man tending to disparage him in his profession will support
an action, although the same words when spoken will not;" and he refers to
King v. *Lake*, Hardres, 471; but that case does not authorize any such doctrine.

[16] Blackstone speaks of blasphemous, immoral, treasonable, schismatical, sedi-
tions or scandalous libels. (4 Bl. Comm. ch. xi.) And Lord Bolingbroke, writing
to Queen Anne, Oct. 17th, 1711, says: "I have discovered the author of another
scandalous libel, who will be in custody this afternoon; he will make the thir-
teenth I have seized and the fifteenth I have found out." In Borthwick on Libel,
25, note, it is said: His Lordship seems to have retained the adjective [infa-
mous] in reference to the usual meaning of the word *libel*, when not qualified, in
the law of Scotland, which is the same [meaning] as it still has in the spiritual
courts of England. It would appear, however, that, even in the courts of common law in England, there was formerly some doubt whether *libel*, or *libellus*, by
itself, was the proper technical expression. This we learn from a note (*a.* p. 4)
in the "Digest of the Law Concerning Libels." "Lord Chief Justice Raymond,"
says the author, "in Curl's case, said that he did not think that *libellus* was
always to be taken as a technical word, and asked whether action would lie *de
quodam libello intitula*—the New Testament—and whether the spiritual court did
not proceed upon a libel? Mr. Justice Fortescue said a libel was a technical
word at common law. Mr. Justice Reynolds' said that *libellus did not, ex vi termini, import defamation*, but was to be governed by the epithet added to it."
2 Stra. 791.

In Thorley's case, 4 Taunt. 355, the expression " written and unwritten slander " is used.

Mr. Heard, in his treatise on libel and slander, § 8, uses the phrase "actionable libel." This implies that there may be a libel which is not actionable. He
also uses the phrase printed libel. In the index to the same treatise is the phrase
" ironical libel."

The Encyclopedia Brittannicæ, voce Libel, uses the phrase " defamatory libel;"

many grounds. Upon the whole, we conclude that the division we have adopted will be found obnoxious to as few objections, and be more convenient, than any other we could have selected. In describing the matter of a slander or libel—that is, the speech or writing which may or may not constitute a slander or a libel, but which is charged to be a slander or libel—we shall designate it speech or writing, as the matter of slander or libel may be intended, but generally, and where both slander and libel are used, shall employ the term language or defamatory matter. Neither judges, advocates, nor text writers confine themselves to the terms slander and libel, but employ the terms libel, slander, scandal, calumny, defamation, detraction, verbal injury, and some others, without any accord as to, and with very little regard for, their definitions or connotations. We shall confine ourselves throughout to the terms slander and libel, and employ them as distinct terms and as marking the division between an offence by means of speech and an offence by means of writing or effigy; but in using the phrase *law of libel,* we desire, noth-

---

and the statute, 6 and 7 Vict., ch. 96, uses the term "defamatory words and libel" in lieu of "slander and libel."

"The high court of the Paris Parliament commenced a prosecution against him for *libellous defamation.*" Westminster Review, July, 1860; Art. The French Press, page 118, Am. Reprint.

"Mr. J. Mackenzie's Narrative, *a false libel,* a defence of Mr. G. Walker, &c., 1690," is the title of a pamphlet published in 1690. And the phrase "*false slander*" is used; *Finch's Law,* 185.

In an ordinance agreed to by both Houses of the English Parliament, 30th September, 1647, the word *libel* seem to be used in the sense of a book or pamphlet. The ordinance runs thus: "That what person so ever shall make, write, print, publish, sell or utter any book, pamphlet, treatise, ballad, *libel,* or sheet of news whatsoever, or cause so to be done, except the same be licensed by both or either House of Parliament," &c. The word *libel* cannot here mean a defamatory publication, as it is not to be supposed the Parliament would in any case license a defamatory publication.

Sometimes any unfair statement is called a libel, and we say it is a libel on humanity, on the goodness of God, &c.

The phrase, "action *for words,*" might seem to be always, as it generally is, employed by the English lawyers, in reference to words *spoken* alone. This, however, is not the case. Thus, Mr. Tomlins, in his Law Dictionary (voce Action II. § 1), says: "Action on the case *for words ;* which is brought for words spoken or *written.*" This passage may be remarked as another instance of the varied meaning of légal phrases. (*Borthwick Libel, v.* 22, *note.*)

ing being said to the contrary, to be understood as meaning and
including as well the law applicable to what we call slander as
to what we call libel.

§ 19. From some cause—perhaps from the fact that language
in writing may amount to a public wrong—it has happened
that the wrong occasioned by writing (libel) has occupied a
larger share of attention than has the wrong occasioned by
speech (slander). Whether this is sufficient to account for the
circumstance or not, these facts remain, that while it is common
to speak of the law of libel, it is quite uncommon to speak of
the law of slander; and while ingenuity has been tortured to
frame a definition of libel or a libel, scarcely any attempts have
been made to frame a definition of slander or a slander.

§ 20. The attempts which have been made to define *libel* or
" a libel " are so many as to be almost innumerable, yet they
have in reality been unavailing; no definition, properly so
called, of libel or a libel exists.[17] The term libel being conno-

---

[17] " It is to be observed that no correct, no logical definition of a libel has
ever been given." (*George on Libel*, 14.)

Lord Brougham, in answer to the question how far it was possible to define
the law of libel said: " It is a subject to which I have paid considerable attention, but I must freely own without any success whatever. I hold it to be hardly
possible to define libels by which guilt may be incurred as tending to a breach
of the peace, to other proceedings of a violent nature, * * and to a variety
of other heads. * * * * Any definitions that I have ever seen
given had one or other of two faults, * * * they were either so
vague as not to specify or define anything, or * * they were only rendered particular and definite by omitting some species of libel * * *
which ought to have been comprehended. * * * I have never yet
seen, or been able myself to hit upon anything like a definition of libel * *
which possessed the requisites of a definition, and I cannot help thinking
that the difficulty is not accidental, but essentially inherent in the nature of the
subject. * * * The latin of libel is not *libellus* but *libellus famosus.*
* * Libel then means, in its original, not "little book" but "a defamatory little book." * * * Libel is an offence of a somewhat vague
description, but sufficiently known in law, and perhaps as well defined as assault
and some others, and I do not believe, from all the experience I have had, that
in practice any considerable difficulty is felt on account of its indistinctness.
(*Report of House of Lords on defamation and libel*, July, 1843.)

At Rome the cards of the races with the names and colors of the riders and
drivers were called *libelli.*

tative, its definition to be complete should unfold the whole
meaning it involves, the whole of what is connoted; should
" select from among the whole of its properties those which
shall be understood to be designated and declared by its name;"
"those which unfold its nature, which are peculiar to it and
which are not found in a like combination elsewhere." This
describes a *real definition* of the kind called *essential*, and before
we can frame such a definition we must know all the properties of our subject, and then select those proper for the purpose. As a libel comprehends a complex aggregate of particulars either not all known or not all agreed upon, it may be
impossible to circumscribe them by a correct and compact general description.

§ 21. The definitions which have been attempted have been
framed as supposed standards by which to determine of any
given proposition whether or not it constitutes a libel; and
experience demonstrating the total worthlessness for any practical purposes of these *supposed* definitions it has come to be
taken for granted, at least by some, that there is that inherent
in the subject which prevents the possibility of its definition.
This, although imputed to libel as a peculiarity, is not so in
fact, the like difficulty attaches to many other terms and particularly to every other wrong. An attempt to frame a concise,
real, essential definition of any other wrong will disclose the
like difficulties as occur in the case of libel.[1]

---

[19] As Cousin said, when asked to state in a single sentence the spirit of German philosophy, "These things do not sum themselves up in single sentences."

We subjoin some specimens of the attempts to define libel:

It is not infamous matter or words which make a libel; for, if a man speak
such words, unless they are *written*, he is not guilty of the making of a libel;
writing is of the essence of a libel. (*Ld. Raym.* 416.) In order to constitute a
libel, the subject-matter complained of must be a subject of visible perception.
But, provided only it be an object of visible perception, a libel does not appear
to be confined to any particular form or shape. By the requisite, which is essential to the existence of a libel, that it be an object of visible perception, *libel* is
distinguished from what is technically called *defamation or spoken slander*.
Again, "The words most nearly synonymous to the word *libelling*, are *defaming,
disparaging, aspersing, slandering.*" (*George on Libel*, p. 35, 36, 41.)

" A libel is a contumely or reproach, published to the defamation of the government, of a magistrate, or of a private person." (*Comyn's Digest.*)

§ 22. It is rare, indeed, that we can frame a real, essential definition, but by a definition is sometimes understood such an explanation of a given term as conveys an idea of its connota-

---

A libel is a malicious *publication* tending to the disrepute of an individual, the breach of the peace, the seditious violation of the good order of government. (*Capel Loft's Essay on Libels*, edit. 1785, p. 6.)

. The American Encyclopedia, voce Libel, refers to the following definition of libel as the best definition: " A libel is any published defamation." And the same article states the difference between libel and slander to consist in this, that libel is published defamation, and slander is spoken defamation. This seems to ignore an oral publication.

Written defamation is otherwise termed libel, and oral defamation slander. (*Burrell, Law Dict.*)

Defamatory words, written and published, constitute a libel. (*Maunder.*)

Libel, a word which has many different meanings, but is chiefly known in this country as the name of a department of the law which, from incidental circumstances, has come to include the naturally distinct heads of written slander, sedition, and outrage against religion. (*Encyc. Brit.* voce Libel.)

A libel has been *usually* treated of as scandal, written or expressed by symbols. Libel may be said to be a technical word deriving its meaning rather from its use than its etymology. (*Russell's Treatise of Crimes and Misdemeanors*, edit. 1819, p. 308.)

In a strict sense it [libel] is taken for a malicious defamation, expressed either in printing or writing; in a larger sense, the notion of libel may be applied to any defamation whatsoever, expressed either by signs or pictures, as by affixing up a gallows at a man's door, or by painting him in a shameful and ignominious manner. (*Hawkin's Pl. Cr.*)

Libell, a criminous report of any man cast abroad or otherwise unlawfully published in writing, but then, for difference sake, it is called an infamous libel— *famosus libellus.* (*Minshœi, A Guide into the Tongues, &c.*, London, 1627.)

Written or printed slanders are libels. (*Bouvier.*)

" All publications injurious to private character or credit of another are libellous." *Addison on Wrongs*—referred to as a good definition, *McNally v. Oldham*, 8 Law Times, Rep. N. S. 604.

" A libel is anything of which any one thinks proper to complain." Essay prefixed to report of Finnerty's Trial; supposed to be from Jeremy Bentham's Writings. It is also quoted thus: " A libel is anything published upon any matter of anybody, which any one was pleased to dislike." Attributed to Bentham, cited in pamphlet, trial of David Lee Child.

A libel is a censorious or ridiculing writing, picture, or sign, made with a mischievous and malicious intent towards government, magistrates, or individuals. (Per Hamilton, arg. *People v. Croswell*, 8 Johns. C. 354; adopted, *Steele v. Southwick*, 9 Johns. 214; *Cooper v. Greeley*, 1 Den. 347.)

A libel is a malicious publication expressed either in printing or writing, or by signs and pictures, tending either to blacken the memory of one dead, or the

tion and enables us to distinguish it from, and prevents our confounding it with, any other term of a *similar* but not the *same* import. When we employ definition in this sense and for this

reputation of one who is alive, and expose him to public hatred, contempt, or ridicule. (Per Ch. J. Parsons, quoted in *Root* v. *King*, 7 Cow. 613.)

A libel is a malicious publication in printing, writing, signs, or pictures, imputing to another something which has a tendency to injure his reputation ; to disgrace or to degrade him in society, and lower him in the esteem and the opinion of the world, or to bring him into public hatred, contempt, or ridicule. (*State* v. *Jeandell*, 5 Harring. [Del.] 475.)

Everything written of another, holding him up to scorn and ridicule, and calculated to provoke a breach of the peace, is a libel. (*Torrance* v. *Hurst*, Walker, 403 ; *Newbraugh* v. *Curry*, Wright, 47.)

Every publication by writing, printing, or painting. which charges or imputes to any person that which renders him liable to punishment, or which is calculated to make him infamous, odious, or ridiculous, is, *prima facie*, a libel, and implies malice in the publisher. (*White* v. *Nicholls*, 3 How. U. S. 266.)

A publication, to be a libel, must tend to injure the plaintiff's reputation, and expose him to public hatred, contempt and ridicule. (*Armentrout* v. *Moranda*, 8 Blackf. 426.)

Any publication. the tendency of which is to degrade and injure another person, or to bring him into contempt, hatred, or ridicule, or which accuses him of a crime punishable by law, or of an act odious and disgraceful in society, is a libel. (*Dexter* v. *Spear*, 4 Mason. 115.)

A libel is a malicious publication expressed either in printing or writing, or by signs and pictures, tending either to blacken the memory of one dead, or the reputation of one who is alive, and expose him to public hatred, contempt, or ridicule. (*Commonwealth* v. *Clapp*, 4 Mass. 163, 168.)

A libel is a censorious or ridiculing writing, picture, or sign, made with a mischievous intent. (*The State* v. *Farley*, 4 M'Cord, 317.)

A publication is a *libel* which tends to injure one's reputation in the common estimation of mankind, to throw contumely or reflect shame and disgrace upon him, or hold him up as an object of hatred, scorn, ridicule and contempt, although it imputes no crime liable to be punished with infamy, or to prejudice him in his employment. So every publication by writing, printing, or painting, which charges or imputes to any person that which renders him liable to punishment, or which is calculated to make him infamous or odious or ridiculous, is, *prima facie*, a libel. (1 *Hilliard on Torts*, ch. vii. § 13.)

Holt in his treatise, p. 213 [223], defines libel as against private persons thus: "Everything, therefore, written of another which.holds him up to scorn and ridicule, that might reasonably (that is according to our natural passions) be considered as provoking him to a breach of the peace, is a libel." Mr. Mence (*Law of Libel*, vol. 1, p. 120), referring to this passage in Holt, says: "This agrees with his two preceding definitions, and with the common acceptation of the term libel, by making it essential that the subject or object of the attack should be some person

3

purpose merely, it ceases to be important whether the definition
adopted be strictly accurate. If we always employ the term in
that one predetermined sense, it serves to avoid confusion and

---

or persons ; but it disagrees with them, by introducing the tendency to provoke
a breach of the peace. It follows that, if this be a correct definition, the other
two must be defective, because, in one of them, the tendency or (as is there said)
the intent to provoke is required only in cases where the object of the slander is
a deceased person, and in that from Lord Coke it is wholly omitted. On the
other hand, if the two former definitions be correct, the third must necessarily be
inaccurate, for an accurate definition is one which neither omits what is essential
nor admits what is superfluous.   *   *   *   And it is to be further observed
that the third definition disagrees with the two former and the common acceptation of the term *libel*, not only by introducing the intent or the tendency to
provoke, but by leaving out the falsehood and malice. For *libel*, in common
acceptation, signifies written slander; and the term slander and all its synonyms,
as defamation, detraction, calumny, even without the epithets malicious and
injurious, imply falsehood and malice."

"The familiar acceptation of the word libel is no less simple and intelligible
[than the term horse-stealing], but the legal and technical use is as if *horse-stealing* stood not only for stealing a horse but for murder, arson, larceny, and other
crimes more or less atrocious; and even for actions not criminal, or of which the
criminality is at least doubtful and not to be measured or ascertained till we have
separated them from the greater crimes with which they are confounded. This
perverse and cabalistic use of language it is that has given birth to so much of
the obscurity with which the law of libel is reproached. And nothing can be
easier than to reform it. We have only to consider written challenges to fight as
a class by themselves; to class blasphemous writings under the head of blasphemy; obscene and grossly indecent or immoral writings under the head of
obscenity; or both these heads, together, under that of offences immediately
against God ; seditious writings under the head of sedition; and all other writings denominated libels under the two distinct heads of libels and censure, as they
are either tainted with falsehood and malice, or criminal by carrying upon them
the manifest intent to provoke a breach of the peace, or by having a tendency,
or of being merely suspected of having a tendency, so to do." And on page 181
he says, "This is blasphemy under the title of libel upon the Christian religion,
classed or confounded, as is obscenity also with crimes (if crimes they be), from
which it differs as much both in kind and degree as murder does from picking a
pocket or robbing a hen-roost." (1 *Mence on Libel*, 125.)

In several of the States, libel has been *defined by statute*. Thus, in Maine,
it is enacted that " a libel shall be construed to be the malicious defamation of a
person, made public either by any printing, writing, sign, picture, representation,
or effigy, tending to provoke him to wrath, or expose him to public hatred, contempt, or ridicule, or to deprive him of the benefits of public confidence and
social intercourse; or any malicious defamation, made public as aforesaid,
designed to blacken and vilify the memory of one that is dead, and tending to

enables us to reason upon it with certainty. Mathematical
science is certain, not because its definitions are true, but because they are certain; and legal science is only uncertain because its definitions are uncertain.[19] We may ensure certainty
by having definitions which, however defective in other respects,
at least admit of our using the terms defined always in one and
the same sense and always so using them. We shall not attempt
to construct real definitions of slander and libel, but to definitely
mark what is meant when those terms are employed. We define slander and libel as *wrongs occasioned by language or effigy*
—that is to say, *slander is a wrong occasioned by speech*, and
libel is a wrong occasioned by writing or effigy.

---

scandalize or provoke his surviving relatives or friends." And in Illinois it is
enacted, "a libel is a malicious defamation, expressed either by printing or by
signs, or the like tending to blacken the memory of one who is dead, or to im-
peach the honesty, integrity, virtue or reputation, or publish the natural defects
of one who is alive, and thereby to expose him or her to public hatred, contempt,
or ridicule." Definitions of the like import are to be found in the statute books
of some other States.

See, *Maine Rev. Stat.*, 1840, ch. 165, § 1; *Iowa Rev. Code of* 1851, ch. 151, art.
2767; *Arkansas Rev. Stat.*, 1837, div. 8, ch. 44, art. 2, § 1, p. 280; *Georgia,
Prince's Dig.*, pp. 643, 644; *Hotchk. Dig.*, p. 739; *Cobb's Dig.*, vol. 2, p. 812;
California Stat., 1850, ch. 99, § 120; *Illinois Rev. Stat.*, 1845, Crim. Code, § 120.

[19] "Mathematics will, in no greater degree than theology or metaphysics, give
us 'certainty by rigid demonstration' without the assumption of those primary
truths which we accept, because we are so constituted that we must accept them."
Westminster Review, October, 1864; art. Dr. Newman's Apologia. The question What is the foundation of mathematical demonstration? was discussed by
Dugald Stewart, and the conclusion at which he arrived was that the certainty
of mathematical reasoning arose from its depending on *definitions*. And further,
that mathematical truth is hypothetical; if the definitions are assumed, the conclusion follows. Mr. Whewell controverts these views. See "The Mechanical
Euclid," &c., and Remarks on Mathematical Reasoning, &c., by the Rev. W. Whewell, M. A., and Edinburgh Review, April, 1838.

"Nothing is harder than a definition. While on the one hand there is for the
most part no easier task than to detect a fault or flaw in the definition of those
who have gone before us, nothing on the other hand is more difficult than to pro-
pose one of our own which shall not also present a vulnerable side." Dean
Trench. See Burrill's Law Dict., voce Definition, and 2 Wooddes. Lect., 196.

CHAPTER II.

Language can have no effect unless published. It must be true or false, commendatory or discommendatory. Must concern a person or thing. Its effect, direct or indirect, or both. Reputation.

§ 23. Language may exist as mere thought, but, before it can have any effect extra the individual with or in whom it originated, it must be expressed; it must come into existence as an expression, by sound, as in speech, or by sign, as in writing or effigy; and not only must it be expressed, it must also be *published*—that is, communicated by the individual with or in whom it originated to some *other*.

§ 24. Language when employed to communicate ideas must assume the form of a proposition or a series of propositions; by a proposition being meant "discourse which affirms or denies something of some person or thing, the subject of the proposition." Every proposition is an assertion, and must be either true or false—that is, it must assert of its subject that which is true, or that which is false, and the assertion may be either of commendation or discommendation.

§ 25. Language must concern either a person or a thing, or both, and it may concern a person in his individual and natural capacity merely, or in some acquired or artificial relation or capacity as a trader, an office-holder, or as the author, owner, or possessor of some certain thing.

§ 26. The effect of the publication of language upon a person, other than the author or publisher of the language, must be direct or indirect, or both.

§ 27. Language cannot directly affect a thing; whatever direct effect it can have must be upon a person.

§ 28. Language, whether it concerns a person or a thing, may have a direct effect upon the person *to whom* it is published, but upon none other. It may directly affect the feelings, health, belief, or opinion of him to whom it is published, and it may influence or excite him towards a particular course of action or forbearance by himself, or in respect of himself or his affairs, or in respect to some other person or some thing, or the affairs of some other person. It may either please or displease him, or cause him to feel pleased or displeased with some other person or thing, or cause him to do some act or to abstain or resolve to abstain from doing some act to the advantage or disadvantage of himself or some other, or cause him to think better or worse of himself or of some other person or some thing. That other person may be either he who makes the communication or he whom the language concerns. All the *direct* effects of the publication of language are personal to the individual to whom the publication is made, and can extend no further. The publication of language can have no *direct effects* other than those we have enumerated; whatever other effects may result from the publication of language must be *indirect* or consequent upon one or other or some of these enumerated direct effects.

§ 29. The kind of effect produced, *i. e.*, the direct or indirect effect, must be the same whether the publication be by sound (speech), or by sign (writing or effigy), but the mode of publication may affect the amount of effect produced.

§ 30. It is scarcely supposable that the publication of language which concerns another or his affairs can produce no direct effect, but it is easy to suppose that it may not produce any indirect effect. The publication may occasion a resolve (a direct effect), and that resolve may never be put into execution (produce no indirect effect), or it may occasion a change in the opinion entertained of another, and that other may never be otherwise in any the least degree affected by that change of opinion. The change of opinion may not prevent or occasion any action different from what would otherwise have been done or forborne; while, however, this is supposable, it is improbable; the possibility, however, of such an occurrence suffices for our purpose. Sometimes, indeed, the direct and indirect effects are apparent, and their extent ascertainable; and again, it may be that neither the direct nor the indirect effect is apparent or its extent ascertainable.

§ 31. It is impossible to anticipate all the indirect effects which may result from the publication of language; experience has made us acquainted with some of them, and to these we shall have occasion to refer by way of illustration.

§ 32. Among the direct effects of the publication of language which we have enumerated is the occasioning the person to whom the publication is made to think well or ill of another. Now, what one thinks of another is the reputation of that other, and hence, when by language one is induced to think ill of another, the reputation of that other suffers disparagement.[20] That others think well of him is as gratifying to a man as that

---

[20] Reputation is the estimate in which an individual is held by public fame in the place where he is known. *Cooper* v. *Greely*, 1 Denio, 347, 365.

"Character is defined by Webster to be the peculiar qualities impressed by nature or habit on a person, which distinguish him from others; these constitute *real character*, and the qualities he is supposed to possess constitute his *estimated character* or *reputation*." Per Welles, J. in *Carpenter* v. *The People*, 8 Barb. 608.

"If the word reputation, when unqualified, does, *ex vi termini*, or, in common parlance, mean general reputation—as we think it does—it is unnecessary to prefix the word general." *French* v. *Millard*, 22 Ohio Rep. 50.

"Reputation is thinking. I repute a man to be good or bad—that is, I think him to be so." Maule, J., Doe dem. *Padwick* v. *Wittcomb*, 15 Jur. 778; 5 Eng. Law & Eq. Rep. 487.

"The mere entry of something that was in a lease is not any expression of opinion or reputation." Cresswell, J., *id.*

"The words character and reputation are often used as synonymous terms, though in fact not synonymous." *Bucklin* v. *Ohio*, 20 Ohio R. 18; *French* v. *Millard*, 22 *id.* 50.

"Character is a term convertible with common report." *Kimmel* v. *Kimmel*, 3 Serg. & R. 337. Gibson, J.

Character and reputation are the same. *Id.*, Duncan, J.

"General character is the estimation in which a person is held in the community where he resides." Marcy, J., *Douglass* v. *Tousey*, 2 Wend. 354.

"Public opinion is the question in common cases where character is in issue." *Boynton* v. *Kellogg*, 3 Mass. R. 192. Parsons, Ch. J.

The word *character* has been variously used in legal proceedings, and sometimes denotes the personal, official, or special character in which a party sues or is sued as executor, officer, &c., but it more frequently refers to reputation or

others think ill of him is distasteful, but their merely thinking well or ill of him by itself can neither benefit nor prejudice him. Unless in consequence of the opinion thus entertained, some act is done or forborne in reference to him or his affairs, which would not otherwise have been done or forborne, he is physically and pecuniarily in nowise better nor worse for such opinion. It cannot affect his person or his property. In the ordinary course of events some indirect effect does always result from the publication of language. The probability or improbability of any indirect effect resulting depends sometimes on the kind of language published, and sometimes on the circumstances of the publication, and sometimes on both the kind of language and the circumstances of the publication.

§ 33. We conclude, therefore, that there may be an injury to the reputation without, and independently of, an injury to the person or property, and that an injury to the reputation does not necessarily imply an injury to the person or the property.[21]

---

common report. (1 Cow. & Hill, notes 460, 1768; *Leddy* v. *Tousey*, 2 Wend. 352; *King* v. *Root*, 4 Wend. 113.) It is seldom used as synonymous with mere inclination or propensity or even secret habit, nor is descriptive of the more qualities of individuals, only so far as others have formed opinions from their conduct. *Safford* v. *The People*, 1 Parker's Crim. R. 478.

General character is the result of general conduct. *Sharp* v. *Scoggin*, Holt's N. P. C. 541; 3 Amer. Law J. N. S. 145.

Proof of general bad character—as that term is generally understood and used in society—does not necessarily and legally prove the fact that the witnesses' character for veracity is bad. *Gilbert* v. *Sheldon*, 13 Barb. 627.

"Chaste character" means actual personal virtue—not mere reputation. *Carpenter* v. *The People*, 8 Barb. 603; *Crozier* v. *The People*, 1 Park. Cr. R. 453; *Safford* v. *The People*, id. 474.

[21] Domat Civil Law, Public Law, Book III., enumerates "defamatory libels" among private offences, and in the same book, title 1, "of crimes and offences," enumerates three kinds of "*goods*," "the third is that good which is called *honor*, and which men value above all other goods." The author then proceeds to inquire what is signified by the term honor, and concludes, "lastly, it signifies reputation." Further on it is laid down that honor may be wounded either by injurious treatment of the honor or by assaulting the reputation, for one may offend another's honor by actions or by opprobrious language, without lessening his reputation, and we may blemish his honor by words, by writing and other attempts against his reputation, or one may attack by one and the same way both the reputation and person of another.

CHAPTER III.[a]

Description of Rights and Duties. Wrongs, Rights, and Duties undefinable. What determines of any act if it be a Wrong. Remedies. Injunction. Original writs.

§ 34. Having in a preceding chapter described slander and libel as wrongs, it is proper to explain what is meant by a wrong, and to that end we must first briefly consider the nature of rights and duties. For the opposite to *a right* is not *a wrong*, but *a duty.*

§ 35. Rights and duties are neither persons nor things, but powers and obligations. A right is a power to do or forbear or require another to forbear. A duty is an obligation, a necessity to do or forbear, or to submit to some act of another.

§ 36. The object of a right or a duty is a transaction. By transaction is meant an act, and the occasion on which the act is enacted.

§ 37. Rights and duties are reciprocal. The act which one has the right, the power, to do or forbear, that no other can or should hinder or compel the doing or forbearing ; but to such doing or forbearing it is the duty, the necessity, of every other to submit ; and what one has the right, the power, to command another to do or forbear, that it is the duty, the necessity, of that other to do or forbear ; what it is the duty of one to do or forbear, that it is the right of some other to have done or forborne ; what it is the duty of one to do, to that it is the duty of every other to submit.

---

[a] For the tenor of this chapter we acknowledge our indebtedness to the general part of " Thibaut's System of Pandekten Rechts," as translated by Lindley ; also to Mr. Maine's admirable book, " Ancient Law," or, an Inquiry into the Origin of Legal Ideas. As to rights and duties, reference may be had to Austin's Lectures on Jurisprudence.

§ 38. Rights and duties pertain solely to persons. A thing cannot have any rights and cannot owe any duties. And as a thing has no rights, no person can owe a duty to a thing.

§ 39. The exercise of a right is always optional; the performance of a duty is always compulsory. One may forego the exercise of a right, or exercise it, at his option, for either way no right of any other suffers; but one cannot, at his option, forego the performance of a duty; because to omit the performance of a duty is to take away a right somewhere, either in society or an individual, the right to have such duty performed. Therefore every act done in exercise of a right is a voluntary [optional] act, and every act done in the performance of a duty is an involuntary [not optional] act. One may in fact perform his duties willingly, but as the performance or non-performance is not optional, performance is properly regarded as involuntary.

§ 40. Rights must be exercised and duties must be performed strictly and in good faith. An act which exceeds the prescribed limits of a right is not the exercise of that right, and an act which falls short of the prescribed limits of a duty is not the performance of that duty.

§ 41. Rights and duties cannot exist in the absence of a supreme power somewhere, which protects the exercise of the one and enforces the performance of the other; that supreme power is called a law, and that branch of it which relates to the rights and duties of individuals in their social relations constitutes the municipal law. In *some* sense, therefore, it is proper to say that rights and duties are the *results of law*, and if this be granted, it must follow that all rights and duties of which the municipal law takes cognizance are legal rights and legal duties. There can be no such right recognized by law as a natural right. A right anterior to or independent of the law can be a right only of superior physical power.

§ 42. Every act must be done either in the exercise of a right or in the performance of a duty, or neither in the exercise

of a right nor in the performance of a duty; and every act
must be either such as the law permits and does not punish or
such as the law does not permit and will punish. Every act
done in the exercise of a right or in the performance of a duty
is a permitted act. Every act done neither in the exercise of a
right nor the performance of a duty is an unpermitted act.
Every act which the law permits is lawful, and every act which
the law does not permit is unlawful.

§ 43. A lawful act cannot amount to a wrong, but every
unlawful act is a wrong; and as every act must be either lawful or unlawful, every act must be either a wrong or not a
wrong. The rule that for every wrong the law provides a
remedy holds true only by postulating that only that act is a
wrong for which the law provides *a* punishment or *a* remedy.
The rule that for every wrong the law provides a remedy is
not universally true, because sometimes although a wrong has
been committed, the subject of the wrong is by some means
estopped from claiming any redress. The formula by which
this rule is expressed is, that one cannot take advantage of his
own wrong. An act may be such as not to be obnoxious to
every remedy, but if it is obnoxious to any remedy it is a wrong.

§ 44. Different laws prescribe different rules of right and duty,
and where there are courts of different jurisdictions that may
be a wrong in one jurisdiction which is not a wrong in another;
as where there are civil and criminal courts, and as in England
where there are common law courts and ecclesiastical courts.
We may sometimes determine of any act whether or not it is a
wrong by inquiring whether or not the law provides for it *any*
remedy or punishment. If there is no remedy we conclude
there is no wrong—meaning, of course, legal wrong. This, it
must be conceded, is an illogical and inverse method of arriving
at the desired conclusion, but we find it oftentimes resorted to,
as the best attainable standard by which to determine of any
act if it be a wrong.[23]

---

[23] "The remedy may always be referred to as illustrating the right and *e con-
verso*." *Van Rensselaer* v. *Jones*, 2 Barb. 656.

§ 45. Wrongs which only affect society in general, and, so far as they affect society in general, are distinguished from wrongs affecting only individuals, by denominating them *crimes*. Hereafter we shall invariably use the term *wrong* to signify an act injuriously affecting only individuals. Wrongs are direct or indirect. Direct wrongs are those where the act done may be *per se* a violation of a right—a blow is of this character. Indirect wrongs are those where the act done cannot be *per se* a violation of a right, and only becomes a violation of a right by reason of.some consequence resulting from that act. The act of publishing language is of this character.

§ 46. We are accustomed to describe law as the supreme power in the State, commanding what is right and prohibiting what is wrong; but this, besides being untrue, does not aid in determining what is a legal right or a legal wrong. So, too, a wrong is correctly enough described, not defined, as an invasion of a right, but unless or until we know what is a right we cannot know when a right has been invaded.

§ 47. If we could catalogue rights and distinguish each by an intelligible and unvarying definition, we should then have no difficulty in ascertaining when a wrong has been done. But the nature of a right forbids any such proceeding. We do indeed find text writers and judges speaking of the right of speech, the rights of the press, and the right of property. Blackstone, and others following him, state that the *absolute natural rights* are the rights of life, liberty and reputation. Text writers also speak of *relative* rights and *tangible* rights, but all these are mere words, entirely illusory, capable of no practical application. The utmost that can be derived from all that has ever been written on this subject is, that a man has *some* rights pertaining to his person, his property and his reputation; the nature of a right is nowhere attempted to be defined or explained, except in the illogical way of stating a rule with a multitude of exceptions, leaving us in doubt as to each particular case which arises whether it comes within the rule or is one of the exceptions.

§ 48. While defining a wrong as an invasion, meaning every

invasion, of a right, text writers have contented themselves
with speaking of the absolute right of property, the absolute
right of reputation, &c.[24]   Now, if the words "*absolute right
of property*" have any meaning, they must mean that one has
such a right to his property that no one may under any circumstances take it from him; and if this be so, and every invasion
of a right be a wrong, it must follow that *every* deprivation of
property is a wrong.   We know this is not true; one may be
deprived of his property in many ways without a wrong being
done.   A man's property may be taken from him directly for
public use on making due compensation, or it may be taken
from him to satisfy his obligations, and it may be indirectly

---

[24] "Rights of persons are divided into *absolute* and *relative.*   1 Ch. Pl. 137.
This classification is recognized by all our elementary writers.   2 *Kent's Com.*
129; 3 *Blacks. Com.* 138." (By the court *Delamater* v. *Russell,* 4 How. Pr. R. 235.)
"The character of individuals is unquestionably one of their absolute and personal rights.   It is therefore unnecessary to make any distinct affirmation that
the protection of it most immediately falls within the common law.   Reputation,
indeed, is not only one of our perfect rights, but that which alone gives a value
to all our other rights." (*Holt on Libel,* p. 15.)   "The security of his reputation
or good name from the arts of detraction and slander are rights to which every ·
man is entitled by reason and natural justice." (1 *Bl. Com.* book 1, ch. 1.)   "The
use of the law consisteth principally in these three things: *   *   *   *
III. For preservation of men's good names from shame and infamy." *Bacon,
The Use of the Law.*   His Lordship says nothing further on the subject in that
essay.

Slander or libel is an infringement of the *absolute* rights of persons. (*Parker
J. Delamater* v. *Russell,* 4 How. Pr. R. 235.)   "Whether reputation be by the
law of nature one of the *absolute* rights of persons or not, the common law of
England does not so consider it.   The law of unwritten slander is incompatible
with it, and in part establishes a different principle.   For it would follow from
that principle, and he evidently means by it, that no man can lawfully say or
publish anything to the disadvantage of another, even though it be true, and he
is prepared to prove its truth." (1 *Mence on Libel,* 132.)   Blackstone and others,
translating *personæ,* person, instead of status or condition, place among the
rights of persons the right to personal security, the reputation, &c., whereas the
right to reputation is among the rights *in rem.   Edinburgh Review,* Oct. 1863, p.
239, Amer. Reprint.   The right which Blackstone styles the right of reputation
is original or innate as opposed to acquired.   This right has no connection with
a natural right in the other sense of the term.   Blackstone has confounded them,
and, supposing the right of reputation to belong to the law of persons, has called
it an absolute right of persons. (2 *Austin's Lect. on Juris.* 268, 476, 3 *id.* 179.)

taken from him in many ways by acts subjecting him to loss, for which the law affords him no remedy. So, too, if the supposed right to reputation be an absolute right, then every invasion of it must be a wrong; but reputation is often invaded without such invasion amounting to "a wrong," hence the inutility for any practical purpose of the definition of a wrong as an invasion of a right. The truth is that a man has the right to the uninterrupted enjoyment of his property to such an extent only, and subject to such conditions, as the general welfare of the community demands, and so of reputation. It must be, therefore, that instead of saying of one he has an *absolute* right to property or reputation, we should say he has a right thus and so, describing it with such limitation and qualification as will make it true that every interference by another with such an enjoyment of it will amount to a wrong. This may be difficult, or it may be impossible; if the latter, as we conceive it to be,[25] let the attempt be abandoned, but it furnishes no reason for describing that as an absolute right which is something else.

§ 49. It is not so proper to say that the law prescribes what is right and prohibits what is wrong as to say that law determines rights by prescribing duties, and independently of any positive enactment all legal duties are comprised in this one prohibition. *No one shall, without a legal excuse, do or forbear any act, by which doing or forbearing there results a breach of the peace, injury to the community, or damage to the person or property of another.*

§ 50. What determines of any given act whether or not it is permitted, *i. e.*, lawful, or unpermitted, *i. e.*, unlawful; whether there is or is not a legal excuse for the doing such act, is the *occasion* upon which it is enacted. The occasion being the entire group of circumstances surrounding the act, including the actor,

---

[25] "The time is passed when ＊ ＊ it was believed that everything was strictly definable, and must be compressed within the narrow limits of an absolute definition before it could be entitled to the dignity of a thorough discussion. The hope of being able absolutely to define things ＊ ＊ betrays a misconception of human language, which itself is never absolute except in mathematics. It misleads." *Lieber's Civil Liberty*, 28.

the patient or person acted upon, the kind of act, the manner
of effecting the act, the motive of the actor, and the consequences of the act. It is the occasion to which we must in
every instance refer to ascertain whether there was or was not
a legal excuse for the act. Everything considered, was the act
lawful or unlawful? was it in exercise of a right or performance
of a duty? As it is manifestly impossible to preconceive or anticipate every possible group of circumstances, so necessarily it
is impossible to catalogue rights and duties—that is, to catalogue the acts which may or may not be done or forborne.

§ 51. The impossibility of framing such a definition of a
right or of a duty as shall enable us to say of any particular act
by itself, that it is lawful or unlawful, is evident. The utmost
we can do is to say that an act done under a certain given state
of circumstances is a permitted act, one the actor *had the right*
to do, or that it is an unpermitted act, one the actor *had not the
right* to do—that is, the doing of which it was his duty to forbear.

§ 52. The law, besides prescribing duties, provides the means
called remedies for protecting rights and redressing wrongs. It
will in some cases interpose by injunction to prevent the perpe-
tration of a wrong, but in no case will an injunction be issued
to stay the publication of an alleged libel.[*]

---

[*] The court of star chamber, which Lord Campbell described as a court of
criminal equity (*Emperor of Austria* v. Day, 7 Jur. N. S. 483), and which description was quoted with approval by Chief Baron Pollock (The Alexandria, MS.), was
in the habit of restraining the publication of certain libels (Hudson's Star Chamber). After the abolition of that court Chief Justice Scroggs, and the other
judges of the King's Bench, prohibited the publication of a periodical called
"The Weekly Packet of Advice from Rome; or, the History of Popery." For
this Scroggs was impeached (8 Howell's State Trials, 198). In *Du Bost* v. *Beresford*, 2 Camp. Rep. 511, Lord Ellenborough said the exhibition of a libelous
painting might be restrained by injunction. That was an *obiter dictum*, and is
said to have excited great astonishment in the minds of all the practitioners in
the courts of equity in England. (Horne's case, 20 Howell's State Trials, 799
note.) In *Burnett* v. *Chetwood*, 2 Merivale's Rep. 441, note, Lord Chancellor
Parker granted an injunction to restrain the publication of a translation of a book
from Latin into English, on the ground that the book in English might have a
hurtful public tendency not likely to occur while the matter remained in Latin.
In *Brandreth* v. *Lance*, 8 Paige, 24, the Chancellor, on demurrer to a bill praying

§ 53. The ordinary mode of remedying a wrong is by an action. Actions were anciently commenced by original writ.[77] These writs differed from each other according to the nature of the wrong to be redressed. These writs were preserved in the Chancery in *The Register of Writs*, which register was printed and published in the reign of Henry VIII. of England.[78] The

---

an injunction to restrain the publication of a libelous pamphlet, dismissed the bill on the ground that the court had no jurisdiction to interfere, no right to "literary or medical property" being invaded; and see *Hoyt* v. *McKenzie*, 3 Barb. Ch. R. 320. In *Clarke* v. *Freeman*, 11 Beavan, 112; 12 Jurist, 149; 17 Law Jour. Rep. Ch. 142, the plaintiff, a physician, applied for an injunction to restrain the defendant from among other things publishing an advertisement so expressed as to raise the inference that certain pills sold by defendant were sold by him on behalf of the plaintiff. The court held the advertisement in question amounted to a libel on the plaintiff, and dismissed the bill; because, to grant the injunction, "would imply that the court has jurisdiction to stay the publication of a libel, and I cannot think it has." This case is questioned in supplement to Drewry on Injunctions, 84, but not on the ground that the court had jurisdiction to restrain the publication of a libel. In deciding *Brandreth* v. *Lance* (*supra*), the Chancellor referred to 2 R. S. 737, s. 1, pt. iv, ch. 11, tit. 6, art. 1. This section confers on courts the power to bind persons to give security to keep the peace in certain cases, and its last clause reads thus: "This section shall not extend to convictions for writing or publishing any libel, nor shall any such security be hereafter required, by any court upon any complaint, prosecution, or conviction for any such writing or publishing." The revisers, in their note to that section, say, in reference to the above-recited clause, that it is *new*, and "it is conceived that this provision virtually takes away from the courts the common law power of binding over a party guilty of publishing a libel." As to the common law power of binding to good behavior, see Hawkins' Pleas Cr., ch. 61, and Viner's Abridgment, tit.—Good Behaviour; Highmore on Bail, 248. By Laws of 1860, ch. 508, § 20, p. 1007, every person in the city of New York shall be deemed guilty of disorderly conduct "who shall use any threatening, abusive, or insulting behavior with intent to provoke a breach of the peace." The courts interfere by injunction to restrain the publication of letters written by a party or his testator to the defendant or others. (2 Story Eq. Juris. §§ 948 to 949; *Woolsey* v. *Judd*, 11 How. Prac. Rep. 49; 4 Duer, 379.) See Appendix, note 1.

[77] One of the earliest refinements in forensic science was that of classifying the various subjects of litigation and allotting to each class an appropriate *formula* of complaint or claim. Such was the practice in ancient Rome almost as early as the law of the twelve tables, and continued until the time of Constantine, who abolished the judicial formulæ. These formulæ in the English law were called *writs*. How, or when, or whence introduced into England is undetermined. Stephens' Pl. ch. 1, and *id.* appendix, note 2.

[78] 4 Reeve's Hist. 426, 432. Original writs were abolished in England by statute. 2 Will. IV., ch. 39.

most ancient writs provided for the most obvious kinds of wrongs, as nuisance, waste, trespass, &c.; but in the progress of society it seems that cases of injury arose new in their circumstances, and not within any of the writs then known, and that the power to issue writs of a new kind was conceived not to exist without the authority of the Parliament; accordingly by the statute of the 13 Edward I., ch. 24, called the statute of Westminster the 2d (say A. D. 1285), it was provided "That as often as it shall happen in the chancery, that in one case a writ is found, and *in a like case* (*in consimilu casu*) falling under the same right, and requiring like remedy, no writ is to be found, the clerks in the chancery shall agree in making a writ," &c. Under the sanction of this act large accessions were made to the existing stock of original writs.[20] These new writs were said to be issued upon *the case*, and the actions commenced by them were designated *actions upon the case*, or *actions of trespass on the case*. Among this class was the action of *trespass on the case for words*—the ancient form of the action—now known as the action of slander or libel, and which is the only *civil* remedy for slander and libel.

§ 54. The consideration of the course of procedure in an action pertains more properly to a subsequent stage of our inquiry. We will here merely remark that the rules by which we determine when a wrong has been committed and the rules of pleading, of evidence and of practice, although they have a certain inter-dependence, are in fact, and, if we would avoid confusion, must ever be regarded as separate and distinct rules. Preliminary to attempting an analysis of the wrongs, slander and libel, we shall in our next chapter consider what is the gist of the action for slander or libel.

---

[20] Although the new writs were to be framed only *in consimilu casu*, "many writs were framed for various kinds of trespasses unknown in former ages." Sullivan's Lectures, Lect. 38; Stephens' Pl. 7. The first reported action of trespass on the case is said to be found 22 Edw. III., Ass. 41. Reeve's Hist. That would be A. D. 1349. We have not verified this statement, and doubt its correctness. The action on the case has its counterpart in the *actio utilis* of the Roman Law. See 2 Austin Lect. Jur. 303.

CHAPTER IV.

WHAT IS THE GIST OF THE ACTION FOR SLANDER OR LIBEL.

History Silent as to the Introduction of the Action for Slander.
Hypothesis Necessary. How the Law Protects Reputation.
Fiction. Pecuniary Loss the Gist of the Actions for Slan-
der and Libel.

§ 55. It is not known with certainty, or, rather, all are not
agreed, either as to the origin of the remedy by action for slan
der or libel, or as to the gist of such an action, and neither
history nor judicial decision furnishes any satisfactory solution
of these doubts. We know, indeed, that all nations have recognized the capacity for injury inherent in language, and have
provided some means for punishing offences arising from an
abuse of the gift of speech; but we seek in vain among these
laws for a clew to the principles by which at this day we may
determine when a wrong by slander or libel has been occasioned,
and when we may properly invoke the remedy, by action for
slander or libel.[30] As the action of trespass on the case owed

---

[30] After a reference to all available authorities on the subject of the ancient
laws against offences by language, and preparing a lengthy note on the subject,
we conclude that however interesting as history, its publication here would not
advance the object of this essay. The curious student may refer to Holt on
Libel, ch. 1, II.; 1 Mence on Libel, ch. 8, 9; Starkie on Slander, note 3 Johns.
Cas. 382; Wilkins' Leg. Anglo-Sax.; Lambard's Saxon Laws; Nicholson's Pre-
fat. ad Leg. Anglo-Sax.; Stiernhook De Jure Vetusto Suconum et Gothorum;
Tacitus' De Mor. Germ.; Saltern De Antiq. Leg. Brit.; Dugdale's Origines Ju-
ridicales; Disney's Ancient Laws against Immoralities; Gurdon's History of
Court Baron and Court Lect.; Petit's Leges Atticæ; Johnson's Institutes of the
Civil Law of Spain; Michaelis' Com. on the Law of Moses; Smith's Translation;
The English Statutes, 8 Edw. I.; 2 Rich. II.; 1 Phil. and Mary; 1 Eliz.; the
publications of the English Record Commissioners; Pitcairn's Criminal Trials in
Scotland. For seventeenth century ideas of the law of libel in Massachusetts,
see Sketches of the Judicial History of Massachusetts; and among the Dutch in

4

its origin to the provisions of the statute, 13 Edward I., A. D. 1285, it seems necessarily to follow that the action of trespass on the case for words must date its origin at some period subsequent to that statute;[31] but it does not thence follow that anterior to the introduction of the action of trespass on the case for words, there existed in England no remedy for wrongs by language. We know that for centuries prior to the statute of 13 Edward I., offences which we at this day designate slander and libel were recognized and punished; but of the time and manner of introducing the remedy by action of trespass on the case for words we know absolutely nothing. The reported decisions in the courts of law in England, printed and in manuscript, reach back at least as far as A. D. 1216, but we find in those reports no reference to an action for words earlier than A. D. 1321.[32] That decision merely serves to inform us that at that time existed the struggle for jurisdiction which probably commenced on the division of the courts into courts temporal and courts ecclesiastical, and which continued certainly until after the reign of the first James of England.

§ 56. Since, then, we can obtain no positive information on the subject of our inquiry, we are driven to hypothesis. Our *unwritten* law is based on the so-called common law of England,

---

New York, see Valentine's Manual of Common Council for 1849, p. 402, 421, and under English rule; Valentine's Manual for 1847, p. 359; and Thomas' Hist. of Printing in America. And see List of Authors following Table of Cases, ante.

[31] Section 53, ante and note 29, ante, Mr. Pomeroy, in his Introduction to Municipal Law, says, § 199: That before the statute "there was absolutely no provision for a vast majority of the legal rights * * which are now the most common and important." And § 201: The effect of the statute "was to extend this action to cases where the injury was *consequential* or indirect."

[32] That case is in the year book of Edward II. (Hil. 14, Edw. II., p. 416); it was an attachment upon a prohibition against proceeding in a court Christian for defamatory words. There is nothing in the report to indicate that it was a novel proceeding. *March*, in his Treatise on Slander, says he could find no action for scandalous words before Edward the Third's time, and only one such action during fifty years of that King's reign; three such actions during the reign of Edward the Fourth; not one in the reign of Henry the Seventh; and only five in thirty-eight years of the reign of Henry the Eighth. At p. 5 he says: Actions for scandal are amongst the most ancient in the law.

and whatever the number of sources which contributed to make up that complex, vaguely understood and imperfectly ascertained set of legal ideas denominated the common law of England, it is certain that so much of it as pertains to the rights of persons is mainly derived from the Anglo-Saxon and Roman civil laws. Of both of those systems of laws history furnishes us ample details. We know that Rome held possession of Britain from about the end of the first half century of the Christian era to about the middle of the fifth century (say from A. D. 45 to A. D. 448), and during this period Roman civil law was administered in England. When the Romans abandoned Britain the Saxons became its masters, and, alternately with the Danes, so continued until the Norman conquest (A. D. 1066). The Saxons introduced their own system of laws. The controlling idea of those laws was the maintenance of the peace and protecting the person and property. They did not, nor does the law at this day, give *directly* any remedy for outraged feelings or sentiments.[83] With few exceptions, these laws de-

---

[83] See *Tilley* v. *Hudson R. R. Co.*, 28 How. 369, 370; *Green* v. *Hudson R. R. Co.*, 32 Barb. 25; *Lehman* v. *City of Brooklyn*, 29 Barb. 234; *Flemington* v. *Smithers*, 2 C. & P. (N. P.)292; *Terwilliger* v. *Wands*, 17 N. Y. 54; *Wilson* v. *Goit*, 17 N. Y. 442; *Bedell* v. *Powell*, 13 Barb. 183; the cases to the contrary were overruled. Mence, commenting on the statement of Holt, that the few actions for slander to be found in the earlier law reports was creditable to the people of those times, remarks that the credit was not due to the good manners but to the fact that "the common law took cognizance only of injuries to the person and property." (1 Mence on Libel, 333.) Perhaps among the reasons why there were so few actions for slander, one may be that the parties themselves undertook to redress the injury without resorting to the law. When King Harold wanted a blood-fine of Reidar, the Icelander, for killing one of his (Harold's) followers, Reidar refused to pay it, because the man brought his death upon himself, by behaving rudely to him. See Den Danske Erobring of England og Normandict; Copenhagen, 1863. The Jesuits sanctioned killing for slander, particularly for slander of one in religious orders, but they held that the killing should be secret, and not open to create scandal. (Pascal Letters, xiii.) In the "Ethica Christiana," by Father Benedict Stattler, published in 1789, it is stated, paragraphs 1889, 1891, and 1892, that a Christian may, to prevent a "contumelia gravis certo provisa * * * * aut calumnia" * * * * murder the "injusti aggresoris aut calumniatoris." Father Stattler's book was published "cum permissu superiorum," and is said to be still in use as a manual for ecclesiastics.

The necessity of protecting character by law could not obtrude itself till so-

signed to remedy every wrong by a pecuniary mulct or fine
(*were*)[M] proportioned and adjusted to the kind and degree of the
wrong committed. In that form of trial which corresponded to
our present jury trial, the question in Saxon times was only the
guilt or innocence of the accused.[M] The penalty (the damages) was fixed by the codes. At a later period, after the Norman Invasion, and when the Anglo-Saxon codes were lost by
desuetude, the courts fixed the amount of damages; this power,
however, when jury trials assumed their present phase, appears
to have been transferred by the court to the jury—the court,
however, retaining its power to regulate the damages.[M] For
ages the courts always regularly revised the allowance by the
jury of damages, and the power is still held and exercised by
the courts, although at the present time it is customary to make
the revision by granting a new trial. Even now the courts not
unfrequently order a reduction of damages, or a new trial, at
the election of the party to whom damages have been awarded.
The Anglo-Saxon[57] codes provide for offences occasioned by

ciety had begun to assume a complicated form. (Borthwick on Libel, 1.) The
coarseness of language indulged in formerly must strike every student of history.
Henry III. (A. D. 1248) spoke of the Aldermen of London as "London boors,"
applied a like epithet to the Bishop of Ely, and dismissed Bishop Aymer by telling him to go to the devil. See Miracles of Simon de Montfort and works of
Roger Bacon. See note 48, post.

[M] Damages correspond to the *Anglo-Saxon were:* 1 Palgrave's Rise, &c.,
Eng. Commonwealth, 205; Bosworth's Anglo-Saxon Dict., tit. *Were* and *Wite*; 2
Lappenburg's History of England (Thorp's Translation), 336.

[M] As to the origin of trial by jury, &c., see Forsyth's Hist. of Trial by Jury.
and Stephen Pl. Appendix, note 40; 2 Reeves' Hist. 270; Fortescue de Laudibus
Legum Angliæ, ch. xxv., xxvi., xxvii., and notes to the edition by Amos; 2 Hallam's Middle Ages, 388–406, note, 11th edit.; Palgrave's English Commonwealth, 272.

[M] See Viner's Abr., tit. Damages—J. K. L. M., as to powers of courts to increase or mitigate damages. The right was denied in an action for slander, because there is in such an action nothing apparent for the judgment of the court
to act upon. *Id.* K. The damages increased for giving plaintiff bad food to eat.
(1 Rolle, 89.) And in cases of maihem. See Jacobs' Law Dict., tit. Maihem. Rolle
Ab., tit. Damages; 2 Sharswood's Blackstone's Comm., 121 *note.*

[57] Sir Francis Palgrave, in his "History of Normandy and of England," which
unhappily he was not spared to complete, objects to the term *Anglo-Saxon* as a

language, but they are all offences which amount to public wrongs or crimes, sedition, or treason, rather than private wrongs or torts. These codes are in fact barren of any provision of a pecuniary fine or penalty for a private injury by language. While the Saxons were yet dominant in Britain, Christianity, which had been early introduced into England and become extinct, was reintroduced through the Church of Rome —say A. D. 596. The introduction of Christianity did not abrogate the Saxon laws, but it at least supplemented upon them many precepts of Christianity, and, beyond a doubt, laid the foundation for the dicta that Christianity is part of the common law of England.[38] The clergy rose to great power in the

---

designation of the English of the ante-Norman period. He denies there was any Anglo-Saxon people or language, properly so called, and says: "If you had asked Alfred what he had in his hand, he would have answered it was an *Englisc-boc*. * * * The name of our nation then, as now, was English." (Vol. iii., p. 631, edit. 1864.) Mr. Palgrave himself employs the term *Anglo-Saxon* in his earlier works.

[38] We do not intend to assert that Christianity *is* parcel of the English common law. Sir Matthew Hale, in *Rex* v. *Taylor* (Ventris, 293; 3 Keble, 621; Tremayne's Pleas of the Crown, 226;) following Lord Coke, uttered a dictum that "Christianity is part of the laws of England." That dictum has been repeated in subsequent cases. See, among others, *Rex* v. *Webster*, Fitzg. 64; 2 Str. 834; *Reg.* v. *Gathercole*, 2 Lewin C. C. 237; *Reg.* v. *Hetherington*, 5 Jur. 529, Q. B.; *Rex* v. *Paine*, 1 East P. C. 5; and Lewis on Authority in Matters of Opinion. Holt says Alfred made Christianity part and parcel of the common law. (Holt on Libel, 32.) See strictures on this dictum, 1 Mence on Libel, 303. We are informed that Jefferson has shown the fallacy of the dictum, but we have not verified this information.

The Dome-Book of Alfred, said by Blackstone to have been extant so late as the reign of King Edward the Fourth, and to have been lost, was supposed by both Hallam and Turner never to have existed. It has since been published by the Record Commissioners, vol. 1, pp. 45-101. It commences with the ten commandments, followed by many Mosaic precepts. After quoting the canons of the Apostolical council at Jerusalem, Alfred refers to the command, "As ye would that men should do unto you, do ye also to them;" adding, "from this one doom, a man may remember that he judge every one righteously he need heed no other doom book."

The Puritan Colony of New England resolved at a "General Court, October 25th, 1639 * * * the worde of God shall be the onely rule to be attended vnto in ordering the affayres of government in this plantatio."

State, they sat in the courts of justice, and took part in the decision of all judicial controversies, and they claimed and exercised a sole jurisdiction over all questions involving considerations of moral right and wrong (*sins*), rather than considerations of legal rights or rights of property ; those rights in fact
which were provided for by the letter of the laws.   The jurisdiction thus claimed and exercised included heresy, adultery,
perjury, and defamation.   This jurisdiction was assumed and
exercised with the avowed design not of compensating the injured party, but for the reformation of the offender.   Reparation
in damages was made only in the cases and for the offences
provided for in the codes.   In the exercise of their powers the
clergy adopted—at least to some extent—the forms of procedure in use in the Roman law.

On the Norman accession William introduced the feudal
system, but professed to respect and continue in force the Saxon
laws.   He separated the courts into courts of different jurisdictions, the clergy no longer sat in the temporal courts, but apart
in courts Christian or Ecclesiastical.   It would seem they were
debarred the exercise of any jurisdiction in controversies in
which money or damages were claimed.   The line of demarcation between the jurisdiction of the temporal and ecclesiastical
courts appears to have been that, where compensation was
sought, resort was to be had to the temporal courts, and where
the reformation of the offender only was desired, then resort
was to be had to the ecclesiastical courts.   And where the
ecclesiastical courts entertained jurisdiction of suits in which
money might be demanded, the temporal courts restrained them
from proceeding therein by the writ of prohibition.   As there
is now, so there must ever have been, a distinction between
language occasioning pecuniary or temporal injury and language
insulting and provoking, and harrowing to the feelings, without
occasioning pecuniary or temporal injury.   This distinction
seems to have been clearly recognized by the statute *circum-
specte agatis*,[20] and leads almost irresistibly to the conclusion

---

[20] The statute thus styled was passed 13 Edward I., stat. iv., ch. 1, A. D. 1285.
The King to his justices sendeth greeting: "Use yourselves circumspectly (*cir-*

that the gist of the action of trespass on the case for words was the pecuniary loss, and not for the injury to the reputation—the defamation. In the early stages of society only that language which put one in peril of punishment, loss of inheritance or of social companionship, could occasion pecuniary loss;[40] but as society progresses, as more faith and reliance have to be placed by men each in the integrity of the other, so increases the power to inflict pecuniary injury by means of language. The theory of the law being to redress all wrongs by a pecuniary fine, whenever it appeared that a pecuniary wrong was occasioned by language, there the temporal courts undertook to afford redress. It may be that at first, in all cases, in order to maintain an action for words in the temporal courts, it was

---

cumspecte agatis) in all matters concerning the Bishop of Norwich and his clergy, not punishing them if they hold pleas in courts Christian of such things as be *meer* spiritual * * * and for laying violent hands on a clerk, and in canons of defamation *it hath been granted already* that it shall be tried in a spiritual court when money is not demanded but a thing done for punishment of sin." By this it appears, said Lord Coke, that the cognizance of defamation was granted by act of Parliament. (2 Inst. 492.) See Appendix D, No. 11, to Ecclesiastical Comm'rs Report, Feb. 27, 1832; and Stephens' Ecclesiastical Statutes, pp. 26–34. The statute 9 Edward II., stat. 1, ch. iv., A. D. 1315, enacted: "In defamation prelates shall correct also in manner above said, the King's prohibition notwithstanding."

It seems of those *defamations* by which the party is *damnified* the spiritual court cannot hold plea. Vin. Ab., tit. Prohibition, D. 5. In Bacon's Abr., tit. Courts Ecclesiastical D, it is said: "No suit can be instituted in an ecclesiastical court for defamatory words in writing, because they may be the subject of an action at law." Comb. 71. This, however, appears not to be correct. In *Ware* v. *Johnson*, 2 Sir Geo. Lee's Cas. in Eccl. Co'ts, 108 (A. D. 1755), the words, "He keeps a whore in his house," was held to be defamation, and that whether the language was in writing or by parol. And see 2 Phil. Eccl. Cas. 106.

The jurisdiction of Ecclesiastical Courts in suits for defamation was abolished by statute. (18 and 19 Vict., ch. 40.)

[40] It is said that formerly no actions were brought for words unless the slander was such as, if true, would endanger the life of the object of it. (Noy, 64; 1 Freem. 277.) But too great an encouragement being given by this lenity to false and malicious slanders, it is now held that for scandalous words of the species before mentioned (that may endanger a man by subjecting him to the penalties of the law, may exclude him from society, may impair his trade, or may affect a peer of the realm, a magistrate, or one in public trust), an action on the case may be had without proving any particular damage to have happened, but merely upon the probability that it might happen. 3 Bl. Com. ch. 8.

necessary to prove a pecuniary loss; but those courts, by laying it down as a rule of evidence that certain words *per se*, and, without any further evidence, were proof of pecuniary loss, facilitated a resort to the temporal courts, and by gradually extending the list of words which were regarded *per se* as evidence of pecuniary loss, so did those courts extend their jurisdiction. Thus, probably, originated the distinction between words actionable *per se* and words only actionable on proof by other evidence than the words themselves of pecuniary loss. It is supposed that formerly the English law recognized no distinction between the effect of written and spoken words. When or why that distinction was introduced is unknown. It may well be that the desire of the temporal courts to enlarge their jurisdiction led them to adopt this distinction, for which they found some warrant in the Roman law.[41]

§ 57. We attempted to explain in Chapter II. the difference between an injury to reputation and an injury to property; and to show that an injury to the reputation did not necessarily imply an injury to the person or property. In Chapter III. we attempted to show that reputation was not an *absolute right*, and in the preceding portion of this chapter we have attempted to show that the temporal courts of common law only recognized injuries involving pecuniary or temporal loss. It nowhere appears that the temporal courts recognized any right to reputation, and it is entirely consistent with all our knowledge of the law to assert that *in theory* at least the temporal courts of England never did, and, as the law in this respect has not been changed, they do not now recognize reputation as a right which the law protects. And if this be so in England, then is it so in the United States. When we consider that "falsely and maliciously to impute, in the coarsest terms and on the most public occasion, want of chastity to a woman of high sta-

---

[41] See note 14, ante. Daniel O'Connell, in 1834, proposed a bill in the English Parliament intended, amongst other things, to assimilate libel to slander as to what language should give a right of action. See this Bill commented upon, XI London Law Mag. 432.

tion and unspotted character, or want of veracity or courage to a gentleman of undoubted honesty and honor, cannot be made the foundation of any proceeding civil or criminal; whereas an action may be maintained for saying that a cobbler is unskillful in mending shoes, or that any one has held up his hand in a threatening posture to another,"[42] it would seem to need nothing more to satisfy the most skeptical that the protection is to the property and not to the reputation. We conclude, therefore, to state as law, that pecuniary loss to the plaintiff is the gist of the action for slander or libel. If the language published has not occasioned the plaintiff pecuniary loss (actual or implied), then no action can be maintained.[43] Let us not be misunder-

---

[42] Report of Committee of House of Lords on Defamation and Libel, July, 1843.

[43] In a note to the "Preliminary Discourse" to the American edition of Starkie on Slander, after referring to the Roman law as making *personal contumely and insult* the essence of the offence of slander, adds: "This, it will be seen, is a circumstance which constitutes a very essential and characteristic distinction between the law of England and that of Rome, and of those countries which have adopted the civil law; * * * for the law of England has from very distant times considered the *temporal injury* to a man's estate and not the contumely or insult of the agent as the ground of compelling reparation in damages." Prelim. Disc. vii. "There must be some certain or probable temporal loss or damage to make words actionable;" this was said of *oral* words by De Grey, C. J., in *Onslow* v. *Horne*, 8 Wils. 177, and this was approved by Lawrence, J., in *Holt* v. *Scholefield*, 6 T. R. 691. And per Bayley, J., in *Whittaker* v. *Bradley*, 7 D. & R. 649: "The principle on which this species of action (action for saying orally plaintiff, an innkeeper, was a bankrupt) is, that the slander has the effect of producing *temporal* damage to the party complaining." To maintain the action there must be *injury* to the plaintiff. Ellenborough, Ch. J., *Maitland* v. *Goldney*, 2 East, 426. An action on the case is not maintainable in any case without showing especial prejudice. *Lowe* v. *Harwood*, Cro. Car. 140 S. C.; Palmer, 529; Ley, 62.

Reputation or fame is under the protection of the law, because all persons have an interest in their good name, and scandal and defamation are injurious to it, though defamatory words are not actionable otherwise than as they are a damage to the estate of the person injured. Wood's Ins. 37; Jacob's Law Dict., voce Reputation or Fame.

"In England, by the common law, defamatory words are not actionable, otherwise than as they are a damage to the estate of the person injured." Wood's Civil Law, 244, note. "I am not certain," says Lord Kames, "that in England any verbal injury is actionable except such as may be attended with pecuniary

stood. We concede all that can be urged as to the value of a
"*good reputation.*" We believe, like Lord Bacon, that "men's
reputations are tender things, and ought to be like Christ's coat,
without seam."[44] We do not intend to deny that the law does
in fact, and to a great extent, protect reputation, but we intend
to be understood as insisting that where the law does protect
reputation it does so indirectly by means of a fiction—an assumption of pecuniary loss. In theory, the action for slander
or libel is always for the pecuniary injury and not for the in-

---

loss or damage. *If not we in Scotland are more delicate.* Scandal, or any imputation
upon a man's good name, may be sued before the commissaries, even when the
scandal is of such a nature that it cannot be the occasion of any pecuniary loss.
It is sufficient to say, I am hurt in my character." *Historical Law Tracts,* p. 225.

"The party injured [by libel] may no doubt bring an action on the case. This
process, however, is not competent unless it is grounded on an actual loss, which
must be shown to have been sustained." Borthwick on Libel, 4. In
Boldroe v. *Porter,* Yelv. 20, the declaration alleged *per quod* the plaintiff was
in danger to lose her goods and life. In Edward's Case, Cro. Eliz. 6, held the
charge actionable, and assigned as the reason that "*by such speech the plaintiff's
good name is impaired.*" In *Button* v. *Heywood,* 8 Mod. 24, Fortescue, J., observed:
"It was the rule of Holt, Ch. J., to make words actionable whenever they sound
to the *disreputation of the person* of whom they were spoken, and this was also
Hale's and Twisden's rule, and I think it a very good rule."

"I will cite rights to forbearances merely. A man's right or interest in his
good name is a right which avails against persons as considered generally and in-
determinately. They are bound to forbear from such imputations against him as
would amount to injuries towards his right in his reputation. But though the
right is a *real* right, there is no subject, thing, or person over which it can be said
to exist. If the right has any subject, its subject consists of the contingent ad-
vantages which he may possibly derive from the approbation of others. 2 Austin's Lect. Juris., 51. Right to reputation may be classed with property. It is a
right to the chance of the favorable opinion and the good offices of others. There
is no obligation to do me good, but an obligation to forbear from lessening the
chance of deriving good from voluntary service, &c. 2 *id.* 479, and 3 *id.* 179,
184.

[44] Lord Bacon's Charge against Lumsden. Good reputation has ever been, as
it is now, of great value as a shield against imputation of crime; by a law of William the Conqueror, if a man of good reputation was charged with theft, he might
clear himself by his single oath. Leges Gul. Conq. 14, in the Ancient Laws and
Institutes published by the English Record Commissioners. See Anthon's Law
Student, Thesis x.: Character, how far a Universal Shield. Also, McNally's
Crim. Ed. 573.

jury to the reputation. There are many such fictions introduced into the administration of the law, by means of which, without changing the rule of law, the law is, in effect, changed.[45] When this is the case this difficulty arises: Shall the rule be stated as it is in theory or as it is in effect? and then this further difficulty, that these two phases of the same rule are sometimes stated as two distinct rules, and the rule being stated sometimes one way and sometimes the other creates confusion and apparent contradiction. It may be that practically it is the same thing whether the remedy is given by law for the injury to the reputation or for the pecuniary injury by means of an attack on the reputation; but in reasoning on this, as on any other subject, it makes all the difference whether we start with the true principle or a false one. With a false premise we *may* arrive at a conclusion which is true, but we can never, under such circumstances, be sure that our conclusion is true.

§ 58. Among the fictions referred to in the last preceding section, perhaps the most noticeable, and the one which best illustrates our meaning, is that by which more than nominal damages are recovered by a parent for the seduction of a daughter. At the present day no lawyer doubts that at common law no action could be maintained for the seduction of a daughter, merely as a daughter, nor merely for the seduction. But at common law, to deprive one of the services of his hired servant gave a cause of action, because it occasioned a pecuniary injury. The common law gave a parent a right to the services of his minor children; then, in order to afford a remedy for seduction, which was not contemplated by the common law, the daughter is styled servant, and the remedy is given in theory, not for the grief and shame of the seduction, but because by means of the seduction the servant was the less able to perform the services required of her, and the parent thereby sustained a pecuniary loss.[46] This was the first step; and where

---

[45] See Maine, Ancient Law, 26.

[46] There can be no doubt that the law is as above stated (*Knight* v. *Wilcox*, 14 N. Y. 413); and yet it is but candid to say that there are dicta to the effect that

the daughter was in fact one of the parent's household, the change from the *status* of daughter to servant was easy enough. The next step was where the infant daughter was not in fact one of the parent's household, but was in the service of another, by her own contract, and not by the contract of the parent; then the action was allowed on these grounds: the daughter, being an infant, could not lawfully contract for her services, therefore the parent could at will rescind the contract and take the daughter to the parental service; but if the parent did so, the servant would be less efficient, and so a pecuniary injury might or did result. The next and final step thus far is, that where the infant daughter was by the contract of the parent the servant of another, still the action can ,be maintained if the seducer by his fraud had procured the making of the contract, and this on the ground that the fraud vitiated the contract and leaves the parent an option to reclaim the daughter's services.[47]

§ 59. By similar processes to those detailed in the last preceding section it has come to pass that the remedy for injuries by language, in theory given only to redress a pecuniary loss, is now applied to and embraces cases in which no pecuniary loss is or can be shown to have occurred. The process by which this result has been arrived at is by adopting the rule of evidence above referred to (§ 56), that certain language is *per se*, and without other evidence, conclusive proof of pecuniary loss; this, however, is only a rule of evidence, and the rule of right remains intact—that a pecuniary loss must be shown to entitle to a remedy. That the rule is so is demonstrated by the case of

---

the mortification and disgrace and wounded feelings constitute the *gravamen* of the action. See *Badgley* v. *Decker*, 44 Barb. 577, and cases there cited.

[47] See *Lipe* v. *Eisenlerd*, 32 N. Y. 229; *White* v. *Nellis*, 31 N. Y. 405; *Dain* v. *Wyckoff*, 18 N. Y. 45; S. C. 7 N. Y. 191; *Mulvehall* v. *Milward*, 11 N. Y. 343; *Bartley* v. *Richtmeyer*, 4 N. Y. 38; *Knight* v. *Wilcox*, 14 N. Y. 413; *Harper* v. *Luffkin*, 7 B. & C. 387; 1 M. & R. 166. This last case is a noticeable instance of how far courts will in effect depart from the rule of law while they uphold it in the letter.

words to which the rule of evidence just referred to does not apply, or to words which are said not to be actionable *per se*, that is, which are not *per se* evidence of pecuniary loss. As to these, it has never been doubted that a pecuniary loss must be shown to entitle the plaintiff to a remedy.[48]

---

[48] *Beach* v. *Ranney*, 2 Hill, 809 ; *Herrick* v. *Lapham*, 10 Johns. 291 ; *Hallock* v. *Miller*, 2 Barb. 630 ; *Hersh* v. *Ringwalt*, 3 Yeates, 508. "The real foundation of the action [for libel] is the right to recover pecuniary satisfaction." (*Viele* v. *Gray*, 10 Abb. Pr. R. 7.) The special damage must be of a pecuniary nature. (*Beach* v. *Ranney*, 2 Hill, 809.) And see note, 33 ante.

CHAPTER V.

Wrongful Acts. Liability. Presumptions of Law. Questions of Law and Fact. Essential Acts in Slander and Libel. Defamatory. Falsity. Voluntary. Involuntary. Intention. Malice.

§ 60. Although we are unable to predicate of any act *per se* whether or not it is *a wrong* (§ 51), we may, at least as to some acts, determine of them *per se* whether or not they are *wrongful.*

§ 61. An act is wrongful which as a necessary or as a natural and proximate consequence occasions hurt of body or pecuniary loss to another than the actor. When the necessary consequences of the act *must* be hurt of body or pecuniary loss, then the act is patently wrongful, or wrongful *per se.* When the act is one the consequences of which are not necessarily hurtful to the person or property of another, but is an act the natural and proximate consequences of which *may* occasion hurt to the person or property of another, then it is latently wrongful. It is wrongful provided that as a natural and proximate consequence there ensues personal hurt or pecuniary loss to another. One and the same act may occasion harm to the person and loss of property of another, and either by its necessary or its natural and proximate consequences, or both. It is not always easy to determine what are necessary and natural and proximate consequences, and to distinguish them from those which are not necessary, not natural, or not proximate (*remote*) consequences. The rules for making this determination and distinction will be hereafter considered. We have here but to remark that the necessary, natural, and proximate consequences of an act are those of which alone the law takes cognizance, and these it is which constitute in legal phraseology damage or injury. Any consequence which is neither necessary nor natural and proximate is disregarded in law.

§ 62. No act, but a wrongful act, can become a wrong; but every wrongful act, in the absence of any excuse for it being shown, is *prima facie* a wrong. It is a wrong provisionally or conditionally; that is to say, it is regarded for *all purposes* as a wrong, unless and until a legal excuse for the doing it is shown. That which does not exist and that which is not shown to exist are the same. A legal excuse not shown to exist is the same as though no legal excuse existed. The burden of showing the existence of a legal excuse or a defence is always upon the doer of the wrongful act.

§ 63. Anything which must be shown to establish a legal excuse or a defence is no part of the essential element of a wrong. In practice, to entitle to a remedy, it is required only to show a wrongful act done, and nothing more appearing, the right to the remedy follows as of course. Reason and expediency alike demand that in this respect the theory should correspond to the practice.

§ 64. Legal excuses are of two kinds—such as constitute an absolute bar or defence to the act, or lsuch as constitute a conditional defence. A legal excuse of the latter kind is a defence, until some additional fact is shown which takes from it the character of a legal excuse. The legal excuse that the language was spoken by a judge as such, or by a witness as such, is of the first or absolute kind. The legal excuse that the language was published to one who was interested to know it and with a belief that it was true is a legal excuse of the second or qualified kind. The excuse exists only provided it does not appear that the language was published not believing it to be true, or published to one not interested to know it.

§ 65. There is this distinction between *legal excuse* and defence. Legal excuse is such a state of facts as prevents a wrong-

ful act amounting to a wrong. Defence includes legal excuse
and more; namely, those cases in which the wrong is admitted
to have been done, but where, from some circumstance, such as
the statute of limitations, or satisfaction, or in the action for
libel the truth of the language published, the plaintiff has forfeited or waived his right of action.

§ 66. The question what constitutes a wrong or when has a
wrong been committed, and the question who is liable therefor,
are essentially distinct questions, and to be determined by different rules.

§ 67. As regards liability, no one is responsible for involuntary acts,[49] nor for any other than *wrongful* acts (§ 62). All
who without legal excuse concur in a wrongful act are alike
liable either jointly or separately. No one can excuse his con-
currence in a wrongful act merely on the ground that in what
he did he acted as agent for another.[50] It sometimes happens

---

[49] A man must will an act before he can be responsible for it. (Wood's Civil
Law, 18.) No action lies for an inevitable accident. (*Harvey* v. *Dunlop*, Hill &
Denio, Sup. 193; see *Center* v. *Finney*, 17 Barb. 94, affirmed 2 Selden's notes, 44.)
No man is liable civilly or criminally for a purely accidental mischief; that is
to say, for the consequences of an act not his own which he was unable to foresee,
or, foreseeing, was unable to prevent. (2 Austin's Lect. Juris. 165, 167.) The
act must be intentionally done; the meaning of which is, that the defendant
should know what he published, for, as in the case put by Starkie, if a servant
should deliver a sealed letter containing the defamatory matter without knowing
its contents, he would not, though the actual instrument of publication, be liable
to an action. (Daly, F. J., *Viele* v. *Gray*, 10 Abb. Pr. R. 7; 18 How. Pr. R. 550.) If
published inadvertently it would not be a libel. (*Rex* v. *Abingdon*, 1 Esp. Cas.
228.) Being the sale of a few copies of a periodical journal containing the libel,
it was for the jury to say if the defendants were cognizant of what they sold.
(*Chubb* v. *Flannagan*, 6 C. & P. 431.) Since intention and will are essential to
every act, and intention, will, and malice to every crime, the absence of any intention or will will prevent any occurrence from being an action, and the absence
of malice * * * will prevent any action from being a crime. (Stephen
Crim. Law, 85.)

[50] If a person does an act with a guilty intent, he is not the agent of any one.
If he does it innocently, he is the agent of some person or persons, and if two have
agreed to employ him, he is the agent of both. Alderson B., *Reg.* v. *Bull*, 7 Law
Times (London), 8.

that those who are in nowise concerned in the actual doing of a wrongful act, or a wrong, are nevertheless liable therefor; this, be it observed, is *not on account of any presumed connection with the act*, but because under the circumstances they are legally responsible for the acts of the actual wrongdoers.[51] It may also occur that the one who actually does the act may not be liable, while for that same act another may be liable.[52]

§ 68. The proposition that one is liable for his wrongful act implies, in terms, liability for the necessary, natural, and proximate consequences of the act. This leaves no room for any question as to the intent with which the act is done. There may or may not be any intent, good or bad; but intent or no intent, the liability is for the act and its consequences, not for the intent. Intent without an act cannot constitute a wrong. The liability may be avoided only by showing some defence. Showing the act to have been done with a good intent would not be a defence. The consequences of an act are incidents to the act and inseparable from the act. Liability for the one is inseparable from liability for the other. The usual ground upon which this liability for the consequences of an act is placed is, that the law presumes every one to intend the necessary and natural consequences of his acts.[53] We object to the phrase, *the law presumes.* The law does not presume.[54] We know it is customary to say that the law presumes every one inno-

---

[51] See *post*, Publisher.

[52] See *ante*, note 49, and *post*, Publisher.

[53] The law presumes a party to intend the injury his acts are calculated to produce. (*Haire* v. *Wilson*, 9 B. & Cr. 643; *Viele* v. *Gray*, 10 Abb. Pr. R. 7, and series of dicta.) A man is as much answerable for the probable consequences of his act as for the actual object. (*Rex* v. *Moore*, 3 B. & A. 194.)

[54] We are not unmindful of the fact that the books are full of such expressions as the law presumes, presumption of law, &c. But the phrase is objectionable and should be reformed. Burrill says the presumption is rather an assumption. (Presump. Ev. 10, 43; and see 6 Lond. Law Mag., 354.) The inference, for it is absurd to call it a presumption. (Stephen Crim. Law, 182.) Counsel: It must be assumed that the trustee will do his duty. Pollock, Ch. B. We must assume nothing either way, but he may not. (*Boulnois* v. *Mann*, 1 Law Reports, Ex. 30.)

5

cent; every one of good repute; every wrongful act to be malicious; every one to intend the consequences of his acts, &c. But it is not so. If one is accused of wrong, the law requires proof of his guilt; not because it presumes him innocent, but because it does not presume him guilty, and requires the fact to be proved. One complaining of injury to his reputation is not required to prove it good because the law presumes it good, but because the law does not presume it bad. On proof of a wrongful act the law will punish it as a wrong, not because it presumes it malicious, but because it does not presume there was any legal excuse for doing the act. It may be a wrong, and if it is not, the burden of showing the legal excuse to exist is on the actor, or whoever is liable for the act. One is liable for the consequences of his acts because the law will not presume the actor intended any other than the consequences of his act, not because the law presumes any intention. It would be as illogical and unfair to presume that one did not intend to do exactly what he has done, as it would be unwise to allow one to say he did not intend what he has done.

§ 69. In every transaction brought before a court of law for adjudication two questions always arise: (1) what are the facts, and (2) what is the law applicable to those facts? The court always decides the questions of law. Some questions of fact are decided by the court and some by the jury.[55] Courts con-

---

<blockquote>
" For twelve honest men have decided the cause
Who are judges alike of the facts and the laws.
</blockquote>

From a political ballad by Alderman Glover, called "Hosier's Ghost." In "Political Ballads of the 17th and 18th Centuries," by W. Walker Wilkins, London, 1860; also to be found in a work entitled "England Under the House of Hanover," by Wright. On the motion for a new trial in the case of the Dean of St. Asaph, Lord Mansfield cited the above lines as thus:

<blockquote>
For twelve honest men have decided the cause
Who are judges of facts, though not judges of laws.
</blockquote>

He attributed the authorship to Mr. Pulteny, and as written on the occasion of the failure of the prosecution against "The Craftsman." (See 21 State Trials, 847, 1046; 17 Id. 625; Forsyth's Hist. of Trial by Jury, 272.)

trol the decisions of juries on questions of fact.[56] (1) By determining whether or not the evidence adduced tends any way to prove the fact in issue; whether there is *some* evidence or *no* evidence. (2) By deciding in some cases that certain established facts warrant or do not warrant certain inferences and requiring the jury to accept such inferences as proved. (3) By deciding what evidence is to be regarded and what disregarded, whether as going to prove or disprove a fact or to affect damages. (4) By granting new trials when they deem the verdict as contrary to or as against evidence, or the damages excessive or inadequate. The connection between one fact and another, as cause and effect, is always a question of fact. It is the degree of probability of such connection which leads courts to determine whether they decide the question, or whether they leave it to the jury to decide. (1) If one event is very generally the cause of a certain other event, the courts lay down the general rule that the proof of the one event is the proof of the other, and do not allow juries to decide contrariwise. (2) If one event is often but not so generally the cause of a certain other event, then the courts leave it to the jury in each case to decide whether or not in that particular case that certain other event has followed.

The necessary consequences of an act always follow the act, and therefore the courts pronounce it a rule of evidence that the proof of the act is proof of its necessary consequences, and the jury may not find otherwise. The natural and proximate consequences of an act do often, but not always, follow the act; therefore the jury decide in each case whether or not those consequences have followed in that particular case.

§ 70. In every slander there are two acts, (1) the composing and (2) the publishing. In every libel there are three acts: (1)

---

[56] The judge put back the jury twice because they offered their verdict contrary to their evidence. (Clayton, 50.) Instances of judges taking questions of fact out of hands of jury. (*Wright* v. *Orient Mut. Ins. Co.*, 6 Bosw. 269; *Well's* v. *Com. Mut. Ins. Co.*, 46 Barb. 413; *Clarke* v. *Rankin*, 46 Barb. 571, and numerous cases.) Juries are *assistants* to the courts in determining some issues of fact. (Forsyth's Hist. Trial by Jury.)

the composing, (2) the writing, and (3) the publishing. The act which is the essential element in the wrongs slander and libel, is a wrongful publication of language, and the general prohibition (§ 49) as applicable to those wrongs would be: *No one shall, without legal excuse, publish language concerning another or his affairs which shall occasion him damage.* In other words: *Every publication of language concerning a man or his affairs which as a necessary or natural and proximate consequence occasions pecuniary loss to another, is prima facie a slander or a libel*—a slander, if the publication be oral; a libel, if the publication be by writing. This, it must be remembered, is not a description, much less a definition of a slander or a libel, but merely a description of what is *prima facie* a slander or a libel.

§ 71. In describing or defining a slander or a libel, it is customary to enumerate among its requisites (1) that the language must be defamatory, (2) and false, and (3) that the publication must be with malice, or made maliciously. We shall endeavor to give sufficient reasons for omitting these three *supposed* requisites from our description.

§ 72. To constitute a slander or libel must the language be defamatory? This question suggests others: What is meant by defamatory? Does defamatory mean more than discommendatory? It appears to us that to say the language must be defamatory, is only stating a portion of what is implied in saying that it must be such language as by a necessary or natural and proximate consequence occasions pecuniary loss to him whom, or whose affairs, they concern. It is scarcely conceivable that any other than discommendatory language can by a necessary or natural and proximate consequence occasion damage; it may therefore not be improper to say that the language must be defamatory, but that alone does not express so much as is implied in the requisite of occasioning *damage.* We shall hereafter have occasion to advert to this subject more in detail.[57]

---

[57] "But if the matter was not in its nature defamatory, the rejection of the

§ 73. To constitute a slander or libel must the language be false ? If the language is true it is a defence ;[58] but it does not thence follow that falsity is an essential element of the wrong. We know that the fact of the language being true is not alone an answer to a prosecution for a libel as a public offence ; the fact, then, of the language being true does not prevent its amounting to a wrong (§ 43). To say that showing the truth of the language published is a defence, and to say the language must be false, are not identical propositions. It may be correct to say one has the right to *speak* the truth,[59] but it is not correct to say one has the right to publish the truth by writing (§ 43). In certain cases, as will hereafter be explained, a cause of action for slander or libel could not be shown without alleging the language to be false ; but in the ordinary case of language concerning the person, no allegation of falsity was required to show a cause of action. In the latter instance the allegation of falsity was not necessary in a civil action, nor even in a criminal prosecution.[60] But where, as often happened, the language was alleged to be concerning the person and also concerning the affairs, then the allegation of falsity became material. The approved precedents of pleadings all contained the allegation of falsity, and thus, probably, falsity came to be

plaintiff cannot be considered the natural result of the speaking of the words. To make the speaking of the words wrongful, they must in their nature be defamatory." (Patteson, J., *Kelly* v. *Partington*, 5 B. & Ad. 645, and to the same effect see *Vicars* v. *Wilcocks*, 1 East, 1 ; *Ashley* v. *Harrison*, 1 Esp. 48 ; Peake, 194.) " We cannot have a definite idea of a design to injure unconnected with some degree of probability that the means made use of would effect the design." (*Durham* v. *Musselman*, 2 Blackf. 99.)

[58] "The truth of the supposed slander is in effect a ground of justification, which must be substantiated by the defendant." (1 *Starkie on Libel*, 9.) To maintain the action the words should be untrue. (Ellenborough, Ch. J., *Maitland* v. *Goldney*, 2 East, 426.)

[59] "Our laws allow a man to speak the truth, although it be done maliciously." (Bronson, J., *Baum* v. *Clause*, 5 Hill, 199 ; and to the like effect, *Foss* v. *Hildreth*, 10 Allen, 76.)

[60] *Rex* v. *Burke*, 7 T. R. 4, and if falsity is alleged it cannot be traversed (*Lewis* v. *Allcock*, 3 M. & W. 188 ; S. C. 6 Dowl. Pr. C. 389) and *post, Pleading.*

regarded as essential to the wrongs and to the descriptions of the wrongs slander and libel.

In those cases in which falsity must be alleged to show a cause of action, then the language cannot, as a necessary or natural and proximate consequence, occasion a pecuniary loss unless it is false; *in such cases, therefore, if not in every case*, the requirement that the publication must, as a necessary or natural and proximate consequence, occasion pecuniary loss, includes the requirement that the language be false. As will appear hereafter, where the language is concerning the person, the plaintiff is not allowed in the first instance, nor, except to disprove a defence of truth, to give any evidence of the falsity of the language published.[61]

§ 74. To constitute a slander or libel must the publication of the language be with malice or maliciously? To answer this question it is material to inquire *what is malice, and what is meant by the term malice as used* in the text-books and the reports.[62]

§ 75. We have seen that every act must be lawful or unlawful (§ 42). Lawful, such as has a legal excuse; unlawful, such as has not a legal excuse. Acts done without lawful excuse are said to be done with malice or to be malicious acts. All acts, whether lawful or unlawful, must be voluntary or involuntary.[63]

---

[61] 2 Starkie on Libel, 59; *Stuart* v. *Lovell*, 2 Starkie's Cas. 93.

[62] How much bad law and bad philosophy of law have arisen from imperfect comprehension of the terms will, motive, intention and negligence, may be seen in the nonsense of English law writers concerning malice. *Edinburgh Review*, Oct., 1863, p. 230, Amer. Reprint.

[63] "I purposely abstain from the use of the words *voluntary* and *involuntary*, on account of the extreme ambiguity of their signification. By a voluntary act is meant sometimes an act in the performance of which the will has had any concern at all—in this sense, it is synonymous to '*intentional*'—sometimes it means uncoerced, and sometimes spontaneous." *Bentham's Principles of Morals and Legislation*, 22, 79, 81, and see 2 Austin's Lect. Juris. 88.

§ 76. A voluntary act is an act done under no legal or other obligation to perform it, and which the actor may do or forbear at his option, as an act done in the exercise of a right. An act done with a consciousness or knowledge of the character of the act, or under such circumstances as that the actor ought to know, and by the exercise of a degree of care proportionate to the exigencies of the occasion the actor might know, the character of the act. A voluntary act does not mean a mere act of volition, but an act of volition coupled with a means of knowing the character of the act about to be performed and an intention to do that very act.[64] It is the act sometimes called an intentional act. Every act is *prima facie*, and without more, a voluntary act; it is regarded for all purposes as a voluntary act unless and until it is shown to be involuntary.

§ 77. An involuntary act is an act done under circumstances which permit to the actor no option as to whether he will do or forbear the act; an act done under some legal obligation to perform it as an act done in discharge of a duty; an act done under duress; an act done unconsciously and without knowledge as to the character of the act, the unconsciousness not being self-imposed; and the act done without the opportunity, by the exercise of a degree of care proportioned to the exigency of the occasion, of knowing the character of the act.

§ 78. Besides, and in addition to the intention of performing any act, there may be an intention in the mind of the actor to accomplish, by means of the act done, certain ends, or to produce certain consequences. Passing over the metaphysical distinctions between *will* and *intent* we may draw a distinct line of demarkation between the intent *to do an act* and the intent *to produce the consequences of the act.* This line we draw.

§ 79. Intent may or may not, in fact, be synonymous with

---

[64] "An act of the will is the same as an act of choosing or choice." Edwards on the Will, pt. 1, § 1; commented on Hazard on the Will, 177. As to will and intention see Stephen Crim. Law, 76.

motive, but we desire it understood that we use intent and motive as synonymous. By intent we mean motive, and if the term motive be employed instead of intent it must be divided as we have divided intent, and a distinction observed between the motive for doing the act and the motive to produce the consequences of the act. The intent or motive which goes towards the doing the act we include in the term voluntary. The intent or motive which refers to the consequences of the act we denominate intent or intention.

§ 80. A voluntary act may be done without any intent to produce its consequences, and an involuntary act may be done with an intent to produce its consequences.[65] In the cases in which there exists any intent to do more than commit the act itself, the intent may be either to produce all or some of the consequences of the act, or to produce an effect not a consequence of the act done. As one is responsible only for the necessary and natural and proximate consequences of his acts, at least any intent to produce any other consequence or effect must be immaterial. If the intent is at all material, it must be the intent to produce the necessary and natural and proximate consequences of the act.

§ 81. The various kinds of intents with which an act may be done are all resolvable into two classes, (1) an intent to injure some one, (2) an intent to benefit some one. The one to be injured or benefited may be the actor or some other. One

---

[65] "Nor does the nature of the resulting effect make any difference to the moral quality or character of the effort. A man's intentions may be most virtuous, and yet the actual consequences of his efforts be most pernicious. * * The moral nature of a volition is not, then, in any way affected by what actually follows that volition." (Hazard on the Will, 154.) "Feeling that *will implies intention*, numerous writers on jurisprudence employ *will* and *intention* as synonymous. They forget that *intention does not imply will*. * * * The agent may not intend a consequence of his act. In other words, when the agent wills the act he may not contemplate the given event as a consequence of the act which he wills." (2 Austin's Lect. Juris. 94.) "It is perfectly manifest that badness or goodness cannot be affirmed of the will, and that a criminal intention may accord with a good disposition." (*Id.* 183.)

and the same act may be done with an intent to injure one and benefit another.

§ 82. Intent may be divided into *general* and *particular*. Particular intent, or the intent with which any certain act may be done, is to be distinguished from the general intent. One may have a general intent to injure or benefit another, and synchronously with that intent may do some act concerning that other without any reference to the general intent, or without any particular intent, or with a particular intent different from or contradictory to the general intent. As a question of probability, the particular intent will follow the general, but not necessarily so ; whether it does or does not is in every case a question of evidence.

§ 83. Intent or intention is a mental conception—an existence. It is a fact,⁎ impalpable, intangible, invisible, but nevertheless a fact. The existence or non-existence of an intent or an intention and its character are always questions of fact. Save the declarations of the individual in whose mind the

---

⁎ The existence of mind is as much a matter of fact as the existence of matter. (Elementary Sketches of Moral Philosophy, by Sidney Smith, Introductory Lecture.) Intention is a fact. (*Clift* v. *White*, 12 N. Y. 538.) A witness may be asked with what *intent* he did an act. (*Seymour* v. *Wilson*, 14 N. Y. 567; *Griffin* v. *Marquardt*, 21 N. Y. 121; *Forbes* v. *Waller*, 25 N. Y. 439.) But his evidence is not conclusive. (*Griffin* v. *Marquardt*, 21 N. Y. 121.) And it seems this question is not permissible in certain cases, as where the intent may be or must be inferred from the act. (*The People* v. *Saxton*, 22 N. Y. 309; *Parker Mills* v. *Jacot*, 8 Bosw. 161; *Ballard* v. *Lockwood*, 1 Daly, 164.) We are not aware of the right to put the question as to intent having been mooted in an action for slander or libel. We suppose it could not properly be put in any action for slander or libel, because we are of opinion the question of mere intent can never be material in those actions. But assuming that intent is or may be material, then the question might be put in connection with a state of facts which discloses a qualified legal excuse. In our opinion the decisions show the rule to be, you may inquire into the intent, directly, as by inquiring of the party, in cases where the intent is material and the act complained of is as consistent with a good intent as with a bad intent, but in no other cases. (See supra, and *Booth* v. *Sweezy*, 4 Selden, 281; *Ellis* v. *The People*, 21 How. Pr. R. 356; *Powis* v. *Smith*, 5 B. & A. 850.)

intent is supposed to exist, we can have no *direct* testimony as to the existence or non-existence of any intent, or its character. Save such declarations we can have none but *indirect* testimony. That indirect testimony is the inference we may draw from his acts.[67]

§ 84. Not technically, but in reality, when the intent is to injure it is a *bad intent*, and bad intent is *malice*.[68] The act by means of which a bad intent is sought to be realized is a *malicious act*, and the act is done *maliciously*.

§ 85. Upon reference to the text-books and reports to dis-

---

[67] The state of a man's mind can only be known by others through his acts, through his own declarations, or through other conduct of his own. (2 Austin's Lect. Juris. 106.) Previous intentions are judged by subsequent acts. (*Dumont* v. *Smith*, 4 Denio, 819, 820.) The intention of an act done must be judged by its necessary consequences. Where these are directly pernicious the intent to work mischief becomes a conclusion of law. (*Safford* v. *Wyckoff*, 1 Hill, 11, referring to *Reg.* v. *Boardman*, 2 Moo. & Rob. 147, 148.) Where the guilt or innocence of the act depends upon the motive of the actor, his conduct and declarations as to other similar transactions about the same time are always admissible to show it. (*Barron* v. *Mason*, 31 Verm. (2 Shaw) 189; *Scanlan* v. *Cowley*, 2 Hilton, 489; *Center* v. *Spring*, 2 Clarke (Iowa), 393.)

[68] "Hardly any word in the whole range of the criminal law has been used in such various and conflicting senses, nor is there any which it is more important to understand correctly." (Stephen Crim. Law, 81.) The etymological meaning of the words malice and malicious is simply wickedness and wicked (*id.* 82), and it will be found in practice impossible to attach to these terms any other meaning. (*id.*) "I apprehend that there is no ground for distinguishing between the legal and the popular sense of the word, and that it means in its legal sense exactly what it means in its popular sense, namely, a mischievous design or intent to do an injury to an individual, or to the public." (Daly, F. J., *Viele* v. *Gray*, 10 Abb. Pr. R. 5; 18 How. Pr. R. 550.) The law presumes from the act an intent to bring about its consequences; "to denominate this intent malice or malice in law, when it may have arisen from a good motive, the defendant believing what he alleges to be true, is to employ the word malice in a sense neither justified by its etymology, its ordinary meaning, nor its previous legal signification." (*Id.*) The difference in the import of the word malice in legal and in common acceptation is commented on 17 Howell's State Trials, 43, 63. And see Sir Thomas Moore's distinction between *Malitia* and *Malevolentia* (1 *id.* 391.), and remarks on the introduction of the words *Falso et malitiose* into indictments for libel. (1 *id.* 30; 6 *id.* 1113.)

cover the meaning *in use* of the terms intent[69] and malice we find :

§ 86. As respects the term *intent*, it is sometimes employed to signify done intentionally, and in that sense is equivalent to will, or to what we have designated voluntary ; sometimes employed to signify an intent to produce the consequences or some certain consequences by means of the act done, and some-times employed to sigpify *bad intent* or *bad motive*. When employed in the sense of *will* or *intentionally* it is sometimes divided into express, tacit, presumed, and fictitious.[70]

§ 87. As respects the term *malice*, it is sometimes employed to signify the absence of legal excuse,[71] sometimes as meaning a bad or wicked motive or intent,[72] sometimes as meaning

---

[69] "If we would know the nature of wrongs, we must try to determine the meaning of *intention* and negligence with precision, for both of them run in a continued vein through the doctrine of wrongs, and one of them, *intention*, meets us at every step in every department of jurisprudence. (2 *Austin's Lect. Juris.* 80.) Unless the import of those terms are determined at the outset, the subsequent speculations will be a tissue of uncertain talk. (3 *Id.* 358.)

[70] See Lindley's Studies of Jurisprudence, 168, § 187, and *id.* App. CIV.

[71] Malice, the doing any act without a just cause. (1 *Chit. Gen'l. Pr.* 46.) Malice in its legal sense always excludes a just cause. (*Jones* v. *Givin*, Gilb. Cas. 185.) It is a technical expression, and means the absence of any excuse. (*Penn.* v. *Lewis*, Addison R. 282.) It is implied in every [wrongful] act for which there is no legal justification, excuse, or extenuation. (*Penn.* v. *Honeyman*, Addison R. 149.) A term of law denoting directly wickedness and exclud-ing just cause or excuse. (1 *Russ. Cr.* 483.) A wrongful act, done intentionally, without just cause or excuse. (*Bromage* v. *Prosser*, 4 B. & C. 247.) If malice be used as a descriptive term, it must be understood of malice in a technical and artificial sense as merely signifying the absence of any legal justification or excuse. (1 *Starkie on Libel*, 3.) If malice be used as descriptive * * * it must be understood in its legal and technical sense as merely denoting that which is inferred from the doing of a wrongful act without lawful justification or excuse. (*Id.* 213.) Malice, the doing any act injurious to another without just cause. (*Bouvier's Law Dict.*, tit. Malice.) See *York's case*, 9 Metc. 93 ; *Darry* v. *The People*, 10 N. Y. 139 ; *Hilliard on Torts*, ch. vii. § 106 ; *Mitchell* v. *Jenkins*, 5 B. & A. 590.

[72] "*Malice*. In criminal law and general practice, wickedness of purpose ; a spiteful or malevolent design against another ; a settled purpose to injure or destroy another. Any formed design of doing mischief. 1 Hale's P. C. 455, Am.

scienter[73] or knowingly, sometimes as meaning intentionally or voluntarily,[74] and often without any definite or ascertainable meaning whatever.[75] The term malice is also divided into *mal-*

---

ed. note; 2 Stra. 766. Any evil design in general. 4 Bl. Com. 198. A disposition or inclination to do a bad thing. 2 Rolle R. 461. General wickedness of heart; inhuman or reckless disregard of the lives or safety of others, as when one coolly discharges a gun or throws any dangerous missile among a multitude of people, or strikes even upon provocation with a weapon that must produce death. 4 Bl. Com. 199, 200. Deliberate disregard of the rights of others, as when one carries on the trade of melting tallow to the annoyance of the neighboring dwellings. Abbott, C. J., 3 B. & C. 584. (*Burrill's Law Dict.*, tit. Malice, and see note 68, *ante.*)

[73] "Maliciously is sometimes equivalent to scienter." (3 *Austin's Lect. Juris.* 327.) A "*conscious violation*" of law. (9 Cl. & Fin. 321; and *Sherwin* v. *Swindall*, 12 M. & W. 787.) In the Code prepared by Messrs. Austin & Lewis for the Island of Malta they employ the phrase "*culpable knowledge*" in lieu of "*implied malice.*" See Appendix A. to House of Lords' Report on Law of Defamation, A. D. 1843.

[74] If I am arraigned of felony and wilfully stand mute, I am said to do it of *malice*, because it is a wrongful act and done *intentionally.* (Bayley J., *Bromage* v. *Prosser*, 4 B. & C. 247.) Any unlawful act done wilfully is malicious. (*Commonwealth* v. *Snelling*, 15 Pick. 337.)

[75] In the English law, in certain cases we have employed the word *malice* to mean intention generally. As malice implies intention, it has been extended to cases in which there is no malice. As I shall show, it does not denote the motive. And it is manifest that the motive to a criminal action may be laudable. The intention of an act, suggested by a blamable motive, lawful. (2 *Austin's Lect. Juris.* 110.) It having been assumed inconsiderately that malice or criminal design is of the essence of *every* crime, the term is extended abusively to negligence * * * it is often confounded with malice as denoting malevolence, insomuch that malevolence (though the motive or inducement of the party is foreign to his guilt or innocence) *is supposed to be* essential to the crime. (3 *Id.* 327.) Malice has also been defined "as the plain indication of a heart regardless of social duty, and fatally bent on mischief" (*U. S.* v. *Cornell*, 2 Mason, 60); improper motives (*Weekerly* v. *Geyer*, 1 S. & R. 35); wilfulness (*Dexter* v. *Spear*, 4 Mason, 115; Holt on Libel, 55); a design formed of doing mischief to another (*Reg.* v. *Mawgridge*, Kely. R. 127); any wicked or mischievous intention of the mind (*Rex* v. *Harvey*, 2 B. & C., 257). *Malice*, as applied to torts, does not necessarily mean that which must proceed from a spiteful, malignant, or revengeful disposition, but a conduct injurious to another, though proceeding from an ill-regulated mind not sufficiently cautious before it occasions an injury to another. (11 S. & R. 39, 40.) Indeed, *in some cases it seems not to require any intention in order to make an act malicious.* When slander has been published, therefore, the proper question for the jury is not whether the *intention* of the publication was

ice in law and *malice in fact*,[76] and *express malice* and *implied malice*.[77] Probably the phrase implied malice is identical with the phrase malice in law, and the phrase express malice with the phrase malice in fact; for among the definitions we find malice in law defined as " The malice which is inferred from the doing a wrongful act without lawful justification or excuse." [78] The distinction between malice in law and malice in fact is supposed to consist in this, that the one is *inferred* and the other *proved.* The attempted distinction is unreal and unsound; there is no distinction between what is inferred and what is proved—*what is inferred is proved.* " We say of a fact, it is proved when we believe its truth by reason of some other

to injure the plaintiff, but whether the tendency of the matter published was so injurious. 10 B. & C. 472; s. c. 21 E. C. L. Rep. 117; and see 3 B. & C. 584; s. c. 10 E. C. L. Rep. 179. (*Bouvier's Law Dict. voce Malice.*)

[76] Malice " has been sometimes divided into legal malice or malice in law, and actual malice or malice in fact. These terms might seem to imply that the two kinds of malice are different in their nature. The true distinction, however, is not in the malice itself, but simply in the evidence by which it is established. In all ordinary cases, if the charge complained of is injurious, and no justifiable motive for making it is apparent, malice is inferred from the falsity of the charge. The law in such cases does not impute malice not existing in fact, but presumes a malicious motive for making a charge which is both false and injurious when no other motive appears. When, however, the circumstances show that the defendant may reasonably be supposed to have had a just and worthy motive for making the charge, then the law ceases to infer malice from the mere falsity of the charge, and requires from the plaintiff other proof of its existence. It is actual malice in either case, the proof only is different." Selden, J., *Lewis* v. *Chapman*, 16 N. Y. 372.

[77] The distinction between express and implied malice is well illustrated in the argument of that distinguished lawyer, Nicholas Hill, in *Darry* v. *The People*, 10 N. Y. 123, as thus: The term *express* malice originally meant malice proved independently of the mere act from which death resulted, and *implied* malice the reverse. They therefore described only different modes of proving actual guilt, not different degrees of it; and they belonged to the law of evidence, not to a definition of homicide. They did not even indicate different degrees of evidence, both kinds when sufficient being conclusive until overcome. And they were applicable to every case where proof of the actual intent was requisite to characterize an offence." He supports these views by a profuse citation of authorities. The opinions in this case should be perused by those who desire more information on the subject of implied malice.

[78] 1 *Starkie on Libel*, 213.

fact from which it is said to follow."[79] Some judges have
avoided this objection by denying that *malice in law* is a
question of fact, and styling it *a conclusion of law* not required
to be proved and not permitted to be denied.[80] If malice in
law is a conclusion of law, then is malice in fact a conclusion of
law ; and if this be so, it is still true that they are not distinguish-
able the one from the other. Whether malice *in fact* is here
employed in the sense of want of legal excuse or in the sense
of bad intent is immaterial on this point. The non-existence
of legal excuse in the one case and the existence of bad intent
in the other can be proved only by inference. No argument
can make it more clear than the mere statement that the non-
existence of a legal excuse does not admit of direct proof, and
can be proved only by inference. As to the proof of malice in
fact or of a bad intent, we have already considered how *intent*
may be proved ; and from the nature of the subject it will con-

---

[79] Mill's Logic, b. 2, c. 1, § 1.

[80] " The malicious intent of the publication is not a question of fact, but a conclusion of law. It is the intent which the law implies, and which the plaintiff is
therefore not required to prove, nor the defendant permitted to deny." (Duer J.
Fry v. *Bennett*, 1 Code Rep. N. S. 243; 5 Sandf. 54.) The only case in which
malice may be proved is where privilege is pleaded. (*Root* v. *Lownds*, 6 Hill,
520 ; *Washburn* v. *Cook*, 3 Denio, 112 ; *Howard* v. *Sexton*, 4 Coms. 157.) " Malice, so far as the law requires it to sustain the action, is implied from the publication of that which is untrue—the law presuming it to exist in such a case.
Therefore, *express malice is not required to sustain the action.*" (*Littlejohn* v. *Greeley*,
13 Abb. Pr. R. 55.) " It is said that malice is involved in the issue. * * *
The answer to this suggestion is that in the action of slander, except in cases of
privileged communications, *express malice* forms no part of the issue. *Legal
malice* only is affirmed or denied, and this results from proof of the transaction
* * * which the law pronounces wrongful, and therefore malicious.—2
Greenl. Ev. § 410, 418, 421." (Gardiner J., *Howard* v. *Sexton*, 4 Coms. 160.)
" In an ordinary action for a libel or for words, though evidence of malice may
be given to increase the damages, it never is considered as essential, nor is there
any instance of a verdict for the defendant on the ground of a want of malice."
(Mansfield, Ch. J., *Hargrave* v. *Le Breton*, 4 Burr. 2425, repeated by Bayley, J.,
in *Bromage* v. *Prosser*, 4 B. & C. 247.) Others say malice must be proved.
" The jury have no more right to find malice in the defendant, without sufficient
evidence, than they have to find any other fact in the plaintiff's favor without
proof." (Woodruff, J., *Liddle* v. *Hodges*, 2 Bosw. 544.) And see *Dolloway* v. *Turrell*, 26 Wend. 396 ; *Cooke on Defamation*, ch. iv.

clusively appear that inasmuch as at the time when this division of malice took place parties to a transaction were not allowed to testify, there could at that time be none other than indirect evidence of bad intent or malice. At that time the existence of bad intent or malice could be proved in no other manner than by inferring it from the acts or declarations of the actor, or by the like means as the proof of, so called, malice in law.

§ 88. Pursuing the subject, and upon reference to the text-books and reports to ascertain whether intent and malice are elements of a wrong, we find some authors and judges laying down the rule that *intent* is the essential ingredient of every wrong.[81] Intent, of course, means bad intent, and this is so universally conceded that all collections of legal maxims include this. "*Actus non facit reum, nisi mens sit rea;*" which is translated: "An act does not make guilty, unless the mind be guilty—that is, unless the intention be criminal;[82] others as-

---

[81] Every wrong supposes intention or negligence on the part of the wrong-doer. (2 *Austin's Lect. Juris.* 2.) Intention, negligence, heedlessness, or rashness, is of the essence of a wrong, is a necessary condition precedent to the existence of guilt (*Id.* 144). Guilt imports that the party has broken a duty (*Id.* 147, 149); it denotes the intention and connotes the act, forbearance or omission, which was the *effect* of his intention (*Id.* 147), and at p. 165, Unlawful intention or un-lawful inadvertence is of the essence of injury. And on examining the grounds of exemption from liability, we find the party is or is presumed to be clear of intention or inadvertence; and (p. 168) the ultimate ground of exemption for ignorance or error of fact is the absence of unlawful intention or unlawful inadvertence. At p. 179, An infant or a person insane is exempted from liability, not because he is an infant or insane, but because it is inferred from his infancy or insanity that the wrong was not the consequence of unlawful intention or inadvertence; and (p. 185) the reason assigned by Blackstone and other writers is hardly worth powder and shot. He tells us that a wrong is the effect of a wicked will. And (says) infants and madmen are exempted, because the act goes not with their will, or is not imputable to a wicked will. * * * He cannot mean to affirm that an infant or madman has not as much *will* as the adult or the sane. [It must be observed that Austin makes a distinction between will and motive. By will, if we interpret him aright, he intends only the mere act of volition.] Intent is the essence of crime. (*Krom* v. *Schoonmaker*, 3 Barb. 647.) The criminality of the act depends altogether upon the intent with which it was done. (*Genet* v. *Mitchell*, 7 Johns. 120; and see 2 Starkie Ev., tit. Intention.)

[82] See Burrill's Law Dict. tit. *Actus*, where he adds, The intent and the act must both concur to constitute the crime. Kenyon, Ch. J. 7 T. R. 514; Broom's

sert that intent is immaterial in civil actions, *except* in the civil
actions for slander and libel ;[83] others, that intent is immaterial
in slander and libel, or immaterial except under certain circumstances ;[84] and others, that the essential element of a slander or
a libel is malice or a malicious intent, the mind must be in

Max. 144. This maxim is exclusively applicable to criminal law *and to civil proceedings* for slander and libel; in [qy. other] civil actions the intent is immaterial
if the act done be injurious to another. (*Id.* 155, 161.) The maxim " *Affectio
tua nomen imponit operi tuo*" [your disposition or intention gives name or character to your work or act] embodies the same principle. Bract. fo. 101b. See
Broom's Maxims, tit. *Actus non facit*, &c., where he says: With respect to libel
and slander the rule is * * * where an occasion exists which if fairly acted
upon furnishes a legal protection to the party who makes the communication
complained of, the *actual* intention of the party affords a boundary of legal liability. See also Burrill's Law Dict. tit. *Voluntas*, citing *Voluntas et proposi-
tum distinguunt maleficia*—Will and purpose characterize crimes. *Crimen non
contrahitur, nisi voluntas nocendi intercedat.* Crime is not contracted unless the
intention of doing harm be present. *Tolle voluntatem et eris omnis actus indiffe-
rens.* Take away *will* and every act will become indifferent. ⟍
   We cannot pass the quotation of a so-called law maxim without entering our
protest against their reception as legal *axioms.* We believe that not a
single law maxim can be pointed out which is not obnoxious to objection. The
old law maxims must be put aside or forgotten, or remembered only as things of
the past and dead, even as we have put aside and forgotten maxims in science,
supplying their places with maxims drawn from a larger experience and more
philosophical analysis. "Perhaps there is a period in every system of law previous to which the formation of maxims will be productive of bad effects, as
leading to the establishment of principles which it is not permitted to controvert,
but which more enlightened views would repudiate." Fortesque de laudibus, &c.,
ch. viii., note to edition by Amos. See Dodderidge's English Lawyer ; Doctor
and Student, Dial. 1, ch. 8, 9; Bacon's Preface to his Maxims. The benefit
which science has received from the use of maxims is of a questionable nature,
and the adoption of these is of a questionable nature whenever the ideas are
confused. (*Locke on the Understanding*, B'k iv., ch. 7.)

   [83] See in note 82, *ante.*

   [84] The secret intention of the publisher is immaterial (*Hankinson* v. *Bilby*, 16
M. & W. 442), " It is an error to suppose that *motive*, except where the words are
privileged, is in any way essential to a cause of action." The motive of the
defendant is wholly immaterial as respects the right of action. It may be a good
or a bad one. (Daly, F. J., *Viele* v. *Gray*, 10 Abb. Pr. R. 6, 7 ; 18 How. Pr. R., 550.)
In an action brought by A against B for slandering the title of the former to
certain slaves by him exposed to public sale, a verdict was found for him ; B
brought his bill praying for relief, and an injunction against the verdict, and it

fault;[38] and some expressly and some by implication assert that this fault in the mind, this bad intent or malice, must be in fact

---

was held that as the loss in the sale of the slaves was caused by B, *even though he was believed to have designed no injury*, he was bound to make reparation, and his bill was dismissed. (*Ross* v. *Pines*, Wythe, 71.) There is no instance of a verdict for the defendant on the ground of want of malice. (Mansfield, Ch. J., *Hargrave* v. *Le Breton*, 4 Burr. 2425; repeated by Bailey, J., *Bromage* v. *Prosser*, 4 B. & C. 247.) If I give a man slanderous words, whereby I damnify him in his name and credit, *it is not material whether I use them upon sudden choler* and provocation, *or of set malice*, but *in an action upon the case I shall render damages alike.* (Bacon Maxims of the Law, Regula VII.)

The *intent* with which an act is done is by no means the test of the liability of a party to an action of trespass. (*Guille* v. *Swan*, 19 Johns. 381; *Percival* v. *Hickey*, 18 *id*. 257; *Tremain* v. *Cohoes Co.*, 2 Coms. 164; *Ruckman* v. *Cowell*, 1 Coms. 507; *Safford* v. *Wyckoff*, 1 Hill, 11.) Bona fides will not protect a magistrate who does an illegal act. (*Prickett* v. *Greatrex*, 1 New Mag. Cas. 548; 7 Law Times, 139.) It is immaterial with what motive a man does a legal act. (*Humphrey* v. *Douglass*, 11 Verm. R. 22); and so of an unlawful act. (*Amick* v. *O'Hara*, 6 Blackf. 258.) Intention held to be immaterial. (*Bullock* v. *Babcock*, 8 Wend. 391; *Baker* v. *Bailey*, 16 Barb. 60.) Intent immaterial if the words are a libel. (*People* v. *Freer*, 1 Caines' Rep. 485.) In a private action for libel the motives are out of the question. (*Root* v. *King*, 7 Cow. 683.) If the words are not actionable *per se*, and have not occasioned any special damage, no amount of malice in the publisher will make them actionable. (*Kelly* v. *Partington*, 3 Nev. & M. 116; 5 B. & Adol. 645; and see 2 Nev. & M. 460; 4 B. & Adol. 700.) "Bad motives in doing an act which violates no legal right of another cannot make that act a ground of action." (*Pickard* v. *Collins*, 23 Barb. 459.)

Where an act in itself indifferent if done with a particular intent becomes criminal, there the intent must be proved and found; but when the act is in itself unlawful (i. e. *prima facie* and unexplained) the proof of justification or excuse lies on the defendant, and in failure thereof the law implies a criminal intent; in the latter case the intention is immaterial and therefore not a question of fact in issue, for the crime consists in publishing a libel: "*a criminal intention in the writer is no part of the definition of the crime of libel at the common law.*" Per Lord Mansfield in Woodfall's case, the words quoted are from the opinion of the twelve English judges delivered in the House of Lords upon questions put to them on the subject of libel. (Journals of the House of Lords, 1792, Appendix 27; and 22 Howell's State Trials, 300.) Except in the cases of privileged communications express malice forms no part of the issue. (*Howard* v. *Sexton*, 4 Coms. 157, and see note (80) *ante*.) "In which case [privileged communication] express malice must be shown, while in other cases express malice forms no part of the issue. *Thorn* v. *Moser*, 1 Denio, 488; *The State* v. *Burnham*, 9 N. Hamp. 34; *Howard* v. *Sexton*, 4 Coms. 157." (W. F. Allen, J., *Bush* v. *Prosser*, 11 N. Y. 355; see *id*. p. 358, and note 85, *post*.)

[38] "To constitute that injury [slander] malice must be proved, not mere gene-

or impliedly in the mind of the defendant in the action.   And
the divisions of will and of malice heretofore referred to (§§ 86,
87) appear to have been designed to meet this requirement in

---

ral ill-will but malice in the special case set forth in the pleadings, to be inferred
from it and the attending circumstances." (Gardiner, J., *Howard* v. *Sexton*, 4
Comst. 161; quoted and approved by Rosekrans, J., *Fry* v. *Bennett*, 28 N. Y. 328; ·
and by W. F. Allen, J., *Bush* v. *Prosser*, 11 N. Y. 357.) " Malice is essential to every
action for libel." (Selden, J., *Lewis* v. *Chapman*, 16 N. Y. 372.) " In *all* cases
malice is essential to the action. Not *imputed* malice merely, but actual malice,
· malice established by proof." (Selden, J., *Bush* v. *Prosser*, 11 N. Y. 358.) To
maintain the action there must be " (1) malice in the defendant; (2) injury to the
plaintiff; (3) that the words should be untrue." (Ellenborough, Ch. J., *Maitland*
v. *Goldney*, 2 East, 426.) The malice of the publication or the intent to defame
the reputation of another is the essence of the offence of libel. (*Com'wealth* v.
Clapp, 4 Mass. R. 163 ; *Com'wealth* v. *Snelling*, 15 Pick. 337.) In order to render
the publisher amenable to the law, the publication· must be *maliciously* made,
but malice will be presumed if the matter be libelous. (Bouvier Law Dict.,
voce Publisher.) "The *criminality* of the charge in the indictment consisted in a
malicious and seditious *intention.* There can be no crime without a wicked mind."
(Kent, J., *The People* v. *Crosswell*, 3 Johns. Cas. 364); and " as a libel is a *defamatory* publication made with a *malicious intent.* (*Id.* 377.) The injury consists in
" *falsely and maliciously* " charging another with, &c. (Kent's Com., part iv., sect.
24, p. 706 of 1 vol. 11th ed., and *id.* p. 617.) "The essential ground of action for
defamation consists of the *malicious intention*, and when the mind is not in fault
no prosecution can be maintained ;" and the story recited from Fox's Martyrology
in *Brook* v. *Montague*, Cro. Jac. 91, is referred to. " The mind must be in fault
and show a malicious intention to defame." (Kenyon, J., *Rex* v. *Abingdon*, 1
Esp. 226.) " By the law of England *malice* is an essential ingredient in every
action on the case for slander." (Borthwick on Libel, 194.) And in a note (*id.*) attributed to Starkie, it is said, Every definition of the subject-matter of an action
for slander to be found in the books of reports or elementary writers, includes
malice as an essential ingredient. Malice is the gist of the action for slander.
(*McKee* v. *Ingalls*, 4 Scam. 30; *White* v. *Nicholls*, 3 How. U. S. Rep. 266.) There must
be a mischievous intention. (George on Libel, 162.) The guilt [gist] of and essential ground of action for defamation consists in the *malicious* intention, and when
the mind is not in fault no prosecution can be· maintained. 2 Kent's Com. 26.
(W. F. Allen, J., *Bush* v. *Prosser*, 11 N. Y. 355.) In the trial of the Seven Bishops, Justices Holloway and Powell both say to make a libel it must be malicious.
" The *main* question is *quo animo* the defendant published the article complained
of. • • •   The plaintiff is bound to show that the defendant was actuated by
malice." (Ellenborough, Chief J., *Tabart* v. *Tipper*, 1 Camp. 350, 351.) "The
gist of an action of slander, for words in themselves actionable, is the *malice*
which produced them; take away this and the suit is not maintainable . in
any shape." (Rossell, J., *Cook* v. *Barkley*, 1 Penn. N. J. Rep. 180, and p. 183
· per Pennington, J.)   " The *quo animo* with which the words were spoken

those cases in which there is no pretence of any bad intent, or
no possibility of any bad intent in the mind of the defendant
in the action. There will be no necessity for any such division
of will or malice if the distinction between the wrong and the
· liability be observed (§ 66). At the same time that courts hold
malice, meaning bad intent, to be a necessary ingredient of slander
and libel, they hold that it is not absolutely necessary to allege
malice in a declaration,[36] and that the introduction of an allegation of malice in a declaration for libel is " rather to exclude
the supposition that the publication had been made on some

was the point in issue, as malice constitutes the gist of the action." " It is said
there need be no express malice except in the case of privileged communications,
that in other words implied or legal malice is all that is required. What is meant
by *implied* malice ? Does it mean malice which the law imputes without any
proof of its existence ? I apprehend not. It means this : that the fact that the
defendant is shown to have published a false charge against another which was
calculated to injure him, *proves* that the defendant was actuated by malicious
motives, unless the circumstances are such as to suggest some other and innocent
motive. This is nothing more than the application of a familiar rule of evidence,
viz., that every person is presumed to intend that which is the natural consequences of his actions. * * * But is malice any more the ground of the action in
cases of privileged communication than in others? Clearly not. It is called for
the sake of convenience express malice in the one case and implied in the other ;
but the malice is the same, the difference is in the proof alone. We may therefore assume that in *all cases* malice is essential to the action. Not *imputed* malice
merely, but actual malice ; malice established by proof." (Selden, J., *Bush* v.
Prosser, 11 N. Y. 358.)

The case of *Mercer* v. *Sparks* (Owen, 51 ; Noy, 35) was cited in *McPherson* v.
Daniels (10 B. & Cr. 266) as an authority for the proposition that in an action for
slander malice need not be alleged; but per Parke, J., "that was after verdict, and
malice must have been proved at the trial." Malice "may be said to be a neces-
sary ingredient in one form or other of all crimes whatever." (Stephen, Crim.
Law, 81.) As to necessity of proving malice in actions for slander and libel, see
George on Libel, 149 ; Jones on Libel, 8, 9, 11, 14, Comyn Dig. Action for Defamation, G ; *Smith* v. *Ashley*, 11 Met. 486 ; *McCorkle* v. *Binns*, 5 Binney, 340 ;
Coxhead v. *Richards*, 2 C. B. 608 ; *Lillie* v. *Price*, 5 Ad. & El. 645 ; *Harwood* v.
Astley, 4 Bos. & Pul. 47 ; and *Hastings* v. *Lusk*, 22 Wend. 416 ; *Steele* v. *South-
wick*, 9 Johns. 214 ; *Root* v. *King*, 4 Wend. 113 ; 1 Saund. 243, *note* 4.

[36] In a complaint for libel it is not necessary to aver express malice. (*Purdy* v.
Carpenter, 6 How. Pr. R. 366.) Maliciously need not be used if words of an equivalent import are used. (*White* v. *Nicholls*, 3 How. U. S. Rep. 266.) The omission
is cured by verdict. (*McPherson* v. *Daniels*, 10 B. & C. 266 ; *Taylor* v. *Kneeland*, 1
Doug. 67.)

innocent occasion than for any other purpose."[87]   And except
to aggravate the damages courts will not allow, on a trial, any
evidence of malice (bad intent) in addition to that which is said
to be inferred, until evidence has been given which counter-
vails or reverses the so-called presumption of malice or malice ·
in law,[88] nor will they allow this presumption nor malice in fact
to be contradicted by any mere denial, or shown not to exist by
proving an actual good intent.   They permit but one way of
evading this malice in law, and that is by showing the existence
of a legal excuse for the act of publication. If the legal excuse shown be a prima facie one only, its effect is merely to
remove the alleged presumption of malice and raise an alleged
presumption of absence of malice, and, as it is said, require
the plaintiff to show malice in fact. This very intricate course
of procedure arises from erroneously treating, in practice, as an
affirmative part of the essential element of a wrong that which
is more properly a *negative* part, not required to establish the
fact of a wrong done, but required only when it is designed to
show that what is a wrongful act, and prima facie a wrong, is
not so in fact (§ 63).   Let a wrongful act stand for a wrong,
unless and until a legal excuse be shown, and we make intelligible and consistent what is now difficult to understand, and
only to be reconciled by a series of fictions.[89]

§ 89. One meaning in which intent or intention is employed
is will. When so employed it corresponds to what we have
described as voluntary. And if instead of saying *intent* is
necessary to constitute a wrong, we say *will* is necessary to

---

[87] Abbott, Ch. J., *Duncan* v. *Thwaites*, 3 B. & C. 585.

[88] In the adjustment of damages malice [*bad intent*] may become an element.
(*Viele* v. *Gray*, 10 Abb. Pr. R. 6; 18 How. Pr. R. 566; *Root* v. *King*, 7 Cow. 638;
Fry v. *Bennett*, 28 N. Y. 327, S. C. 3 Bosw. 200; *Taylor* v. *Church*, 1 E. D. Smith,
279; and 4 Selden, 452; *Littlejohn* v. *Greeley*, 13 Abb. 57; *Bush* v. *Prosser*, 11
N. Y. 359; and see *post*, Damages.)

[89] Mr. Stephen, after referring to the manner in which the word "malicious"
operates in shifting the burden of proof from the prosecutor to the prisoner, and
stating that legal fictions are matters of regret, says, "it would be better to throw
the law into a different shape, and to enact specifically that persons who do acts
of which the natural consequence is to kill, &c., shall be punished instead of
introducing the question of intent at all. (Stephen Crim. Law, 804.)

constitute a wrong, and then keep in view the distinction between will or voluntary and intent, we at once remove very much of the difficulty which has been supposed to be inherent in the law relating to slander and libel. It is conceded, at least by some, that in civil actions other than those for slander and libel, intent, in the sense of intending the consequences of an act, is immaterial; why should the civil actions for slander and libel be exceptions? Certainly the burden of proving them to be exceptions lies upon those who insist that they are not within the rules which govern every other civil action.

§ 90. One meaning of malice is absence of legal excuse. This is the sense in which the term is most frequently employed, and it is, we conceive, the only sense in which it is properly employed.[90] Substitute "absence of legal excuse" for "malice" in many opinions in the reports which are difficult to be understood, and they will become easily intelligible, and accord with the principles we venture to propound.

To illustrate, that what is called malice in fact really means nothing more nor less than absence of legal excuse, suppose A. has untruely said B. is a thief, under circumstances that A. believing B. to be a thief, would constitute a legal excuse. A familiar instance of this is the case of giving, as it is termed, the character of a former employé. In the case supposed the material inquiry is: what was A's belief? To answer this inquiry, and only for the purpose of answering this inquiry, it may be material to ascertain what feeling or intention A. had towards B.; if the intention is found to be friendly, it is a link in the chain of evidence that A. spoke believing what he said. If the intention of A. towards B. was unfriendly, it is a link in the chain of evidence that A. spoke rather from that intent or for some purpose other than from his belief; and being spoken not in a belief of its truth, the speaking was out of the pale of legal excuse, and was wrongful, not merely or in anywise because of the intent, which may have been good or bad, but because the speaking was not in the manner prescribed to constitute a legal excuse, namely, from belief. If in such a case

---

[90] See note 71, *ante.*

A. was allowed to testify, and was to admit that he did not
believe to be true what he said concerning B., but that he spoke
without any intent to injure or with a good intent towards B. or
any other, that testimony would not constitute any defence;
admitting that he did not believe what he spoke, would take
away the legal excuse.

§ 91. The intent—meaning the intent to effect certain consequences—with which an act is done is material on the question of the amount of damages; the absence of a bad intent
will mitigate the damages; the presence of a bad intent will
aggravate them. The intent of the actor is sometimes mate- ·
rial as a link in the chain of evidence to determine whether or
not some certain act was or was not done under circumstances
constituting a legal excuse, as where the legal excuse is dependent upon the question: what was the belief of the actor? With
these exceptions, we conceive that intent is never material and
that intent is never an essential element of a wrong. No
amount of good intent will excuse an act otherwise wrongful,
and no amount of bad intent will make wrongful that which is
otherwise a permitted act. If intent is not an essential element
of a wrong, neither, in the sense of bad intent, is malice. If
the term malice is to be retained in use as a technical term, it
must be only in the sense of want of legal excuse.

§ 92. This view is not, we are pleased to say, any innovation
or novel doctrine; it is but a return to the old paths, from which
the departure has been very wide. Holt, after referring to the
objections urged against the law of libel, says[91]: "It is urged
that the motive of many publications which the law decrees
libels, may be innocent and even laudable; and that without
the proof of malice, or, what is equivalent to malice, the mere
act of composing or publishing a libel ought not to be the subject of punishment. This objection only becomes specious from
the misapprehension of the term *malice*. Malice, in legal understanding, implies no more than willfulness.[92] The first in-

<hr/>

[91] Holt on Libel, conclusion of ch. iii., b'k 1, p. 55; and see comments on this,
2 Mence on Libel, 25.

[92] See *Dexter* v. *Spear*, 4 Mason, 115.

quiry of a civil judicature, if the fact do not speak for itself as
a *malum in se*, is to find out whether it be willfully committed;
*it searches not into the intention or motive any further or other-
wise than as they are the marks of a voluntary act;* and having
found it so, it concerns itself no more with a man's design or
principle of acting, but punishes without scruple what manifestly to the offender himself was a breach of the command of
the Legislature. The law collects the intention from the act
itself—the act being in itself unlawful [wrongful], an evil intent is inferred, and needs no proof by extrinsic evidence. That
mischief which a man does he is supposed to mean, and he is
not permitted to put in issue a meaning abstracted from the
fact. 'The crime consists in publishing a libel; a criminal intention in the writer is no part of the definition of the crime of
libel at common law.' 'He who scattereth firebrands, arrows,
and death (which if not an accurate is a very intelligent description of a libel) is *ea ratione* criminal.' It is not incumbent
on the prosecution to prove his intent, and on his part he shall
not be heard to say, 'Am I not in sport.' To determine,
therefore, the guilt of a civil act, and to inflict punishment on
the offender, there is no need of knowing his motives. Human
laws require no justification in imposing penalties for an act
prohibited by the magistrate, in its consequences injurious, and
which has indubitable marks of being voluntarily committed."
This exhibits and illustrates our view that the intent which the
law regards is that intent which enters into the question: was
the act voluntary? and this it determines by the knowledge
of the actor, did he know or ought he to have known, that his
act would produce an injury, if he had this knowledge, or might,
but for his own misfeasance or omission, have had this knowledge, he is liable for his act and its consequences. And it is
altogether immaterial whether we say he is liable for the act
and its consequences, or say he is liable for the act because it
was voluntary, and for the consequences because he must be
presumed to have intended them. The latter mode of statement
is the more usual, but we think less correct, and may have contributed to the confusion which pervades our subject.

CHAPTER VI.

PUBLICATION—PUBLISHER.

A Publication is Necessary. Meaning of the term Publica-
·tion. The Language Published must be Understood. The
Publication may be Orally or in Writing. What amounts
to an Oral and what to a Written Publication. Publica-
tion of Effigy. Requisites of an Oral Publication. Requi-
sites of a Written Publication. Time of Publication.
Place of Publication. Who is a Publisher. Republica-
tion and Repetition—Distinction between. Joint Publi-
cation. Liability for Publications. Voluntary and In-
voluntary Publications. Liability of Principal and Agent.
Newspaper Publisher. Bookseller.

§ 93. As heretofore observed (§ 23), for language to affect
another than its author the language must be published; that is

---

⁹² To publish, means not only a "giving out," but a "taking in." In English
we have only one word to express the idea, in the German they have two words.
They say of a book *herausgegeben* that it is "given out," but not that it is published until sales of it have been effected.

"Publication [of a writing] is nothing more than doing the last act for the
accomplishment of the mischief intended by it." (*Rex* v. *Burdett*, 4 B. & Ald.
126.)

"The sense in which the word published is used in law, is an uttering of the
libel. Though in common parlance that word may be confined in its meaning to
making the contents known to the public, yet the meaning is not so limited in
law. The making it known to an individual only is indisputably, in law, a publishing. (*Id.*)

The mode of publication of writings in early times was by scattering them in
the highways. The conclusion of "The Outlaw's Song of Trail-lebaston," temp.
Edward II., is as follows :

Escrit estoit en parchemyn pur mont remember
E gitté en haut chemyn qe um le dust trover.

to say, it must be communicated to some other than its author. There must be a publication.[94]

§ 94. Publication is an ambiguous term, employed to signify sometimes the matter published, sometimes an act of publishing only, and sometimes an act of publishing such as may sub-

---

[It was written on parchment to be better remembered, and cast on the high. way that people may find it.] See Political Songs of England from John to Edward II. Edited and translated by Thomas Wright, Camden Society, 1839. (Astor Library.) And see London Quarterly Review, April, 1857.

This method of publication seems to have continued at least until the sixteenth century. John Fox mentions " A libel or book entitled the Supplication of Beggars, thrown and scattered at the procession in Westminster, on Candlemas day (2d February, 1526), before King Henry the Eighth, for him to read and peruse ;" and again, Wolsey immediately went to his Majesty (Henry Eighth) complaining of divers seditious persons having scattered abroad books. The like mode of publication was adopted by Burdet, tried " for conspiring to kill the king and the prince by casting their nativities, foretelling the speedy death of both, and *scattering* letters containing the prophecy among the people." 9 Foss's Judges of England, and Croke Car. 121.

The meaning and etymology of the word *Trail-lebaston* is discussed in 9 Foss's Judges of England, and note to Political Songs of England, and claimed to be different from that given in the Law Dictionaries.

That the mode of publication of libels among the Romans was by scattering them on the highways may be inferred from the provisions in the Codes in reference to the finding and finders of libels. The 4th resolution in Halliwood's Case, in Coke's fifth report commences, " If any one *find* a libel." (See 2 Starkie on Libel, 226.)

A new method of framing and dispersing libels was invented, says Hume, by the leaders of popular discontent : petitions to Parliament were drawn up stating particular grievances, presented and immediately printed.

A most cowardly and atrocious, yet ingenious, method of defaming is mentioned by Hazlitt in his " Essay on Wills," and referred in the London Quarterly Review for October, 1860, as thus : " A wealthy nobleman hit upon a still more culpable device for securing posthumous ignominy. He gave one lady of rank a legacy ' by way of compensation for injury he feared he had done her fair fame ;' a large sum to the daughter of another, a married woman, ' from a strong conviction that he was the father ;' and so on through half a dozen more items of the sort, each leveled at the reputation of some one from whom he had suffered a repulse ; the whole being nullified (without being erased) by a codicil."

[94] There must be a publication. (*Lyle* v. *Clason*, 1 Cai. 581 ; *Weir* v. *Hass*, 6 Ala. 881.)

ject the publisher to legal liability.   Ordinarily the context will
disclose in which of these several senses the term is employed.

§ 95. Every communication of language by one to another
is a publication.   But to constitute an *actionable publication*,
that is, such a publication as may confer a remedy by civil
action, it is essential that there be a publication to a *third person*, that is, to some person other than the author or publisher
and he whom or whose affairs the language concerns.   No possible form of words can confer a right of action for slander or
libel, unless there has been a publication to some third person.[95]
The husband or wife of the author or publisher, or the husband
or wife of him whom or whose affairs the language concerns, is
regarded as a third person.[96]

---

[95] 2 Starkie on Libel, 13, 14, citing 1 W. Saund. 132, note 2; *Phillips* v. *Jan-
son*, 2 Esp. Cas. 226; Hicks' Case, Hob. 215; *Rex* v. *Wegener*, 2 Stark. Cas. 245.
Where the defendant, knowing that letters addressed to the plaintiff were opened
and read by his clerk, wrote and sent a letter directed to the plaintiff which was
opened and read by his, plaintiff's, clerk, this was held to be a publication. (*Dela-
croix* v. *Thevenot*, 2 Starkie's Cas. 63.) Where a letter, folded but not sealed, was
delivered to a third person to be conveyed to the plaintiff, and was so conveyed
without being read by any one, held there was no publication. (*Clutterbuck* v.
Chaffers, 1 Starkie's Cas. 471.) Where a writing is sent to the plaintiff, and he,
in the presence of a third person, repeats the contents of such writing to the
writer, who admits having sent such a writing, this is not a publication of the
writing to the third party. (*Fonville* v. *Nease*, Dudley (S. C.), 303.)
  The delivery of a writing by the governor of a colony to his attorney-general, not for an official purpose, is an actionable publication. (*Wyatt* v. *Gore*,
Holt, 299.) So is the delivery of a writing to any third person. (*Ward* v.
Smith, 6 Bing. 749.)

[96] A sealed letter, addressed and delivered to the wife, containing a libel on
her husband, is a publication. (*Schenck* v. *Schenck*, 1 Spencer, 208; *Wenman* v.
Ash, 13 Com. B. 836.
  Gibbons wrote defamatory matter of Trumbull and had fifty copies printed in
pamphlet form in Massachusetts. Forty-five copies he retained and five copies
he sent to his wife in New Jersey, indorsing four of them with the names of certain persons, acquaintances of the wife, but without any instructions to the wife
as to how she should dispose of the copies so sent her. The wife delivered two of
the copies in New Jersey to the persons whose names were indorsed thereon, and
the others she delivered in New Jersey to Trumbull, who exhibited them to

§ 96. There cannot properly be said to be a communication of language by one to another unless that other understands the signification or meaning of the language sought to be communicated. When we say the language must be understood by the one to whom it is published, we mean only that the matter published must be in a language which the person to whom it is published can interpret to some meaning. To one who does not understand the language in which a publication is made, it is as to him nothing more than unmeaning sounds or signs and not language (§ 1).[77]

§ 97. The publication of language may, in reference to the place at which the publication is made, be either in the vernacular or in a foreign language. Where the language published is the vernacular to the place of publication, it requires no proof that those who heard or read it understood it ; but it may be shown that those who heard or read such language did not in fact understand its signification. Where the language published is one foreign to the place of publication it will not be assumed that those who heard or read it understood it, but it may be shown that such hearers or readers did, in fact, understand what they heard or read.[98] Where the matter published is in a

___

various persons. On Trumbull suing Gibbons in New York for libel, it was contended for defendant (1) that there was no publication by defendant, (2) or no publication within the State. The second point was overruled, and as to the first it was held that *the delivery of the manuscript to be printed* was a publication, and although a delivery to a wife in confidence would not be a publication, yet in the case then before the court the wife acted as the agent of her husband, and her delivery of the pamphlets amounted to a publication by the defendant. (*Trumbull* v. *Gibbons*, 3 City Hull Recorder, 97.)

[77] "Scandalous words, if they be spoken in an unknown tongue which none of the auditors understand, will not bear an action because they do no injury." (Danvers Abr. 146, pl. 1, 2.) "Where slander is published in a foreign language it is necessary to show that the hearers understood the language " (2 Starkie on Slander, 52 ; *Fleetwood* v. *Curley*, Hob. 267; Viner's Abr. tit. Actions for Words, A. b.), for the slander and damage consist in the apprehension of the hearers. (Cro. Eliz. 496, pl. 16.)

[98] *Amann* v. *Damm*, 8 Com. B. N. S. 597. But in Ohio it is held that where words are spoken in German in a German county, it will be presumed they were

language which he who hears or reads it understands, it will be assumed he understood it in the sense which properly belongs to it.   In all cases of doubt, the question whether or not the third person to whom the publication was made understood the language employed, is a question of fact.   How such third person understood the language, that is to say, the sense in which he understood it, is ordinarily a question of interpretation.   In our courts a witness cannot be asked how he understood the language, or what he understood by the language.[99]

§ 98. The publication of language may be orally or in writing. The distinction between these two modes of publication is material to be observed, as it marks the boundary line between slander and libel. That alone is a libel which " has an existence *per se* off the tongue." [100]

§ 99. Where language has not been reduced to writing, its communication from one to another must be an oral publication. Where the language has been reduced to writing, its communication from one to another may, according to the circumstances of the communication, amount to either an oral publication or a publication in writing.

§ 100. As respects oral language, speech, we must distinguish between the sound itself and the signification of the sound. As respects language in writing, we must distinguish

---

understood, and no averment that they were understood is necessary. (*Bechtell* v. *Shatter*, Wright, 107.) And as to Welsh words see what is said 1 W. Saund. 242, n. 1.

[99] *Smart* v. *Blanchard*, 42 N. H. 137; *Wright* v. *Paige*, 36 Barb. 438; *Gibson* v. *Williams*, 4 Wend. 320; *Van Vechten* v. *Hopkins*, 5 Johns. 211.   A witness who has heard a conversation cannot be asked " What did you understand by that," without previously laying a foundation for such a question by showing that something had previously occurred in consequence of which the words would convey a meaning different to their ordinary meaning; having done so, the witness may then be asked " What did you understand," &c. (*Daines* v. *Hartley*, 3 Ex. 200; 11 Law Times, 271: see 2 Starkie on Libel, 52; *Fleetwood* v. *Curley*, Hob. 267.) See *post, Construction.*

[100] Holt on Libel, 254 .

between the writing, the paper, or other substance written upon; the writing, the characters inscribed upon the paper, or other substance written upon; and the signification of those inscribed characters, the subject-matter of the writing.

§ 101. The possession of a writing, the material written upon, may be parted with, and the writing itself, the material written upon, may be passed from hand to hand without any communication of either the characters inscribed upon such material written upon, or of the signification of such characters. As, for example, the delivery of a sealed letter to another. Such a parting with the writing does not of itself, and without more, amount to a publication of any kind. Thus where a folded letter was delivered to a third person to deliver to him whom the subject-matter of the letter concerned, and the third person delivered the letter as addressed, without reading its contents, it was held that there was not any publication to such third person.[101]

§ 102. The characters inscribed upon a paper may be communicated by one to another without any parting with the possession of the writing, the material written upon, itself; as by an exposure of the writing, 'the material written upon, in such a manner as that the characters inscribed upon it may be seen and read by another, this would be a publication in writing.

§ 103. The subject-matter of a writing, the signification of the characters inscribed upon a paper, may be communicated

---

[101] *Clutterbuck* v. *Chaffers*, 1 Starkie's Cas. 471.

Throwing a sealed letter, addressed to the plaintiff or a third person, into the enclosure of another, who delivers it unopened to the plaintiff himself, is not a publication. (*Fonville* v. *Nease*, Dudley, S. C. 303.)

Sending to the person whom the writing concerns a letter sealed up is no publication; and a letter is always to be understood as being sealed up, unless otherwise expressed. (*Lyle* v. *Clason*, 1 Cai. 581; *Phillips* v. *Jansen*, 2 Esp. 625.) See 1 W. Saund. 132, *note* 2.

Nor would it amount to a publication, though the plaintiff afterwards repeated the contents of it publicly, and the defendant avowed himself the author of it. (*Fonville* v. *Nease*, Dudley, S. C. 303.)

orally by one to another; and if this be done without any parting with the possession of the writing itself, and without any
exposure of such writing to any other person; as where one
reads the contents of a writing to another without parting with
the writing itself, and without permitting the other to read the
contents of such writing. This we *suppose* would amount only
to an oral publication.[102]

§ 104. Parting with the possession of a writing, the material written upon, in such a condition and under such circumstances as that the characters inscribed upon it may be and are
seen and read and understood by another, is a publication in
writing. It amounts to a publication if or provided the subject-
matter be read and understood.[103]

§ 105. An exposure by one person to another of a writing,
the material written upon, without parting with the possession
of such writing, but permitting the writing, the characters inscribed, to be read by the other, is a publication in writing.

---

[102] The writer's reading to a stranger his letter to the plaintiff, before dis-
patching it, is a publication. (*Snyder* v. *Andrews*, 6 Barb. 43; *McCombs* v.
Tuttle, 5 Blackf. 481; *Van Cleef* v. *Lawrence*. 2 City Hall Recorder, 41.) Query,
the kind of publication.

[103] Posting a writing in a public place, and taking it down before any one had
read it, would not be a publication. (2 Starkie on Libel, 16, note n.)

A publication by delivery of letters containing the defamatory matter, or by
posting the writing on a church door, are termed *constructive publications* in
Baldwin v. *Elphinstone*, 2 W. Black. Rep. 1037, referring to Rastell's Entries tit.
Action sur le case, 13; *Penson* v. *Gooday*, 3 Cro. 97, 327.

By section 17 of statute 38 Geo. III., ch. 78, the printer or publisher of every
newspaper or other such paper is required to deliver a copy of the paper at the
stamp office, it was held that such delivery was a publication. (*Rex* v. *Amphlitt*,
4 B. & Cr. 35.)

If A. sends a manuscript to the printer of a periodical publication, and does
not restrain the printing and publishing of it, and. he prints and publishes it in
that publication, A. is the publisher, and liable to an action. (*Burdett* v. *Cobbett*,
5 Dowl. 301. See *Bond* v. *Douglas*, 7 Car. & P. 626.)

Printing, * * unless qualified by circumstances, is *prima facie* a publishing, the manuscript must be delivered to the compositors. (*Baldwin* v. *Elphinstone*, 2 W. Black. Rep. 1037; Holt on Libel, 293; *Trumbull* v. *Gibbons*, 3 City
Hall Recorder, 97.)

§ 106. Effigy resembles a writing, the material written upon, as distinguished from the subject-matter of a writing. An exposure of an effigy or a parting with the possession of it in such a condition that it may be seen by another is a publication.

§ 107. The requisites of *an oral publication* are: (1) that the language be spoken to or in the presence of at least some one third person (§ 95). No possible form of words can be the basis of an action for slander if at the time of their utterance the only persons present are the speaker and the person whom or whose affairs the language concerns.[104] (2) The third person present must *hear* the language spoken.[105] Whether the third person present at the speaking did or did not hear the language spoken is, in every case, a question of fact. And this is not the less the rule, because where the speaking is in the presence of a third person, under such circumstances that he might have heard what was spoken, he may, as a rule of evidence, be assumed to have heard it, unless it be shown that he did not hear.[106] The burden is on him who alleges a publication to establish that the third person heard the language spoken. (3) The third person must understand the language (§ 96). When hereafter we speak of an oral publication, or a publication orally, we shall intend a publication with the requisites above mentioned.

§ 108. The requisites of *a publication in writing* are (1) that the writing, the material written upon, be so exposed as that

---

[104] Uttering slanderous words in the presence of the person slandered only is not actionable. (*Sheffill* v. *Van Deusen*, 13 Gray, 304); and see note 95, *ante.*

[105] "If none heard the words it is no slander." Viner's Abr. tit. Actions for Words. L. *b.* 4; and see cases cited, 1 Caines' R. 582.

[106] The word "publish," as applied to speech, implies that the language was spoken in the presence and hearing of others. (*Watts* v. *Greenlee*, 2 Dev. 115; Viner's Abr. tit. Actions for Words, L. *b.* 4; *contra, Burton* v. *Burton*, 3 Iowa, 316.) In slander it is sufficient if the words are laid to have been spoken "in the presence" of others. (*Brown* v. *Brashier*, 2 Penns. 114.) Or in the presence and hearing of divers persons, or of certain persons named. (*Burbank* v. *Horn,* 39 Maine, 233), and see 1 W. Saund. 242, *n.* 1.

the subject-matter of the writing is *read* by at least some one third person (§ 101). No possible form of language in writing can be the basis of an action for libel if read only by the writer and the person whom or whose affairs the language concerns.[107] (2) The subject-matter of the writing must be *understood* by at least some one third person by whom it is read (§ 96). When hereafter we speak of a publication in writing, we shall intend a publication with the requisites above mentioned.

§ 109. The publication must be *prior* to the commencement of the action, and a publication prior to the commencement of the action should be proved.[108] Where a witness called to prove publication was unable to say whether the speaking the words referred to was before or after the date when the action was commenced, it was decided that his testimony was not admissible.[109] But it was held not to be a ground for arresting the judgment that it appeared on the face of the record that the writ issued prior to the alleged publication.[110]

§ 110. The place of publication may be within or without the territorial limits of the State or country within which redress is sought. The decisions, so far as they go, all hold, that as a question of jurisdiction, it is immaterial whether the publication was within or without the territorial limits of the State or country within which redress is sought, and this on the ground that the wrong follows the person and may be redressed by civil action in any court having jurisdiction of the person at the time redress is sought. It is conceded, however, that as regards *crimes* no redress can be had in one State for a crime enacted within the territorial limits of another State, because a crime is a violation of the law of the State within which it is

---

[107] But delivery to the party libelled is a sufficient publication to support an indictment. (*Phillips* v. *Jansen*, 2 Esp. 624.)

[108] *Taylor* v. *Sturgingger*, 2 Rep. Con. Ct. 367.

[109] *Steward* v. *Layton*, 3 Dowl. Pr. Cas. 480.

[110] *Scovel* v. *Kingsley*, 7 Conn. R. 284.

enacted. This concession implies that for a wrong committed in one State there can be no remedy in another; because the right to a remedy is based on a violation of some general prohibition of the law, and not like a remedy on contract for a breach of a private convention between the parties, which of course 'follows the persons of the parties to the convention.[111]

[111] Mr. Stephens, in his "Treatise on Criminal Law," insists that a crime and a tort differ only as regards their consequences.

No court "administers justice in general" (*De Bode* v. *Reg.*, 13 Ad. & El., N. S. 386), and "the laws of a State have no force *proprio vigore* beyond its territorial limits." (*Hoyt* v. *Thompson*, 1 Selden, 340.) "If two persons fight in France, and both happening casually to be here [in England], one should bring an action of assault against the other, it might be doubtful whether such an action could be maintained here [in England]. * * * It might perhaps be triable only where both parties at the time were subjects." (*Mostyn* v. *Fabrigas*, 20 State Tr. 82; 1 Smith's Leading Cases.) In *Molony* v. *Dows* (8 Abb. Pr. R. 316) it was held at *nisi prius*, but after elaborate argument and deliberation, that an action for an assault in California could not be maintained in the courts of the State of New York. In *McIvor* v. *McCabe* (16 Abb. Pr. R. 319), it was held that the courts of New York had jurisdiction of an action for a personal injury committed in New Jersey by one citizen of that State upon another. As to actions for tort committed in a foreign country, see *Scott* v. *Seymour*, 6 Law Times Rep. N. S. 607.

To maintain an indictment for libel, the publication must be proved to have been made in the county laid in the indictment, all matters of crime being local. (Holt on Libel, 299; citing *Rex* v. *Johnson*, 7 East, 65.) In *Trumbull* v. *Gibbons*, 3 City Hall Recorder, 97, the libel was printed in Boston and published in New Jersey, but held the courts of New York had jurisdiction; and see *Glen* v. *Hodges*, 9 Johns. 67; *Smith* v. *Bull*, 17 Wend. 323.

If one of our citizens goes into Canada and slanders his neighbor, an action will lie in this State. (*Lister* v. *Wright*, 2 Hill, 320.)

An action for slander will lie, in Indiana, for words spoken in another State actionable at common law. (*Offutt* v. *Earlywine*, 4 Blackf. 460; *Linville* v. *Earlywine*, 4 Blackf. 469; *Stout* v. *Wood*, 1 id. 71.) And the same in Connecticut. (*Langdon* v. *Young*, 33 Verm., 4 Shaw, 136.)

In an action of slander brought in Indiana, it will be presumed, until the contrary be proved, that they were spoken in that State. (*Worth* v. *Butler*, 7 Blackf. 251.)

It is sometimes necessary to show a publication in a particular county. Where the defendant wrote letters in Ireland, and sent them to Middlesex county, England, to be printed and published, and the letters were there published, it was held to be a publication by the defendant in Middlesex county. (*Rex* v. *Johnson*, 7 East, 65; and to the like effect *Rex* v. *Middleton*, Str. 77.) Where A. wrote a letter and sent it by mail to B., in the county of B., and it was again sent by

The effect of the place of publication upon the construction of the language published, and as a question of *venue*, and as affecting the liability, will hereafter be considered.

§ 111. The *person who makes a publication* is a publisher. In the text books, and in reference to slander and libel, the term publisher is employed sometimes to signify the person who actually makes a publication, and sometimes the person who, not being the actual publisher, is liable for the publication; *is liable, as publisher.* We shall always employ the term publisher in the sense of and to signify the person who actually makes the publication.

§ 112. *Republication* is a second or subsequent publication of the *same language.* *Repetition* is a publication of language of *the same import* or meaning, as the language of a previous publication. Repetition is a *subsequent publication* independent and distinct from the first publication. There may be a republication of a writing, the material written upon, there may be a repetition of the subject-matter of a writing, and there may be a repetition of oral language (speech), but there cannot be a republication of oral language.

§ 113. Speech is but sound, a mere vibration of the atmosphere, cognizable only by the auditory sense. From its nature it necessarily follows that the *same* sound cannot be repeated; a *similar* or a *like* sound may be produced, undistinguishable in every respect from the first, and of the like character and signification, but that will not be the same sound. One who re-

---

mail to the county of M., at which county B. received and read it, held to be a publication in the county of M. (*Rex* v. *Watson,* 1 Camp. 215; and see *Rex* v. *Girdwood,* East's P. C. 1116, 1120; Case of the Seven Bishops, 4 State Trials, 304; *Rex* v. *Burdett,* 4 B. & A. 717; 2 Starkie on Slander, 39–43; *Commonwealth* v. *Blanding,* 3 Pick. 304.)

In an action for suspending a lamp before the plaintiff's house, intimating that it was a house of ill-fame, the parish in which the declaration states the house to have stood and the tort to have been committed, is to be considered as venue merely, and not as local description, and it is immaterial whether there be any such parish in existence. (*Jefferies* v. *Duncombe,* 2 Camp. 3; 11 East, 226.) And see *Mersey Navigation Company* v. *Douglas,* 2 East, 497.

peats a word previously spoken does not utter the identical
word, but a similar or like word; he repeats *a like* sound of *the
same signification* as the first. The two sounds are separate
and distinct, although each has the same meaning. Hence each
publication of oral language is a new, distinct, and separate
publication.

§ 114. As respects oral publications, the person who actually
makes the publication, the publisher, and the person liable as
the publisher, must be always one and the same person. Every
speaker is the publisher of what he speaks, and is solely liable
therefor. That the words spoken have been previously published by another, can neither relieve the subsequent speaker
from his liability for the publication made by him, nor impose
any liability on the previous publisher. The act of publication
is as to each publisher an entirely distinct act. Each person
can be liable only for the publication made by him. If one
makes an oral publication, and another repeats it, the first publisher is not liable for the repetition.[112] Besides that, the repetition is not a repetition of the same language (§ 113). The
repetition is neither a necessary nor a natural and proximate
consequence of the first publication.

§ 115. As respects a publication by writing, a libel, not only
the publisher but all who in anywise aid or are concerned in the
production of the writing are liable as publishers; the publication of the writing is the act of all concerned in the production
of the writing (§ 113). Thus, if one composes and dictates, a
second writes, and a third publishes, all are liable as publishers,
and each is liable as a publisher.[113]

<hr>

[112] Where A. uttered a slander of B. the wife of C., and B. repeated the slander
to C., in consequence of which C. refused to cohabit with B., held that no action
could be maintained against A.; the publication was not A.'s, and A. was not responsible for the consequences of it. (*Parkins* v. *Scott*, 6 Law Times Rep. N. S. 894.)
The person who originates the slander can only be liable for the special damage
occasioned by his own communication of it. (*Cates* v. *Kellogg*, 9 Ind. 506; *Dixon*
v. *Smith*, 5 Hurl. & Nor. 450.)

[113] All concerned in making a libel are alike liable. "The law denominates
them all makers." (Holt on Libel, 288, 289; 2 Starkie on Slander, 225; Bishop's

§ 116. The mere composing or writing any certain form of words, and keeping the writing and its contents confined to the custody and to the knowledge of the composer or writer, so that it is not communicated to any other person, does not render the composer or writer liable either to indictment or to civil action, for there is no publication. So, having or retaining possession of a writing, no matter by whom written, cannot amount to a wrong by the person so having or retaining possession of such writing ; for as to him, at least, there is no publication.[114] The

---

Crim. Law, § 931 [814], citing *Rex* v. *Drake*, Holt, 425; *Rex* v. *Paine*, 5 Mod. 163; *Rex* v. *Bear*, Carth. 407; *Rex* v. *Williams*, 2 Camp. 646.) "All persons who concur and show their assent or approbation to do an unlawful act, are guilty; so that murdering a man's reputation by a scandalous libel may be compared to murdering his person; and if several are assenting and encouraging a man in that act, though the stroke was given by one, yet all are guilty of homicide." (Quoted by Kent, Ch. J., in *Dole* v. *Lyon*, 10 Johns. 461.)

The publisher is equally responsible with the author of a libel. (*Dexter* v. *Spear*, 4 Mason, 115.) Printer and editor are both liable. (*Watts* v. *Fraser*, 7 Car. & P. 369.) The responsibility of the writer of a private letter for the publication of its contents, is not limited to the consequences of a communication of them to the person to whom the letter is addressed, but extends to the probable consequences of thus putting the letter in circulation. (*Miller* v. *Butler*, 6 Cush. 71.)

Where, in case for oral and written slander, to support the count on the latter, a reporter to a newspaper was called, who proved that he had written down from the defendant's mouth (who said at the time it would make a good case for the newspapers) the statement which he afterwards sent to the editor, and that a paragraph, which afterwards appeared, was in substance the same ; held. that what was so published in consequence of what passed with the defendant might be considered as published by the defendant; but to prove that what was published was the same as that given to the editor by the reporter, could only be done by producing the written paper itself. (*Adams* v. *Kelly*, 1 Ry. & M. 158.)

Two persons having participated in the composition of a libelous letter written by one of them, which was afterwards put into the post-office, and sent by mail to the person to whom it was addressed; such participation was held to be competent and sufficient evidence to prove a publication by both. (*Miller* v. *Butler*, 6 Cush. 71.) And see *Rex* v. *Cooper*, 15 Law Jour. Rep. Q. B. 206.

[114] Until publication, possession of a libel is no more than the possession of a man's thoughts. (*Rex* v. *Almon*, 5 Burr. 2689.) So long as the writer retains possession of the writing he has a *locus penitentiæ* ; but "The moment a man delivers a libel from his hands, and ceases to have control over it, there is an end of his *locus penitentiæ* ; the *injuria* is complete, and the libeler [the writer] may

composer and the writer of matter which is afterwards published is liable as publisher for such publication.[115] And this liability, *as we suppose*, is not to be qualified by the circumstances under which the publication occurred. It would be no excuse to say that the writing was kept guarded and concealed, and was taken from him by force, or obtained from him by fraud or by the procurement of the party whom or whose affairs it concerns.[116] If the matter written is of an injurious tendency, and any injury ensues from its publication, the composer and the writer is liable, not because of any imputed or presumed malice in making the publication, but because unless such a writing had been created the injury occasioned by it could not have happened; creating the writing and preserving it were wrongful acts, for the necessary or natural and proximate consequences of which the author is liable.

§ 117. The material written upon, and the subject-matter inscribed upon such material, are substantial entities. The very identical writing may be passed from hand to hand, and each such passage is as well a separate and distinct publication as a republication of such writing. Every person concerned in making such a publication is liable not alone for the consequences of that publication, but for the consequences of any subsequent publication of the *same writing*. One and the same writing may be many times published at the same or at several and distinct places, and may have many publishers; and many persons may be liable as publishers at one and the same time or at several times. The subject-matter of a writing cannot be

be called upon to answer for his act" (*Rex* v. *Burdett*, 4 B. & Ald. 148; Holroyd, J.); and see 5 Mod. 167; Holt on Libel, 294; 2 Starkie on Slander, 228; *Rex* v. *Rosenstein*, 2 Car. & P. 414.

[115] Holt on Libel, 289; *Bond* v. *Douglass*, 7 C. & P. 626; *Miller* v. *Butler*, 6 Cush. 71; *Burdett* v. *Cobbett*, 5 Dowl. 301; *Giles* v. *The State*, 6 Geo. 276.

[116] Where the plaintiff sent his agent to the office of the defendant, the publisher of a newspaper, to purchase a copy of the paper, held that a sale to such agent was a publication to a third person. (*Brunswick* v. *Harmer*, 14 Q. B. 185; see *King* v. *Waring*, 5 Esp. Cas. 13; *Smith* v. *Wood*, 3 Camp. 323; *Thorn* v. *Moser*, 1 Denio, 488; *Griffiths* v. *Lewis*, 7 Ad. & Ell. N. S. 61; contra, see *Sutton* v. *Smith*, 13 Miss. 120.)

republished apart and separate from a republication of the writing, the material written upon. Apart from the material on which the matter is inscribed, it is as impossible to republish the same subject-matter of a writing as it is to republish the same sound or oral language or speech. If one copies the subject-matter of a writing upon another piece of material, the copy is no more the SAME subject-matter as the subject-matter copied from, than is the repetition of a sound au uttering of the same sound. The copy is not the same writing but another—a second and independent writing, having *the like* but not *the same* subject-matter. A publication of this copy would have no other connection with the original than that it contained *the like* subject-matter. The persons liable for the publication of the first writing would not be liable for the publication of the second or the copy, and the persons responsible for the publication of the second writing would not be responsible for the publication of the original writing. The publication of the second writing is neither a necessary nor a natural and proximate consequence of the publication of the first writing, nor is a publication of the first writing a necessary or a natural and proximate consequence of the publication of the second writing. It may be urged that but for the publication of the first writing the second might not, or perhaps could not, have come into existence. The author of the second writing could not have possessed the material or knowledge requisite for its production. The same objection would apply, and with equal force, to an oral publication. If the first speaker had not uttered the words the second speaker could not have repeated them. We know such an objection would be unavailing. Again, it may be urged that the one who dictates the language forming the subject-matter of a writing, which is afterwards published by another, is responsible for such publication, either solely or jointly with the publisher, or that the writing first published is equivalent to a dictation of the language of the second writing; but this is not so; the dictation, to incur any responsibility for a subsequent publication of the language dictated, must be made with *an intent or a request* that the language so dictated shall be subsequently published (§§ 115, 118).

§ 118. There may be a joint publication by writing, but, for the reasons heretofore stated (§ 113), there cannot be a joint oral publication. If two or more utter the *like* words, either simultaneously or separately, it is not a joint publication, but a several publication by each, for which each must be sued separately, and for which they cannot be sued jointly.[117] Within this rule husband and wife are considered as separate individuals. If husband and wife utter the like words, either simultaneously or separately, there are two publications—a separate publication by each. For the words uttered by the husband he must be sued alone ; for the words uttered by the wife, the husband and wife must be sued together.[118] Two or more may agree together (conspire) in composing a set of words which one or both shall speak ; that is to say, two or more may conspire to injure another by an oral publication of language ; for this the remedy would be, not an action for slander, but an action for a conspiracy to defame.[119]

§ 119. Where the publication is the joint act of two or more, they may be sued jointly or separately ; if sued separately, the plaintiff can have but one satisfaction, but may elect *de melioribus damnis.* Thus, where A. brought an action of libel against B., who pleaded *puis darrein continuance,* that he was a partner with C. in the printing and publishing the newspaper which contained the libel, and that A. brought a previous action against C. for the same identical publication, and recovered a judgment which had been satisfied, &c. On demurrer this

---

[117] A joint action cannot be maintained against two or more persons for slander. (*Webb* v. *Cecil,* 9 B. Mon. 198 ; *Forsyth* v. *Edmiston,* 2 Abb. Pr. R. 481 ; 5 Duer, 658 ; *Chamberlaine* v. *Willmore,* Palm. 313 ; 1 Bulst. 15 ; 2 W. Saund. 117 a.)

It is impossible for three men to make arbitrament by word of mouth, because it cannot be jointly pronounced. (Lawson's Case, Clayt. 17, A. D. 1668.)

[118] There must be separate actions or words spoken by a husband and a wife. (*Penters* v. *England,* 1 M'Cord, 14 ; *Malone* v. *Stillwell,* 15 Abb. Pr. R. 425.)

[119] See 2 Hilliard on Torts, 444, 458 *n. ;* 8 Barr. 237 ; 10 *id.* 369 ; 11 Met. 856.

was held a good plea, and that the plaintiff could have but one satisfaction, but might elect *de melioribus damnis.*[120]

§ 120. A publication, the act of publishing, must be upon some occasion (§ 50), and must be voluntary or involuntary (§ 67). Liability as publisher depends upon the occasion and upon whether, as to the person sought to be charged, the publication was voluntary or involuntary, and generally upon the principles to which reference has heretofore been made (§§ 50, 67, 68, 70). In the text books and reports much is said on the subject of privileged publications, employing the term publication to mean as well the act of publishing as the matter published; and these privileged publications are divided into such as are *absolutely* privileged and such as are *conditionally* privileged. Reserving the subject of privileged publication to be hereafter considered at length, we limit ourself here to stating that *all involuntary* and *some voluntary* publications are privileged.

§ 121. Where a closed paper is given to an employé to deliver to another, it becomes the duty of the employé to deliver such paper as directed, without inspecting its contents, and in making the delivery without ascertaining the contents of the paper, he performs a duty ; and, as the performance of a duty is an involuntary act (§ 39), and cannot amount to a wrong (§ 42), if it happen that the paper contained defamatory matter, the employé incurs no liability. The act of publishing *defamatory matter* was as to him *involuntary.* He did not know, and was not under any obligation to know, the contents of the paper carried and delivered by him. He could have known the contents of the paper only by a violation of his duty; having simply performed his duty, no liability attached to him.[121]   But

---

[120] *Thomas* v. *Rumsay,* 6 Johns. 26 ; *Brown* v. *Hirley,* 5 Up. Can. Q. B. R. (O. S.) 734 ; *Webb* v. *Cecil,* 9 B. Mon. 198.

[121] In Nutt's case, as reported Barnard. 306, it is said : if a servant carries a libel for his master, he certainly is liable for what he does, though he cannot so much as read or write. Mr. Starkie (2 Starkie on Slander, 29, note *f*), refer-

if, in such a case, the employé does in fact know the contents of the paper, he cannot excuse himself by saying he carried and delivered it as agent or employé (§ 67). Ordinarily it would be said that the non-liability of the employé, in the instance above put, arose from the absence of *malice* on his part in making the publication; but this can only mean that he had a legal excuse for performing the act, namely, that the act, so far as it was wrongful, was as to him involuntary. This is the

ring to this dictum, says: " It is impossible not to dissent from this doctrine, so expressed, without the qualification added that the servant had some reason to know that he was discharging an illegal mission." To constitute a publication such as will render the publisher liable to an action, the publication must be *knowingly*. (*Layton* v. *Harris*, 3 Harring. 406.) Intentional. (*Viele* v. *Gray*, 10 Abb. Pr. R. 12; 18 How. Pr. 'R. 567). One is not liable for a publication *inadvertently*. (*Rex* v. *Abingdon*, 1 Esp. Cas. 228.) As by delivering by *mistake* a paper out of his study. (5 Mod. 167; Holt on Libel, 290.) Or if it be stolen from him. See *Weir* v. *Hoss*, 6 Ala. 881; *Barrow* v. *Lewellin*, Hob. 62; 1 Hill. Torts, 321, note 7. Reading a libel in the presence of another without knowing it before to be a libel, with or without malice, does not amount to a publication. (4 Bac. Abr. 458; Holt on Libel, 290.) But if he who has either read a libel himself or has heard it read by another, do afterwards maliciously read or repeat any part of it in the presence of others, or lend or show it to another, he is guilty of an unlawful publication of it. (Hawk. P. C. c. 73, § 10; Holt on Libel, 291.) Reading a libel by command of his father or master is not an actionable publication—so said Comyn's Dig. tit. Libel, B. 2, and cited George on Libel, 162.

If a man deliver *by mistake* a libellous paper out of his study, he would probably be held liable civilly, for the publication was by his carelessness. (*Mayne* v. *Fletcher*, 4 M. & Ry. 312.)

" The mere act of communicating that which is slanderous will not subject a party even to civil liability without some degree of culpability on his part. If, for instance, a servant or agent were in the ordinary course of his duty to deliver a sealed libel, without any knowledge of its contents, though he were thus the actual instrument of publication, yet if he acted but as the agent of another, without any reason for suspecting that any wrong was intended, he would not subject himself to any civil, still less to any criminal responsibility." (Starkie on Libel, 226, [227].)

In an action against the defendant for publishing libels, it appearing that five packets, addressed to individuals and enclosed in one addressed to him, had been received at the coach-office where he was porter, and he delivered them; held that if the jury found that he did so in the course of his business, and in ignorance of the contents, he was not liable; but, being *prima facie* liable, it was for him to show such ignorance. (*Day* v. *Bream*, 2 M. & Rob. 54.)

true ground for the decisions in which the non-liability is said to be the absence of malice. Those that cannot be explained on this ground were either erroneously decided or decided upon erroneous grounds. The true ground for the decision in *Smith* v. *Ashley*[122] was that there was no " *conscious violation* " of law or " *culpable knowledge*."[123] The work of fiction published had nothing on its face to indicate that it reflected upon any individual or his affairs ; the publisher did not know, and had no means of knowing, that it reflected on any individual or his affairs ; in so far, therefore, as it did reflect upon any individual, it was as to the publisher an involuntary act, equally as much as the unconscious delivery by an employé of defamatory matter by the direction of his employer. This subject will be further discussed hereafter, when we come to treat of defences.

§ 122. Upon the principles of law condensed in the expression *respondeat superior*, one is responsible not only for what he does or omits to do in his own proper person, but also for all that his *agents* may do or omit to do in and about his business. Every one is charged with the duty to exercise such a vigilance in the selection of agents, animate and inanimate, as are competent and adequate to the performance of the business they may be required to transact and the ends they may be designed to accomplish ; he must exercise such a control over them that in the transaction of his business they neither do or omit to do any act amounting to a wrong. He cannot

---

[122] An action for a libel cannot be maintained against the publisher of a newspaper, if he has no knowledge, at the time of publication, that the article complained of is libellous. Hence, if he publishes an article which he believes to be a fictitious narrative, or mere fancy sketch, and does not know that it is applicable to any one, he cannot be held responsible, although it was intended by the writer to be libellous, and to apply to the party who brings the action. In such case, the writer only is answerable to the party libeled. (*Smith* v. *Ashley*, 11 Met. 367.)

[123] See note 73. *ante*. " He who shall be convicted in the said case either ought to be a contriver of the libel, or a procurer of the contriving of it, or a *malicious* publisher of it, *knowing it to be a libel*." (9 Co. 59, Mo. 813 ; George on Libel, 107.)

escape this liability by omitting to exercise this vigilance; for such omission is itself negligence. It is upon this principle, and not upon any presumption of malice, that an employer or principal is held responsible for the act of his servant or agent.[124]

§ 123. The proprietor of a newspaper is responsible for all that appears in its columns, although the publication may have been made, without his knowledge, in his absence, and contrary to his orders. His liability is not on the ground of his being the publisher, nor of being presumed to be the publisher, but because he is responsible for the acts of the actual publisher.[125]

---

[124] Legal criminality is merely legal responsibility, and may exist where there is no moral criminality whatever. (Holt on Libel, 53.)   Malice, in legal understanding, implies no more than *wilfulness* (id. 55, note 74 *ante*), and between *negligence* and *wilfulness* there is no difference but of degree.   (*Bramwell B. Mangan* v. *Atterton*, 1 Law Reports, Ex. 240.)   Negligence embraces acts of commission as well as of omission, and diligence implies action as well as forbearance to act.   (*Grant* v. *Mosely*, 29 Ala. 302.)   But the only principle on which a man can be rendered liable for the wrongful acts of another, is that such a relation exists between them that the former, whether he be called principal or master, is bound to control the conduct of the latter whether he be agent or servant.   The maxim of the law is respondeat superior.   (*Blackwell* v. *Wiswall*, 14 How. Pr. R. 258.)

In an action for a libel contained in a letter: Proof that it was written by defendant's daughter, who was authorized to make out his bills and write his general letters of business, is not sufficient, unless it can be shown that such libel was written with the knowledge of or by the procurement of the defendant. (*Harding* v. *Greening*, 1 Moore, 477; 1 Holt N. P. 531; 8 Taunt. 42.)   Writing the letter was not within the scope of the daughter's authority to act for her father. (*Id.*)   A parent is not liable as such for the wrongful acts of his child. (*Tifft* v. *Tifft*, 4 Denio, 175, and see *Moon* v. *Towers*, 8 Com. B. N. S. 611.)

If an attorney introduces slanderous matter into the pleadings, without the direction of his client, the client is not responsible.   (*Hardin* v. *Cumstock*, 2 A. K. Marsh, 480.)

[125] The proprietor of a newspaper is responsible for whatever appears in its columns.   It is unnecessary to show that he knew of the publication, or authorized it.   (*Huff* v. *Bennett*, 4 Sand. 120.)   For he is liable even though the publication was made in his absence and without his knowledge by an agent to whom he had given express instructions to publish nothing exceptionable, personal, or abusive, which might be brought in by the author of the libel.   (*Dunn* v. *Hall*, 1 Carter (Ind.), 344; 1 Smith, 228.)   And see *Curtis* v. *Mussey*, 6 Gray (Mass.), 261.

124. The liability of the proprietor of a newspaper is shared
in common with the proprietor of a printing press, a printer,
book publisher, and bookseller. The proprietor of a bookstore
is liable for the contents of every book and paper sold in his
store.[126]

An action for a libel lies against the proprietor of a gazette edited by another,
though the publication was made without the knowledge of such proprietor.
(*Andres* v., *Wells*, 7 Johns. 269.)

But if a printing press and newspaper establishment be assigned to a person
merely as security for a debt, and the press remain in the sole possession and
management of the assignor, the ownership of the person holding the security or
lien is not such as will render him liable to an action as proprietor. (*Id.*)

A receiver of a newspaper establishment, appointed to take charge thereof,
and continue the publication of the newspaper, would be responsible for any
defamatory matter published in the newspaper while the same was under his
control. (*Marten* v. *Van Schaick*, 4 Paige, 479.) A receiver was appointed to
carry on the publication of a newspaper in *Dayton* v. *Wilkes*, 17 How. Pr. R. 510.

The editor and publisher of a newspaper is answerable in law, if its contents
are libellous, unless the libellous matter was inserted by some one without his
order and against his will. (*The Commonwealth* v. *Kneeland*, Thacher's Crim.
Cas. 346.)

Rex v. *Gutch*, 1 Moo. & Mal. 433, on the trial of defendant for publishing
a libel in a newspaper of which he was the proprietor, it was contended on his
behalf that he was not liable, because he took no part in the publication of the
newspaper; but he was held liable and the court said: A person who derives
profit from and who furnishes means for carrying on the concern, and entrusts the
conduct of the publication to one whom he selects, and in whom he confides,
may be said to cause to be published what actually appears;" and see *Rex* v.
Alexander, 1 Moo. & Mal. 437.

[126] "It is not material whether the person who disperses libels is acquainted
with their contents or otherwise, for nothing would be more easy than to publish
the most virulent papers with the greatest security, if the concealing the purport
of them from an illiterate publisher would make him safe in dispersing them.
(2 Starkie on Slander, 30, note *s.*; Moore, 627; Wood's Inst. 431; Bac. Abr. tit.
Libel, 458.) See note 121 *ante*.

Nutt's Case, Fitzg. 47; Barnard. 306: The defendant was tried for publishing
a libel. It appeared in evidence the defendant kept a pamphlet shop, and that
the libel was sold in defendant's shop, by her servant, for her account, in her
absence, and that she did not know the contents of it, nor of its coming in or
going out. This was held to be a publication by the defendant, but a jury was
withdrawn.

Rex v. *Dodd*, 2 Sess. Cas. 33: The defendant was tried for publishing a libel.
It was insisted for the defendant that she was sick, and that the libel was taken

CHAPTER VII.

CONSTRUCTION OF LANGUAGE.

Actionable quality of language dependent upon its construction. All language ambiguous or unambiguous. Difficult to determine what is and what is not ambiguous. Points upon which ambiguity arise. Causes of ambiguity. Ambiguity, how explained. Different effect of language concerning a person and of language concerning a thing. Materiality of questions, what person or thing affected, and whether the person is affected as an individual merely, or in some acquired capacity. Principles of construction; before verdict—after verdict. Examples of construction. Divisible matter.

§ 125. Language as a means for effecting a wrong must be either such as *is actionable* or such as *is not actionable*. To which of these divisions any particular language is to be referred, depends upon the construction of the language in question. Anterior, therefore, to an inquiry into what language is and what language is not actionable, it is proper to consider at least the principal rules by which alleged defamatory language is construed.

---

into her house without her knowledge; this was held no excuse, the law presumed her acquainted with what her servant did.

Rex v. Almon, 5 Burr. 2689, the liability of booksellers was much discussed, and the court expressed an opinion that the sale of a libel in a bookseller's shop was *prima facie* evidence of a publication, though not so conclusive but that it might be rebutted by circumstances. It is said (2 Starkie on Slander, 34): "But the defendant may rebut the presumption by evidence that the libel was sold contrary to his orders, or clandestinely; or that some deceit or surprise was practiced upon him; or that he was absent under circumstances which entirely negative any presumption of privity or connivance." And reference is made to *Rex* v. *Almon,* supra, and to Woodfalls' Case, where the defendant was imprisoned at the time of the publication by his servant, and without his privity. In *Rex* v. *Fisher,* 1 Moo. & Mal. 483, it is said the presumption arising from proprietorship of a newspaper may be rebutted, and an exemption established. If the publi-

§ 126. Language may be ambiguous or unambiguous.[127] It is not easy in every case to determine what is ambiguous and what is unambiguous language. Language may be unambiguous on its face, which, by reason of some circumstances connected with it, is in fact ambiguous. This is always the case with language used ironically. When language is unambiguous on its face it must be construed as unambiguous, unless its ambiguity be shown ; and on the one who asserts the ambiguity of language unambiguous on its face, is the burden of establishing the ambiguity.[128]

---

cation is made without the consent of the writer, the offence is not complete as to him. (*Weir* v. *Hoss*, 6 Ala. 881. See Holt on Libel, 294.) As if the writing be stolen from him. (*Mayne* v. *Fletcher*, 9 B. & C. 382.)

In *Chubb* v. *Flanaghan*, 6 Car. & P. 431, it was held that if a publication consists in merely selling a few copies of a periodical in which the libel was contained among the articles, it was a question for the jury whether the defendant *knew* what he was selling.

[127] " Words or signs may be divided into three classes : (1) those which bear an obvious and precise meaning on the face of them ; as if A. say to B., you *murdered* C. ; (2) those which on the face of them are of dubious import, and are capable either of a criminal or innocent meaning ; as if A. says to B., you were *the death* of C. ; (3) those which are *prima facie* and abstractedly innocent, and which derive their offensive quality from some collateral or extrinsic circumstance ; as if A. says to B., you *did not murder* C., which words, from the ironical manner of speaking them, may convey to the hearers as unequivocal a charge of murder as the most direct imputation." (1 Starkie on Slander, 46.)

[128] " Where the words of themselves impute a larceny, and are unaccompanied by an explanation showing the hearers that they were not so intended, the defendant must show that they referred to a transaction that was not larceny, and were so understood by all who heard them. And where the plaintiff had taken wood through mistake, and the defendant, knowing the excuse for taking it, persists in charging him with stealing, in reference to such taking, he cannot fall back and rest upon the plaintiff's innocence." (*Phillips* v. *Barber*, 7 Wend. 439.)

" As doubtful or apparently innocent words may by circumstances be shown to be actionable, so may words apparently actionable be explained by circumstances to have been intended and understood in an innocent sense. Thus, though the defendant should say, Thou art a murtherer, the words would not be actionable if the defendant could make it appear that he was conversing with the plaintiff concerning unlawful hunting, when the plaintiff confessed that he killed several hares with certain engines, upon which the defendant said, Thou art a murtherer, meaning a murtherer of hares so killed. 4 Co. 13." (1 Starkie on Slander, 98.)

§ 127. When language is ambiguous, the ambiguity may be either (1) whether the language concerns a person or a thing, or (2) what person or what thing it concerns, or (3) if it concerns a person does it concern him as an individual merely or in some acquired capacity, as in an office, trade or profession; (4) what is the import or signification of the language, and (5) is the charge or matter divisible or indivisible.

§ 128. The ambiguity may be patent or latent, that is to say the ambiguity may be inherent in the language and apparent upon its face, or the ambiguity may arise by reason of the language in question being connected with some other language or event in such a manner as that its accustomed signification is affected and changed by such other language or event.

§ 129. The ambiguity of language unambiguous upon its face is shown, and the ambiguity of language in every case is explained, by introducing the other language or event which exhibits or which explains the ambiguity, and by alleging the supposed true meaning of the language in question. The manner by which ambiguity is shown and explained is by allegations in pleading, termed averments, colloquia, and innuendoes, the nature and offices of which several allegations will be considered under the head of Pleading.[129]

---

[129] An *averment* is to ascertain that to the court which is generally or doubtfully expressed, so that the court may not be perplexed of *whom*, or of *what*, it [the language] ought to be understood, and to add matter to the plea to make doubtful things clear. A *colloquium* serves to show that the words were spoken in reference to the matter of the averment. An *innuendo* is explanatory of the subject-matter sufficiently explained before, and it is explanatory of such matter only; for it cannot extend the sense of the words beyond their own meaning unless something is put upon the record for it to explain. (*Van Vechten* v. *Hopkins*, 5 Johns. 220.)

It seems that in some instances where the language is unambiguous on its face the plaintiff will not be allowed to treat it as ambiguous and give it a meaning different from that it ordinarily bears. Thus the words spoken of a dyer were "Thou art not worth a groat," the plaintiff alleged that at E., where the words were spoken, they were all one as calling him Bankrupt. The court held the averment idle, because the words in themselves imply a plain and intelligible sense. (*Meade* v. *Axe*, Mar. 15, pl. 37; and see *McCluskey* v. *Cromwell*, 1 Kernan, 601.)

§ 130. Whether the language concerns a person or a thing, *i. e.* the affairs of a person (§§ 25, 27, 28), is material in this respect: that language when it concerns a person, and is discommendatory, is always, in the absence of any evidence to the contrary, regarded as *uncalled for*, as published without any lawful excuse, and as not to be believed or considered as true unless its truth be established; or, as the phrase is, such language is presumed to be malicious and false. But as to language concerning a thing no such presumption is indulged; and upon those who allege language concerning a thing to be false and malicious is the burden of establishing those conclusions by other evidence than that afforded by the mere publication of the language. And besides, to give a cause of action for language concerning a thing, special damage must in all cases be alleged and proved.[130]

While a distinction has been actually maintained between language concerning a person and language concerning a thing, the essential grounds of the distinctions seems not to have been clearly, nor indeed rightly, apprehended. That branch of the law of libel known as " Slander of Title," has been regarded as something distinct from Slander and Libel, properly so called, whereas in reality slander of title is but a portion of that division of the law relating to wrongs by language which includes language concerning things.[131] The rules relating to

---

[130] See *Swan* v. *Tappan*, 5 Cush. 104; *Ingram* v. *Lawson*, 6 Bing. N. C. 212; 8 Scott, 571; *Evans* v. *Harlow*, 5 Q. B. 624; *Kendall* v. *Stone*, 1 Selden, 14, reversing S. C. 2 Sand. 269; *Hargrave* v. *Le Breton*, 4 Burr. 2422; *Smith* v. *Spooner*, 3 Taunt. 246; *Bailey* v. *Dean*, 5 Barb. 297; *Linden* v. *Graham*, 1 Duer, 670; *Tobias* v. *Harland*, 4 Wend. 537; *McDaniel* v. *Baca*, 2 Cal. 326.

[131] Debated if *slander of title* within statute 21 Jac. 1, ch. 16, actions on the case *for slander*, held by three judges against one. that it was not; " that action in the case for slander" referred to the person of a man and not to the title of lands. For this is not properly a slander but a cause of damage. (*Lowe* v. *Harwood*, Cro. Car. 140.) " An action for slander of title is not properly an action for words spoken or libel written and published, but an action on the case for special damage sustained by reason of the speaking or publication of the slander of the plaintiff's title. This action is ranged under that division of actions in the Digests and other writers on the text law, and is so held by the courts at `

slander of title apply to all language concerning things, but where the language concerns both a person and a thing, it is governed by the rules which relate to language concerning the person. The question whether the language concerns a person or a thing arises in cases of alleged privileged publications in the form of criticisms on books, works of art, or places of public entertainment. It must be determined in those cases whether in point of fact the language of the criticism was concerning the thing, the book, the work of art, or the proprietor of the place; and according to the decision of that question will the language be, or not be, actionable. We shall advert to this hereafter, in treating of defences.

§ 131. What person or what thing the language concerns is material; as upon the answer to that question depends whether the party complaining has, or has not, any right to redress. Of course unless the language concerns either the person or the affairs of the party complaining, no wrong can have been done him of which he can rightfully complain.[122]

the present day. *Malachy* v. *Soper*, 3 Bing. N. C. 371; 3 Scott, 723." (Heard on Libel, § 59.) " An action of slander of title is a sort of metaphorical expression." (Maule, J., *Pater* v. *Baker*, 3 C. B. 831.) "The cause of action is denominated slander of title by a figure of speech, in which the title to land is personified and made subject to many of the rules applicable to personal slander, when the words in themselves are not actionable." (Gardiner, J., *Kendall* v. *Stone*, 1 Selden, 14.)

[122] In action for scandalous words it is requisite that "the person scandalized be certain." (*James* v. *Rutledge*, 4 Rep. 17 b.) "No writing whatever is to be esteemed a libel unless it reflects upon some particular person." (Hawk, P. C., c. 73, § 9.) After quoting the foregoing sentence, Holt (Holt on Libel, 246) adds: "This is unquestionably true, as it relates to the action on the case for slander, in which the party complaining must show himself to be meant by the libel." (Holt on Libel, 247; *Harvey* v. *Coffin*, 5 Blackford, 566.) It is not material whether the person is described nominally or indirectly, provided his identity be ascertained. (*Sumner* v. *Buel*, 12 Johnson, 475.) Identity is presumed from identity of name. (*Jackson* v. *Goes*, 13 Johnson, 518; *Jackson* v. *King*, 5 Cow. 237; *Jackson* v. *Cody*, 9 Cow. 140; *Hamber* v. *Roberts*, 18 Law Jour. R. (N. S.) 250, C. P.; *Hatcher* v. *Rocheleau*, 18 N. Y., 86; but see *Jackson* v. *Christman*, 4 Wend. 277.) Where the language is not applicable to the plaintiff (does not concern the person) no averment or innuendo can make it so. (*Solomon* v. *Lawson*, 8 Q. B. 823; *Ingram* v. *Lawson*, 6 Bing. N. C. 212; 8 Scott, 571; *Dottarer* v. *Busbey*, 4 Har. 208; *Swan* v. *Tappan*, 5 Cush. 104; Vin. Abr., Act. for Words ,H. b. 12, 13.) Where the language is applicable to the plaintiff, although not so upon its face to maintain

8

§ 132. When the language concerns a person, it is material further to inquire whether it concerns him as an individual merely, or in some acquired capacity, as in an office, trade or profession, because language which would not be actionable if it concerned one as an individual merely, may be actionable if it concerns him in his office, trade, or profession.

an action therefor he must by *averment* introduce such facts as make it apparent that persons who knew him would, on hearing or reading such language, perceive its application to him. (*Miller* v. *Maxwell*, 16 Wend. 9.) He cannot show the application of the language to himself by an innuendo alone. (*Wilson* v. *Hamilton*, 9 Rich. Law (So. Car.), 882 ; *Maxwell* v. *Allison*, 11 S. & R. 343 ; *Turner* v. *Merryweather*, 7 C. B. 251 ; *Tyler* v. *Tillotson*, 2 Hill, 507.) Thus it is not sufficient to allege that the defendant said, " R. saw *a young man* (meaning the plaintiff) ravishing a cow." (*Harper* v. *Delph*, 3 Ind. 225.) Or, W. *or somebody* altered the indorsement on a note. (*Ingalls* v. *Allen*, Breeze, 233.) I know of but one man who owes me enmity enough to do such a thing, and you know whom I mean. (*Robinson* v. *Drummond*, 24 Ala. 174.) A. was supervisor of an election, at which there was false swearing. (*Lewis* v. *Soule*, 3 Mich. 514.) And held that the postmaster of J. could not maintain an action for words spoken of a missing letter containing the resignation of one M.: " I do not think M.'s resignation has gone to Washington. I have no doubt it was embezzled at J." (*Taylor* v. *Kneeland*, 1 Doug. 67.) For the words, "All the bravery you (A.) ever showed was, sleeping with your sisters," held that the sisters of A. could not sue. (*Mallison* v. *Sutton*, 1 Smith, 364.) For calling W. a bastard, the mother of W. could not sue for the imputation upon her without proper averments connecting the allegation with her. (*Maxwell* v. *Allison*, 11 S. & R. 343.) An action may be supported for language in which the plaintiff is described directly or indirectly, though his name is not given. Thus, with proper averments, one may bring an action for the words concerning on their face " his *friend*" (*Clark* v. *Creitzburgh*, 4 M'Cord, 491); or the " surgeon of whiskey memory" (*Miller* v. *Maxwell*, 16 Wend. 9); or the " man at the sign of the Bible" (*Steele* v. *Southwick*, 9 Johns. 214); or, O. B. (*O'Brien* v. *Clements*, 16 M. & W. 159); or " desperate adventurers" (*Wakley* v. *Healey*, 18 Law Jour. 241, C. P.). " The writer in the *Register* who was deprived of a twopenny justice-ship for malpractice in packing a jury" (*Hix* v. *Woodward*, 12 Conn. 262); and see "One who edits the *Times*" (*Tyler* v. *Tillotson*, 2 Hill, 507); "Filly Horse" (*Weir* v. *Hoss*, 6 Ala. 881). Where B. had been accused of stealing a tray of biscuits, and A. said in the hearing of B. and of other persons, that if they did not look out he would make the tray of biscuits roar, held, that with proper averments connecting B. with this language of A., B. might maintain an action against A. (*Briggs* v. *Byrd*, 11 Ired. 353.) The words "I am a true subject, and thou servest no true subject," spoken to the servant of I. S., held sufficient to give a right of action to I. S. (Vin. Abr., Act. for Words, C. b. 1.) And so of the words, "Thy master, Mr. Browne, hath robbed me." (*Id.* 3.) If A. says to B., One of us two is perjured, and B. says to A., It is not I, and A. says again, It is not I, B. may maintain an action. (*Id.* 4.) For

§ 133. The different effect which in certain cases is attributed to *written* as distinguished from *oral* language, does not extend to the construction of language with a view to determine its proper meaning. For the purpose of its construction, language is to be regarded not merely in reference to the words employed,

the words "Thy son hath robbed" me, the son of the person spoken to may maintain an action if he be the only son; and if one say to a son, thy father, or to a wife, thy husband hath robbed me, the father or the husband may have an action. (*Id.* 6; II. *b;* K. *b;* and see *Ralph* v. *Davye,* Sty. 150; *Brent* v. *Ingram,* Cro. Eliz. 36; *Anderson* v. *Stewart,* 8 U. C. Q. B. R. 243.) For the words "Your boys stole my corn," "your children are thieves," either of the sons in the one case, and of the children in the other, may sue. (*Maybee* v. *Fisk,* 42 Barb. 326; *Gidney* v. *Blake,* 11 Johns. 54.) And for the words, A. or B. killed T. S., either A. or B. may sue. (*Falkner* v. *Cooper,* Carth. 66.) Where the language affects a particular class of men, as for instance men of the gown, it gives no right of action to an individual of that class. (*Ryckman* v. *Delavan,* 25 Wend. 186; rev'g *White* v. *Delavan,* 17 Wend. 49.) And see *Ellis* v. *Kimball,* 16 Peck, 132; *Le Faun* v. *Malcolmson,* 1 Ho. of Lords Cas. 637. Thus where Ensign Sumner brought an action against Buel for defamatory matter published by Buel, reflecting on the character of the officers generally of the regiment to which the plaintiff belonged, it was held by a majority of the court that the action could not be maintained, and that the appropriate remedy in such a case was indictment. (*Sumner* v. *Buel,* 12 Johns. 475.) An information may issue in such a case. See *Rex* v. *Baxter,* 12 Mod. 139; L'd Raym. 879; *Rex* v. *Osborne,* 2 Barnard. 138; Kel. 230 Pl. 183; *Rex* v. *Griffin,* Rep. temp. Hardwicke, 89; *Rex* v. *Horne,* Cowper, 672; Holt on Libel, 249; Cooke on Defamation, 215. Where the defamatory matter is concerning a class, as an unincorporated fire company, the members of the class cannot maintain a joint action. (*Giraud* v. *Beach,* 8 E. D. Smith, 337.) A man may be libelled, not by name, or any specific description of himself, but under some such description of persons as includes him with others—as all the brewers in a designated portion of a city. (*Ryckman* v. *Delavan,* 25 Wend. 186; rev'g *White* v. *Delavan,* 17 Wend. 49; and see *Le Faun* v. *Malcolmson,* 1 Ho. of Lords Cas. 637.) And "a scandal published of three or four or any one or two of them is punishable at the complaint of one or more or all of them." (Holt on Libel, 247; *Harrison* v. *Berington,* 8 C. & P. 807.) Thus where there was an indictment against sixteen persons for conspiracy, and I. S. said the defendants were those who helped to murder W. N., held, either of the sixteen defendants might have his action (Vin. Abr., Act. for Words, C. *b.* 5); and see *Forbes* v. *Johnson,* 11 B. Monr. 48; *Chandler* v. *Holloway,* 4 Port. 17; and see *post,* Parties. Where the intention to apply defamatory remarks to the prosecutor is rendered doubtful and ambiguous by the defendant having left blanks for names, or from his having given merely the initials or introduced fictitious names, it is always a question for the opinion and judgment of the jury whether the prosecutor was the party really aimed at. (2 Starkie on Slander, 32; *The State* v. *Jeandell,* 32 Penn. State Rep. 475; *Mix* v. *Woodward,* 12 Conn. 262; *Ryckman* v.

but according to the sense or meaning which, all the circumstances of its publication considered, the language may be fairly presumed to have conveyed to those to whom it was published. The language is always to be regarded with reference to what has been its effect, actual or presumed, and the sense is to be arrived at with the help of the cause and occasion of its publication.[132] The court or the jury is to place itself in the situation of the hearer or reader, and determine the sense or meaning of the language in question according to its natural and popular construction.[134]

Delavan, 25 Wend. 186.) For this purpose the judgment and opinion of witnesses who, from their knowledge of the parties and the circumstances, are liable to form a conclusion as to the defendant's intention and application of the libel, is evidence for the information of the jury. (2 Starkie on Slander, 321), and he adds in a note; Lord Ellenborough held that the declarations of spectators while they looked at a libelous picture, publicly exhibited in an exhibition-room, was evidence to show that the figures portrayed were meant to represent the parties alleged to have been libeled. (*Du Bost* v. *Beresford*, 2 Camp. 512); and see Starkie on Evidence, part iv., p. 861. In New York a witness is not allowed to state his conclusion from the facts as to the intention of the defendant to apply the words or libel to the party or circumstances as alleged. (*Van Vechten* v. *Hopkins*, 5 Johns. 211; *Gibson* v. *Williams*, 4 Wend. 320.) In some other States witnesses have been allowed to testify as to the sense in which they understood the words, and the application of the words to the plaintiff. (*Morgan* v. *Livingston*, 2 Rich. 573; *Miller* v. *Butler*, 6 Cush. 71; *Leonard* v. *Allen*, 11 Cush. 241; *McLaughlin* v. *Russell*, 17 Ohio, 475; *Goodrich* v. *Davis*, 11 Met. 473; *Goodrich* v. *Stone*, 11 Met. 486; *Allensworth* v. *Coleman*, 5 Dana, 315; *White* v. *Sayward*, 33 Maine, 322; *Mix* v. *Woodward*, 12 Conn. 262; *Smart* v. *Blanchard*, 42 N. H. 137; *Smawley* v. *Stark*, 9 Ind. 386; *Tompkins* v. *Wisener*, 1 Sneed, 458; *Commonwealth* v. *Buckingham*, Thacher's Crim. Cas. 29.) But the rule adopted in New York appears to have been followed in *Snell* v. *Snow*, 13 Met. 278; *Rangler* v. *Hummell*, 37 Penn. St. Rep. 130; *Briggs* v. *Byrd*, 11 Ired. 353.

[13] In actions for words we are to consider the words *themselves* and the *causa dicendi*, for sometimes in the first case they will bear an action, and yet when the *causa dicendi* is considered they will not. (Barclay, J., Mar. 20, p. 45.) "In case of slander by words, the sense of the words ought to be taken, and the sense of them appears by the cause and occasion of speaking them; for *sensus verborum ex causa dicendi accipiendus est.*" (4 Co. 18.) The construction which it behooves a court of justice to put on a publication which is alleged to be libelous, is to be derived as well from the expressions used, as from the whole scope and apparent object of the writer. (Van Buren, Senator, *Spencer* v. *Southwick*, 11 Johns. 592.)

[134] " Words are now construed by courts as they always ought to have been, in the plain and popular sense in which the rest of the world naturally under-

It is said that words to confer a cause of action for slander or libel ought to be in the affirmative,[135] and that actions for slander do not lie upon inferences,[136] but negative or ironical language may be shown to be in fact affirmative, and if so found, has the like effect as affirmative words.[137] "The law

stand them." (*Roberts* v. *Camden*, 9 East, 93.) "It is quite clear, from all the modern authorities, that a court must read these words in the sense in which ordinary persons, or in which we ourselves, out of court, reading this paragraph, would understand them." (Tenterden, C. J., *Harvey* v. *French*, 1 Cr. & M. 11.) We cannot pervert the words and alter the ordinary construction of them. (*Bonyon* v. *Trotter*, Sty. 231.) The words must be understood by the court in the same sense in which the rest of mankind would ordinarily understand them. (*Woolnoth* v. *Meadows*, 5 East, 463; *Spencer* v. *Southwick*, 11 Johns. 579.) We "ought to expound words according to their general signification" (Pratt, C. J., *Button* v. *Heyward*, 8 Mod. 24), or acceptation (*Fallenstein* v. *Booths*, 13 Mis. 427; *Ogden* v. *Riley*, 2 Green, 186); their popular sense (*Duncan* v. *Brown*, 15 B. Monr. 186; *Hancock* v. *Stephens*, 11 Humph. 507); their most obvious meaning (*Hogg* v. *Wilson*, 1 N. & M. 216), or common import (*Thirman* v. *Mathews*, 1 Stew. 384; *Hogg* v. *Dorrah*, 2 Port. 212), as understood by the hearer (*Dorland* v. *Patterson*, 23 Wend. 422; *Butterfield* v. *Buffum*, 9 N. Hamp. 156; *McGowan* v. *Manifee*, 7 Monr. 314); and according to the ideas they are calculated to convey (*Demarest* v. *Haring*, 6 Cow. 76; *Truman* v. *Taylor*, 4 Iowa, 424); according to their natural meaning and common acceptation (*Wright* v. *Paige*, 36 Barb. 438). The jury are to be guided in forming their opinion [on the meaning of the alleged defamatory matter] by the impression which the words or signs used were calculated to make on the minds of those who heard or saw them, as collected from the whole of the circumstances. (1 Starkie on Slander, 60.) Words are to be taken in that sense in which they are generally understood, and when that puts upon them a guilty sense they are actionable. (*Pike* v. *Van Wormer*, 6 How. Pr. R. 99; *Dias* v. *Short*, 16 id. 322; *Walrath* v. *Nellis*, 17 id. 72; *Hughley* v. *Hughley*, 2 Bailey, 592; *Tuttle* v. *Bishop*, 30 Conn. 80.) The words are to be taken in their natural meaning and according to common acceptation (*Carroll* v. *White*, 33 Barb. 618), and the vulgar intendment of the bystanders. (*Somers* v. *House*, Holt, 39.)

[135] *Weblin* v. *Meyer*, Yelv. 158.

[136] Jenk. 302 Pl. 72. To sustain an action plaintiff must show (1) that the words used either "of themselves or by reference to circumstances, are capable of the offensive meaning attributed to them; (2) that the defendant did, in fact, use them in that sense." (1 Starkie on Slander, 44.) "Words imputing crime must be precise." (*Id.*) See note 163, *post*.

[137] Words calculated to induce the hearers to suspect that the plaintiff was guilty of the crime alleged, are actionable. (*Drummond* v. *Leslie*, 5 Blackf. 453.) It is not necessary that the words in terms should charge a crime. If such is the necessary inference, taking the words altogether, and in their popular meaning, they are actionable. (*Morgan* v. *Livingston*, 2 Rich. 573; *Case* v. *Anderson*, 33

cannot be evaded by any of the artful and disguised modes in which men attempt to conceal libellous ·or slanderous meanings;"[188] and the fact of language being ungrammatical, or

---

Verm. 182; *Colman* v. *Godwin*, 3 Doug. 90; 2 B. & C. 285; *Commonwealth* v. *Runnels*, 10 Mass. 518.) " A libel in hieroglyphics is as much a libel as an open Invective. Not only an allegory but a rebus or an anagram may be a libel." (Holt on Libel, 245.) The man that is painted with a fool's cap or coat, or with horns, or whose picture is drawn with asses' ears, is certainly abused. (1 Wood's Inst. 445; Holt on Libel, 244; *Du Bost* v. *Beresford*, 2 Camp. 512; *Mezzara's Case*, 2 City Hall Recorder, 113.)

"I know what I am, and I know what Snell is; I never buggered a mare." These words held to import a charge of buggery against Snell. (*Snell* v. *Webbling*, 2 Lev. 150.) But the words, " I never came home and poxed my wife," held not capable of being construed as a charge that the party to whom the words were addressed had gone home and poxed his wife. (*Clerk* v. *Dyer*, 8 Mod. 290.) And so the words, " A man that would do that would steal," held not to amount to a charge of stealing. (*Stees* v. *Kemble*, 27 Penn. 112.)

The defendant wrote a pamphlet called " Advice to the Lord Keeper, by a Country Parson," wherein he would have him love the church as well as the Bishop of Salisbury, manage as well as Lord Havesham, be brave as another Lord, &c. The defendant was found guilty, and upon motion in arrest of judgment, it was urged that no ill thing was said of any person, and all he said was good of them; but by the court; the words were laid to be *ironical*, and the jury have found them to be so, and the motion was refused. (*Reg.* v. *Browne*, Holt, 425; 11 Mod. 86, recognized; *Andrews* v. *Woodmansee*, 15 Wend. 232; *Boydell* v. *Jones*, 4 M. & W., 446; 7 Dowl. Pr. Cas. 210.) So where the words were, " You are no thief." (4 Rep. 19; Cro. Jac. 65 ; 2 Bulst. 188 ; L'd Raym. 236.) You will not play the Jew nor the hypocrite. (*Rex* v. *Brown*, Popham, 139; Hob. 215.) " An honest lawyer." (*Boydell* v. *Jones*, 4 M. & W. 446 ; 7 Dowl., P. C. 210.) They being alleged to have been spoken ironically, and so found by the jury, held to be actionable.

[188] Shaw, Ch. J., *Commonwealth* v. *Child*, 13 Pick. 198. The court will regard the use of fictitious names and disguises in a libel in the sense that they are commonly understood. (*The State* v. *Chace*, Walk. 384.) " If, therefore, obscure and ambiguous language is used, or language which is figurative or ironical, courts and juries will understand it according to its true meaning and import; and the sense in which it was intended, is to be gathered from the context and from all the facts and circumstances under which it was used." (Shaw, Ch. J., *Commonwealth* v. *Kneeland*, 20 Pick. 206; and see *Vanderlip* v. *Roe*, 23 Penn. State Rep. (11 Harris), 82.)

A defamatory writing expressing only one or two letters of a name, in such a manner that from what goes before and follows after it, must necessarily be understood to signify a certain person in the plain, obvious, and natural construction of the whole, is to be understood as if the name were written in full. (*Reg.*

such as is not usually found in any dictionary,[139] will not suffice to prevent the law taking cognizance of such language, or of the meaning it properly conveys.[140]

---

v. *Hurt*, Hawk. Pl. Cr. 194; *Rex* v. *Woodfall*, Lofft. 776; Holt on Libel, 243.) If in a libel asterisks be put instead of the name of the party libelled, it is sufficient that the plaintiff should be so designated that those who know him may understand that he is the party meant. It is not necessary that all the world should understand that the plaintiff is the party intended. (*Bourke* v. *Warren*, 2 C. & P. 307); and see in note 140, *post*, and note 132, *ante*.

[139] One "cannot protect himself from an action by the mere grammatical structure of the phrase." (Cowen, J., *Cornelius* v. *Van Slyck*, 21 Wend. 70.) "The etymology of words, or the grammatical construction of sentences, will be fallacious if followed as the only guides in the interpretation of language." (Borthwick on Libel, 142.) "Here is three *cockels* in this place we *now* them well, he is a *nare*, he cheats and *rongs* the country, and is the cur of a son of a whore." The indictment for these words was demurred to because the words were not intelligible, but the court overruled the demurrer, and said " it would be hard that a court of justice must not understand what is *spelt* badly, when all the world besides make no scruple to find the signification of the words." (*Rex* v. *Edgar*, 2 Sess. Cas. 29, Pl. 33.) " Common sense is not to be deemed a stranger to legal process, but as very influential in ascertaining the force and effect of words and sentences which, although technical, are to receive a sensible construction." (Parker, Ch. J., *Commonwealth* v. *Runnels*, 10 Mass. 518.)

[140] Courts take judicial notice of the meaning of words and idioms in the vernacular language. (1 Greenl. Ev., § 5, citing: 6 Vin. Ab. 491, Pl. 6, 7, 8; Tit. Court C.; *Hoyle* v. *Cornwallis*, 1 Stra. 387; *Page* v. *Faucet*, Cro. El. 227; *Harvey* v. *Brand*, 2 Salk. 626; and see note 142, *post*.) And no colloquium or innuendo is necessary to point their meaning. (*Elam* v. *Badger*, 23 Ill. 498; *Forbes* v. *King*, 1 Dowl. P. C. 672; *Hoare* v. *Silverlock*, 12 Adol. & Ell., N. S. 624; *Horner* v. *Taunton*, 5 Hurl. & Nor. 661; *Edgar* v. *McCutchen*, 9 Miss. 768.) Thus, in *Hoare* v. *Silverlock* (12 Ad. & El., N. S. 624), the court took judicial notice, without an innuendo, of the reproachful meaning of the term " frozen snake;" and so in *Ashley* v. *Billington* (Carth. 231), of the term "Jezebel," and so of the terms " Empirick" and "Mountebank." (Vin. Abr., Act. for Words, 8. a. 12.) In *King* v. *Lake* (2 Ventr. 18), the court said they could not take notice of "milk your purse," because it had not become an idiom. See as to "Man Friday," " Gambling Fracas." (*Forbes* v. *King*, 1 Dowl. 672.) Shooting out of a leather gun. (*Harman* v. *Delany*, 2 Stra. 898.) " Bogus pedlar" was said not to have acquired a meaning sufficiently definite to allow the court to take judicial notice of its import. (*Pike* v. *Van Worner*, 6 How. Pr. R. 101; 5 *id*. 175.) The law does not take notice of what a "cozener" is (*Walcot* v. *Hind*, Hutt. 14); or the meaning of "tan money." (*Day* v. *Robinson*, 1 Ad. & El. 554.) Woolcomber, held not to need an innuendo to show it means one who buys wool to work with. (Anon. Lofft, 322.) Truckmaster, a word said not to be found in

§ 134. Whenever language charged to be defamatory has any reference to or is connected with any other language or event, which affects its meaning, it must be construed in relation to such other language or event; and this, although on the face of the alleged defamatory matter there is no reference to any other language or event. In the absence, however, of any proof to the contrary, matter which has on its face no reference to any other language or event, will not be presumed to have any such reference, and must be construed as standing alone.[141]

---

any dictionary, was used without an innuendo; it was left to jury to decide if used in libellous sense. (*Homer* v. *Taunton*, 5 Hurl. & Nor. 661.)

The court is to inform itself of the meaning of English words, although unusual and peculiar to a particular place (Parke, B., *McGregor* v. *Gregory*, 2 Dowl., N. S. 769; 11 M. & W. 287; Com. Dig., Act. for Defam. C.), as healer of felons (Rolle Abr. 86); or Welsh words (Hobart, 126), *Daffa-down-dilly*, by averment meaning *ambo dexter* (*Pearce's Case*, Cro. Car. 382); and where particular English words have acquired some sense different from their natural one, an averment by way of inducement of that acquired sense is necessary; an innuendo without such an averment would be insufficient (*McGregor* v. *Gregory*, 2 Dowl. N. S. 769); so held of the terms *black sheep* and *black legs* (*id.*); and see notes 142, 146, *post*.

[141] Explanatory circumstances known to both parties, speaker and hearer, are to be taken into the account as part of the words. (*Dorland* v. *Patterson*, 28 Wend. 422, citing *Andrews* v. *Woodmansee*, 15 *id.* 232; *Miller* v. *Maxwell*, 16 *id.* 9; and see *Hankinson* v. *Bilby*, 2 Car. and Kir. 440; *Perry* v. *Mann*, 1 Rhode I. 263.) Words otherwise actionable explained at the time of publication by referring to a known and particular transaction are to be construed accordingly. (*Dole* v. *Rensselaer*, 8 Johns. Cas. 458; *Aldrich* v. *Brown*, 11 Wend. 596; *Trabue* v. *Mays*, 8 Dana, 138; *Emery* v. *Miller*, 1 Denio, 208; *Thompson* v. *Bernard*, 1 Camp. 48; *Shecut* v. *M'Dowel*, Const. Rep. 35; *Christie* v. *Cowell*, Peake, 4; *Pegram* v. *Styron*, 1 Bailey, 595.) Words which do not necessarily import anything injurious, may do so when taken in connection with other charges (*Beardsley* v. *Tappan*, 1 Blatch. C't Co't Rep. 588), or according to the common understanding of them. (*Cooper* v. *Perry*, Dudley, 247.) The defendant may show the language related to some transaction (*Ceely* v. *Hoskins*, Cro. Car. 509; *Norton* v. *Ladd*, 5 N. H. 203), or was uttered in connection with other words, which controlled its meaning. (*Stevens* v. *Handley*, Wright, 123; *Williams* v. *Cowley*, 18 Ala. 206; *Hays* v. *Mitchell*, 7 Blackf. 117; *Robinson* v. *Keyser*, 2 Foster (N. H.), 323.)

Where the language is *prima facie* actionable, the burden is on the defendant to show that they are not actionable. (2 Starkie on Slander, 85; *Penfold* v.

It is impossible to anticipate or catalogue all the circumstances which may affect the meaning of language, but among
them are the circumstances of time, place, and usage,[142] and
some others to be presently mentioned.

Westcote, 2 N. R. 335; *Christie* v. *Cowell*, Peake's Cas. 4; Sel. N. P. 1250; *Bissel*
v. *Cornell*, 24 Wend. 354; *Watson* v. *Nicholas*, 6 Hump. 174.)

[142] "Libel * * * has been variously construed at various times; being a
mere legal reason, and therefore variable not only according to all the circumstances of the times, but according to the ability and information of the judges.
In ignorant and despotic times it had not the same limits and precision as in the
days of liberty and science." (Holt on Libel, 43.) "In judging of the meaning
of language, our juries have been directed to attend to the criteria of the time,
the place, when and where, and the person by and to whom the language has
been employed." (Borthwick on Libel, 142.)

"Precedents in actions for words are not of equal authority as in other actions;
norma loquendi is the rule for the interpretation of words, and this rule is different in one age from what it is in another. The words which an hundred years
ago did not import a slanderous sense, may now, and *vice versa*." (*Harrison* v.
Thornborough, 10 Mod. 196; cited *Beardsley* v. *Dibblee*, 1 Kerr, 246.) And it is
the duty of courts to take notice of the mutations in language. (*Vanada's Heirs*
v. *Hopkins*, 1 Marshall Ken. R. 287.) The precedents in Croke's reports are be-
ginning to be considered apocryphal." (Gibson, J., *Bash* v. *Sommer*, 20 Penn. St.
R. 159.) "Many of those cases [in Cro. Jac. and Cro. Car.] could not be supported at the present day. I do not mean to cast any doubt upon the cases
quoted from Bacon's Abridgement and Comyn's Digest." (Pollock, C. B., *Tozer*
v. *Mushford*, 6 Ex. 539; and see *Beardsley* v. *Dibblee*, 1 Kerr, 260; *Foster* v.
Small, 3 Whart. 143; *Bloss* v. *Tobey*, 2 Pick. 320.) Bridgeman, Ch. J., said he
was not satisfied to go by precedents, because he held that to be scandalous now
which was not twenty years ago. That it is use makes words have force, and
words that are actionable now, hereafter may not be so. (Carth. 55.) "The
opinions of later times have been in many instances different from those in former
days in relation to words." (Holt, Ch. J., *Baker* v. *Pierce*, 6 Mod. 23.)

In the time of Charles the Second of England, it was held actionable to call
one a Papist or to say he went to Mass (*Row* v. *Clargis*, L'd Raym. 482; 2
Salk. 696; *Walden* v. *Mitchell*, 2 Vent. 265; *Cutler* v. *Friend*, 2 Show. 140); but
held otherwise in the reign of King James. (*Ireland* v. *Smith*, 2 Brown, 166.)
So in England, to write of one that he was a "*Man Friday*," was held not actionable (*Forbes* v. *King*, 1 Dowl. P. C. 672; 1 Cr. & M. 435; 2 Law Jour. Rep. N. S.
Ex. 109), for the reason as stated in *Hoare* v. *Silverlock*, 12 Adol. & El. N. S. 624,
that being a black man might be a great misfortune, but was no crime; while in
the United States it has been held actionable to call one a Mulatto. (*King* v.
Wood, 1 N. & M. (So. Car.) 184; *Eden* v. *Legare*, 1 Bay, 171; *Atkinson* v. *Hartley*,
1 McCord, 203; contra *Barrett* v. *Jarvis*, 1 Hamm. 83, note; see Borthwick on
Libel, 176; Trench's English Past and Present; Mills' Logic, Bk iv. ch. v.—The
history of variations in the meaning of terms.)

§ 135. In allowing extraneous circumstances to affect the construction of language, courts inquire whether or not the hearer or reader of the language knew such circumstances. If the hearer or reader was acquainted with those extraneous circumstances, the construction will be with reference to them, not because it is important how the hearer or reader understood the language, but because those circumstances form a proper element in determining the meaning to be attributed to the language in question. If the hearer or reader was not acquainted with those extraneous circumstances, then they will not be taken into consideration in determining the meaning of the language. The hearer or reader not being acquainted with those circumstances which affect the meaning of the language, its effect upon such hearer or reader is as if no such circumstances existed, and the language is to be construed without reference to such circumstances. The circumstance that the act charged is physically or legally impossible, does not always prevent the language being actionable. The alleged test in such a case is the knowledge possessed by those to whom the language is published. Thus where the defendant attributed to the plaintiff sexual intercourse with a dog, and of having given birth to a litter of pups in consequence of such intercourse, it was held not to be a defence—that such a result was impossible. But *semble* that it might have been a defence if it had been shown that the defendant and those who heard the words knew that such a result was impossible.[148]

The word "*screwed*," or "*strained*," does not of itself import sexual intercourse, but in certain localities it may have that import. (*Mills* v. *Van Horn*, 17 Ind. 245; Vin. Abr. Act. for Words, L. b. 7.) In London, England, *pimp* signifies *common bawd*. (*Dimmock* v. *Fawcet*, Cro. Car. 393, pl. 5.) *Healer of felons* means, in some localities, *aider of felons; limir* means *thief*, and *outputter* means *receiver of felons* (Vin. Abr., Act. for Words, L. b. 1, 6), and see *id.* 4, 7, as to the word *champertor* and the phrase *cut him out of doors;* and see note 140, *ante*.

[148] *Kennedy* v. *Gifford*, 19 Wend., 296. Courts cannot say judicially whether it be possible for a woman to have connection with a dog, or to have pups by him, but as it is not popularly believed to be impossible, the people not being presumed to know scientific facts, the injury to the plaintiff will be the same in either case, and the action will lie. (*Ausman* v. *Veal*, 10 Ind., 355.)

In *Fenn* v.*Dixe*, Jo. 444, pl. 5, the words were of a brewer and his beer. "I

To charge A. with the murder of B., although B. was alive at the time, would be actionable; but *semble* not so if those to whom the publication was made knew that B. was alive.[144] So,

will give my mare a peck of malt, and lead her to the water and let her drink, and she shall piss as good beer as any Tom Fenn (the plaintiff) brews." One reason assigned for holding the words not to be actionable, was that the words were impossible to be true in the understanding of any man.

" Thou art a bastard-bearing whore, and hadst two bastards." It was objected that these words spoken of a married woman were not actionable, because a married woman cannot have a bastard, but held actionable because they purported that she was not married when she had the bastards. (*Stevens* v. *Ask*, Sty. 424.)

These words concerning a churchwarden, " Who stole the bell ropes, you scamping rascal ?" Not actionable, because the property of the bell ropes was in the plaintiff as churchwarden, and as he could not steal his own property, the words imputed no felony. (*Jackson* v. *Adams*, 2 Bing. N. C. 462.) " If a man says to a miller who keeps a corn mill, thou hast stolen three pecks of meal, an action lies ; for, although the corn was delivered to him to grind, nevertheless, if he steal it, it is felony, being taken from the rest." (1 Rolle's Abr., 73, s. 16, cited *Nichols* v. *The People*, 17 N. Y. 117; and see *Hume* v. *Arrasmith*, 1 Bibb, 165.)

In an action for slander the words were, "You are a thief; you robbed Mr. L. of £30." The words were spoken in the hearing of B. and of several strangers. B. knew that the words did not mean to impute felony, but meant to impute that the plaintiff had improperly obtained £30 from Mr. L. to compromise an action for a distress. *Held*, that under these circumstances the question to be left to the jury *was not what the defendant meant by the words he spoke, but what reasonable men, hearing the words, would understand by them*. *Semble*, also, that if *all* the persons present when the words were spoken had known that the words did not impute felony, that would have been an answer to the action. (*Hankinson* v. *Bilby*, 2 Car. & Kir. 440; 16 M. & W. 442.) The mere fact that the defendant charged the plaintiff with theft, in regard to an article of property which had been either loaned or sold to the plaintiff, but which sale or loan was not known to those in whose presence he made the charge, will not be a ground of showing either that the act charged was impossible or that the charge was not seriously made. (*Smith* v. *Miles*, 15 Verm., 245.)

[144] So held, *Sergart* v. *Carter*, 1 Dev. & Bat. 8; *Snag* v. *Gee*, 4 Coke, 16. " You have killed A.; you have poisoned him," are slanderous words, though, at the time they were spoken, A. was living in a distant part of the country. (*Eckart* v. *Wilson*, 10 S. & R., 44; and see *Tenney* v. *Clement*, 10 N. H. 52; *Carter* v. *Andrews*, 16 Pick. 1; *Stone* v. *Clark*, 21 Pick. 51; *Stallings* v. *Newman*, 26 Ala. 300.) Wilt thou murder my sister as thou didst thy wife, actionable although the wife was alive. (*Brown* v. *Charlton*, Keb. 359, pl. 52.) Thy father says thou hast murdered thy husband. Judgment was arrested after verdict for plaintiff for these words, because it was not alleged that the husband was dead at the time the words were spoken. (*Boldroe* v. *Porter*, Yelv. 20.) Words actionable *per se*

semble, one tenant in common of chattels cannot be guilty of larceny of the chattels held in common; and therefore to charge one of several tenants in common with larceny of a chattel held in common, would be actionable, unless those to whom the publication was made knew of the tenancy in common.[145]

§ 136. In the case of all oral, and of some written publications, it may be possible to prove whether or not the hearer or reader was acquainted with such extraneous circumstances, but in the majority of cases it would be impossible to make such proof. Some circumstances are of such general notoriety that every person is presumed to be acquainted with them, and then all language must be construed in reference to them.[146] With circumstances of less general notoriety the knowledge of the hearer or reader is in every case a question of proof, and the

---

are not so when spoken of a transaction not amounting to the crime charged if known to the hearers to be so spoken. (*Parmer* v. *Anderson*, 38 Ala. 78; *Hankinson* v. *Bilby*, 2 Car. & K. 440; *Perry* v. *Man*, 1 Rhode Island, 263; *Kennedy* v. *Gifford*, 19 Wend. 296; *Williams* v. *Stott*, 1 Cr. & M. 675; 3 Tyrw. 688); and see *post*, note 354.

[145] *Carter* v. *Andrews*, 16 Pick. 1; *Stone* v. *Clarke*, 21 Pick. 51; and see note 143, *ante.*

[146] "It is the duty of the jury to construe plain words and clear allusions to matters of universal notoriety, according to their obvious meaning and as everybody else who reads must understand them. But the defendant may give evidence to show they were used on the occasion in question in a different or qualified sense. If no such evidence is given, the natural interpretation of the words and the obvious meaning to every man's understanding, must prevail." (Lord Mansfield, *Rex* v. *Horne*, 2 Cowper, 672.)

"You are a soldier; I saw you in your red coat doing your duty; your word is not to be taken." These words, spoken of an upholsterer, held actionable, it being known to be a common practice for tradesmen to protect themselves from arrest by their creditors by a counterfeit listing. (*Arne* v. *Johnson*, 10 Mod. 111.)

In an action for *libel* for writing to a client of the plaintiff, a barrister, " He would give her ill counsel and stir up a suit; he would *milk her purse* and fill his own large pockets," per Vaughan, C. J., " Saying he will milk your purse, taken annunciatively, signifies no more than milking a bull; the phrase is not come to an idiom." (*King* v. *Lake*, 2 Ventr., 18.) Mr. Parry, in his edition of Lord Campbell's Libel Act, says (p. 13) it is doubtful if this decision could now be supported, and we agree with him. See note 140, *ante.*

burden of making such proof rests upon him who claims that the hearer or reader possessed such knowledge.

§ 137. The construction to be put upon any language spoken or written must be that which is consistent with the whole of the speech or writing. Thus the language of any part of a writing is to be construed with reference to the entire writing, and the language of any part of an oral discourse is to be construed with reference to the entire discourse. Hence words which, standing alone, would be actionable, may not be actionable when taken in connection with their context.[147]

§ 138. Formerly the condition in life of the person spoken of materially affected the construction, and words concerning "great men of the realm" were held actionable, which would not have been so held when published concerning private persons. Language defaming these "great men" was called *scandalum magnatum*. In the United States no such distinction of persons is known.[148] How far the condition in life of the parties will affect the damages will hereafter be considered.

---

[147] The sense is to be gathered from the whole of the words or writing. (2 Starkie on Slander; *Cooke* v. *Hughes*, 1 R. & M. 112; *Carter* v. *Andrews*, 16 Pick. 1.) The construction which it behooves a court of justice to put on a publication is to be derived as well from the expressions used as from the whole scope and apparent object of the writer. (*Cooper* v. *Greely*, 1 Denio, 358; citing *Spencer* v. *Southwick*, 11 Johns. 592; *Fidler* v. *Delavan*, 20 Wend. 57.) "God forbid that a man's words should, by strict and grammatical construction, be taken *by parcels*, against the manifest intent of the party upon consideration of all the words which import the true cause and occasion which manifest the true sense of them." (4 Co. 18.)

A defendant should be tried by all that he has published in the same pamphlet or paper. (*Morehead* v. *Jones*, 2 B. Munroe, 210.) Brittridge brought an action for the words, "Mr. Brittridge is a perjured old knave, *and* that is to be proved by a stake parting the lands of Martin and Wright." The judgment was arrested, on the ground that the latter words explained the former as not meaning judicial perjury. (4 Co. 18; Yelv. 10, 34; Mo. 666.)

[148] For information as to scandalum magnatum, the reader is referred to Starkie on Slander; Holt on Libel. *Secundem gradum dignitatis*, &c., was the rule of the Roman law, and is the rule in Scotland and in France. Borthwick on Libel, 176, 177 n., Inst. Lib. IV., tit. 4; Code Criminel, tit. 111, art. 1; Black. Com. B'k III., c. vii., s. 5; Selwy's N. P. 1155; Barrington on Penal Statutes; 3 Reeve's Hist. of the Common Law.

§ 139. The sense in which the publisher meant the language cannot be material. The dicta which apparently sanction such a rule will, on a comparison with their context, be found in reality to be, not what did the defendant mean, but what properly may he be taken to have meant. How might the language be understood by those to whom it was published. It cannot, therefore, be correct to say that the language is to be construed in the sense in which the publisher intended it to be understood. "When a party has made a charge that clearly imputes a crime, he cannot afterwards be permitted to say, I did not intend what my words legally imply." [149]

§ 140. Where the language is *ambiguous*, in that case the

---

[149] Woodworth, J., *McKinly* v. *Rob*, 20 Johns. 351. Words having naturally none of their own carry that signification to the hearer that he is used to put upon them, whatever be the sense of him that uses them. (Locke, Conduct of the Understanding, § 35.)

The question in an action for words is not what the party using them considered their meaning by any secret reservation in his own mind, but what he meant to have understood as their meaning by the party to whom he uttered them." (*Read* v. *Ambridge*, 6 C. & P. 308.)

"The effect of the words used, and not the meaning of the party in uttering them, is the test of their being actionable or not." That is, first ascertain the meaning of the words themselves, and then give them the effect any reasonable bystander would affix to them." (*Hankinson* v. *Bilby*, 16 M. & W. 442.) "The secret intent of the publisher is immaterial." (*Id.*) The injury caused by slander depends on the effect of the words on the hearers. (*Hawks* v. *Patton*, 18 Geo. 52.)

The speaker "is accountable for the import of the words as they will naturally be understood by the hearer." (*Dorland* v. *Patterson*, 23 Wend. 424; citing *Harrison* v. *Thornborough*, 10 Mod. 196; *Gidney* v. *Blake*, 11 Johns. 54.) "It was not enough that the defendant could point the slander in his own mind, so long as it appears to have been pointless in the minds of the hearers." (*Id.*) It is the sense in which the hearers understood the words on which the jury are to pronounce. (*Demarest* v. *Haring*, 6 Cow. 76; *Kennedy* v. *Gifford*, 19 Wend. 296.) "Language shall be construed and understood in the sense in which the writer or speaker intended it." (*Commonwealth* v. *Kneeland*, 20 Pick. 206.) If the words impute a crime, it is not necessary to allege an *intention* to charge such crime. (*Galloway* v. *Courtney*, 10 Rich. Law, 414.)

"Nor by the term *meaning* are we to understand what the defendant intended to express; for he may have designedly written that which, in its literal sense, should be imperfect. But we are to understand the meaning which he intended others should believe him to have—the sense in which he designed his production should be received by others. (George on Libel, 36.)

manner in which it was or might be understood by those to whom it was published is material, and will control in determining the meaning; but where the language is *unambiguous*, it is to be construed in its ordinary sense, and without reference to how those to whom it was published understood it, or what was intended by the publisher.[150]

---

[150] A man is to some extent responsible for the hearing of the bystanders, if he uses language which imputes crime, with an explanation; if the bystanders did not hear the explanation, he is liable to an action. (*Maybee* v. *Fisk*, 42 Barb. 336; see, however, apparently contra, *Shecut* v. *M'Dowell*, 3 Brevard, 38.) But the understanding of the bystanders cannot be shown to make words actionable *per se*, which, as alleged in the declaration, are not actionable *per se*. (*Smith* v. *Gafford*, 33 Ala. 168.)

"Taken by itself, and without more, the understanding of a person who hears an expression is not the legal mode by which it is to be explained. If words are uttered or printed, the ordinary sense of those words is to be taken to be the meaning of the speaker." (*Daines* v. *Hartley*, 3 Ex. 200.) "There can be no doubt that words may be explained by bystanders to import something very different from their obvious meaning. The bystanders may perceive that what is uttered is uttered in an ironical sense, and therefore that it may mean directly the reverse of what it professes to mean. Something may have previously passed which gives a peculiar character and meaning to some expression; and some word which ordinarily is used in one sense may, from something that has gone before, be restricted and confined to a particular sense, or may mean something different from that which it ordinarily and usually does mean." (*Id.*)

"We are to understand words in the same sense as the hearers understood them." (*Button* v. *Heyward*, 8 Mod. 24.) "In a common sense according to the vulgar intendment of the bystanders." (*Somers* v. *House*, Holt, 39.) "Words uttered must be construed in the sense which hearers of common and reasonable understanding would ascribe to them, even though particular individuals, better informed on the matter alluded to, might form a different judgment." (*Hankinson* v. *Bilby*, 16 M. & W. 442.) Language imputing an indictable offence is actionable or not, according to the sense in which *it may fairly be understood* by those who hear or read it, and who are *not* acquainted with the matter to which they relate, or which may render them a privileged communication. (*Id.*) To accept the understanding of the words by the hearer or reader as their true meaning "would be to make the defendant's liability depend, not on his own malicious intent and purpose, in using the language, which might be quite innocent and free from blame, but upon the misconception or morbid imagination of the person in whose hearing they were spoken." (Heard on Libel, § 268, citing *Snell* v. *Snow*, 13 Metc. 278; *Van Vechten* v. *Hopkins*, 5 Johns. 211; *Gibson* v. *Williams*, 4 Wend. 320; *Allensworth* v. *Coleman*, 5 Dana, 315.) The judgment of the witness is not to be substituted for the judgment of the jury. (Heard on Libel, § 269.) "Words are to be taken in that sense that is most natural and

§ 141. The construction of language as actionable or not actionable, is sometimes determined by the knowledge or imputed knowledge of the person spoken of; thus the words "that thief A. hath stolen my goods and delivered them to Bacon," held not to give any right of action to Bacon, it not being alleged he knew the goods were stolen.[151] So of the words he received goods that were stolen and will be hanged for them.[152] You have passed counterfeit money.[153] So to allege that one got his sister with child, or had carnal intercourse with his daughter, does not impute incest without an allegation that the plaintiff was guilty of the act charged with a knowledge of the relationship.[154] Without an allegation of knowledge, it was held not actionable to charge, "He hath gotten much wealth by trading with pirates,"[155] or "He was confederate with Campion the Jesuit,"[156] or "He poisoned Smith,"[157] or "He is a maintainer of thieves,"[158] or "He offered, or was about to offer for sale, unwholesome meal."[159]

§ 142. It is customary to concede (1) that *formerly* courts construed language in *mitiori sensu*, and (2) that the practice of so construing language has been abandoned.[160] These proposi-

---

obvious, and in which those to whom they are spoken will be sure to understand them. (*Id.*, § 163.)

[151] *Bacon's Case*, Dal. 41, pl. 21.

[152] *Ratcliff* v. *Long*, Palm. 67; in *Miller* v. *Miller*, 8 Johns. 74, held that where the offence charged was concealing stolen goods, it was not necessary to allege that the plaintiff knew the goods were stolen.

[153] *Pike* v. *Van Wormer*, 6 How. Pr. R. 171; *Church* v. *Bridgman*, 6 Miss. 190.

[154] *Lumpkins* v. *Justice*, 1 Smith (Ind.) 322; *Griggs* v. *Vickroy*, 12 Ind. 549.

[155] *Crook* v. *Averis*, Golb. 252; 2 Bulst. 216.

[156] *Brown* v. *Lisle*, Cro. Eliz. 251.

[157] *Jacob* v. *Miles*, Vin. Abr., Act. for Words, E. b.; and see *March* v. *Davison*, 9 Paige, 580, and *post*, § 144, subd. x.

[158] *Ball* v. *Bridges*, Cro. Eliz. 746; and see *Tabbs* v. *Matthew*, 1 Bulst. 109.

[159] *Hemmenway* v. *Woods*, 1 Pick. 524. See note 144, *ante*.

[160] Where words are ambiguous, so as they may be expounded in good or ill part, no action lies, for they shall be expounded in the best sense. (Anon. Cro. Eliz. 672.) "The law strains not to hurt but to heal." (*Coots* v. *Gilbert*,

tions require some qualification. Alleged defamatory matter comes before the court for construction in the form of a pleading,

Hob. 77, Pl. 100); and "where words are indifferent, and are equally liable to two distinct interpretations, we ought to construe them in *mitiori sensu*, but we will never make any exposition against the plain, natural import of the words." (Pratt, C. J., *Button* v. *Heyward*, 8 Mod. 24; and see *Naber* v. *Miecock*, Skin. 183.) The maxim for expounding words in *mitiori sensu* has for a great while been exploded. (Fortescue, J., *Button* v. *Heywood.* 8 Mod. 24; *Roberts* v. *Camden*, 9 East, 93; and see *Wakley* v. *Healey*, 7 Com. B. 591; *Ogden* v. *Riley*, 2 Green, 186; *Duncan* v. *Brown*, 15 B. Monr. 186; *Fallenstein* v. *Boothe*, 13 Mo. R. 427; *Demarest* v. *Haring*, 6 Cow. 76; *Pike* v. *Van Wormer*, 6 How. Pr. R. 99; *Backus* v. *Richardson*, 5 Johns. 476.) "The earlier English judges discouraged the action of slander by all sorts of evasions." (Gibson, J., *Bash* v. *Sommer*, 20 Penn. St. R. 159; and see *Harrison* v. *Thornborough*, 10 Mod. 196.) "We will not give more favor unto actions on the case for words than of necessity we ought to do, where the words are not apparently scandalous, these actions being now too frequent." (Coke, C. J., *Crofts* v. *Brown*, 3 Bulst. 167.) In *Alsop* v. *Alsop* (5 Hurl. & N. 534), the court say actions for slander are not to be encouraged; and to the like effect see *Bennett* v. *Williamson*, 4 Sandf. 67. "Although slanders are to be suppressed yet the judges had resolved that actions for scandals should not be maintained by any strained construction." (Wray, C. J., *Stanhope* v. *Blith*, 4 Co. 15.) Ch. J. Holt said, that whenever words tended to take away a man's reputation, he would encourage actions for them, because so doing would contribute to the preservation of the peace; and he repeated a story attributed to Justice Twisden, of a man who, failing in his action for words, said, if he thought he should not have recovered damages he would have cut the defendant's throat. (*Baker* v. *Pearce*, L'd Raym. 959; 6 Mod. 24; Cas. temp. Holt, 654; and see *ante*, note 33.) One who couches his slander in ambiguous terms, in the hope of blasting the reputation of his neighbor, without incurring any legal responsibility, cannot claim an indulgent construction of his words. (*Gibson* v. *Williams*, 4 Wend. 320.)

Starkie (1 Starkie on Slander, 47) refers to the following cases as specimens of the doctrine of *benignior sensus*: "Thou art as arrant a thief as any in England, for thou broken up J. S.'s chest, and taken away £40." After verdict for plaintiff held not actionable. (*Forster* v. *Browning*, Cro. Jac. 687.) "Thou art a lewd fellow; thou didst set upon me by the highway, and take my purse from me, and I will be sworn to it." After judgment for the plaintiff, held on error not actionable. (*Holland* v. *Stoner*, Cro. Jac. 315.) "Thou art a thievish rogue, and hast stolen bars of iron out of other men's windows;" held not actionable. (Cro. Jac. 204.) "J. D. was robbed of £40, and Alice Bagg (the plaintiff) and J. S. had it, and for which they will be hanged;" after judgment for plaintiff, held not actionable. (*King* v. *Bagg*, Cro. Jac. 331.) And so of "Thou dost lead a life in manner of a rogue; I doubt not but to see thee hanged for striking Mr. Sydman's man, who was murdered." (*Barrons* v. *Ball*, Cro. Jac. 331.)

and then of course is governed by the rule for construing pleadings,
that the pleader is supposed to have stated his case in the manner most favorable to himself.[161] We think that an examination
of the decisions will disclose the fact that what are regarded as
constructions in *mitiori sensu* are usually a more or less rigor-
ous application of this rule of pleading. The words admitting
of two constructions, the one actionable and the other not actionable, where the pleader failed to point the language to the
actionable meaning, courts have refused to put the actionable
meaning on the language, supposing that if the language had
such a meaning the pleader would have pointed it out. The
rule requiring certainty in the allegations of a pleading was no
doubt carried to excess,[162] but we take it to have always been
and to be still the rule, that where a party makes a charge of
slander it is for him to show that the words have a slanderous
sense,[163] and that where the language is equally susceptible of

---

[161] The law will not assume in favor of a party any thing he has not averred
(*Cruger* v. *Hudson River R. R. Co.*, 2 Kernan, 201), or that the pleading is less
strong than the facts warrant (*id.*). A pleading is to be construed in its popular
sense (*Woodbury* v. *Sackrider*, 2 Abb. Pr. R. 405; *Munn* v. *Morewood*, 5 Sandf.
557); according to what it says, and not what the pleader intended. (*Gould* v.
Glass, 19 Barb. 185; and see *Allen* v. *Patterson*, 3 Selden, 480; *Sheddon* v. *Patrick*, 28 Eng. Law & Eq. R. 68.) The court will not, in support of a pleading,
infer a criminal intention where the pleader has not ventured directly to aver its
existence. (*Bartholomew* v. *Bentley*, 15 Ohio, 670.) " It is a clear principle that
the language of an indictment [a pleading] must be construed by the rules of
pleading, and not by the common interpretation on ordinary language, for nothing
indeed differs more widely in construction than the same matter when viewed
by the rules of pleading and when construed by the language of ordinary life."
(Per Erle, J., in *Reg.* v. *Thompson*, 16 Q. B. 832, 846; 4 Eng. Law and Eq. R. 287,
292.)

[162] Action for the words *Home dit:* Sir Th. Holt hath taken a cleaver and
stricken his cook upon the head, so that one side of the head fell upon one shoulder and the other upon the other shoulder, et [the declaration] ne averr que le
cook fuit mort, et pur ceo fuit adjudge nemy bon. (Rolle R. 286.)

[163] Tindal, Ch. J., *Edsall* v. *Russell*, 5 Scott N. R. 801; 2 Dowl. N. S. 614; 4
M. & G. 1090; 12 Law Jour. Rep. N. S. C. P. 4; note 136, *ante.*   " Either the
words themselves must be such as can only be understood in a criminal sense, or
it must be shown in a colloquium in the introductory part that they have that
meaning, otherwise they are not actionable." (*Holt* v. *Scholefield*, 6 T. R. 691.)
Words to be actionable should be unequivocally so. (*Harrison* v. *Stratton*, 4

both a harmless and an injurious meaning, it is the duty of the pleader and not of the court to point out the injurious meaning, and that if he fails to do this the court will not put upon the language the injurious meaning. Although there may be no rule to put on ambiguous language its non-actionable sense, certainly there is no rule by which courts put on ambiguous language the actionable sense. The rule is that the natural meaning is to be taken,[164] and if in that view the language will bear a non-actionable meaning equally as well as an actionable one, courts will adopt the non-actionable construction. Where the meaning is doubtful, the pleader may by an innuendo point the language to the sense in which he wishes it to be understood. Where the alleged defamatory matter stated that A. was a prostitute, and that she was under the patronage or protection of the plaintiff, but there was no innuendo pointing an injurious meaning, the language was held not actionable. The court held, in effect, that it would not take the worst or most injurious sense when the words may properly receive a harmless as well as an offensive construction.[165]

§ 143. Where language may be taken in a double sense, the court, after a verdict, will *usually* construe it in that sense

---

Esp. Cas. 218.) Where there is no *colloquium*, the plaintiff must be held to allege that the words were used in their natural and ordinary signification (*Edgerly* v. *Swain*, 32 N. Hamp. 478); and they will be so construed, and not in *mitiori sensu*. (*Chaddock* v. *Briggs*, 13 Mass. 248; *Bloss* v. *Tobey*, 2 Pick. 320.) Where the words have two meanings, one of them harmless, and the other injurious, the innuendo may properly point out the injurious meaning. (*Joralemon* v. *Pomeroy*, 2 N. Jersey, 271; *Griffith* v. *Lewis*, 8 Q. B. 841; 7 Law Times, 177; *Gosling* v. *Morgan*, 32 Penn. St. R. 273.)

[164] Words "are not to be taken in the more lenient or the more severe sense, but in the sense which fairly belongs to them, and which they were intended to convey. (L'd Ellenborough, *Rex* v. *Lambert*, 2 Camp. N. P. Cas. 398.) See note 134, *ante*.

[165] *More* v. *Bennett*, 33 How. Pr R. 180; and see *Dolloway* v. *Turrell*, 26 Wend. 383. In *Edsall* v. *Russell*, 5 Scott, N. R. 801; 2 Dowl. N. S. 614; 4 Man. & G. 1090, the words were, "He made up the medicines wrong through jealousy, because I would not allow him to use his own judgment." There being no innuendo that the defendant meant to impute that the medicines occasioned any injury, the court refused to put that meaning upon them, and held the words not actionable. And see *Forbes* v. *King*, 1 Dowl. 672; *Kelly* v. *Partington*, 5 B. & Adol. 645.

which will support the verdict.[166] If the language admits of a
harmless as well as an injurious meaning, which is the meaning

---

[166] In *Burgess* v. *Boucher*, 8. Mod. 240, it is said that after verdict the court will
always construe the words to support the verdict, and the dictum is repeated by
Starkie without qualification. (2 Starkie on Slander, 108.) But such a rule as
was pointed out by Best, C. J., in *Goldstein* v. *Foss*, 6 B. & Cr. 154; 9 D. & R. 197 ;
4 Bing. 489; Moo. & P. 402; 2 Y. & Jer. 146 would practically deprive a party
of the right to move in arrest of judgment; and see *Forbes* v. *King*, 1 Dowl. Pr.
Cas. 672. In *Ceely* v. *Hoskins* (Cro. Car. 509), the words were, "Thou art forsworn in a court of record, and that I will prove." It was contended after verdict for plaintiff that the action would not lie, because it was not said in what
court of record he was forsworn, nor that he was forsworn in giving any evidence to a jury ; that it might be intended only that he was forsworn, not judicially, but in ordinary discourse in some court of record ; held the words must be
taken as an accusation of perjury ; the court add ; to say such an one is a murderer without saying whom he murdered, or when, an action lies, and it shall not
be intended that he was a murtherer of hares, unless such foreign intendment be
shown or discovered in pleading. In *Baal* v. *Baggerly* (Cro. Car. 326), the words
were, "Thou hast forged a privy seal and a commission ! why dost thou not
break open thy commission ?" after verdict for plaintiff it was contended that
the words were not actionable, but by the court being found guilty, the words
are to be intended according to the vulgar interpretation, that the king's privy
seal was meant, the counterfeiting whereof is treason. In *Somers* v. *House* (Holt,
39), the words were, "You are a rogue, and broke open a house at Oxford; and
your grandfather was forced to bring over £30 to mend the breach ;" after verdict
for plaintiff, it was urged in arrest of judgment that the word rogue was not
actionable, that *breaking open* a house was but a trespass, and *mending the breach*
might be *repairing;* but the court held the contrary, for taking all the words
together, one who heard them could not but understand a felonious breaking ; the
court would take the words in a common sense according to the vulgar intendment of the bystanders. In *Baker* v. *Pierce* (L'd Raym. 959 ; 6 Mod. 234 ; Holt,
654), the words were, "Baker stole my boxwood, and I will prove it." After
verdict for plaintiff, it was urged in arrest of judgment, that the words mean
wood growing, of which only a trespass could be committed. That to say you
are a thief, and have stolen my timber, or my apples, or my hops, is not actionable, for it imports only a trespass ; but the court ordered judgment for the plaintiff, and denied the authority of the case of *Mason* v. *Thompson* (Hutt. 38), in
which the words " I charge thee with felony in taking forth from J. D.'s pocket,
and I will prove it," were held not actionable. In 3 Salk. 325 ; 2 Vent. 172 ; 2
Lev. 51 ; 2 Sir T. Jo. 235, the words were "he is a clipper and coiner ;" after
verdict for plaintiff, it was moved in arrest of judgment that it was not a charge
of clipping and coining money, but held a clipping and coining of money must
be intended. Where the words were spoken by a married woman, charging a
theft of *her* goods, to support a verdict it was held that she meant a theft of her
goods before marriage. (*Powell* v. *Plunkett*, Cro. Car. 52.)

to be attached to it will be resolved by the verdict.[167] It is not sufficient to show by argument that the language will admit of some other meaning than that which obviously the jury have attached to it,[168] and therefore, after verdict for plaintiff, language which admits of an innocent and an injurious meaning will be construed to have its injurious meaning.[169] After verdict all averments on the side of the successful party which were involved in the issue tried, will be taken to have been duly proved unless the contrary appear upon the record,[170] and thus

[167] *Ford* v. *Primrose*, 5 D. & Ry. 287; *Giddins* v. *Mirk*, 4 Geo. 364; *O'Connor* v. *Lloyd*, 2 Hudson & Br. 626; *Chapman* v. *Smith*, 13 Johns. 78; *Sherwood* v. *Chase*, 11 Wend. 38.

[168] *Woolnoth* v. *Meadows*, 5 East, 463; *Roberts* v. *Camden*, 9 East, 93.

[169] " Words or signs will, after a verdict for the plaintiff, be considered by the courts to have been used in their worst sense." (1 Starkie on Slander, 60, repeated; Heard on Libel, § 173, citing *Southee* v. *Denny*, 1 Ex. 195; *Sloman* v. *Dutton*, 10 Bing. 402; 4 M. & Sc. 174; *Wakley* v. *Healey*, 7 Com. B. 591; *Tomlinson* v. *Brittlebank*, 4 B. & Adol. 630; 1 Nev. & M. 455; *Francis* v. *Roose*, 3 M. & W. 191; *Hughes* v. *Reese*, 4 M. & W. 204; *Rowcliffe* v. *Edmonds*, 7 M. & W. 12; *Digby* v. *Thompson*, 4 B. & Adol. 821; 1 Nev. & M. 485; *Daines* v. *Hartley*, 8 Ex. 200; *Read* v. *Ambridge*, 6 C. & P. 308; *Shipley* v. *Todhunter*, 7 C. & P. 680; *Chaddock* v. *Briggs*, 13 Mass. 248; *Goodrich* v. *Davis*, 11 Metc. 473; *Brown* v. *Lamberton*, 2 Binney, 35; *Bloom* v. *Bloom*, 5 Serg. & R. 391; *Cornelius* v. *Van Slyck*, 21 Wend. 70; *Butterfield* v. *Buffum*, 9 N. Hamp. 156; *Hamilton* v. *Smith*, 2 Dev. & B. 274; *Hancock* v. *Stephens*, 11 Hump. 509; *Goodrich* v. *Woolcott*, 3 Cow. 231; *Walton* v. *Singleton*, 7 Serg. & R. 451; and see *Beers* v. *Story*, Kirby, 12.)

One of the reports commenced, " Wilful and corrupt perjury;" held that, after verdict, this must be taken as a description of the nature of the charge, not as an imputation, by the publisher, of the perjury in fact. (*Lewis* v. *Levy*, 1 Ellis, B. & E. 537.)

Publishing in writing that the plaintiff had realized the fable of the frozen snake; after verdict for plaintiff, the court refused to arrest the judgment, as the jury might have understood the words " frozen snake " to impute a charge of ingratitude to friends, although not so explained by innuendo. (*Hoare* v. *Silverlock*, 12 Ad. & Ell. N. S. 624.)

[170] *Gates* v. *Bowker*, 18 Verm. (3 Washb.), 23; *Cass* v. *Anderson*, 33 Verm. (4 Shaw), 182; *Hoyle* v. *Young*, 1 Wash. 150; *Ramsey* v. *Elms*, 3 Jur. 1180. But nothing more will be presumed after verdict than is necessary to support the allegations. (*Sweetapple* v. *Jesse*, 2 Nev. & M. 36; 5 B. & Adol. 27.) Where the words taken by themselves do not necessarily import a charge of crime, yet where it is alleged in the innuendo that the defendant meant by the words that the act was maliciously done, they will be taken, after verdict, to have been in-

after verdict for plaintiff, if the language published may in its ordinary acceptation and without the aid of extrinsic circumstances be reasonably understood as having an actionable meaning, judgment will not be arrested upon the ground that the inducement and innuendoes do not sufficiently apply the language to the plaintiff, or because the innuendoes in so far as they apply the language to the plaintiff are unwarranted.[171] If the innuendoes are unwarranted in any other respect it is a ground for arresting the judgment, of which hereafter.

§ 144. We will here give some few additional illustrations of the manner in which the courts have construed certain language; many more illustrations will be found in the next succeeding chapter:

a. Adultery.—A charge of violating the seventh commandment held not to import a charge of adultery.[172]

b. And—For.—A distinction has been taken between saying, Thou art a thief, *for* thou hast stolen such a thing, as a tree, which could not be felony, and the saying, Thou art a thief, *and* hast stolen such a thing, since in the former case the subsequent words show the reason of calling the plaintiff a thief, and that no felonious imputation was meant; but in the latter, the action lies for calling him a thief, and the addition, Thou hast stolen, is another distinct sentence by itself, and not the reason of the former speech, nor any diminution thereof.[173] To say one has been in jail *for* stealing, in some cases held not to imply that the party stole, and in others that it did. In the latter class of cases

---

tended to import such a charge. (*Tuttle* v. *Bishop*, 30 Conn. 80; and see *Kennedy* v. *Gifford*, 19 Wend. 256; *Beers* v. *Strong*, Kirby, 12; *Ramsey* v. *Elms*, 3 Jurist, 1189.)

[171] *Wakley* v. *Healey*, 18 Law Jour. (C. P.) 241; 7 C. B. 591.

[172] *Farnsworth* v. *Storrs*, 5 Cush. 412.

[173] Cro. Jac. 114; Bull. N. P. 5; Hob. 77, 106; Cro. Eliz. 857; Browl. 2, Godb. 241; Hard. 7; All. 31; Sty. 66; 1 Starkie on Slander, 99. This distinction was referred to and its correctness questioned by Holt, Ch. J., *Baker* v. *Pierce*, 6 Mod. 23, where it is said *and* and *for* have the same meaning; and see *Lewis* v. *Acton*, Yelv. 84.

it was said he could not be imprisoned *for* stealing if he did not steal.[174]

c. Arson.—The words " Thou set fire to those buildings, and thou wilt never be easy till thou hast told of it," does not impute arson.[175] So of the words " he fired his house ; "[176] he burnt my barn ;[177] he set the store on fire, and none but him ;[178] T. burned the mill himself ;[179] but the words, He set fire to and burnt my factory, were construed to mean a wilful burning ;[180] and the words, "Public opinion says you was the author of it (firing a stable), and what public opinion says I believe to be true," held to amount to a charge of arson ;[181] and so of the words, "I have every reason to believe he burnt the barn, and I believe he burnt the barn."[182]

d. Bawdy House.—Your house is no better than a bawdy house, is equivalent to charging that the party kept a bawdy house ;[183] but public house, or house of ill fame, cannot be so construed.[184] Whore house is equivalent to bawdy house or house of ill fame.[185]

[174] Vin. Abr., Act. for Words, P. a. 2.

[175] *Rigby* v. *Heron*, 1 Jur. 558.

[176] *Anon.*, 11 Mod. 220.

[177] *Barham* v. *Nethersoll*, Yelv. 21.

[178] *McNab* v. *McGrath*, 5 Up. Can. Q. B. Rep. O. S. 516.

[179] *Tibbetts* v. *Gooding*, 9 Gray (Mass.), 254.

[180] *Tuttle* v. *Bishop*, 30 Conn. 80.

[181] *Gage* v. *Shelton*, 3 Rich. 242. It is the general opinion of the people in J.'s (plaintiff's) neighborhood that he burnt C.'s gin house, held actionable. (*Waters* v. *Jones*, 3 Port. 442.)

[182] *Logan* v. *Steele*, 1 Bibb, 593; I believe A. (plaintiff) burnt the camp ground, held actionable. (*Giddens* v. *Mirk*, 4 Geo. 364.) My watch was stolen in Polly Miller's bar; I have reason to believe that Tina M. took it and Polly Miller, her mother, concealed it, actionable. (*Miller* v. *Miller*, 8 Johns. 174.)

[183] *Huckle* v. *Reynolds*, 7 C. B. (N. S.) 114.

[184] *Dodge* v. *Lacey*, 2 Carter (Ind.) 212. House of ill fame, means the house is one of bad reputation, not that it is a bawdy house, unless there is an inducement that the defendant was in the habit of using the words "house of ill fame," to convey the idea of "bawdy house." (*Id.*)

[185] *Wright* v. *Paige*, 36 Barb. 438.

e. Bigamy.—The words "he was married to a woman (naming her) and kept her till he got sick of her, and then sent her away, having all this time two wives," amount to a charge of bigamy.[186]

f. Blackleg.—The term blackleg does not necessarily mean a cheating gambler.[187]

g. Clipper.—Where the words were, Thou art a clipper *and* shall be hanged for it, or, Thou art a clipper *and* thy neck shall pay for it,—it was held that the word clipper taken in connection with the words which followed it, meant a clipping of money—a felony.[188] .

h. Conspiracy.—A libel which was alleged to be concerning a false charge of felony, made through feelings of religious bigotry, by the plaintiff against one D. S., went on to allege that plaintiff was aided in making said charge by one C. R., who were stated to "have been for some time back employing every means to win the confidence of this young gentleman, their intended victim (meaning thereby that plaintiff and said C. R. had been contriving some plan to assail the character of said D. S.), as taking him on country visits, and inviting him to the continent, with the hope, it is alleged, of getting him altogether to themselves, and destroying his prospects the more easily, by some foul charge, which he might not find means of contradicting, there being no one else of the company. They had met with a direct refusal, it seems, to their invitation to the continent, and therefore, rather prematurely, opened their present plot (meaning said charge of felony). Affidavits are, we understand, shortly to be laid before the law officers of the Crown, charging the above facts, together with certain conversations between the pair of Romanists, who have trained this ingenious manœuvre (meaning the charge of

[186] *Parker* v. *Meader*, 32 Verm. (3 Shaw) 300.
[187] *Barnett* v. *Allen*, 3 Hurl. & N. 376.
[188] *Walter* v. *Beaver*, 3 Lev. 166; Cro. Jac. 255, 276; 1 Lev. 155.

felony aforesaid)." Held that the language did not amount
to a charge of conspiracy.[189]

i. Convicted Felon.—Plaintiff having been convicted of selling
liquor in violation of law, was termed in a printed circular a " *convicted felon ;* " held that if these terms, taken in
connection with the context and the evidence, were understood to mean only an offender against the license law,
they were no cause of action.[190]

j. Embracery.—Saying that A., on a certain trial, handed papers
to one of the jury, and that he ran away, or the judge
would have put him in prison for it,—or that he handed
papers to the jury to influence or bribe them,—imputes
embracery, and is actionable *per se.*[191]

k. Forgery.—The term forgery does not necessarily mean a felonious forgery,[192] as to say one forged words and sentiments
for Silas Wright ;[193] and to deny having signed a note, or
authorized his name being indorsed, does not import a
charge of forgery ;[194] nor does a charge, if you have any
letters from them, you forged them ;[195] or, I never put my
name on the back of the note, but he must have done
it.[196] A charge of altering books may impute forgery.[197]
Exhibiting a note and saying, " Do you think it is G.'s
handwriting," may import a charge of forgery ;[198] and
so the words, " He altered the note to get better security, to bind me to pay it.[199] The words, I would give five

[189] *O'Connell* v. *Mansfield,* 9 Irish Law R. 179.
[190] *Perry* v. *Mann,* 1 Rhode Island, 263.
[191] *Gibbs* v. *Dewey,* 5 Cow. 503.
[192] *Alexander* v. *Alexander,* 9 Wend. 141. See § 167, *post.*
[193] *Cramer* v. *Noonan,* 4 Wis. 231.
[194] *Andrews* v. *Woodmansee,* 15 Wend. 232.
[195] *Mills* v. *Taylor,* 3 Bibb, 469.
[196] *Atkinson* v. *Scammon,* 2 Fost. 40.
[197] *Gay* v. *Homer,* 13 Pick. 535.
[198] *Gorham* v. *Ives,* 2 Wend. 534.
[199] *Harmon* v. *Carrington,* 8 Wend. 488.

dollars if I could write as well as that,—I never signed the note,[200] do not necessarily impute forgery. But a letter charging plaintiff with having subscribed defendant's name to a receipt without authority, and to defraud him out of the money, and adding, It is not my purpose to call hard names—the statute fixes the name and punishment, imputes forgery.[201]

l. Fornication.—To allege that a woman is not a decent woman,[202] or a bad character, a loose character,[203] or has raised a family of children to a negro, does not amount to a charge of fornication ;[204] but to say of an unmarried woman she had a child and buried it in the garden, imputes fornication.[205]

m. Kill—Killed—Killing.—The words kill, killed, and killing, unexplained, have a felonious signification.[206] The words, " I think the business ought to have the most rigid inquiry, for he murdered his first wife, that is, he administered improperly medicines to her for a certain complaint, which was the cause of her death," after verdict for plaintiff, held actionable as imputing a charge of manslaughter.[207]

n. Knave.—Imports dishonesty.[208]

o. Known.—Stating plaintiff is about to commence an action, but that he will not bring it to trial in a particular county

---

[200] *Andrews v. Woodmansee*, 15 Wend. 232.

[201] *Snyder v. Andrews*, 6 Barb. 43.

[202] *Dodge v. Lacey*, 2 Carter (Ind.), 212.

[203] *Vanderlip v. Roe*, 25 Penn. St. Rep. (11 Harris), 82.

[204] *Patterson v. Edwards*, 2 Gilman, 720.

[205] *Worth v. Butler*, 7 Blackf. 251. See § 172, *post.*

[206] *Carroll v. White*, 33 Barb. 620; *Button v. Hayward*, 8 Mod. 24; *Cooper v. Smith*, Cro. Jac. 423; *Hays v. Hays*, 1 Hump. (Tenn.) 402; *Taylor v. Casey*, Minor (Ala.), 258; *Ecart v. Wilson*, 10 Ser. & R. 44; *Johnson v. Robertson*, 4 Porter, 486; *Chandler v. Holloway, id.* 18; *Edsall v. Russell*, 5 Scott N. R. 801; 2 Dowl. N. S. 614; 4 Man. & G. 1090.

[207] *Ford v. Primrose*, 5 Dowl. & R. 287. See § 168, *post.*

[208] *Harding v. Brooks*, 5 Pick. 244.

because he is *known* there, amounts to a charge that the plaintiff is in bad repute in that county.[209]

p. Larceny.—The words, A man that would do that would steal, do not impute a larceny;[210] but to say one was whipped for stealing hogs, does.[211] You will steal, imputes a charge of larceny.[212] The words "he is mighty smart after night," and "put him in the dark and he would get it all," spoken with reference to a dispute which existed between plaintiff and defendant, relative to the division of a certain tan-yard; held not to impute the crime of larceny, and not actionable.[213] I have reason to suppose that many of the flowers of which I have been robbed are growing on your premises, held to amount to a charge of larceny.[214]

q. Liar.—The words "this is not the first time the idea of false-hood and B. (plaintiff) have been associated in the minds of many honest men," imports that B. is a liar.[215]

r. Made away with.—A charge of making away with does not amount to a charge of larceny.[216]

s. Murder.—To say one is *guilty* of the death of another imports a charge of murder. The word *guilty* implies a malicious intent, and can be applied only to something which is universally allowed to be a crime. But to say one was the *cause* of another's death does not import a crime, for a

[209] *Cooper* v. *Greely,* 1 Denio, 347.
[210] *Stees* v. *Kemble,* 27 Penn. State R. 112; and see *Stolen,* p. 142, *post.*
[211] *Holly* v. *Burgess,* 9 Ala. 728.
[212] *Cornelius* v. *Van Slyck,* 21 Wend. 70.
[213] *Kirksey* v. *Fike,* 29 Ala. 206.
[214] *Williams* v. *Gardiner,* 1 M. & W. 245; and see note 145, *ante.*
[215] *Brooks* v. *Bemiss,* 8 Johns. 455.
[216] The words, "Uncle Daniel must settle for some of my logs he has made away with," do not of themselves amount to a charge of larceny. (*Brown* v. *Brown,* 2 Shep. 317.)

physician may be the cause of a man's death, and very innocently.[217]

t. Packing.—The charge of " packing a jury " imports the corrupt selection of a jury.[218]

u. Perjury.—To publish a direct and positive contradiction of what a witness, at a certain trial, had sworn that A. had said; *held*, not to amount to a charge of perjury.[219] Nor do the words, Thou wert detected of perjury, imply being guilty of perjury.[220] Words charging a grand juror with having " forsworn himself by neglecting or refusing to present an offence within his knowledge," do not amount to a charge of perjury or any indictable offence.[221] To say one is forsworn, was indicted for it, and compounded for it, imputes perjury ; for the alleged compounding is equivalent to a confession of the indictment being true.[222] And to say, Thou art forsworn, and I will set thee on the pillory, or I will have his ears cropt, imply perjury.[223] Loss of life was occasioned by the collision of two steamboats. An inquest was afterwards held, and a person named Granger, who was on board of one of the steamboats at the time of the accident, gave his evidence. The defendant, in giving an account of the accident and inquest, stated — " Had requisite means been employed, the lives of the two children might have been saved, in spite of the story of Mr. Granger, who swore through thick and thin, and who, although asleep at the moment of the

---

[217] *Peake* v. *Oldham*, Cowp. 275.

[218] *Miz* v. *Woodward*, 12 Conn. 262.

[219] *Stecle* v. *Southwick*, 9 Johns. 214.

[220] Vin. Ab., Act. for Words, P. *a.* 21. The words, Thou didst take a false oath before Justice Scawen, may mean not a justice of the peace named Scawen, but one named Justice Scawen. (*Garnett* v. *Derry*, 3 Lev. 166), note 680, *post.*

[221] *McAnnally* v. *Williams*, 3 Sneed, 26.

[222] *Gilberd* v. *Rodd*, 3 Bulst. 304.

[223] *Williams* v. *Bickerton*, Het. 63 ; Vin. Ab., Act. for Words, F. *a.* 11. I could prove J. S. perjured, if I would imply that J. S. committed perjury. (*Id.*)

accident, had yet sufficient time to dress himself and assist his wife:" *held*, that the language did not charge Granger with perjury.[224] The following was published by A.: "Charge 4. Refusing to correct G. C. in his statement as a witness before Esq. B., when I believe he, J. C., knew his, G.'s, statement was not true." *Held*, that this writing, when shown by proper innuendos to have been applied by A. to the testimony of G. C., on the trial of a cause, imputed perjury to G. C., and was actionable.[225]

v. Pilfering.—The term pilfering imports a crime.[226]

w. Plundered.—The term plundered does not import a felonious taking.[227]

x. Poison.—Saying of a surgeon that he did poison the wound of his patient, may mean that he poisoned the wound to cure it. But if it be charged that he poisoned the wound to get money, that is different.[228]

y. Prostitute.—She is a bad girl and unworthy to be employed, will not support an innuendo, a prostitute.[229] "If I am not misinformed she is a prostitute," is the same as saying she is a prostitute.[230]

z. Robbed—Robbing.—The *prima facie* meaning of robbed is to impute a crime, an unlawful taking;[231] but the words, You have robbed me of one shilling tan money, amount only to a charge of embezzlement.[232] Robbing is a word of an

---

[224] *Reg.* v. *Marshall*, 2 Jur. 254 ; and see note 147, *ante*.

[225] *Coombs* v. *Rose*, 8 Blackf. 155.

[226] *Beckett* v. *Sterrett*, 4 Blackf. 499 ; *contra*, see *Carter* v. *Andrews*, 16 Pick. 1.

[227] *Carter* v. *Andrews*, 16 Pick. 1.

[228] Vin. Abr., Act. for Words, *R. a.* 10, 40.

[229] *Snell* v. *Snow*, 13 Met. 278.

[230] *Treat* v. *Browning*, 4 Conn. 408.

[231] *Tomlinson* v. *Brittlebank*, 1 Nev. & M. 455; *Jones* v. *Chapman*, 5 Blackf. 88; Heard on Libel, § 38.

[232] *Day* v. *Robinson*, 1 Ad. & El. 554.

uncertain signification.[233]   The words, "He robbed the treasury and bought a farm with it, were held not to impute felony.[234]

a. a. Shaving Purposes.—Shaving as applied to promissory notes means buying notes at a discount, beyond the debt and interest, which is neither dishonorable nor discreditable.[235]

b. b. Steal—Stolen.—The natural and obvious meaning of steal is a felonious taking or larceny.[236] The term stolen imputes a larceny.[237]   Stealing unexplained, *ex vi termini*, imports felony.[238]   Stealing and feloniously stealing are not the same; in common parlance, stealing does not always import felony.[239]   If the article alleged to have been stolen is of the kind of which felony can be committed, the term steal or stolen imputes a larceny, otherwise if the article alleged to have been stolen could not be the subject of a felony.[240]   Thus it has been held not actionable to say, You stole my wood,[241] or my apples;[242] or a load of hoppoles;[243] or a tree;[244] or a dog;[245] or a bee-tree;[246] or wild bees;[247] or a sable caught in a trap;[248] or marl, earth, or

[233] *Palmer* v. *Edwards*, Rep. of Cas. of Prac. in C. P. 160.
[234] *Allen* v. *Hillman*, 12 Pick. 101.   See § 170, *post*.
[235] *Stone* v. *Cooper*, 2 Denio, 293.
[236] *Dunnell* v. *Fiske*, 11 Metc. 551.   See § 170, *post*.
[237] *Burbank* v. *Horn*, 39 Maine (4 Heath), 233; *Coleman* v. *Playsted*, 36 Barb. 26; contra, *Dunnell* v. *Fisk*, 11 Metc. 551; *St. Martin* v. *Desnoyer*, 1 Min. 156.
[238] Powell, J., *Baker* v. *Pierce*, 6 Mod. 23.
[239] Holt, Ch. J., *Baker* v. *Pierce*, 6 Mod. 23.
[240] *Cock* v. *Weatherby*, 5 Sme. & M. 383.   See note 143, *ante*.
[241] Meaning standing timber.   *Robins* v. *Hildredon*, Cro. Jac. 65; *Idol* v. *Jones*, 2 Dev. 162; Heard on Libel, 87, note 3; contra, *Phillips* v. *Barber*, 7 Wend. 489.
[242] *Clark* v. *Gilbert*, Hob. 331.
[243] *Guilderslew* v. *Ward*, Cro. Eliz. 225; *Dexter* v. *Taber*, 12 Johns. 239.
[244] *Cook* v. *Gilbert*, Hob. 77.   See *Bryan* v. *Wikes*, Cro. Car. 572.
[245] *Findlay* v. *Bear*, 8 Serg. & R. 571.
[246] *Cock* v. *Weatherby*, 5 Sme. & M. 833.
[247] *Wallis* v. *Mease*, 3 Binn. 546; *Gillet* v. *Mason*, 7 Johns. 16.
[248] *Norton* v. *Ladd*, 5 N. Hamp. 203.

furze;[249] because felony cannot be committed of such things. A charge of having stolen boards,[250] or "my box-wood,"[251] held to impute a larceny; and a charge of stealing the property of A., deceased, imports a larceny from the personal representatives of A.[252] He will steal, and I can prove it, is equivalent to saying he had stolen;[253] and to allege, I will venture anything he has stolen the book, is equivalent to a charge of stealing the book.[254] To say, You are as bad as your wife when she stole my cushion, is not a charge of stealing, without an averment that the wife had committed felony.[255]

c. c. *Suffer.*—To *suffer*, held to import suffer death, as where the defendant said, "I will make you *suffer* for a witch, it was held to mean suffer death for a witch.[256]

d. d. *Taken.*—Words which charge the taking of the personal property of another, may be slanderous or not, according to circumstances.[257] Ordinarily, *taken* is not equivalent to stolen;[258] but where the words were, I have lost a calf-skin,

---

[249] *Ogden* v. *Riley*, 2 Green, 186; *Clarke* v. *Gilbert*, Hob. 331.

[250] *Burbank* v. *Horn*, 39 Maine (4 Heath), 233.

[251] After verdict for plaintiff. *Baker* v. *Pierce*, 6 Mod. 23.

[252] *Bash* v. *Sommer*, 20 Penn. St. R. 159.

[253] *Cornelius* v. *Van Slyck*, 21 Wend. 70.

[254] *Nye* v. *Otis*, 8 Mass. 122.

[255] *Upton* v. *Pinfold*, Comyn's R. 268. The words, "I expect Murphy will have plenty of bacon to sell, as he has killed some of my hogs," after verdict for plaintiff, were held to amount to a charge of hog-stealing. (*Murphy* v. *Antley*, 2 Boston Monthly Law Rep. N. S. 520.) R. S. was attainted of felony, and defendant said, You (plaintiff) have done as ill and worse; it will not cost you as much to be quit as it cost him. Court doubted if actionable. (Smith's Case, Cro. Eliz. 31.)

[256] *Stephens* v. *Corben*, 3 Lev. 394.

[257] *Watson* v. *Nicholas*, 6 Hump. 174.

[258] *Robertson* v. *Lea*, 1 Stew. 141; *Coleman* v. *Playstead*, 36 Barb. 26. The words, Thou hast picked my pocket, and *taken away* ten shillings, held not actionable, although the charge of picking the pocket without more would be. (Humfries' Case, cited Godb. 287.) Taking away implies a lawful

* * Bornman must have taken it, they were held to impute a larceny.[259]

e. e. Thief.—To call one thief is not actionable unless it is intended to impute to him a felony.[260] Unexplained, it will be construed in a felonious sense,[261] but subject to explanation by the context.[262] To say of one, he is a *thieving* person, is the same as saying he is a thief.[263]

f. f. Threatening Letters.—A charge of sending threatening letters, and that the plaintiff had been indicted therefor, must mean that they were unlawful threatening letters.[264]

g. g. Unnatural Offence.—To allege that one has been with a

---

taking. (*Foster* v. *Browning*, Cro. Jac. 688, pl. 2; Wilks' Case, Vin. Abr., Act. for Words, R. a. 3); see *Dotterer* v. *Bushey*, 16 Penn. St. Rep. 204.

[259] *Bornman* v. *Boyer*, 3 Binn. 515. He is a thief, for he hath *stolen* corn from Mr. Kay, held actionable (*Smith* v. *Ward*, Cro. Jac. 673), for corn threshed and not in the sheaf shall be intended; but if the words had been *hath taken away* instead of *hath stolen*, no action would lie—a lawful taking would be intended. (*Foster* v. *Browning*, Cro. Jac. 688, pl. 2.) Thou art as arrant a thief as any in England, for thou hast broken up J.'s chest and *taken away* £40; not actionable. (*Id.*) Thou art a thief, for thou takest my boasts by reason of an execution, and I will hang thee. (Wilks' Case, Vin. Ab., Act. for Words, R. a. 3.)

[260] *Brite* v. *Gill*, 2 Monroe (Ky.), 66; *Quinn* v. *O'Gara*, 2 E. D. Smith, 388.

[261] *Penfold* v. *Westcote*, 2 New Rep. 335; *Curtis* v. *Curtis*, 10 Bing. 477; *Fisher* v. *Rotereau*, 2 M'Cord, 189; *Dudley* v. *Robinson*, 2 Iredell, 141. The words, He is a thief and a liar, and I can prove it, import a charge of larceny and are actionable. (*Robinson* v. *Keyser*, 2 Foster (N. Hamp.), 323.)

[262] *Thompson* v. *Bernard*, 1 Camp. 48; *Christie* v. *Powell*, Peake's Cas. 4; *McKee* v. *Ingalls*, 4 Scam. 30; *Ogden* v. *Riley*, 2 Green, 186; Vin. Abr., Actions for Words, G. a. 1, 2. To say, "Thou art as very a thief as any in Warwick gaol," no thief being then in the gaol, would not be actionable, but if a thief is in the gaol at the time, the words would be actionable. (Fenner, J., Bulst. 40.)

[263] *Alley* v. *Neely*, 5 Blackf. 200.

[264] *Harvey* v. *French*, 1 Cr. & M. 1, affirmed 2 M. & Sc. 591. "Threatening letters. The grand jury have returned a true bill against a gentleman named French," construed to mean that the grand jury had found a true bill against French for sending threatening letters, but that the words would not bear the meaning that French had sent threatening letters to extort money. (*Id.*)

beast,[265] was seen *ravishing* a cow, amounts to a charge of buggery;[266] but an allegation that one was seen *a foul* of a cow, or "*with a* heifer,"[267] do not amount to a charge of buggery. To say of one, his character is infamous, he would be a disgrace to any society; I will publish his in- famy; delicacy forbids me bringing a direct charge, but it was a male child who complained to me; held to impute unnatural practices without an innuendo.[268]

h. h. Whore.—To assert that " A. is a whore, or else she would never ride with B.," is to assert that A. is a whore.[269]

i. i.—To say, there is strong reason to believe,[270] or there is a rumor,[271] or if report be true,[272] a certain fact occurred, is equivalent to an allegation that such fact occurred; and so to say, I would venture anything,[273] or public opinion says so, and what public opinion says I believe to be true,[274] or I have every reason to believe,[275] is equivalent to a posi- tive allegation.

j. j.—To say of one, he is thought no more of than a horse thief and a counterfeiter, is to call him a horse thief and a counterfeiter;[276] and when it is said of one, he has com- mitted an act for which he could be transported, it must be understood he has been guilty of a crime punishable by transportation.[277]

k. k.—To charge, he has broken open my letters in the post- office, do not import an unlawful breaking open.[278]

---

[265] *Woolcott* v. *Goodrich*, 5 Cow. 714.
[266] *Harper* v. *Delph*, 3 Ind. 225.
[267] *Id.* ; *Johnson* v. *Hedge*, 6 Up. Can. Q. B. Rep. 337.
[268] *Woolnoth* v. *Meadows*, 5 East, 463. See note 137 on page 118, *ante.*
[269] *True* v. *Plumley*, 36 Maine, 466.
[270] *Turner* v. *Merryweather*, 12 Law Times, 474; 7 C. B, 251.
[271] *Kelly* v. *Dillon*, 5 Porter (Ind.), 426.
[272] *Smith* v. *Stewart*, 5 Barr, 372.
[273] *Nye* v. *Otis*, 8 Mass. 122.
[274] *Gage* v. *Shelton*, 3 Rich. 242; and see note 181, *ante.*
[275] *Logan* v. *Steele*, 1 Bibb, 593; and see note 182, *ante.*
[276] *Nelson* v. *Musgrave*, 10 Mo. R. 649.
[277] *Curtis* v. *Curtis*, 4 Mo. & S. 337; 10 Bing. 477.
[278] *McCuen* v. *Ludlam*, 2 Har. 12.

10

l. l.—Thou canst not *read* a declaration, construed to mean from ignorance, not blindness.[279]

m. m.—The words " we again assert the cases formerly put by us on record, we assert them against [the plaintiff]; we again assert they are such as no gentleman or honest man would resort to." Construed not to be a mere denial of some assertion made by plaintiff, but as an accusation against the plaintiff.[280]

n. n.—"He was an United Irishman, and got the money of the United Irishmen into his own hands and ran away with it," imputes a breach of trust, not a felony, and not actionable.[281]

§ 145. What allegations are divisible? One rule whereby to test whether a charge is divisible or not, is to inquire if the measure of damages would be different for the whole or for a part; and if it would, then the charge is divisible, and part may be justified.[282] Another rule would be to inquire if a part of the charge would sustain an action. Where the charge was that the plaintiff, a proctor, had been suspended three times for extortion, held divisible, and that the defendant might justify as to one suspension.[283] Where the alleged defamatory matter professed to give a report on an election petition, and commented on a party bail for one of the petitioners, and stated " he is hired for the occasion," held divisible.[284] The charge was acts of barbarity to a horse, and "beating out one of his eyes, and that plaintiff had ordered the person having charge of the horse, not to let any one see it," held divisible.[285] So of the words; Ware hawk, you must take care of yourselves there,

[279] *Powell* v. *Jones*, 1 Lev. 297.
[280] *Hughes* v. *Rees*, 4 M. & W. 204.
[281] *McClurg* v. *Ross*, 5 Binn. 218; and see *Caldwell* v. *Abbey*, Hardin, 520; *Huron* v. *Smith*, 4 B. Monr. 385.
[282] *Clarkson* v. *Lawson*, 6 Bing. 587; *Cooper* v. *Lawson*, 1 Perr. & D. 15; *Churchill* v. *Hunt*, 2 B. & A. 685.
[283] *Clarkson* v. *Lawson*, 6 Bing. 587.
[284] *Cooper* v. *Lawson*, 1 Perr. & D. 15.
[285] *Weaver* v. *Lloyd*, 2 B. & Cr. 678 ; 4 D. & R. 230.

mind what you are about;[296] and where the charge was that plaintiff had killed his adversary in a duel, and that a portion of the night preceding the duel was spent in practicing with a pistol, held to be divisible allegations;[297] and where the charge was that the plaintiff had, by furious driving, caused the death of a party and then commented in terms held to be actionable on the fact of the plaintiff, on the same evening, attending a public ball, held that the charges were divisible;[298] so of the words, she is a forsworn whore and a perjured whore,[299] and Thou are a roguish knave and a thief.[300] Where the charge was that plaintiff was in prison and unable to pay his rent, and a mere man of straw, held not divisible, but one charge of insolvency.[301] Allegations of time, and space, and number, are divisible.[302]

---

[296] *Orpwood* v. *Barkes*, 4 Bing. 261 ; S. C. sub. nom. *Orpwood* v. *Parkes*, 12 Moore, 492.

[297] *Helsham* v. *Blackwood*, 11 C. B. 111 ; 5 Eng. Law & Eq. R. 409.

[298] *Churchill* v. *Hunt*, 2 B. & A. 685 ; 1 Chit. 480.

[299] *Wales* v. *Norton*, Hard. 7.

[300] *Bailey* v. *Maynard*, 2 Bulst. 134.

[301] *Enton* v. *Johns*, 1 Dowl. Pr. C. N. S. 602.

[302] *Monkman* v. *Shepherdson*, 3 Perr. & D. 182 ; 11 Ad. & El. 411 ; so said in argument, *Page* v. *Hatchett*, 6 Law Times, 218 ; and as to divisible allegations, see *McGregor* v. *Gregory*, 2 Dowl. Pr. C. N. S. 769 ; 11 M. & W. 289 ; *Nelson* v. *Patrick*, 3 C. B. 772 ; *Mountney* v. *Watton*, 2 B. & Ad. 673 ; *Tapley* v. *Wainwright*, 5 B. & Adol. 395, cited, *Dunckle* v. *Wil*.*s*; 6 Barb. 523 ; *Vessey* v. *Pike*, 8 C. & P. 512 ; *Berry* v. *Adamson*, 2 C. & P. 503 ; *O'Connell* v. *Mansfield*, 9 Ir. Law R. 179 ; *Edwards* v. *Bell*, 1 Bing. 403 ; *Lewis* v. *Walter*, 4 Dowl. & R. 810 ; 3 B. & Cr. 138 ; *Johns* v. *Gittings*, Cro. Eliz. 239 ; Vin. Abr. Act. for Words, *F. a.* 43 ; Heard on Libel, 286, note 2.

CHAPTER VIII.

Language must be such as does or does not occasion damage. What is meant by actionable per se, and actionable by reason of special damage. What language concerning a person as such, published orally, is actionable per se. What language concerning a person as such, published in writing, is actionable per se. What language concerning one in an acquired capacity, is actionable per se. What language is actionable by reason of special damage. What language concerning the affairs of a person, his property or his title thereto, is actionable.

§ 146. All language concerning a person or his affairs, which, as a necessary or natural and proximate consequence, occasions him pecuniary loss, is *prima facie* actionable (§§ 57, 59, 70). Language must be either (1) such as necessarily, in fact, or by a presumption of evidence, occasions damage to him whom or whose affairs it is concerning, or (2) such as does not necessarily, or as a necessary consequence, but does by a natural and proximate consequence, occasion damage to him whom or whose affairs it is concerning, or (3) such as neither as a necessary nor as a natural and proximate consequence occasions damage to him whom or whose affairs it is concerning.[299] The loss which ensues as a *"necessary consequence,"* is termed damage; the loss which ensues as a *"natural and proximate consesequence,"* is termed *" special damage."* One and the same set of words may both necessarily occasion damage and also occasion damage as a natural consequence.

---

[299] In the jurisprudence of Louisiana, a distinction is not made between words actionable and words not actionable, as the basis of damages in a suit for slander, where no special damages are proved. (*Feray* v. *Foote,* 12 La. Ann. 894.)

§ 147. Language of the first of these classes is commonly termed libellous *per se*, or actionable *per se*, because its publication confers a *prima facie* right of action, and is *prima facie* a wrong without any evidence of damage other than that which is implied or presumed from the fact of publication. Probably language of this class might more correctly be termed injurious *per se*, or language which imports damage.

§ 148. The publication of language of the second of these classes does not, *per se*, confer a *prima facie* right of action, and is not, *per se*, a *prima facie* wrong. It confers a right of action only in those cases in which, as a natural and proximate consequence of the publication, loss (special damage) has in fact ensued to him whom or whose affairs the language was concerning.

§ 149. The publication of language of the third of these classes cannot in any event amount to a wrong, and cannot in any event confer a right of action.

§ 150. We attempted to explain in Chapter IV., that pecuniary loss, actual or presumed, is the gist of the action for slander or libel, and we stated (pp. 55, 56) the basis, as we suppose, of the distinction between words actionable *per se* and words only actionable by reason of special damage, to consist solely of a rule of evidence; the rule by which courts decide what words[204] shall be considered by their publication *necessarily* to occasion pecuniary loss or damage. The courts, while exercising this power, have failed to promulgate a formula which can be applied with any degree of certainty, to distinguish the cases in which damage is necessarily implied, from the cases in which no such implication occurs, and in which to give a right of action special damage must be proved.

§ 151. As the injurious, or presumed injurious effect of language depends upon whether (1) the language concerns a per-

---

[204] Words mean written or spoken words (*Minter* v. *Stewart*, 2 How. (Mis.) 183), and an action for written slander may be an action for "slanderous words" within the Vermont Judiciary Act (*Parsons* v. *Young*, 2 Verm. 434), but see note 131, *ante*.

son or a thing (2) or the person as such or in some acquired capacity, or (3) in certain cases, whether the language be published orally or by writing, it will be necessary to consider the topic of actionable language under the following heads :

I.—What language concerning a person, as such, published orally, is actionable *per se*.

II.—What language concerning a person, as such, published in writing, is actionable *per se*.

III.—What language concerning one in an acquired capacity or special character, as in a business, profession, or office, or as partner, or as heir at law, is actionable *per se*.

IV.—What language is actionable by reason of special damage.

V.—What language concerning things, as the affairs of a person, his property, or his title thereto, is actionable.

§ 152. What language concerning a person, as such, published orally, is actionable *per se ?*   Although it has been said that " The law of England defines with much greater distinctness than is usually found in other codes, the limits of the civil action for oral slander in the absence of special damage,"[295] it is nevertheless true that " There is not perhaps so much uncertainty in the law upon any subject, as when words shall be in themselves actionable."[296]   " The line of demarcation seems never to have been satisfactorily defined,"[297] and is " more satisfactorily determined by an accurate application of the principles upon which actions on the case for words depend, than by a reference to adjudged cases, especially those in the more ancient authors."[298]   The diversity of opinion as to what words should be treated as imputing damage, or actionable *per se*, arose from a wavering in the minds of the judges between two oppo-

---

[295] Prelim. Discourse to Starkie on Slander, XXX. (30), note v.

[296] Spencer, J., *Brooker* v. *Coffin*, 5 Johns. 192.

[297] Borthwick on Libel, 5 ; Lord Holt said it was not worth while to be learned on the subject. *Baker* v. *Pierce*, 6 Mod. 24.

[298] 1 Comyn's Dig. 273, note, 4th edit.

site inconveniences. · The fear of encouraging a spirit of vexatious litigation, by affording too great a facility for this species of action, was contrasted with the mischief resulting to the public peace from refusing legal redress; and according as the former or latter of these considerations preponderated, so was the rule of decision rigid or relaxed.[299]

§ 153. Several of the States provide by statute what words shall be actionable; thus, in Mississippi, Virginia, and Georgia, it is enacted that all words which from their usual construction and common acceptation are considered as insults and breaches of the peace, shall be actionable. In Tennessee, imputing adultery or fornication, or calling one coward or poltroon for not fighting a duel, is actionable. In Arkansas and Illinois, to impute adultery, fornication, or false swearing, or having sworn [or affirmed in Illinois] falsely in common acceptation, whether in a judicial proceeding or not, is actionable. In Missouri, to impute · adultery or fornication, is actionable. In Indiana, to impute to a female incest, fornication, adultery, or whoredom, or to impute to any one incest, or an infamous crime against nature with man or beast, is actionable. In Florida, a *charge by any* citizen of that State against another, imputing incest, fornication, or adultery, is actionable. In North Carolina, any words spoken of a female which amount to a charge of incontinency, are actionable; and in Maryland, all words tending to the injury of the reputation for chastity of a *feme sole*, are actionable.[300]

In the absence of any statutory provision on the subject, all language concerning a person in his individual capacity merely, when published orally, is actionable *per se*, which,

' I. Charges an indictable offence involving moral turpitude; or,

II. Charges the being afflicted with certain diseases.

§ 154. In New York, oral language is actionable *per se*,

[299] 1 Starkie on Slander, 12.
[300] See concluding paragraph of note 18, *ante*, and note 482, *post*.

when it imputes a charge which if true will subject the party
charged to an indictment for a crime involving moral turpitude,
or subject him to an infamous punishment.   This was the rule
laid down by Justice Spencer, in *Brooker* v. *Coffin*,[301] and as to
which Justice Bronson said, that although it was not entirely
satisfactory to his mind, he felt bound to follow it.[302]   It was
proposed by counsel to modify the rule as stated above by altering *or* into *and,* but the court refused to yield to the suggestion,[303] and the rule, as laid down in *Brooker* v. *Coffin,* has been
followed in numerous cases in New York and other States.[304]
In reference to the above rule it has been remarked that "when
the courts say the words are actionable if they subject the party
to indictment and *infamous* punishment, provided they be
true, we clearly understand what is the extent of the rule;"
but when they add, " or subject the party to an indictment for
an offence involving *moral turpitude,* we are left in doubt what
charges are embraced within the sentence ; it lacks precision."[305]
And again, " This element of moral turpitude is necessarily
adaptive; for it is itself defined by the state of public morals,
and thus far fits the action to be at all times accommodated to
the common sense of the community."[306]   Chief Justice Par-

---

[301] 5 Johns. 188.

[302] *Young* v. *Miller,* 3 Hill, 22.

[303] *Widrig* v. *Oyer,* 13 Johns. 124.

[304] *Wright* v. *Paige,* 36 Barbour, 438 ; *Quin* v. *O'Gara,* 2 E. D. Smith, 388 ;
Martin v. *Stillwell,* 13 Johnson, 275 ; *Burtch* v. *Nickerson,* 17 Johnson, 219 ;
Van Ness v. *Hamilton,* 19 Johns. 367 ; *Gibbs* v. *Dewey,* 5 Cow. 503 ; *Dem-*
arest v. *Haring,* 6 Cow. 88 ; *Crawford* v. *Wilson,* 4 Barb. 504 ; *Alexander* v. *Alex-*
ander, 9 Wend. 141 ; *Hoag* v. *Hatch,* 23 Conn. 590 ; *Andres* v. *Hoppenheafer,* 3
Serg. & R. 255 ; *Todd* v. *Rough,* 10 Serg. & R. 18 ; *McCuen* v. *Ludlam,* 2 Harri-
son (N. J.), 12 ; *Johnson* v. *Shields,* 1 Dutcher, 118 ; *Giddens* v. *Mirk,* 4 Ga. 360 ;
Burton v. *Burton,* 3 Iowa, 316 ; *Gage* v. *Shelton,* 3 Rich. 242 ; *Kinney* v. *Hosea,* 3
Harr. 77 ; *Coburn* v. *Harwood,* Minor, 93 ; *Perdue* v. *Burnett,* Minor, 138 ; *Hil-*
house v. *Peck,* 2 Stew. & Por. 395 ; *Johnston* v. *Morrow,* 9 Porter, 525 ; *Taylor* v.
Kneeland, 1 Doug. (Mich.), 67 ; *Beck* v. *Stitzel,* 21 Penn. St. R. 522 ; *Billings* v.
Wing, 7 Verm. 439 ; *The State* v. *Burroughs,* 2 Halst. 426 ; 1 Amer. Lead. Cas.
113, 3d ed.

[305] Daniel, J., *Skinner* v. *White,* 1 Dev. & Bat. 471 ; and see *Brady* v. *Wilson,*
4 Hawks, 93 ; *Wall* v. *Hoskins,* 5 Ired. 177 ; *Shipp* v. *McCraw,* 3 Murph. 463.

[306] Lowrie, J., *Beck* v. *Stitzel,* 21 Penn. St. Rep. 522.

ker refused to adopt the rule as laid down in *Brooker* v. *Coffin*, *supra*, and laid down the rule as thus: an accusation is actionable whenever an offence is charged which, if proved, may subject the party to a punishment, though not ignominious, and which brings disgrace upon him.[307]

The same learned judge, in another case, laid down the rule as thus: " Words imputing crime in the party against whom they are spoken, which if true would subject him to disgraceful punishment, are actionable without special damage.[308]

§ 155. The following offences, among others, have been held to involve *moral turpitude :* keeping a bawdy house,[309] removing land marks,[310] selling spirituous liquor to a slave,[311] paying money to secure election as a justice of the peace,[312] opening a letter addressed to another,[313] altering the owner's

---

[307] *Miller* v. *Parish*, 8 Pick. 383.

[308] *Chaddock* v. *Briggs*, 13 Mass. 248 ; and to the like effect, *Bloss* v. *Tobey*, 2 Pick. 320 : " Words to be actionable must charge an offence subject to corporal or infamous punishment." (*Elliott* v. *Ailsberry*, 2 Bibb, 473 ; *McGee* v. *Wilson*, Lit. Sec. Cas. 187.) Words are not actionable *per se* when " they impute no crime which could be visited by infamous punishment." (*Buck* v. *Hersey*, 31 Maine, 558; *Gosling* v. *Morgan*, 32 Penn. State Rep. 273.) The charge of a misdemeanor to be actionable *per se* must be one which " implies some heinous offence involving moral turpitude." (*Mills* v. *Wimp*, 10 B. Monroe, 417.) An indictment lies for many acts not involving moral turpitude. (*Quinn* v. *O'Gara*, 2 E. D. Smith, 388.)

Words charging an offence involving moral turpitude and indictable, although not subjecting the offender to infamous punishment, are actionable in themselves. (*Perdue* v. *Burnett*, Minor, 138.)

Any words which, according to their natural import, impute a crime or misdemeanor, which is punishable in the temporal courts by corporal punishment, are actionable in themselves. (*Demarest* v. *Haring*, 6 Cow. 76.)

" An action will lie for all words spoken of another, which impute to him the commission of a crime involving moral turpitude, and which is punishable by law." Heard on Libel, 25.

[309] *Martin* v. *Stillwell*, 13 Johns. 275; *Brayne* v. *Cooper*, 5 M. & W. 249.

[310] *Young* v. *Miller*, 3 Hill, 24 ; *Todd* v. *Rough*, 10 S. & R. 18 ; *Dial* v. *Holter*, 6 Ohio (N. S.), 228.

[311] *Smith* v. *Smith*, 2 Sneed, 473.

[312] *Hoag* v. *Hatch*, 23 Conn. 585.

[313] *Cheadle* v. *Buell*, 6 Ham. 67 ; contra, *McCuen* v. *Ludlam*, 2 Harr. 12 ; and see *Hillhouse* v. *Peck*, 2 Stew. & Port. 395.

marks on animals,[314] soliciting one to commit murder,[315] indecent exposure of the person,[316] embracery,[317] making a false
declaration of a right to vote,[318] and counterfeiting.[319]

§ 156. In some of the States it seems that all oral language
which imputes an indictable offence or an offence punishable
at law, is actionable *per se*; thus it is said, "All that is essential to the maintenance of the action for slander is that the
words shall impute the commission of a punishable offence."[320]
To be actionable the effect of the language must be "to charge
some crime or offence punishable by law;"[321] "a charge of
crime or some punishable offence,"[322] or "words imputing to
another a crime punishable by law,"[323] or an indictable offence.[324]
While in other States it is held that words, to be actionable,
must impute not only an indictable offence, but an indictable
offence for which corporal punishment may be inflicted as the
immediate penalty.[325]

§ 157. Judging from the language of many English dicta,
the rule in England would seem to be that all oral language is
actionable *per se*, which imputes a crime or indictable offence.
"An action lies for any words which import the charge of a
crime for which the party may be indicted."[326] "The test is,

[314] *Perdue* v. *Burnett*, Minor, 138.
[315] *Demarest* v. *Haring*, 6 Cow. 76.
[316] *Torbitt* v. *Clare*, 9 Irish Law R. 86.
[317] *Gibbs* v. *Dewey*, 5 Cow. 503; see *ante*, § 144, subd. *j*.
[318] *Crawford* v. *Wilson*, 4 Barb. 505.
[319] *Howard* v. *Stephenson*, 2 Const. Rep., 2d series, 408; *Thirman* v. *Matthew*,
1 Stew. 384. See Arson, Forgery, Larceny, Perjury, Homicide.
[320] McKinney, J., *Poe* v. *Grever*, 3 Sneed, 666. "Words which impute trespass, assault, battery, and the like, are not actionable *per se*, and yet these
offences are punishable by indictment." (*Smith* v. *Smith*, 2 Sneed, 478; *Dudley*
v. *Horn*, 21 Ala. 379; *Billings* v. *Wing*, 7 Verm. 444.)
[321] *Dunnell* v. *Fiske*, 11 Metc. 552.
[322] *Edgerley* v. *Swaine*, 32 N. Hamp. 481.
[323] *Tenney* v. *Clement*, 10 N. Hamp. 57.
[324] *Kinney* v. *Hosea*, 3 Harring. 77.
[325] *Birch* v. *Benton*, 26 Miss. (5 Jones) 153; *Billings* v. *Wing*, 7 Verm. 144.
[326] *Mayne* v. *Digle*, Freeman, 46. Words, to be actionable in themselves, must
charge some *scandalous* crime; they must be such as to impute to the party an

whether the crime is indictable or not."[327] "Where an offence of a criminal nature is imputed by the slander for which the party is liable to indictment or punishment by the common or statute law, those words are actionable *per se*.[328] "It is well known that words are not actionable unless they impute some crime or indictable offence."[329] "The words, to be actionable, must impute a criminal offence; that is, the words, if true, must be such that the plaintiff would be guilty of a criminal offence."[330] While other decisions seem to require that an offence must be imputed—which would not only subject the party charged to imprisonment, but to an infamous punishment. To make the words actionable *per se* "there must not only be imprisonment, but an infamous punishment;"[331] and therefore in that case it was held that the words "Thou art one of those that stole my Lord Shaftesbury's deer" were not actionable *per se*, because, although the offence of deer stealing was punishable by imprisonment, it was not an *infamous* punishment. "The words [to be actionable] must contain an express imputation of some crime liable to punishment, some capital offence, or other infamous crime or misdemeanor."[332] Mr. Starkie says: "Perhaps it may be inferred, generally, that to impute any crime or misdemeanor for which corporal punishment may be inflicted

---

offence for which he may be indicted. (*Walmsley* v. *Russell*, 6 Mod. 200.) In *Smale* v. *Hammon*, 1 Bulst. 40, it was said where the words spoken do tend to the infamy, discredit or disgrace of the party, they shall be actionable, but this dictum was said to go too far. (*Holt* v. *Scholefield*, 6 T. R. 691.) In *Scobell* v. *Lee* (2 Show. 82), it was held not actionable to call one *regrator*, because *regrating*, although criminal, was not punishable by loss of life or limb.

[331] Comyn Dig. Act. for Defam. F. 20.

[328] 2 Saund. Pl. and Ev. 898, 2d Eng. Ed.

[329] Tyndal, Ch. J. *Edsall* v. *Russell*, 5 Sc. N. R. 815; 2 Dowl. N. S. 648; 4 M. and G. 1099; 12 Law Jour. N. S. C. B. 7.

[330] Alderson, B. *Heming* v. *Power*, 10 M. and W. 570.

[331] Holt, Ch. J., *Turner* v. *Ogden*, 2 Salk. 696.

[332] De Grey, Ch. J., *Onslow* v. *Horne*, 3 Wilson, 186. This rule, says Mr. Heard (Heard on Libel, 16), is universally referred to as the correct rule, and was repeated in *Holt* v. *Scholefield*, 6 T. R. 694, and in *Beardsley* v. *Dibblee*, 1 Kerr, 258, and adopted in *Shaffer* v. *Knitzer*, 1 Binney, 542; *Andres* v. *Koppenheafer*, 3 Serg. & R. 257; *Bloom* v. *Bloom*, 5 *id.* 392; *Pelton* v. *Ward*, 3 Caines, 79; *Smith* v. *Smith*, 2 Sneed, 478; *Johnson* v. *Shields*, 1 Dutcher, 119.

in a temporal court is actionable, without proof of special damage. Where the penalty for an offence is merely pecuniary, an action will not lie for charging such offence; even though in default of payment imprisonment should be prescribed, imprisonment not being the primary and immediate punishment for the offence."[233]

§ 158. It has been supposed that the gist of the action for slander was the peril of prosecution to which a person was exposed by the charge, and therefore that for charging an offence which has been pardoned or atoned for, or which is barred by the statute of limitations, no action can be maintained. Thus it is said, "The ground of the matter being actionable is, that a charge is made which, if it were true, would endanger the plaintiff in point of law."[234] The better opinion is, that the action of slander " is always for the loss of character and not the danger of punishment,"[235] or the hazard of a criminal prosecution.[236] " It is a great slander to be once a criminal; and although a pardon may discharge the punish-

---

[233] 1 Starkie on Slander, 43; 6 Mod. 104. This view of the law is adopted in *Billings* v. *Wing*, 7 Verm. 439; *Wagaman* v. *Byers*, 17 Md. 183; and in a note at page 90 of Metcalf's edition of Yelverton's Reports; but is questioned 1 Amer. Lead. Cas., 112, 2d ed., and in *Smith* v. *Smith*, 2 Sneed, 478. Saying that plaintiff went to mass was held actionable, because it was by statute an offence punishable by fine and imprisonment. (*Sir Lionel Walden* v. *Mitchell*, 2 Vent. 265.) And concealing a felony was held actionable at a time when such an offence was punishable by fine only. (*Newlyn* v. *Fasset*, Yelv. 154.) But the words thou art a common barretor, it was said would not support an action because the punishment was merely fine and binding to good behavior. (*Heake* v. *Moulton*, Yelv. 90.)

[234] Parke, B., *Heming* v. *Power*, 10 M. & W. 569. See *Harvey* v. *Boies*, 1 Penn. 14; *Andres* v. *Hoppenheafer*, 3 Serg. & R. 258; *Dalrymple* v. *Lofton*, 1 M'Mullan, 118. " The grounds of action are to be found in the degradation of the party in society, or his liability to criminal animadversion. * * * The party's jeopardy, in a legal point of view, is regarded by the law as the principal ground of action." (1 Starkie on Slander, 18.) But criminal liability is not always the peculiar and exclusive ground of action; instances are to be found of remedy for imputations which could not subject the party to any future penalty. (*Id.* 19.)

[235] *Van Ankin* v. *Westfall*, 14 Johns. 233; *Shipp* v. *McCraw*, 3 Murph. 466.

[236] *Eastland* v. *Caldwell*, 2 Bibb, 24; *Smith* v. *Stewart*, 5 Barr, 372; *Beck* v. *Stitzel*, 21 Penn. St. R. 524; *Poe* v. *Grever*, 3 Sneed, 604.

ment, yet the scandal of the offence remains."[337] It is in this
view that it has been held actionable, subject to justification on
the ground of truth,[338] to say of one, " He was a thief and stole
my gold ;"[339] or, " He is a returned convict ;"[340] or, " He is a
convict and has been in the Ohio penitentiary ;"[341] or, " You
have been cropped for felony;"[342] or, " Thou wast in Laun-
ceston gaol for coining and burnt in the hand for it ;"[343] or,
" Robert Carpenter (the plaintiff) was in Winchester gaol and
tried for his life, and would have been hanged had it not been
for Leggett, for breaking open the granary of farmer A. and
stealing his bacon ;"[344] or, " He was whipped for stealing
hogs ;"[345] or, " He was put in the roundhouse for stealing
ducks at Crowland ;"[346] or, " Thou hast been in gaol for stealing a pan."[347] For the words, " Thou wert in gaol for robbing
on the highway," the court was divided if actionable or not ;[348]
a charge of committing a statutable offence was held actionable, although intermediate the speaking the words and the
commencement of the action the statute was repealed.[349]

§ 159. Where the offence is charged to have been committed in a foreign state, it will be actionable if it appear that
the offence charged is one by the law of that state punishable
by indictment, and involving moral turpitude.   Where the

---

[337] *Boston* v. *Tatham*, Cro. Jac. 622, and see *Cuddington* v. *Williams*, Hobart,
81.
[338] *Baum* v. *Clause*, 5 Hill, 196; *Van Ankin* v. *Westfall*, 14 Johns. 233; and
see *post*, Defences.
[339] *Boston* v. *Tatham*, Cro. Jac. 622.
[340] *Fowler* v. *Dowdney*, 2 Moo. & Rob. 119; and see the reporter's note to this
case.
[341] *Smith* v. *Stewart*, 5 Barr, 372.
[342] *Wiley* v. *Campbell*, 5 Monr. 396.
[343] *Gainford* v. *Tuke*, Cro. Jac. 536.
[344] *Carpenter* v. *Tarrant*, Rep. temp. Hard. 839, cited by L'd Ellenborough
Roberts v. *Camden*, 9 East, 97.
[345] *Holley* v. *Burgess*, 9 Ala. 728.
[346] *Beavor* v. *Hides*, 2 Wils. 300.
[347] *Showell* v. *Haman*, Cro. Jac. 153.
[348] *Smale* v. *Hammon*, 1 Bulst. 40.
[349] *French* v. *Creath*, Breese, 12.

offence charged is one punishable by indictment at common
law it will be presumed to be indictable everywhere; but if
the offence charged be one created by statute or punishable by
indictment by statute, then, as courts cannot take judicial
notice of the statutes of foreign states, to make the charge
actionable the statute relating to the offence charged must be
pleaded and proved like any other fact.[350] Thus it is actionable
per se, to charge one with stealing in a foreign state or country,[351] or with murder,[352] and an action may be maintained for
charging a crime committed in another state, which it would
not be actionable to charge the commission of in the state in
which the action is commenced.[353]

§ 160. "No charge upon a plaintiff, however foul, will be
actionable without special damage, unless it be of an offence
punishable in a temporal court of *criminal* jurisdiction,"[354] and

[350] *Offutt* v. *Earlywine,* 4 Blackf. 460; *Linville* v. *Earlywine,* id. 469; *Langdon* v.
Young, 33 Verm. 136; *Stout* v. *Wood,* 1 id. 71; *Barclay* v. *Thompson,* 2 Penns.
148; *Poe* v. *Grever,* 3 Sneed, 644. Thus the stealing of bank notes not being
indictable at common law, to charge a theft of bank notes in South Carolina, was
held not to be actionable in North Carolina, unless it was shown that, by the laws
of South Carolina, such stealing was subject to an infamous punishment. (*Wall*
v. *Hoskins,* 5 Iredell, 177.) A. and B. being in North Carolina, A. charged B.
with stealing a note from him in Virginia, and it appearing that stealing notes
was a larceny in Virginia, the charge was held to be actionable. (*Shipp* v.
McCraw, 3 Murph. 463.)
[351] As to say in Canada, Old Smith (plaintiff) is a damned thief, he stole a cow in
the States (United States). (*Smith* v. *Collins,* 3 Up. Can. Q. B. R. 1; and see
Johnson v. *Dicken,* 25 Missouri, 315; *Cofret* v. *Burch,* 1 Sneed, 400.)
[352] Words charging the commission of murder in Ireland are actionable without proving murder to be an indictable offence in that country. (*Montgomery* v.
Deeley, 3 Wis. 709.) To charge one with administering poison in a foreign country, with intent to kill, is actionable, *semble* the court will presume such an
offence to be indictable. See *Langdon* v. *Young,* 33 Verm. 136.
[353] *Van Ankin* v. *Westfall,* 14 Johns. 233; and see *Stout* v. *Wood,* 1 Blackf. 71.
[354] 1 Starkie on Slander, 21, and he proceeds to establish this proposition by
referring to the cases in which it has been decided that to say a man is "forsworn," or has "taken a false oath," is not actionable unless the charge connects
it with some judicial proceeding. Without this connection he says the charge
only imputes a breach of morality, for which no action lies. [See *Perjury,* post.]
Besides the older authorities there is cited *Hopkins* v. *Beedle,* 1 Cai. 347; *Stafford*
v. *Green,* 1 Johns. 505; *Ward* v. *Clark,* 2 id. 10; *Watson* v. *Hampton,* 2 Bibb's R.

therefore held not actionable *per se* to charge a breach of trust[855] or a malicious trespass,[856] or of burning, destroying, and suppressing a will,[857] or attempting to procure, or causing or procuring a miscarriage,[858] or with incest,[859] or adultery,[860] or crime

---

319; *Jacobs* v. *Fylee*, 3 Hill, 572. To these we add *Hopwood* v. *Thorn*, 8 C. B. 293; *Bute* v. *Gill*, 2 Monr. 65; *Dorsey* v. *Whipps*, 8 Gill, 457; *Holt* v. *Schofield*, 6 T. R. 694; *Wyant* v. *Smith*, 5 Blackf. 293; *Tebbetts* v. *Goding*, 9 Gray, 254; *Edgerly* v. *Swain*, 32 N. H. 478; *Wright* v. *Lindsay*, 20 Ala. 428; *Barham* v. *Nethersall*, Yelv. 21; and see Heard on Libel, § 28. A charge of having "broken open and read a letter" sent by mail, held not actionable, because the offence, although indictable, is not, morally speaking, a crime. (*Hillhouse* v. *Peck*, 2 Stew. & Port. 395; and see *McCuen* v. *Ludlam*, 2 Harr. 12; *Cheadle* v. *Buell*, 6 Ham. 67.)

Where the words on their face charge a criminal offence, but are shown by their context or otherwise, not to have that meaning, they are not actionable; thus the words they are highwaymen, robbers, and murderers, being shown to relate to a transaction not amounting to a criminal offence, were held not to be actionable. (*Van Rensselaer* v. *Dole*, 1 Johns. Cas. 279.) And see § 134 and note 147, *ante.*

It has been held that a charge by a married woman of having stolen her goods, is not actionable [she having no separate estate], as a married woman could not have goods of her own. (1 Rolle Abr. 74; 6 Bac. Abr. 238; 1 Starkie on Slander, 77.) But where a married woman said my turkeys are stolen, Charnell hath stolen them, it was held Charnell might have his action. (*Charnell's Case*, Cro. Eliz. 279.) And so where a married woman said, thou hast stolen my faggots. (*Stamp* v. *White*, Palmer, 358; and see *Powell* v. *Plunkett*, Cro. Car. 52.)

By the statutes of Illinois, no child under the age of ten years can be punished for larceny; but an action may be maintained by such child for slanderous words accusing her of theft. (*Stewart* v. *Howe*, 17 Ill. 71; and see *Redway* v. *Gray*, 31 Verm. (2 Shaw) 292; *Dukes* v. *Clark*, 2 Blackf. 20; *Bash* v. *Somers*, 20 Penn. (8 Harris) 159. See notes 143, 144, 240, and § 144, subd. bb. *ante.*

[855] *McClurg* v. *Ross*, 5 Binn. 218.

[856] *Wilcox* v. *Edwards*, 5 Blackf. 183.

[857] *O'Hanlon* v. *Myers*, 10 Rich. Law (S. C.), 128; and see 3 Salk. 327.

[858] Not within the exceptions of the statute (*Bissell* v. *Cornell*, 24 Wend. 354; *Abrams* v. *Foshee*, 3 Clarke, 274; *Smith* v. *Gafford*, 31 Ala. 43), and held not actionable to charge an attempt to commit a robbery. (*Russell* v. *Wilson*, 7 B. Monr. 261.)

[859] *Eure* v. *Odom*, 2 Hawks, 52; and as to charge of incest, see *Starr* v. *Gardner*, 6 Up. Can. Q. B. Rep. O. S. 512; *Watts* v. *Greenlee*, 2 Dev. 115; *Gallwey* v. *Marshall*, 9 Exch. 294, *ante*, § 141.

[860] *Wagaman* v. *Byers*, 17 Md. 183; *Castlebury* v. *Kelly*, 26 Geo. 606; see *ante*, § 144, subd. a., and *post.*

against nature,[361] or with cheating,[362] or " mismarking " cattle,[363] or living by imposture.[364]

§ 161. A purpose or intent to do an unlawful act without any act being done, is not punishable criminally, and therefore within the rule stated in the last preceding section (§ 160), it is not actionable orally to charge one with a mere intent to commit an offence,[365] " and this rule seems in all times to have been adhered to with more consistency than is generally observable in decisions relating to slander." [366] Thus it has been held not actionable to say of one, Thou hast procured J. S. to come thirty miles to commit perjury against his father * * * and hast given him £10 for his pains; or, Harris hath procured and *suborned* one Smith to come thirty miles to commit perjury against his father * * * and given Smith £10 for that purpose;[367] or, Thou wouldst have killed me,[368] or She would have cut her husband's throat;[369] or, Thou wouldst have taken my purse from me on the highway;[370] or, Thou wouldst have murdered me;[371] or, Sir Harbert Crofts keepeth men to rob me;[372] but for the words, He sent his man A. to kill me, the

---

[361] *Coburn* v. *Harwood*, Minor, 93; *Estes* v. *Carter*, 10 Iowa. 400; see *ante*, §§ 144, 153, and *post.* Where the crime against nature is indictable, to charge the commission of it is actionable. (*Goodrich* v. *Woolcot*, 3 Cow. 231; 5 Cow. 714.)

[362] *Odiorne* v. *Bacon*, 6 Cush. 185; *Richardson* v. *Allen*, 2 Chit. 657; *Werback* v. *Trone*, 2 Watts & Ser. 408. Thou hast cheated me of several pounds, held actionable. (*Surman* v. *Shilletto*, 3 Burr. 1688.)

[363] *Williams* v. *Karnes*, 4 Humph. 9; *Johnston* v. *Morrow*, 9 Port. 525.

[364] *Willy* v. *Elston*, 18 Law Jour. 320, C. P.; 13 Jur. 706; 7 Dowl. & L. 143; 8 C. B. 142.

[365] *McKee* v. *Ingalls*, 4 Scam. 30; *Seaton* v. *Cordray*, Wright, 101; *Harrison* v. *Stratton*, 4 Esp. 218.

[366] 1 Starkie on Slander, 23.

[367] *Harris* v. *Dixon*, Cro. Jac. 158; Yelv. 72.

[368] Potts' Case, Vin. Ab. Act. for Words, Q. a. 8; cited as Dr. Poe's Case, 2 Bulst. 206.

[369] *Scott* v. *Hilliers*, Lane, 98; but it being added, and did attempt it, the latter words were held actionable.

[370] Godb. 202.

[371] *Tettal* v. *Osborne*, cited in *Storrer* v. *Audley*, Cro. Eliz. 250. He *sought* to murder me, held actionable, because *sought* implies more than a mere intent. (Cro. Eliz. 808.)

[372] *Crofts* v. *Brown*, 3 Bulst. 167.

court were divided if actionable or not;[373] and the words, He will lie in wait to rob J. S. within two days, were held actionable.[374] From the fact that in England a mere intent may constitute the crime of treason, a charge of treasonable intention has there been held to be actionable; thus, for saying "he is a Jacobite, and for bringing in the Prince of Wales and popery to the destroying of our nation," held an action could be maintained.[375]

§ 162. It has been said the cases are uniform on the point that for an imputation of evil *inclinations* or *principles* no action lies, unless it affects the plaintiff in some particular character, or produces special damage.[376] But unless by *inclinations* and *principles* are meant *intentions* (§ 161), or the assertion be limited to oral language, the dictum seems to be unwarranted. It was held actionable to publish in writing that plaintiff had openly avowed the opinion that government had no more right to provide by law for the support of the worship of the Supreme Being than for the support of the worship of the Devil;[377] or that plaintiff would put his name to anything that T. would request him to sign, that would prejudice D.'s character;[378] and the words, "He would rob the mail for one hundred dollars," spoken of a postmaster, were held actionable.[379]

§ 163. It is held, in some cases, that words which denote *the opinion* or *the suspicion* entertained by the publisher, are not equivalent to a direct charge, and therefore are not actionable;[380] thus, where the words were, "I have a suspicion that you, B., have robbed my house, and therefore I take you into custody," it was held the judge rightly directed the jury that if they believed the defendant meant to impute only a suspicion

---

[373] *Bray* v. *Andrews*, Moore, 63; Dal. 66.

[374] *Sidman* v. *Mayo*, 3 Bulst. 261.

[375] *Prin* v. *Howe*, 1 Bro. Parl. Cas. 64; and see *Eaton* v. *Allen*, 4 Rep. 16.

[376] 1 Starkie on Slander, 24; *Harrison* v. *Strutton*, 4 Esp. 218.

[377] *Stow* v. *Converse*, 3 Conn. 325.

[378] *Duncan* v. *Brown*, 15 B. Monr. 186.

[379] *Craig* v. *Brown*, 5 Blackf. 44.

[380] Words which denote opinion or suspicion are not actionable. (Comyn's Dig. Act. for Defam. F. 13; cited in *Hodgson* v. *Scarlett*, 1 B. & Ald. 233.)

11

of felony, and not an absolute charge of felony, their verdict must be for the defendant.[361] The words "she ought to have been transported," were held not actionable because they expressed only *the opinion* of the speaker.[362] But the words, He ought to be hanged as much as A., who was in fact hanged, were construed to charge an offence which deserved hanging, and actionable;[363] and it was held actionable to say of one, if you had your deserts you had been hanged before now;[364] and so of the words, He hath deserved his ears to be nailed to the pillory,[365] but not actionable to say: Thou deservest to be hanged;[366] or, Thou shouldst have sat on the pillory if thou hadst thy deserts;[367] or, Thou hast done that for which thou deservest to be hanged.[368] But the words, You have done things with the company for which you ought to be hanged, and I will have you hanged before the first of August, were held actionable;[369] and so of the words, "I know enough he has done to send him to the penitentiary."[390] It was held not to be actionable to say of one, "He is a great rogue, and deserves to be hanged as well as Gale," who was condemned to be hanged. Because the words show opinion merely, and perhaps

---

[361] *Tozer* v. *Mashford*, 4 Eng. L. & Eq. R. 451; 6 Exch. 639; 20 Law Jour. Rep. (N. S.) Ex. 224. The words, "I will take him to Bow street (a police court so called) on a charge of forgery," held not actionable, as not amounting to a charge of felony. (*Harrison* v. *King*, 4 Price, 46; 7 Taunt. 431.)

[362] *Hancock* v. *Winter*, 7 Taunt. 205. The words, I will transport him for felony, were held actionable. (*Tempest* v. *Chambers*, 1 Stark. Cas. 67.)

[363] *Read* v. *Ambridge*, 6 Car. & P. 308; and see *Davis* v. *Noak*, 1 Stark. Cas. 372.

[364] Downs' Case, Cro. Eliz. 62.

[365] *Jenkinson* v. *Mayne*, Cro. Eliz. 384.

[366] *Heake* v. *Moulton*, Yelv. 90.

[367] Anon., Moore, 243.

[368] *Fisher* v. *Atkinson*, Vin. Abr. Act. for Words, G. a. 5.

[369] On the ground that they imputed the commission of a crime punishable by hanging (*Francis* v. *Roose*, 8 M. & W. 191). "I will have him transported for perjury and forgery," with special damage held actionable. (*Floyd* v. *Jones*, 2 Barnard. 101.)

[390] *Johnson* v. *Shields*, 1 Dutcher, 116. A general charge of having been guilty of crime without naming the particular crime, seems sufficient (*Curtis* v. *Curtis*, 4 Moo. & S. 337); but held not sufficient to say he had been guilty of conduct unfit for publication. (*James* v. *Brook*, 10 Jur. 541.)

the speaker might not think Gale deserved hanging.[301] It was
held not actionable to say, I will take him to Bow street (a
police office so called) on a charge of forgery.[302] It was held
actionable for one to say he supposed the plaintiff was guilty
of a crime;[303] or, I *think* he is a horse stealer.[304] It seems
no more than the expression of an opinion to say, "Two dyers
have gone off, and for aught I know Harrison will be so too
within this time twelve month." Yet these words were held
to be actionable;[305] so of the words, "All is not well with
Daniel Vivian; there are many merchants who have lately
failed, and I expect no otherwise of Daniel Vivian";[306] and so
of the words, "I am thoroughly convinced you are guilty of
the death of D. D."[307] But held not actionable to express a
supposition or belief that one went to a certain place for the
purpose of persuading another to commit adultery with
him.[308]

§ 164. One may charge another with the commission of an
offence as well by way of a question as by a direct assertion,[399]
as, Is H. the man who broke jail?[400] what art thou? a bankrupt;[401] when will you bring home the nine stolen sheep you

<hr/>

[301] *Bush* v. *Smith,* 2 Jones, 157.
[302] *Harrison* v. *King,* 4 Price, 46; 7 Taunt. 431.
[303] *Dickey* v. *Andrews,* 32 Verm. 55.
[304] *Stitch* v. *Wisedome,* Cro. Eliz. 348.
[305] *Harrison* v. *Thornborough,* 10 Mod. 11.
[306] 3 Salk. 326.
[307] *Peake* v. *Oldham,* Cowper, 275; 2 W. Black. 960.
[308] *Dickey* v. *Andrews,* 32 Verm. 55, and as to a charge of inciting one to com
mit a crime (see *Passie* v. *Mondford,* Cro. Eliz. 747; *Lady Cockaine's Case,* Cro.
Eliz. 49; *Eaton* v. *Allen,* 4 Co. 16). The dicta and decisions that words denoting
opinion are not actionable, must have their origin in the *supposed* distinction between matters of fact and matters of opinion. See this distinction discussed in a
case of misrepresentation, *Haight* v. *Hoyt,* 19 N. Y. 468, in an Essay on the influence of authority in matters of opinion, by George Cornewall Lewis, and in the
review of that work—*Edinburgh Review,* April, 1850; also in Whateley's Logic;
and see the distinction noticed, *Root* v. *King,* 7 Cow. 629.
[399] *Gorham* v. *Ives,* 2 Wend. 534; *Sawyer* v. *Eifert,* 2 Nev. & M. 511.
[400] *Hotchkiss* v. *Oliphant,* 2 Hill, 510.
[401] *Jordan* v. *Lyster,* Cro. Eliz. 273, pl. 1.

stole from I. S.?[402] have you brought the £40 you stole?[403] wilt
thou murder my sister as thou didst thy wife?[404] who stole the
bell-ropes?[405] Asking as to a forgery, whether the witness did
not think it was in G.'s handwriting, and asserting that he had
shown it to some persons who said it was in G.'s handwriting,
would seem to show an intent to impress a belief of G.'s guilt
of the forgery.[406]

§ 165. In some of the older cases it was held that "adjective words," or "words spoken adjectively," do not confer a
right of action. But, as was well said by Lord Coke, "sometimes adjectives will maintain an action and sometimes not."[407]
Thus it was held not actionable to call one "conjuring knave,"[408]
or "murderous villain,"[409] or "pocky whore,"[410] or "rebellious
knave;"[411] but held actionable to call one a "traitorous
knave,"[412] or a "traitor knave."[413] We conceive the true rule
to be, that when the word imputes an act it is actionable, and
when it imputes an intention or inclination only it is not actionable.[414] Thus it has been held not actionable to call one a
"thievish knave," or to say to one "thou hast thievishly
taken my money," because the word *thievish* or *thievishly*
implies an inclination only;[415] but to call one a thieving rogue

[402] *Hunt* v. *Thimblethorp*, Moore, 418.
[403] *Mayott* v. *Gibbons*, 2 Rolle R. 166.
[404] *Brown* v. *Charlton*, Keb. 359, pl. 52.
[405] *Jackson* v. *Adams*, 2 Scott, 599; 2 Bing. N. C. 402. The words in this case
were held not actionable. See in note 143, *ante.*
[406] *Gorham* v. *Ives*, 2 Wend. 534.
[407] 4 Coke, 19.
[408] *Killick* v. *Barns*, 2 Bulst. 138.
[409] Ld. Raym. 236. So "murderous quean" held not actionable. (Vin. Ab.,
Act. for Words, I a. 4.)
[410] Gulford's Case, 2 Rolle R. 71; and "pocky rascal," see Vin. Abr., Act. for
Words, G. b. 5.
[411] *Ward* v. *Thorne*, Cro. Eliz. 171; *Booth* v. *Leach*, Lev. 90.
[412] *Id.*
[413] *Selby* v. *Carryer*, 2 Bulst. 210.
[414] 1 Starkie on Slander, 71, and § 162, *ante.*
[415] Vin. Abr., Act. for Words, I. a. 4, 11; *Robins* v. *Hildredon*, Cro. Jac. 65.

was held actionable because *thieving* implies an act.[416] "Thieving puppy" was held actionable,[417] and so were "thievish pirate,"[418] "bankrupt knave," "pocky knave,"[419] and "bankrupt skrub."[420] "Bankrupt rogue" was held not actionable when spoken of an individual as such;[421] but those words, when spoken of one in trade (a shoemaker), were held actionable.[422] "Bankruptly knave" was said not to be actionable because the phrase implies only bankrupt-like knave.[423] And so "Cuckoldy rogue" was held actionable.[424] A participle, it is said, implies an act done, and therefore held actionable to call one a "murdering rogue,"[425] or a "buggering rogue,"[426] or to say he is robbing or ravishing.[427]

§ 166. Words charging a burning amounting to *arson*, whether at common law or by statute, are actionable;[428] but

---

[416] *Hunt* v. *Merrychurch*, 2 Keb. 440; *Dorrell* v. *Grove*, Freem. 279.

[417] *Little* v. *Barlow*, 26 Geo. 423; *Pierson* v. *Stiortz*, 1 Morris, 186, and see *post*, note 452.

[418] Vin. Abr., Act. for Words, I. a. 12.'

[419] *Inglebath* v. *Jones*, Cro. Eliz. 99; but it was doubted in *Robinson* v. *Meller*, Cro. Eliz. 843, if "bankrupt knave" was actionable, and the phrase was held not actionable when spoken of a tanner. (*York* v. *Cecil*, Browl. 16.) The words "base, beggarly bankrupt knave" were held actionable in *Still* v. *Finch*, Cro. Car. 381; and so of the words bribing knave spoken of an attorney. (*Yardley* v. *Ellis*, Hob. 8.)

[420] *Wilson* v. *Crow*, Sty. 75.

[421] *Loyd* v. *Pearse*, Cro. Jac. 424.

[422] *Langley* v. *Colson*, Godb. 151.

[423] *Selby* v. *Carrier*, Cro. Jac. 345; but said otherwise, *Booth* v. *Leach*, Lev. 90. See Vin. Abr., Act. for Words, I. a. 3.

[424] The words were spoken in London, and held actionable as implying his wife was a whore. 1 Str. 471.

[425] *Green* v. *Lincoln*, Cro. Car. 318.

[426] *Collier* v. *Bourn*, 2 Keb. 377; or "perjured knave," *Staverton* v. *Relfe*, Yelv. 160; or "perjured rogue," *Orton* v. *Fuller*, Lev. 65; but where the words were, Thou art a perjured knave, that is to be proved by a stake that parts the lands of J. S. and J. D., it was doubted if they were actionable. (*Brechcley* v. *Atkins*, Yelv. 10.)

[427] Sybthorp's Case, 1 Rolle Abr. 176; 1 Starkie on Slander, 72.

[428] *Brady* v. *Wilson*, 4 Hawks, 93; *Case* v. *Buckley*, 15 Wend. 327; *Jones* v. *Hungerford*, 4 Gill & Johns. 402; *House* v. *House*, 5 Har. & Johns. 124; *Wallace* v. *Young*, 5 Monr. 155. Saying, He [plaintiff] has been at different times close about where C.'s gin-house was burned, in disguise, held not to amount to a

charging one with burning his own store,[429] or the barn of another, is not actionable.[430] But to charge one with burning his own store to defraud the insurers would be actionable.[431]

§ 167. A general charge of *forgery* made orally is actionable ;[432] and so to charge, " You are a rogue, for you forged my name," [433] or " you signed my name without my permission." [434] But held not actionable to say, " Thou hast forged my hand," or " thou art a forger." [435] The writing charged to have been forged must it seems be one which if genuine would operate as the foundation of another's liability.[436] It has been held actionable to charge the forgery of a deposition,[437] a warrant,[438] a peti-

---

charge of arson, and not actionable. (*Waters* v. *Jones*, 3 Port. 442.) See *ante*, § 144, subd. *c.*

[429] *Bloss* v. *Tobey*, 2 Pick. 310; *McNab* v. *McGrath*, 5 Up. Can. Q. B. Rep. O. S. 516; or a building belonging to the wife of plaintiff, but occupied by plaintiff. (*Redway* v. *Gray*, 81 Verm. 292.)

[430] *Barham* v. *Nethersall*, Yelv. 21; charging one with burning a school-house was held actionable (*Wallace* v. *Young*, 5 Monr. 155); and so of a gin-house. (*Waters* v. *Jones*, 3 Port. 442.)

[431] 1 Am. Lead. Cas. 117, 3d ed.; and see *Tebbetts* v. *Goding*, 9 Gray, 254; contra, *Redway* v. *Gray*, 81 Verm. 292.

[432] *Alexander* v. *Alexander*, 9 Wend. 141; *Andrews* v. *Woodmansee*, 15 Wend. 232; *Nicholls* v. *Hayes*, 13 Conn. 155; *Arnold* v. *Cost*, 8 Gill & Johns. 219. Thou hast forged *a deed* or bond actionable, but thou hast forged a writing not actionable (*Motley* v. *Slany*, Keb. 273; *Austie* v. *Mason*, Cro. Eliz. 554; *Reynell* v. *Sackfield*, 2 Bulst. 132; *Aier* v. *Frost*, Rolle R. 431; S. C. *Frost* v. *Ayer*, 3 Bulst. 265; *Andrews* v. *Bird*, Het. 81), unless with an innuendo, a deed. (Anon. Sid. 16; and see *Goodale* v. *Castle*, Cro. Eliz. 554.) You have falsely forged your father's hand, and thereby falsely have procured your father's tenants to pay rents to you which were due to your sister, held not actionable. (*Venard* v. *Woton*, Cro. Eliz. 166.) See *ante*, § 144, subd. *k.*

[433] *Jones* v. *Hearne*, 2 Wils. 87.

[434] *Creelman* v. *Marks*, 7 Blackf. 281.

[435] Vin. Abr., Act. for Words, G. *a.* 20.

[436] *Jackson* v. *Weisiger*, 2 B. Monr. 214. You say you were authorized by P. to draw bills on him. You never were authorized; if you have any letters from him they are forged. These words held not actionable. *Mills* v. *Taylor*, 3 Bibb, 469.

[437] *Atkinson* v. *Reding*, 5 Blackf. 39; or forging writs. (*Hungerford* v. *Watts*, 4 Lev. 181; *Sale* v. *Marsh*, Cro. Eliz. 178; contra, *Halley* v. *Stanton*, Cro. Car. 268.)

[438] *Stone* v. *Smalcombe*, Cro. Jac. 648; *Thomas* v. *Axworth*, Hob. 2.

tion to the legislature for a grant of land; [439] and so of a letter containing these words, " I have to inform you I have received your money, and want you to come and receive it. [440]

§ 168. A general charge of being a murderer, [441] or of having killed another, is actionable. [442] Thus held actionable to say " thou hast killed a man; " [443] " you killed my brother; " [444] " you killed one negro and nearly killed another; " [445] " George Button is the man who killed my husband; " [446] " I will call him in question for poisoning his own aunt, and make no doubt but to prove he hath poisoned his aunt; " [447] and the words " he killed my child; it was the saline injection that did it," with an innuendo that it was meant to charge the plaintiff with felo-

---

[439] *Alexander* v. *Alexander*, 9 Wend. 14.

[440] *Reeks* v. *Cooper*, 3 Hawks, 587. See § 144, subd. *k*, *ante*.

[441] *Dudley* v. *Robinson*, 2 Iredell, 141; Vin. Abr., Act. for Words, G. *a.* 11, *ante*, § 144, subd. *m. s.*; but the words, Thou art a murderer and a bloody fellow, and I am afraid of you, were held not actionable. (*Id.* 25.) To call one murderer because he murdered a dog, not actionable; *dictum*, *Waggoner* v. *Richmond*, Wright, 173; see notes 128, 166, *ante*; and the words " They are highwaymen, robbers, and murderers," appearing to be spoken in reference to a transaction not involving robbery or murder, were held not actionable. (*Van Rensselaer* v. *Dole*, 1 Johns. Cas. 279.)

[442] *Johnson* v. *Robertson*, 4 Port. 486; *Chandler* v. *Holloway*, id. 18. It need not be alleged the party charged to have been killed is in fact dead. (*Carroll* v. *White*, 33 Barb. 618; see *ante*, notes 144, 354, and § 144, subd. *m. s.*)

[443] *Cooper* v. *Smith*, Cro. Jac. 423; *Banfield* v. *Lincoln*, Freem. 278.

[444] *Taylor* v. *Casey*, Minor, 258. Thou art a rogue and rascal, and hast killed thy wife, held actionable. (*Wilner* v. *Hold*, Cro. Car. 489.)

[445] *Hays* v. *Hays*, 1 Hump. 402.

[446] *Button* v. *Hayward*, 8 Mod. 24. Held actionable to say, Thou didst poison thy husband (*Gardiner* v. *Spurdance*, Cro. Jac. 438); or T. (plaintiff) killed thy husband (Toose Case, Cro. Jac. 306); or, Thou hast killed a man (*Godfrey* v. *More*, Cro. Eliz. 317); or, Thou hast killed my wife (Talbot's Case, Cro. Eliz. 823); or, Thou hast killed thy wife (*Wilner* v. *Hold*, Cro. Car. 489).

[447] *Webb* v. *Poore*, Cro. Eliz. 569. See *ante*, § 144, subd. *x*. Not actionable to say, " It could be proved by many violent presumptions that he (plaintiff) was the death of P." (*Weblin* v. *Meyer*, Yelv. 153); or, " I doubt not but to see thee hanged for killing Mr. Sydman's man who was murdered." (*Anon.*, Jenk. 302.) It was held actionable to say, Thou hast murdered A. thy late servant (if A. is not dead, or if there were no such person, the scandal is the greater); (*Green* v. *Warner*, 3 Keb. 624); or, Thou didst kill thy master's cook. (*Cooper* v. *Smith*, Cro. Jac. 423; and see *Barons* v. *Ball*, id. 331.)

niously killing a child by improperly and with gross negligence and culpable want of caution administering the injection.[448]

§ 169. A general charge of being a thief[449] is actionable, as to call one "a hog thief,"[450] "a bloody thief."[451] It is actionable to say of one he is a "thieving person, he stole and ran away;"[452] or "he is a thief, he stole my wheat and ground it and sold the flour to the Indians;"[453] or "you are a thief, you have robbed me of my bricks."[454] The charge is not the less actionable because made indirectly.[455] Thus it was held actionable to say "tell him (plaintiff) he is riding a stolen horse, and has a stolen watch in his pocket;"[456] or, "I saw him take corn from A.'s crib twice, and look round to see if any person saw him measuring;"[457] or, "You get your living by sneaking about when other people are asleep. What did you do with the sheep you killed? Did you eat it? It was like the beef you got the negroes to bring you at night. Where did you get the little wild shoats you always have in your pen? You are an infernal roguish rascal;"[458] or, "There is the man who stole my horse and fetched him home this morning."[459] A charge by one partner against his copartner of "pilfering" out of the

[448] *Edsall* v. *Russell*, 5 Scott N. R. 801 ; 2 Dowl. N. S. 614 ; 4 Man. & G. 1090 ; and see *Carroll* v. *White*, 83 Barb. 615, and *ante*, § 144. The words " That rogue Davies, the apothecary, hath poisoned my uncle ; I will have him digged up again, and haug him," held actionable. *Davies* v. *Okeham*, Sty. 245.

[449] *Dudley* v. *Robinson*, 2 Iredell, 141 ; and see *ante*, note 417 ; or of having been a thief,.*ante*, note 337 ; and see *ante*, § 144, subd. p. r. z. bb. dd. ee.

[450] *Hogg* v. *Wilson*, 1 N. & M. (So. Car.), 216.

[451] *Fisher* v. *Rottereau*, 2 McCord, 189.

[452] *Alley* v. *Neely*, 5 Blackf. 200 ; and see *ante*, note 417.

[453] *Parker* v. *Lewis*, 2 Greene (Iowa), 311.

[454] *Sloman* v. *Dutton*, 10 Bing. 402 ; 4 M. & Sc. 174. Ayres is a thief and hath stolen my apple trees, actionable. Ayres Case, 2 Brownl. 280.

[455] *McKennon* v. *Greer*, 2 Watts, 352 ; *Mayson* v. *Sheppard*, 12 Rich. Law (So. Car.), 254. I believe he will steal, and I believe he did steal, amount to a charge of larceny. (*Dottarer* v. *Bushey*, 16 Penn. St. R. 204 ; and *ante*, § 144, subd. bb.)

[456] *Davis* v. *Johnston*, 2 Bailey, 579.

[457] *Jones* v. *McDowell*, 4 Bibb, 188.

[458] *Morgan* v. *Livingston*, 2 Rich. 573.

[459] *Bonner* v. *Boyd*, 3 Har. & J. 278.

store, held actionable ;[460] and held actionable to say of one "he *took* my wood, and is guilty of any and everything that is dishonest;"[461] or, "he robbed the United States mail;"[462] and it is actionable to charge one having the custody of goods with stealing them;[463] but held not actionable to charge a weaver with stealing filling sent to his house to be woven into cloth.[464] ;

§ 170. A charge of larceny, that is, the taking *animo furandi* the personal property of another, the subject of larceny, is actionable;[465] thus the words, "You have stolen my belt,"[466] or "my boards,"[467] or "my tea,"[468] were held actionable. And so of the words "You robbed me, for I found the thing you done it with;"[469] or, "You robbed W. ;"[470] but the words "He robbed the treasury and bought a farm with it,[471] or "Bear witness he

---

[460] *Becket* v. *Sterrett*, 4 Blackf. 499. Actionable to say, She is as very a thief or a worse thief than any that robbeth by the highway. (*Ratcliffe* v. *Shubley*, Cro. Eliz. 224.)

[461] *Dottarer* v. *Bushey*, 16 Penn. St. Rep. 204.

[462] *Jones* v. *Chapman*, 5 Blackf. 88.

[463] *Gill* v. *Bright*, 6 Monr. 130.

[464] *Haun* v. *Smith*, 4 B. Monr. 385; but see *ante*, in note 143, and § 144. To charge one with stealing cotton held actionable, although the charge was made in allusion to cotton which the plaintiff had to gin for the defendant's brother (*Stokes* v. *Stuckey*, 1 McCord, 562); and as an overseer of an estate may be guilty of stealing the goods of his employer intrusted to him, it was held actionable to charge an overseer with stealing corn of his employer. (*Wheatley* v. *Wallis*, 3 Har. & J. 1.)

[465] *Galloway* v. *Courtney*, 10 Richard. 414; *Blanchard* v. *Fisk*, 2 N. H. 398; *Bonner* v. *Boyd*, 3 Har. & Johns. 278; *Wheatley* v. *Wallace*, 3 id. 1; *Stokes* v. *Stuckey*, 1 M'Cord, 562; *Gill* v. *Bright*, 6 Monroe, 130; *Gaul* v. *Fleming*, 10 Ind. 253; and see *ante*, § 144, subd. p. z. *bb, dd; ee*, and note 354. A charge of taking clothes animo furandi from a dead body, held actionable. (*Wonson* v. *Sayward*, 13 Pick. 402.)

[466] *St. Martin* v. *Desnoyer*, 1 Min. 156; and so of the words, Thou hast stolen my goods, and I will have thy neck. (*Fleming* v. *Jales*, 2 Brownl. 280.)

[467] *Burbank* v. *Horn*, 39 Maine (4 Heath), 232.

[468] *Coleman* v. *Playstead*, 36 Barb. 26.

[469] *Rowcliffe* v. *Edmonds*, 7 M. & W. 12.

[470] *Tomlinson* v. *Brittlebank*, 1 Nev. & M. 455; 4 B. & Adol. 630. Thou hast robbed the church, and thou hast stolen the lead off from the church, held actionable. (*Benson* v. *Morley*, Cro. Jac. 153.) And so of the words: He hath robbed the church. (Sibthorpe's Case, Jones, 366.)

[471] *Allen* v. *Hillman*, 12 Pick. 101, and see in § 144, note 232.

hath stolen my cloth," held not actionable.[472] Charging plaintiff with having stolen a barrel of pork may or may not be
actionable, according to the circumstances of the publication;[473] but *semble* to render them non-actionable it must
appear that the facts could not in any view amount to a felony.[474] Where the words were " I have lost a calf-skin out of
my cellar. * * * There was no one in the cellar but
you, Bornman and Gray. I do not blame you nor Gray, but
Bornman must have taken it," they were held actionable.[475]
Charging one with stealing a key out of the lock of a door,
held actionable.[476]

---

[472] *Bury* v. *Wright*, Yelv. 120.

[473] *Phillips* v. *Barber*, 7 Wend. 439; and see § 144. You (plaintiff) have
stolen a file of bills out of my desk, with an innuendo that by file of bills was
intended a file of unsatisfied accounts, held not actionable. (*Blanchard* v. *Fisk*,
2 N. Hamp. 398)

[474] *Laurie* v. *Wells*, 7 Wend. 175; *Alexander* v. *Alexander*, 9 *id.* 141; *Case* v.
Buckley, 15 *id.* 327. B. spoke of A., that A. and B. and one C. sat down to
gamble in a house in D., and while there, C. took from his pocket-book a five dollar bill and proposed to bet one dollar; that after the bill was put down on a
chance it was missing, and search was made for it but it could not be found,
whereupon the parties agreed to submit to a search, which was made but the bill
was not found; that after this search, all the parties went out of the house to
search for the missing bill: near the window they found a pocket-book with the
clasp unfastened, and in it was the missing bill; that C. took out the bill and
handed the pocket-book to A., who took it, and then said, " Boys, don't tell this
on me, for if you do it will ruin me." Held that these words did not, of themselves, import a charge of larceny. (*Prichard* v. *Lloyd*, 2 Carter, 154.)

[475] *Bornman* v. *Boyer*, 3 Binn. 515; *ante*, § 144, subd. *dd.*

[476] *Hoskins* v. *Tarrence*, 5 Blackf. 417, this decision was on the hypothesis
that stealing a key out of the lock of a door is larceny. It was so held in *Rex*
v. *Hedges*, 1 Leach C. C. 201, 4 ed., but is said to be " clearly wrong." Heard on
Libel, p. 37, note 4. Actionable to say: You never thought well of me since G.
[plaintiff] did steal my lamb (Grove's Case, Cro. Eliz. 289); or, I dealt not so un-
kindly by you [plaintiff] when you stole a sack of corn. (*Cooper* v. *Hakewell*, 2
Mod. 58.) J. W. [plaintiff] was in question for stealing a mare, and hue and cry
went out after him, and he durst not show his face hereabouts, doubtful if actionable. (*Gray* v. *Wayle*, Sty. 159.) A. said to B. [the defendant], My sheep were
feloniously stolen away; B. replied, I know who took them—It was J. S.; held actionable. (*Helly* v. *Hender*, 3 Bulst. 83.) Go follow suit against W. [the plaintiff]
for stealing thy two kine, and hang him—held actionable. (*Willymote* v. *Welton*,
Cro. Eliz. 904.) So were the words, " He is infected of the robbery and murder

§ 171. A direct charge of perjury is actionable *per se*,[477] and it is actionable to say of one, " The Reverend Thomas Smith is a perjured man,"[478] or " He perjured himself,"[479] or " He committed perjury by swearing in his vote at the school district meeting;[480] and where the defendant, speaking of an allegation in an affidavit made by the plaintiff, said it was not true and plaintiff had perjured himself, were held to be actionable if the intent was to impute perjury.[481] The words " he swore a false

lately committed, and doth smell of the murder. (*Hawley* v. *Sidenham*, Vin. Abr. Act. for Words, P. *a.* 14.) You might have known your own sheep and not have stolen mine, court divided if actionable or not. (*Thompson* v. *Knott*, Yelv. 144.) Thou [plaintiff] hast stole my mare or was consenting to it, held not actionable; the plaintiff might consent and yet be faultless, and the latter part of the sentence controlled the first. (Anon., Noy, 172.) S. [plaintiff] did steal a mare, or else G. is forsworn, not actionable, not being a direct charge of stealing. (*Sparkham* v. *Pye*, Cro. Jac..532.)

[477] *Newbit* v. *Statuck*, 35 Maine (5 Red.), 315; *Bell* v. *Farnsworth*, 11 Humph. 608; *Eccles* v. *Shannon*, 4 Harring. 193; *Cook* v. *Bostwick*, 12 Wend. 48; *Hopkins* v. *Beadle*, 1 Cal. 347; *Commons* v. *Walters*, 1 Port. 377; *Hall* v. *Montgomery*, 8 Ala. 510; *Haws* v. *Stanford*, 4 Sneed, 520; *Lee* v. *Robertson*, 1 Stew. 138; *Chapman* v. *Gillett*, 2 Conn. 40; as to perjured knave, see note 420, *ante*. A., speaking with reference to a complaint preferred by him before the grand jury against B., said that " he went before the grand jury and asked them if they wanted any more witnesses, and they said they had witnesses enough to satisfy them;" *held*. actionable, if he thereby meant to impute the perjury to B. (*Rundell* v. *Butler*, 7 Barb. 253.) Saying of plaintiff he was under a charge of prosecution for perjury, and that G. W. (an attorney of that name) had the attorney-general's directions to prosecute the plaintiff for perjury, held actionable after verdict for plaintiff. (*Roberts* v. *Camden*, 9 East, 93.) And saying " I would not swear to what C. W. has for the town of R.; P. W. is honestly mistaken but C. W. is wilful," imputes perjury to C. W. and is actionable. (*Walrath* v. *Nellis*, 17 How. Pr. R. 72.) See *ante*, § 144, subd. *u.* A charge of subornation of perjury is actionable (Cro. Jac. 158; *Beers* v. *Strong*, Kirby, 12); as, You have caused this boy to perjure himself. (Brownl. 2.)

[478] *Cummin* v. *Smith*, 2 S. & R. 440.

[479] *Sanford* v. *Gaddis*, 13 Ill. 329. I will prove thee a perjured knave, actionable. (*Slaverton* v. *Relfe*, Yelv. 160.) O. [plaintiff] says I am a perjured rogue; he is a perjured rogue as well as I—held actionable. (*Orton* v. *Fuller*, Lev. 65.) If I list I can prove him perjured—held not to impute perjury, and therefore not actionable. (Davis' Case, Hutt. 127.)

[480] *Crawford* v. *Wilson*, 4 Barb. 504.

[481] *Cook* v. *Bostwick*, 12 Wend. 48. The words " he has delivered false evidence and untruths in his answer to a bill in chancery," held not actionable. (1 Rolle Abr. 70; 3 Inst. 167.)

oath," or " he swore a lie," or " he swore false," are not action-able *per se*, nor can an action be maintained for them merely by an innuendo that they imputed or were intended to impute, perjury.   There must be an averment and colloquium of a *judicial* proceeding.[462]   To say of one, he is " mainsworn," was held actionable when spoken at a place where mainsworn meant perjured.[463]   A charge of being forsworn is not action-able *per se ;* it imports only " false swearing," and not " per-jury."   But a charge of " false swearing " may convey to the minds of the hearers an imputation of perjury, and when it does such a charge is actionable *per se ;*[464] as where, after a charge of false swearing, the defendant added " I will attend

---

[462] *Packer* v. *Spangler*, 2 Binn. 60; *Sheely* v. *Biggs*, 2 Har. & J. 363; *Power* v. *Miller*, 2 McCord, 220; *Martin* v. *Melton*, 4 Bibb, 99; *Slader* v. *Wilson*, 10 Ire. 92; *Beswick* v. *Chappel*, 8 B. Mon. 486; *Roella* v. *Follow*, 7 Blackf. 377; *Vaughan* v. *Havens*, 8 Johns. 109; *Chapman* v. *Smith*, 13 Johns. 78; *Hopkins* v. *Beadle*, 1 Cal. 347; *Phincle* v. *Vaughan*, 12 Barb. 215; *Barger* v. *Barger*, 18 Penn. State Rep. 489; *Blair* v. *Sharp*, Breese, 11; *McManus* v. *Jackson*, 28 Miss (7 Jones) 56; *Watson* v. *Hampton*, 2 Bibb, 319; *Shinloub* v. *Ammerman*, 7 Ind. 347; *Mebane* v. *Seilars*, 3 Jones' Law (N. C.), 199; *Harris* v. *Woody*, 9 Mis. 113; *Horn* v. *Foster*, 19 Ark. 346; *Harvey* v. *Boies*, 1 Penn. 12; *Dalrymple* v. *Lofton*, 2 Speer, 588; *Shaffer* v. *Kuitzer*, 1 Binn. 537; *Hall* v. *Montgomery*, 8 Ala. 510; *Walrath* v. *Nellis*, 17 How. Pr. R. 72; *Ward* v. *Clark*, 2 Johns. 10; *Stafford* v. *Grier*, 1 Johns. 505; *Robertson* v. *Lea*, 1 Stew. 141, but see *Rue* v. *Mitchell*, 2 Dall. 58; *Canterbury* v. *Hill*, 4 Stew. & Porter, 224; *Smale* v. *Hammon*, 1 Bulst. 40; *Lewis* v. *Soule*, 3 Mich. 514; *Hall* v. *Weedon*, 8 Dowl. & R. 140; Colomes Case, Cro. Jac. 204. " Mr. H.'s oath is not to be taken, for he has been a forsworn man.   I can bring people to prove it, and they that know him will not sit in the jury-box with him." without any colloquium, referring the words to the conduct of the plaintiff as a juryman, and no special damage, held not in themselves actionable, and judgment arrested. (*Hall* v. *Weedon*, 8 D. & R. 140.)   " Stanhope hath but one manor, and that he got by swearing and forswearing." (*Stanhope* v. *Blith*, 4 Co. 15.)   In Arkansas, by statute, to charge a person with having sworn falsely or sworn a lie is actionable, without an averment or proof of special damage, or a *colloquium*. (*Carlock* v. *Spencer*, 2 Eng. 12; *McGough* v. *Rhodes*, 7 Eng. 625.) And so in Mississippi.   *Crawford* v. *Mellton*. 12 S. & M. 328.   See *ante*, § 153.

[463] Hob. 12.

[464] *Sherwood* v. *Chace*, 11 Wend. 38; *Crookshank* v. *Gray*, 20 Johns. 344; *McClaughry* v. *Wetmore*, 6 Johns. 82; *Jacobs* v. *Tyler*, 3 Hill, 572; *Coons* v. *Robinson*, 3 Barb. 625; *Morgan* v. *Livingston*, 2 Rich. 573; *Hillhouse* v. *Dunning*, 6 Conn. 391.   Defendant said, Thou art a *forsworn* fellow; plaintiff answered, Will you say that I am perjured ? defendant said, Yes, if you will have it so—held not actionable. (*Levermore* v. *Martin*, Cro. Eliz. 297.)

to the grand jury about it;"[485] or, "If you had your deserts you would have been dealt with in the time of it;"[486] or, "For which you now stand indicted;"[487] or, "To my injury $600;"[488] or, "and done it meaning to cut my throat;"[489] or, "and I will put him through for it if it costs me all I am worth."[490] And held actionable to say of one, "Thou art a forsworn man. I will teach thee the price of an oath, and will set thee on the pillory;"[491] or, "You swore a lie, and I can prove it," used in reference to a judicial proceeding in which the plaintiff had testified as a witness;[492] or, under similar circumstances, the words, "He swore a lie."[493] Where the charge is of false swearing before a particular court or tribunal, or in a particular proceeding, naming it, the charge is actionable if the court or tribunal named is one authorized to administer an oath, or if the proceeding named is a judicial proceeding; thus it has been held actionable to say of one, he swore false before the grand jury;[494] or, "Thou art a forsworn knave, and I will prove thee to be forsworn in the spiritual court;"[495] or, "Thou wast forsworn before my Lord Chief Justice in evidence;"[496] or, "before a justice of the peace;"[497] or, "in Ilston Court," a court leet so named;[498] or, "I had a lawsuit with A., and B. (the plaintiff)

[485] *Gilman* v. *Lowell*, 8 Wend. 573.
[486] *Phincle* v. *Vaughan*, 12 Barb. 215.
[487] *Pelton* v. *Ward*, 3 Cai. 73.
[488] *Jacobs* v. *Tyler*, 3 Hill, 572.
[489] *Coons* v. *Robinson*, 3 Barb. 625.
[490] *Crone* v. *Angell*, 14 Mich. 340.
[491] 1 Starkie on Slander, 91.
[492] *Lewis* v. *Black*, 27 Mass. (5 Cush.) 425; *Rhineheart* v. *Potts*, 7 Ired. 403; *Rainey* v. *Thornbury*, 7 B. Monr. 475; *Sherwood* v. *Chace*, 11 Wend. 88.
[493] *Harris* v. *Purdy*, 1 Stew. 231; and see *Wilson* v. *Harding*, 2 Blackf. 190; *Gibbs* v. *Tucker*, 2 A. K. Marsh, 219; and 6 T. R. 691.
[494] *Pernelly* v. *Bacon*, 20 Miss. 330.
[495] *Shaw* v. *Thompson*, Cro. Eliz. 609; and see *Rex* v. *Foster*, Russ. & R. Cr. Cas. Res. 459; Stat. 40 Geo. 4, ch. 76. False swearing before an ecclesiastical tribunal is not perjury in Pennsylvania. (*Harvey* v. *Boies*, 1 Penn. St. R. 12.) contra in Connecticut. (*Chapman* v. *Gillet*, 2 Conn. 40.)
[496] Le. 127.
[497] *Gurneth* v. *Derry*, 3 Lev. 166; 4 Coke, 17.
[498] *Marshal* v. *Dean*, Cro. Eliz. 720.

swore falsely against me, and I have advertised him as such;"[499] or, "You swore false at the trial of your brother John."[500] Held not actionable to say of one, "Thou wert forsworn at Whitechurch court;"[501] or, "Thou art a false and forsworn knave, and that I will prove, for thou forswore thyself against Peter Rumball in the hundred court."[502] An arbitration is a judicial proceeding, and false swearing in such a proceeding is perjury; therefore, to charge false swearing in such a proceeding is actionable;[503] but perjury cannot be predicated of evidence in a controversy relative to pre-emption rights before the registers, &c., of the land office, and therefore a charge of false swearing in such a controversy is not actionable.[504] Ordinarily words are actionable which imply in their customary import that a false oath has been taken in a judicial proceeding,[505] as, you swore false in court,[506] and this, although the proceeding referred to never had any existence.[507] Saying of one, he swore to a damned lie, but I am not liable because I have

---

[499] *Magee* v. *Stark*, 1 Hump. 506. The words, I had a lawsuit, imply a judicial proceeding. (*Id.*)

[500] *Fowle* v. *Robbins*, 12 Mass. 498. The words were held actionable after verdict; and see Cro. Car. 378; but the words, you swore falsely on the trial of a case between me and A. before Squire J., were held not actionable. (*Dalrymple* v. *Lofton*, 2 Speer, 588.)

[501] Cro. Car. 378, because it did not appear that Whitechurch court was a court of record, and for the same reason the words "He has forsworn himself in a Leake court," were held not actionable. (1 Rolle Abr. 39; 6 Bac. Abr. 207) But the words, " A. C. is a forsworn man, and hath taken a false oath in his deposition at Tiverton, where he waged his law against me," were held actionable because the forswearing appeared to amount to perjury. (Cro. Jac. 204.)

[502] *Core* v. *Morton*, Yelv. 27. So ruled after verdict.

[503] *Moore* v. *Horner*, 4 Sneed, 491; *Ross* v. *Rouse*, 1 Wend. 475; *Bullock* v. *Koon*, 9 Cow. 30; and see *Sanford* v *Gaddis*, 13 Ill. 329.

[504] *Hall* v. *Montgomery*, 8 Ala. 510.

[505] *Cass* v. *Anderson*, 33 Verm. 182.

[506] *Hamilton* v. *Dent*, 1 Hayw. (N. C.) 116; see *ante*, note 500.

[507] *Bricker* v. *Potts*, 12 Penn. St. R. 200; *Henry* v. *Hamilton*, 7 Blackf. 506. And though an affidavit for a warrant be insufficient to justify the granting of it, an action may be maintained for imputing perjury in making the affidavit, if any fact set forth in it be material to the application. (*Dayton* v. *Rockwell*, 11 Wend. 140; and see *Bell* v. *Farnsworth*, 11 Humph. 608.)

not said in what suit he testified, was held not actionable.[508] To say to a witness whilst giving his testimony on a trial in court, "that is a lie;"[509] or, "I believe you swear false. It is false what you say;"[510] or, "You have sworn a manifest lie,"[511] is actionable.

Swearing falsely as to immaterial matter does not amount to perjury, and therefore to charge false swearing as respects matter which is immaterial to the issue involved, cannot in any event or under any circumstances, be actionable;[512] thus, saying of one that on a certain trial he testified to what was false, that the matter so testified to was immaterial, but that he, the party testifying, showed great disregard for the truth, was held not actionable.[513] The test of materiality is not whether the witness believes his testimony to be material, but whether if false he can be indicted for perjury. If the testimony is in fact immaterial, it cannot be perjury, though it may be false, and whatever may be the opinion of the witness.[514] Another essential element of perjury is, that the oath alleged to have been broken was administered by competent authority, and therefore to charge the breach of an oath not administered by competent authority would not be actionable.[515]

§ 172. Ordinarily, and in the absence of any statutory provision, words published orally charging a woman with want of

---

[508] *Muchler* v. *Mulhollen*, Supp. to Hill & Denio's Rep. 263.

[509] *Mowrr* v. *Watson*, 11 Verm. 536.

[510] *Cole* v. *Grant*, 3 Harr. 327.

[511] *Kean* v. *McLaughlin*, 2 S. & R. 469; *McClaughry* v. *Wetmore*, 6 Johns. 82, contra *Badgley* v. *Hedges*, 1 Penn. 233.

[512] *Horn* v. *Foster*, 19 Ark. 346; *Darling* v. *Banks*, 14 Ill. 46; *Wilson* v. *Oliphant*, Wright, 153; *Crookshank* v. *Gray*, 20 Johns. 344; *Ross* v. *Rouse*, 1 Wend. 475; *Dayton* v. *Rockwell*, 11 Wend. 140; *Power* v. *Price*, 12 Wend. 500; S. C., 16 Wend. 450; *Roberts* v. *Champlin*, 14 Wend. 120; *Wilson* v. *Cloud*, 2 Speer, 1; *Owen* v. *McKean*, 14 Ill. 459; *McGough* v. *Rhodes*, 7 Eng. 625.

[513] *Stone* v. *Clark*, 21 Pick. 51; and see *McKinley* v. *Rob*, 20 Johns. 351; *Smith* v. *Smith*, 8 Ired. 29; *Wilson* v. *Cloud*, 2 Speer, 1.

[514] *Ross* v. *Rouse*, 1 Wend. 475. Perjury may be alleged in swearing to a promise within the statute of frauds, and therefore false swearing as to such a promise may be actionable. (*Howard* v. *Sexton*, 4 Selden, 157.)

[515] *Jones* v. *Marrs*, 11 Humph. 214; and see *Vansteenburgh* v. *Kortz*, 10 Johns. 167; *Niven* v. *Munn*, 13 Johns. 48; Cro. Car. 378; 1 Rolle Abr. 39.

chastity are not actionable *per se;*[516] as, thus, except in the City of London and Borough of Southwark it is not actionable to call a woman a whore,[517] or prostitute, or common prostitute,[518] or to charge an unmarried woman with having had a

---

[516] 1 Starkie on Slander, 28; *Byron* v. *Elmes,* 2 Salk. 693; *W.* v. *L.,* 2 Nev. & M. 204; *Berry* v. *Carter,* 4 Stew. & Port. 387; *Elliot* v. *Ailsbury,* 2 Bibb, 473; contra in Connecticut (*Frisbie* v. *Fowler,* 2 Conn. 707), in Kentucky since the statute of 1811 (*McGee* v. *Wilson,* Litt. Sel. Cas. 187; *Smalley* v. *Anderson,* 2 Monr. 56), in Illinois (*Spencer* v. *McMasters,* 16 Ill. 405), in Missouri (*Moberly* v. *Preston,* 8 Mis. 462; *Stieber* v. *Wenzel,* 19 Mis. 513), in Ohio (*Malone* v. *Stewart,* 15 Ohio, 319; *Wilson* v. *Robbins,* Wright, 40; *Wilson* v. *Runyon, id.* 351; *Sexton* v. *Todd, id.* 317), in Maryland (*Terry* v. *Bright,* 4 Md. 430), in Alabama (*Sidgreaves* v. *Myatt,* 22 Ala. 617; but see *Barry* v. *Carter,* 4 Stew. & Port. 387), in Indiana (*Shields* v. *Cunningham,* 1 Blackf. 86; *Worth* v. *Butler,* 7 *id.* 251; *Rodeburgh* v. *Hollingsworth,* 6 Ind. 639), in North Carolina (*McBrayer* v. *Hill,* 4 Ired. 136; *Snow* v. *Witcher,* 9 *id.* 346), in South Carolina (*Watts* v. *Greenlee,* 2 Dev. 115; *Freeman* v. *Price,* 2 Bailey, 115), in Iowa (*Beardsley* v. *Bridgman,* 17 Iowa, 290; *Cleveland* v. *Detweiler,* 18 *id.* 299; *Cox* v. *Bunker,* Morris, 369; *Dailey* v. *Reynolds,* 4 G. Greene, 354; *Freeman* v. *Taylor,* 4 Iowa, 424; *Smith* v. *Silence, id.* 321.)

[517] 12 Mod. 106; Holt R. 40; Keb. 418; Sid. 97; *Robertson* v. *Powell,* 2 Selw. N. P. 1224; *Alsop* v. *Alsop,* 5 Hurl. & Nor. 534: *Williams* v. *Holdridge,* 22 Barb. 397; *Linney* v. *Mahon,* 13 Texas, 449; *Underhill* v. *Welton,* 32 Verm. 40; *Boyd* v. *Brent,* 3 Brev. 241; contra *Pledger* v. *Hatchcock,* 1 Kelly, 550; *Cox* v. *Bunker,* 1 Morris, 269. Drunken whore held actionable (*Williams* v. *Greenwade,* 3 Dana, 432); and so was whore. (*Smith* v. *Silence,* 4 Iowa, 321; *Kelly* v. *Dillon,* 5 Ind. 426; *Clarke* v. *Mount,* Opinions in the Mayor's Co't, 18.) The following words have been held actionable: You are a whore. I can have a better whore for a groat; you get your living by your tail; or, You are a whore, and have played the whore with so many men you cannot number them; or, Thou art a whore and hast been carted; or, Thou art a whore and hast been in Bridewell; or, Thou art a whore, and hast emptied thy cask in the country; or, Thou art a whore, and thy plying place is in Cheapside, where thou gettest 40s. a day. (Vin. Abr. Act. for Words, D. a. 45, 39, 42.) The words import more than the bare calling a woman whore. (*Hicks* v. *Joyce,* Sty. 394.) Common whore held actionable. (*Green* v. *How,* Sty. 323.) And held actionable to call one a whore who held a copyhold *dum casta vixerit.* (*Bays* v. *Boys,* Sid. 214.) But held not actionable to say to or of a woman, "You are a whore, and keep a man to lie with you" (*Gascoigne* v. *Ambler,* 2 L'd Raym. 1004); or, "She is a whore, and had a bastard by her father's apprentice." (*Graves* v. *Blanchard,* 2 Salk. 696; and see Anon., *id.* 694.) Calling a woman "whorish bitch," actionable in Alabama. (*Scott* v. *McKinnish,* 15 Ala. 662.) To call a woman a strumpet is not equivalent to calling her a whore. (*Williams* v. *Bryant,* 4 Ala. 44.) See in note 641, *post.*

[518] *Brooker* v. *Coffin,* 5 Johns. 188; *Wilby* v. *Elston,* 8 C. B. 142; 7 Dowl. & L. 143; 1 Starkie on Slander, 28. See *ante,* § 144, subd. *y.*

bastard,[519] or to call a woman a bawd,[520] or to charge an unmarried woman with fornication,[521] or a married woman with adultery,[522] or a woman with being of a wanton and lascivious disposition,[523] or to say of a woman, she was hired to swear the child on me; she has had a child before this, when she went to Canada; she would come damned near going to the state prison.[524] But it has been held actionable to say of a woman, she is a "loose woman,"[525] or to charge conduct amounting to open and gross lewdness,[526] or to say of a married woman, she slept with one not her husband,[527] or to charge an unmarried woman with being in the family way;[528] and adding, I can prove it by A. that she has been taking camphor and opium pills to produce an abortion;[529] or, she had two or three little

---

[519] Vin. Abr. Act. for Words, D. a. 19, 23; *Graves* v. *Blanchard*, 2 Salk. 696, in note 517 *ante ;* and saying to a married woman, "Thou bold culloblne, bastard-bearing whore, thou didst throw thy bastard into the dock at Whitechapel, held not actionable. (*Colabyn* v. *Viner*, Jones, 356.) So saying of a woman, She had a child, and either she or somebody else made away with it, was held not actionable. (*Falkner* v. *Cooper*, Carth. 55.)

[520] *Cavel* v. *Birket*, Sid. 438; contra, *Hicks* v. *Hollingshead*, Cro. Car. 261.

[521] *Buys* v. *Gillespie*, 2 Johns. 115; such a charge is actionable in Kentucky (*Smaliey* v. *Anderson*, 2 Monr. 56), in Ohio (*Wilson* v. *Robins*, Wright, 40), in North Carolina (*McBrayer* v. *Hill*, 4 Ired. 186), in Indiana (*Rickett* v. *Stanley*, 6 Blackf. 169), and in New Jersey (*Joralemon* v. *Pomeroy*, 2 N. Jersey, 271). Charging an unmarried woman with being "a bad character," and guilty of fornication, held actionable in Iowa. (*Dailey* v. *Reynolds*, 4 Greene, 354.) And see *ante*, § 144, subd. *l.*, and *post*, note 571.

[522] *Woodbury* v. *Thompson*, 3 N. Hamp. 194; *Stanfield* v. *Boyer*, 6 Har. & J. 248; contra, *Miller* v. *Parish*, 8 Pick. 384; and see *Walton* v. *Singleton*, 7 S. & R. 449. To charge a woman with fornication or adultery, or incontinence in any form, is not actionable at common law. (Heard on Libel, p. 46, citing in addition to the cases already noted. *Ayre* v. *Craven*, 2 Adol. & El. 2; 4 Nev. & M. 220; *Evans* v. *Gwyn*, 5 Q. B. 844.)

[523] *Lucas* v. *Nichols*, 7 Jones' Law, N. C. 32.

[524] *Brooker* v. *Coffin*, 5 Johns. 188.

[525] *Adecock* v. *Marsh*, 8 Ired. 360.

[526] *Underhill* v. *Welton*, 32 Verm. 40.

[527] *Guard* v. *Risk*, 11 Ind. 156.

[528] *Smith* v. *Minor*, Coxe, 16; *Miles* v. *Van Horn*, 17 Ind. 245; contra, see *Shepherd* v. *Wakeman*, Sid. 79; Lev. 87.

[529] *Miles* v. *Van Horn*, 17 Ind. 245. "It's my soul's opinion that nothing else

ones to A. ;[530] or, her child is A.'s and A. was keeping her unmarried for his own purposes ;[531] or charging sexual intercourse
with a dog ;[532] and where the defendant said of the plaintiff
that B. told him that on Sunday, at the camp-meeting, he
scared the plaintiff and a man up from behind a log; that they
broke and run, and that he (B.) got her (plaintiff's) parasol and
handkerchief, held that these words were actionable ;[533] but
saying of a woman, she went down the river to the *goose house*,
without averring any special meaning to goose house, was held
not actionable.[534]

§ 173. The following words and phrases published orally of
an individual as such, have been held actionable *per se :* Bogus
peddler,[535] dealer in counterfeit money,[536] knave,[537] pickpocket,[538]
sheepstealer,[539] traitor,[540] common barretor or champertor,[541] re-

---

kept that girl in the house last winter but taking medicine to banish the young
baker," innuendo that plaintiff had taken medicine to procure an abortion, held
actionable. (*Miller* v. *Houghton*, 10 Up. Can. Q. B. R. 348.) And held actionable to say of a woman, "She procured or took medicines to kill the bastard
child she was like to have, and she did kill or poison the bastard child she was
like to have." (*Widrig* v. *Oyer*, 13 Johns. 124.)

[530] *Symonds* v. *Carter*, 32 N. Hamp. 458, and *ante*, note 519.

[531] *Richardson* v. *Roberts*, 23 Geo. 215. She (plaintiff) is not chaste. I have
kept her, and had criminal intercourse with her; or, " I have had sexual intercourse with her," held not actionable. (*Berry* v. *Carter*, 4 Stew. & Port. 387.)
The words, I have lain with her and pockified her, held actionable. (*Neal* v. *Mal-
lard*, 2 Show. 312.)

[532] *Cleveland* v. *Detweiler*, 18 Iowa, 299, and see *ante*, note 143.

[533] *Proctor* v. *Owens*, 18 Ind. 21.

[534] *Dyer* v. *Morris*, 4 Mis. 214.

[535] *Pike* v. *Van Wormer*, 6 How. Pr. R. 101; 5 *id.* 175.

[536] *Pike* v. *Van Wormer*, 6 How. Pr. R. 99.

[537] Knave imports dishonesty, and is actionable. *Harding* v. *Brooks*, 5 Pick.
244; contra, see Weeks' case, 1 Sid. 149, Latch, 150, and Monthly Law Rep.,
Oct., 1862, p. 716.

[538] *Stebbing* v. *Warner*, 11 Mod. 255, and see note 258, *ante*.

[539] *Parret* v. *Parret*, 3 Bulst. 303; Vin. Abr. Act. for Words, I. *a.* 5.

[540] Dal. 17.   *Bellingham* v. *Minors*, Cro. Eliz. 133.

[541] Vin. Abr. Act. for Words, II. *a.* 7; *Heake* v. *Moulton*, Yelv. 90; *Box* v.
Barnaby, Hob. 117, but maintainer of suits is not actionable. (*Id.*) See contra,
Portman v. *Stowell*, Mo. 43.

ceiver of stolen goods,[542] counterfeiter.[543] I charge you with felony;[544] you are a rogue, and I will prove you a rogue, for you forged my name;[545] concealing stolen goods,[546] purchasing stolen goods, knowing them to have been stolen.[547] Hog thief.[548] He is a rogue, and has stolen my sheep.[549] You have altered the marks of four of my hogs;[550] he killed a horse.[551] You have removed my land-marks; cursed is he that removeth a land-mark.[552] She put poison in a barrel of drinking-water to poison me.[553] You are a vagrant,[554] a corn-stealer,[555] concealer of felony.[556] He is a rogue and villain; he has ruined many families, and the curses of widows and children are on him; he has

---

[542] *Dias* v. *Short*, 16 How. Pr. R. 322. To charge one with having received stolen goods is not actionable, unless the receiving was with a guilty knowledge (*id.*); and *Patterson* v. *Collins*, 11 Up. Can. Q. B. R. 63. See *Dorsey* v. *Whipps*, 8 Gill, 457; *Cox* v. *Humphreys*, Cro. Eliz. 877; *Steventon* v. *Higgins*, 2 Keb. 338; *Dawes* v. *Bolton*, Cro. Eliz. 888.

[543] *Howard* v. *Stephenson*, 2 Rep. Conn. C't, 408; *Thirman* v. *Matthews*, 1 Stew. 384. The law takes notice of the word counterfeit, as importing a felony. (*Stone* v. *Smalcombe*, Cro. Jac. 684.)

[544] Vin. Abr. Act. for Words, G. a. 3; Jones, 32; *Smith* v. *Hodgeskins*, Cro. Car. 276; Poph. 210; *Paine* v. *Prestny*, Sty. 235.

[545] *Jones* v. *Hearne*, 2 Wils. 87.

[546] *Miller* v. *Miller*, 8 Johns. 74; and see *Newlyn* v. *Fassett*, Yelv. 154.

[547] *Alfred* v. *Farlow*, 8 Adol. & El. N. S. 854; *Mayo* v. *Sample*, 18 Iowa, 306; Brigg's Case, Godb. 157; and see *Dorsey* v. *Whipps*, 8 Gill, 457.

[548] *Cheatwood* v. *Mayo*, 5 Munf. 16.

[549] *McAlexander* v. *Harris*, 6 Munf. 465.

[550] *Perdue* v. *Burnett*, Minor, 138; contra, *Williams* v. *Karnes*, 4 Humph. 9; *Johnston* v. *Morrow*, 9 Porter, 525.

[551] *Gage* v. *Shelton*, 3 Rich. 242. He cut my horse's throat is actionable. (*Yearly* v. *Ashley*, 4 Har. & J. 314.) He poisoned my cow, held actionable. (*Burton* v. *Burton*, 3 Iowa, 316,) contra of He poisoned my horse. (*Chaplin* v. *Cruikshanks*, 2 Har. & J. 247.)

[552] *Young* v. *Miller*, 3 Hill, 21.

[553] *Mills* v. *Wimp*, 10 B. Monr. 417.

[554] *Miles* v. *Oldfield*, 4 Yeates, 423.

[555] Vin. Abr. Act. for Words, G. a. 24; Anon. Cro. Eliz. 563.

[556] Thou art a concealer of felony, and it lieth in my power to hang thee. Vin. Abr. Act. for Words. G. a. 21; Yelv. 154. M. hath stolen sheep, and Nichols by agreement hath taken a meadow to help him to cloak and escape the felony, held actionable, although not alleged that Nichols knew of the felony for taking the meadow to cloak the felony implied he had notice of it. (*Nichols* v. *Budget*, Mo. 428.) And see, *Rich* v *Holt*, Cro. Jac. 268.

wronged my father's estate, and cheated my brother.[557]   She produced a false heir, or a bogus baby;[558] she *kept* a bawdy house,[559] or she keeps a whore-house;[560] indecent exposure;[561] bribery to secure election;[562] breaking open a letter addressed to another, and taking out money and using the money so taken.[563]   You have committed an act for which I can transport you.[564]   I know enough he has done to send him to the penitentiary.[565]   I am thoroughly convinced that you are guilty (innuendo of the death of D.), and rather than you should go without a hangman I will hang you.[566]   Fraudulently destroying a vote;[567] signing name to a note without authority;[568] he has been excommunicated,[569] whoremonger,[570] fornication, when or where punishable by indictment.[571]   He hath got M. N. with

[557] *Marshall* v. *Addison*, 4 Har. & McllLen. 537.

[558] *Weed* v. *Bibbins*, 32 Barb. 315.

[559] The offence, although past, is still punishable. (*Newton* v. *Masters*, 2 Lev. 283; *Martin* v. *Stillwell*, 13 Johns. 275; Vin. Abr. Act. for Words, H. a. 8.)   See *ante*, note 144, subd. *d.*   A charge of keeping a bawdy house was held not actionable.   Anon. Cro. Eliz. 643.

[560] *Wright* v. *Paige*, 36 Barb. 438.   See *ante*, note 144, subd. *d.*

[561] *Torbett* v. *Clare*, 8 Ir. Law Rep. 86.

[562] *Bendish* v. *Lindsay*, 11 Mod. 194; *Hoag* v. *Hatch*, 23 Conn. 585, or to procure an appointment under the government. (*Purdy* v. *Stacy*, 5 Burr. 2698.   See *Lindsey* v. *Smith*, 7 Johns. 359; *Chipman* v. *Cook*, 2 Tyler, 456.)

[563] *Cheadle* v. *Buel*, 6 Ham. 67; see *McCuen* v. *Ladlam*, 2 Harr. 12; *Bell* v. *Thatcher*, Freeman, 276; *Hillhouse* v. *Peck*, 2 Stew. & Port. 395.

[564] *Curtis* v. *Curtis*, 4 Mo. & Sc. 337; 10 Bing. 477.

[565] *Johnson* v. *Shields*, 1 Dutcher, 116.

[566] *Peake* v. *Oldham*, Cowp. 275; 2 W. Black, 960.

[567] *Dodds* v. *Henry*, 9 Mass. 262.

[568] *Creelman* v. *Marks*, 7 Blackf. 281.

[569] The defendant, a minister, pronounced in church that the plaintiff had been excommunicated, and refused to proceed with the service until plaintiff left the church, held actionable. (*Barnabas* v. *Traunter*, Vin. Abr. Act. for Words, D. a. 15.)

[570] Vin. Abr. Act. for Words, D. a. 26; see note 598, *post.*

[571] 2 Sid. 21; *Joralemon* v. *Pomeroy*, 2 N. Jersey, 271.   In Kentucky a man may maintain an action of slander for words charging him with having been guilty of fornication (*Morris* v. *Barkley*, 1 Litt. 64; see, also, *Phillips* v. *Wiley*, 2 *ib.* 153); and so in Pennsylvania, though he be a married man (*Walton* v. *Singleton*, 7 S. & R. 449), but not so in Ohio. (*Wilson* v. *Robbins*, Wright, 40; and see *Dukes* v. *Clarke*, 2 Blackf. 20.) And for such a charge a woman may main-

child.[572] He should [would] have been hanged for a rape, but it cost him all the money in his purse.[573] You will lie with a cow again as you did. If you had your deserts you deserve to be hanged.[574] You (plaintiff) are as great a rogue as your master, who is a rogue for that he stole rugs.[575] Adultery in certain States in which it is punishable as a crime.[576] Incontinence.[577]

§ 174. The following words and phrases published orally of an individual as such, have been held *not* actionable *per se:*—Adulterer,[578] bawd,[579] bankrupt,[580] blackleg,[581] cheat,[582] common filcher,[583] companion of cut throats,[584] enchanter,[585] liar,[586]

tain an action in Missouri, Indiana and New Hampshire. (*Moberly* v. *Preston*, 8 Mis. 462; *Abshire* v. *Cline*, 3 Ind. 115; *Symonds* v. *Carter*, 32 N. H. 458;) and see note 521, *ante*.

[572] *Marston* v. *Dennis*, 2 Sid. 1657. Sir John Lenthall lay with me, and had the use of my body *by force*, held actionable; the majority of the court being of opinion that the words *by force* imputed a rape (Lenthall's Case, Litt. Rep. 337, and see *Taylor* v. *Tally*, Palmer, 385, where a charge that T. *ravished* H.'s wife, was held actionable.) The words, He had the use of my wife's body *by force*, with allegation of special damage that in consequence of the words plaintiff was arrested on a charge of rape, and put to expense in making his defence, held actionable. (*Harris* v. *Smith*, Vin. Abr. Act. for Words, D. a. 9.)

[573] *Redfern* v. *Todd*, Cro. Eliz. 589.

[574] *Poturite* v. *Barrel*, Sid. 220.

[575] *Apton* v. *Penfold*, Comyn's R. 267.

[576] *Steber* v. *Wensel*, 10 Mis. 513; *Farnsworth* v. *Storrs*, 5 Cush. 412; *Richett* v. *Stanley*, 6 Blackf. 169. See *ante*, note 172, and *post*, note 578.

[577] *Watts* v. *Greenlee*, 2 Dev. 115. See *ante*, note § 153, and *post*, note 884.

[578] Vin. Abr. Act. for Words, G. a. 12; D. a 27.

[579] Vin. Abr. Act. for Words, H. a. 9.

[580] Vin. Abr. Act. for Words, H. a. 6.

[581] *Barnett* v. *Allen*, 3 Hurl. & Nor. 376.

[582] *Chase* v. *Whitlock*, 3 Hill, 139; *Stevenson* v. *Hayden*, 2 Mass. 406; Vin. Abr. Act. for Words, G. a. See note 621, *post*.

[583] Vin. Abr. Act. for Words, G. a.

[584] Vin. Abr. Act. for Words, G. a.

[585] Vin. Abr. Act. for Words, H. a.

[586] *Smalley* v. *Anderson*, 4 Monr. 367; *King's Case*, 4 Inst. 181; and see note 215, *ante*.

rogue,[597] arrant rogue,[598] damned rogue,[599] you are a rogue and cheated J. S. out of £100,[600] sacrilege,[601] scoundrel,[602] sorcerer,[603] swindler,[604] varlet,[605] villain,[596] witch,[597] whoremaster,[598] bastard.[599] He is father of a bastard.[600] He cozened J. S. of one hundred marks.[601] He cozened the Earl of H. of as much as he (plaintiff) is worth.[602] You cozened me of £1,200 at one time.[603] Your master (plaintiff) is a cozening, cheating knave, and a rogue to boot, and cozened and cheated all the parish and all persons he deals with.[604] Those two rascals (plaintiff and his brother) killed my hogs and converted them to their own use.[605] The library has been plundered by C. (the plain-

---

[597] *Articta* v. *Articta*, 15 La. Ann. 48; *Idol* v. *Jones*, 2 Dev. 162; *Quinn* v. *O'Gara*, 2 E. D. Smith, 388. " Your father was a horse-stealing rogue, and you (plaintiff) are a great rogue," not actionable (*Bellamy* v. *Barker*, 1 Strange, 304). Rogue, rascal, scoundrel, and the like, are not actionable. 1 Starkie on Slander, 24.

[598] Vin. Abr. Act. for Words, G. *a.*

[599] *Oakley* v. *Farrington*, 1 Johns. Cas. 129; *Caldwell* v. *Abby*, Hard. 529. God-damned rogue, not actionable. *Ford* v. *Johnson*, 21 Geo. 399.

[600] *Winter* v. *Sumvalt*, 3 Har. & J. 38. Saying one was a rogue of record, was held actionable. Sty. 220.

[601] *Gawdy* v. *Smith*, Sid. 376.

[602] *Quinn* v. *O'Gara*, 2 E. D. Smith, 388.

[603] Vin. Abr. Act. for Words, H. *a.*

[604] *Chase* v. *Whitlock*, 3 Hill, 139; *Saville* v. *Jardine*, 2 H. Black, 531; *Odiorne* v. *Bacon*, 6 Cush. 185; *Stevenson* v. *Hayden*, 2 Mass. 406. See *post*, notes 666, 667.

[605] Vin. Abr. Act. for Words, G. *a.*

[596] Vin. Abr. Act. for Words, G. *a.*

[597] Vin. Abr. Act. for Words, H. *a.* " Heretic " or " Papist," not actionable. *Id.* D. *a.*

[598] *Witcher's Case*, Keb. 119; Vin. Abr. Act. for Words, D. *a.* But actionable with special damage. *Crass* v. *Matthew*, Cro. Jac. 323; 2 Bulst. 80.

[599] Not actionable unless special damage. Vin. Abr. Act. for Words, D. *a.* 16, 17, 18, 21, 22, 31; *Nelson* v. *Staff*, Cro. Jac. 432.

[600] Unless the bastard is chargeable to the parish. *Salter* v. *Brown*, Cro. Car. 436; *Randle* v. *Real*, Cro. Jac. 473.

[601] *Somerstaile's Case*, Goldsb. 125.

[602] *Tut* v. *Kerton*, 1 Bulst. 172.

[603] *Townsend* v. *Barker*, Sty. 388. Thou hast no more than thou has got by cozening, not actionable. *Broomfield* v. *Snoke*, 12 Mod. 307.

[604] *Tamlin* v. *Hamlin*, Show. 181.

[605] *Sturgenegger* v. *Taylor*, 2 Brevard, 480.

tiff).[606] He killed and salted one of my hogs.[607] He de-
frauded a meal man of a horse.[608] He robbed the treasury
and bought a farm with it.[609] He embezzled goods.[610] He
attempted to commit a robbery.[611] He passed counterfeit
money.[612] He cut off the tail of my horse.[613] He harbored
my negroes.[614] He whipped his wife,[615] or his mother.[616] He is
a mulatto and akin to negroes.[617] He gave a free pass to a
negro.[618] He (plaintiff) is a brabbler and a quarreller, for he
gave his champion counsel to make a deed of gift of his goods,
to kill me and then to fly out of the country, but God preserved me.[619] His (plaintiff's) boys did frequently come to our
house and hire our negroes and take the dogs and go down
into the river bottom and killed cattle no more theirs than
mine.[620] You cheated the lawyer of his linen and stood bawd
to your daughter to make it up with him; you cheat everybody,
you cheated me of a sheet, you cheated T. S., and I will let
him know it.[621] She secreted one shilling under the till stating
these are not times to be robbed.[622] She is an hermaphrodite.[623]
He is a bloodsucker, and not worthy to live in a common-

---

[606] *Carter* v. *Andrews*, 16 Pick. 1.

[607] *Clay* v. *Barkley*, Ky. Dec. 79.

[608] *Richardson* v. *Allen*, 2 Chit. 654.

[609] *Allen* v. *Hillman*, 12 Pick. 101.

[610] *Caldwell* v. *Abbey*, Hard. 529; and see *Williams* v. *Stott*, 1 Cr. & M. 675; 3
Tyrw. 688.

[611] *Russell* v. *Wilson*, 7 B. Monr. 261.

[612] *Church* v. *Bridgman*, 6 Miss. 190.

[613] *Gage* v *Shelton*, 3 Rich. 242.

[614] *Croskeys* v *O'Driscoll*, 1 Bay, 481; *Skinner* v. *White*, 1 Dev. & Bat. 471.

[615] *Birch* v. *Benton*, 26 Miss. 153; *Dudley* v. *Horn*, 21 Ala. 379.

[616] *Speaker* v. *McKinzie*, 26 Miss. 255.

[617] *Burrett* v. *Jarvis*, 1 Ham. 83, note. But such a charge was held actionable.
Eden v *Legare*, 1 Bay, 171; *Atkinson* v. *Hartley*, 1 McCord, 203; *King* v. *Wood*,
1 N. & M. 184.

[618] *McManus* v. *Jackson*, 28 Miss. 56.

[619] *Eaton* v. *Allen*, 4 Co. 16.

[620] *Porter* v *Hughey*, 2 Bibb, 232.

[621] *Davis* v. *Miller*, 2 Strange, 1169; and see note 582, *ante.*

[622] *Kelly* v. *Partington*, 2 Nev. & M. 460.

[623] The words were spoken of one who taught dancing, and held not actionable

wealth, and his child, unborn, is bound to curse him.[624] Thy credit hath been called in question and a jury being to pass upon it, thou foistedst on a jury early in the morning, and the lands thou hast are gotten by lewd practices.[625] Thou wast the cause that J. S. did hang himself, and that R. N. did cut his own throat, and thou beginnest with no man but thou undoest him;[626] drunkenness;[627] he got drunk on Christmas day.[628]

§ 175. With respect to a charge of having a disease, it is actionable to charge one with having the venereal disease,[629] or gonorrhœa,[630] or leprosy,[631] or *semble*, falling sickness,[632] but not the itch or small pox.[633] To call one leprous knave was held actionable.[634] But it has been held not actionable to charge one with *having had* any of the diseases above indicated;[635] thus it was held not actionable to say of one, Thou art a base fellow and *hadst* [*or*, hast had] the French pox,[636] or to say of a

---

because men as well as women taught dancing (*Weatherhead* v. *Armitage*, 2 Levinz, 233). But in Ohio it has been held actionable to call a woman an hermaphrodite. (*Malone* v. *Stewart*, 15 Ohio, 319.)

[624] *Thimmelthorp's Case*, Noy, 64.

[625] *Nichols* v. *Badger*, Cro. Eliz. 348; see *ante*, § 144, subd. *j*.

[626] *Anon.* Dal. 89.

[627] *Buck* v. *Hersey*, 31 Maine, 558; *O'Hanlon* v. *Myers*, 10 Rich. Law (So. Car.) 128. But held actionable when charged against a preacher or settled minister (*McMillan* v. *Birch*, 1 Binn. 178; *Chaddock* v. *Briggs*, 13 Mass. 248), or a female. (*Brown* v. *Nickerson*, 5 Gray, 1.)

[628] *Warren* v. *Norman*, Walker, 387.

[629] *Bloodworth* v. *Gray*, 7 M. & G. 334; 8 Sc. N. S. 9; *Goldman* v. *Stearns*, 7 Gray, 181; *Williams* v. *Holdridge*, 22 Barb. 398; *Hewit* v. *Mason*, 24 How. Pr. R. 366; Vin. Abr. Act. for Words, D. a. 56; II. a. 3, 4, 5, 9; U. a. 15; *Nichols* v. *Guy*, 2 Carter, 82.

[630] *Watson* v. *McCarthy*, 2 Kelly, 57; *Williams* v *Holdridge*, 22 Barb. 398.

[631] *Id.*

[632] Spoken of a lawyer. *Taylor* v. *Perkins*, Noy, 117.

[633] See *Villers* v. *Monsley*, 2 Wils. 403, and notes 141 *ante*, and 676 *post*.

[634] *Taylor* v. *Perkins*, Cro. Jac. 144.

[635] *Carslake* v. *Mapeldora*, 2 T. R. 474; *Bloodworth* v. *Gray*, 7 M. & G. 334; 8 Sc. N. S. 9; *Pike* v. *Van Wormer*, 5 How. Prac. R. 171.

[636] *Smith's Case*, Noy, 157; *Dutton* v. *Eaton*, All. 81. But in *Miller's Case*, Cro. Jac. 430, the words Mrs. Miller is a whore and *hath had* the pox, were held actionable.

woman, "I have kept her common these seven years, she hath given me the bad disorder and three or four other gentlemen."[687] The reason assigned for these decisions is, that to charge the having such a disease is actionable because the disease, being contagious, the *having* it renders the person an improper member of society, but there is no reason why the company of a person who *has had* a contagious disease should be avoided; and therefore, to say one *has had* such a disease is not actionable. A distinction is taken between having had a disease and having been guilty of a crime, the stain of which remains.[688] These decisions assume that it is the fact of the disease being *contagious* which renders the charge of having it, actionable. We are not satisfied that this assumption is warranted. The charge of leprosy certainly involved more than a mere charge of having a contagious disease. The leper lost his civil rights and all ecclesiastical privileges, he was at once cast off by society and excommunicated by the church. The physician held out to him no hope of being cured, and the priest no hope of being saved; and besides, leprosy impeded the descent.[689] And there was a writ *de leproso amovendo* commanding the sheriff to remove him to a solitary place. Even at this day, in those countries in which leprosy prevails, the slightest ascertained taint of the disease entails upon the sufferer a compulsory exclusion tantamount to banishment from the rest of the community, or even to perpetual detention in a lazaret; and strange to say, it seems, that leprosy is not a contagious disease,[640] although beyond doubt it was so

---

[687] *Curslake* v. *Mapeldora*, 2 T. R. 473.

[688] There is this difference of scandal in the past tense, when it touches the mind and when it touches the body. If it be a scandal to the mind and the affections as perjury, felony, &c., then the mind that remains is slandered; but if it be of an *accidental* infirmity or disease of the body it is otherwise, for none now will forbear his company though he had the plague in times past. Coke, Ch. J.; see *Smith's Case*, Noy, 157; *Dutton* v. *Eaton*, All. 31. As to charges in the past tense, see § 158, *ante*.

[689] Hale's Hist. Com. Law, ch. VI.

[640] Report on Leprosy by the Royal College of Physicians, prepared for Her Majesty's Secretary of State to the Colonies. London, 1867.

esteemed at the period when the dicta we have above referred to were pronounced. The charge, too, of having the *lues venerea*, was something more than a charge of having a contagious disease, at least it involved a charge of lewdness. That the bare fact of the disease being contagious was not the ground for making the charge actionable, seems to be apparent from this: Lues venerea, vulgarly called pox, was formerly called the French pox, or the great pox, to distinguish it from *variola* or small pox. Now the small pox is a contagious disease, but it has never been held actionable to charge one with having the "small pox," and we find in the reports that when the charge was simply of having the pox—without any other words or facts—to indicate that the French pox was intended, the charge was held not actionable.[641] To such an extent was this distinction carried that where the charge was simply of having the pox, it was held the meaning of French pox could not be given to the word by an innuendo, without an averment which warranted it.[642] Notwithstanding the dicta above referred to, probably a better reason for holding a charge of having the leprosy or *lues venerea* is that those diseases were supposed to be ineradicable from the system, and their taint hereditary. If this reason is the true one, then the charge of *having had* should be actionable equally with a charge of *having* such a disease.

---

[641] It was held not actionable to say of a man, Hang him, he is full of the pox (*Bonner's Case*, 4 Coke, 17), or of a woman, You are a pocky whore, go to the leech [doctor] for the pox (———— v. *Farm*, Vin. Abr. Act. for Words, Y. a. 23), or, Thou art a scurvy pocky whore (*Hunt* v. *Jones*, Cro. Jac. 499), because it was not apparent that French pox was intended, but it was said in another case that when the word pox was coupled with the word whore, the French pox would be intended (Sid. 50; *Clifton* v. *Wells*, 12 Mod. 633; *Garford* v. *Clark*, Cro. Eliz. 857; and see note 517, *ante*). So saying of one, He *caught* the pox, was held not actionable, as not implying the French pox, but saying he got the pox by a yellow-haired wench (*Syn* v. *Hockley*, Sid. 324), or He is rotten with the pox (*Davies* v. *Taylor*, Cro. Eliz. 648), or Thy pocky wife, her nose is eaten with the pox (*Brooke* v. *Wise*, Cro. Eliz. 878), or The pox haunts you twice a year (*Preckington's Case*, Vin. Abr. Act. for Words, Y. a. 17), or You were laid for the pox (*Austin* v. *White*, Cro. Eliz. 214), or Thou art burnt and hast the pox (*Box's Case*, Cro. Eliz. 2), was held actionable because French pox is implied. Webster, in his Dictionary, says that the word pox, without an epithet, imports *lues venerea*; strumpet equivalent to whore. *Cook* v. *Wingfield*, 1 Stra. 555 contra, note 517, *ante*.

[642] *Bonner's Case*, Mo. 573; 4 Coke, 17.

§ 176. What language published in writing concerning an individual as such, is actionable *per se ?* That language in writing is actionable *per se* which denies " to a man the possession of some such worthy quality as every man is *a priori* to be taken to possess," [643] or, which "tends to bring a party into public hatred or disgrace," [644] or " to degrade him " [645] " in society," [646] or, expose him to "hatred, contempt or ridicule," [647] or " which reflects upon his character," [648] or " imports something disgraceful to him," [649] or " throws contumely " on him, [650] or "contumely and odium," [651] or " tends to vilify him," [652] or " injure his character or diminish his reputation," [653] or which is "injurious to his character," [654] or to his "social character," [655] or shows him to be "immoral or ridiculous," [656] or " induces an ill opinion of him," [657] or " detracts from his character as a man of good morals," [658] or alters his "situation in society for the worse," [659] or "imputes to him a bad reputation " [660] or " degra-

---

[643] George on Libel, 17.

[644] Tenterden, Ch. J., *Woodward v. Dowsing*, 2 M. & R. 74.

[645] Holroyd, J., *id.*

[646] Bayley, B., *Forbes v. King*, 1 Dowl. 627.

[647] *Parmeter v. Coupland*, 6 M. & W. 105; *Gathercole v. Miall*, 15 M. & W. 319; *Miller v. Butler*, 6 Cush. 71; *Shattuck v. Allen*, 4 Gray, 540; *Com'wealth v. Wright*, 1 Cush. 46; *Hillhouse v. Dunning*, 6 Conn. 391; *McGregor v. Thwaites*, 3 B. & C. 24; *Clement v. Chivis*, 9 B. & C. 172; 4 Man. & R. 127; *Clark v. Binney*, 2 Pick. 113; *Cooper v. Stone*, 24 Wend. 434; *Colby v. Reynolds*, 6 Verm. 489; *Johnson v. Stebbins*, 5 Ind. 364; *Lansing v. Carpenter*, 9 Wis. 540.

[648] *O'Brien v. Clement*, 15 M. & W. 435; *Johnson v. Stebbins*, 5 Ind. 364.

[649] *Digby v. Thompson*, 4 B. & Adol. 821; 1 Nev. & M. 485.

[650] *Bell v. Stone*, 1 Bos. & P. 331; *Obaugh v. Finn*, 4 Pike, 110.

[651] *Riggs v. Denniston*, 3 Johns. Cas. 198.

[652] *Shipley v. Todhunter*, 7 C. & P. 680.

[653] 2 Leighs N. P. 1360; *Dunn v. Withers*, 2 Humph. 512; *Melton v. The State*, 3 *id.* 380.

[654] *Cockayne v. Hodgkison*, 5 C. & P. 543.

[655] 1 Am. Lead. Cas. 138; 3d ed.

[656] *The State v. Farley*, 4 M'Cord, 317.

[657] *Hillhouse v. Dunning*, 6 Conn. 391.

[658] *Young v. Miller*, 3 Hill, 21; *Quinn v. O'Gara*, 2 E. D. Smith, 388.

[659] 1 Starkie on Slander, 169; and see *Turner v. Merryweather*, 7 C. B. 251; *Wakley v. Healey*, *id.* 594; *Gregory v. Reg.*, 15 Q. B. 957; *Capel v. Jones*, 4 C. B. 259; *Prior v. Wilson*, 1 C. B. N. S. 95.

[660] *Cooper v. Greely*, 1 Denio, 347.

dation of character,"[661] and all defamatory words injurious in their nature.[662] But to sustain an action for libel the plaintiff must either show special damage or "the nature of the charge must be such that the court can legally presume he has been degraded in the estimation of his acquaintances, or of the public, or has suffered some other loss either in his property, character or business, or in his domestic or social relations, in consequence of the publication.[663]

§ 177. It is actionable to charge one in writing with being a villain,[664] liar,[665] rogue, rascal,[666] swindler,[667] drunkard, cuckold and tory;[668] the author or publisher of a libel or slander;[669] a

---

[661] *McCorkle* v. *Binns*, 5 Binney, 340.

[662] *Chaddock* v. *Briggs*, 13 Mass. 248. For some definitions of libel see *ante*, note 18; *The State* v. *Avery*, 7 Conn. 267; *Williams* v. *Karnes*, 4 Humph. 9; *Clark* v. *Binney*, 2 Pick. 113; *Baron* v. *Beach*, 5 N. Y. Legal Observer, 448.

[663] *Cooper* v. *Stone*, 2 Denio, 299; repeated *Bennett* v. *Williamson*, 4 Sand. 65. "There must be some certain or probable temporal loss or damage to make words actionable; but to impute to a man the mere defect or want of moral virtue, moral duties or obligations, which renders a man obnoxious to mankind, is not actionable. (De Grey, Ch. J., *Onslow* v. *Horne*, 3 Wils. 177, approved by Lawrence, J., *Holt* v. *Scholefield*, 6 T. R. 691.) But is said (1 Starkie on Slander, 2), "an action lies in respect of any wilful communication, *oral* or *written*, to the damage of another in law or in fact, made without lawful justification or excuse." "A person cannot say anything disparaging of another that has not a tendency to injure him morally or professionally." (Tyndal, Ch. J., *Doyley* v. *Roberts*, 3 Bing. N. C. 835; 5 Scott, 40.)

[664] *Bell* v. *Stone*, 1 Bos. & P., 331.

[665] *Brooks* v. *Bemis*, 8 Johns. 455, approved *Moore* v. *Bennett*, 33 How. Pra. R. 180; and see *ante*, note 215. Liar and knave, see King's Case, 4 Inst. 181. A charging that one shot out of a leather gun, meaning that he was guilty of falsehood, held actionable. (*Harmon* v. *Delancy*, 2 Str. 89, and *post*, note 679.)

[666] Rogue, rascal, swindler, villain, are libellous. Cooke on Defam. 2. "I look upon him as a rascal," actionable. (*Williams* v. *Karnes*, 4 Humph. 9.) Felon, debauchee, and seducer, are actionable. (*Millett* v. *Hulton*, 4 Esp. Cas. 248.)

[667] *I'Anson* v. *Stuart*, 1 T. R. 748; see note 594, *ante*.

[668] *Giles* v. *The State*, 6 Geo. 276.

[669] *Andreas* v. *Koppenheafer*, 3 Ser. & R. 255; *Colby* v. *Reynolds*, 6 Verm. 489; *Viele* v. *Gray*, 10 Abb. Prac. Rep. 1; *Russell* v. *Ligon*, Vin. Abr. Act. for Words, II. a. 27; *Clark* v. *Binney*, 2 Pick. 113. Held actionable to publish "a report circulated by B. (the plaintiff) against C., stating he, C., made him, B.,

hypocrite, and using the cloak of religion for unworthy purposes;[670] a miserable fellow, it is impossible for a newspaper
article to injure to the extent of six cents, and that the community can hardly despise him worse than they now do;[671] or with
having kidnapped a free colored man and hurried him into
slavery;[672] or, paid money to procure an appointment to
an office, or received money for offices;[673] or, of having been
deprived of the ordinances of the church;[674] or with being
thought no more of than a horse-thief and a counterfeiter;[675] or,
with stinking of brimstone and having the itch;[676] or, with voting twice on the same ballot for the election of State officers;[677]
with infracting a patent,[678] with falsehood,[679] dishonesty,[680] smug

---

pay a note twice, and proved by B. to be false. (*Shelton* v. *Nance.* 7 B. Monr.
128.) "A report has gone abroad through the instrumentality of S. W. (the
plaintiff), stating that R. W. had a load of falsely-packed cotton bales, which
report is a direct falsehood," was held actionable. (*Woodburn* v. *Miller*, Cheves,
194.) "His slanderous reports nearly ruined some of our best merchants," held
actionable. (*Cramer* v. *Noonan*, 4 Wis. 231.) Formerly a libeler was disqualified
from making a will. See Swinburn on Wills, Pt 1, § 7, *et seq.*; Redfield on
Wills, ch. 111, § 14 a., p. 118, and the author or publisher of a libel could receive no benefit under the will of the person libelled. See Domat's Civil Law,
Bk I., p't II., title 1, § 111, subd. vii. *Gardiner* v. *Helvin*, 3 Lev. 248.

[670] *Thorley* v. *Kerry*, 4 Taunt. 355.

[671] *Brown* v. *Remington*, 7 Wis. 462.

[672] *Nash* v. *Benedict*, 25 Wend. 645.

[673] *Weed* v. *Foster*, 11 Barb. 203; and see *Purdy* v. *Stacey*, 5 Burr. 2698.

[674] *McCorkle* v. *Binns*, 5 Binn. 340.

[675] *Nelson* v. *Musgrave*, 10 Mis. 648.

[676] *Villers* v. *Munsley*, 2 Wils. 403. In this case the words complained of were:

> Old Villars, so strong of brimstone you smell,
> As if not long since you had got out of Hell.
> But this damnable smell I no longer can bear,
> Therefore I desire you would come no more here.
> You old stinking, old nasty, old itchy, old toad,
> If you come any more you shall pay for your board.
> You'll therefore take this as a warning from me,
> And never enter the doors while they belong to L. P.

[677] *Walker* v. *Winn*, 8 Mass. 248.

[678] *Watson* v. *Trask*, 6 Ham. 531.

[679] *Cooper* v. *Stone*, 24 Wend. 434; *Lindley* v. *Horton*, 27 Conn. 58; *Woodburn*
v. *Miller*, Cheves, 194; *Shelton* v. *Nance*, 7 B. Monr. 128, and *ante*, note 665.

[680] *Hart* v. *Reed*, 1 B. Monr. 166; *Taylor* v. *Church*, 1 E. D. Smith, 279, S. C.
on Appeal, 8 N. Y. 452; *Fowles* v. *Bowen*, 30 N. Y. 20; and see *Henderson* v.

gling,[681] blasphemy,[682] false swearing,[683] insanity,[684] or being fit
for a lunatic asylum, and unsafe to go at large;[685] being guilty
of gross misconduct in insulting females, &c.;[686] with want of
chastity;[687] as engaged in serving writs on the anti-renters and
catching Indians;[688] or for charging that plaintiff, a married
man, went through the ceremony of marriage with an actress;[689]
and to publish an obituary notice of a living person, was held
actionable.[690] Plaintiff having defendant's bond, the validity
of which had been long litigated, and advertised it for sale, a
statement of the circumstances under which it was given,·con-
cluding with "his object is either to abstract money from the
pocket of an unwary purchaser, or what is more likely, by this
threat of publication to extort money from me;" held to be
actionable.[691] And held actionable to charge one with an unauthorized publication of private letters;[692] or with entering into
a corrupt agreement to benefit himself at the expense of the
public, and if elected to the Senate would use his influence to

---

Hale, 19 Ala. 154.   Actionable to publish of one that he had been detected in
cheating at cards.   *Livingston* v. *Cheatham*, Pamphlet Report; Holt on Libel,
239, note.   *Detected* implies guilt, note 220, *ante.*

   [681] *Stillwell* v. *Barter*, 19 Wend. 487.

   [682] *Stow* v. *Converse*, 3 Conn. 325, note 708, *post.*

   [683] *Steele* v. *Southwick*, 9 Johns. 214.   The words were: "Our army swore ter-
ribly in Flanders, said Uncle Toby; and if Toby were here now, he might say
the same of some modern swearers; the man (meaning A. the plaintiff) is no
slouch at swearing to an old story;" *held*, that these words, if they did not import
a charge of perjury, were libellous, as they held up the plaintiff to contempt and
ridicule, as being so thoughtless or so criminal as to be regardless of the obligation of an oath."

   [684] *Southwick* v. *Stevens*, 10 Johns. 443; *Morgan* v. *Lingen*, 8 Law Times Rep.
N. S. 800; *Rex* v. *Harvey*, 2 B. & C. 258; *Rex* v. *Creevey*, 1 M. & S. 273; see,
however, *Mayrant* v. *Richardson*, 1 Nott & McCord, 348.

   [685] *Perkins* v. *Mitchell*, 31 Barb. 461.

   [686] *Clement* v. *Chivis*, 9 B. & Cr. 172; 4 M. & R. 127.

   [687] *Bodwell* v. *Osgood*, 3 Pick, 379.

   [688] *Hallock* v. *Miller*, 2 Barb. 632.

   [689] *Rex* v. *Kinnersley*, 1 W. Black, 294; and see *Caldwell* v. *Raymond*, 2 Abb.
Pra. R. 193.

   [690] *McBride* v. *Ellis*, 9 Rich. Law, S. C. 313.

   [691] *Robertson* v. *McDougall*, 4 Bing. 670.

   [692] *Bacon* v. *Beach*, 5 N. Y. Legal Observer, 448.

defeat the public interest and benefit himself;[602] or imputing to one who is an author a disregard of justice and propriety as a man, and as being infatuated with vanity, mad with passion, and the apologist from force of sympathy of another stigmatized with ingratitude and perfidy, and as having published as true statements falsified and encomiums retracted.[604] So it was held actionable to publish of one that he was "as versatile as Monroe Edwards [a noted forger] in circumventing the law of right,[605] or that he was prominent in the corrupt legislation of last winter;[606] or of one soliciting charity that she prefers unworthy claims;[607] or of one that, although aware of the death of a person occasioned by his improperly driving a carriage, he attended a public ball on the evening of the same day;[608] or of one who had contracted to relay a road with *new* material that he had used *old* material;[609] and held actionable where a public officer published, in a report of an official investigation into his conduct, the following comments upon the testimony of a witness before the commissioners of inquiry : " I am extremely loath to impute to the witness, or his partner, improper motives in regard to the false accusations against me ; yet I cannot refrain from the remark that, if their motives have not been unworthy of honest men, their conduct in furnishing materials to feed the flame of calumny has been such as to merit the reprobation of every man having a particle of virtue or honor. They have both much to repent of for the groundless and base insinuations they have propagated against me."[700]

---

[602] *Powers v. Dubois*, 17 Wend. 63.

[604] *Cooper v. Stone*, 24 Wend. 434.

[605] *Cramer v. Noonan*, 4 Wis. 231.

[606] *Littlejohn v. Greeley*, 13 Abb. Pra. R. 41.

[607] *Hoare v. Silverlock*, 12 Q. B. 624.

[608] *Churchill v. Hunt*, 1 Chit. R. 480.

[609] *Baboneau v. Farrell*, 27 Eng. Law & Equity R. 339; 15 Com. B. 360; 24 Law Jour. R., N. S., C. P. 9; 1 Jur., N. S., 114.

[700] *Clark v. Binney*, 2 Pick. 113. It was held actionable to publish, If any person can ascertain that I. D. (the plaintiff) was married previous to 10 August, 1799, with an innuendo meaning that he was married prior to the date mentioned, and had another wife then living, he being then married to E. his present wife. (*Delaney v. Jones*, 4 Esp. 191.)

§ 178. It is not actionable to charge one in writing with terms of general abuse,[701] or with a breach of conventional etiquette,[702] or with an intention to put money into Wall Street for shaving purposes.[703] So the words, "the Rev. John Robinson and Mr. James Robinson, inhabitants of this town, not being persons that the proprietors and annual subscribers think it proper to associate with, are excluded this room," published by posting a paper on which they were written, purporting to be a regulation of a particular society, held not to be actionable.[704] It was held not libellous to publish of one who was a druggist, "The above druggist refusing to contribute his mite with his fellow-merchants for watering Jefferson Avenue, I have concluded to water the avenue in front of his store for one week."[705] And held not actionable to publish of one that was engaged in a "gambling fracas" arising out of a dispute at *play*, there being no averment that illegal play was intended.[706] Where a paragraph in a newspaper merely stated that a bill had been drawn, and that the acceptance had been forged or obtained by fraud, but threw no imputation on the drawer (the plaintiff), nor insinuated that the plaintiff had practised the fraud or committed the forgery, it was held not to amount to a libel on the plaintiff.[707] And where it was stated that the plaintiff purchased a newspaper and gave his note for it; that he was unable to pay the note, and begged for delay; and that subsequently, when sued upon it, he pleaded the statute of limitations successfully; held that, there being no charge of dishonesty, the publication was not libellous.[708]

---

[701] *Tappen* v. *Wilson*, 7 Ham. 190.

[702] *Clay* v. *Roberts*, 8 Law Times, N. S. 397.

[703] *Stone* v. *Cooper*, 2 Denio, 293.

[704] *Robinson* v. *Jermyn*, 1 Price, 11.

[705] *The People* v. *Jerome*, 1 Manning's Mich. R. 142.

[706] *Forbes* v. *King*, 1 Dowl. 672.

[707] *Stocking* v. *Clement*, 4 Bing. 162.

[708] *Bennett* v. *Williamson*, 4 Sand. 60. Where the charge was, "This Major Noah, the knight of the broken seal, who converted to his own use property known to be stolen, meaning he obtained possession of a political letter addressed to another person, which he had published," the jury failed to agree. (*Noah's Case*, 3 City Hall Recorder, 18.) Opening a letter and detaining it merely from

§ 179. There is a distinction as to its actionable quality between language concerning an individual as such, and language concerning one in certain capacities or special characters. Heretofore in this chapter the attention has been solely directed to language concerning an individual as such; we have now to consider what language concerning one in certain acquired capacities or special characters is actionable *per se ?* Language which is actionable, if published of an individual as such, does not cease to be actionable because published of one in a special character; and all language which is actionable as concerning an individual as such, must also be actionable when it concerns him in any special character of the kind presently to be mentioned. Our present inquiry is limited to that language which, not being actionable when published of an individual as such, becomes actionable when published, and because it is published, of him in some special character or relation. The effect of the special character of the publisher, and of the person to whom the publication is made, will be considered under the head of defences. Where the language is actionable as concerning an individual as such, it is unimportant and unnecessary, except in some cases as affecting the amount of damages, to inquire further whether such language is also actionable as concerning him in some special character; thus, where an action was for language alleged to be concerning the plaintiff generally and concerning him as an attorney, the language being actionable as concerning the plaintiff generally, it was held that he might sustain the action without proof of his being an attorney.[708]

§ 180. The distinction maintained between oral and written language, as regards its actionable quality when published concerning an individual as such, is not recognized in regard to language concerning one in a special character. As respects language concerning one in a special character, it makes no difference in regard to its actionable quality, whether it be pub-

---

curiosity or political motives, held to be a trespass only, and not a felony. (*Rex v. Godfrey,* 8 C. & P. 563.)

[708] *Lewis v. Walter,* 4 D. & Ry. 810; 3 B. & C. 138.

13

lished orally or in writing.[710] Because the language in writing
which concerns one in a special character, is usually actionable
when published concerning the individual as such, and without
reference to his special character; it is almost exclusively in
respect to oral language that questions arise as to whether it is
or is not actionable as affecting one in a special character.

§ 181. In connection with our present inquiry, it must be
remembered that no special character which one may occupy
can enhance his rights to protection, for that would be in dero-
gation of the rule to which reference has heretofore been made
(§ 138). Whatever may be the special character, the right
must be the same as the right of every other individual, the
right that no one shall, without legal excuse, publish language
concerning another or the affairs of another which shall occasion him damage (§§ 70, 49), that is, pecuniary loss. But
although one by virtue of his special character has no right
superior to that of an individual as such, and who does not
possess any special character, yet it must be obvious that one
may occupy a position in society which will render it easier to
occasion him damage than to occasion damage to one not so
situated. The position of a person may render him peculiarly
obnoxious to injury. It is this special susceptibility to injury
alone, that creates the distinction between the actionable quality of language when it concerns one in a special character and
when it concerns him only as an individual. It is not every
special character the possession of which renders its possessor
more than ordinarily susceptible to injury by language, and
this being so we have to ascertain which are the special characters that have such an effect. It is not possible to particularize the special characters which entail this greater degree of
liability to injury, but it may be stated generally that every
legal occupation or position from which pecuniary benefit may
or possibly can be derived, will create in the follower of such
occupation, or the holder of such position, that peculiar or

---

[710] Holt on Libel, 218. But he adds, "though defamation when written may
be actionable under certain circumstances when the same words if spoken would
not." See in note 15, *ante*, and note 711, *post.*

special susceptibility to injury by language to which reference
has already been made; and hence results this rule that language concerning one in any such lawful occupation or position
may. as a necessary consequence, occasion him damage which
would not have that consequence if it concerned him as an individual merely; and therefore, as heretofore (§ 132) observed,
language which would not be actionable if it concerned only,
an individual as such, may be actionable if it concerns him in
his special character.[711] The rule which makes language concerning one in a special character sometimes actionable, when
the same language concerning one as an individual merely
would not be actionable, is in reality nothing more than a
phase of the rule (§ 134) that language connected with any
fact affecting its meaning or effect, must be construed in connection with such fact. The language being connected with
the fact of the special character of the person whom it concerns, must be construed in reference to such special character.

§ 182. Limiting ourselves for the present to occupations, we
conclude that subject only to the conditions (1) that the occupation is one in which a person may lawfully be engaged, and
(2) that it is an occupation which does or reasonably may yield,
or may be expected to yield, *pecuniary* reward, there is no employment—call it business, trade, profession or office, or what
you will[712]—so humble or so exalted but that language which
concerns the person in such his employment will be actionable,
if it affects him therein in a manner that may, as a necessary
consequence, or does as a natural and proximate consequence,

---

[711] *Brown* v. *Smith*, 13 C. B. 596. "For the reason that from the nature of
the case it is evident damage must ensue." (*McMillen* v. *Birch*, 1 Binn. 178.)
"The law has always been very tender of the reputation of tradesmen, and
therefore words spoken of them in the way of their trade will bear an action
that will not be actionable in the case of another person; and if bare words are
so, it will be stronger in the case of a public newspaper which is so diffusive."
(*Harman* v. *Delany*, 2 Str. 898.)

[712] Business includes trade and more. "Trade has a more restricted meaning
than business." (*Harris* v. *Amery*, 1 Law Rep. 154, C. P.) The word Business
embraces everything about which a person can be employed. (*Parker Mills* v.
Com'rs of Taxes, 23 N. Y. 244.)

prevent him deriving therefrom that pecuniary reward which probably he might otherwise have obtained.[713] We state the rule much broader than usual. Ordinarily it is said that the language must concern one in his business, profession, or office, and then is discussed what occupations are comprised within the terms business or profession, and what kind of office is intended. In one case[714] it was said *obiter* that to call a woman who taught children to read and write (a school-teacher or school-mistress) a whore was not actionable, because she was not in a *business* or *profession*. For the same reason, Lord Hale, in another case, was for denying the right to recover to a *letter-carrier* charged with breaking open letters. The tenor of his Lordship's remarks were, that if such an action could be maintained, a man should not speak disparagingly of his cook or his groom but an action would be brought.[715] It was said of a renter of tolls that he was not in a business or profession in which he could be slandered or libelled,[716] and the like was held of a stock broker.[717] On the other hand, it has

---

[713] *Foulger* v. *Newcomb*, 2 Law Rep. 327, *Ex.* See note 715, *post.*

[714] *Wharton* v. *Brook*, 1 Vent. 21. Where I. S. said to A., who kept a stable and received horses at livery (a livery-stable keeper), "Thou buyest nothing but rotten hay to poison men's horses," it was held that A. could not maintain an action therefor because he was not of any trade allowed in law. (*Jones* v. *Joice*, Vin. Abr. Act. for Words, U. a. 7.) Livery-stable keeping is recognized as a business in which one may be libelled. See *Southam* v. *Allen*, Raym. 231; *Alexander* v. *Angle*, 1 Cr. & J. 143.

[715] 1 Vent. 275. "The humility of the employment or occupation seems no objection to the action, either in law or in reason." (1 Starkie on Slander, 128; and see Cooke on Defam. 21; *Terry* v. *Hooper*, Lev. 115.) In *Cockaine* v. *Hopkins*, 2 Lev. 214, the plaintiff alleged that he used the art of buying and selling and gained great profit thereby, and that defendant said of him, He is a *runagate*, whereby he, plaintiff, lost his customers, but did not allege special damage; after verdict for plaintiff, judgment was arrested because, as the court said, runagate was not equivalent to bankrupt, and as plaintiff did not allege what trade he followed, it might be a *tinker* or *pedlar*, who are rogues by statute. This presuming that plaintiff's trade is unlawful was done in *Morris* v. *Langdale*, 2 Bos. & Pul. 284; but at this day the presumption would be the other way. See *post*, note 727.

[716] *Bellamy* v. *Burch*, 16 M. & W. 590; 8 Law Times, 413; and see *Sellars* v. *Killew*, 7 Dowl. & R. 121; 4 B. & C. 55.

[717] *Morris* v. *Langdale*, 2 Bos. & Pul. 284.

been held that the business need not be one which renders him who follows it liable as a trader to the bankrupt law,[718] and that the same rule applies to a mere trader or retail dealer as to a merchant.[719] It was supposed formerly that the rule was limited to occupations by which the person whom the language concerned obtained his livelihood or "daily bread;" but such a limitation, if it ever existed, no longer prevails. It is now held to be sufficient if the person whom the language concerns habitually (as distinguished from occasionally) acts in or pursues the occupation to derive an emolument from it.[720] Where it was objected against the plaintiff's right to recover that it was not alleged he got his living by his occupation, the objection was overruled.[721]

§ 183. We mentioned in the last preceding section (§ 182) as one of the conditions to the right of action for language concerning one in his occupation, that the occupation must be a lawful one. It is a universal rule, of which very numerous examples are to be found in the reports, that one engaged in an unlawful pursuit cannot recover for work done or goods sold by him, nor for any injury he may sustain in such occupation;[722]

[718] *Whitaker* v. *Bradley*, 7 D. & R. 649; S. C. *Whittington* v. *Gladwin*, 5 B. & C. 180; 2 Car. & P. 146.

[719] *Gates* v. *Bowker*, 8 Verm. (3 Wash.) 23; *Ostrom* v. *Calkins*, 5 Wend. 264; *Carpenter* v. *Dennis*, 3 Sandf. 305.

[720] *Baboneau* v. *Farrell*, 15 C. B. 360; *Bryant* v. *Loxton*, 11 Moore, 344; *Davis* v. *Davis*, 1 Nott & M'C. 290. "The action seems to extend to words spoken of a person in any lawful employment in which he may gain his livelihood." (1 Starkie on Slander, 127.) "It does not appear to be necessary that the party should gain his living in the character to which the slander is applied, but it is sufficient if he habitually act in that character and derive emolument from it. (*Id.* 129.)

[721] *Dobson* v. *Thorstone*, 3 Mod. 112.

[722] *Timmerman* v. *Morrison*, 14 Johns. 369; *Allcott* v. *Barber*, 1 Wend. 526; *Smith* v. *Tracy*, 2 Hall, 465; *Bailey* v. *Mogg*, 4 Denio, 60; *Finch* v. *Gridley*, 25 Wend. 469; *Smith* v. *Wileoz*, 24 N. Y. 353; S. C. 19 Barb. 581, and 25 Barb. 841; *Cundell* v. *Dawson*, 4 C. B. 476; *Best* v. *Bauder*, 29 How. Pr. R. 489; *Ferdon* v. *Cunningham*, 20 id. 154; *Cope* v. *Rowland*, 2 M. & W. 149; *Smith* v. *Mawhood*, 14 M. & W. 452; *Seneca County B'k* v. *Lamb*, 26 Barb. 595; *Barton* v. *Port Jackson Plank Road*, 17 Barb. 397; *Griffith* v. *Wells*, 3 Denio, 227; *Bell* v. *Quinn*, 2 Sandf. 146; *Taylor* v. *Crowland Gas Co.*, 10 Ex. 293; 18 *Jur.* 912; 26 Eng. Law & Eq. R. 460; *Cowan* v. *Milbourn*, 2 Law. Rep. 230, *Ex.*; 2 Pars. on Cont. 259; Story on Contr. 620.

hence, for language concerning a person in an unlawful occupation, an action is not maintainable. Thus it was held that pugilistic exhibitions being illegal, one could not maintain an action for language affecting him as proprietor of a tennis court where such exhibitions were made;[723] and *semble* one who practices as a physician without being duly licensed, cannot maintain an action for language concerning him as a physician.[724] The fact, however, that a person is engaged in an unlawful occupation is no reason for his not being allowed his action for any language concerning him as an individual, or concerning him in any other and lawful occupation in which he may be engaged.[725] If the language be actionable as concerning the person as an individual merely, it is unimportant and unnecessary to inquire further whether he is in any or in what occupation, legal or otherwise.[726] If the illegality of the occupation proceeds from the fact that the person following it is not duly licensed, the burden is on the publisher to show that the person whom the language concerns was unlicensed.[727]

§ 184. As to the kind of office which one must hold to render actionable language which concerns him in such office, it is laid down by Starkie, but as we conceive erroneously, that " words are equally actionable whether the office be lucrative or merely confidential."[728] Pecuniary loss is the gist of the action

---

[723] *Hunt* v. *Bell*, 1 Bing. 1.

[724] *Marsh* v. *Davison*, 9 Paige, 580, referring to a statute since repealed.

[725] *Yrisarri* v. *Clement*, 2 C. & P. 223; 3 Bing. 432; 11 Moore, 308; *Greville* v. *Chapman*, 1 D. & M. 553. In *Manning* v. *Clements*, 7 Bing. 362; 5 M. & P. 211, the plaintiff alleged he was a manufacturer of bitters, and defendant was allowed to introduce evidence of the illegality of such manufacture (namely, that the alleged bitters were another and a prohibited article), not as a justification, but in contradiction of plaintiff's allegation.

[726] *Harwood* v. *Astley*, 4 Bos. & P. 47; 1 New Rep. 47.

[727] *Fry* v. *Bennett*, 28 N. Y. 324; *Smith* v. *Joyce*, 12 Barb. 25.

[728] 1 Starkie on Slander, 119. He states that the whole class of cases in which recovery has been had for words affecting one in office not lucrative, "seems to rest on more dubious principles than any other." At page 122 he says—erroneously as we conceive—"the danger of exclusion from office gives rise to the action." And at page 118 he says the ground of action is "somewhat different" according as the office is confidential or lucrative. And at page 124 he says

for slander or libel (§ 57); and as no pecuniary loss can result from language concerning one in an office which yields no pecuniary emolument, words not otherwise actionable cannot become so because they concern one in such an office.[789] Whatever may have been the doctrine and practice of the Court of Star-chamber, or of the common law courts under the statutes *scandalum magnatum*, we believe that no court, proceeding according to the common law and independently of any statute, has sanctioned the doctrine as laid down by Starkie. Wherever language concerning one in an office merely honorary, has in a common law court and independently of any statute, been held actionable, it will be seen that the language would have been actionable had it been published of an individual as such.

§ 185. Another relation or special character in which one may be injuriously affected by language, is that of partner. Language may concern partners or one or some of several partners in their or his individual capacity merely, or it may *touch* them or him in their or his partnership business. As respects language concerning one who is a partner, and which concerns him as an individual merely, the fact of his being a partner, unless, perhaps, as affecting the damages, has no significance. Language concerning partners in their partnership business may be actionable *per se*, or actionable only by reason of the special damage. That language touching the business which would be actionable *per se* if published concerning one who is not a partner, would also be actionable *per se* as concerning partners or one who is a partner. Actionable language concerning part-

---

"the action appears to extend to all offices of *trust* or profit without limitation, provided they be of a *temporal* nature." This word *temporal* is used as the converse of *spiritual*, to take away the ecclesiastical jurisdiction.

[789] *Gallwey* v. *Marshall*, 9 Ex. 204. In that action the language [oral] imputed incontinence to a clergyman. The court, in deciding against the plaintiff, said: We should have no doubt of the plaintiff's right to recover if the declaration had averred that he was *beneficed*, or was in the actual receipt of professional *temporal emolument*, * * as the charge would have caused the loss of the benefice or the emoluments. In the absence of any averment of plaintiff having any office of temporal [pecuniary] profit, we are not satisfied this action will lie. There is no authority that it will where there is no actual damage.

ners and which touches them in their partnership business, is
an injury to their joint business, and is a joint and several injury for which both may sue jointly or either may sue separately.   Thus where the language imputed to two persons who
were partners as wool-staplers, that they had been guilty of
fraud in a sale of wool, and they sued jointly, alleging special
damage to their trade, the action was sustained.[730]   For words
charging partners with making an assignment to defraud their
creditors, an action by one partner was allowed;[731] and where
the *firm* was charged with insolvency, the language used being
" J. T. & Co. are down," held a joint action might be maintained.[732]   In such a joint action no damages are recoverable
for the injury to the feelings of the partners.[733] Where language
concerns one only of several partners but touches him in his
partnership business, there is an injury to the partnership business for which the partner whom the language concerns may
sue alone or all the partners may unite with him.   Thus where
the language was of one of several partners as bankers, and
imputed to him insolvency, and for this he alone brought suit
alleging damage to the partnership business, it was pleaded in
abatement that the plaintiff carried on his business jointly with
A. B., and that the alleged damage accrued to A. B. jointly
with the plaintiff alone.   On general demurrer the plea was
overruled, but a question was raised whether a special demurrer might not have been interposed to the declaration for unit-
ing damages which accrued to the plaintiff with damages which
accrued to his partner.   In other words, as the damage to the
business was jointly to the plaintiff and his partners, was it
proper for plaintiff to allege them in his declaration ?   It was
assumed that on the trial the jury would separate the dam-

---

[730] *Cook* v. *Batchelor*, 3 Bos. & Pul. 150; see note to *Goldstein* v. *Foss*, 2 Car.
& P. 252.

[731] *Odiorne* v. *Bacon*, 6 Cush. 185.

[732] *Titus* v. *Follett*, 2 Hill, 318; and see *Foster* v. *Lawson*, 3 Bing. 452; *Le Fanu*
v. *Malcomson*, 1 Cl. & Fin. N. S. 637; *Maitland* v. *Goldney*, 2 East, 426; *Beardsley*
v. *Tappan*, Ms. decided in U. S. Circuit Co't Sout. Dist. N. Y., October, 1867.
See *Corporations*.

[733] *Haythorn* v. *Lawson*, 3 Car. & P. 196.

ages;[734] and in other cases, one of several partners sustained an action for libel on him in his business.[735] Where the language published purported to give information as to the credit and standing of a mercantile firm and charged one member with dishonesty, a joint action by all the partners was sustained.[736] Where the partners unite in the action, or where the partner whom the language concerns sues alone, in either case the language being of the kind called actionable *per se* (§§ 146, 147), the action may be maintained without any allegation or proof of special damage;[737] but where a partner whom the language does not personally concern sues alone for language personally concerning his partner, in that case the action cannot be maintained unless there be an allegation and proof of special damage. A recovery by the partner whom the language personally concerns would not bar an action by his partner, and probably would not bar a separate action by all the partners; nor would a recovery by all the partners be a bar to a separate action by the partner whom the language personally concerns.[738]

§ 186. The circumstance of one being heir presumptive has been held to give an actionable quality to language concerning him in that character. Starkie devotes a chapter to a partial review of the cases in which, on the ground that it may cause his disinherison, it has been held actionable to call a presumptive heir bastard, and he concludes that, although such decisions carry the doctrine of presumptive loss to a great extent, they seem to be warranted by the application of sound and general principles. He does not state what those principles are, and for ourselves we can discover no principle which will support such decisions. It certainly is not a *necessary* con-

---

[734] *Robinson* v. *Marchant*, 7 Q. B. (Adol. & Ell. N. S.) 918.

[735] *Fidler* v. *Delavan*, 20 Wend. 57; and see *Solomon* v. *Medex*, 1 Stark. Cas. 191; *Harrison* v. *Bevington*, 8 Car. & P. 708, and *Davis* v. *Ruff*, Cheves, 17. This last-named case is commented on in *Taylor* v. *Church*, 1 E. D. Smith, 287.

[736] *Taylor* v. *Church*, 1 E. D. Smith, 279; S. C. 8 N. Y. 452.

[737] *Id.*; 2 Saund. Pl. & Ev. 117 a, 117 b. 6 ed.; and see *Foster* v. *Lawson*, 3 Bing. 452; 11 Moore, 360.

[738] *Taylor* v. *Church*, 1 E. D. Smith, 287.

sequence that one should disinherit his presumptive heir because
it has been said of him that he is a bastard.

§ 187. One being a candidate for an office or for employment does not have the effect to make language concerning
him in that character actionable *per se*, otherwise than as it
would be actionable *per se* if it concerned him as an individual
merely.[739] If the language concerning a candidate for office or
employment occasions him special damage, as the failure to
obtain such office or employment, it will be actionable; thus if
a clergyman is to be presented to a benefice, and one to defeat
him says to the patron, He is a heretic, or a bastard, or excommunicated, and he thereby loses his presentment, he may have
his action;[740] and where a lawyer was a candidate for the office
of steward of a corporation, and the electors being assembled
to make an election, one of them said to the others, He (said
candidate) is an ignorant man and not fit for the place, by
means of which he was refused, the court inclined to the opinion that the words were actionable, but no judgment was
given.[741] The fact of one being a candidate for an office or for
employment, in many instances affords a license or legal excuse
for publishing language concerning him as such candidate, for
which publication there would be no legal excuse did he not
occupy the position of such a candidate. The consideration of
language concerning one as a candidate for office or for employment, falls more appropriately under the head of legal
excuses or defences, and it will be there discussed.

§ 188. As regards the kind of language concerning one in
an occupation or office which will confer a right of action, it
has been said: " Words are actionable when spoken of one in
an office of profit, which may *probably* occasion the loss of his

---

[739] *Powers* v. *Dubois,* 17 Wend. 63; *Prinn* v. *Howe,* Brown's Cas. Parl. 64;
Littlejohn v. *Greely,* 13 Abb. 41; *Hunt* v. *Bennett,* 4 E. D. Smith, 647; 19 N. Y.
173.

[740] *Davis* v. *Gardiner,* 4 Rep. 17 a.

[741] *Sanderson* v. *Rudden,* Mar. 146. Words which will cause others not to vote
for him of whom they were spoken, at an election at which he is a candidate, are
actionable. (*Brewer* v. *Weakley,* 2 Overt. 99.)

office, or where spoken of persons touching their respective professions, trades and business, and do or may probably tend to their damage.[742] "If the words be of *probable* ill consequence to a person in a trade or profession or an office;"[743] Bayley, B., objected to this rule that the words *probably* and *probable* were too indefinite, and unless considered equivalent to "having a *natural* tendency to" and as confined within the limits of showing the want of some necessary qualification or some misconduct in the office, it went beyond what the authorities warranted.[744] But, "How is a *natural* stronger [more definite] than a *probable* tendency?"[745] To maintain an action for words spoken, they must impute some matter in relation to the party's particular trade or vocation, and which, if true, would render him unworthy of employment.[746] "Every authority which I have been able to find either shows the want of some general requisite, as honesty, capacity, fidelity, &c., or connects the imputation with the plaintiff's office, trade or business;"[747] or his office of trust and place of honor, provided they be of a temporal nature;[748] and "We ought not to extend the

---

[742] De Grey, Ch. J., *Onslow* v. *Horne*, 2 Wils. 186.

[743] Same case, as reported 2 W. Bl. R. 753.

[744] *Lumby* v. *Allday*, 1 Cr. & J. 301 ; 1 Tyrw. 217.

[745] Williams, J., *James* v. *Brook*, 9 Q. B. 7; and see *Sibley* v. *Tomlins*, 4 Tyrw. 90.

[746] *Kinney* v. *Nash*, 3 N. Y. 177 ; *Fowles* v. *Bowen*, 30 N. Y. 24.

[747] Bayley, B., *Lumby* v. *Allday*, 1 Cr. & J. 301; 1 Tyrw. 217; approved *Ayre* v. *Craven*, 2 Adol. & El. 2 ; 2 Nev. & M. 220; and see *Jones* v. *Littler*, 7 M. & W. 433 ; *Southee* v. *Denny*, 1 Ex. 196 ; *James* v. *Brooke*, 9 Q. B. 7.

[748] *How* v. *Prinn*, Holt, 652 ; S. C. *Prinn* v. *Howe*, Brown's Cas. Parl. 64 ; 1 Starkie on Slander, 124. "A distinction is usually taken between an office of profit and an office of honor, but the distinction is not a sound one, and though it may apply to an action for words. it does not extend to an action for libel." If a person be in an office of profit, it is libellous to impute to him either inability, want of integrity, or anything which amounts to it. But if the office be an office of honor, it is said no action lies except the import of the words be a charge of dishonesty. In either case charging a man with inclinations and principles which show him unfit for an office of trust or honor is libellous, without charging him with any act. Any imputations against a person who is in the enjoyment of an office, either public or private, of honor, profit or trust, which imports a charge · of unfitness to administer the duty of the office, are libels." (Holt on Libel, 208.) Words which charge a breach of a public trust are actionable. See *Kinney* v. *Nash*, 3 N. Y. 178.

limits of actions of this nature beyond those laid down by our predecessors."[749] Although every lawful lucrative occupation is, as regards the actionable quality of language, governed by the same general principles, yet the kind of occupation affects the application of the principles, and the identical language which may be not actionable as concerning one in some certain occupation, may be actionable as concerning one in some other occupation. The test in every case by which to decide if the language be actionable, meaning actionable *per se*, is, does it necessarily occasion damage; and because the language which may necessarily occasion damage in one occupation will not have that effect in some other, it happens that in every case regard must be had to the character of the occupation. Numerous illustrations of this are to be found in the subsequent part of this chapter. We select one instance: In the case of a merchant the keeping of account books is or is considered to be a requisite to the successful prosecution of his business, and therefore to charge one who is a merchant with keeping false books has been held to be actionable,[750] but the like charge concerning a farmer was held not actionable, because the keeping of books was not considered requisite to the conduct of his business, although in addition to his business of farmer he sawed logs for reward and dealt in lumber.[751]

---

[749] Pollock, Ch. B., *Gallwey* v. *Marshall*, 9 Ex. 294.

[750] *Backus* v. *Richardson*, 5 Johns. 476; and the like charge against a blacksmith held actionable. *Burtch* v. *Nickerson*, 17 Johns. 217; and see *Crawfoot* v. *Dale*, Vent. 263; and Viner's Abr. Act. for Words, U. a. 22.

[751] *Rathbun* v. *Emigh*, 6 Wend. 407. Where the defendant said of the plaintiff, a mercer, " He hath deceived in a reckoning, and his debt-book which he keepeth is a false debt-book," judgment went against the plaintiff, because the book might be kept by the defendant's servant, and he, defendant, not have knowledge of it. (Brook's Case, Godb. 231.) In *Backus* v. *Richardson* (5 Johns. 476), the court said the words " You keep false books " implied knowledge in plaintiff; and in *Todd* v. *Hastings* (Vent. 117), it was held that to charge a trader with keeping " *false books* " would be construed to mean " false *debt* books." Keeping books of account is necessary in this country where credit is generally given, as well by the mechanic as by the merchant and professional man. (*Burtch* v. *Nickerson*, 17 Johns. 217.) Mechanics " generally sell on credit, and their success and reputation depend upon their character for fair dealing." (*Rathbun* v. *Emigh*, 6 Wend.

§ 189. One of the essential elements of the actionable quality of language concerning one in his occupation or office, is the fact that the person whom the language concerns is in such occupation or office (§ 181); it necessarily follows that to render language concerning one in his occupation or office actionable *per se*, the person whom the language concerns must follow such occupation or hold such office at the time the language is published. No language concerning one in any special character, published after he has ceased to occupy that character, can be actionable as concerning him in such special character. The general rule is that in an action for language concerning one in a special character, it must be shown that he maintained that special character at the time the language was published.[702] Where the plaintiff had been commissioner to make a treaty with the Indians, and after his commission had terminated the defendant charged him orally with hiring and bribing the Indians to sign such treaty, held that no action could be maintained.[703] Where plaintiff was twice constable, once in 1843 and again in 1846, and during the latter period one said of him orally that while constable in 1843 he had made a false return, held that the words would not support an action.[704] If a man has been a merchant and leaves off merchandising for a time, and another calls him bankrupt, an action lies; for though he does not use the trade of a merchant at the time of the speaking the words, yet he *remains a merchant*, and may resume the trade at his pleasure;[705] but where the plaintiff alleged he had

---

407.) Another reason why a charge of keeping false books of account was held actionable was, that such books, if generally reputed correct, were receivable as evidence of their contents. (*Crawfoot* v. *Dale*, Vent. 263.)

[702] *Smayles* v. *Smith*, Browl. 1; *Reignald's Case*, Cro. Car. 563; *Bellamy* v. *Burch*, 16 M. & W. 590; 8 Law Times, 413; *Allen* v. *Hillman*, 12 Pick. 101; *Forward* v. *Adams*, 7 Wend. 204; *Oram* v. *Franklin*, 5 Blackf. 42: *Harris* v. *Bailey*, 8 N. Hamp. 216.

[703] *Forward* v. *Adams*, 7 Wend. 204.

[704] *Edwards* v. *Howell*, 10 Ired. 211; but it was said plaintiff might have recovered on proof of special damage.

[705] *Gardner* v. *Hopwood*, Yelv. 159; and see Vin. Abr. Act. for Words, U. *a*. 19. An attorney who has not taken out his annual certificate, although he is by statute disabled from recovering his fees, nevertheless continues an attorney, and

for many years used the trade of a drover, but without alleging
he was a drover at the time of the publication, it was held he
did not show a cause of action.[756] Whether or not the plaintiff
occupied the special character alleged, and whether or not he
continued in such special character until the time of the publi- •
cation complained against, are questions of fact. A person   •
shown once to have been in any certain office, profession, or
trade, is presumed to continue therein.[757] The decisions which
are sometimes referred to as exceptions to the rule that the person whom the language concerns must maintain his special
character at the time the language is published, are really not
exceptions to that rule, they are cases which follow another
and different rule because comprehended in a different class.
On examination they will be found to range themselves under
the division relating to language concerning an individual as
such; and the true ground on which in such cases the actions   •
were sustained, was of the language being actionable as affecting the individual as such, without regard to his having occupied the special character to which the language refers. Thus
where one had been senator, and after his term of office had
ceased it was published of him in writing that he had been
guilty of corrupt conduct in his office of senator, the action
was sustained;[758] and so where one had been constable, and
after he quitted that office it was said of him that while in
office he was a healer of felons, or of one that when in office
as a justice he was a bribing justice.[759]

---

may maintain an action for language concerning him as an attorney. (*Jones* v.
Stevens, 11 Price, 235; *Pearce* v. *Whale*, 5 B. & C. 38.)

[756] *Collis* v. *Malin*, Cro. Car. 282; *Gray* v. *Medcalfe*, Yelv. 21.

[757] *Tuthill* v. *Milton*, Yelv. 158; *Collis* v. *Malin*, Cro. Car. 282; *Jordan* v. *Lyster*, Cro. Eliz. 273; *Moore* v. *Syme*, 2 Rolle R. 84; *Dod* v. *Robinson*, All. 63; *Forward* v. *Adams*, 7 Wend. 204; *Bellamy* v. *Burch*, 16 M. & W. 590; *Fry* v. *Bennett*, 28 N. Y. 324; but see *M'Leod* v. *Murphy*, 3 Car. & P. 311.

[758] *Cramer* v. *Riggs*, 17 Wend. 209; and see 7 Wend. 204; *Littlejohn* v. *Greely*,
13 Abb. Pra. R. 41; *Walden* v. *Mitchell*, 2 Vent. 266.

[759] *Pridham* v. *Tucker*, Yelv. 153. To say of a commissioner appointed to take
testimony, he hath taken bribes (*Moor* v. *Foster*, Cro. Jac. 65), and charging an
officer of a court of record with taking bribes, held actionable. (Anon. Dal. 43;
Lee v. *Swan*, Yelv. 142.)

§ 190. To render language concerning one in a special character or relation actionable, " it must touch him " in that special character or relation ; for unless it does, it must be judged in regard to its actionable quality by the rules which apply to language concerning an individual as such. That the language " must touch " the person whom it concerns in his special character, means only that it must concern him in such special character, and affect him therein. It is not sufficient that the language disparages him generally, or that his general reputation is thereby affected ; it must be such as if true would disqualify him or render him less fit properly to fulfill the duties incident to the special character he has assumed. It is not enough that the language " tends to injure the person in his office, profession, or trade, it must be spoken [published] of him in his official or business character." [760] It must "touch him in his office, profession, or trade." [761] Thus, saying of a justice of the peace " there is a combined company here to cheat strangers, and Squire Van Tassel has a hand in it.—I don't see why he did not tell me the execution had not been returned ·in time, so that I could sue the constable ; " [762] or,

[760] *Van Tassel* v. *Capron,* 1 Denio, 250; *Sibley* v. *Tompkins,* 4 Tyrw. 90; *Doyley* v. *Roberts,* 3 Bing. N. S. 835 ; *Ridway* v. *Gray,* 31 Verm. (2 Shaw) 292; *Buck* v. *Hersey,* 31 Maine (1 Red.) 558. It seems, however, that where one is in business, words spoken of him in his private character will bear an action, if they are such as must necessarily affect him in his business ; thus, to say of a brewer, he had been locked up in a sponging-house [a private jail, kept by deputy-sheriffs where persons arrested for debt, on paying for the indulgence, have the option of remaining instead of going to the debtor's prison], was held actionable, because the words were held necessarily to affect his credit as a trader. (*Jones* v. *Littler,* 7 M. & W. 423.) And see *Bell* v. *Thatcher,* Freem. 277; *Fowler* v. *Bowen,* 30 N. Y. 23; *Starr* v. *Gardner,* 6 Up. Can. Q. B. R. (O. S.) 512. So in *Davis* v. *Ruff,* Cheves, 17, it is said that words affecting the pecuniary credit of a merchant need not be averred nor proved to have been used in relation to his occupation as a merchant, for in their nature they strike at the root of mercantile character.

[761] *Kinney* v. *Nash,* 3 Coms. 177; *Van Tassel* v. *Capron,* 1 Denio, 250 ; Comyn's Dig. Act. for Defam. D. 27. Whether words were spoken of a man in a certain capacity, is a question of fact for the jury. (*Skinner* v. *Grant,* 12 Verm. 456; *Sibley* v. *Tomlins,* 4 Tyrw. 90; *Doyley* v. *Roberts,* 3 Bing. N. S. 835; *Tomlinson* v. *Brittlebank,* 1 Har. & W. 573.)

[762] *Van Tassel* v. *Capron,* 1 Denio, 250.

"Squire Oakley is a damned rogue,"[702] was held to impute misconduct as a man and not as a magistrate, and not to be actionable. For a like reason it was held not actionable to say of one
who kept a public garden, "He is a desperate man, a dangerous man. I am afraid to go to his house alone; I am afraid of
my life;"[704] and these words of a pork butcher, "Who stole F.'s
pigs? You did, you thief; you poisoned them with mustard
and brimstone," were, after verdict, held not to have any necessary connection with his trade, and were not calculated to
injure him in it, and therefore not actionable.[705] The words,
"He has defrauded his creditors, and been horse-whipped off
the course at D.," spoken of an attorney but not in his character of an attorney, held not actionable.[706] And the same decision was made in reference to these words spoken of an attorney: "I have taken out a judge's order to tax A.'s bill. I
will bring him to book, and have him struck off the roll.[707] I
will take him to Bow Street on a charge of forgery."[708] And
saying of a livery-stable keeper, "You are a regular prover
under bankruptcy; you are a regular bankrupt maker; if it
was not for some of your neighbors your shop would look
queer," was held not to be a charge in the way of his trade nor
actionable.[709] Where words imputing incontinency and not in
themselves actionable were spoken of one in respect of his situation as clerk in a gas company, held that not imputing any
misconduct in his capacity of clerk, they were not actionable.[710]
A charge against the plaintiff, laid to be spoken of him in his

---

[702] *Oakley* v. *Farrington*, 1 Johns. Cas. 129; and held not actionable to say of
a justice: "He is a logger-headed, a slouch-headed, and a bursen-bellied hound."
(1 Keb. 629.) Calling one who is a cooper varlet and knave is not actionable—
the words do not touch him in his trade. (*Coles* v. *Kettle*, Cro. Jac. 204.)

[704] *Ireland* v. *McGarvish*, 1 Sandf. 155.

[705] *Sibley* v. *Tomlins*, 4 Tyrw. 90.

[706] *Doyley* v. *Roberts*, 3 Bing. N. S. 835.

[707] *Phillips* v. *Jansen*, 2 Esp. Cas. 624.

[708] *Harrison* v. *King*, 4 Price. 46; 7 Taunt. 431.

[709] *Alexander* v. *Angle*, 1 Cr. & J. 143; 4 Tyrw. 9.

[710] *Lumby* v. *Allday*, 1 Cr. & J. 301; 1 Tyrw. 217. The words were, "You
are a fellow, a disgrace to the town, unfit to hold your situation for your conduct
with whores."

trade of a staymaker, of criminal intercourse with a female employed by him in his trade, held not to affect him in his trade and not actionable.[771] And so it was held that a charge of adultery against a physician did not *necessarily* touch him in his profession, and was not actionable without its being shown that the charge was connected with the plaintiff's profession;[772] and the same was held of these words of a physician: "He is so steady drunk he cannot get business any more;"[773] or, he is a two-penny bleeder;[774] or, he gave my child too much mercury; or, he made up the medicines wrong through jealousy, because I would not allow him to use his own judgment.[775] Saying of a woman who gained her livelihood by teaching girls to dance, "She is as much a man as I am; she got I. S. with child; she is an hermaphrodite," was held not actionable, no special damage being properly alleged, and because girls are taught to dance as frequently by men as by women.[776] It was held actionable to call a school-mistress a dirty slut;[777] or to charge, by writing, a school-teacher with making a false report to the school visitors and with general untruthfulness,[778] or with want of chastity.[779] It was held actionable to say of a shop-keeper, he had nothing but rotten goods in his shop;[780] or to charge in writing that the place of business of a trader (a coach-builder) was not respectable;[781] or, that a ship of which the

---

[771] *Brayne* v. *Cooper*, 5 M. & W. 249.

[772] *Ayre* v. *Craven*, 2 Adol. & El. 2; 4 Nev. & M. 220. In *Parrett* v. *Carpenter*, Noy, 64, it was held not actionable *per se* to charge a clergyman with adultery; but that case, it was said in *Galwey* v. *Marshall*, 9 Ex. 294, has been overruled; and saying of a clergyman that he had two wives was held actionable. (*Nicholson* v. *Lynes*, Cro. Eliz. 94.) See note 886, *post*.

[773] Anon. 1 Ham. 83, note.

[774] *Foster* v. *Small*, 3 Whart. 138.

[775] *Edsall* v. *Russell*, 4 M. & G. 1090.

[776] *Weatherhead* v. *Armitage*, 2 Levinz, 233. In *Malone* v. *Stewart*, 15 Ohio, 319, it was held actionable to call a married woman an hermaphrodite.

[777] *Wilson* v. *Runyon*, Wright, 651.

[778] *Lindley* v. *Horton*, 27 Conn. 58.

[779] *Bodwell* v. *Osgood*, 3 Pick. 379.

[780] *Bennett* v. *Wells*, 12 Mod. 420.

[781] *Barrett* v. *Long*, 3 Ho. Lords Cas. 395; 16 Eng. Law & Eq. R. 1.

14

plaintiff was owner and master, and which he had advertised for a voyage to the East Indies, was not seaworthy, and that Jews had bought her to take out convicts.[792]

§ 191. In those trades or professions in which ordinarily credit is essential to their successful prosecution, there language is actionable *per se* which imputes to one in any such trade or profession, a want of credit or responsibility or insolvency, past, present, or future;[793] as, to say of a tradesman, He is not able to pay his debts; or, He owes more than he is worth;[794] he will break shortly.[795] He is a pitiful fellow and a rogue; he compounded his debts at 5s. in the pound.[796] He is indebted to me, and if he does not come and make terms with me I will make a bankrupt of him and ruin him.[797] He is a bankrupt.[798] He was a bankrupt.[799] He is a bankrupt, and unable

---

[792] *Ingram* v. *Lawson*, 6 Bing. N. C. 212. The words were held to be more than a libel on the ship, and to constitute a libel on the plaintiff in his trade, for which he might recover without proof of malice or special damage.

[793] *Seycroft* v. *Dunker*, Cro. Car. 317; *Harrison* v. *Thornborough*, 10 Mod. 11; *Southam* v. *Allen*, T. Raym. 231; *Sewall* v. *Catlin*, 3 Wend. 291; *Read* v. *Hudson*, 1 L'd Raym. 610; *Ostrom* v. *Calkins*, 5 Wend. 263; *Davis* v. *Lewis*, 7 T. R. 17; *Dobson* v. *Thornistone*, 3 Mod. 112; *Chapman* v. *Lamphire*, 3 Mod. 155; *Mott* v. *Comstock*, 7 Cow. 654; *Whitaker* v. *Bradley*, 7 D. & R. 649; S. C., *Whittington* v. *Gladwin*, 5 B. & C. 180; 2 C. & P. 146; *Lewis* v. *Hawley*, 2 Day, 495; Anon., Lofft, 322; *Hull* v. *Smith*, 1 M. & S. 287; *Else* v. *Ferris*, Anthon, 23; *Brown* v. *Smith*, 20 Eng. L. & Eq. R. 243; 13 C. B. 596; 22 Law Jour. R. N. S. C. P. 151; 17 Jur. 807; 1 Com. Law Rep. 49; *Jones* v. *Littler*, 7 M. & W. 423; *Carpenter* v. *Dennis*, 3 Sand. 305; *Phillips* v. *Hoeffer*, 1 Penn. St. Rep. 62; *Prettyman* v. *Shockley*, 4 Harring. 112; *Griffiths* v. *Lewis*, 15 Law Jour. 249, Q. B.

[794] Vin. Abr. Act. for Words, U. a. 11, 12, 13, 20, 21, and to publish in writing concerning one engaged in a business in which credit was essential, "Had to hold over a few days for the accommodation of L. (plaintiff)." *Lewis* v. *Chapman*, 19 Barb. 252; S. C. 16 N. Y. 369.

[795] Hill's case, Lat. 114; *Dobson* v. *Thornistone*, 3 Mod. 112.

[796] Spoken of a pawnbroker, and special damage alleged. *Stanton* v. *Smith*, 2 L'd Raym. 1480. This case was questioned 3 Bing. N. C. 840, but sustained *Jones* v. *Littler*, 7 M. & W. 423.

[797] *Brown* v. *Smith*, 13 C. B. 596; 1 Com. Law Rep. 49; 22 Law Jour. Rep. N, S. C. P. 151; 20 Eng. Law & Eq. R. 243.

[798] Spoken of a grazier. (Anon., 1 Bulst. 40.) Of a dyer. (*Squire* v. *Johns*, Cro. Jac. 558.) Of a shoemaker, who bought and sold leather. (*Stanley* v. *Osbaston*, Cro. Eliz. 268; and see Vin. Abr. Act. for Words, U. a. 18, 19, 35, 36, 38, I. a.)

[799] *Hull* v. *Smith*, 1 M. & S. 287.

to pay his just debts.[790] The sheriff will sell him out one of these days, and claims against him not sued will be lost.[791] He must fail; his time is come.[792] He is not worth a penny and will run away.[793] He will be a bankrupt.[794] He is next door to breaking.[795] He is broken and run away, and will never return.[796] I heard he was run away.[797] I have heard of no failures, but understand there is trouble with S.[798] Two dyers are gone off, and for aught I know H. will be so too, within this time twelve months.[799] H. will lose his debt; M. (plaintiff) is unable to pay it.[800] He came a broken merchant from Ham-

---

[790] Spoken of a drover, whose business was to purchase droves of cattle and drive them to market and sell them. (*Lewis* v. *Hawley*, 2 Day, 495.) An innkeeper is a trader. (*Ombony* v. *Jones*, 19 N. Y. 241.) The words, "You have been a pauper ever since you have lived in the parish; you are now a pauper. I have paid £20 a year towards your maintenance; you will be in the bankrupt list in less than twelve months," spoken of an innkeeper, held actionable. (*Whittington* v. *Gladwin*, 5 B. & C. 180; 2 Car. & P. 146; S. C., *Whitaker* v. *Bradley*, 7 D. & R. 649.) So it is actionable to say of an innkeeper, He is broke, and there is neither entertainment for man or horse. (*Southam* v. *Allen*, T. Raym. 231.)

[791] Spoken of a farmer. (*Phillips* v. *Hoeffer*, 1 Penn. St. Rep. 62.)

[792] Spoken of a distiller, the course of whose business was to purchase grain on credit. (*Ostrom* v. *Calkins*, 5 Wend. 263.)

[793] Anon., Lofft, 322. He is about to run away and defraud his creditors. (*Prettyman* v. *Shockley*, 4 Harring. 112.)

[794] In *three days*. (*Thompson* v. *Trenge*, 2 Rolle R. 438.) Or in six months. (*Else* v. *Ferris*, Anthon N. P. 23.) He will be bankrupt, without saying when, said not to be actionable. Vin. Abr. Act. for Words, O. *a*.

[795] Spoken of a laceman [a dealer in lace]. (*Read* v. *Hudson*, 1 L'd Raym. 610.)

[796] Spoken of a carpenter. (*Chapman* v. *Lamphire*, 3 Mod. 155.) And spoken of a farmer. (*Dobson* v. *Thornistone*, 3 Mod. 112.) To say of a merchant, he is broke, is actionable. (*Leycroft* v. *Dunkin*, Cro. Car. 31.)

[797] Spoken of a tailor. (*Davis* v. *Lewis*, 7 Term R. 17.) Spoken of a carpenter. (3 Mod. 312.)

[798] Spoken of a merchant. (*Sewell* v. *Catlin*, 3 Wend. 291.) To say of a banker, he suspended payment, is actionable. Dictum in *Forster* v. *Lawson*, 3 Bing. 452.

[799] *Harrison* v. *Thornborough*, 10 Mod. 11.

[800] Spoken of a merchant. (*Mott* v. *Comstock*, 7 Cow. 654.) It was held not actionable to say to a creditor of a merchant (the plaintiff), You were best to call for it [your money] in, and take heed how you trust him. (Vin. Abr. Act. for Words, U. *a*. 17.)

burgh.[801]   All is not well with V.; there are many merchants
who have lately failed, and I expect no otherwise of V.[802] There
is no bottom to you.   I would put you through, but you won't
stand ; you will burst or fail before I have a chance.[803]   Thou
art a beggarly fellow, and not worth a groat.[804] They have
been sued ; report says J. B.'s wife (J. B. being one of the plaintiffs) is about to apply for a divorce, and that J. B. has put his
property out of his hands; if so, their store will be closed
soon.[805]

§ 192. Language of one in his trade or profession is actionable *per se* when it imputes to him fraud, want of integrity, or
misconduct in the line of the business or profession " whereby
he gains his bread." [806] Thus it was held actionable to say of a
weaver, He is a rogue and villain, and taketh the goods of his
customers and pawneth them, and he is not a man to be
trusted ;[807] of an auctioneer and appraiser, He is a damned
rascal, and has cheated me out of £100 on the valuation ;[808] of
a trader, He was guilty of dishonestly using old materials instead of new in doing a certain piece of work ;[809] of a corn-

---

[801] *Scycroft* v. *Dauker*, Cro. Car. 317.

[802] Vivian's Case, 3 Salk. 326.

[803] Spoken of one engaged in buying and selling woodenware. *Carpenter* v.
Dennis, 3 Sandf. 305.

[804] *Simpson* v. *Barlow*, 12 Mod. 591.

[805] *Beardsley* v. *Tappan*, 1 Blatch. Cir. C't R. 588.

[806] *Baboneau* v. *Farrell*, 15 C. B. 360; *Bryant* v. *Loxton*, 11 Moore, 344; *Davis*
v. *Davis*, 1 Nott & McCord, 290; *Chipman* v. *Cook*, 2 Tyler, 456; *Rush* v. *Cave-
naugh*, 2 Barr, 187; *Brown* v. *Mims*, 2 Rep. Con. C't, 235; *Foot* v. *Brown*, 8
Johns. 64; *Riggs* v. *Deniston*, 3 Johns. Cas. 198; *Thomas* v. *Jackson*, 3 Bing. 104;
10 Moore, 425; *Odiorne* v. *Bacon*, 6 Cush. 185; *Gay* v. *Horner*, 13 Pick. 535;
Ludwell v. *Hole*, 2 L'd Raym. 1417; *Davis* v. *Miller*, 2 Strange, 1169; *Obaugh* v.
Finn, 4 Pike, 110; *Boydell* v. *Jones*, 4 M. & W. 446; 7 Dowl. (P. C.) 210; *Sempsey* v. *Levy*, 2 Jur. 776; Vin. Abr. Act. for Words, U. a. 25, 26. " Any charge of
dishonesty against an individual in connection with his business, whereby his
character in such business may be injuriously affected, is actionable." (*Fowles* v.
Bowen, 30 N. Y. 24.)

[807] Vin. Abr. Act. for Words, U. a. 4.

[808] *Bryant* v. *Loxton*, 11 Moore, 344.

[809] *Baboneau* v. *Farrell*, 1 Jur. N. S. 114; 15 C. B. 360; 24 Law Jour. R. N. S.
9, C. P.; 28 Eng. Law & Eq. R. 339.

factor, You are a rogue and a swindling rascal; you delivered me one hundred bushels of oats worse by six pence a bushel than I bargained for;[810] of a limeburner, He is a cheating knave;[811] of a bailiff, You did cozen your master of a bushel of barley, or, he hath deceived his master by buying and selling;[812] of a butcher, That he used false weights;[813] of a jeweler, He is a cozening knave in selling me a sapphire for a diamond;[814] of a goldsmith, He sold me a chain of copper for gold; of one who sold chamois skins, He will cozen you and sell you lamb skins instead of chamois skins; of a brewer, that he makes or sells unwholesome beer; of a tradesman, that he adulterates the article in which he deals; of one who took children to board, that he starved a child entrusted to his care.[815] And actionable to charge the agent of a stage company, that he (plaintiff) and B., his sub-agent, had altered waybills and books to screen the plaintiff (innuendo charging forgery), and that plaintiff and B. were together to cheat the company, and they would cheat them out of more than the company can make.[816] Actionable to charge by writing a steamboat agent with being an impertinent person and withholding newspapers intrusted to him for the defendants.[817] And it was held

---

[810] *Thomas* v. *Jackson*, 3 Bing. 104; 10 Moore, 425; and to charge a merchant with being a swindler is actionable. (*Herr* v. *Bamburg*, 10 How. Pra. R. 128.)

[811] *Terry* v. *Hooper*, Raym. 87; Lev. 115.

[812] Vin. Abr. Act. for Words, U. a. 5, and note 464, *ante*.

[813] *Griffiths* v. *Lewis*, 15 Law Jour. 249, Q. B.; and see *Prior* v. *Wilson*, 1 C. B. N. S. 95. The way in which Messrs. P. (the plaintiffs) do things at Guilford—inserting the wedge—innuendo inserting a wedge to falsify the weight.

[814] Vin. Abr. Act. for Words, I. a. 9, and several cases there referred to.

[815] Vin. Abr. Act. for Words, U. a. 27, 30, 28, 81, 29; Freem. 25. Charging a brewer with filthy and disgusting practices in preparing his malt, is actionable. (*White* v. *Delavan*, 17 Wend. 49; *Ryckman* v. *Delavan*, 25 Wend. 186.) See *Wood* v. *Brown*, 1 Marsh. 522; 6 Taunt. 169. In that case, a declaration which alleged that defendant published of plaintiff, a brewer, that his beer was of a bad quality and deficient in measure, was held bad on general demurrer.

[816] *Gay* v. *Homer*, 13 Pick. 535.

[817] *Keemle* v. *Sass*, 12 Mis. 499. The language being published in writing was actionable as concerning the plaintiff as an individual merely.

actionable to publish orally of a land surveyor, who sur-
veyed by mathematics, as distinguished from one who measured
with a pole, He is a cozening and shifting and a cheating knave;
and it was said that the same words of a shoemaker, a butcher,
or a baker would not be actionable, because the goodness or
deceit of their wares may be discerned by the eye, but deceit
in land measuring could be discovered only by persons skilled
in the art;[816] but not actionable to say of a workman, He has
received forty days' wages for work that might have been done
in ten days, and is a rogue for his pains;[819] nor to say of a
smith, Thou art a cozening rogue, and in one tire of wheels
which thou didst send to J. S. thou didst cozen him of a noble;
for the words import he cozened in the price only, and not in
the ill making of the wheels. And for saying of men in trade
who sell things that they cozen in the price, is no disgrace, for
every trader cozens in the price when he sells for more than the
thing is worth.[820] Actionable to publish orally of a merchant's
clerk, That he (plaintiff) had become such a notorious liar that
he (defendant) could place no confidence in him; that he had
strong reason to doubt his honesty, and had written S. to employ an officer to watch him.[821] And the following words
spoken of the plaintiff as clerk of the firm of defendant and his
partner, " Your man (plaintiff) is plotting to blow me (defendant) and the concern (said firm) up," were held actionable.[822] So
it has been held actionable to publish orally of an attorney, He
is a forging rogue,[823] a cheat,[824] a damned rascal;[825] he will play

---

[816] *Blunden* v. *Eustace*, Cro. Jac. 504; *London* v. *Eastgate*, 2 Rolle R. 72.

[819] *Lancaster* v. *French*, 2 Stra. 797.

[820] Vin. Abr. Act. for Words, S. *a.* 24. Thou didst cozen a woman of her goods,
held not actionable. (*Enquæt* v. *Browne.* Cro. Eliz. 99.) And held not actionable to say of an innkeeper, He is a caterpillar and lives by *robbing* his guests.
Robbing not construed feloniously. Vin. Abr. Act. for Words, U. *a.* 84.

[821] *Fowles* v. *Bowen*, 30 N. Y. 20; and see *Brown* v. *Orvis*, 6 How. Pra. R. 378.
Where the words affect one as merchant's clerk, special damage need not be alleged. *Butler* v. *Howes*, 7 Cal. 87.

[822] *Ware* v. *Clowney*, 24 Ala. 707.

[823] Anon., 1 Comyn R. 262.

[824] *Rush* v. *Cavanaugh*, 2 Barr. 187.

[825] *Brown* v. *Minns*, 2 Rep. Con. Ct. 235.

on both sides or he deals on both sides,[826] a bribing knave, and has taken twenty pounds of you to cozen me;[827] he is not a man of integrity, and is not to be trusted; he will take a fee on both sides ;[828] he is a cheater, I will have him barred of his practice;[829] he deserves to be struck off the roll;[830] he is a false knave, a cozening knave, and has gotten all that he has by cozenage; he has cozened all those that have dealt with him; he arresteth without taking out writs; he is a knave in his practice;[831] he offered himself as a witness to divulge the secrets of his clients;[832] he is a rogue for taking your money, and has done nothing for it; he has not entered an appearance for you; he is no attorney at law, he don't care to appear before a judge; what signifies going to him, he is only an attorney's clerk and a rogue, he is no attorney.[833] Is M. your attorney? * * He will overthrow your cause.[834] I marvel you will employ such a knave as Nicholls, you will have but disgrace by it; he is a proclaimed knave;[835] he is the falsest knave in England;[836] he is a base rogue, and maintains his family by his knavery;[837] he is an extortioner, and cozened A. in a bill of costs;[838] he keepeth many markets and stirreth up men to suits, and promises if he do not recover in their cause he will take no charges, and he once promised me that if he did not recover in a cause he would take no charges of me, yet

---

[826] *Brown* v. *Hook*, Browl. 5; Vin. Abr. Act. for Words, S. a. 2. 4; *Shire* v. *King*, Yelv. 32; S. C. *King* v. *Shore*, Cro. Eliz. 914.

[827] *Yardley* v. *Ellis*, Hobart, 8, 9; 1 Rolle R. 53.

[828] *Chipman* v. *Cook*, 2 Tyler, 456.

[829] *Taylor* v. *Starkey*, Cro. Car. 192.

[830] Dictum, *Phillips* v. *Jansen*, 2 Esp. 624.

[831] *Jenkins* v. *Smith*, Cro. Jac. 586; *Bell* v. *Thatcher*, Freeman, 277.

[832] *Riggs* v. *Denniston*, 3 Johns. Cas. 198.

[833] *Hardwick* v. *Chandler*, 2 Str. 1138.

[834] *Martyn* v. *Burlings*, Cro. Eliz. 589; Golds. 128.

[835] *Webb* v. *Nicholls*, Cro. Car. 459.

[836] Anon., Mo. 61; Dal. 63.

[837] *Shaw* v. *Wakeman*, Vin. Abr. Act. for Words, S. a. 2.

[838] *Stanley* v. *Boswel*, Cro. Eliz. 608.

he afterwards took charges of me;[839] he deserves to have his ears nailed to the pillory.[840] Thou art a paltry fellow; thy credit is fallen, for thou dealest on both sides and dost deceive many that trust thee.[841] He suppressed a will;[842] he is a cozener, and hath cozened me of twenty shillings.[843] He is a cozener, and cozened his clients, and for that cause was discharged the court.[844] He is a base, cheating, cozening knave, and hath cheated me as never any man was cheated.[845] He took corruptly five marks of B. T., being against his own client, for putting off an assize against him.[846] Thou art a common barretor, a Judas, a promoter.[847] He sets people together by the ears, and we shall have him indicted for a common barretor.[848] You are a knave; you were attorney for my mother against my husband, and set her on to sue him, and made him spend £1,000, and such knaves as you are have made my husband spend almost all his estate.[849] And actionable to say of a counsellor, He will deceive you; he revealed the secrets of my cause.[850] It is actionable to publish in writing of an attorney employed to defend a prisoner, that on the trial he sent important witnesses away without the knowledge of his client or of counsel;[851] or that he has been reprimanded for sharp practice.[852]

[839] *Smith* v. *Andrews*, Sty. 183.
[840] *Jenkinson* v. *Wray*, Mo. 41.
[841] *Shire* v. *King*, Yelv. 32; S. C., *King* v. *Shore*, Cro. Eliz. 914.
[842] *Godfrey* v. *Owen*, Palm. 21.
[843] *Litman* v. *West*, Het. 123.
[844] *Mead* v. *Perkins*, Cro. Car. 261.
[845] *Jeffryes* v. *Payhem*, Cro. Car. 510.
[846] *Smaylcs* v. *Smith*, Browl. 1.
[847] *Taylor* v. *Starkey*, Cro. Car. 192.
[848] *Annison* v. *Blofield*, Carth. 848.
[849] *Hilton* v. *Playters*, All. 18.
[850] *Snag* v. *Grey*, Cro. Eliz. 358.
[851] *Sanford* v. *Bennett*, 24 N. Y. 20.
[852] *Boydell* v. *Jones*, 4 M. & W. 446. Held not actionable to say of an attorney, he is a paltry lawyer (*Rich* v. *Holt*, Cro. Jac. 267); but actionable to say, He is a pettyfogging, blood-sucking attorney. (*Armstrong* v. *Jordan*, Carlisle Assizes, 1826.)

§ 193. Language of one in a business or profession which imputes to him ignorance generally in his business or profession, or such ignorance as unfits him for its proper exercise, is actionable;[**] as to say of a physician or an apothecary, "It is a world of blood he has to answer for in this town through his ignorance; he did kill a woman and two children. He was the death of J. P.; he killed his patient with physic;[**] or, Dr. A. killed my children; he gave them teaspoon doses of calomel, and it killed them. . . . They died right off the same day;[**] or, He has killed the child by giving it too much calomel;[**] or, He has killed six children in one year;[**] or, He is a drunken fool and an ass, he never was a scholar;[**] or, I wonder you had him to attend you; do you know him? He is not an apothecary; he has not passed any examination; he is a bad character, none of the medical men here will meet him; several have died that he has attended, and there have been inquests held upon them;[**] or, He killed my child, it was the saline injection that did it;[**] or, He is an empirick and a mountebank;[**] or a quack;[**] or, He is a quack, and if he shows you a diploma it is a forgery;[**] or, His treatment of a patient was rascally;[**] and so it has been held actionable to say of a mid-

---

[**] *Jones* v. *Powell*, 1 Mod. 272; *Procd* v. *Johnes*, Cro. Car. 382; *Camp* v. *Martin*, 23 Conn. 86; *Day* v. *Buller*, 3 Wils. 59; *Garr* v. *Selden*, 6 Barb. 416.

[**] *Tutty* v. *Alewin*, 11 Mod. 221, and see note 448 *ante.*

[**] *Secor* v. *Harris*, 18 Barb. 425.

[**] *Johnson* v. *Robertson*, 8 Porter, 486; see dictum *March* v. *Davison*, 8 Paige, 580. To charge a physician with having killed a patient with physic, held not actionable. (*Poe* v. *Mendford*, Cro. Eliz. 620.)

[**] *Carroll* v. *White*, 33 Barb. 615.

[**] *Cawdry* v. *Telley*, Godb. 441.

[**] *Southee* v. *Denny*, 1 Ex. 196; 17 Law Jour. R. 151, Ex. Alleging that a physician is not entitled to practice as not being duly licensed, may be actionable. See *Collins* v. *Carnegie*, 3 Nev. & M. 703; 1 Ad. & El. 695.

[**] The words impute manslaughter. (*Edsall* v. *Russell*, 4 M. & G. 1090.)

[**] Vin. Abr. Act. for Words, S. *a.* 12. Publishing in writing of a barrister that he was a quack lawyer and a mountebank and an imposter, is actionable. (*Wakley* v. *Healey*, 7 C. B. 591.)

[**] *Pickford* v. *Gutch*, Dorchester Assizes, 1787.

[**] *Moises* v. *Thornton*, 8 Term. R. 303.

[**] *Camp* v. *Martin*, 23 Conn. 86.

wife, Many have perished for want of her skill [*i. e.* for her want of skill].[865] She is an ignorant woman, and of small practice, and very unfortunate in her way; there are few she goes to but lie desperately ill, or die under her hands.[866] She is no midwife but a nurse, and if I had not pulled her from Mrs. J. S. she had killed her and her child.[867] She lays no woman, but Dr. Chamberlayn or his lady does her work.[868] And it has been held actionable to say of a schoolmaster, Put not your son to him, for he will come away as very a dunce as he went.[869] He has no knowledge in grammar or in the Latin tongue, nor knows how to educate his scholars in the Latin tongue, with an allegation of loss of scholars.[870] So it has been held actionable to say of an attorney, He hath no more law than Mr. C.'s bull, or than a goose;[871] he cannot *read* a declaration;[872] what, does he pretend to be a lawyer? he is no more a lawyer than the devil;[873] or of a barrister, He is a dunce, and will get little by law, he was never but accounted a dunce;[874] or of a shoemaker, that he is a cobbler;[875] or of a watchmaker, that he knows not how to make a good watch.[876]

§ 194. It is not actionable to charge one in a business or profession with want of skill or ignorance in a particular trans-

[865] Flower's Case, Cro. Car. 211.
[866] *Wharton* v. *Brook*, Vent. 21; *Wharton* v. *Clover*, 2 Keb. 489.
[867] *Whitehead* v. *Fownes*, Freem. 277.
[868] *Gyles* v. *Bishop*, Freem. 278.
[869] Het. 71.
[870] *London* v. *Eastgate*, 2 Rolle R. 72.
[871] *Baker* v. *Morfue*, Sid. 327.
[872] *Powell* v. *Jones*, 2 Keb. 710; 1 Mod. 272. It implies ignorance, not a defect of sight.
[873] *Day* v. *Buller*, 3 Wils. 59.
[874] *Proed* v. *Johnes*, Cro. Car. 382.
[875] Vin. Abr. Act. for Words, U. *a*; 16.
[876] *Redman* v. *Pyne*, 1 Mod. 19; but to say of a watchmaker, he is a bungler, and knows not how to make a good piece of work, would be actionable. (*Id.*) Where A., the author of a work, sold the copyright to the defendant, who afterwards published a new edition as edited by A., containing mistakes and errors, held, if this was calculated to injure A.'s reputation as an author, he might maintain an action. (*Archbold* v. *Sweet*, 5 C. & P. 219; 1 M. & Rob. 162.)

action.[877] Thus it was held not to be actionable to say of an attorney in a particular suit, "He knows nothing about the suit; he will lead you on until he has undone you."[878] It is said, however, that it is actionable to charge ignorance or unskilfulness if it amounts to gross ignorance or unskilfulness.[879] This seems only another mode of imputing such ignorance as unfits the person for the proper exercise of his art, or with misconduct therein.

§ 195. It is actionable to publish orally of a minister of the gospel : that he preaches lies in the pulpit;[880] he made a seditious sermon,[881] he hath two wives,[882] he is a drunkard,[883] or incontinent,[884] or guilty of incest,[885] or he has a bastard,[886] or he is a perjured priest.[887] The following words were held not actionable, spoken of one who was a minister at the time of the

---

[877] *Garr* v. *Selden*, 6 Barb. 416 ; *Camp* v. *Martin*, 23 Conn. 86 ; *Southee* v. *Denny*, 1 Ex. 196.

[878] *Foot* v. *Brown*, 8 Johns. 64.

[879] *Secor* v. *Harris*, 18 Barb. 425, and *Sumner* v. *Utley*, 7 Conn. 257 ; *Johnson* v. *Robertson*, 8 Port. 486 ; *Camp* v. *Martin*, 23 Conn. 86.

[880] *Drake* v. *Drake*, Sty. 363; and see *Cranden* v. *Walden*, 3 Lev. 17; Bishop of Norwich Case, Cro. Eliz. 1; *Dod* v. *Robinson*, Aleyn, 63, and *Gallwey* v. *Marshall*, 9 Ex. 294.

[881] *Phillips* v. *Badly*, 4 Rep. 19 a.

[882] *Nicholson* v. *Lyne*, Cro. Eliz. 94.

[883] *McMillan* v. *Birch*, 1 Binn. 178; *Chaddock* v. *Briggs*, 13 Mass. 248; contra see *Buck* v. *Hersey*, 31 Maine (1 Red.) 558; *O'Hanlon* v. *Myers*, 10 Rich. Law (So. Car.) 128. In *Dod* v. *Robinson*, Aleyn, 63, the words were: You are a drunkard, a whoremaster, a common swearer and a common liar, and you have preached false doctrine, and deserve to be degraded. These words were held actionable.

[884] *Demarest* v. *Haring*, 6 Cow. 76. It seems that in England to render such a charge actionable, the person affected must be beneficed, or in the actual receipt of professional emolument as a preacher, lecturer, or the like. (*Gallwey* v. *Marshall*, 9 Ex. 294 ; 24 Eng. Law & Eq. R. 463 ; and see note 577 *ante*.)

[885] Spoken of a *paid* preacher or lay exhorter of the Methodist Church. (*Starr* v. *Gardner*, 6 Up. Can. Q. B. Rep. O. S. 512.)

[886] Special damage being alleged. (*Payne* v. *Beamnorris*, Lev. 248.) He is a lewd adulterer, and hath two children by the wife of O. S., spoken of a clergyman, held not actionable. (*Parret* v. *Carpenter*, Noy, 64, and *ante*, note 772.) And so of the words. You are an old rogue, rascal, and contemptible fellow (*Musgrove* v. *Borey*, Stra. 946.)

[887] *Hogg* v. *Vaughan*, Sty. 6.

publication, and who had been a draper in partnership with
H. P., and who had a controversy with H. P. as to the partnership accounts : " I do not go by reports, I go by a knowledge of
facts. Mr. H. (the plaintiff) is a rogue, and I can prove him to be
so by the books at S. He pretends to say he has been as good as
a father to H. P., when in fact he has been robbing him. He has
cheated P. of £2,000. I will so expose him that he will not be
able to hold up his head in T. pulpit. * * * I wonder how any
respectable person can countenance such a man by their presence. I have been advising some persons to go to the Wesleyan
chapel as they would hear plain honest men."[698] So the following words spoken of a clergyman were held not actionable :
" Dr. P. (plaintiff) placed before me a bill, I signed it ; I do
not know for what amount it was, for I was completely pigeoned
by Dr. P." (plaintiff).[699] In the same case the following words
spoken of a clergyman, held to touch him in his professional
character, and to be actionable: " The very day I came into
residence, Dr. P. (plaintiff) sent for me ; I went and dined
with him, and the wine must have been drugged, for I took but
two glasses and was quite stupefied. While in this condition
Dr. P. put a bill into my hands, and requested me to sign it,
saying, C. just put your name to this ; I wish to have it as a
security for the payment of £130 per annum for reading for
you. I answered, Give me a pen and I will sign it. Immediately I had signed it, Dr. P. snatched it up and said, This will
be quite safe. The bill I think was drawn for £2,500, but having been stupefied with the wine I do not rightly remember.
You cannot suppose I can meet a man who so cheated me at my
first coming ? " It is actionable to charge a Protestant arch-
bishop with having sought by means of a bribe to induce a

---

[698] *Hopwood* v. *Thorn*, 8 C. P. 293.

[699] *Pemberton* v. *Colls*, 1011 ; 16 Law Jour. 403, Q. B. To charge a bishop with
being a wicked man (*Thomas* v. *Hughes*, 2 Mod. 159), or a bankrupt, said to be
actionable (Holt on Libel, 233, note); and held actionable to publish in writing
that the plaintiff, a clergyman, had caused a misunderstanding in his congregation by personal invectives from the pulpit against a young lady of spotless reputation. (*Edwards* v. *Bell*, 8 Moore, 467.)

Romish priest to abandon his religious creed.[800] It was held not actionable to charge a Roman Catholic priest with having imposed certain penance, there being nothing to show that enjoining such penance affected his character as such priest.[801]

§ 196. As regards language concerning one in an office, the same general principles apply as to language concerning one in a business or profession. Language concerning one in office which imputes to him a want of integrity or misfeasance in his office, or a want of capacity generally to fulfil the duties of his office, or which is calculated to diminish public confidence in him,[802] or charges him with a breach of some public trust.[803] But as in the case of one in trade, the language to be actionable must touch him in his office.[804] To charge a judge with erring in judgment or disregarding public sentiment, or with any impropriety which would not furnish a cause of impeachment, is not actionable *per se ;* but to charge that he had "abandoned the common principles of truth," or "lacked capacity as a judge," or made the office of clerk of his court a subject of private negotiation, is actionable *per se.*[805] So it is actionable *per se* to charge that a judge improperly put his official signature to the jurat of a paper in the form of an affidavit,[806] or procured one to take a false oath,[807] or took a bribe,[808] or acted unjustly in his office,[809] or to charge that he is a lewd

---

[800] *Tuam* v. *Robeson,* 5 Bing. 17 ; 2 M. & P. 32.

[801] *Hearne* v. *Stowell,* 12 Adol. & El. 719.

[802] *Lansing* v. *Carpenter,* 9 Wis. 540.

[803] *Kinney* v. *Nash,* 8 Conn. 177, and authorities there referred to.

[804] *McGuire* v. *Blair,* 2 Law Reporter, 443, and *ante,* § 190. So that charging a justice with misfeasance in trying a cause, not within his jurisdiction, was held not actionable as not affecting him as justice. (*Oram* v. *Franklin,* 5 Blackf. 42 ; see, however, *Carter* v. *Andrews,* 16 Pick. 1 ; *Stone* v. *Clark,* 21 *id.* 51.)

[805] *Robbins* v. *Treadway,* 2 J. J. Marsh. 540.

[806] *Dollaway* v. *Turrill,* 26 Wend. 383 ; 17 *id.* 426.

[807] *Chetwind* v. *Mecston,* Cro. Jac. 308.

[808] *Colton's Case,* Mo. 695. In *Lindsey* v. *Smith,* 7 Johns. 360, an action was sustained for the words, "Lindsey had been feed by Abner Wood, and I could do nothing when the magistrate was in that way against me."

[809] I have often been with him for justice, but could never get any at his hands but injustice. *Isham* v. *York,* Cro. Car. 14. Actionable to say of a judge, his sentence was corruptly given. See *Chaddock* v. *Briggs,* 13 Mass. 253 ; *Chipman* v. *Cook,* 2 Tyler, 456.

or false,[900] or corrupt,[901] or a partial,[902] or half eared, and will
hear but one side, or that he cannot hear of one ear,[903] or that
he perverted justice,[904] or made use of his office to worry one
out of his estate,[905] or, He is forsworn and not fit to sit upon a
bench,[906] or, He did seek my life and offered ten shillings to the
under-sheriff to empanel a jury that might find me guilty.[907]
But held not actionable to publish orally of a justice, He is a
blood-sucker and seeketh after blood, if a man will give him a
couple of capons he will take them;[908] or, You robbed the poor
and are worse than a highwayman.[909] It is not actionable to
say of a mayor, He is a rogue and rascal;[910] or of an alderman,
When he puts on his gown Satan enters it;[911] or of an under-
sheriff, Thou didst serve an execution and keep in thy hands
the money collected.[912] But it is actionable to charge a sheriff
with malpractice in his office;[913] or to say of a constable, He is
not worthy of his office, for he and his company the last time

---

[900] *Wright v. Moorhouse*, Cro. Eliz. 358.

[901] *Cæsar v. Curseny*, Cro. Eliz. 305. You are a rascal, a villain, and a liar,
spoken of a magistrate in the execution of his office, the words import a charge
of corruption. (*Aston v. Blagrave*, 1 Strange, 617; 2 L'd Raym. 1369.) And so
of the term rogue. *Kent v. Pocock*, 2 Str. 1108.

[902] *Kemp v. Housgoe*, Cro. Jac. 90.

[903] *Masham v. Bridges*, Cro. Car. 223, and *Alleston v. Moor*, Het. 167.

[904] *Delaware v. Pawlet*, Mo. 409.

[905] *Newton v. Stubbs*, 3 Mod. 71.

[906] *Carn v. Osgood*, 1 Levinz, 280; S. C., *Kerle v. Osgood*, 1 Vent. 50; and see
Pepper v. Gay, 2 Lutw. 1288; *Stutley v. Bulhead*, 4 Rep. 16 a, 19 a; *Lassels v.
Lassels*, Mo. 401; *Hollis v. Briscow*, Cro. Jac. 58; *Burton v. Tokin*, Cro. Jac. 143;
Beamond v. Hastings, Cro. Jac. 240.

[907] *Bleverhasset v. Baspoole*, Cro. Eliz. 313.

[908] *Hilliard v. Constable*, Mo. 418. Held actionable to publish in writing of a
justice that he had been chairman of a finance committee, and had audited
accounts, containing items nominally to furnish lodgings for the judges, but in
reality for the accommodation of the magistrates; innuendo that plaintiff had
conducted himself corruptly in his office of justice. (*Adams v. Miredew*, 3 Y. & J.
219, overruling S. C., 2 Y. & J. 417.)

[909] *Palmer v. Edwards*, Rep. of Cas. of Prac. in C. B. 160.

[910] *Reg v. Lang'ey*, 6 Mod. 125; 2 Salk. 697.

[911] 2 Starkie on Slander, 314.

[912] *Oceeo v. Copshill*, Cro. Eliz. 854.

[913] *Dole v. Van Rensselaer*, 1 Johns. Cas. 330.

he was constable stole five of my swine and eat them;[914] or to publish in writing of a police officer that he had been guilty of blackmailing and had been dismissed for that cause.[915] But held not actionable to publish orally of a police officer, I saw a letter respecting an officer of the *L.* police, who had been guilty of conduct unfit for publication, there being no allegation of special damage and the charge not being connected with his official character.[916] It is actionable to publish orally of the director of a public company, that he had sold the property of the company and pocketed the money;[917] or of a town clerk acting as moderator of a town meeting, that he had fraudulently destroyed a vote;[918] or of an administrator, that he had been guilty of fraud in the appraisement of the estate of the decedent;[919] or of a juror, that he agreed with another juror to determine the amount of damages to be given in a certain cause in which he acted as juror, by the result of a game of draughts.[920] A churchwarden holds a temporal office, and to charge him with cheating the parish, is actionable.[921] It is actionable to publish in writing of a court commissioner, that he will act in his judicial office according to the views of the persons "whose tool and toady he is, and that the past would warrant the depriving him of his office;"[922] of an overseer, that when out of office he advocated low rates, and that he (defendant) would

[914] *Taylor* v. *Howe,* Cro. Eliz. 861. Doubtful if actionable to say of a constable, Thou art a cozening knave, and has cozened the parish in rates to £30. (*Thomas' Case,* Het. 36.)
[915] *Edsall* v. *Brooks,* 17 Abb. Pra. R. 221 ; 2 Robertson, 29.
[916] *James* v. *Brook,* 9 Q. B. 7; 16 Law Jour. 17 Q. B. ; 10 Jur. 541.
[917] *Johnson* v. *Shields,* 1 Dutcher, 116.
[918] *Dodds* v. *Henry,* 9 Mas. 262.
[919] *Beck* v. *Stitzel,* 21 Penn. St. R. (9 Harris), 522.
[920] *Commonwealth* v. *Wright,* 1 Cush. 46. The charge was in writing. Held actionable to publish orally of a juryman, Thou art a common juryman, and hast been the overthrow of one hundred men by thy false means. Vin. Abr. Act for Words, F. *a.* 23.
[921] *Townsend* v. *Barker,* Sty. 394; *Woodruff* v. *Wooley,* Curt. 1; *Strode* v. *Holmes* Sty. 338; and see *Hutton* v. *Beck,* Cro. Jac. 339; *Hopton* v. *Baker,* 2 Bulst. 218; *Willis* v. *Shepherd,* Cro. Jac. 419.
[922] *Lansing* v. *Carpenter,* 9 Wis. 540.

not trust him (plaintiff) with £5 of his private property;[923] or of an overseer, that he had been guilty of illiberal and illegal practices towards paupers, in compelling them to procure goods from a particular person, and threatening him with the penalties of the act against such practices;[924] or of a postmaster, who resided in the house used as the post-office, that the house in which the post-office is kept is of such a low character that a decent lady dare not enter.[925] And actionable to publish orally of a postmaster that he opened a letter, took money out of it, and appropriated it to his own use, and kept and embezzled letters;[926] or that he would rob the mail for five hundred dollars— yes, he would rob the mail for five dollars.[927] It is not actionable to charge a member of Parliament with want of sincerity;[928] or a member of the legislature, in reference to the future discharge of his functions, with being a corrupt old tory.[929] It is actionable to publish in writing of a member of Congress, " He is a fawning sycophant, a misrepresentative in Congress, and a grovelling office-seeker; he has abandoned his post in Congress in pursuit of an office;"[930] or of a lieutenant-governor, that he was in a beastly state of intoxication while in the discharge of his duty in the senate, and was an object of loathing and disgust;[931] or a commissioner of bankrupts, with being a

---

[923] The jury found that the words imputed dishonesty. *Cheese* v. *Scales*, 10 M. & W. 448.

[924] *Woodward* v. *Downing*, 2 M. & Ry. 74.

[925] *Johnson* v. *Stebbins*, 5 Ind. (Porter), 364.

[926] *Hays* v. *Allen*, 3 Blackf. 408. See contra, *M'Cuen* v. *Ladlum*, 2 Harr. 12, and notes 663, 708 *ante*, and *Taylor* v. *Kneeland*, 1 Doug. 67.

[927] *Craig* v. *Brown*, 5 Blackf. 44.

[928] *Onslow* v. *Horne*, 2 W. Black. 750; 3 Wils. 177. The words complained of were: " As to instructing our members to obtain redress, I am totally against that plan; for as to instructing Mr. Onslow (the plaintiff), we might as well instruct the winds, and should he (the plaintiff) ever promise his assistance, I should not expect him to give it us." One of the reasons for holding the words not actionable was, they did not charge the plaintiff with any breach of his duty, his oath, or any crime or misdemeanor whereby he had suffered any temporal loss, in future office, or in any way whatever.

[929] *Hogg* v. *Dorrah*, 2 Port. 212.

[930] *Thomas* v. *Croswell*, 7 Johns. 264.

[931] *Root* v. *King*, 7 Cow. 613; 4 Wend. 113.

misanthropist, and violent partisan, stripping unfortunate debtors of every cent, and then depriving them of the benefit of the act.[892]

§ 197. We have already directed attention to the distinction between patently and latently wrongful acts, and to the rule of law that the necessary and natural and proximate consequences of an act are those alone for which the actor is responsible [§ 61]; and we have pointed out the difference between language being actionable *per se* and actionable only by reason of special damage [§ 146]. So far, this chapter has been solely devoted to language actionable *per se;* we have now to consider what language *concerning a person* is actionable, because and only because its publication has occasioned *special damage.* " Undoubtedly, all words are actionable if a special damage follows."[893] " Any words are actionable by which the party has a special damage."[894] " To make words actionable, they must be such that special damage may be the fair and natural result of them."[895] "There must be some limit to liability for words not actionable *per se,* both as to the words and the kind of damages, and a clear and wise one has been fixed by law."[896] The limitation is, that special damage must ensue. But what is meant by 'special damage? Special damage is a term ambiguously employed; properly, it connotes the natural and proximate but not necessary consequences of a wrongful act;[897] but it is frequently used to indicate any or all

---

[892] *Riggs* v. *Denniston,* 3 Johns. Cas. 198.

[893] Heath, J., *Moore* v. *Meagher,* 1 Taunt. 39; and see among other cases, *Wilby* v. *Elston,* 13 Jur. 706; 8 C. B. 142; 7 Dowl. & L. 143; *Barnes* v. *Trundy,* 31 Maine (1 Red.), 321; *McCuen* v. *Ludlam,* 2 Harr. 12; *Bentley* v. *Reynolds,* 1 McMullan, 16.

[894] Comyn's Dig., Act. for Defam. D, 30.

[895] Taunton, J., *Kelly* v. *Partington,* 3 Nev. & M. 116; 5 B. & Adol. 645.

[896] Strong, J., *Terwilliger* v. *Wands,* 17 N. Y. 61.

[897] Such damages as are the *natural,* although not the necessary result of the injury, are termed special damages. (*Vanderslice* v. *Newton,* 4 N. Y. 132.) The special damage must be the immediate, not the remote consequence of the publication. (*Beach* v. *Ranney,* 2 Hill, 309; *Sewell* v. *Catlin,* 3 Wend. 291.) " The damage must be the natural and proximate consequence of the wrongful act com-

15

loss which, not being a necessary consequence, is the subject of other proof than the mere commission of the act · complained of, and without regard to whether such loss is or is not a natural or natural and proximate consequence of such act. The term is employed in the latter sense when it is said that language which occasions *special damage* is not actionable unless it be defamatory,[258] which is equivalent to saying, that language which as a natural and proximate consequence occasions loss, is not actionable unless it is injurious [defamatory]. If the language is not injurious [defamatory] in its nature, it cannot as a *natural* consequence occasion loss, and it may well be that none other than language defamatory in its nature [disparaging] can as a natural and proximate consequence occasion loss. It may be correct to say that " to make the words wrongful they must in their nature be defamatory,"[259] provided the rule thus expressed be understood as being subordinate to and implied in the more comprehensive rule, that to render actionable that language which is not actionable *per se*, the language must occasion special damage, in the proper sense of that term.[260] The real question must always be, was the damage complained of a natural and proximate consequence of the publication.[261] For " it is a rule equally consistent with good sense, good logic, and good law, that a person who would recover damages for an

---

plained of." (2 Smith's Lead. Cas. 534, 6th ed.) " I have always understood that the special damage must be the natural result of the thing done." (Patteson, J., *Kelly* v. *Partington*, 5 B. & Adol. 546;) and see *Haddou* v. *Lott*, 15 C. B. 411; 24 Law Jour. Rep. N. S. 49 C. P.; 29 Eng. Law and Eq. R. 215.

[259] "The special damage will not help you if the words are not defamatory." (Blackburn, J., *Young* v. *McCrae*, 3 Best & S. 264 ; 7 Law Times, N. S. 354.)

[260] Patteson, J., *Kelly* v. *Partington*, 5 B. & Adol. 645.

[261] " I cannot agree that words laudatory of a person's conduct would be the subject of an action if they were followed by *special damage*. They must be defamatory or injurious in their nature." (Littledale, J., *Kelly* v. *Partington*, 3 Nev. & M. 117; 5 B. & Adol. 645.) "The words must be defamatory in their nature ; and must in fact disparage the character, and this disparagement must be evidenced by some positive loss arising therefrom directly and legitimately as a fair and natural result." (Strong, J., *Terwilliger* v. *Wands*, 17 N. Y. 61); and see *Hallock* v. *Miller*, 2 Barb. 633.

[261] Denman, Ch. J., *Knight* v. *Gibbs*, 3 Nev. & M. 467; 1 Adol. & El. 48.

injury occasioned by the conduct of another, must show as an
essential part of his case, the relation of cause and effect between the conduct complained of and the injury sustained." [942]

§ 198. What is special damage? Special damage consists [943]
in the loss of marriage, loss of consortium of husband and
wife, [944] loss of emoluments, profits, customers, employment or
gratuitous hospitality, [945] or by the being subjected to any other
inconvenience or annoyance occasioning or involving an actual
or constructive pecuniary loss, [946] as where the plaintiff, an unmarried woman, in consequence of a charge of incontinence,
was refused civil treatment at a hotel or tavern. [947] A charge
of incontinence against an unmarried woman, whereby she
loses her marriage, is actionable, as to say of the plaintiff,

[942] *Olmstead* v. *Brown*, 12 Barb. 662.

[943] " As to what constitutes special damage, Starkie mentions the loss of marriage, loss of hospitable gratuitous entertainment, preventing a servant or bailiff
from getting a place, the loss of customers by a tradesman, and says that in general whenever a person is prevented by the slander from receiving that which
would otherwise be conferred upon him, though gratuitously, it is sufficient."
Terwilliger v. *Wands*, 17 N. Y. 60; citing Starkie on Slandor, 195, 202; Cooke
on Defam. 22, 24. Plaintiffs being refused employment (*Strong* v. *Forman*, 2
Car. & P. 592), or insurance upon a ship of which he was master (*Shipman* v.
Burrows, 1 Hall, 399), is special damage.

[944] *Lynch* v. *Knight*, 5 Law Times, N. S. 291: *Parkins* v. *Scott*, 6 *id.* 394.

[945] *Moore* v. *Meagher*, 1 Taunt. 39; *Williams* v. *Hill*, 19 Wend. 305.

[946] " All the cases proceed upon the assumption that the plaintiff has sustained
some pecuniary loss in consequence of the slander. It is not sufficient that she
has fallen into disgrace, contempt, and infamy, and lost her credit, reputation,
and peace of mind, or the society or good opinion of her neighbors, unless she
has been injured in her estate or property." *Woodbury* v. *Thompson*, 3 N.
Hamp. 194; and see *ante*, notes 43, 48; *Kelly* v. *Partington*, 3 Nev. & M. 116; 5
B. & Adol. 645; *Keenholts* v. *Decker*, 8 Denio, 346; *Foulger* v. *Newcomb*, 2 Law
Rep. 380, Ex. " One essential element of a good cause of action for defamation
is damage," but in *Terwilliger* v. *Wands*, 17 N. Y. 61, and *Wilson* v. *Goit*, *id.* 442,
the whole tenor of the opinions imply that loss of reputation is the gist of the
action, and in the first named case it is said, " It is injuries affecting the reputation only, which are the subject of the action." "The special damage must flow
from impaired reputation." This, however, may mean only that the language
must be defamatory. See *ante*, note 43.

[947] *Olmstead* v. *Miller*, 1 Wend. 510.

Anne Reston hath had a child, and if she has not a child, she
has made away with it;[948] or, You ought not to marry M., the
plaintiff, for before God she is my wife, and therefore if you do,
you will live in adultery, and your children will be bastards.[949]
Loss of a wife is the same to a man as loss of a husband is to
a woman, and therefore, where defendant called the plaintiff a
whoremaster, whereby he lost his marriage, it was held he could
maintain his action;[950] and so saying of one who was a wid-
ower that he had kept his wife basely, and starved her or
denied her necessaries, whereby he lost his marriage, was held
actionable;[951] and calling plaintiff bastard, whereby he lost his
marriage, was held actionable.[952]   As to loss of customers,
where it was said of an innkeeper, I (defendant) saw Cook lie
with Collins' (plaintiff's) wife, whereby plaintiff lost his customers, it was held that an action could be maintained;[953] and
so where it was said of an innkeeper, that a person had died in
his house of the plague, whereby his (plaintiff's) guests left his
house, it was held he might maintain his action.[954]   Words

---

[948] *Reston* v. *Pomfreicht*, Cro. Eliz. 639.

[949] *Shepherd* v. *Wakeman*, Sid. 79; Lev. 87. Saying of a woman, she was a
man, not a woman, with special damage held actionable. (*Pye* v. *Wallis*, cited
Curt. 55.) See *Hermaphrodite.*

[950] *Matthew* v. *Crass*, Cro. Jac. 323; 2 Bulst. 86; and see *Sell* v. *Facy*, 2 Bulst.
276; *Southall* v. *Dawson*, Cro. Car. 269; *contra*, see Witcher's Case, Keb. 119.
In *Taylor* v. *Tally*, Palmer, 385, defendant said of plaintiff that he, plaintiff, had
ravished the wife of H.; and plaintiff alleging that thereby he lost his marriage,
the words were held actionable.

[951] Anon. Mar. 2; *Wicks* v. *Shepherd*, Cro. Car. 155.

[952] *Nelson* v. *Staff*, Cro. Jac. 422.

[953] *Collins* v. *Matthews*, 3 Keb. 242.

[954] Comyn's Dig., Act. for Def. D. 29; as to loss of customers, see *Evans* v.
Harris, 1 Hurl. & Nor. 251; 38 Eng. Law and Eq. R. 347; Vin. Abr. Act. for
Words, U. a. 13; *Barrow* v. *Gibson*, L'd Raym. 831; 1 Str. 560; Bull. N. P. 7;
1 Lev. 140; *Trenton Ins. Co.* v. *Perrine*, 3 Zabr. 402. Action by a butcher for
saying a cow, the carcass of which he had to sell, died of calving, by which he
lost his customers, judgment was given for the plaintiff, but reversed on error,
the alleged loss of customers being too general; but held that had it been laid
the plaintiff *exposed the meat for sale*, and by reason of the words he lost the sale,
the action could have been maintained. *Rice* v. *Pidgeon*, Comb. 161, and *Tassan*
v. *Rogers*, 2 Salk. 693. " A distinction has been made between *particular* damage

imputing incontinence to a dissenting minister, whereby the persons frequenting his chapel refused to permit him to preach, and discontinued giving him certain reward as they usually had, and but for the publication complained of would have done, were held actionable.[555] Where the declaration alleged that plaintiff being the proprietor of certain rooms adapted for a dancing academy, defendant falsely and maliciously published of the building and rooms, and of plaintiff as proprietor thereof, that " the magistrates having refused to renew a music and dancing license to the proprietor, all such entertainments there carried on are illegal, and the proprietor renders himself thereby indictable for keeping a disorderly house, and every person found on the premises will be apprehended and dealt with according to law," by means of which premises plaintiff was prevented from letting said rooms ; held on demurrer that the declaration disclosed a cause of action.[556]

§ 199. It seems that where the person to whom the publication is made is by reason of the charge induced to act upon it •

and *general* damage; thus, in an action for slandering a man in his trade, when the declaration alleges that he thereby lost his trade, he may show a general damage to his trade, though he cannot give evidence of particular instances." (Creswell, J., *Rose* v. *Groves*, 5 M. & G. 618.)

[555] *Hartley* v. *Herring*, 8 Term. R. 130.

[556] *Bignell* v. *Buzzard*, 3 Hurl. & Nor. 217. In *Dibdin* v. *Swan*, 1 Esp. Cas.[?] 28, the plaintiff was the proprietor of a place of amusement called Sans Souci, where he sang certain songs, supposed to be composed by himself; he sued the defendant, the proprietor of a newspaper called the World, for publishing in that paper that such songs were not composed by the plaintiff; that on the first night when plaintiff sang there had been a very thin audience, and that composed of persons admitted by orders [for free admission], and that the applause was only from the persons so admitted. The report does not state the result of the case but merely the charge of Lord Kenyon that the editor of a newspaper may fairly and candidly comment on any place or species of public entertainment, but it must be done fairly and without malice or view to injure the proprietor. That if so done, however severe the censure, the justice of it screens the editor from legal animadversion; but if the comment be unjust, malevolent, or exceeding the bounds of fair opinion, it is actionable. As to comments on theatrical performances, see *Fry* v. *Bennet*, 5 Sand. 54; 3 Bosw. 200; 28 N. Y. 324; *Gregory* v. *Duke of Brunswick*, 6 M. & G. 953.

to the prejudice of the person whom it may concern, it is immaterial whether the person to whom the publication was made believed or disbelieved in the truth of the charge; thus, where a charge was made to a mistress against a female (the plaintiff) in her employ, in consequence of which she dismissed the plaintiff from her employ, on the trial she testified that such dismissal was not because she believed the charge to be true, but because she was afraid she should offend the defendant, her landlord, by retaining plaintiff in her employ; held, that the special damage being the consequence of the charge, the action was maintainable, the court could not speculate upon motives of witnesses.[857]

§ 200. Mere apprehension of loss is not such special damage as will maintain an action; as where defendant said of plaintiff that he had two bastards, and the alleged special damage was that, by reason of the words, a contention arose between plaintiff and his wife, and he was in danger to be divorced.[858] And where the defendant said of plaintiff she is with child by T. S., and the alleged special damage was that in consequence of the words the father of plaintiff *threatened* to turn her out of his house, this was held not to amount to such special damage as would support an action.[859] Where the plaintiff alleged that she was a single woman and chaste, and that her mother meant to give her £150 and her brother £100, and that by reason of the defendant's charging her with incontinence, they did not give her these sums, it was doubted if the action was main-

---

[857] *Knight* v. *Gibbs*, 3 Nev. & M. 467; 1 Adol. & El. 43. I do not know that the belief of the party is at all material. I may not believe a charge, and yet I may not have the courage to keep a person who is suspected by others. I think it better that we should lay it down generally, that if the words are slanderous and are acted upon to the prejudice of the party slandered, an action may be maintained. (*Id.*) To the like effect see *Gillett* v. *Bullivant*, 7 Law Times, 490. *Contra* is a dictum, *Wilson* v. *Goit*, 17 N. Y. 445. An action of slander would plainly be perverted if allowed where the slanderous words were not credited by any individual.

[858] *Randle* v. *Beal*, Cro. Jac. 473; *Salter* v. *Brown*, Cro. Car. 436.

[859] *Barnes* v. *Strudd*, 2 Keb. 451.

tainable, and no judgment was rendered.[960] Again, where the plaintiff alleged that by reason of the publication he had incurred the ill-will of his mother-in-law, who had previously promised him £100, held that no cause of action was shown.[961] Where the injury to the plaintiff is the result in part only of the defendant's act, subject to the qualifications hereafter to be mentioned, it will not give a right of action against the defendant; thus, where the plaintiff was discharged from his employment partly on account of the publication by the defendant and partly for other causes, it was held that the plaintiff could not recover.[962] And where the plaintiff alleged that in consequence of the words he (the plaintiff) refused to marry his betrothed, and so he lost his marriage, it was held the loss of marriage did not under such circumstances constitute special damage.[963] Where the plaintiff alleged that by reason of the language published by the defendant all honest persons refused to marry their daughters to him (the plaintiff), held that the plaintiff did not disclose a cause of action.[964] As the law gives no remedy for outraged feelings or sentiments [§ 56], a sickness induced by mental distress in consequence of the language published, followed by inability to transact business and expense for medical attendance, does not constitute special damage, and for words not actionable *per se* which occasion such results, no action can be maintained.[965] If, after a recovery has been had in an action for slander or libel, special damage occurs, no action can be

[960] *Bracebridge* v. *Watson*, Lilly Ent. 61.
[961] *Harris* v. *Porter*, Curt. 1.
[962] *Vickars* v. *Wilcocks*, 8 East, 1; 2 Stark. Ev. 637.
[963] *Carter* v. *Smith*, Vin. Abr. Act. for Words, D. *a.* 10.
[964] *Norman* v. *Simons*, Vin. Abr. Act. for Words, D. *a.* 12.
[965] *Terwilliger* v. *Wands*, 17 N. Y. 54; *Wilson* v. *Goit*, 17 N. Y. 442; *Alsop* v. *Alsop*, 5 Hurl. & Nor. 534; *Bedell* v. *Powell*, 13 Barb. 183. These decisions overrule *Brandt* v. *Towsley*, 13 Wend. 253; *Fuller* v. *Fenner*, 16 Barb. 333; *Olmstead* v. *Brown*, 12 Barb. 657; *Underhill* v. *Welton*, 32 Verm. (3 Shaw), 40. That plaintiff was shunned by her neighbors and turned out of the moral reform society, was held not to constitute special damage. (*Beach* v. *Ranney*, 2 Hill, 309; and see *ante*, note 946.) Loss of a wife's services from illness occasioned by the publication of language not actionable *per se*, is not special damage, so as to give a right of action to the husband. *Wilson* v. *Goit*, 17 N. Y. 442; and see *Guy* v.

maintained therefor, the first recovery is a bar to any subsequent action.[966]

§ 201. It has been very generally reputed and accepted for law that the illegal act of a third party cannot constitute special damage;[967] in other words, that one illegal [wrongful] act cannot be a natural and proximate consequence of another illegal [wrongful] act. This idea appears very frequently in the reports in the expression that special damage must be the natural *and legal* consequence of the act complained of. The case usually referred to in support of this proposition is one in which the defendant asserted that plaintiff had cut his master's cordage, in consequence of which the plaintiff's master, although under a binding contract to employ him for a term which had not then expired, discharged him, it was held the plaintiff could not recover; that such discharge did not constitute special damage, because it was not a natural and *legal* consequence of the publication; that the defendant was no more answerable for the discharge than if in consequence of the words spoken other persons had assaulted the plaintiff; and that if in such a case plaintiff could recover, for the refusal of a third person to perform his legal contract, he might twice recover for the same cause— once in the action for the slander, and again in an action against the third person for the breach of his contract.[968] It was sufficient to sustain this decision that the discharge was not a *natural* consequence of the publication; the residue of the decision is *obiter*, and is not sustainable either on principle or precedent. Subsequently, in an action for words whereby one who was under a contract to marry the plaintiff broke his contract and refused to marry her, it was urged against the maintenance of the action that the plaintiff had her remedy on the contract to

Gregory, 9 Car. & P. 584; *Dongale* v. *Gardiner*, 4 M. & W. 5; *Beach* v. *Ranney*, 2 Hill, 309.

[966] Bull. N. P. 7, citing *Fittler* v. *Veal*, Cas. K. B. 542; Cooke Defam. 24.

[967] *Bentley* v. *Reynolds*, 1 McMullin, 16.

[968] *Vickars* v. *Wilcocks*, 8 East, 1. This is one of the cases selected by Mr. Smith as a leading case, and appears with an elaborate note in 2 Smith's Leading Cases. This case is commented upon in a note, 1 Starkie on Slander, 207.

marry her, that the breach of the contract was an *illegal* act of
the contracting party, and that the breach of said contract was
not special damage, because not a *legal* consequence of the publication, but the action was sustained.[669] These decisions, although
apparently conflicting, are not so in reality; for obviously an
illegal act, equally with a legal act, *may* be the natural consequence of a publication, and where, as in the case of a promise
to marry, the breach of it, although illegal, is nevertheless a
natural consequence of the publication, in that case the illegal
act constitutes special damage; but where the breach of a contract is not a natural, or, if a natural, is not a proximate consequence of the publication, in such a case, the breach of contract does not constitute special damage, not because such
breach is an illegal act, but because it is not a natural and proximate consequence of the publication.[670] Where the defendant
published language concerning one, an actress, in the employ of
another, the proprietor of a theatre, in consequence of which
such employee refused to fulfill her engagement with her employer (the plaintiff), and whereby the plaintiff, as he alleged,
lost profits in his business, it was held that the action could not
be maintained.[671] That the damages were too remote is usually
assigned, and is one of the expressed grounds for the decision;
another and a sufficient ground would be, that her refusal to
fulfill her engagement was not a natural result of the publication.

§ 202. Ordinarily the repetition [§ 112] of defamatory

---

[669] *Moody* v. *Baker,* 5 Cow. 351.

[670] There are many cases where a recovery has been had for illegal acts of
third persons induced by the defendant's act, as for preventing workmen from
continuing their work, enticing away wives, servants, apprentices, or tenants,
&c. See in note 2, *ante,* and *Green* v. *Button,* 2 Cr. M. & R. 707; *Lumley* v. *Gye,*
2 Ell. & Black. 216.

[671] *Ashley* v. *Harrison,* 1 Peake's Cas. 194. In an action for fraudulently selling plaintiff diseased sheep, held it was not special damage that in consequence
of a report that plaintiff had purchased defendant's diseased sheep, one A. refused
to complete a contract he had with plaintiff for a supply of meat, or that plaintiff's customers had left him. (*Crain* v. *Petrie,* 6 Hill, 523.)

language by another than the first publisher is not a natural
consequence of the first publication, and therefore except
under circumstances to be presently referred to, the loss resulting from the repetition of defamatory language does not constitute special damage, and is not attributable to the first publisher.[672] Thus where it was alleged that defendant said of
plaintiff, "He is a rogue and a swindler; I know enough
about him to hang him," and it was alleged as special damage
that one B. who was about to sell goods to plaintiff on credit
had by reason of *defendant's* representation refused to trust
plaintiff, on the trial the proof was that defendant spoke the
words to one C., who repeated them to B., and that it was in
consequence of that repetition, and nothing else, that B. refused
to trust plaintiff, it was held the defendant was not liable for
the consequences of the repetition, and that the plaintiff could
not recover.[673] In some instances the circumstances of the
case may be such as render the repetition of the language by
another than the first publisher a link in the chain of natural
consequences of the first publication, and the loss by such repetition to the person whom the language concerns a natural
and proximate consequence of the first publication, and therefore special damage for which the first publisher is responsible.
Where a police magistrate, after disposing of a charge before
him, said to a police officer (the plaintiff) who had been examined as a witness in the matter, that he was not to be believed,
and this being heard by another officer present was by him

---

[672] *Stevens* v. *Hartley,* 11 Metc. 542; *Olmstead* v. *Brown,* 12 Barb. 657; *Keenholts* v. *Becker,* 3 Denio, 346; *Terwilliger* v. *Wands,* 17 N. Y. 58, and note 112,
ante.

[673] *Ward* v. *Weeks,* 7 Bing. 211. The decision seems to have been put on the
ground of a variance, the allegation being that the injury was in consequence of
a publication by the defendant, and the proof being that the injury was in consequence of a publication by another. Where words were spoken to a servant of the
plaintiff imputing incontinence to the plaintiff, and the plaintiff alleged for special
damages that in consequence of the words J. S. who was in communication of marriage with her refused to marry her, the plaintiff failed to sustain her action, because the words were not spoken to J. S. (*Holwood* v. *Hopkins,* Cro. E. 787.) In
Moody v. *Baker,* 5 Cow. 351, it was held that the declarations of the man that he was
not influenced in his refusal to marry by the words published, were not admissible.

reported to the plaintiff's employers, the police commissioners, and they in consequence dismissed the plaintiff from their employment, it was held, in an action against the magistrate, that such dismissal was special damage.[974] Where the plaintiff was governess in the family of A., and the defendant published language to the plaintiff's father imputing to her having had a child by A., this language the plaintiff's father repeated to A., who thereupon dismissed her from his service, alleging as a reason that although he knew the charge to be false, it would be injurious to the plaintiff and would be unpleasant both to the plaintiff and himself A. that she should remain in his family, it was held that the dismissal was a natural consequence of the defendant's first publication, for which he was liable.[975] And so where the plaintiff was a clerk in the employ of C. & S., who were partners, and the defendant, a former employer of plaintiff, published to C., one of said partners, language imputing dishonesty to the plaintiff, this language C. repeated to S., his partner, and it was held the defendant was liable for the consequences of the repetition.[976] In each of the two cases lastly referred to, the court evidently having in view the supposed rule of law above referred to [§ 201], that special damage must be a *legal* consequence of the act complained of, lays a marked stress upon the fact that the repetition was privileged, that is to say that the father in the one case and the employer and partner in the other, was justified in making the repetition, and that in neither case could the plaintiff have maintained an action against the one making the repetition, and the whole tenor of these decisions lead to the inference that unless the repetition had been justifiable as regards the person making it, the defendant would not have been responsible for its consequences.[977] The repetitions, however, were justifiable

[974] *Kendillon* v. *Maltby*, 1 Car. & Marsh. 402.
[975] *Gillett* v. *Bullivant*, 7 Law Times, 490.
[976] *Fowler* v. *Bowen*, 30 N. Y. 22.
[977] "Occasions may doubtless occur where the communication of slanderous words by a person who heard them will be *innocent ;* and it is certainly reasonable that when repeated on such an occasion and damages result, the first speaker

only in part; they were justifiable as to the persons making them, but not as to the first publisher; they illustrate the principle [§§ 67, 121] that the actual publisher may not be liable, while another, not the actual publisher, is liable. In the case of *Ward* v. *Weeks*, above referred to, the court dwelt on the fact that the defendant had not requested the person to whom he made the publication to repeat the language, intimating indirectly at least that if the defendant had made such a request he would have been liable for the repetition; most probably that would have been the result,[78] but such a request would not have justified the repetition [§ 67]. It seems plain, therefore, that it is not the fact of the repetition being or not being justifiable that determines the liability of the first publisher, but the test in every case must be whether or not the repetition was a *natural* consequence of the first publication. It was natural and to be expected that a father, when told of the seduction of his daughter, should seek out the supposed seducer and tax him with his offence; it was natural and to be expected that a partner, when informed that one in the employ of himself and partner was dishonest, should communicate the information to his copartner, therefore it was that in both cases the first publisher was held to be liable for the repetition.

§ 203. We have already [§ 130] adverted to a distinction between language concerning a person and language concerning a thing. Thus far, in this chapter, we have confined ourselves exclusively to language concerning a person; our present business is with language concerning things. As respects language concerning things, no such distinction exists between the effect of oral and written language, as is maintained with respect to language concerning persons [§ 18]. By things we intend whatever is external to the person; therefore, as here used, things include whatever one may or may be entitled to own, possess, or enjoy.

---

should be held responsible for the damages, as flowing directly and naturally from his own wrong." (*Terwilliger* v. *Wands*, 17 N. Y. 58, cited *Fowles* v. *Bowen*, 30 N. Y. 22.)

[78] *Keenholts* v. *Becker*, 3 Denio, 346.

§ 204. As a thing has no rights, and as no one owes any duty to a thing [§ 38], no wrong can be done to a thing, and language which merely concerns a thing cannot be actionable. In other words, one may, *in good faith,* speak or write whatever he may please concerning a thing, and with any intention towards the thing, and for such speaking or writing no action can be maintained. The thing cannot complain; it has no right which can be invaded. But although things have no rights, persons may have a right in or to a thing, the right of property, and this right may be invaded by language concerning the thing. When this invasion occurs, the language which effects it is actionable. A loss of or injury to the property is not an invasion of the right of property, unless the loss is occasioned by a wrongful act [§§ 48, 49]. A loss occasioned by a lawful act does not amount to a wrong, and does not confer a right of action [§ 62]. Where, therefore, by reason of an exercise of the right of speech or writing concerning a thing, the owner of the thing sustains a loss, he cannot have any redress therefor, as no wrong has been done. Thus an action cannot be maintained by a manufacturer or dealer against another, simply for publishing that the article he manufactures, or in which he deals, is not a good article, or is a bad article, or is not so good as, or is inferior to an article manufactured or sold by some other person.[910] But rights must be exercised in good faith; bad faith in an act done in the assumed exercise of a right makes the act wrongful [§§ 40, 42]. Good faith, in this connection, means an *honest belief in the truth and fitness* for the occasion of the matter published, and bad faith is the converse of this; namely, the absence of such honest belief, or the *disbelief in the truth and fitness* for the occasion of the matter published. As, then, the existence of this *belief* or of this *disbelief* determines whether the publication was or was not made with a legal excuse, it becomes necessary to ascertain the belief of the publisher; and this involves the question of his intent in making the publication. Not as already explained [§§ 90, 91], because the intent

[910] *Tobias* v. *Harland,* 4 Wend. 537; *Young* v. *McCrae,* 3 Best & Sm. 264; 7 Law Times N. S. 854; *Carr* v. *Duckett,* 5 Hurl. & N. 783.

is essential to constitute a cause of action, but because it is a
link in the chain of evidence of the existence or the absence of
a legal excuse. Proof that the publisher, while pretending to
exercise the right of speaking or writing concerning a thing,
was in reality designing and intending to injuriously affect the
owner of the thing, while it would not of itself constitute bad
faith, would be a circumstance from which bad faith might properly be inferred. Although the language concerns only a thing,
yet if it appears to have been published without lawful excuse,
i. e. maliciously [§ 91], it will be actionable if pecuniary loss
is a necessary or natural 'and proximate consequence of the
publication, and hence we may deduce this rule, that language
concerning a thing is actionable when published maliciously,
i. e. without lawful excuse [§ 91], if it also occasions damage
to the owner of the thing [§ 146].⁹⁸⁰

---

⁹⁸⁰ "I am far from saying if a man falsely and maliciously makes a statement
disparaging an article which another manufactures or vends (although in so doing
he casts no imputation on his personal or professional character), and thereby
causes an injury and special damage is averred, an action might not be maintained." (Cockburn, C. J., *Young* v. *McCrae*, 3 Best & Sm. 264.)

In *Swan* v. *Tappan*, 5 Cush. 105, the words were "alleged to be of and concerning the plaintiff's books," and nothing else, without any allegation of special
damage. The action was held not maintainable, but the court intimated that if
special damage had been alleged the action could have been sustained. In *Ingram* v. *Lawson* (6 Bing. N. C. 212; 8 Scott, 571), it was held that the language
was concerning the plaintiff personally, but that if the language had been concerning the plaintiff's ship, the action could have been maintained if special damage had been alleged. And as to words reflecting on a steamboat, see *Hamilton*
v. *Walters*, 4 Up. Can. Q. B. Rep. O. S. 24, and in Yates' Pleadings and Forms, p.
436, is the form of a plea to a declaration for slander of the plaintiff's ship. In
Young v. *McCrae* (3 Best & Sm. 264), Cockburn, J., observed: "I am far from
saying there can be no action for a *false* reflection on goods. Such an action,
however, would be more in the class of actions for false representations than
actions of libel." An intentional false statement by defendant in regard to articles manufactured by plaintiff, for the purpose of preventing sales, by plaintiff, of
such articles, and thereby preventing such sales, constitutes a cause of action.
(*Snow* v. *Judson*, 38 Barb. 212, citing *Benton* v. *Pratt*, 2 Wend. 385; *White* v. *Mer-
ritt*, 3 Selden, 352; *Gallager* v. *Brunel*, 6 Cowen, 346.)

A declaration for libel stated that the plaintiff, before and at, &c., carried on the
business of an engineer, and was the inventor and registered proprietor (under
2 & 3 Vict., c. 17) of an original design for making impressions on metal articles,
and sold divers articles on which the design was used. That plaintiff, before and

§ 205. Malice and damage are both essential requisites to
sustain an action for language concerning a thing. To these
requisites is usually added a third, that the language must be

at, &c., had sold and had on sale in the way of his said trade, articles and goods
called "self-acting tallow syphons, or lubricators," and that defendant published
a libel of and concerning plaintiff, and of and concerning him in his said trade,
and of and concerning said design, and plaintiff as the inventor, &c., thereof,
and manufacturer of the articles with the said design thereon, and of and concerning the said goods which he had so sold and had on sale, and plaintiff as the
seller, as follows: "This is to caution parties employing steam power, from a
person" (meaning plaintiff) "offering what he calls self-acting tallow syphons or
lubricators" (meaning said design, and meaning said goods and articles which he,
plaintiff, had so sold and had on sale as aforesaid), "stating that he is the sold
inventor, manufacturer, and patentee, thereby monopolizing high prices at the
expense of the public. R. Harlow (meaning defendant), "takes this opportunity
of saying, that such a patent does not exist, and that he has to offer an improved
lubricator," &c. "Those who have already adopted the lubricators" (meaning,
&c., same innuendo as before), "against which R. H. would caution, will find that
the tallow is wasted instead of being effectually employed as professed." No
direct averment connected the tallow syphon with the registered design mentioned in the first part of the inducement. No special damage was alleged. Held,
that the words were not a libel on the plaintiff, either generally or in the way of
his trade, but were only a reflection upon the goods sold by him, which was not
actionable without special damages. (*Evans* v. *Harlow*, 5 Q. B. 624.)

Publishing of a newspaper that it was a vulgar, ignorant, and scurrilous journal, was held not actionable, but it was held actionable to say that it was low in
circulation—such a charge being calculated necessarily to produce damage.
(*Heriot* v. *Stuart*, 1 Esp. Cas. 437.)

Plaintiff was possessed of certain shares in a silver mine, touching which
shares certain claimants had filed a bill in chancery, to which plaintiff had demurred. Held, that, without alleging special damage, plaintiff could not sue the defendant for falsely publishing that the demurrer had been overruled; that the
prayer of the petition (for the appointment of a receiver) had been granted, and
that persons duly authorized had arrived at the mine. Held, also, that an allegation that the plaintiff was injured in his rights, that the shares were lessened in
value, that divers persons believed that he had no right to the shares, that the
mine could not be worked, and that he had been prevented from disposing of his
said shares, and from working the mine in so ample a manner as he otherwise
would have done, and was prevented from gaining divers profits which would
otherwise have accrued to him, was not a sufficient special damage. (*Malachy* v.
Soper, 3 Bing. N. C. 871; 3 Scott, 723.)

In an action for misdescribing the plaintiff's vessel in a publication of the defendants, called "The Shipping Register," it appearing that the plaintiffs had
requested the surveyor of the defendants to examine the ship, held that they could
maintain no action against them for what they did in consequence of his report,

false. It is true the language must be false, not because it is
an additional requisite to malice and damage, but because it is
comprised in the requirement of damage. Language concerning a thing which is not false, *i. e.* which is true, cannot, as a
necessary or natural consequence, occasion pecuniary loss.
Language concerning a thing is *prima facie* or presumptively
lawful ; and, therefore, with regard to it, there is neither any
assumption or presumption of its being untrue or false, nor of
its occasioning damage, nor of its being without lawful excuse
[malicious] [§ 130] ; and therefore it is, that one complaining of
an injury by reason of language concerning a thing, in order
to establish his right to maintain an action, has to allege and
prove that the publication was made without lawful excuse
[maliciously], that the language was untrue, and that he has
sustained pecuniary loss as a necessary or as a natural and
proximate consequence of the publication.

§ 206. What is ordinarily designated slander of title, is
comprised within the division of language concerning things.
Slander of title is publishing language, not of the person, but
of his right or title to something. All the preceding observations upon language concerning things apply to actions for
slander of title ; thus, in an action for slander of title, no distinction is made with regard to the medium of the publication,
as whether oral or written ;[981] and to sustain the action, the
publication must be made maliciously ; the language must be
false, and must occasion, as a natural and proximate conse-

---

the remedy was against him if he made a false report. (*Kerr* v. *Shedden*, 4 C. &
P. 528.)

The foregoing cases seem to imply that the fact of loss, or special damage, as
it is termed, will render actionable language concerning a thing ; we state it otherwise in the text, and we suppose it to be otherwise. In *Carr* v. *Hood*, 1 Camp.
355, n., Lord Ellenborough, speaking of language concerning a thing (a book),
says: "I speak of fair and candid criticism ; this every one has the right to publish, although the author may suffer loss from it. Such a loss the law does not
consider as an injury, because it is a loss which the party ought to sustain."

This subject will be further considered under the head of Defences.

[981] *Malachy* v. *Soper*, 3 Bing. N. C. 371 ; 3 Scott, 723.

quence, a pecuniary loss to the plaintiff.[982] Where the assignee of a lease which contained a proviso for re-entry in case . the rent reserved by it was in arrear, exposed the lease for sale, there being at the time rent in arrear, the lessee appeared at the time and place appointed for the sale, and announced that such assignee had no title and could not make a title, in consequence of which announcement, persons who came to bid for the lease refused to bid ; the lessee afterwards offered £100 for the lease, which was refused ; he brought ejectment and recovered the possession of the premises. Intermediate the attempted sale and the recovery in the ejectment, the assignee sued the lessor for slander of title ; the court on the trial was of opinion that under the circumstances the plaintiff could not maintain the action, but left the question of malice in making the publication to the jury, and they found that it was malicious. The court, however, directed a nonsuit.[983] It is supposed that the nonsuit was set aside, and that the plaintiff had judgment on the ground that the question of malice having been left to the jury as a question of fact, and found against the defendant, the court could not disregard the finding and say there

---

[982] *Kendall* v. *Stone*, 1 Selden, 14, rev'g S. C. 2 Sandf. 269 ; *Like* v. *McKinstry*, 41 Barb. 186. There must be malice which the plaintiff must prove. (*Smith* v. *Spooner*, 3 Taunt. 246 ; *Hill* v. *Ward*, 13 Ala. 310.) Malice is not to be presumed. (*McDaniel* v. *Baca*, 2 Cal. 326.) There must be malice either express or implied. (*Hargrave* v. *Le Breton*, 4 Burr. 2422.) But all malice is implied. (§ 87, *ante*.) To support an action for slander of title, special damages must be shown. (*Bailey* v. *Dean*, 5 Barb. 297 ; *Linden* v. *Graham*, 1 Duer, 670; *Watson* v. *Reynolds*, 1 Mo. & Malk. 1, and note 992, *post*.) There must, too, be a want of probable cause ; and, if what the defendant said or did, was in pursuance of a claim of title, for which he has some ground, he is not responsible. (*Bailey* v. *Dean*, 5 Barb. 297.) The existence of probable cause is no answer to the action, nor does the want of it necessarily prove malice. (*Kendall* v. *Stone*, 2 Sand. 269.) Mere assertions, threats, and designs, made against a grantee of real estate, and against the party in possession, cannot be deemed a cloud upon the title. If the owner is injured by any such false claims or representations, he can probably maintain an action for damages. (*Re Madison Ave. Bapt. Church*, 26 How. Pra. R. 72.)

[983] *Smith* v. *Spooner*, 3 Taunt. 246. The attorney of a party who would be justified in making objections to a title, is not liable to an action, if he *bond fide*, though without authority, state only what his principal might have stated. (*Watson* v. *Reynolds*, 1 M. & Malk. 1.)

16

was no malice.[964]   The defendant, a surveyor appointed under
Stat. 7 and 8 Vict., ch. 84, attended a sale of some unfinished
houses, of which the plaintiff was the lessee for a term of years.
The roadway to these houses, although of sufficient width
according to the above statute, was at that time in an
unpaved state and unfit for traffic.   At such sale the defendant
made the following announcement: "I shall not allow the
houses to be finished until the roads are made good.   I have no
power to compel any one to make the roads, but I have power
to stop the buildings until the roads are made."   Some time
after such sale, the defendant, on being asked why he pursued
Mr. Pater, replied, "I pursue Mr. Pater because I am not able
to pursue Mr. Agar, the ground landlord."   Upon this state of
facts, held, that there was no evidence to support the allegation
of malice.[965]   Where one mortgaged his estate, and afterwards
committed an act of bankruptcy, subsequently the property
was offered for sale by the assignee of the mortgagor, the defendant, the attorney of the mortgagee, stopped the sale by
stating that the mortgagor had committed an act of bankruptcy, and which was untrue, that a docket had been made
out for a commission, in an action for losing the sale, held that
although the defendant went beyond the truth, there was no
material variance and no difference made with respect to plaintiff's title, and there being no proof of malice, the action could
not be maintained.[966]   The plaintiff being about to sell an estate, the defendant wrote a letter to the intending purchaser,
imputing insanity to Y., the person from whom the plaintiff
derived his title, and stating that the title would be disputed; in
consequence of which letter the proposed purchaser refused to
purchase.   It appeared on the trial that Y. had married a sister of the defendant, and that a term of years in the estate in
question was vested in the defendant as trustee, to secure a
jointure to Y.'s wife.   The judge on the trial ruled that if
defendant believed, upon *such grounds as would persuade a man*

[964] 1 Starkie on Slander, 318.
[965] *Pater* v. *Baker*, 11 Jurist, 370; 16 Law Jour. R. 124 C. P.; 3 C. B. 831.
[966] *Hargrave* v. *Le Breton*, Burr. 2422.

of sound sense and knowledge of business, that Y. was insane, the defendant would be entitled to a verdict.. A verdict 'was taken for the plaintiff; the court above, on granting a new trial, condemned this ruling as unsound, and stated, " If what the defendant wrote was most untrue, but nevertheless *he believed it*, if he was acting under the most vicious of judgments, yet if he exercised that judgment *bonâ fide*, it was a sufficient justification. * * The jury must arrive at their conclusion through the medium of malice or no malice in the defendant. The *bonâ fides* of the publication, and not what a man of rational understanding would have done, is the question to be canvassed." [987] The defendant who was the ground landlord and remainder-man of leasehold premises, of which the plaintiff was assignee of the lessee, stated at an auction at which the lease and assignment were put up for sale, that all the covenants in the lease had been broken, that he had commenced ejectment to recover the possession of the premises, and that it would cost £70 to repair the premises, in consequence of which the lease brought less than it otherwise would. On the trial it appeared that some only of the covenants in the lease had been broken, and the judge directed the jury, that the only question was whether what the defendant stated was untrue, and if it was, the plaintiff was entitled to recover. On motion for a new trial, the ruling at the trial was held erroneous, and that the proper question was, whether so much of the defendant's statement as was false was also malicious. [988] An order having been made by the Court of Chancery, requiring G., the plaintiff, to pay a sum of money, the defendant registered the order pursuant to Statute 1 and 2 Vict., ch. 110, whereby it became a lien on the real estate of the plaintiff, and prevented him raising, by a sale or mortgage of his estate, the money ordered to be paid, held the action could not be maintained, there being no proof of malice. [989] And where the defendant published a notice cautioning all persons not to purchase of the

---

[987] *Pitt* v. *Donovan*, 1 M. & Sel. 639.

[988] *Brook* v. *Rawl*, 4 Exch. 521.

[989] *Gibbs* v. *Pike*, 1 Dowl. N. S. 409; 6 Jur. 465.

plaintiff a certain tract of land, alleging that the plaintiff obtained the title to said land from the defendant by means of false pretences, and that the defendant intended to institute a suit to annul plaintiff's pretended title, was held not on its face to show malice.[990] Some of the old cases hold that one claiming title in himself cannot give a right of action, that to render the charge actionable it must assert a title in a stranger.[991] This distinction no longer prevails. So formerly it seems to have been supposed that the only ground of damage was a loss of the sale or leasing of the property, the title to which was assailed; it is, however, well settled at this day that any damage which is a natural and proximate consequence of the language will support an action.[992] The action cannot be maintained unless there is *special* damage.[993] Where, prior to the publication of the language complained against, the plaintiff and one W. had contracted for the sale of a lot of land—in consequence of the publication, W. wished to be released from his contract, and plaintiff released him—plaintiff sued, charging the loss of a sale to W. as the special damage, held that the rescinding of the contract with W. was not special damage, and that no action could be maintained.[994] Perhaps plaintiff being prevented from raising money by mortgage on his lands, is such damage as may entitle him to maintain an action.[995] Where the alleged slander consists in the defendant claiming title in himself, the fact of his not having a title is not *per se* evidence

[990] *McDaniel* v. *Baca*, 2 Cal. 326.

[991] Jenkins Cent. 247; *Pennyman* v. *Rabanks*, Cro. Eliz. 427; S. C., Mo. 410; *Lovett* v. *Weller*, 1 Rolle R. 409; *Gerard* v. *Dickinson*, 4 Rep. 18; *Snrade* v. *Badley*, 3 Buls. 75; S. C., 1 Rolle R. 244; and see Vin. Abr. Act. for Words, L. (B. 2), 8; Anon. Sty. 414.

[992] *Malachy* v. *Soper*, 3 Bing. N. C. 371; 3 Sc. 723; *Tasburgh* v. *Day*, Cro. Jac. 485.

[993] *Watson* v. *Reynolds*, 1 Mo. & Malk. 1; *Lowe* v. *Harwood*, Sir W. Jones, 196; S. C., Cro. Jac. 140; Pal. 529; *Cane* v. *Goulding*, Sty. 169; *Sneade* v. *Badley*, 3 Bulst. 75; S. C., 1 Rolle R. 244; *Brook* v. *Rawle*, 4 Exch. 521; *Pater* v. *Baker*, 3 C. B. 831, and *ante*, in note 982.

[994] *Kendall* v. *Stone*, 5 N. Y. 14, rev'g S. C., 2 Sandf. 269.

[995] *Linden* v. *Graham*, 1 Duer, 670. In that case the action was not maintained, because the damage was not stated with sufficient certainty, and as to how the damage must be alleged, see *Malachy* v. *Soper*, 3 Bing. N. C. 371; *Tilk* v.

of malice.[996] But the defendant having no title is a circumstance from which malice may be inferred.[997] Where the defendant in fact made the publication under the advice of counsel, but did not at the time of making the publication, state that he was acting under such advice, held that the fact of his acting under such advice did not *per se* shield him from an action;[998] but it was a circumstance to be considered in determining whether or not the publication was made maliciously.[999]

§ 206. The action for slander of title is not restricted to language affecting real property, it lies for slander of title to personal property; thus, where at a public sale of rye the defendant attended, and in the presence and hearing of the persons there assembled, said: "I forbid selling the rye; it is mine," in consequence of which persons were deterred from bidding, and the rye sold for less than it would otherwise have done, it was held an action could be maintained.[1000]

§ 207. As one cannot cloak his wrong-doing by the use of ironical language [§ 133], so neither can one with impunity attack a person by *pretending* to attack a thing; for although the words may be professedly concerning a thing, yet if they are in reality concerning a person, they will be judged by the rules governing language concerning the person.[1001] Whether certain

---

Parsons, 2 Car. & P. 201; *Delegal* v. *Highley*, 8 Car. & P. 444. A general allegation that the plaintiff's property has been lessened in value, or that people believe he has no title, or that he has been prevented from selling, is not sufficient.

[996] *Hill* v. *Ward*, 13 Ala. 310.

[997] *McDaniel* v. *Baca*, 2 Cal. 326.

[998] *Like* v. *McKinstry*, 41 Barb. 186.

[999] *Hill* v. *Ward*, 13 Ala. 310.

[1000] *Like* v. *McKinstry*, 41 Barb. 186; and see *Green* v. *Button*, 1 Gale, 349; 2 C. M. & R. 707; 1 Tyrw. & G. 118; *Malachy* v. *Soper*, 3 Bing. N. C. 371; 3 Scott, 723; *Carr* v. *Duckett*, 5 Hurl. & N., 783; *Hill* v. *Ward*, 13 Ala. 310; and slander of title to a slave. *Pines* v. *Wythe*, 71.

[1001] *Carr* v. *Hood*, 1 Camp. 355, n. In *Tobias* v. *Harland*, 4 Wend. 537, the court said that words disparaging an article made or dealt in by the plaintiff, were not actionable unless they imputed deceit or malpractice in the making or vending, or a want of skill in the manufacture. In reference to this dictum it must be observed that words imputing to plaintiff deceit or want of skill, do not concern the thing but the person, and are therefore within the rules relating to personal defamation.

language concerns a person or a thing is sometimes a question difficult to determine; but it is always a question of fact, and like every other question of fact, to be determined sometimes by the court and sometimes by the jury [§ 69]. The language which on its face concerns a person, may indirectly affect a person other than the person whom on its face the language concerns. It may affect one as concerning him personally, and affect another as concerning a thing. The language heretofore referred to [§ 201] concerning an actress, whereby she refused to perform her engagement, was as to her concerning the person, but as to her employer it was concerning a thing, namely, his right of property in or to her services.

CHAPTER IX.

Privileged publications generally. Repetition. Truth. Legislative proceedings and reports thereof. Judicial proceedings. Parties to proceedings. Counsel. Witnesses. Judges. Reports of judicial proceedings. Quasi judicial proceedings. Church discipline. Seeking advice or redress other than judicially. Giving information or advice generally. Master and servant. Candidates for office or employment. Insanity. Drunkenness. Infancy. Accord and satisfaction. Previous recovery. Apology. Freedom of the Press. Criticism.

§ 208. The actionable language referred to in the preceding chapter is to be understood as *primâ facie* actionable only, that is to say, it is actionable when published without any legal excuse for making the publication.[1002] We have, in previous chapters [§§ 64, 65], referred to the kinds of legal excuses and the distinction between legal excuses and defences, and [§ 50] stated that it is the occasion which determines of every act, and consequently of the act of publication, whether or not it admits of a legal excuse or defence. When the occasion really or apparently furnishes a legal excuse for making the publication, in that event the publication is termed a privileged publication [§ 120], or a privileged communication. Privileged

---

[1002] To every libel there may be an implied justification from the occasion. (*Weatherstone* v. *Hawkins*, 1 T. R. 110.) " Whether the circumstances under which a communication is made constitute it a privileged communication or not is a question which the court has assumed the jurisdiction to decide. But it is more a question of fact in each particular case than a question of law. The court is to consider whether the occasion is such as to make the communication one of a privileged character. That being so, it by no means follows that we can derive much aid in one case from another, the circumstances of which are not exactly the same." Maule, J., *Wenman* v. *Ash*, 13 C. B. 836 ; and see *Darby* v. *Ouseley*, 86 Eng. Law and Eq. R. 518.

publication is the better term, because the phrase privileged
communication has another meaning, namely, a communication made under circumstances which either entitles or obliges
the person to whom the communication is made to withhold
the disclosure of the matter communicated.[1008] The term privileged communication, when hereafter employed, will be as a
synonym for privileged publication.

§ 209. Privileged publications are usually divided into absolutely privileged and conditionally privileged.[1004] By an absolutely privileged publication is not to be understood a publication for which the publisher is in no wise responsible, but it
means a publication in respect of which, by reason of the occasion upon which it is made, no remedy can be had in a civil action
of slander or libel. A conditionally privileged publication is a
publication made on an occasion which furnishes a *primâ facie*
legal excuse for the making of it; and which is privileged unless
some additional fact is shown which so alters the character of the
occasion as to prevent it furnishing a legal excuse. The additional fact which in the majority of cases is required to be
shown to destroy this conditional privilege is malice, meaning

---

[1003] As to the distinction between communications privileged from being given
in evidence and privileged from being a cause of action for slander or libel, see
remarks of Bushe, C. J., *Black* v. *Holmes*, 1 Fox & Sm. 85.

[1004] *Perkins* v. *Mitchell*, 31 Barb. 467; *Warner* v. *Paine*, 2 Sandf. 198. Privileged communications are of four kinds, to wit: where the publisher of the
alleged slander acted in good faith in the discharge of a public or private
duty, legal or moral, or in the prosecution of his own rights or interests; anything said or written by a master concerning the character of a servant who has
been in his employment; words used in the course of a legal or judicial proceeding; and publications duly made in the ordinary mode of parliamentary proceedings. (*White* v. *Nichols*, 3 How. U. S. Rep. 266.) Absolutely privileged
communications are of two kinds: (1) proceedings in courts of justice; (2) memo-
rials and petitions to the legislature. (*Cook* v. *Hill*, 3 Sandf. 341.) Courts are
not inclined to extend the doctrine of absolutely privileged communications. (*Id.*)
A conditionally privileged publication must be made "in good faith, believing
the statements it contains to be true, or having probable cause to believe them
to be true." If there was no probable cause for the communication, the law implies that it was made with malice. If, however, it appears that there was probable cause, the communication is privileged, no matter how much actual malice
dictated it. (*Ib.*)

bad intent, in the publisher, *i. e.* an intent to injure the person whom or whose affairs the language concerns, and therefore by a conditionally privileged publication is very generally understood one which rebuts the presumption of malice, meaning absence of legal excuse, which in cases where no legal excuse is apparent, arises from the mere fact of publication.[1005] And therefore it has been said: "Instead of the expression 'privileged communication,' it is more correct to say that the communication was made on an occasion which rebuts the presumption of malice."[1006] The proper meaning of a privileged communication is only this: that the occasion on which the communication was made rebuts the inference *primâ facie* arising from a statement prejudicial to the character of the plaintiff, and puts it upon him to prove that there was malice in fact, that the defendant was actuated by motives of personal spite or ill-will independent of the occasion on which the communication was made.[1007] The description of cases recognized as privileged communications must be understood as exceptions to the rule [that every defamatory publication implies malice],

---

[1005] "In general an action lies for the malicious publication of statements which are false in fact and injurious to the character of another (within the well known limits as to verbal slander), and the law considers such publication as malicious unless it is fairly made by a person in the discharge of some public or private duty, whether legal or moral, or in the conduct of his [the publisher's] own affairs, in matters where his interest is concerned. In such cases the occasion prevents the inference of malice which the law draws from unauthorized communications, and affords a qualified defence depending upon the absence of actual malice. If fairly warranted by any reasonable occasion or exigency, and honestly made, such communications are protected for the common convenience and welfare of society, and the law has not restricted the right to make them within any narrow limits." (Parke, B., *Toogood* v. *Spyring*, 1 Cr. M. & R. 181; and to the like effect see *Coxhead* v. *Richards*, 2 C. B. 569; *Blackham* v. *Pugh*, 2 C. B. 611; *Bennett* v. *Deacon*, 2 C. B. 628; *Taylor* v. *Hawkins*, 16 Q..B. 308; *Kine* v. *Sewall*, 3 M. & W. 297; *Swan* v. *Tappan*, 5 Cush. 104.)

[1006] Erle, J., *Gilpin* v. *Fowler*, 9 Ex. 615.

[1007] *Wright* v. *Woodgate*, 2 Cr. M. & R. 573. Where the writer is acting on any duty, legal or moral, towards the person to whom he writes, or where he has by his situation to protect the interest of that person, that which he writes under such circumstances is a privileged communication, and no action will lie for what is thus written, unless the writer be actuated by malice. (*Cockayne* v. *Hodgkisson*, 5 Car. & P. 543.)

and as being founded upon some apparently recognized obligation or motive, legal, moral, or social, which may fairly be presumed to have led to the publication, and therefore, *primâ facie* relieves it from the just implication from which the general rule of the law is deduced. The rule of evidence as to such cases is accordingly so far changed as to impose it on the plaintiff to remove those presumptions flowing from the seeming obligations and situations of the parties, and to require of him to bring home to the defendant the existence of malice as the true motive of his conduct.[1008] And it has been said: Few rules of law are of greater practical importance than that which requires proof of express malice where the words are spoken under circumstances which make the communication privileged. The malice required to deprive communications of this sort of the protection arising out of the occasion of the speaking of the words, must be such as to induce the court, or any reasonable person, to draw the inference that the occasion has been taken advantage of to give utterance to an unfounded charge.[1009] Privileged communications comprehend all statements made *bonâ fide* in performance of a duty, or with a fair and reasonable purpose of protecting the interest of the person making them,[1010] or the interest of the person to whom they are made.[1011] A communication made *bonâ fide* upon any subject-matter in which the party communicating has an interest, or in reference to which he has a duty, is privileged if made to a person having a corresponding interest or duty, although it contain criminatory matter, which without this privilege, would be slanderous and actionable.[1012] We venture with much hesitation to suggest the rule as to privilege to be: one may publish by speech or writing whatever he may honestly believe is essential to the protection of his own rights, or to the rights of another, provided the publication be confined solely to those

---

[1008] *White* v. *Nicholls*, 3 How. U. S. Rep. 266.

[1009] *Manby* v. *Witt*, 18 C. B. 544.

[1010] *Somerville* v. *Hawkins*, 3 Eng. Law and Eq. R. 503; 10 C. B. 583; 15 Jur. 450.

[1011] *Pattison* v. *Jones*, 8 B. & C. 578.

[1012] *Harrison* v. *Bush*, 5 El. & Blac. 344.

persons whom the publisher honestly believes can assist him in the protection of his own rights, or to those whom he honestly believes a knowledge of the matter published will enable to assert their rights or to protect their rights from invasion.

§ 210. It will be convenient, prior to considering the several occasions which give rise to privileged publications, to discuss the supposed privilege under.certain conditions of *repeating* defamatory matter. It already appears that the publication of defamatory matter cannot be justified on the ground that it is but a repetition [§ 114].[1013] For a long period, how-

---

[1013] One who repeats a slander is responsible. *Evans* v. *Smith*, 5 Monr. 363; *Kenney* v. *McLoughlin*, 5 Gray, 3; *Clarke* v. *Munsell*, 6 Metc., 373; *Hampton* v. *Wilson*, 4 Dev. 468. It is no defence to an action for defamatory matter published in a newspaper that it was the communication of a correspondent, or copied from another newspaper. *Talbutt* v. *Clark*, 2 Moo. & R. 312; *Sanford* v. *Bennett*, 24 N. Y. 20; *Miles* v. *Spencer*, 1 Holt R. 533; *Parker* y. *McQueen*, 8 B. Monr. 16; or that it had been previously published, and the plaintiff had failed to prosecute the previous publisher; *Rex* v. *Holt*, 5 T. R. 436; *Curtis* v. *Mussey*, 6 Gray (Mass.), 261; see *Poppenheim* v. *Wilkes*, 1 Strobhart, 275; or that when the charge was made the plaintiff did not deny it. *Fuller* v. *Dean*, 31 Ala. 654. In *Reg.* v. *Newman*, 18 E. L. & E. R. 122, the defendant on the trial offered to put in evidence the Dublin Review, of a date prior to the alleged libel, in order to show that the charge contained in the libel had been published a considerable time before the alleged libel, and that the publisher had not been prosecuted; this evidence was rejected, and the rejection was made one of the grounds for a motion for a new trial, and per Coleridge, J., "It has been said that probably the libel was true because another libel was published by another person. Upon that principle it might have been argued that the statements in the Dublin Review were true because they had previously appeared in some other publication. Such evidence is far too vague to be received. The fallacy of the learned counsel's argument consists in the prosecutor's alleged submission to the previous libel. The utmost that can be said is that he did not prosecute the parties. That might have arisen from various considerations. He might not be able to fix on a particular person, or upon any one of character, or he might be prevented from proceeding by his poverty, or by a variety of other circumstances. Besides, it is not always considered expedient to institute proceedings in respect to the first charge." Nor is it any justification that prior to the publication complained against, there was a rumor or report current and generally believed that the plaintiff was guilty of the offence imputed. *Hampton* v. *Wilson*, 4 Dev. 468; *Haskins* v. *Lumsden*, 10 Wis. 359; *Moberly* v. *Preston*, 8 Mis. R. 462; *Cude* v. *Redditt*, 15 La. An. 492; *Dane* v. *Kenney*, 5 Foster, N. H. 318; *Lewis* v. *Niles*, 1 Root, 346; *Woolcott* v. *Hall*, 6 Mass. 514; *Alderman* v. *French*, 1 Pick. 1; or that

ever, it was tacitly conceded that such a repetition could be
justified by declaring the name of the previous publisher. The
origin of the error is generally attributed to a dictum in the
Earl of Northampton's case, A. D. 1613.[1014] That case was an
information under the statutes of *scandalum magnatum* in the
Star Chamber, against Goodrich, Cox, Varner, Minor, Lake,
and Ingram, for publishing defamatory language concerning
the Earl of Northampton. · The defendants all appeared in
court; Goodrich confessed to the publication, but alleged in justification that he was not the first author, and vouched said
Cox, who in like manner confessed and vouched said Varner,
who in like manner confessed and vouched said Minor, who in
like manner confessed and vouched said Lake, who in like manner confessed and said he heard the words from one Spoket,
who said he heard them from said Ingram, who in like manner
confessed and said he heard the words from two English fugi-
tives at Leghorn. The court intimated that *the defence of the
language being a repetition would be available in the case of a
common person*, but not in the case of a peer, and all the defendants were punished by fine and imprisonment. The error
so far gained ground that subsequently [1015] we find it held that
a plaintiff in an action for slander, where the slander appeared to be a repetition, was required in his declaration to
negative that the defendant had in fact heard spoken the language he was charged with publishing. Passing over a long
interval we find, A. D. 1796, Lord Kenyon, then Chief Justice
of the King's Bench, referring approvingly to the Earl of

---

the defendant spoke the words as merely giving the report. *Wheeler* v. *Shields*,
2 Scam. 348; *Smalley* v. *Anderson*, 4 Monr. 867. Perhaps a defendant may give
in evidence under the general issue the existence of rumors against the plaintiff's character, to show that he has sustained no injury, or in mitigation.
Waithman v. *Weaver*, 1 D. & R. 10; *Treat* v. *Browning*, 4 Conn. 408; *Nelson* v.
Evans, 1 Dev. 9; *Calloway* v. *Middleton*, 2 A. K. Marsh. 372; *Binns* v. *Stokes*, 27
Mis. (5 Cush.) 239. Neither particular reports, nor public reputation of the slander, nor of kindred charges against the plaintiff, are admissible. *Inman* v. *Foster*, 8 Wend. 602; *Kennedy* v. *Gifford*, 19 Wend. 296; *Mapes* v. *Weeks*, 4 Wend.
659; *Watson* v. *Buck*, 5 Cow. 499.

[1014] 12 Rep. 132; Moore, 821.
[1015] *Crawford* v. *Middleton*, 1 Lev. 82.

Northampton's case, but he introduced this qualification that
to render the repetition justifiable, the defendant must ·at the
time of the repetition, mention the name of the previous publisher, and that to name the previous publisher for the first
time in the defendant's plea [1016] was not a justification. This
qualification was repeated in a subsequent case, A. D. 1805.[1017]
This other qualification was also introduced, that if the first publisher *retracted* what he had published; one who subsequently
and with a knowledge of such retraction repeated the matter,
was not legally excused by naming the prior publisher.[1018] It
long continued to be conceded as law that no action could be
maintained for the repetition orally of defamatory matter, if at
the time of the repetition the name of the previous publisher
was mentioned; thus, in A. D. 1829, in an action for slander,
the plea that the language was a repetition of words previously
spoken by A., and that A. was named as the author at the time
of the publication was overruled, not because naming the
author was no defence, but because the plea did not allege that
A. spoke the words maliciously, nor that the defendant believed
them to be true, nor that they were spoken on a justifiable occasion.[1019] In Connecticut, it seems, that giving the name of the
author was never allowed as a defence, but the fact was received in mitigation;[1020] subsequently it was held not receivable in that State, even in mitigation.[1021] In Pennsylvania,
giving the name of the previous publisher was held to rebut
the inference of malice,[1022] and to amount to a mitigating circumstance.[1023] In Maine, Indiana, and some other States, it

---

[1016] *Davis* v. *Lewis*, 7 T. R. 17; and see *Church* v. *Bridgman*, 6 Missouri, 190.

[1017] *Woolnoth* v. *Meadows*, 5 East, 463.

[1018] *Maitland* v. *Goldney*, 2 East, 426.

[1019] *McPhearson* v. *Daniels*, 10 B. & C. 263; and see *Moberly* v. *Preston*, 8 Missouri, 462. In *Lewis* v. *Walter*, 4 B. & A. 605, it was said there must be a just
reason for the repetition.

[1020] *Leister* v. *Smith*, 2 Root, 24.

[1021] *Austin* v. *Hanchett*, 2 Root, 148; *Treat* v. *Browning*, 4 Conn. 408.

[1022] *Binns* v. *McCorcle*, 2 P. A. Brown's R. 79; *Hersh* v. *Ringwalt*, 3 Yeates,
508.

[1023] *Kennedy* v. *Gregory*, 1 Binney, 85; *Morris* v. *Duane*, 1 Binney, 90 n. In
New Jersey, naming the previous publisher was received in mitigation. *Cook* v.
Barkley, 1 Penn. N. J. Rep. 169, A. D. 1807.

has been held that in an action for slander, giving the name of the previous publisher of the words is a justification of the repetition.[1024] Thus far we have had reference only to actions for slander; the first case in which the question appears to have been raised in an action for libel, was in the Supreme Court of Pennsylvania, A. D. 1803.[1025] It was there held that giving the name of the author was no excuse for the publication of a libel. The like ruling was made A. D. 1813, in the Supreme Court of New York.[1026] The first mention of the point arising in an action for libel in the English courts was in A. D. 1817, when it was held not to be a defence that the defamatory matter was communicated to the defendant by a third person.[1027] In a subsequent case for publishing an alleged libel, purporting to be an account of a trial, the plea was that the alleged libel had been previously published in the H. Journal, and that G. H. M. then and still was the publisher thereof; on demurrer the plea was held bad, as the defendant in his repetition had only named the journal from which the alleged libel was copied, and had not given the name of the publisher, and it was intimated by the court that the defence of the publication being a repetition, and

---

[1024] Unless it be proven that the repetition was malicious. *Haynes* v. *Leland,* 29 Maine (16 Shep.), 233; *Abrams* v. *Smith,* 8 Blackf. 95; *Jones* v. *Chapman,* 5 Blackf. 88; *Crane* v. *Douglass,* 2 Blackf. 86; *Cummerford* v. *McAvoy,* 15 Ill. 311; *Johnston* v. *Lance,* 7 Iredell, 448. Disclosing name of author at time of repetition held a defence. *Kelly* v. *Dillon,* 5 Ind. (Porter), 426; *Trabue* v. *Mayo,* 3 Dana, 138; *Robinson* v. *Harvey,* 5 Monr. 519; *Parker* v. *McQueen,* 8 B. Monr. 16. Giving name of author is evidence of want of malice. *Miller* v. *Kerr,* 2 M'Cord, 285; *Church* v. *Bridgeman,* 6 Miss. 190; and see *Easterwood* v. *Quinn,* 2 Brevard, 64; *Smith* v. *Stewart,* 5 Barr. 372; *Saxton* v. *Todd,* Wright, 317; *Haine* v. *Welling,* 7 Hum. 253; *Farr* v. *Roscoe,* 9 Mich. 353. The defence of giving name of author must be specially pleaded. *Brooks* v. *Bryan,* Wright, 760. In slander, evidence that the defendant had been told by a third person that the plaintiff was guilty of the crime imputed to him is inadmissible. *Mapes* v. *Weeks,* 4 Wend. 659; *Austin* v. *Hanchett,* 2 Root, 148. In slander, it is no justification that defendant *after* speaking the words and before the commencement of the action, disclosed to plaintiff the author of the words. *Skinner* v. *Grant,* 12 Verm. 456. In *Scott* v. *Peebles,* 2 Smo. & M. 546, it was held to be no defence to an action for slander that the defendant heard the matter from a person out of the jurisdiction of the court. See *Evidence in Mitigation.*

[1025] *Runkle* v. *Meyers,* 3 Yeates, 518.

[1026] *Dole* v. *Lyon,* 10 Johns. 447.

[1027] *Miles* v. *Spencer,* 1 Holt, N. P. 533.

that the previous publisher was named at the time of the repetition, did not apply to libel.[1028] The first case in which the dictum in the Earl of Northampton's case appears to have been altogether repudiated, was one before Judge Betts in New York, A. D. 1825.[1029] It may now be considered as settled in New York and in England, that neither in the action for slander nor for libel is it any legal excuse that the alleged defamatory matter had been previously published by another, whose name was mentioned at the time of the repetition.[1030]

§ 211. It is now universally conceded that to show the truth of the matter published is a complete defence to an action either of slander or libel. A publication of the truth is absolutely privileged.[1031] We do not pretend to vindicate the rule making truth a defence, either as just in its practical operation or sound

---

[1028] *Lewis* v. *Walter*, 4 B. & A. 605, A. D. 1821.

[1029] *Chevalier* v. *Brush*, Anthon's Law Student, 186; this was followed by *Mapes* v. *Weeks*, 4 Wend. 659; *Inman* v. *Foster*, 8 Wend. 602; *Hotchkiss* v. *Oliphant*, 2 Hill, 510; and see *Johnston* v. *Laud*, 7 Iredell, 448; *Dole* v. *Lyon*, 10 Johns. 447; *Clarkson* v. *McCarty*, 5 Blackf. 574; *Moberly* v. *Preston*, 8 Mis. 462.

[1030] *McGregor* v. *Thwaites*, 3 B. & C. 24; 4 D. & R. 695; *De Crespigny* v. *Wellesly*, 5 Bing. 392; *Bennett* v. *Bennett*, 6 C. & P. 588; *Fidman* v. *Ainslie*, 10 Exch. 63; 28 Eng. Law and Eq. R. 567; nor does it make a defence that the defendant believed the matter published to be true, *id.* ; *Saus* v. *Joerris*, 14 Wis. 663; or that plaintiff himself had previously published the same matter. *Cook* v. *Ward*, 6 Bing. 409.

[1031] Truth is a good defence in an action for libel or slander. (*Ante*, notes 58, 59; and see Stat. 6 and 7 Vict., ch. 96; *Perry* v. *Mann*, 1 Rhode Island, 263; *Root* v. *King*, 7 Cow. 613, and 4 Wend. 113; 1 Stark. on Sland. 229; *Lake* v. *Hutton*, Hob. 253; *J'Anson* v. *Stuart*, 1 T. R. 748); but it must be pleaded and cannot be given in evidence under the general issue, either in bar or in mitigation. (*Underwood* v. *Parkes*, Str. 1200; *Andrews* v. *Van Deuser*, 11 Johns. 38; *Van Ankin* v. *Westfall*, 14 Johns. 233; *Shephard* v. *Merrill*, 13 Johns. 475; *Snyder* v. *Andrews*, 6 Barb. 43; *Wagner* v. *Holbrunner*, 7 Gill, 296; *Smith* v. *Smith*, 8 Ired. 29; *Kelly* v. *Dillon*, 5 Porter (Ind.), 426; *Arrington* v. *Jones*, 9 Port. 139; *Douge* v. *Pearce*, 13 Ala. 127; *Kay* v. *Fredrigal*, 8 Barr, 221; *Thompson* v. *Bowers*, 1 Doug. 321; *Taylor* v. *Robinson*, 29 Maine (16 Shep.), 323; *Teagle* v. *Deboy*, 8 Blackf. 134; *Wagstaff* v. *Ashton*, 1 Harring. 503; *Bodwell* v. *Swan*, 3 Pick. 376; *Alderman* v. *French*, 1 Pick. 1; *Updegrove* v. *Zimmerman*, 13 Penn. State Rep. (1 Harris), 619; *Scott* v. *McKinnish*, 15 Ala. 662; *Eagan* v. *Gantt*, 1 McMullan, 468; *Rumsey* v. *Webb*, 1 Car. & M. 104; *Else* v. *Evans*, Anthon N. P. 23; *Burns* v. *Webb*, 1 Tyler, 17; *Samuel* v. *Bond*, Litt. Sel. Cas. 158; *Treat* v. *Browning*, 4 Conn. 408; *Bisbey* v. *Shaw*, 2 Kernan, 67; *Sheahan* v. *Collins*, 20 Ill. 325;

in principle.   Neither the justice nor expedience of this rule is
universally nor even generally conceded.[1082]   The maxim, that a

---

Hawes v. *Stanford*, 4 Sneed, 520; and see *Sidgreaves* v. *Myatt*, 22 Ala. 617.)   The
defendant may prove in mitigation such facts as show a ground of suspicion not
amounting to actual proof of the charge (*Wagner* v. *Holbrunner*, 7 Gill, 296), or
which tends to a proof of the truth, yet falls short of it (*Snyder* v. *Andrews*, 6
Barb. 43; *Bisbey* v. *Shaw*, 2 Kernan, 67; *Scott* v. *McKinnish*, 15 Ala. 662), or which
rebut the presumption of malice.   (*Kennedy* v. *Dear*, 8 Porter,· 90; *Arrington* v.
Jones, 9 Porter, 139; *Hart* v. *Reed*, 1 B. Monr. 166; *Chapman* v. *Calder*, 14 Penn.
St. Rep. (2 Harris), 365; *Abshire* v. *Cline*, 3 Ind. 115; and see *Moseley* v. *Moss*,
6 Gratt. 534.)   Evidence of general bad character may be admitted under the
general issue.   (*Smith* v. *Smith*, 8 Ired. 29; *Taylor* v. *Richardson*, 29 Maine, 323.)
An action of slander for charging a man with having the venereal disease, and,
with that disease upon him, contracting marriage, and communicating that disease to his wife, cannot be maintained, if the plaintiff immediately after his marriage had the disease in fact, even by proof that his wife, whom he married without knowing that she had the disease, communicated it to him.   *Golderman* v.
Stearns, 7 Gray, 181.   In slander for calling plaintiff a whore, the words
were laid to have been spoken in 1842; plea, that plaintiff, while unmarried, in
1834, had carnal connection with one A.   Replication, that plaintiff, at the time
mentioned in the plea, was betrothed to said A.; that afterwards she was lawfully married to him; that she lived with him a virtuous life until August, 1836,
when he died; and that she had ever since continued to live in innocent and virtuous widowhood.   Held, on general demurrer, that the replication was insufficient.   (*Alcorn* v. *Hooker*, 7 Blackf. 58.)   Where the charge is of a crime of
which the plaintiff was convicted, it is no answer to a plea of the truth of the
charge, that the plaintiff was pardoned.   (*Baum* v. *Clause*, 5 Hill, 196; see *ante*,
§ 158.)

Semble.—The provision of the Constitution of the State of New York, as to
the defence of truth in prosecutions for libel, does not apply to civil actions.
(*Dolloway* v. *Turrill*, 26 Wend. 383.)   See further under heads *Pleading*, *Evidence*.

It is said that where a crime is charged, and the defence of truth is sustained,
the plaintiff may be put upon his trial for the offence without the intervention of
a grand jury.   (*Cook* v. *Field*, 3 Esp. R. 133.)   Many instances have occurred
where the plaintiff's action for slander imputing the commission of a crime, have
occasioned the prosecution and conviction of the plaintiff for the imputed offence.
See *Pigot's Case*, Cro. Car. 383; and note *t*, 1 Stark. Slan. 237.

Wm. Parks, the first printer in Williamsburg, Virginia, published (A. D. 1736)
of a member of the House of Assembly, that he had been convicted of sheep
stealing; Parks being arraigned before the House, stated the charge to be true,
and that being found the fact, he was discharged.   See Thomas's History of
Printing in America.

[1082] " I am quite clear that the truth ought not to be made decisive [as a de-
fence] either in civil or criminal proceedings; for cases may be put where the

man shall not profit by his own wrong,[1033] ordinarily adduced as an apology for the rule under consideration, if it applies in any case, certainly has no application where the truth consists in the misfortune and not in the wrong-doing of the person whom the publication concerns. The rule allowing truth as a defence in a civil action for libel appears to be an innovation,

---

truth instead of being a justification, would not even be any mitigation; nay, where it would be an aggravation. Lord Brougham, Evidence, Rep. of Ho. of Lords on Libel, &c., July, 1843; and see in the same report the opinions of other lawyers and judges to the like effect; and see 2 Kent's Com. 25; Borthwick on Libel, 252; 29 Parl. Hist. 575; Preliminary Discourse to Starkie on Slander, xliv.

[1033] Blackstone gives as a reason the merit of the defendant in having exposed the truth. (3 Black. Com. ch. 8.) This is combated by Starkie, who contends for the ground that the plaintiff cannot take advantage of his own wrong. 1 Starkie on Slander, 230, 232; and see Preliminary Discourse to Starkie on Slander.

If the words be true they are no slander, and may be justified. 2 Wils. 301; 11 Mod. 99. If the defendant * * prove the words to be true, no action will lie, * * for then it is no slander or *false tale.* 3 Black. Com. ch. 8. The defendant is justified in law and exempt from all civil responsibility, if that which he publishes be true. 1 Starkie on Slander, 229.

In *Rex* v. *Roberts,* Ms. 8 Geo. 11, A. D. 1735, L'd Hardwicke, Ch. J., says, "It is said that if an action was brought, the fact, if true, might be justified, but I think that is a mistake, such a thing was never thought of in the case of *Harman* v. *Delany,* (1 Str. 898.) I never heard such a justification in an action for a libel even hinted at; the law is too careful in discountenancing such practices; all the favor that I know truth affords in such a case is, that it may be shown in mitigation of damages." It is added in a note by the editor of the American edition of Starkie on Slander (vol. 1, p. 233), "In the time of Lord Hardwicke, it was denied, not only by him but by others, that the truth could be given in evidence in bar of a recovery;" and in a subsequent note (vol. 1, p. 235), until 1792, when the judges of England gave their opinion in Parliament upon questions put to them on the Libel Bill, the only authorities for the position that a defendant might plead the truth of a libel in justification, were the dicta of Hobart, C. J., in *Lake* v. *Hutton,* Hob. R. 253, and of Holt, C. J., in an anonymous case, 11 Mod. 99; and the acquiescence of the bar and the court in *J'Anson* v. *Stuart,* 1 T. R. 748. Since then are the cases of *King* v. *Parsons,* A. D. 1799, in which L'd Kenyon observed that it was competent for a defendant in an action for libel to plead the truth in justification, and *Plunket* v. *Cobbett,* A. D. 1804, in which Lord Ellenborough remarked, "in case the libel had been true the defendant could have justified it on the record." Another reason assigned for making truth a defence is, that truth disentitles to damages. (Blackburn, J., *Campbell* v. *Spottiswoode,* 8 Law Times Rep. N. S. 201; 3 Best & S. 769; *Fairman* v. *Ives,* 5 B. & A. 646.)

17

and of comparatively modern introduction.[1084] Probably its origin was in this wise: Until the statute of the fourth year of Queen Anne, A. D. 1706, only a single plea was permitted in a civil action, and there is no record prior to that statute of a plea of truth in an action for libel. At least until A. D. 1702, truth was admitted in mitigation under the general issue of not guilty,[1085] but between that date and A. D. 1716, probably after the statute of Anne allowing several pleas, at a meeting of the judges of England, the rule was settled not to allow the truth to be given in evidence in mitigation, but requiring that it should be pleaded. From this we infer that no such plea existed prior to that time, and the requiring the truth to be specially pleaded was evidently to prevent a surprise upon the plaintiff, and to enable him to be prepared with his reply. Notwithstanding this rule requiring truth to be specially pleaded, we find that at least until A. D. 1735, truth was regarded only as matter of mitigation. The system of pleading then in vogue knew no such thing as a plea in mitigation; in that system every plea was either in abatement or in bar, and when truth was required to be pleaded it was almost of course to regard it as a plea in bar, and thus, as we suppose, the truth, when specially pleaded, became a defence. The truth, however, which is admitted as a defence is the truth of the defamatory matter in substance and in fact, and in the sense in which it was used and was intended to be understood. If A. says of X. that he is a thief, and C. publishes that A. said X. was a thief, in a certain sense C. would publish the truth, but not in the sense which would constitute a defence; C.'s publication would in fact be but a repetition of A.'s words, which, as we have seen, would not be a defence. [§ 210.] The truth, which in such a case would amount to a defence, would be that X. was a thief. Again, if A., speaking ironically, says of X. that he is an honest man, meaning and conveying the idea that X.

[1084] Selwyn's N. P. 986; Borthwick on Libel, 246. Truth, it is said, was at all times a defence in an action for *slander.* 1 Stark. on Slander, 284; 3 Blac. Com. ch. 8. This, however, seems doubtful. See *Smith* v. *Richardson*, Willes, 20; Bull. N. P. 7.

[1085] *Smith* v. *Harrison*, Raym. 727.

is a dishonest man, it would not be a justification of these words
to allege that it was true X. was an honest man, but to constitute a defence the allegation required would be that it was true
X. was a dishonest man. We shall give some illustrations of
the requirements of a justification on the ground of truth, and
the subject will be further illustrated under the head of Pleading.

§ 212. Where defamatory allegations, whether published
orally or in writing, are divisible [§ 145], but not otherwise,
the defendant is permitted to justify on the ground of truth,
one or some of them, less than the whole.[1036] But whether he
justify the whole or a part only, the justification as to so much
as is intended to be justified must go the whole length of the
charge in all its material allegations. The justification must
always be as broad as the charge, and of the very charge attempted to be justified.[1037] A charge that the plaintiff, a
brewer, *caused* his establishment to be supplied with unwhole-

---

[1036] See *ante*, notes to § 145, and *Stiles* v. *Nokes*, 7 East, 493; *Andrews* v.
Thornton, 8 Bing. 431; 1 M. & Sc. 670; *Gregory* v. *Duke of Brunswick*, 6 Sc. N.
R. 809; *Vessey* v. *Pike*, 3 C. & P. 512; *Van Derveer* v. *Sutphin*, 5 Ohio N. S.
293; *O'Connell* v. *Mansfield*, 9 Ir. Law R. 179; *Smith* v. *Parker*, 18 M. & W.
459; *Fero* v. *Ruscoe*, 4 Coms. 162. A declaration for a libel commencing "horse-
stealer," and followed by a statement of facts, and concluding that the defendant
published it with intent to cause it to be believed that the plaintiff had been
guilty of feloniously stealing a horse; plea, except as to the word horse-stealer,
a justification, stating circumstances inducing suspicion that the plaintiff had
been guilty of the fact; held, on demurrer, that the plea was insufficient.
(*Mountney* v. *Watton*, 2 B. & Ad. 673.)

[1037] *Weaver* v. *Lloyd*, 2 B. & C. 678; 4 D. & R. 230; *Bissell* v. *Cornell*, 24 Wend.
354; *Stillwell* v. *Barter*, 19 Wend. 478; *Fidler* v. *Delavan*, 20 Wend. 57; *Torrey* v.
Field, 10 Verm. 353; *Crump* v. *Adney*, 1 Cr. & M. 362; *Burford* v. *Wible*, 32 Penn.
St. R. 95; *Wilson* v. *Beighler*, 4 Iowa, 427; *Van Derveer* v. *Sutphin*, 5 Ohio N. S. 293;
Powers v. *Skinner*, 1 Wend. 451; *Cooper* v. *Barber*, 24 Wend. 105; *McKinly* v. *Rob*,
20 Johns. 351. The plea must justify the same words as those contained in the
declaration. (*Skinner* v. *Grant*, 12 Verm. 456; *Ormsby* v. *Douglass*, 2 Abb. Pra.
Rep. 407.) "There is no such thing as a half-way justification. When several
distinct things are charged [§ 145, *ante*], the defendant may justify as to one,
though he may not be able to do so as to all; but as to any one charge the justification will either be everything or nothing. If the charge be of stealing a
horse, it is not half a defence, nor any part of one, to show the plaintiff took the
horse by a mere trespass." *Fero* v. *Ruscoe*, 4 Coms. 165.

some water, is not proved to be true by showing that the establishment *was* supplied with unwholesome water. To establish
the truth of the charge, it must be shown the plaintiff *caused*
the supply.[1038] To a charge against the plaintiff, a schoolmaster, that the decay of the school under his management was
attributable to his violent conduct, it was held, on special
demurrer to the plea, not a sufficient justification to allege that
the plaintiff had been guilty of violent conduct toward some
of his scholars; to have amounted to a justification, it should
have been shown that the decay of the school was occasioned
by the violent conduct of the plaintiff.[1039]   A charge that

---

[1038] *Fidler* v. *Delavan*, 20 Wend. 57.   A charge that plaintiff was a "*cheat*"
and "*swindler*" was held justified by the fact that he sold goods for the purpose
of preventing their seizure under an attachment for the benefit of his creditors.
(*Odiorne* v. *Bacon*, 6 Cush. 185.)

[1039] *Smith* v. *Parker*, 15 M. & W. 459.   To a declaration for a libel, charging
that, by hypocritical cant, &c., plaintiff and his associates effected the incorpo-
ration of the Manhattan Bank, in which plaintiff's share of the profits was several thousand dollars; and that plaintiff, as a member of the senate, advocated
the bill entitled "An Act for supplying the City of New York with pure and
wholesome water," knowing that it contained a clause authorizing the company
to carry on banking business, and when he knew that the other members of
the legislature were ignorant of that fact, &c., the defendant pleaded in justification, that the plaintiff was a senator on second April, 1798; that such a law was
passed, and that, at the time of passing said law (first April, 1798), plaintiff, as
senator, advocated the bill, knowing at the time that it contained such clause,
&c.; and that a large majority of the members of the legislature were ignorant
of that fact, &c.; and that, at the time and place first above mentioned, plaintiff
held, and was owner of a large portion of the stock created by the said law, to
wit, five thousand dollars; all which acts of the plaintiff were hypocritical and
deceptive, and contrary to his duty as a senator, &c.   The plaintiff replied, that
at the time he advocated the said law as a senator, he did not hold, and was not
owner of any stock created by it; nor had he any interest whatever in the stock,
&c.   On a general demurrer to the reply the plea was held to be bad, as not being an answer to the declaration, and that the defendant having committed the
first fault in pleading, the plaintiff was entitled to judgment. (*Spencer* v. *Southwick*, 11 Johns. 573; rev'g 10 Johns. 259, where the replication was held to be
bad.)   Held that a charge of incest could not be justified by alleging that plaintiff told the defendant her brother had had sexual intercourse with her. (*Abshire*
v. *Cline*, 3 Ind. 115; and see *Long* v. *Brougher*, 5 Watts, 437, and in note 1030,
ante.)   It is not every act of illicit intercourse on the part of a female that will
justify calling her a whore. (*Smith* v. *Wyman*, 4 Shep. 13.)   The defendant, in
a case of slander, admitted in his answer that, while he was conducting his own

●

plaintiff had stolen defendant's shingles is not justified by the fact that plaintiff sold defendant's shingles without his authority, and afterward denied that he knew anything respecting them ; to constitute a justification of such a charge, a felonious taking must be shown.[1040] And where the charge was that plaintiff had begotten a bastard child, innuendo that he had committed adultery with the child's mother, it was held that to allege an adulterous intercourse with the mother of the bastard was not stating a sufficient justification.[1041] So a charge of selling intoxicating liquor contrary to law, is not justified by showing a sale of intoxicating liquor. The charge that the sale was contrary to law, is not answered.[1042] Nor is a charge that plaintiff had one night gone nine miles from home, to four different colliers' shanties, and that she had gone to bed to the colliers, justified by showing, that plaintiff had committed fornication with one collier elsewhere than at the shanties referred to in the charge.[1043] A charge of criminal intercourse with A. cannot be justified by showing a criminal intercourse with B.[1044]

---

cause before a justice, and examining the plaintiff as a witness, he interrogated him: "Do you say I put you on Williams' land ?" that the witness answered, "I do," and that the defendant replied, "That's a lie." The answer further alleged that plaintiff's answer to defendant's question, and his statement that the defendant put witness on Williams' land, were untrue. Held, that the answer was not good as a justification. (*Lewis* v. *Black,* 27 Miss. (5 Cush.) 425.) A charge that plaintiff's ship was unseaworthy and had been bought by Jews to take out convicts, is not justified by showing the ship was unseaworthy. (*Ingram* v. *Lawson,* 5 Bing. N. C. 66.) The justification should be of the *meaning*, not of the words merely. (*Snow* v. *Witcher,* 9 Ired. 346 ; *Fidler* v. *Delavan,* 20 Wend. 57.) The charge must be directly met, and not argumentatively or by inference. (*Id.*) Where the charge was that the plaintiff had *bolted*, it is not a justification to say he *quitted*. (*O'Brien* v. *Bryant,* 16 M. & W. 168 ; 4 D. & L. 341 ; 16 Law Jour. Rep. 77, Ex.; and see *Wachter* v. *Quenzer,* 29 N. Y. 547.)

[1040] *Shepherd* v. *Merrill,* 13 Johns. 475.

[1041] *Holton* v. *Muzzy,* 30 Verm. 365.

[1042] *Holton* v. *Muzzy,* 30 Verm. 365.

[1043] *Burford* v. *Wible,* 32 Penn. St. R. 95, and see *Rieke* v. *Stanley,* 6 Blackf. 169 ; *semble,* a defendant cannot justify a charge that the plaintiff had criminal intercourse with a certain woman at a certain place, by pleading that he had such intercourse with her at another place. (*Sharp* v. *Stephenson,* 12 Ired. 348.)

[1044] *Watters* v. *Smoot,* 11 Ired. 315, and see *Pallet* v. *Sargent,* 36 N. H. 496 ; *Randall* v. *Holsenbake,* 3 Hill, S. C. 175 ; *Ridley* v. *Perry,* 4 Shepl. 21.

So a charge of committing one offence is not justified by showing the commission of another offence, although of the same
or even greater enormity.[1045] A charge of stealing one kind of
chattel cannot be justified by showing theft of another kind of
chattel. A charge that plaintiff stole "a pot and waiter" is
not justified by the fact that he stole a waistcoat pattern.[1046] A
charge of stealing a dollar from A. cannot be justified by
proof of stealing a dollar from B.[1047] To prove a forgery to
the amount of $80, is not a justification of a charge of forgery
to the amount of $250, or any other sum.[1048] A charge of the
crime against nature with a *mare*, is not justified by showing a
commission of that crime with a *cow*.[1049] A charge that A., a
commissioner to examine witnesses, returned the examination
of *divers* witnesses that were never sworn, is not justified by
proof of a return of the examination of *one* witness who had
not been sworn.[1050] Nor is a charge that the plaintiff carried
on smuggling as a business, justified by proof of a single act of
smuggling.[1051] So a charge of smuggling *during* the war, is
not justified by showing a smuggling before the war.[1052] And
where the charge was that plaintiff was a bankrupt in April,

[1045] *Slow* v. *Converse*, 4 Conn. 17; *Torrey* v. *Field*, 10 Verm. 353; *Andrews* v.
Van Deuzer, 11 Johns. 38. Charging plaintiff with being a whore is not justified by the fact that she is a "reputed thief." (*Smith* v. *Buckecker*, 4 Rawle,
295.) It is no justification of a charge of horse-stealing and counterfeiting that
plaintiff was thought no more of than a horse-thief. (*Nelson* v. *Musgrave*, 10
Mis. 648.) A charge of hardness toward the poor, dissoluteness of morals, &c.,
purporting to be conclusions from instances of bad conduct previously narrated
in the publication, cannot be justified by proof of other instances. *Bartholemy*
v. *The People*, 2 Hill, 248.

[1046] *Eastland* v. *Caldwell*, 2 Bibb, 21; *Hilsden* v. *Mercer*, Cro. Jac. 676. A
charge of perjury on one occasion cannot be justified by showing that plaintiff
committed perjury on some other occasion, or in some other respect, than that
alleged. *Whittaker* v. *Carter*, 4 Ired. 461; *Starr* v. *Harrington*, 1 Smith, 360;
1 Cart. 515; *Randall* v. *Holsenbake*, 3 Hill, S. C. 175.

[1047] *Self* v. *Garner*, 15 Mis. 480.
[1048] *Stiles* v. *Comstock*, 9 How. Pra. R. 44.
[1049] *Andrews* v. *Van Deuzer*, 11 Johns. 38.
[1050] *Fysh* v. *Thorougood*, Cro. Eliz. 623.
[1051] *Stillwell* v. *Barter*, 19 Wend. 487.
[1052] *Stillwell* v. *Barter*, 19 Wend. 487.

in the twelfth year of James the First, it was held not to be a justification to show that plaintiff was a bankrupt in the fifteenth year of James the First.[1053] It is not a justification of several charges to prove the truth of one of them.[1054] A charge in these words: "thou hast played the thief with me, and hast stolen my cloth and a half yard of velvet," is not justified by showing that plaintiff was defendant's tailor, and that he, defendant, delivered to plaintiff a yard and a half of velvet to make defendant hose, and plaintiff made them too narrow, by reason of which defendant said, "Thou hast stolen part of the velvet which I delivered to you."[1055] A charge against an attorney, "You are a paltry lawyer, and use to play on both hands," is not justified by showing that plaintiff had exhibited articles of the peace against R., and had afterwards promised R. that he should not be molested on account of those articles, and that notwithstanding he had endeavored to prosecute R. upon those articles."[1056] A charge that plaintiff, a public minister, had traitorously betrayed the secrets of his own government, is not justified by the fact that the plaintiff disclosed the instructions given to him as such minister, although coupled with the additional fact that he was censured by his government for making such disclosures.[1057] A charge that plaintiff, a counsellor-at-law, had offered himself as witness in order to divulge the secrets of his client, is not justified by the fact that in a private conversation out of court the plaintiff disclosed a secret of his client, nor by the fact that plaintiff offered himself as a witness to divulge matters communicated to him by his client, but which were not privileged publications in the sense of publications he was privileged from disclosing [§ 208].[1058] A charge that plaintiff, a clergyman, had asserted

[1053] *Upsheer* v. *Betts*, Cro. Jac. 578. Where the libel imputed the continuance of a judgment, held not sufficient to allege there was a judgment. *McNally* v. *Oldham*, 8 Law Times, N. S. 604.

[1054] *Powers* v. *Skinner*, 1 Wend. 451.

[1055] *Johns* v. *Gittens*, Cro. Eliz. 239; and see *Bellingham* v. *Mynors*, Cro. Eliz. 153.

[1056] *Rich* v. *Holt*, Cro. Jac. 267.

[1057] *Genet* v. *Mitchell*, 7 Johns. 120.

[1058] *Riggs* v. *Denniston*, 3 Johns. Cas. 198.

that the blood of Christ had nothing to do with our salvation, more than the blood of a hog, is not justified by the fact that plaintiff had denied the divinity of Christ and the doctrine of the atonement; and asserted that Christ was a creature, a perfect man, but there was no more virtue in his blood than that of any creature.[1059] So a charge, "But this is not the first time the idea of falsehood and M. B. (plaintiff) have been associated together in the minds of many honest men," is not justified by the fact that more than seven persons believed plaintiff not to be a man of truth, but addicted to falsehood.[1060] Charging the plaintiff, a proctor, with having been suspended *three* times, is not justified by the fact that he had been *once* suspended.[1061] Where the charge is of a crime committed under aggravating circumstances, the aggravating circumstances must be justified; it is not sufficient to justify as to the commission of the crime. Thus where the alleged libel charged that the plaintiff had been tried for murder in a duel, and that " he had spent nearly the whole of the night preceding the duel in practicing pistol firing," held that to constitute a justification it must be shown not only that the plaintiff had been tried for murder, but that he spent nearly the whole of the night preceding the duel in practicing pistol firing.[1062] The charge against the plaintiff was *inter alia* " he has robbed me *to a serious amount.*" The pleas were the general issue, and as to the words "he has robbed me," that plaintiff had robbed defendant of a loaf of bread of the value of three pence. On the trial the plaintiff proved the charge, and the defendant proved the stealing by plaintiff of the loaf of bread. The judge directed the jury to give some damages for the words *to*

[1059] *Skinner* v. *Grant,* 12 Verm. 456.

[1060] *Brooks* v. *Bemiss,* 8 Johns. 455.

[1061] *Clarkson* v. *Lawson,* 6 Bing. 587; 4 M. & P. 356, and see *Goodburne* v. *Bowman,* 9 Bing. 532; 3 M. & Sc. 69; *Biddulph* v. *Chamberlayne,* 6 Eng. Law & Eq. R. 347; 17 Q. B. 351; *Skinner* ads. *Powers,* 1 Wend. 451. A charge of stealing "hogs" is not justified by the fact that plaintiff stole one hog. *Swan* v. *Rary,* 3 Blackf. 298.

[1062] *Helsham* v. *Blackwood,* 5 Eng. Law. & Eq. R. 409; 11 C. B. 111; 20 Law Jour. Rep. N. S. 187, C. P., and see *Churchill* v. *Hunt,* 2 B. & A. 685.

a serious amount, which were not covered by the plea. The jury gave the plaintiff forty shillings damages, and the court above refused to disturb the verdict.[1063] The charge that plaintiff had been imprisoned on a *charge* of high treason, is not justified by the fact that plaintiff was arrested on suspicion of high treason.[1064] And a charge that the plaintiff, a commissioner in bankruptcy, had been guilty of *wilful* misconduct in his office, is not justified by showing misconduct consistent with rectitude of intention.[1065]

§ 213. A justification on the ground of truth need not go further than the charge,[1066] and it is sufficient to justify so much of the defamatory matter as is actionable,[1067] or so much as constitutes the sting of the charge; it is unnecessary to repeat and justify every word of the alleged defamatory matter;[1068] it is sufficient if the substance of the libellous charge be justified.[1069] Thus, where the alleged libel was that a serious misunderstanding had taken place amongst the Independent Dissenters of M. and their pastor, the plaintiff, in consequence of some "*personal invective*" from the pulpit by the latter, and that the matter was to be taken up seriously, held that a plea, alleging that the plaintiff had spoken from the pulpit of a young lady, naming her, that her conduct was a bad example, and disgrace to the school, and that she did more harm than good, was a sufficient justification; that such expressions clearly constituted

---

[1063] 1 Starkie on Slander, 484.
[1064] Cooke on Defam. 116.
[1065] *Riggs v. Denniston*, 3 Johns. Cas. 198.
[1066] *Sanford v. Gaddis*, 13 Ill. 329.
[1067] *Clarke v. Taylor*, 4 Bing. N. C. 654; and see *Wilson v. Nations*, 5 Yerg. 211. Where the plea justifying a libel gave no answer to particular scurrilous terms used in it; held that, not containing any ground of imputation against the plaintiff distinct from that which was the gist of the libel, and the truth of which was justified by the plea, the plea was sufficient, and a rule to enter judgment *non obstante veredicto* refused. *Morrison v. Harmer*, 3 Bing. N. C. 758.
[1068] *Edwards v. Bell*, 1 Bing. 403; *Moore v. Terrill*, 1 N. & M. 559; *Cooper v. Lawson*, 1 Per. & D. 15; *Clark v. Taylor*, 2 Bing. N. C. 654; 3 Scott, 95; *Morrison v. Harmer*, 3 Bing. N. C. 758; 5 Scott, 410.
[1069] 1 Stark. on Slan. 483.

"*personal invective.*"[1070] Where the charge was that the plaintiff had been guilty of fornication, it was held sufficient as a
justification to allege that plaintiff was a strumpet, as being a
strumpet included the offence of fornication.[1071] And where the
charge was that in consequence of the plaintiff being in bad repute in the county of O., he would not like to bring his action
for libel in that county, held sufficient as a justification to allege
that the plaintiff had the reputation in the county of O. of "a
proud, captious, censorious, arbitrary, dogmatical, malicious,
illiberal, revengeful, and litigious man, and therefore was in bad
repute, and would not like to bring his suit there."[1072] And to
a charge that plaintiff signed defendant's name to a note without his (defendant's) permission, it was held sufficient as a justification to allege that defendant did sign defendant's name to a
note without his (defendant's) permission.[1073] Where the declaration alleged that plaintiff was cashier to Q., and that defendant, in a letter addressed to Q., falsely wrote and published of
plaintiff the words, "I conceive there is nothing too base for him
to be guilty of." A plea in justification, that plaintiff signed
and delivered to defendant an I. O. U., and afterwards, on
having sight thereof, falsely and fraudulently asserted that the
signature was not his; and that the alleged libel was written
and published solely in reference to this transaction, was, on
demurrer, held a sufficient justification, as the alleged libel must
be understood with reference to the subject-matter.[1074]

[1070] *Edwards* v. *Bell,* 1 Bing. 403. In an action of slander by a single woman,
under the act of 1808, Rev. Sts. of North Carolina, c. 110, where the words
charged were "that she had lost a little one," "A. B. is a credit to her," the said
A. B. being notoriously an incontinent person, and "she better be listening to
the report about herself losing a little one," it was held, that it was sufficient to
plead that plaintiff was an incontinent woman. (*Snow* v. *Witcher,* 9 Ired. 346.)
But the justification should extend to every part of the defamatory matter which
could by itself form a substantive ground of action. (*Cooper* v. *Lawson,* 8 Adol.
& Ell. 751.)

[1071] *Clark* v. *Munsell,* 6 Metc. 373, *ante* in note 641.

[1072] *Cooper* v. *Greely,* 1 Denio, 347.

[1073] *Creebman* v. *Morley,* 7 Blackf. 281.

[1074] *Tighe* v. *Cooper,* 90 Eng. Com. Law Rep. (7 Ell. & Bl.) 639.

§ 214. To justify a charge of perjury on the ground of truth, it must not only be alleged that the plaintiff's testimony was false, but that it was wilful or corrupt.[1075] It would be no justification of such a charge to allege that the false testimony was given by mistake.[1076]

§ 215. Where the meaning of the defamatory matter is pointed by an innuendo, a justification on the ground of truth must justify in the sense imputed by the innuendo.[1077] Thus, where the plaintiff, an apothecary, was charged with administering medicine to a child, with an innuendo that he had feloniously killed the child, a plea that the plaintiff did injudiciously, indiscreetly and improperly, and contrary to his duty, administer medicine to the child, and that the death of the child was caused or accelerated by the said medicine, was held bad on demurrer, as confessing without justifying the innuendo.[1078]

§ 216. Although the truth of the defamatory matter is admitted as a defence, a mere *belief in the truth* of the matter published, however honestly that belief may be entertained, will not of itself constitute any defence.[1079] Belief or disbelief

[1075] *Mitchell* v. *Borden,* 8 Wend. 570; *Clark* v. *Dibble,* 16 Wend. 601; *Gage* v. *Robinson,* 12 Ohio, 250; *Bissell* v. *Cornell,* 24 Wend. 354.

[1076] *Fero* v. *Ruscoe,* 4 Coms. 162; *Torrey* v. *Field,* 10 Verm. 353; *The State* v. *Burnham,* 9 N. Hamp. 34; *Jenkins* v. *Cockerham,* 1 Ired. 309. It is not a justification of a charge of false swearing that the defendant had good reason for publishing the words, and made the publication from good motives and justifiable ends. (*Thompson* v. *Bowers,* 1 Doug. 321.)

[1077] *Mitchell* v. *Borden,* 8 Wend. 570; *Clarke* v. *Dibble,* 16 Wend. 601; *Gage* v. *Robinson,* 12 Ohio, 250.

[1078] *Edsall* v. *Russell,* 2 Dowl. N. S. 641; 5 Sc. N. S. 801. Where an intent is charged, it must be justified. *Gage* v. *Robinson,* 12 Ohio, 250; *Riggs* v. *Denniston,* 3 Johns. Cas. 198.

[1079] However honestly the party who publishes a libel believes it to be true, if it is untrue in fact, the law implies malice, unless the occasion justifies the act; and whether the occasion justifies the act, is a question of law. *Darby* v. *Ouseley,* 36 Eng. Law & Eq. R. 518; *Holt* v. *Parsons,* 23 Texas, 9. A *bona fide* belief in the truth of the alleged libel is no defence. *Campbell* v. *Spottiswoode,* 3 Best & Smith, 769; 8 Law Times Rep. N. S. 201; and see *Moore* v. *Stevenson,* 27 Conn. 14; *Woodruff* v. *Richardson,* 20 Conn. 238; *Fry* v. *Bennett,* 3 Bosw. 200; *Smart* v. *Blanchard,* 42 N. Hamp. 137; *Watson* v. *Moore,* 2 Cush. 133; *Hotchkiss* v. *Por-*

in the truth of the matter published can be material only upon an inquiry into the intent with which a publication is made [§·90].

§ 217. Legislative proceedings are privileged. It is obviously necessary to the efficient discharge of the duties of a legislator, that in the performance of those duties he should be allowed unlimited license of speech, and be 'unfettered with any apprehension of being made responsible for the consequences of any utterances he may deem it fitting and necessary to make in his official capacity ; accordingly we find it everywhere wisely provided that for what a legislator says as a legislator, and within the legislative chamber, he can never be challenged in any tribunal other than the body of which he is a member. This immunity, enjoyed by the members of the British Parliament in virtue of custom and statutes, is guaranteed to members of Congress by the Federal Constitution, and to members of the State legislatures by State constitutions and statutes.[1000] The proceedings of the English Parliament

---

ter, 30 Conn. 314; *Gilmer* v. *Ewbank*, 13 Ill. 271; *Duncan* v. *Brown*, 15 B. Monr. 186; *Grimes* v. *Coyle*, 6 B. Monr. 301. Defendant cannot show that it was generally admitted for many years that the plaintiff was guilty of the crime charged. (*Long* v. *Brougher*, 5 Watts, 439); or that plaintiff was reported by her own sister to be guilty of the offence imputed. (*Smith* v. *Buckecker*, 4 Rawle, 295.) No suspicion, however strong, will amount to a justification. (*Powell* v. *Plunkett*, Cro. Car. 52; *Moyer* v. *Pine*, 4 Mich. 409.) Common fame is no ground for justifying an extra judicial charge. (Hutt. 13; Bridg. 62; Brownlow, 2.) A defendant cannot justify a charge of theft by showing that he has just grounds for believing the plaintiff to be a very dishonest man. (*Woodruff* v. *Richardson*, 20 Conn. 238.) The publication in a newspaper of rumors is not justified, but may be mitigated, by the fact that such rumors existed. (*Skinner* ads. *Powers*, 1 Wend. 451.) In mitigation of damages, in an action for a libel, the defendant was allowed, under the general issue, to show that he copied the statement from another newspaper; but was not allowed to show that it appeared concurrently in several other newspapers. (*Saunders* v. *Mills*, 6 Bing. 213; 3 M. & P. 520.) In an action for a libel in the defendant's newspaper, held that he could not show that it was copied from another paper, against the proprietor of which damages had been recovered, but he might show that he had omitted many of its parts reflecting on the plaintiff. (*Crevy* v. *Carr*, 7 C. & P. 64.)

[1000] 2 Hume's Hist. of England, 280; Statutes, 4 Hen. VIII.; 1 W. & M. st. 2, ch. 2. The constitution of New York (Const. of 1846, Art. III., § 12) enacts, "For any speech or debate in either house of the legislature, the members shall not be questioned in any other place." This provision is repeated in exactly the same words, 1 Rev. Stat. of New York, 154, § 11.

are *in theory* conducted with closed doors, and although in fact reporters and others are usually present during the debates, yet persons so present are supposed to be concealed, and the fact of their presence to be unknown to the House. All persons not members are liable to be expelled on a member or the clerk of the House rising and stating, " Mr. Speaker, there are strangers present." This intimation is always made prior to a division, and all persons not members, nor officers of the House, without exception, retire. It is a part of the same theory which forbids the publication, unless by order of the House, of any of its proceedings, and which makes any publication of its proceedings without such order a criminal contempt. Congress has never asserted, at least as directly as the British Parliament, the right to sit with closed doors, or to control the publication of its proceedings. The twelfth rule of the House of Representatives provides for clearing the galleries in cases of disorderly conduct, and the fourteenth rule provides for the admission, by the Speaker, of stenographers wishing to take down the debates.[1081] The immunity accorded to speech in leg-

---

A member of the legislature is not liable to an action of slander for words spoken in the discharge of his official duties, even though spoken maliciously. (*Coffin* v. *Coffin*, 4 Mass. 1, 31. But see *Commonwealth* v. *Blanding*, 3 Pick. 810, 314.) But this privilege is not extended to words spoken unofficially, though in the legislative hall, and while the legislature is in session. (*Coffin* v. *Coffin*, 4 Mass. 1.) Thus where one member informally communicated to another, within the representatives' hall, and while the house was in session, that the statement which he had just made to the house upon some question lately under consideration, and likely again to be acted upon, was founded upon misrepresentation, and that his informant was a person not to be believed, using some slanderous expression in regard to the informant, it was held, that the slander was not privileged by the place or occasion. (*Ib.*)

[1081] The constitution of the State of New York of 1777, § xv., enacted that: The doors both of the Senate and Assembly shall at all times be kept open to all persons, except when the welfare of the State shall require their debates to be kept secret. * * This provision was repeated in the constitution of 1823, Art. 1, § 4, but not in the constitution of 1846. The Revised Statutes of New York (1 R. S. 153, § 4) provide: The doors of each house are to be kept open, except when the public welfare shall require secrecy. The Constitution of the United States, Art. I., § 5, subd. 3, provides: That each house [of the legislature] shall keep a journal of its proceedings, and, from time to time, publish the same, excepting such parts as may in their judgment require secrecy. The constitu-

islative assemblies extends to any record such assemblies may
make of their proceedings, and to all documents read in such
assemblies; it extends also to all petitions or addresses presented to the legislature, and to such a prior publication of any
such documents as may be necessary to their preparation and
completeness.[1062]

§ 218. The immunity which is accorded to a legislator
while in the performance of his duties, does not extend so far
as to justify his repeating, not in his official capacity, any
defamatory matter he may have written or spoken while in the
discharge of his duties; and therefore for any repetition by a
legislator outside of the legislative chamber of what he may
have spoken within it, he is liable in like manner as any other
individual.[1063]

---

tions of New York of 1777, § xxxv., and of 1823, Art. I., § iv., required both
branches of the State legislature to keep a journal of their proceedings, and to
publish the same; and the Revised Statutes of New York (1 R. S. 153, § 3)
enact: Each house is required to keep a journal of its proceedings, and to publish the same, except such parts as may, in its judgment, require secrecy.

[1062] Where a petition to Parliament, containing defamatory matter, was referred to a committee, held that no action would lie for printing and distributing a number of copies for the use of the members. *Lake* v. *King*, 1 Mod. 58;
1 W. Saund. 131 *b*. See *post*, note 1092.

[1063] The defendant, in a speech in the House of Lords, accused the prosecutor
(an attorney) of improper conduct in his profession. This speech the defendant
afterwards printed in several newspapers. For this publication an information
was filed against the defendant, and he was convicted, the publication being held
not to be privileged. Lord Kenyon said "That a member of Parliament had
certainly a right to publish his speech, but that speech should not be made a
vehicle of slander against any individual; if it was, it was a libel." (*Rex* v.
Lord Abinger, 1 Esp. 226; Peake Cas. 310.) In *Rex* v. *Creevy*, 1 Man. & S. 278,
the defendant, a member of the House of Commons, had made a speech in his
place in Parliament containing a charge against an individual. An incorrect
report of this speech having been published, the defendant procured the publication of a correct version of his speech; this publication was held not to be
privileged. Semble, a *bona fide* publication by a member of the House of Commons to his constituents, of a speech delivered by him in his place in Parliament,
is privileged. (*Davison* v. *Duncan*, 7 Ell. & Bl. 229; 3 L'd Campbell's Lives of
the Chief Justices, 167.) Horne Tooke applied for a criminal information against
a bookseller for publishing a copy of a report made by a committee of the House
of Commons. The rule was discharged, partly because the report did not appear
to bear the meaning imputed to it, and partly because the court doubted its right
to interfere. (*Rex* v. *Wright*, 8 Term Rep. 293.)

§ 219. The English Parliament, as does Congress and our State legislatures, print for the use of its members reports of their proceedings in the bodies of their Houses and in their committees, and these are privileged. The English Parliament also print additional copies for sale to the public. These additional copies are printed by the printer to the Parliament Houses, at the public expense, and sold by such printer, the proceeds of the sales being returned to the public treasury. The publication of these additional copies was held by the Court of Queen's Bench not to be privileged, and where a report so printed and sold contained defamatory matter, the printer and publisher was held to be liable therefor in an action for libel.[1084] In consequence of that decision a statute was passed legalizing the publication by the orders of the Parliament Houses of the reports of their proceedings.[1085] In the State of New York, the publication in a newspaper of legislative proceedings and debates is, by statute, conditionally privileged.[1086] While it has been very generally and perhaps universally conceded that it would be proper to legalize, by statute, the publication without the order of Parliament of fair and true reports of the proceedings, it has, until recently, been generally admitted, that as no such statute has been enacted, and inasmuch as any report of the proceedings in Parliament is *per se* a wrongful and unpermitted act, the publisher is liable for the consequences of the publication of any such report, and

---

[1084] In *Stockdale* v. *Hansard*, 9 Adol. & El. 1; 2 M. & Rob. 9; 3 Per. & D. 330; 7 Car. & P. 731, it was held to be no defence, in an action for libel, that the defamatory matter was contained in a report of parliamentary proceedings and was published by order of the House of Commons. As to this case see May's Law and Practice in Parliament, 156, and Report to the House of Commons of a Select Committee on the Publication of Printed Papers, May, 1837, with an Appendix of the orders and proceedings of the two Houses of Parliament relating to the publication of Parliamentary Reports and papers and review of the legal authorities upon the jurisdiction of Parliament on matters of privilege.

[1085] 3 and 4 Vict., ch. 9. Defendant may, under the general issue, prove an order to publish, and the absence of malice, which entitles him to a verdict.

[1086] Laws of New York, 1854, ch. 130. See *post*, Freedom of the Press, and note 1122.

cannot shield himself by the plea that the matter published was a true report of the proceedings in Parliament.[1067]

[1067] Lord Campbell: " I think it should be declared and enacted that a fair and faithful report of proceedings in either House of Parliament, from which strangers are not excluded, is justifiable, and cannot be made the subject of any action or prosecution." Lord Denman: "I cannot help entertaining a strong opinion that no faithful report of a debate ought to expose the publisher to an action or to a criminal proceeding. As the law now stands, the fact of the report being a faithful one is nothing like a justification, but it ought to be." (Report from Committee of House of Lords on the Law of Defamation and Libel, July, 1843.)

In connection with this branch of our inquiry we cannot refrain from a reference to the case of *Wason* v. *Walter*, reported in the London Times of 19th, 20th, and 21st December, 1867. The plaintiff, a member of the bar, sent a petition to Earl Russell for presentation to the House of Lords, praying an inquiry into a complaint he alleged against the Lord Chief Baron of the Court of Exchequer. In the debate on the presentation of this petition, the friends of the Lord Chief Baron cast imputations upon the plaintiff. A report of this debate, and a leading article in reference thereto, appeared in the London Times of which the defendant was the proprietor. For the publication of this report and leading article the action was brought. The defences were, that the report was a true report, and that the leading article was a just and fair comment upon the proceedings in the debate. It was admitted that the matter was libellous in its character, and the only questions were, (1) Was it a defence to say the matter was a correct report of a proceeding in Parliament? and (2) Was it the subject of criticism? The Lord Chief Justice charged the jury: The report being faithful and correct, " I am prepared to direct you, in point of law, that the report is a privileged communication, and one which is not the subject-matter of an action." And after stating that the question was then for the first time directly presented for adjudication, and that some dicta supported his ruling, he added: " The cases have not hitherto gone the length of establishing the law I am now laying down, but I find nothing which to my mind satisfactorily contradicts the position I adopt." And again: "There may be dicta which may possibly have a different tendency, but, I think, with the larger and more enlightened views relative to the law of libel which have gradually developed themselves in our day, the time has come when the proposition I have put, ought to be affirmatively announced." As to the second point, the charge was: "I am of opinion that the debate in the House of Lords upon the plaintiff's petition was a matter of public interest and concern upon which a public writer was perfectly justified in making such comments as the circumstances warranted." The plaintiff tendered a bill of exceptions to this charge. The jury gave a verdict for the defendant. The Lord Chief Justice has shown by his charges in all the cases of libel tried before him, that he favors the greatest latitude of newspaper criticism. For his views on the right of criticism, reference may be had, in addition to the above case, to the case of *Dr. Hunter* v. *The Publisher of the Pall Mall Gazette*, printed in pam-

§ 220. Defamatory matter published in or to a court of criminal jurisdiction, may constitute the wrong called "*malicious prosecution*," [668] but never the wrong called[slander or libel. Thus where the defendant went before a justice of the peace, and demanded a warrant against the plaintiff for stealing his ropes, the justice said, "Be advised, and look what you do," and the defendant replied, "I will charge him with flat felony, for stealing my ropes from my shop;" in an action of slander for speaking these words, the court agreed that the words being spoken to a justice of the peace, on an application for a warrant which was lawful, would not support an action, for if they would, no other would come to a justice of the peace to inform him of a felony.[1089] Every one having reasonable and probable grounds for suspecting that a crime has been committed, has the right to communicate his suspicions to the magistrate having jurisdiction of criminal offences. The existence of reasonable and probable ground for the suspicion is absolutely necessary to create this right; a communication made without these grounds is inexcusable, and is a malicious prosecution, for which, however, no remedy can be had in an action for slander or libel. This results from the rules of pleading and the classification of actions into several different *forms* [§ 53] or *causes of action*, and operates even in those States

pblet form and in the Pall Mall Gazette of Nov. 27, 28, 29, 30, Dec. 1, 3, 1866. In the above referred to case of *Wason* v. *Walter*, the plaintiff gave the following neat definition of libel: "Defamation, without legal excuse."

[668] It is "malicious prosecution," and not what we term "slander or libel," which corresponds to "calumny" in the civil law. In the Roman law calumny signified an unjust prosecution or defence of a suit, and a calumniator was one who unjustly accused others in a court of law. See Domat's Civil Law, B'k III., tit. 5, § 2, div. 14, note, edit. by Strahan. Calumny is still employed in this sense in the courts of Scotland, and in the Ecclesiastical and Admiralty Courts of England. See Dunlap's Adm. Pra. 291, and *post*, note 1092.

[1089] *Ram* v. *Lamley*, Hutt. 113. An action of slander does not lie for a charge of a criminal offence made to a magistrate upon which a warrant issues, although the accused be discharged after examination. (*Schock* v. *McChesney*, 2 P. A. Browne's R. 6, App.) And see *post*, note 1091.

18

where it has been expressly enacted that all forms of action are abolished.[1090]

§ 221. The right of appealing to the civil tribunals is more extensive than the right of appealing to the criminal tribunals; for, as to the former, every one has the right, with or without reasonable cause for so doing, to prefer his complaint to them; and whatever he may allege in his pleading as or in connection with, his grounds of complaint, can never give a right of action for slander or libel. The immunity thus enjoyed by a party complaining, extends also to a party defending; whatever one may allege in his pleading by way of defence to the charge brought against him, or by way of counter-charge, counter-claim, or set-off, can never give a right of action for slander or libel. The rule as thus laid down has been doubted by some, and it has been said that if the tribunal to which the complaint be made has no jurisdiction of the subject-matter, or if the defamatory matter be irrelevant to the matter in hand, or if the party complaining or defending maliciously inserts defamatory matter in his pleading, that in such cases the party aggrieved may maintain his action for slander or libel.[1091] Notwithstanding the dicta to the contrary,

---

[1090] This result is brought about as thus: If the plaintiff shows on the face of his [declaration] complaint that the publication was made to a court of criminal jurisdiction, he does not show a cause of action unless he alleges *inter alia* that the publication was made without reasonable or probable cause. But if the [declaration] complaint does not disclose that the publication was made to a court of criminal jurisdiction, then it would be a complete defence that the publication was made to a court of criminal jurisdiction; which defence could not be avoided by replying or proving on the trial that the publication was without reasonable or probable cause, as that would be in the one case a *departure*, in the other a *variance.* See *Torrey* v. *Field*, 10 Verm. 353.

[1091] "Words that might otherwise import a slander, being necessarily used in a judicial procedure, cannot subject the party to any censure or penalty, either in respect to parties, objections to witnesses, or challenges to jurymen, that being understood as done in vindication of one's right; but yet, if things that are injurious, quite foreign to the cause, be charged in the libel" (i. e., the summons or declaration), "such pursuer shall suffer as a slanderer; for the cover of a judicial procedure cannot protect him, since the design of injuring is evident, and the more public and solemn it is, the injury is so much the more heinous."

we believe the better and the prevailing opinion to be, that for
any defamatory matter contained in a *pleading* in a court of
civil jurisdiction, no action for libel can be maintained; the
power possessed by courts to strike out *scandalous* matter from
the proceedings before them, and to punish as for a contempt,
is considered a sufficient guarantee against the abuse of this

---

(Borthwick on Libel, 215, n.) If he (a party appealing to a court of competent
jurisdiction) approaches the council with other than pure views; if under the
mask of vindicating his violated rights, seeking a redress for injuries, or removing a public grievance, he calumniates the man against whom he prefers his
complaint, I can discover no legal or even plausible ground to shield him from
answering as a libeller; and the opinion of the court from 4 Co. 14, in the case of
Buckley v. *Wood*, I consider as very apposite to this case. It is dictated by
sound principles of law and solid sense. (The Chancellor in *Thorn* v. *Blanchard*,
5 Johns. 525.) No action of slander or libel lies for defamatory matter in a
pleading (Vin. Abr. Act. for Words, C, a. 19; *Dawling* v. *Wenman*, 2 Show. 446;
S. C. *Dawling* v. *Venman*, 3 Mod. 108; *Cox* v. *Smith*, 1 Lev. 119; *Brown* v. *Mi-
chel*, Cro. Eliz. 500; *Hoar* v. *Wood*, 3 Metc. 198; *Gosslin* v. *Cannon*, 1 Harrington, 3; *Briggs* v. *Byrd*, 12 Ired. 377; *Shelford* v. *Gooding*, 2 Jones, N. C. 175;
Lea v. *White*, 4 Sneed, 111), as in a bill in equity (*Forbes* v. *Johnson*, 11 B. Monr.
48), or a writ or declaration (*Hardin* v. *Cumstock*, 2 A. K. Marsh. 480), although
the charge be groundless. (*Hill* v. *Miles*, 9 N. Hamp. 9.) Where one addresses a
complaint to persons competent to redress the grievance complained of, no action
will lie against him, whether his statement be true or false, or his motives innocent or malicious. (*Thorn* v. *Blanchard*, 5 Johns. 508.) And it is at least doubtful
whether a want of jurisdiction in the court to which a complaint may be exhibited, will make it a libel, because the mistake of the court is not imputable to
the party but to his counsel. (*Id.*; *Lake* v. *King*, 1 W. Saund. 132; Hawk. Pl.
Cr. 73, § 8; contra, *Buckley* v. *Wood*, 4 Co. 14.) So no action lies for words
spoken on giving a party in charge to a constable, or in preferring a complaint
to a magistrate. (*Johnson* v. *Evans*, 3 Esp. 32.) But the privilege is confined
strictly to communications which are necessary for obtaining redress, or forward-
ing the ends of justice. Thus where A. obtained a warrant to search the house
of B. for goods suspected to be stolen, and in accompanying the officer to execute
the warrant told the officer that B. had robbed him, held that this statement was
not privileged. (*Dancaster* v. *Hewson*, 2 Man. & R. 176.) See *Lathrop* v. *Hyde*,
25 Wend. 448, where, under a similar state of circumstances, the action was held
maintainable, the jury finding express malice. And where the defendant, before
making any complaint to a magistrate, made a charge against the plaintiff to C.,
a constable, adding that he should require C. to serve the warrant on the plaintiff, held this was not a privileged communication; and where, after the plaintiff
had been acquitted before the justice, the defendant repeated the charge against
the plaintiff, held this was not a privileged communication. (*Burlingame* v.

privilege ;   but whatever may be the reason, it seems certain
that where there is a perversion of the right, " the policy of

---

Burlingame, 8 Cow. 141.) Whatever may be said, or written, by a party to a
judicial proceeding, or by his attorney, solicitor, or counsel therein, if pertinent
and material to the matter in controversy, is privileged, and lays no foundation
for a private or public prosecution. The protection is absolute, and no one shall
be permitted to allege that it was said or written with malice. But if a party
or his agent pass beyond the prescribed limit to asperse or vilify another, he is
without protection, and must abide the consequences. As where a person acting
as counsel in a justice's court prepared and presented a declaration, charging the
defendant with a trespass, and alleging that the defendant was "reputed to be
fond of sheep,". "in the habit of biting sheep," and that "if guilty, he ought to
be shot ; " *held*, that an indictment therefor, as a libel, alleging malice, was good.
(*Gilbert* v. *The People*, 1 Denio, 41.) If a party institute proceedings in a court
of justice as a pretence, and merely to promulgate slander, or to serve any other
improper purposes, an action may be maintained for any libellous matter contained in it. (*Hill* v. *Miles*, 9 N. Hamp. 9.) Where words accusing the plaintiff
of a felony were spoken to a justice, on an application for a warrant for felony,
the question whether they are actionable or not depends upon the question
whether they were made in good faith or not, and that question should be left to
the jury. (*Bunton* v. *Worley*, 4 Bibb, 38 ; and see *Marshall* v. *Gunter*, 6 Rich.
419 ; *Briggs* v. *Byrd*, 12 Ired. 377.) A letter addressed to a judge before whom a
proceeding is pending, being an irregular and improper proceeding is not privileged. (*Gould* v. *Hulme*, 3 C. & P. 625.) For such a letter the writer may be
punished as for a contempt. (*Ex parte* MacGill, 2 Fowl. 474 ; *Eagleton* v. *Duchess
of Kingston*, 8 Ves. 467.) An affidavit made before a magistrate to enforce the
law against a person accused therein of a crime, does not subject the accuser to
an action for a libel, though the affidavit be false and insufficient to effect its object. (*Hartsock* v. *Reddick*, 6 Blackf. 255.) Under statute 5 & 6 Vict. c. 109,
the vestry, on precept from the justices, are to return a list of parishioners liable
to serve as constables, and to give notice when and where objections will be
heard by the justices, who are empowered to strike out of the list the names of
persons not liable to serve. Plaintiff's name was inserted in the list of persons
liable to serve, and he attended a session to be sworn in, when the defendant, a
parishioner, objected to him, and made a statement to the justices, in the presence
of other persons, imputing perjury to plaintiff. In an action for slander the
jury found that defendant made the statement *bona fide*, believing it to be
true. Held, that the statement was properly made before the justices, and was a
privileged communication. *Kershaw* v. *Bailey*, 1 Exch. 743 ; 17 Law Jour. R.
129, Ex. ; and see 10 Law Times, 289, and *ante*, note 1089.

    1091 *Henderson* v. *Broomhead*, 4 Hurl. & N. 577 ; *Astley* v. *Younge*, 2 Burr. 817.
The action of slander does not lie for a criminal charge made by an affidavit be
fore a magistrate, the plaintiff's remedy being by an action for malicious prosecution or arrest, or for maliciously suing out a search-warrant. (*Sanders* v

the law stops in and controls the individual right of redress " by action of libel.[1098]

§ 222. The protection which is accorded to *a pleading* extends to every other proceeding in a civil action, and therefore for anything contained in *an affidavit* made in the course of an action or proceeding, no action for libel can be maintained. Thus, where an attorney sued his client for professional services, the client gave notice, under the general issue, that he would prove that the attorney conducted the prosecution and defence of the several suits, and attended to the other professional business in the declaration mentioned, in so careless, unskillful, and improper a manner, as to render such service of no value; the attorney moved to strike out the notice as false, the client resisted this motion upon an affidavit of his own, stating that the attorney had revealed confidential communications of the client relative to a portion of the business to a third person, to the client's prejudice. For the allegations in this affidavit the attorney brought an action of libel against the client, and in his declaration set out the facts to the effect as stated above, and charged that the allegations of the affidavit were false, malicious, and impertinent, a demurrer to the declaration was sustained, and it was held that the affidavit was pertinent to

Rollinson, 2 Strobh. 447.) No proceeding according to the regular course of justice, will make a complaint or other proceeding amount to a libel for which an action can be maintained; and a distress-warrant is a proceeding given to the party by law, for the purpose of enforcing a legal right, and comes directly within the reason of the rule. (*Bailey* v. *Dean*, 5 Barb. 297.) When a requisition is presented for the arrest of a fugitive from justice, with the proper vouchers, according to the act of Congress, it is the duty of the executive to cause the fugitive to be arrested and delivered to the agent appointed to receive him, and the governor has no power to entertain an application to recall or modify such warrant, and an affidavit to support such an application is not a privileged communication. (*Hosmer* v. *Loveland*, 19 Barb. 111.) A complaint to the grand jury, containing a charge of perjury, is privileged, although before its presentation it was exhibited to various persons, by whom it was signed. (*Kidder* v. *Parkhurst*, 3 Allen (Mass.), 393. See *Lake* v. *King*, 1 Mod. 58; *Vanderzee* v. *McGregor*, 12 Wend. 545; *Sands* v. *Robison*, 12 S. & M. 704.)

[1098] *Thorn* v. *Blanchard*, 5 Johns. 530.

the motion, and the truth or falsity could not be questioned in
an action for libel.[1094]

§ 223. The due administration of justice requires that a witness should speak, according to his belief, the truth, the whole
truth, and nothing but the truth, without regard to consequences, and he is encouraged to do this by the consciousness
that, except for any wilfully false statement of a material fact,
which is perjury, no matter that his testimony may in fact be
untrue, or that he be actuated by malice, or that loss ensues by
reason of his testimony, in no event can an action of slander
be maintained against him for any statement made as a witness.[1095] As where the plaintiff brought an action against one

---

[1094] *Garr* v. *Selden*, 4 Coms. 91, rev'g 6 Barb. 416. In *Doyle* v. *O'Doherty*, 1
Carr. & M. 418, it was held that in an affidavit in answer to the application of
the plaintiff for a criminal information against the defendant for sending a chal-
lenge, the defendant was justified in stating any matters, however defamatory and
otherwise libellous, to prevent the court making the rule absolute, and that no
action could be sustained for anything contained in such an affidavit.

A., in opposing a motion for an injunction against him, contradicted a material fact in the moving affidavit of W., and swore that W. knew its falsity, and
had been guilty of perjury; *held*, that an action for libel could not be maintained
by W. for the allegation in A.'s affidavit. (*Warner* v. *Paine*, 2 Sandf. 195), and
see *Suydam* v. *Moffatt*, 1 Sandf. 495. No action can be maintained for defamatory
matter in an affidavit used in the course of a cause, even where the party defamed is not a party to the cause. (*Henderson* v. *Broomhead*, 4 Hurl. & N. 569;
Revis v. *Smith*, 18 C. B. 126; *Dawling* v. *Venman*, 3 Mod. 109.)

[1095] No action lies for words spoken as a witness. (*Weston* v. *Dobniet*, Cro.
Jac. 432; *Damport* v. *Sympson*, Cro. Eliz. 520; *Astley* v. *Younge*, 2 Burr. 807;
Lewis v. *Few*, 5 Johns. 13.) Although the words are spoken maliciously and
without reasonable or probable cause, and the plaintiff has suffered damage
in consequence. (*Revis* v. *Smith*, 36 Eng. L. and Eq. Rep. 268; 18 C. B. 126.)
The witness is not bound to determine the materiality of the evidence, and he
may answer, without liability for so doing, questions put to him, and not objected to or not ruled out by the court. The fact that the testimony is irrelevant, or that the witness is influenced by malice, will not render him liable to an
action for slander. (*Calkins* v. *Sumner*, 13 Wis. 193.) In *Barnes* v. *McCrate*, 32
Maine (2 Red.), 442, it is said the witness is not liable if the answers are pertinent and responsive. No action will lie against a witness for damage sustained
by the falsity of his testimony (*Smith* v. *Lewis*, 3 Johns. 157; *Grove* v. *Branden-
burg*, 7 Blackf. 234; *Cunningham* v. *Brown*, 18 Verm. 123; *Dunlap* v. *Gladding*,
31 Maine, 435); as where an action was brought against a witness for swearing

L., and the defendant being produced as a witness at the trial, testified that the plaintiff was a common liar, by reason whereof the jury gave the plaintiff but small damages. After verdict for the plaintiff, in an action for slander, it was moved in arrest of judgment that the action did not lie, for if it did, every witness might be charged upon such a suggestion, and judgment was given for the defendant.[1096]

§ 224. A party to a proceeding in a court of justice may ordinarily conduct the prosecution or defence in person or by counsel or attorney,[1097] in either case whatever a party may reasonably believe necessary successfully to maintain his suit or his defence, that he may speak, in the course of the proceeding, without being subject to an action for slander. The plaintiff was a witness on the trial of a cause in which the defendant was a party; on her testifying to a particular fact, the defendant immediately, in open court, exclaimed, "That is a lie, and I can prove it," and soon after added, "and I think I have proved it," for this plaintiff sued, and it was held no action would lie, the words being uttered "in the progress of a trial, and in the course of justice."[1098] Where the defendant, having made a criminal complaint against the plaintiff, was questioned by him, with regard to it during its pendency, and answered, in the

that a jewel was worth no more than £180, whereas it was worth £500, a verdict being found for the plaintiff, judgment was arrested. (*Damport* v. *Sympson*, Cro. Eliz. 520; see cases collected Vin. Abr., Act. on the Case for Deceit.) No action lies for suborning a witness to testify falsely. (*Smith* v. *Lewis*, 8 Johns. 157; *Bostwick* v. *Jervis*, 2 Day, 447.) In slander for charging the plaintiff, in the presence of "sundry persons," with larceny, the defendant pleaded that he spoke the words in giving testimony as a witness in a certain cause. Held, that the defendant might, on the trial, prove what the testimony which he gave was, and that the plaintiff, if he meant to proceed for speaking the words on some other occasion than that named in the plea, should have new assigned. (*Nelson* v. *Robe*, 6 Blackf. 204.)

[1096] *Harding* v. *Bullman*, Brownlow, 2; Hutt. 11.

[1097] In New York State, every person of full age and sound mind may appear by attorney * * in every action * * by or against him in any court, or may at his election prosecute or defend such action in person. (2 R. S. 276, § 11.)

[1098] *Badgley* v. *Hedges*, 1 Penn. N. J. Rep. 233.

presence of the magistrate, that he believed the charge true : *held*, that if the defendant believed in good faith, that it was necessary for him to answer the plaintiff, the answer was privileged.[1099] So it has been held that if a servant summon his master before a court of conscience for wages, and the latter, in his necessary defence, utter words imputing felony to the former, no action will lie.[1100] Where the plaintiff, in an action for slander, alleged that he took an oath in the King's Bench to bind the defendant to good behavior, and thereupon the defendant falsely and maliciously said "there is not a word true in that affidavit, and I will prove it by forty witnesses." The jury found the words false and malicious and for the plaintiff, but judgment was arrested on the ground that what defendant said was in his justification and defence in a legal and judicial way.[1101] A party, who is not a barrister or counsellor, conducting a cause on his own behalf or on behalf of another, has the same privilege as counsel as to what he may say.[1102] The defendant, while advocating his own cause before a referee, and while summing up the cause, called plaintiff among other things a perjured scoundrel ; in an action for these words a verdict was taken for the plaintiff, on motion in arrest of judgment the verdict was sustained, and judgment ordered for the plaintiff. The

---

[1099] *Allen* v. *Crofoot*, 2 Wend. 515. No statement in the course of judicial proceedings, which a party may reasonably deem necessary to his cause, will be held libellous, however defamatory it may in its nature be; and it makes no difference with regard to such privileged statements whether they are or not malicious, provided they may be reasonably deemed necessary to the case. *Lea* v. *White*, 4 Sneed (Tenn.), 111 ; *Vausse* v. *Lee*, 1 Hill, S. C. 197 ; *Gosslin* v. *Cannon*, 1 Harring. 3 ; *Marshall* v. *Gunter*, 6 Rich. 419 ; *Warner* v. *Paine*, 2 Sandf. 195.

[1100] *Trottman* v. *Dunn*, 4 Camp. 211. An action for libellous words spoken or sworn in a court of justice, in a man's own defence, against a charge upon him in that court, will not lie. (*Astley* v. *Younge*, 2 Burr. 807 ; 2 L'd Ken. 536 ; *Badgley* v. *Hedges*, 1 Penn. N. J. Rep. 233.)

[1101] *Boulton* v. *Clapham*, W. Jones, 431 ; Mar. 20, cited by Holroyd, J., in *Hodgson* v. *Scarlett*, 1 B. & A. 244, and commented upon in *Hastings* v. *Lusk*, 22 Wend. 419 ; and see *Kean* v. *McLaughlin*, 2 S. & R. 470.

[1102] *Ring* v. *Wheeler*, 7 Cow. 725 ; *Hastings* v. *Lusk*, 22 Wend. 410 ; and *Hoar* v. *Wood*, 3 Metc. 193, where the defendant was conducting a prosecution on behalf of the people, upon a complaint preferred by himself.

court said that to arrest the judgment, it must be held that counsel are protected for words spoken by them on the trial of a cause, although they may have been false, and uttered wil-fully and maliciously, and were irrelevant, and although neither the evidence nor the circumstances afford a suspicion to warrant the accusation.   But the court thought the rule could not be carried to that extravagant length.[1103]

§ 225. The right which a party to a proceeding in a court of justice has to speak all that he may reasonably believe to be necessary for the successful maintenance of his action or defence, is enjoyed by one conducting a proceeding for another, whether he be conducting it as counsel, attorney, or otherwise. A party was alleged to have kept a sum of money which, by his contract, he ought not to have kept; counsel, in reference to this matter, used the language, " This gentleman has de-frauded us," and was interrupted by the court before he had finished his sentence.   Held, first, that the words were not actionable ; secondly, that they were not irrelevant to the mat-ter before the court.[1104]   " A counsellor hath a privilege to en-force anything which is informed him by his client, and to give it in evidence, it being pertinent to the matter in question, and not to examine whether it be true or false, for a counsellor is at his peril to give in evidence that which his client informs him, being pertinent to the matter in question; but matter not perti-nent to the issue, or the matter in question, he need not deliver,

---

[1103] *Ring* v. *Wheeler*, 7 Cow. 725; *Hastings* v. *Lusk*, 22 Wend. 410.

[1104] *Needham* v. *Dowling*, 15 Law Jour. C. P. 9.   An attorney acting as an ad-vocate is privileged as to statements made in the trial of his client's cause, in the same way as counsel.   An attorney, in defending his client from a charge of assault in turning out the plaintiff from certain premises in which he had agreed to sell wine under an agreement with J., stated that J. had sufficient reasons for determining the agreement; that he had been plundered by the plaintiff to a frightful extent.   Held, a privileged statement.   (*Mackay* v. *Ford*, 5 Hurl. & Nor. 792.)   A master is not liable to an action of slander for words spoken while acting as counsel for his slave, while he is on trial before a competent tribunal, provided the words are material and pertinent to the matter in question.   (*Shel-fer* v. *Gooding*, 2 Jones' Law (N. C.), 175.)   As to the privilege of counsel, see Vin. Abr., Act. for Words, B. a. 2.

for he is to discern in his discretion what he is to deliver and
what not, and although it be false, he is excusable, it being
pertinent to the matter.   But if he give in evidence anything
not material to the issue which is scandalous, he ought to aver
it to be true, for it shall be considered as spoken maliciously
and without cause, which is a good ground for an action." [1105]
" If a counsellor speak scandalous words of one in defending his
client's cause, an action doth not lie against him for so doing;
for it is his duty to speak for his client, and it shall be intended
to be spoken according to his client's instructions." [1106]   " If a
man should abuse this privilege, and under pretence of pleading his cause, designedly wander from the point in question,
and maliciously heap slander upon his adversary, I will not say
he is not responsible in an action at law." [1107]   Counsel is not
liable to answer for defamatory matter uttered by him in the
trial of a cause, if the matter is applicable and pertinent to the
subject of inquiry, but this privilege of counsel must be understood to have this limitation, that he shall not avail himself of his
situation to gratify private malice by uttering slanderous expressions against party, witness, or third persons, which have no
relation to the subject-matter of the inquiry, [1108] and " if a counsel, in the course of a cause, utter observations injurious to
individuals and not relevant to the matter in issue, it seems
to me that he would not therefore be responsible to the
party injured in a common action for slander, but that it
would be necessary to sue him, in a special action on the case,
in which it must be alleged and proved that the matter was
spoken maliciously, and without reasonable and probable cause;"
and semble, that although it be lawful for a counsel in the discharge of his duty to utter matter injurious to individuals, yet
the subsequent publication of such slanderous matter is not

[1105] *Brook* v. *Montague*, Cro. Jac. 90.

[1106] *Wood* v. *Gunston*, Sty. 462; per Glyn, J., in *Hodgson* v. *Scarlett*, 1 B. &
A. 232; L'd Ellenborough said· *Wood* v. *Gunston* carried the privilege too far.

[1107] Tilghman, Ch. J., *McMillan* v. *Birch*, 1 Bin. 178.

[1108] *Jennings* v. *Paine*, 4 Wis. 358; *Hoar* v. *Wood*, 3 Metc. 193; *Hodgson* v.
Scarlett, 1 B. & A. 232; Holt N. P. 621; *Parker* v. *Mitchell*, 11 Barb. 469.

justifiable, unless it be shown that it was published for the purpose of giving the public information which it was fit and proper for them to receive, and that it was warranted by the evidence.[1109]

§ 226. The right of an accused person to say all that he may honestly consider necessary for his defence is not confined to proceedings in a court of justice; it extends to every occasion upon which one is called upon to defend himself from any charge against him. Thus, words spoken in good faith, and within the scope of his defence, by a party on trial before a church meeting, are privileged, and do not render him liable to an action, although they disparage private character.[1110] Where the defendant expressed an opinion founded upon the statements of others that the plaintiff had maliciously killed his (defendant's) horse. For expressing this opinion the defendant was arraigned *before the church.* In self-defence he produced certificates of the persons upon whose authority he had spoken. For this the plaintiff sued, but offering no direct proof of malice, it was held the action was not maintainable.[1111] So where R. & Co. received a written order for an iron target, which order purported to come from the defendant; R. & Co. sent the target to the defendant, who returned it, stating that he had never ordered it, and requested to see the written order upon which R. & Co. had acted; the order was sent to the defendant, and he wrote R. & Co. that he firmly believed it was written by the plaintiff. It was submitted on behalf of the defendant that the communication was a [conditionally] privileged one. It was left to the jury to say whether the defendant had written that the plaintiff was the author of the order sent to R. & Co. *bonâ fide* and without malice, believing his statement to be true; the jury found in the affirmative, a verdict was entered for plaintiff with £5 damages, with leave to the defendant to

---

[1109] Holroyd, J., *Flint* v. *Pike*, 6 D. & R. 528; 4 B. & C. 473.

[1110] *York* v. *Pease*, 2 Gray (Mass.), 282.

[1111] *Dunn* v. *Winters*, 2 Humph. 512.

move to enter the verdict for him, and on motion the verdict was entered for the defendant.[1112]

§ 227. No action for slander or libel can be maintained against a judge, or one exercising judicial functions, for anything he may say or write in his judicial capacity upon the trial or upon the determination of a cause or matter pending before him; if improper, it may be a ground for his impeachment or for an application for his removal, but not for an action of slander or libel.[1113] Thus, no action lies against a coroner for words spoken maliciously in the course of an inquest before him.[1114]

[1112] *Croft* v. *Stevens*, 7 Hurl. & N. 570; see *post*, § 240.

[1113] *Rex* v. *Skinner*, Loft. 1099. Neither party, witness, counsel, jury, or judge, can be made to answer for words spoken in office; although, if they be opprobrious and irrelevant to the case, the court will notice them as a contempt, and examine on an information, and punish accordingly. (*Id.*; *Henderson* v. *Broomhead*, 4 Hurl. & N. 564; *Kendillon* v. *Maltby*, 2 Moo. & Rob. 438; *Moore* v. *Ames*, 3 Caines, 170.) In *Entick* v. *Carrington*, 19 State Trials, 1062, Lord Camden remarks, "No man ever heard of an action against a conservator of the peace as such." Quoted, *South* v. *The State of Maryland*, 18 How. U. S. Rep. 403, and see Vin. Abr. Act. Case Deceit, Q. *b.* 1.

[1114] *Thomas* v. *Churton*, 6 Law Times Rep. N. S. 320. And *semble*, there would be no action although the words were spoken without probable cause. (*Id.*) And per Cockburn, Ch. J.: "I should not wish to lay down the broad proposition that in no case is a judge liable for words uttered by him as a judge." "A public officer, who is not a mere volunteer, but compelled to act in a judicial capacity, is not amenable, either civilly or criminally, for a mistake in law or error of judgment, when his motives are untainted with fraud or malice." (*Teall* v. *Felton*, 1 Coms. 547.)

Words spoken in discharge of official duty are not actionable. (*Goodenow* v. *Tappan*, 1 Ham. 60.) *Aliter*, if spoken under pretence of official duty, wantonly and with malice. The question of intention is to be left with the jury. (*Ib.*) Thus, in an action against the defendant, a ward-beadle, for words spoken by him before an inquest, but not in answer to any inquiries of the jury nor in the presence of the jury only, held that it was a question for the jury whether the words were spoken by the defendant in the discharge of his official duty. (*Wilson* v. *Collins*, 5 C. & P. 373.) In an action for libel against one, a justice of the peace, for defamatory matter contained in an official certificate by him to the grand jury, held the publication was conditionally privileged. (*Sands* v. *Robison*, 12 S. & M. 704.) A report of the grand jury, under any part of § 2992 of the Code of Iowa, held not a privileged communication; but where it was made in good faith, and in the discharge of a supposed public duty, it does not furnish ground to sustain an action for libel. (*Rector* v. *Smith*, 11 Iowa (3 With.), 302.)

For wherever duties of a judicial nature are imposed upon a
public officer, the due execution of which depends upon his own
judgment, he is exempt from all responsibility by action, for
the motives which influence him and the manner in which said
duties are performed. If corrupt, he may be impeached or indicted, but he cannot be prosecuted by an individual to obtain
redress for the wrong which may have been done.[1115] No public officer is responsible in a civil suit for a judicial determination, however erroneous it may be, and however malicious the
motive which produced it.[1116] No action will lie for defamatory
matter contained in a presentment of a grand jury.[1117] The
plaintiff (Captain Jekyll) having preferred certain charges
against Colonel Stewart, an officer in the same regiment with
plaintiff, Colonel Stewart was tried by a court martial, and the
president of the court, Sir John Moore, delivered to the judge
advocate a written opinion, as the decision of the court, and in
such opinion, after stating that the court found Colonel Stewart
not guilty of the charges imputed to him, added: "The court
cannot pass without observation the malicious and groundless
accusations that have been produced by Captain Jekyll against
an officer whose character, during a long period of service, has
been irreproachable." For this addition to the decision Captain
Jekyll brought an action for libel against the president of the
court. The plaintiff was nonsuited, and a new trial being
moved for, it was refused on the ground that the language complained of formed part of the judgment of acquittal.[1118] In

[1115] *Rochester White Lead Co.* v. *The City of Rochester*, 3 Coms. 466. See Cooke on Defam. 63.

[1116] *Weaver* v. *Devendorf*, 3 Denio, 117; *Vail* v. *Owen*, 19 Barb. 22; *Brown* v. *Smith*, 24 *Id.* 419; and see *Hill* v. *Sellick*, 21 Barb. 207; *Harman* v. *Brotherson*, 1 Denio, 537. But an officer who violates a ministerial duty, though his office is primarily judicial, is liable therefor. *Wilson* v. *Mayor of New York*, 1 Denio, 595; *Rochester White Lead Co.* v. *City of Rochester*, 3 Coms. 463. Words spoken by the mayor of a city are privileged. (*Rector* v. *Smith*, 11 Iowa, 302.)

[1117] Bac. Abr. tit. Libel, 446, Mo. 627; Hawk. Pl. Cr. c. 73, § 8; and see ob-servations in *Johnson* v. *Sutton*, 1 T. R. 493.

[1118] *Jekyll* v. *Moore*, 2 New R. 341; and see *Kendillon* v. *Maltby*, 1 Car. & M. 402; 2 Moo. & Rob. 438; *Warden* v. *Bailey*, 4 Taunt. 67; 4 M. & S. 400. And

another case of an action brought for defamatory matter contained in a report of a military court of inquiry appointed to
investigate charges against the plaintiff, it was held that the report was a privileged publication, and could not be given in
evidence.[1119]   So it was held that the defendant, being governor
in council of Fort St. George, was justified in publishing, according to the fact, that the court of directors had resolved to
dismiss the plaintiff from the service for a gross violation of the
trust reposed in him as commanding officer of the Molucca
Islands, and that he (the defendant) had been ordered to erase
his name from the army list.[1120]

§ 228. With regard to the right of a judicial officer, we suppose a difference exists between a judge of a court of record
and a judge of a court not of record, or one who is not, indeed,
a judge in the strict sense of the term, but who merely executes
judicial functions; as respects the first, his being a judge, without more, constitutes a complete defence to an action for anything said or written by him as such judge; but as respects the
second, the privilege arises only in cases in which he had jurisdiction.   "If magistrates while occupying the bench, under
pretence of *giving advice*, publicly hear slanderous complaints
over which they have no jurisdiction, although their names may
be in the commission of the peace, a report of what passed be-

---

where, upon a proceeding on the game laws in Scotland, after the defendant
had confessed, and had appealed to the leniency of the court for a mitigation of
the penalty, it was asserted by the defendants, two of the justices, that "he was
a thief, and had been known to steal bee-hives and leather;" held, on appeal,
that subordinate judges were responsible for words spoken, if malice was clearly
made out, the privilege being confined only to members of Parliament and judges
of the supreme courts; the judgment of the court of session, as far as the inter-
locutor of relevancy was concerned, was therefore affirmed, but the House not
being satisfied that there was evidence of malice, the cause was remitted to
another jury. (*Allardice* v. *Robertson*, 1 Dowl. N. S. 495.)

[1119] *Oliver* v. *Bentinck*, 3 Taunt. 456.

[1120] *Home* v. *Bentinck*, 4 Moore, 563; 8 Price, 226, and note *Id.* 244. A communication to a governor respecting an officer under his command is *quasi* judicial and privileged. (*Gray* v. *Pentland*, 2 S. & R. 23; 4 S. & R. 420.)

fore them is as little privileged as if they were illiterate mechanics in an ale-house."[1121]

§ 229. Independently of any statute, certainly in the State of New York, and probably in every other State, "the publication of the proceedings upon a judicial trial fairly reported and without express malice, is not actionable."[1122] The like rule obtains in England, but as both there and in New York some limitations are imposed upon the rule, it is necessary, in order to show in what these limitations consist, to examine somewhat in detail the authorities upon the subject. The initial principle seems to be that the public good requires that the proceedings in courts of justice should be conducted openly. Accordingly it is in New York provided by statute that "the sittings of every court within this State shall be public, and every citizen may freely attend the same."[1123] Although there is no such law in England, it is the custom there to hold the courts with open doors. And it is said to be a rule of law that "every one is supposed or presumed to be cognizant of

<hr/>

[1121] Pollock, Ch. B. *Lewis* v. *Levy*, 1 El. B. & E. 537; 36 Law Jour. Rep. 282, Ex.; and see as to necessity of tribunal having jurisdiction, *Hosmer* v. *Loveland*, 19 Barb. 111; *Howard* v. *Thompson*, 21 Wend. 819; *King* v. *Root*, 4 Wend. 113; *O'Donaghue* v. *McGovern*, 23 Wend. 26; *Hastings* v. *Lusk*, 22 Wend. 410; *Fawcett* v. *Charles*, 13 Wend. 473; *Harrison* v. *Bush*, 5 Ell. & Bl. 344; *Milam* v. *Burnsides*, 1 Brev. 295; *Moloney* v. *Bartley*, 3 Camp. 210; *McGregor* v. *Thwaites*, 3 B. & C. 24.

[1122] *Edsall* v. *Brooks*, 17 Abb. Pra. R. 227; 26 How. Pra. R. 426. In New York the publication of judicial proceedings is protected by statute, which enacts: —No reporter, editor, or proprietor of any newspaper shall be liable to any action or prosecution, civil or criminal, for a fair and true report in such newspaper of any judicial, legislative, or other public official proceedings of any statement, speech, argument, or debate, in the course of the same, except upon actual proof of malice in making such report, which shall in no case be implied from the fact of publication. (Laws 1854, ch. 130, § 1.) Nothing in the preceding section contained shall be so construed as to protect any such reporter, editor, or proprietor, from an action or indictment for any libellous comments or remarks superadded to and interspersed or connected with such report. (*Id.* § 2.)

[1123] 2 Rev. Stat. 274, § 1. "No law insures the publicity of the courts of justice, either in England or the United States." Lieber on Civil Liberty, 134; enlarged ed. of 1859.

the proceedings in the courts of justice,"[1124] and hence " it is of great consequence that the public should know what takes place in the courts."[1125] A publication of the proceedings of a court " only extends that publicity which is so important a feature of the administration of the law in England, and thus enables to be witnesses of it not merely the few whom the court can hold, but the thousands who can read the report,"[1126] and " we ought to make as wide as possible the right of the public to know what takes place in a court of justice."[1127] It is conceded that some " inconveniences and mischief " results or may result from the publication of the proceedings in courts of justice,[1128] but " the balance of public benefit from the publicity is great."[1129] " Those who are present hear all [that takes place], relevant or irrelevant, and those who are absent may * * have all that is said reported to them. * * When once you establish that a court is a *public* court, a fair and *bonâ fide* report of all that takes place there may be published.[1130] For being a true account of what took place in a court of justice which is open to all the world, the publication of it [cannot be] unlawful."[1131] But, " it must not be taken for granted that the publication of every matter which passes in a court of justice, however truly represented, is under all circumstances and with whatever motive published justifiable, but that doctrine must be taken with some grains of allowance."[1132] For as a judicial proceeding is privileged on principles of public convenience, the privilege is limited in respect to the *subject-matter* of the report, and as to the *manner* of the reporting,[1133] and the " con-

---

[1124] Willard's Eq. Juris. 251.

[1125] Campbell, Ch. J., *Hearne* v. *Stowell*, 12 Adol. & El. 718 ; 4 Per. & D. 696.

[1126] Wilde, B., *Popham* v. *Pickburn*, 7 Hurl. & N. 891. On its being remarked to Lord Mansfield, that few persons attended the courts merely to watch the proceedings, he replied, " No matter, we sit every day in the newspapers."

[1127] Pollock, Ch. B., *Ryalls* v. *Leader*, 1 Law Rep. 298, Ex.

[1128] *Flint* v. *Pike*, 4 B. & C. 473. Littledale, J.

[1129] Campbell, Ch. J., *Hearne* v. *Stowell*, 12 Adol. & El. 718 ; 4 Per. & D. 696.

[1130] Bramwell, B., *Ryalls* v. *Leader*, 1 Law Rep. 298, Ex.

[1131] Eyre, Ch. J., *Curry* v. *Walter*, 1 B. & P. 525.

[1132] *Stiles* v. *Nokes*, 7 East, 493.

[1133] 1 Stark. Slan. 263.

dition necessarily annexed to the immunity is, that the proceeding be fairly, impartially, and correctly reported, and even in that case it will be for the court to consider whether it was lawful to publish it.[1184] "Matters may appear in a court of justice that may have so immoral a tendency, or be so injurious to the character of an individual that their publication would not be tolerated."[1185]   And therefore it is said, "There is no privilege when the subject-matter is *blasphemous* or *defamatory of an individual*."[1186]   Thus where on the trial of Carlile for publishing Paine's Age of Reason, the defendant read the whole of the book to the jury, and afterwards his wife published a full report of the trial, containing an entire copy of the Age of Reason as read to the jury; for this publication a criminal information was granted against Mrs. Carlile, the court observing that although as a general proposition it was certainly lawful to publish the proceedings of courts of justice, yet it must be taken with this qualification, that what is contained in the publication must neither be *defamatory of an individual*, tending to excite disaffection, nor calculated to offend the morals of the people.[1187] Although in the course of a trial it may become necessary for the purposes of justice to hear or read matter of defamatory or immoral tendency, it is not yet competent to any person, under the pretence of publishing that trial, to re-utter or circulate such matter.   It is observed in the Sixth Report of the English Criminal Law Commissioners, that these qualifications destroy all the supposed privilege.   Our explanation is this: Truth is not a defence to a criminal prosecution for libel, and therefore where a report of a trial contains blasphemous, indecent, or defamatory matter, it is not the less the subject of a criminal prosecution because it is a fair or true report of a judicial proceeding. In a subsequent case,[1188] Maule, J., said: "I think it is impossible at this day to say that a fair account of proceedings in a

[1184] Littledale, J., *Flint* v. *Pike*, 4 B. & C. 473; 1 Stark. Slan. 263.
[1185] Maule, J., *Hoare* v. *Silverlock*, 9 C. B. 20.
[1186] 1 Stark. Slan. 263.
[1187] *Rex* v. *Carlile*, 3 B. & Ald. 167.
[1188] *Hoare* v. *Silverlock*, 9 C. B. 20.

court of justice, *not being ex parte*, but on the hearing of both
sides, is not, *generally speaking*, a justifiable publication. *I do
not lay it down as a universal proposition;* but as a general
rule, it may be assumed that the publication of a fair account
of what passes in a court of justice, not *ex parte*, is justifiable,
unless there is something to take it out of that rule." " No
case has decided that a report of proceedings in a court of justice implicating the reputation of a third person is under any
[all] circumstances privileged." [1139] " There is no *dictum* to be
met with in the books, that a man, under the pretence of publishing the proceedings of a court of justice, may discolor and
garble the proceedings by his own comments and constructions,
so as to effect the purpose of aspersing the character of those
concerned." [1140] But we ought to protect a fair and *bona fide*
statement of the proceedings in a court of justice, [1141] and perhaps
the result of the authorities is that : a fair report of a trial or a
proceeding in a court of justice, conducted publicly in the presence of the parties concerned, is conditionally privileged. [1142]

§ 230. When it is said that a fair report of a trial in a court
of justice is privileged, what is meant by a fair report ? In one
case it is said : "*If* a party is to be allowed to publish what passes
in a court of justice, he must publish *the whole case*, and not merely state the conclusion which he himself draws from the evidence," [1143] and where in a report of proceedings under a commission of lunacy, it was stated, " The plaintiff's testimony, being
unsupported, failed to have any effect upon the jury, * * Mr.
Jervis commented with cutting severity on the testimony of Mr.

[1139] *Ryalls* v. *Leader*, 1 Law Rep. 298, Ex.
[1140] Spencer, J., *Thomas* v. *Croswell*, 7 Johns. 264.
[1141] *Ryalls* v. *Leader*, 1 Law Rep. 298, Ex.
[1142] A fair account of what takes place in a court of justice is privileged.
Hearne v. *Stowell*, 12 Adol. & El. 718 ; 4 Per. & D. 696 ; *Turner* v. *Pullman*, 6
Law Times Rep. N. S. 130 ; *Rex* v. *Wright*, 8 T. R. 298 ; *Chambers* v. *Payne*, 2
C. M. & R. 156 ; *Cincinnati, &c. Co.* v. *Timberlake*, 10 Ohio, N. S. 548 : *Flint* v.
Pike, 4 B. & C. 84 ; *Saunders* v. *Mills*, 6 Bing. 213 ; *Lewis* v. *Levy*, 1 El. B. & E.
587 ; 36 Law Jour. R. 282 ; Q. B. *Andrews* v. *Chapman*, 3 C. & K. 286 ; *Smith* v.
Scott, 2 C. & K. 580.
[1143] Abbott, Ch. J., *Lewis* v. *Walter*, 4 B. & A. 612.

O," the statement was held not privileged, and it was said that the proceedings themselves ought to have been set out, not merely the result of them.[1144] Yet again it has been said, that an abridged report may be a " fair report," [1145] and where in an action against the publisher of a newspaper for a libel, on the plea of not guilty, it appeared that the libel purported to be the account of a trial of a former action, brought by the present plaintiff against other parties for a libel, and after stating the libel in the original action, and the facts proved by the then defendants, and the summing up of the judge, it stated that the jury found a verdict for the plaintiff, with £20 damages. No evidence was given as to any such trial having taken place in fact, or whether the report was fair or not. It was left to the jury to say whether the report, although it contained some allegations injurious to the plaintiff, was, if taken altogether, with the statement of the verdict being in his favor, injurious to the plaintiff on the face of it; and the jury having found for the defendant, the court refused a rule for a new trial.[1146] The report is not privileged if it in anywise discolors or garbles the proceedings, or adds [unwarranted] comments or insinuations.[1147] As where

[1144] Roberts v. Brown, 10 Bing. 519; 4 M. & Sc. 407; and see Delegal v. Highley, 3 Bing. N. S. 950; where the matter complained against professed to be a report of proceedings in a court of justice, did not profess to state facts as deposed to by the witness, but only as stated by the counsel for the prosecution—held not-to be a fair report, and not privileged. (Saunders v. Mills, 6 Bing. 213.) And where the report stated that the evidence before the magistrate entirely negatived the story of the plaintiff, which story was the statement of the plaintiff in which the imputed perjury was contained,—Held not to be privileged; and a plea justifying this report on the ground that it was a fair and correct report of the proceedings which had taken place, was held bad after verdict. (Lewis v. Levy, 1 Ellis, B. & E. 537.) The editor of a newspaper has the right to publish the fact that an individual has been arrested, and upon what charge, but he has no right, while the charge is in the course of investigation before the magistrate, to assume that the person accused is guilty, or to hold him out to the world as such. (Usher v. Severance, 2 App. 9.)

[1145] Turner v. Sullivan, 6 Law Times Rep. N. S. 130. A report in substance true, it seems is not privileged. Flint v. Pike, 4 B. & C. 473.

[1146] Chalmers v. Payne, 2 C. M. & R. 156.

[1147] Thomas v. Croswell, 7 Johns. 264; Stiles v. Nokes, 7 East, 493; S. C. sub nom. Carr v. Jones, 3 Smith, 491; Flint v. Pike, 4 B. & C. 473.

the report was headed "Shameful conduct of an attorney,"[1148] or " Extorting money to hush up a complaint,"[1149] or " Black-mailing by a policeman,"[1150] or " Horse-stealing,"[1151] it was held not to be privileged. Where a statement defamatory of the plaintiff was copied from a previous publication, and published by the defendant, prefaced by the word "Fudge," the court left it to the jury to say whether that word was added to vindi-cate the character of the plaintiff, or merely to create an argu-ment in favor of the defendant, in case proceedings should be taken against him for the publication.[1152] In another case the report was headed "Wilful and corrupt perjury," and it was said by the court "That (the heading) is merely stating the charge. It may be a heading entirely innocent, simply indica-ting what is to follow, and it would be a question for the jury whether it is a fair and *bonâ fide* report of· the proceedings."[1153]

§ 231. While it is considered a principle of public conven-ience to allow or even to encourage reports of the proceedings on a trial, reports of preliminary proceedings *have been* discouraged and regarded as having " a tendency to pervert the public mind, and to disturb the course of justice."[1154] In England, the

---

[1148] *Clement* v. *Lewis*, 3 Brod. & B. 297, affirming *Lewis* v. *Clement*, 3 B. & Ald. 702.

[1149] *Stanley* v. *Webb*, 4 Sandf. 21.

[1150] *Edsall* v. *Brooks*, 17 Abb. Pra. R. 221; 26 How. Pra. R. 426.

[1151] *Mountney* v. *Wotton*, 2 B. & Ad. 673.

[1152] *Hunt* v. *Algar*, 6 C. & P. 245.

[1153] *Lewis* v. *Levy*, 1 Ell. B. & E. 537. In *Barber* v. *Bennett*, *MS.*, the report of a proceeding before a magistrate was headed " Suspicion of stealing money." The defence was a fair report, and on demurrer the Superior Court of New York held that the heading did not prevent the report being a privileged publication.

[1154] L'd Ellenborough, *King* v. *Fisher*, 2 Camp. 563; and see *Charlton* v. *Wal-ton*, 6 Car. & P. 385; also *Rex* v. *Fleet*, 1 B. & A. 379, where a criminal informa-tion was granted against the defendant for publishing the minutes of a coroner's inquest. It was said to be highly criminal to publish *ex parte* accounts. Courts and judicial officers have always claimed and exercised the right to dictate whether or not the proceedings before them should be published. In the time of Edward the Third, Luolus de Thacstead, a notary public, was committed to the Tower for merely attending in court to take a note of the proceedings between Joannes de Bourne and Ricardus de Potesgrave, and in *Flint* v. *Pike*, 4 Barn. & C. 473, Lit-

magistrate has the power of conducting preliminary examinations privately, and a report of such a proceeding would not be

---

tledale, J., said it was for the court to consider whether it was lawful to publish a report of the proceedings. Lord Eldon interdicted the publication of the proceedings on the application of the poet Shelley for the custody of his children. (See Memoir of Shelley, by T. L. Peacock, and Fraser's Magazine, No. 342, 361.) So recently as A. D. 1867, a justice of the Superior Court of the City of New York prohibited the publication of proceedings had before him, and his course was approved by the other justices of that court. A coroner may prohibit the publication of proceedings had before him (*Garrett* v. *Ferrand*, 6 B. & C. 611), and so may a committing magistrate. (*Cox* v. *Coleridge*, 1 B. & C. 37.) See Borthwick on Libel, 119, 121, note; Holt on Libel, ch. ix. The cases are more numerous where the publication of the proceedings have been prohibited pending the proceedings. A disregard of such a prohibition is a contempt. In one case, Lord Eldon remarked that when he first came into Westminster Hall, the law was well understood that it would be a contempt to publish the proceedings of the court before they were finished. (*Knight* v. *Knight*, 1 Jac. & Walk. 167.) In *Rex* v. *Clement*, 4 Barn. & Ald. 218, Lord Tenterden ordered that there should be no publication of the proceedings until the several indictments against the defendant had been tried; and he fined a newspaper proprietor £500 for disobedience to this order, in publishing an account of the first trial before the second had begun. The courts upheld the action of Lord Tenterden. Lord Campbell, in his Lives of the Chief Justices, vol. iii. p. 208, gives it as his opinion that this transaction tarnished the fame of Lord Tenterden, and that the order forbidding the publication was "imprudently" made. See *Rex* v. *Gilham*, 1 M. & M. 165. In New York, by statute (2 Rev. Stat. 278, § 10), "Publishing a false or grossly inaccurate report of the proceedings of a court of record is a criminal contempt." Any publication prejudicing the merits of a cause before it is heard is a contempt. (2 Atk. 479.) The validity of plaintiff's marriage coming in question in a suit, her father, pending the suit, advertised in a newspaper, offering a reward to any one who would produce legal proof of the marriage—held a contempt. (*Pool* v. *Sacheverel*, 1 P. Wms. 675.) The printers of a newspaper were committed for publishing that certain parties to a suit had turned "affidavit men." (*Roach* v. *Garvan*, 2 Atk. 469; 2 Dick. 794.) In that case reference was made to the case of a printer of a newspaper punished for publishing of a certain cause, that it was "a hue and cry after charitable uses," and to the case of Capt. Perry, punished for printing and publishing his brief before the cause came on. A party was committed to prison for publishing an advertisement reflecting on an answer in the cause. (See *Cann* v. *Cann*, 2 Dick. 795; 2 Ves. 520; *Ex parte Crow*, 2 Turn. & Ven. Pra. 231, 232.) Where an injunction order appointing a receiver had been granted, the party obtaining the order caused printed copies of it to be dispersed among the tenants, to prevent them paying rents except to the receiver; Lord Hardwick refused to adjudge it a contempt, but expressed his disapproval of the proceeding. (*Baker* v. *Harf*, 2 Atk. 488.) Publishing disparaging comments upon the court, or its officers, or its proceedings, is a contempt. Thus the New York Common Council, being en-

privileged.   But if a preliminary proceeding is carried on *fori-bus apertis*, it would be privileged.   We are not prepared to lay

joined by a preliminary injunction from certain official action, passed resolutions declaring the injunction illegal, proclaiming a resolution to disregard it, and imputing dishonesty to the judge who granted it; held, the resolution was a contempt. (*The People* v. *Compton*, ▶ Duer, 512; affirmed, *The People* v. *Sturtevant*, 9 N. Y. 263; and see *Morrison* v. *Moat*, 4 Edw. 25.)   And where an officer of a corporation had a verdict against him in an action for a malicious prosecution, which verdict was sustained by the court, the corporation voted him a sum of money, and passed a resolution to the effect that in instituting the prosecution in question he had been actuated by motives of public justice; this was held a reflection upon the court, and a contempt.   (*Rex* v. *Watson*, 2 Term R. 199.)   Pending the trial of one Nixon, in the Oyer and Terminer, New York City, April, 1864, an article appeared in the New York Tribune, headed, "A judicial outrage," and which was supposed to reflect upon the conduct of the judge (G. G. Barnard) presiding on the trial of Nixon.   The article was supposed to have been written by Horace Greeley, and an order issued for him to show cause before Judge Barnard why he should not be attached for contempt.   Instead of showing cause, he moved for a writ of prohibition, which being denied the following order was made:

"*In the Matter of Horace Greeley upon an Order to show cause why he should not answer for a Contempt of Court.*—It is ordered by the court, that the said Horace Greeley, now here appearing by I. T. Williams, Esq., his counsel, answer (and the answer under oath is waived) the following interrogatories, and have until Monday next, being the 25th day of April inst., at 11 o'clock A. M., to file answers thereto, and be then heard in this court in defence of the accusation that he published a grossly inaccurate report of the proceedings of this court in the Daily Tribune of April 14, 1864, in the language contained in and recited in interrogatory the first.

"*Interrogatory the First.*—Did you write in manuscript the following matter, which appeared in page 4, in column 2 thereof, in the New York Daily Tribune of Thursday, April 14, 1864, to wit?

["A judicial outrage." Here follows the article, portions of which contain the alleged contempt.]

"*Interrogatory Second.*—If not, did you write in manuscript any *part* thereof?

"*Interrogatory Third.*—If not, did you see the same in manuscript or in proof before it was published?

"*Interrogatory Fourth.*—If not, were you or not the responsible editor of the Tribune on the 14th day of April, 1864 ?

"*Interrogatory Fifth.*—If you did not write or see before publication the said matter, do you know who is the author, or writer, or composer thereof, or did you not know that it was to be published?

"*Interrogatory Sixth.*—If you know the said author or writer, please name him.

"Then follows a statement or report of the transactions in court, which were reported and commented on in the Tribune, and a disclaimer from the court of any complaint as to the editorial comments, but only as to what purports to be a report of the proceedings in court."

To these interrogatories Mr. Greeley made and filed the following statement:

"Horace Greeley, in the above-entitled proceedings referred to, protesting against the jurisdiction of this court over his person, and over the proceedings now being taken, and insisting that they are irregular and without warrant of law, and further insisting that he ought not to be asked, and cannot legally be compelled, to answer questions upon a charge which is in its nature criminal, and for which he may be exposed to indictment, both as a misdemeanor for a contempt as well as for a libel, and further insisting that the said article, in the order to show cause in these proceedings referred to, is not a report of the proceedings of a court, but, on the other hand, is simply an edito-

down the law that the publication of preliminary inquiries before magistrates is invariably lawful, but we are not prepared
to lay down the law that the publication of such inquiries is
invariably unlawful.   There is no distinction between one court
and another as respects the right of publishing reports of their
proceedings, provided the proceedings be had publicly, and not

rial criticism, based upon a report of such proceedings contained in a newspaper called the Evening
Express, published two days before said editorial article was published, to wit, on the 12th day of
April instant.

"For answer to the interrogatories filed and served on him, says that he is now, and ever since
its foundation has been, the principal editor of the newspaper called the Tribune, and is one of its
proprietors, by being a stockholder of the corporation that publishes the same.   That as such editor
and proprietor he is subject to all the responsibilities that justly pertain to that relation.   Believing
that this avowal is a substantial answer to all the interrogatories propounded to him, he most respectfully declines to answer any questions that may expose any of his associates in the editorship and
publication of said newspaper to the discipline of this tribunal, preferring to abide the consequences,
be they what they may."

The court being satisfied that no disrespect was intended, discharged Mr.
Greeley.

As to contempts by publications reflecting on courts, &c., see *Re Van Hook*, 3
City Hall Recorder, 64; *Re Spooner*, 5 Id. 109; *Re Strong*, Id. 9; *Re Yates*, 4 Johns.
317; 6 Johns. 337; *Re Eliz. Mayer*, 2 Barnard. 43; *Ex parte Jones*, 13 Ves. Jr.
237; *Re Crawford*, 18 Law Jour. 225, Q. B.; 13 Jur. 955; *Ex parte Turner*, 3.
Mont. D. & G. 523; *Re Van Sandau*, 1 De Gex, 55; *Birch* v. *Walsh*, 10 Ir. Law
R. 93; *Rex* v. *Lee*, 5 Esp. 123; *Rex* v. *Hart*, 1 Camp. 359; 1 Hawk Pl. Cr. ch:·
73; *Moulton* v. *Clapham*, Sir W. Jones, 431; March on Slander, 20; *Hollings-*
worth v. *Duane*, Wallace's R. 77; *Bayard* v. *Passmore*, 3 Yeates, 438; *Respub-*
lica v. *Oswald*, 1 Dallas, 319; *Richmond* v. *Dayton*, 10 Johns. 393; *Folger* v. *Hoog-*
land, 5 Johns. 235; *Re Bronson*, 12 'Id. 460; *The People* v. *Freer*, 1 Cai. 485; *The*
People v. *Few*, 2 Johns. 290; 2 Stark. Slander, ch. xiii.; Solicitor's Journal, 1864,
page 142; An Inquiry into the Doctrine lately Propagated concerning Attach-
ments for Contempts, &c., by an English Constitution Crown Lawyer, London,
1769. (Historical Soc. Lib. N. Y.) See a pamphlet entitled Rights of Corporations and Reporters, published at Columbia, South Carolina, A. D. 1857, containing the report of the case of *Robert W. Gibbs* v. *Edward I. Arthur* and *John Bur-*
dell. The City Council held, in 1855, a public meeting. The plaintiff, the editor
of one of the city papers, being present, was asked by the mayor whether ho had
come to take notes of the proceedings. The plaintiff answering in the affirmative,
the mayor ordered him to leave, which on the plaintiff's refusing to do, he was,
on the mayor's orders, ejected by a police officer. The plaintiff sued the mayor
and the officer, and the defence interposed was in the first instance that the
mayor acted on a resolution of the City Council forbidding the presence of reporters at their meetings, and subsequently the defence was set up that the City
Council had authorized the publication of their proceedings in a paper other than
that with which the plaintiff was connected. Both these defences failed, and the
plaintiff recovered damages for being ejected.

ex parte.[1155] And where a preliminary examination is publicly conducted, in the presence of the accused, there seems to be no reason why the same rule should not apply to such a proceeding as to a trial. No privilege can be claimed for a report of an *ex parte* proceeding,[1156] but probably it is now settled that a fair report of a proceeding before a magistrate, not being *ex parte*, is privileged. It being shown that the proceeding is judicial, in a public court, and not *ex parte*, a fair report of it is privileged. Thus, in an action for libel, it appeared that the defamatory matter was published in a fair report of proceedings before two judges at chambers, on applications under the Bankrupt Act, 5 & 6 Victoria, chapter 122, and it was held that the proceeding was judicial, and the report privileged.[1157] And in respect of proceedings in jail under the same statute, and before a registrar in bankruptcy, it was held that the jail was a public court, and the proceedings judicial, and the report being a fair one, was privileged, although it affected a person not a party to the proceedings.[1158] A report of the proceedings before a grand jury have been held not to be privileged.[1159] The register of protests of bills and notes in Scotland, established by statute, was held a public document, to which every one had a right of access, and the publication of which was privileged.[1160] Where

---

[1155] *Lewis* v. *Levy*, 36 Law Jour. R. 282, Q. B.; 1 El. B. & E. 537.

[1156] Publishing the contents of an *ex parte* affidavit, made to obtain the plaintiff's arrest, is not privileged as a report of judicial proceedings. (*Cincinnati, &c., Co.* v. *Timberlake*, 10 Ohio, N. S. 548.) Report of *ex parte* preliminary proceedings not privileged. *Duncan* v. *Thwaites*, 3 B. & C. 556; 5 D. & R. 447; *Rex* v. *Lee*, 5 Esp. 123; *Currie* v. *Walter*, 1 B. & P. 523; *Huff* v. *Bennett*, 4 Sandf. 127; *Stanley* v. *Webb*, 4 Sandf. 21; 8 N. Y. 209; *Matthews* v. *Beach*, 5 Sandf. 256; *Hoare* v. *Silverlock*, 9 C. B. 20.

[1157] *Simpson* v. *Robinson*, 12 Adol. & El. N. S. 511; *Smith* v. *Scott*, 2 Car. & K. 580.

[1158] *Ryalls* v. *Leader*, 1 Law Rep. 296, Ex.

[1159] *McCabe* v. *Cauldwell*, 18 Abb. Pra. R. 377. The true ground for this decision was that a proceeding before a grand jury is a secret *ex parte* proceeding, although it seems to rest on the assumption that a grand jury is not a "judicial body." As to report of a coroner's inquest, see *East* v. *Chapman*, M. & M. 46. The publication of a report of commissioners appointed to inquire into corporations, held not to be privileged. (*Charlton* v. *Walton*, 6 C. & P. 385.)

[1160] *Fleming* v. *Newton*, 1 Cl. & Fin. N. S. 363.

one who had been convicted of murder and sentenced to death, while on the scaffold and just before his execution, made a speech, in which he reflected upon one of the counsel who de-fended him on his trial, it was held that a report of this speech published in New York by the defendant, in a newspaper of which he was editor, was not privileged either at common law or by the statute.[1161]

§ 232. Where the judicial proceeding is public, and not *ex parte*, the report of what takes place is not the less privileged because published pending the proceeding, and before it has terminated; thus where a declaration for libel set out, in three separate counts, reports of three separate days' proceedings, respectively, (on two adjournments,) before a magistrate; the report of the first day stating that the plaintiff was charged with perjury, and an adjournment, but reserving the report; the report of the second day also stating an adjournment in language intimating that there would be a report of the pro-ceedings of the day to which the adjournment was; and the third stating the discharge of the party charged; and the jury found generally that the reports were fair and correct. Held, that the reports of the first two meetings did not lose the priv-ilege by reason of the proceedings there reported not being final.[1162] And in the same case, if we correctly interpret the re-port, it was held that the privilege of publishing a report of pre-liminary proceedings is not lost by the fact that the proceeding terminates in the discharge by the magistrate of the party ac-cused.

§ 233. By becoming a member of a church the individual tacitly consents to submit to the church discipline.[1163] The pro-

---

[1161] *Sanford v. Bennett*, 24 N. Y. 20. If a highwayman shall at the gallows arraign the justice of the law, and of those who condemned him, he who publishes [the highwayman's language] shall not go unpunished. (4 Read. Stat. Law, 154; Dig. LL. 32.)

[1162] *Lewis v. Levy*, 1 El. B. & E. 537.

[1163] *Remington v. Congdon*, 2 Pick. 310; *Jarvis v. Hathaway*, 3 Johns. 180; Holt on Libel, 236; *Shelton v. Nance*, 7 B. Monr. 128; *Whittaker v. Carter*, 4 Ired. 461.

ceedings of the church to enforce its discipline are *quasi judicial*, and therefore those who complain, or give testimony, or act, or vote, or pronounce the result, orally or in writing, acting in good faith and within the scope of the authority conferred by this jurisdiction, and not falsely or colorably making such proceedings a pretence for covering an intended scandal, are protected by law.[1164] One Miss Mary Jerom was the daughter of Quaker parents, and she was educated in that persuasion. She having acted in disobedience to the rules of the congregation, by frequenting places of public diversion and otherwise, she was warned to discontinue such practices, whereupon she absented herself from *the meetings*, and declared that she no longer regarded herself as one of their body. After various fruitless attempts to reclaim her, the society proceeded in the usual way to a sentence of expulsion, which was reduced to writing, approved at a monthly meeting, and read by the defendant Hart, as clerk of the meeting, at a subsequent meeting for worship. This sentence of expulsion recited that the prosecutrix was born of Quaker parents, and educated in that society, but that, not regarding the truth they professed, she had imbibed erroneous notions ; divers part of her conduct was inconsistent with a life of self-denial, and the futile attempts made to reclaim her ; then declared her not a member of the society, until by repentance she acknowledged scripture doctrine. Miss Jerom, hearing of this sentence, sent her servant to the defendant for a copy, which he sent her under cover. After failing in an application for a criminal information, Miss Jerom procured the defendant to be indicted, tried, and convicted, for libel. On motion for a new trial, the court held that, no express malice being shown, the jury ought to have been directed to acquit the defendant, and ordered a new trial.[1165] A vote passed by a board of trustees of a church,

---

[1164] *Farnsworth* v. *Storrs*, 5 Cush. 412; *Fairchild* v. *Adams*, 11 Cush. 549; *Smith* v. *Youmans*, 3 Hill (So. Car.) 85. If words, actionable in themselves, be spoken between members of the same church, in the course of their religious discipline, and without malice, no action will lie; and the jury are to decide whether there be malice or not. *Jarvis* v. *Hathaway*, 3 Johns. 180.

[1165] *Rex* v. *Hart*, 1 W. Blacks. 386; 2 Burns' Eccles. Law, 779.

censuring C., a former treasurer of such church, for obstinately retaining the church funds received by him as such treasurer in his hands, and refusing to pay them over, is privileged; but if published maliciously, will support an action.[1106] A communication of a church member, complaining of the conduct of his clergy, addressed to their common superior, is privileged.[1107] And if a selectman, acting in his official capacity, accuse a member of the church of voting twice on the same ballot, it is privileged.[1108]

§ 234. The privilege extended to proceedings to enforce church discipline, applies only to cases where both parties are members of the church. A complaint, to a church, against one of its members by one who is not a member, is not privileged; neither would such a complaint by a member against one who is not a member, be privileged;[1109] but if the party accused voluntarily submits himself to the discipline of the church, all the proceedings are privileged. Where a vote of excommunication from a church has been passed, and the offender thereby declared to be no longer a member, a subsequent reading of the sentence by the pastor, in the presence of the congregation, is privileged.[1110]

§ 235. The publication of defamatory matter is not privileged, because made at a public meeting.[1111] But at meetings of public bodies, having certain duties to perform, what is said

<hr />

[1106] *Holt* v. *Parson*, 23 Texas, 9. In an action for libel, the defendant pleaded that the words were used without malice, in a complaint to a church, of which both parties were members, for the purpose of bringing the plaintiff to trial before a committee thereof. The plaintiff replied that the charge was made wilfully and maliciously; to which replication the defendant demurred. Held, that the replication was sufficient, although it contained no averment of want of probable cause. (*Dial* v. *Holter*, 6 Ohio (N. S.) 228.)

[1107] *O'Donoghue* v. *McGovern*, 23 Wend. 26.

[1108] *Bradley* v. *Heath*, 12 Pick. 163.

[1109] *Coombs* v. *Rose*, 8 Blackf. 155.

[1110] *Remington* v. *Congdon*, 2 Pick. 310.

[1111] *Farnsworth* v. *Storrs*, 5 Cush. 412.

[1112] *Lewis* v. *Few*, 5 Johns. 1; Anthon, 75; *Davison* v. *Duncan*, 7 El. & Bl. 229; 3 Campbell's Ch. Justices, 64, *note*.

in the exercise of such duties, pertinent to the matter in hand, and within the jurisdiction of the meeting, is privileged. This privilege has not, it would seem, always been recognized. Where, at a meeting of a board of public officers, the commissioners of the New York Central Park, and in the course of a debate as to employing the plaintiff to do certain work for said commissioners, the defendant, a member of the board, objected to the employment of plaintiff on the ground that he had published an obscene libel; held, that the charge, being pertinent to the subject under discussion, was privileged, and to entitle the plaintiff to maintain an action in respect of it, he must establish that the charge was made without reasonable or probable cause.[1173] The plaintiff being one of the overseers, and the defendant assistant overseer of a township, a rate was made on a railway company, against which they appealed. Shortly before the hearing of the appeal, a meeting of the overseers was called to consider the matter, when it was resolved to abandon the rate, and a vestry meeting was called to choose fresh overseers and consider the propriety of removing the defendant from his office. At that meeting the plaintiff imputed to the defendant neglect of duty in collecting the rates, and having made a rate which the overseers were obliged to give up, to which the defendant retorted by saying that the plaintiff had sold the rate-payers to the railway company, and had received a bribe from them for that purpose. After the meeting a person remarked to the defendant that he ought not to have said what he did without some foundation for it; to which the defendant replied that he believed there was reason for thinking that the plaintiff had had communications with the officers of the railway company. An action having been brought for the words used by the defendant at the meeting, query, whether the words were spoken under circumstances which rendered them a privileged communication? but held, assuming they

---

[1173] *Viele* v. *Gray*, 10 Abb. Pr. R. 1; 18 How. Pr. R. 550. At a meeting of the proprietors of a fishery, a charge made by one proprietor against another, of having violated the law regulating the fishery, was held to be privileged. (*Bennett* v. *Barr*, 8 Law Times Rep. N. S. 857.)

were, there was evidence of malice proper to be left to the jury.[1174] But it was held not to be a justification of a charge of official misconduct against a town officer that the charge was made in open town meeting, by the defendant, an inhabitant of the town, while animadverting on the conduct of the plaintiff as such officer, relative to a subject then before the meeting, in which the defendant was interested as a qualified voter.[1175] And where a resolution introduced into a county medical society, for the expulsion of a member, upon the ground that he had procured his admission by false pretences, and without the legal qualifications, was held not to be privileged, because the society had no power to expel a member for such a cause.[1176] Where the defendant, one of the selectmen of the town, while he was acting as a public officer, and at an election in an open town meeting, charged the plaintiff with having put two votes into the ballot-box, it was held that the charge was privileged, principally on the ground that the defendant had a duty to perform, and that the charge was made in the performance of his duty.[1177]

§ 236. Nor is the publication of defamatory matter privileged because made in a true report of the proceedings of a public meeting, for "there is no analogy between the proceedings at a public political meeting, and the proceedings in a court of justice;"[1178] and therefore it has been held that a publication of defamatory matter made in a report of proceedings at a public meeting called to petition parliament against making a grant in support of a Roman Catholic college, was not privileged.[1179] And where the defamatory matter was contained in

---

[1174] *Senior* v. *Medland*, 4 Hurl. & N. 843.

[1175] *Dodds* v. *Henry*, 9 Mass. 262.

[1176] *Fawcett* v. *Charles*, 13 Wend. 473.

[1177] *Bradley* v. *Heath*, 12 Pick. 163.

[1178] *Lewis* v. *Few*, 5 Johns. 1. We understand that the legislature of Wisconsin has recently passed a law declaring true reports of proceedings at public meetings privileged, and a bill for the like purpose is now before the British parliament.

[1179] *Hearne* v. *Stowell*, 12 Adol. & El. 719; 4 Per. & D. 696.

a report of the proceedings of a vestry meeting, it was held not to be privileged; thus, an English statute 18 and 19 Vict. ch. 120, provided for the appointment of a medical officer in each parish, who was to report from time to time to the vestry, and such reports were to be published annually, in the month of June. A report was made to the vestry in February, and in the same month published by the defendant in a newspaper of which he was the editor and proprietor, in and as part of the proceedings of the vestry. This report contained a charge of misconduct on the part of the plaintiff; he sued the defendant for libel, and it was held that the publication, being a true report of what took place at the vestry, did not render it privileged.[1180] But in another case, a report of the condition of town schools, made and published as required by law, by the superintending school committee, and charging the prudential committee of the district with unlawfully employing a teacher, and putting her in charge of a school, taking possession of the school-house, and forcibly excluding the general committee and the teachers employed by them, but not imputing corrupt motives, held privileged.[1181] And so it was held that the publication, by a member of the Massachusetts Medical Society, of a true account of the proceedings of that society in the expulsion of another member for a cause within its jurisdiction, and of the result of certain suits subsequently brought by him against the society and its members, on account of such expulsion, is privileged; although it speaks of the expelled member as "the offender," and remarks that "the society has vindicated its action in this case, and its right to act in all parallel cases.[1182]

§ 237. The right to seek redress is not limited to seeking it in a court of justice.[1183] Every one who is aggrieved, or who

---

[1180] *Popham* v. *Pickburn*, 7 Hurl. & N. 891. Query, would the publication have been privileged had it been made by the defendant after the report had been published by the vestry, as required by the statute? (*Id.*)

[1181] *Shattuck* v. *Allen*, 4 Gray, 540; and see *Haight* v. *Cornell*, 15 Conn. 74.

[1182] *Barrow* v. *Bell*, 7 Gray, 301.

[1183] *Padmore* v. *Lawrence*, 11 Adol. & El. 380; 8 Per. & D. 209; *Kine* v. *Sewell*, 3 M. & W. 297; *Robinson* v. *May*, 2 Smith, 2. Semble, that words spoken

has reasonable and probable cause to believe himself aggrieved, may, *in good faith*, seek redress from any body, officer or person having jurisdiction, power, or authority to redress the wrong or supposed wrong. Whatever is spoken or written in such a pursuit for redress is privileged. For defamatory matter published in seeking relief other than from a court of justice, the action is said to be analogous to an action for malicious prosecution, with a distinction or supposed distinction which may be illustrated as thus: that redress for malicious prosecution cannot be had in an action in form for slander or libel [§ 220], while for defamatory matter published in seeking redress from any source other than a court of justice, redress may be had in the form of an action for slander or libel, *with the additional allegation*, either that the application was without reasonable or probable cause, or in bad faith [maliciously],

---

to a police officer engaged in an endeavor to detect a crime, are privileged. (*Smith* v. *Kerr*, 1 Barb. 155. See, however, *Dancaster* v. *Hewson*, 2 M. & R. 176.) Plaintiff assaulted the defendant on the highway; defendant, meeting a constable, requested him to take charge of the plaintiff, and the constable refusing to arrest the plaintiff unless the defendant would charge him with felony, the defendant did so; held, on demurrer to the defendant's plea setting up these circumstances, that they did not render the charge of felony a privileged publication. (*Smith* v. *Hodgkins*, Cro. Car. 276; and see *Allen* v. *Crofoot*, 2 Wend. 515; *Lathrop* v. *Hyde*, 25 Wend. 448.) In *Johnson* v. *Evans*, 3 Esp. 32, plaintiff, a female, had been in the employ of defendant, and on discharging her, some difference arose, the defendant charging the plaintiff with endeavoring to cheat him respecting her wages, and said, "She is a thief, and tried to rob me of part of her wages." Defendant sent for a constable to give plaintiff in charge, and repeated these words to the constable, but did not give plaintiff in charge; the only publication proved was to the constable, and plaintiff was nonsuited. In an action of slander against the defendant, for charging the plaintiff with theft, where it appeared that the words spoken were only expressions of suspicion, founded upon facts detailed by him at the time, made prudently and in confidence to discreet persons, in good faith, with a view to their aiding him to detect the offender and recover the property stolen, it was held that they were not slanderous, but justifiable and proper. (*Grimes* v. *Coyle*, 6 B. Monr. 301.) The defendant having some cause to suspect the plaintiff of dishonesty, went to plaintiff's relations and made to them a charge of theft against the plaintiff; and it appearing that the object in making the communication was rather to compromise the felony than to promote inquiry, or to enable the relations to redeem the plaintiff's character, the publication was held not privileged. (*Hooper* v. *Truscott*, 2 Bing. N. R. 457.)

or was made to a forum not having jurisdiction of the subject-matter; or, again as thus: to an action in form of slander or libel, it is a defence merely to show the publication was made to a court of justice, but it is not a defence merely to show that the publication was made upon an application for redress other than to a court of justice, unless it be also shown that the forum addressed had jurisdiction and the application was honestly made—*i. e.* in good faith and with reasonable and probable cause. To support malicious prosecution, besides showing that the prosecution has terminated, it must be shown that the publication was without probable cause and with malice, *i. e.* bad motive; bad motive alone will not support the action if there was probable cause; while to support an action for a publication in seeking redress extra-judicially, it is sufficient to show either want of jurisdiction in the forum addressed, or want of probable cause or bad motive; for the right to appeal to a court of justice *is general and without reference to the motive* wherever probable cause exists; but the right to such relief, extra-judicially, *is limited to seeking it with probable cause and with a good motive.* In a case where the defendant had written defamatory matter to the superior of the plaintiff, an ecclesiastic, it was alleged in the complaint that the publication was made maliciously; the plea was in effect merely that the publication was made in seeking redress from an officer having jurisdiction to grant relief. On demurrer, the plea was overruled, and it was held that to constitute a defence, the plea should have gone on and alleged reasonable and probable cause for making the complaint, and that it was made with good motives.[1184] It has been held that an action of libel is not maintainable in respect of defamatory matter contained in a petition to the sovereign,[1185] or to parliament,[1186] or to the legislature,[1187] or to the lieutenant-governor of a province (Canada),[1188]

[1184] In *O'Donaghue* v. *McGovern*, 23 Wend. 26, and in *Perkins* v. *Mitchell*, 31 Barb. 461; a distinction is made between a complaint made to a court of justice and a complaint made elsewhere.

[1185] *Hare* v. *Mellor*, 3 Lev. 138.

[1186] *Lake* v. *King*, 1 Lev. 240, and *ante*, note 1087.

[1187] *Reid* v. *Delorme*, 2 Brevard, 76.

[1188] *Stanton* v. *Andrews*, 5 Up. Can. Q. B. Rep. 211, O. S.

or to the governor of a State.[1189] Nor can an action of libel be maintained for defamatory matter contained in a memorial presented to a board of excise,[1190] or in a petition to a council of appointment praying the removal of the plaintiff from office; [1191] or in a memorial to the Post-office Department charging fraud on the plaintiff, a successful bidder for post-office patronage ; [1192] or in letter to the Secretary of War, with the intent to prevail on him to exert his authority to compel the plaintiff (an officer in the army) to pay a debt due from him to defendant ; [1193] or in a letter to the superior officer of the plaintiff, having power to remove him, and charging him with fraud in his office ; [1194] or in a letter written to a bishop informing him that a report was current in a parish in his diocese, that the plaintiff, the incumbent of a district in that parish, had assaulted a schoolmaster.[1195] So no action for slander or libel can be maintained for charges preferred to a lodge of Odd Fellows by one member of that

---

[1189] *Gray* v. *Pentland*, 2 S. & R. 23 ; 4 *Id.* 420.

[1190] *Vanderzee* v. *McGregor*, 12 Wend. 545.

[1191] *Thorn* v. *Blanchard*, 5 Johns. 508. Where the complaint is to a person competent to redress the grievance, no action lies against the publisher, whether his statement be true or false, or his motives innocent or malicious. (*Id.*) See *Harrison* v. *Bush*, 32 Eng. Law & Eq. R. 173 ; 5 El. & Bl. 344 ; *Harris* v. *Harrington*, 2 Tyler, 129.

[1192] *Cook* v. *Hill*, 3 Sandf. 341. A letter of complaint written to the Postmaster General, *bona fide*, of even imaginary grievances, would be privileged ; and the defendant, under the general issue, may show that it was written under such circumstances as would make it a protected communication. (*Woodward* v. *Lander*, 6 C. & P. 548.)

[1193] *Fairman* v. *Ives*, 5 B. & A. 643 ; 1 D. & R. 252.

[1194] *Howard* v. *Thompson*, 21 Wend. 319 ; *Blake* v. *Pilford*, 1 M. & Rob. 198. A petition of parties interested, to the proper authorities, against the appointment of one on the ground of his bad character, as disqualifying him for the appointment, is not actionable as a libel. (*Harris* v. *Harrington*, 2 Tyler, 129.) A letter from an inhabitant of a school district, to the school committee, complaining of a school teacher, is conditionally privileged. (*Bodwell* v. *Osgood*, 3 Pick. 379 ; and see *Maitland* v. *Bramwell*, 2 Fost. & F. 623.)

[1195] *James* v. *Boston*, 2 C. & K. 4. If written merely with the honest intention of calling the attention of the bishop to a rumor in the parish, which was bringing scandal on the church, and not from any malicious motive ; and it is not material that the writer of the letter did not live in the district to the incumbent of which the letter refers. (*Id.*) And see *O'Donaghue* v. *McGovern*, 23 Wend. 26.

20

lodge against another, and for an offence which the lodge under its rules had the right to investigate.[1196] The trustees of the College of Pharmacy in New York, appointed a committee to inquire and report upon the capacity of the plaintiff as drug inspector of the port of New York, with a view upon the facts reported to petition for the removal of the plaintiff from his office. The committee made a written report to the board of trustees, who forwarded it to the Secretary of the Treasury,— held that the report was privileged.[1197] The defendant, the deputy-governor of Greenwich Hospital, wrote and printed a large volume, containing an account of the abuses of the hospital, and reflecting with much asperity upon many of its officers; he distributed copies of this book to governors of the hospital *only ;* an application for a criminal information against the defendant was denied, with the observation that the distribution had been only to persons competent to redress the grievances complained of.[1198]

§ 238. The condition, or one of the conditions, upon which

[1196] *Streety* v. *Wood*, 15 Barb. 105. Where A. accused B. of theft before certain members of a lodge of Odd Fellows, of which both were members, and in an action for slander by A., B. attempted to justify what he said, by showing that it was the duty of Odd Fellows to keep their lodge pure, the justification was held to be insufficient. (*Holmes* v. *Johnson*, 11 Ired. 55.) Defendant, who was a sergeant in a volunteer corps, of which plaintiff also was a member, represented to the committee by whom the general business of the corps was conducted, that plaintiff was an unfit person to be permitted to continue a member of the corps; that he was the executioner of the French king, &c. Lord Ellenborough held the communication privileged. (*Barbaud* v. *Hookham*, 5 Esp. 109.)

[1197] *Van Wyck* v. *Aspinwall*, 17 N. Y. 190, affirming S. C. *sub nom. Van Wyck* v. *Guthrie*, 4 Duer, 268: and see *Haight* v. *Cornell*, 15 Conn. 74.

[1198] *Rex* v. *Baillie*, 21 State Trials, 1; Andr. 229. In another case the plaintiff had been a general commanding a corps of irregular troops during the war in the Crimea. Complaint having been made of the insubordination of the troops, the corps commanded by the plaintiff was placed under the superior command of V. The plaintiff then resigned his command, and V. directed S. to inquire and report on the state of the corps, and referred S. to the defendant for information. Defendant, in a conversation with S., made a defamatory statement in respect to the plaintiff on his giving up the command of his corps; held that it was properly left to the jury to say whether the communication was relevant to the inquiry. (*Beatson* v. *Skene*, 5 Hurl. & N. 838.) See *Dickson* v. *Earl Wilton*, 1 F. & F. 419.

the privilege now under consideration exists, is that the body, officer, or person appealed to has jurisdiction, power, or authority to grant the relief. This is stated in nearly all of the cases cited to the last preceding section [§ 237]. In addition to those cases we refer to a case where the defendant, a physician, gave a certificate that the plaintiff was insane, on which to base proceedings under a statute to have the plaintiff confined in an asylum; for the charge contained in this certificate the plaintiff brought an action against the defendant, and it was held that he could justify only by showing that the provisions of the statute under which the certificate purported to have been given had been strictly complied with. And by the court, "Where one intervenes voluntarily in a special proceeding not known to the common law, and not resulting in a judgment according to its forms, he must see that jurisdiction is acquired, and that there is in reality a proceeding in court, before he can claim any privilege."[1199] A letter written to the Secretary of State, complaining of the conduct of the plaintiff as clerk to a board of magistrates, was held not to be privileged because addressed to an officer not having power to redress the wrong complained of.[1200] The case lastly referred to was affirmed in the Exchequer Chamber, but in a subsequent case it is said that a communication made *bona fide* for the purpose of obtaining redress, is privileged though made to a tribunal having no *direct* authority in respect of the matter complained of, as

---

[1199] *Perkins* v. *Mitchell*, 31 Barb. 461; and see *Hosmer* v. *Loveland*, 19 Barb. 111.

[1200] *Blagg* v. *Sturt*, 10 Q. B. 899; 11 Jur. 181; 8 Law Times, 135; 16 Law Jour. 39, Q. B. In an action for libel it appeared that the defendant had lodged at the plaintiff's house, and on leaving missed a memorandum book and other articles, whereupon he wrote a letter to the plaintiff's wife, in which he accused the plaintiff of having taken the missing articles, and threatened to expose him if he did not return them; the jury found that there was no malice in fact,— *Held*, nevertheless, that sending the letter to the wife was not a privileged publication—she had no authority or power to redress the supposed wrong. (*Wenman* v. *Ash*, 22 Eng. Law & Eq. R. 509; 13 C. B. 836; 22 Law J. Rep. (N. S.) C. P. 190; 17 Jur. 579; 1 Com. Law Rep. 592.) A letter written merely confidentially is not thereby privileged. (*Brooks* v. *Blanchard*, 1 Cr. & M. 779; 3 Tyrw. 844.)

where the plaintiff was a justice of the peace for the county,
and in the habit of acting at petty sessions held in a borough.
The defendant, an elector and inhabitant of the borough,
signed a memorial addressed to the Secretary of State for the
Home Department, complaining of the conduct of plaintiff as
a justice during an election for a member to represent the borough in parliament, and praying that he would cause an inquiry to be made into the conduct of plaintiff, and that on the
allegations contained in the memorial being substantiated, he
would recommend to her Majesty that plaintiff be removed
from the commission of the peace. The jury having found
that the memorial was *bonâ fide*, it was held that it was a privileged communication, inasmuch as plaintiff had both an
interest and a duty in the subject-matter of the communication; and the Secretary of State had a corresponding duty, a
justice of the peace being appointed and removed by the sovereign.[1201]

§ 239. Where the privilege now under consideration may be
exercised by word of mouth, orally, it also may be exercised by
writing; unless, perhaps, where it is shown that it is exercised
by writing rather than orally to serve some unworthy purpose;
thus where an alleged libel consisted of charges made by the
defendant against the plaintiff, a constable, contained in a letter
to a meeting of rate-payers, it was held that inasmuch as the
charge, if made orally, would have been privileged, it was privileged when made in writing, unless the plaintiff could establish that the defendant wilfully absented himself from the

---

[1201] *Harrison* v. *Bush*, 82 Eng. Law & Eq. R. 173; and see *Fairman* v. *Ives*,
5 B. & A. 643; 1 D. & R. 252. In *Rex* v. *Bayley* (3 Bac. Abr. tit. Libel, A 2,
cited 5 B. & A. 647), the defendant had addressed a letter to General Willes and
the four principal officers of the guards, to be by them presented to the King,
stating that the prosecutor had obtained from him [defendant] a warrant for the
payment of money due him [defendant] from the government under promise of
paying the defendant such money, and that the prosecutor had received the money and not paid it over to defendant. The court held this not a libel, but a representation of an injury shown up in a proper way for redress; yet neither the
officers nor the King could give the defendant *direct* assistance in obtaining payment of the money wrongfully withheld.

meeting as a pretence for writing.[1202]   So where the defendant
is privileged to present a petition or memorial for redress, he
does not forfeit his privilege by presenting the petition or memorial to different individuals to obtain their signatures thereto, nor, as it seems, by printing such petition or memorial, provided the presenting for signatures or the printing be done
with a *bonâ fide* intent to carry out the purpose of the petition
or memorial, and not otherwise.[1203]

§ 240. Every one has the right to publish all that he has
reasonable and probable cause to believe necessary to protect
his person, his property, or his reputation from loss or injury.
As where the defendant advertised that his wife had eloped
from him, and cautioned all persons from trusting her, a motion for a criminal information against him for making this
publication was denied, because the advertisement was the only
means he could adopt to protect himself.[1204]   So where A., who
had dealt with the defendant, a butcher, suddenly ceased to
deal with him, alleging as a reason that defendant had made
charges against him, A., for meat which had not been delivered at A.'s house, the defendant wrote a letter to A., protesting his innocence of the alleged overcharge, and stating in
effect that the meat had been improperly disposed of by the
defendant's servants.   For writing this letter, the plaintiff—

[1202] *Spencer* v. *Ameston*, 1 M. & Rob. 470.

[1203] *Vanderzee* v. *McGregor*, 12 Wend. 455; *Cook* v. *Hill*, 3 Sandf. 341; *Rex* v.
Baillie, 21 State Trials, 1; Andr. 229; *Van Wyck* v. *Aspinwall*, 17 N. Y. 190.
and *ante*, note 1198.   Where in an action of slander against the defendant, a surveyor, employed by a committee to investigate the truth of reports against the
plaintiff, as having executed improperly contract work for them, which the defendant alleged on such inquiry to be the case, held that such report was not a
privileged communication, it being found by the jury that the reports originated
with the defendant and were false. (*Smith* v. *Matthews*, 2 M. & Malk. 151.)   An
officer of the navy has no right to make communications, except to the government, upon subjects with which he becomes acquainted in his professional capacity; and, therefore, a letter written to Lloyd's Coffee-house, about the conduct of the captain of a transport-ship, by a lieutenant who was superintendent
on board, was held not to be a privileged communication. (*Harwood* v. *Green*,
2 Car. & P. 141; and see *Robinson* v. *May*, 2 J. P. Smith, 3.)

[1204] *Rex* v. *Enes*, Andr. 229, and see *ante*, § 226; and *Koenig* v. *Ritchie*, 3 Fost.
& F. 413.

whose wife was a servant in the family of A.—brought an action for libel; it was held that if by the letter the defendant meant *bonâ fide* to defend himself, it was a conditionally privileged publication;[1205] and where Q., having had no previous knowledge of B., a trader, sold him goods to the amount of £62 10*s.*, at two months' credit,—upon going to B.'s shop at the expiration of the credit, A. found that the whole stock in trade, including a portion of the goods sold by him, had been sold by auction the previous day, by B.'s desire, and at a reduction of 30 per cent., and that the proceeds were in the hands of S., the auctioneer. Upon inquiry, A. could not learn where B. was to be found. He thereupon went to his attorneys, and they, on his behalf, served on S. a notice not to part with the proceeds of the sale, the said B. having committed an act of bankruptcy. B. had, in fact, committed no act of bankruptcy, the goods having been sold for the purpose of his retiring from business. Held, by Tindal, C. J., Coltman, J., and Erle, J. (Cresswell, J., *dissentiente*), that A. had such an interest in serving the notice as to render it a privileged communication, if it was served with good faith and under the *bonâ fide* belief that B. had committed an act of bankruptcy.[1206] Where the defendant published an advertisement as follows: "Ten guineas reward. Whereas, by a letter received from the West Indies, an event is stated to be announced by a newspaper that can only be investigated by these means,—this is to request that if any person can ascertain that J. D. (the plaintiff, describing him) was married previous to 9 A. M. on, &c., and will give notice to J. (the defendant), he shall receive the reward,"—held that if the publication was with the *bonâ fide* view of finding out the fact referred to, it was privileged, and the jury found a verdict for the defendant.[1207] And where the libel was contained in an advertisement stating the issuing of process

---

[1205] *Coward* v. *Wellington*, 9 C. & P. 531.

[1206] *Blackham* v. *Pugh*, 15 Law Jour. Rep. 290, C. P.; 2 C. B. 611.

[1207] *Delany* v. *Jones*, 4 Esp. 191. In *Lay* v. *Lawson*, 4 Adol. & El. 798, L'd Denman, referring to *Delany* v. *Jones*, said, "I have great doubt whether, there, the interest which the wife had in the inquiry could justify the offering a reward in a newspaper." See *Finden* v. *Westlake*, 1 Mo. & Malk. 461.

against the plaintiff, and that he could not be found, and offering a reward for such information as should enable him to be taken; plea, that a *capias* had been issued and delivered to the sheriff, and that the plaintiff kept out of the way, and that the advertisement had been inserted at the request of the party suing out the writ, to enable the sheriff to arrest; held a sufficient defence.[1208]

§ 241. Every one who believes himself to be possessed of knowledge which, if true, does or may affect the rights and interests of another, has the right, in good faith, to communicate such his belief to that other. He may make the communication *with* or *without* any previous request, and whether he *has* or *has not* personally any interest in the subject-matter of the communication, and although no reasonable or probable cause for the belief may exist. The right is founded on the belief. If A. believes that B. is or is intending to rob C., he has the right to communicate his belief to C., without waiting for C. to inquire on the subject; and if in so doing he injures B., B. is without redress. The exigencies of society require that such a right should exist. A.'s duty to B. is simply not *unnecessarily* to injure him. This right must be exercised as every other right is required to be exercised, in good faith [§ 40]; and all communications made in the exercise of this right are conditionally privileged [§ 209].[1209] The existence of this right,

---

[1208] *Lay* v. *Lawson*, 4 Ad. & El. 795.

[1209] For words " spoken in good faith, to those who have an interest in the communication, and a right to know and act upon the facts stated," no action can be maintained without proof of express malice. (Shaw, C. J., *Bradley* v. *Heath*, 12 Pick. 163.) [If the words are spoken in good faith, no malice can be proved. To prove malice would be to prove that the words were not spoken in good faith.] The law respects communications made in confidence, notwithstanding they may be false and erroneous, and prove injurious to the party. This rule applies equally to words written and spoken. Note to *Wyatt* v. *Gore*, Holt's N. P. 299; and see *ante*, note 1202. And one part of a publication may be privileged, because made to a person interested, and another part not privileged; thus where plaintiff and defendant were jointly interested in property in Scotland of which C. was manager, defendant wrote to C. a letter, principally about the property and the conduct of the plaintiff with reference thereto, and

as will presently be shown, in cases where the communication is made by one having no personal interest in the subject-matter of the communication, and *without* any previous request has been questioned, nevertheless we feel justified in laying it down for law that the right exists as well where *there is not* as where *there is* a previous request, and whether the publisher *has or has not* any such personal interest. The right, as we conceive, in no wise depends either upon the fact of a previous request or upon the interest of the publisher, although the fact that the communication is made *officiously*, as it is termed, *i. e.* unsolicited, or by one having no interests involved, may in *some* cases have a tendency to disclose the motive of the publisher in making the publication. The right, where the publisher is interested, or where the communication is made upon the request of the party in interest, seems never to have been doubted; thus where the language published imputed habits of intemperance to the plaintiff, a dissenting minister, was held privileged because spoken in answer to inquiries.[1210] So a letter written to persons who employed A. as their solicitor, conveying charges injurious to his professional character in the management of certain concerns which they had entrusted to him, and in which B., the writer of the letter, was likewise interested, was held to be a privileged publica-

---

containing a charge against the plaintiff with reference to his conduct to his mother and his aunt; held, that so much of the letter as related to the property was privileged, but the remainder was not. (*Warren* v. *Warren*, 1 Cr. M. & R. 250.) And see *Humphreys* v. *Stillwell*, 2 Fost. & F. 590.

[1210] *Warr* v. *Jolly*, 6 C. & P. 497. A communication made *bona fide* upon any subject-matter in which the party communicating has an interest, or in reference to which he has a duty, is privileged, if made to a person having a corresponding interest or duty, although it contains criminatory matter which without this privilege would be slanderous and actionable. (*Harrison* v. *Bush*, 5 El. & Bl. 344; 32 Eng. Law & Eq. R. 173.) Where a party has a mutual interest with another, he is justified in prevailing on him to become party to a suit, and expressions of angry and strong animadversion on the conduct of the party impeached, unless malicious, are privileged; and, in the case of words, the jury merely take into consideration the whole conversation, to see whether particular words, which may be actionable in themselves, are qualified so as not to convey the primary meaning. (*Shipley* v. *Todhunter*, 7 C. & P. 680.)

tion.[1211]   And where A., being tenant of B., was desired by B.·
to inform him if he saw or heard anything respecting the game,
A. wrote a letter to B., informing B. that his game-keeper (the
plaintiff) sold game,—held, that if A. had been so informed,
and believed the fact so to be, this was a privileged communi-·
cation, and that the game-keeper could not maintain any
action for libel.[1212]   So where the plaintiff had requested his ,
friend R. A. to open a correspondence with the defendant in
reference to certain charges made by the defendant concerning
the plaintiff, held that letters written by the defendant to R. A.
were privileged communications.[1213]   But where in an action
for libel it appeared that the plaintiff was churchwarden and
defendant clergyman of the same parish, and that differences
having arisen between them in that relation, the plaintiff requested that the defendant's future communications should be
by letter to the plaintiff's clerk.   The defendant afterwards
applied by letter to the clerk for rent which he conceived to be
due him from the plaintiff.   The clerk answered that defendant denied his liability, and in reply the defendant wrote the
clerk, " This attempt to defraud me of the produce of the land
is as mean as it is dishonest,"—held that the communication
was not privileged in itself; that it was a question for the jury
whether the language was justified by the occasion, but that the
judge was right in directing the jury that the communication
was actionable.[1214]   An attorney having at plaintiff's desire
written the defendant demanding payment of an alleged debt,
the defendant sent a letter to the attorney containing gross imputations on the plaintiff's character, wholly unconnected with
the demand made upon him; held not a privileged communica-

[1211] On the trial a juror was withdrawn. *McDougall* v. *Claridge*, 1 Camp. 267.

[1212] *Cockayne* v. *Hodgkinson*, 5 C. & P. 543.

[1213] *Hopwood* v. *Thorn*, 8 C. B. 293.

[1214] *Tuson* v. *Evans*, 3 Per. & D. 396.   Where, in an action for defamation, it
appears that a defendant, authorized by his relation to the party addressed to
make a "privileged communication," in professing to do so makes a false charge,
the inference of malice is against him, and the burden is put on him to show
that he acted *bona fide*.   (*Wakefield* v. *Smithwick*, 4 Jones' Law (N. C.), 327; and
see *Cole* v. *Wilson*, 18 B. Monr. 212.)

tion, although the jury found that the letter was written *bonâ
fide;* and negatived malice in fact.[1215] A., the plaintiff, was
party to a suit in chancery by B., his next friend, who was answerable for the costs of the suit. A. expressed a desire to
change his solicitor in that suit, which coming to the knowledge of the defendant, he wrote a letter to B., in which,
amongst other things, he stated that A. had been apprenticed
to a civil engineer, and had had a present made him of his in-
dentures, because he was worse than useless in the office; in action of libel by A., held that the letter was a privileged publication.[1216] The owner of a building which has been set on
fire may caution the persons employed by him therein against
a particular person, suspected of being the incendiary; and his
statements to them, if made in good faith for this purpose, are
privileged communications, although they contain an unfounded
criminal charge against the suspected person.[1217] An insurance
company, of which the defendant was president, made an insurance against fire on the property of one Graves in the occupation of the plaintiff; an application was made to the company to alter the policy; the application was refused, and notice given that the policy would be cancelled. Graves inquired
the reason for this, and was told by the defendant that the company would not insure any building occupied by plaintiff, as a
building insured by the company and occupied by the plaintiff
had been burned under very suspicious circumstances, adding,
" What would you think of a man being seen round the store at
two or three o'clock in the morning before the fire ?" this was
held to be a privileged communication.[1218] The defendant had
the right to give to Graves a reason for the company refusing
to insure the building owned by him, and Graves was interested
to know the opinion the defendant entertained concerning the
plaintiff. So where the plaintiff was secretary of the Brewers'
Insurance Company, and he being charged with misconduct

[1215] *Huntley* v. *Ward,* 6 C. B. N. S. 514; and see *ante,* note 1200.

[1216] *Wright* v. *Woodgate,* Tyr. & Gr. 12.

[1217] *Lawler* v. *Earle,* 5 Allen, 22.

[1218] *Liddle* v. *Hodges,* 2 Bosw. 537, affirmed 18 N. Y. 48.

was called upon to attend a board of directors, for the purpose of explanation, but declined to do so; whereupon the directors, after hearing the charges, passed a resolution that he had been guilty of gross misconduct, and dismissed him. The defendant, a director of that company and also of the London Necropolis Company, of which the plaintiff was auditor, communicated the fact of the plaintiff's dismissal "for gross misconduct" at a board meeting of the latter company, and proposed a resolution to dismiss him, and in answer to an inquiry from the chairman, said that the misconduct consisted in "obtaining money from the solicitors of the company under false pretences, and paying a debt of his own with it;" in an action for slander it was held that the publication was conditionally privileged.[1219] The defendant being a competitor with the plaintiffs for a contract with the Navy Board for African timber, the plaintiffs obtained the contract. Defendants then agreed to supply plaintiffs with a portion of the timber, and made no objection to taking their bills in payment. Afterwards this agreement was rescinded, and defendant wrote to a merchant who was to supply the timber to carry out the agreement, and of whom the defendant was a creditor, and the sole correspondent in London, reflecting on the plaintiff's mercantile character, and putting said merchant on his guard against them. In an action for libel in making this communication, a verdict having been found for the defendant on the ground of privilege, the court granted a new trial.[1220] The plaintiff was a dealer in beer, buying it of a brewer and selling it to publicans. Plaintiff wishing to open an account with the defendant, a brewer, one L., became his [plaintiff's] surety for the price of such beer as defendant should from time to time supply to plaintiff, he [defendant] promising to inform L. of any

---

[1219] *Harris* v. *Thompson*, 13 C. B. 329; 24 Eng. Law & Eq. R. 370.

[1220] *Ward* v. *Smith*, 6 Bing. 749. In *Van Spike* v. *Cleyson*, Cro. Eliz. 541, it is said not to be actionable for one man to tell another *confidentially* not to trust another, if done only by way of counsel. Words of a tradesman that he would soon be a bankrupt, when spoken in confidence and friendship as a caution, held not to be actionable unless the jury found there was malice. (*Herver* v. *Dowson*, Bull. N. P. 8.)

default made by plaintiff in his payments. After plaintiff and
defendant had dealt together for some time, defendant went to
L. and spoke in very abusive terms of plaintiff, saying he
wished to cheat him, and that he had returned as unmerchant-
able, beer he [plaintiff] had adulterated, and that he was a
rogue, &c. At this time there was a balance due defendant
from plaintiff for beer, in respect of which L. was liable on his
guarantee. Lord Ellenborough inclined to think the communication conditionally privileged; he refused, however, to nonsuit the plaintiff, and a juror was withdrawn.[1221] Plaintiff was
engaged to superintend the works of a railway company, and
subsequently, at a general meeting of the proprietors, the engagement was not continued, but a former inspector was rein-
stated. Afterwards a vacancy occurred in the situation of engineer to the commissioners for improving the river Wear, and
the plaintiff became a candidate. The defendant wrote to C.,
introducing D. as a candidate, and C. having written defendant informing him that another person [the plaintiff] had succeeded in obtaining the appointment, the defendant wrote an
answer to C. reflecting on the conduct of the plaintiff whilst
superintendent of the railway works. It appeared that defendant and C. were both shareholders in the railway company,
and that defendant managed C.'s affairs in the railway. Held,
not a privileged publication.[1222] A party is justified in giving
his opinion *bonâ fide* of the respectability of a tradesman *in
answer to an inquiry concerning him;*[1223] thus it is said that
the owner of a public-house cannot maintain an action against
a neighboring publican for giving a bad character of such
house to a person who, being in treaty for purchasing it, applied
to the defendant for information, provided (as is stated) there is
some evidence of the truth of the assertion.[1224] In an action

---

[1221] *Dunham* v. *Bigg*, 8 Camp. 260; and see *Rex* v. *Jenneaur*, 8 Bac. Abr. tit.
Libel, 452; 2 Brownl. 151; 2 Burns' Eccles. Law, 179; *Wilson* v. *Stephenson*, 2
Price, 282.

[1222] *Brooks* v. *Blanchard*, 1 Cr. & M. 779.

[1223] *Storey* v. *Challands*, 8 C. & P. 234; otherwise where there is no inquiry.
(*Id.*)

[1224] *Humber* v. *Ainge*, Manning's Index, tit. Libel, pl. 13. Where a person

for slander by the plaintiffs, bankers at M., the charge was that in answer to a question from one Watkins, whether he [defendant] had said that plaintiffs' bank had stopped, defendant's answer was, " It was true; he had been told so." The proof was that Watkins met defendant and said, " I hear that you say the bank of B. & S. [plaintiffs] has stopped. Is it true?" Defendant answered, " Yes, it is; I was told so," and added, " It was so reported at C., and nobody will take their bills, and I have come to town in consequence." Watkins said, " You had better take care what you say; you first brought the news to town, and told Mr. John Thomas of it." Defendant repeated, " I was told so." It further appeared that defendant had in fact been told there was a run on plaintiffs' bank, but not that it had stopped or that nobody would take the plaintiffs' bills. It was held on the trial that the publication of the words alleged was proved, and the jury were instructed that if they thought the words were not spoken maliciously, the defendant ought to have a verdict. The jury found for the defendant. On plaintiffs' motion a new trial was ordered. On granting the new trial, the court discussed at length the question of malice, and the supposed distinction between malice in fact and malice in law, and stating that there was no instance of a verdict for the defendant on the ground of want of malice, held that instead of instructing the jury that if the words were not spoken maliciously they should find for the defendant, it should have been left to the jury as a previous question whether the defendant understood Watkins as asking for information for his own guidance, and that defendant spoke what he did merely out of honest advice to regulate the conduct of Watkins, then the question of malice in fact would have been proper as a second question to the jury, if their minds were in favor of the defendant upon the first. * * In granting a new trial the court

authorized to make a privileged communication stated false matter, and the court left it to the jury to say whether " In communicating what he had heard and believed to be true," he acted in good faith, and there was no evidence that he had heard anything, nor none as to how he believed, it was held to be error. (*Wakefield* v. *Smithwick*, 4 Jones' Law (N. C.), 327.)

does not mean to say that it may not be proper to put the
question of malice as a question of fact for the consideration of
the jury; for if the jury should think that when Watkins
asked his question the defendant understood it as asked to obtain
information to regulate his [Watkins'] conduct, it will range
under the cases of privileged communication, and the question
of malice in fact will then be a necessary part of the jury's inquiry; but it was not left to the jury to consider whether the
question was understood by the defendant as an application for
advice, and if not so understood the question of malice was
improperly left to the jury.[1225] Where a party interested in a
building contract, on which the plaintiff had been engaged,
applied to the defendant to recommend a surveyor to measure the work, when the defendant stated that he had seen the
plaintiff take away some of the materials, upon which the
plaintiff's employer applied to the defendant if he had seen the
plaintiff taking them away, when he alleged that he had seen
the plaintiff taking them, and that he hallooed to him; held,
that the judge properly directed the jury to say, first, whether
the words imputed felony; and secondly, that even if they did
the plaintiff was not entitled to recover, unless malice were expressly shown, or the jury believed, from the circumstances,
that the defendant was actuated by malicious motives.[1226]
Where A. had sold goods to B., and afterwards and before the
delivery of the goods, C., *without* being asked or solicited in
any way to do so, made representations to A. injurious to the
credit of B. The representations were held not to be privileged, because made without any previous request.[1227] And
where A., seeing that apartments were to let at a house occupied by B., inquired who was the landlord of C. (a neighbor of
B.'s); C. told him, and added that B. had not paid his rent,
and that if A. moved in his goods they would be seized. B.
having sued C. for slander, the judge, at the trial, told the jury
" he thought it was a privileged communication by C., unless

[1225] *Bromage* v. *Prosser*, 4 B. & C. 247; 6 Dowl. & R. 296.
[1226] *Kine* v. *Sewell*, 3 M. & W. 297.
[1227] *King* v. *Watts*, 8 C. & P. 614; and see *Pattison* v. *Jones*, 8 M. & R. 101.

they were of opinion it was made maliciously; that the question for them was, did the defendant honestly believe, at the time he spoke the words, that the statement contained in them was true, or was he actuated by malice in making such statement?—held that there was no misdirection. But the court' granted a new trial, not being satisfied of the fact whether C.'s statements were made officiously or in answer to A.'s inquiries.[1228] Whether a caution not to trust another *bonâ fide* given to a tradesman, *without any inquiry on his part*, is a privileged communication, was discussed in *Bennett* v. *Deacon*,[1229] and it was held by Tindal, Ch. J., and Erle, J., that it was, and by Coltman and Cresswell, JJ., that it was not. The effect of a previous inquiry was very elaborately discussed in a case where C., the mate of a ship, wrote to the defendant falsely charging his captain [the plaintiff] with having endangered the vessel and lives of the crew by continued drunkenness. The vessel was at this time in port, and likely to continue there a few days. The defendant, who was slightly acquainted with the owner of the vessel, but was not interested in the vessel, and had no inquiry made of him, believing in the truth of the letter, showed it to the owner, who, in consequence, dismissed the captain. In an action for libel by the captain, upon these facts appearing on the trial the chief justice directed the jury, that if the defendant acted honestly and *bonâ fide*, the publication was justifiable, and their verdict must be for the defendant, if otherwise for the plaintiff; the jury found a verdict for the defendant. On a motion for a new trial, after the case had been twice argued at the request of the court, held, by Tindal, C. J., and Erle, J., that the publication was justifiable, and that the direction to the jury was right; per Coltman, J., and Cresswell, J., that the direction was wrong; the court being equally divided, the motion for a new trial was denied, and the defendant had judgment.[1230] The defendant

---

[1228] *Chapman* v. *Wright*, 1 Arn. 241.

[1229] 2 Com. B. 628; and see *Lewis* v. *Chapman*, 16 N. Y. 369.

[1230] *Coxhead* v. *Richards*, 15 Law Jour R. 278, C. P.; 10 Jur. 984; 2 C. B. 569. Our opinion is that the Chief Justice and Justice Erle were right, and Justices

being tenant to A. of a house, B., the agent of A. directed the plaintiff to do some repairs at the house. The plaintiff did the repairs, but in a negligent manner, and during the progress of the work got drunk ; circumstances occurred which induced the defendant to believe that the plaintiff had entered his [defendant's] cellar, and taken his cider deposited there. Two days afterwards defendant met the plaintiff in the presence of D., and charged him with having got drunk and spoiled the work, and broken into his [defendant's] cellar. The defendant afterwards told D., in the absence of plaintiff, he was certain plaintiff had broken open the door. On the same day, the defendant complained to B. that plaintiff had been negligent with the work, had got drunk, and, as he thought, had broken open his cellar door. In an action of slander for these three several publications, held that the first and third publications were conditionally privileged, and the second was not privileged.[1221]

Cresswell and Coltman wrong. The importance of the principle involved justifies the reiteration of our conclusion that the material question in such a case is, Was the communication made *bona fide* to protect the interests of the person spoken to, without regard to its effect upon the party spoken of, and without any ill-will towards or desire to injure the person spoken of; if yea, it is privileged, and the absence or presence of a previous request is only material as evidence of the intent. This is conceded to be the law in the case of an employer giving what is termed a character to an ex-employé, and we shall show [§ 245] this latter act comes within the general rule of a communication made to protect the interests of the persons to whom the communication is made. On the argument of *Coxhead* v. *Richards*, 2 C. B. 591, Sir T. Wilde, for the plaintiff, says: "The cases as to characters of servants are not in point. Judges may have been wrong in supposing that a former master stands in a peculiar position. *It may be said that the servant authorizes the master to libel him*" [note 1258, *post*]. But right or wrong the cases proceed upon that distinction. [Erle, J.: In those cases it is perfectly immaterial whether the party was a volunteer; the sole question is, whether the information was given honestly and *bona fide*. Cresswell, J.: Mr. Justice Bayley deals much more clearly with the principle upon which this class of cases proceeds than Lord Tenterden does, in *Pattison* v. *Jones*.] And at page 609, Erle, J., denies that the relation of master and servant is the material one in cases of privileged communication. The action of the defendant in the case now before us seems to be as consistent with a natural and praiseworthy impulse to protect the interest of the ship-owner, and to protect the lives of the persons committed to the plaintiff's care, as with a desire to injure the plaintiff, and should not be considered as by itself evidence of malice.

[1221] *Toogood* v. *Spyring*, 1 Cr. M. & R. 181 ; 4 Tyrw. 582.

Where the defendant, a son-in-law, addressed a letter to his
mother-in-law, about to marry the plaintiff, containing slanderous imputations against him ; held, that the occasion justified
the writing, and that the jury were to say whether the defendant acted *bonâ fide*, and under a belief of the truth, although
the imputations were false, and that such communications were
to be regarded liberally, unless a clearly malicious intention
was manifest in the act.[1232]   But a letter to a woman containing
defamatory matter concerning her suitor, cannot be justified on
the ground that the writer was her friend and former pastor, and
that the letter was written at the request of her parents, who
assented to all its contents.[1233]   So if one not having been inquired of, write to the family of a woman that the man she is
about to marry has been imprisoned for larceny, the communication is not privileged.[1234]   But where the wife of A., prior to
her decease, made a request to B., after her [A.'s] decease, to
look to and advise her daughters. The wife of A. died, and he
remarried. B. told the daughters of A.'s deceased wife that
their step-mother was a loose woman, and that they ought to
leave their home ; this was held to be a privileged publication.[1235]   The plaintiffs, printers at M., had been employed by

---

[1232] *Todd* v. *Hawkins*, 8 C. & P. 88 ; 2 M. & Rob. 20.   The court having instructed the jury "that confidential communications, made in the usual course of
business, or of domestic or friendly intercourse, should be liberally viewed by
juries," held that the charge was right. (*Stallings* v. *Newman*, 26 Ala. 300.) A
grand jury had an indictment for theft of money before them, and a brother of
the man who had lost the money, returning from the court, stated that fact in
answer to inquiries made of him, and said that the general opinion was, that, if
a certain person swore what he had stated, the accused would be convicted.
This brother was afterwards sued for slandering the accused, by saying that "he
believed he stole the money," and it appeared that the words laid in the declaration, if spoken at all of the plaintiff, were spoken in a private conversation with a
brother of the defendant, both being brothers of the man whose money had been
stolen, and were overheard by one who had been employed to listen. Held,
that the occasion, and the relationship between the parties, afforded a *prima
facie* justification, sufficient to defeat the action, in the absence of any other
proof of malice than what arose from the mere speaking of the words. (*Faris*
v. *Starke*, 9 Dana, 128.)
[1233] *Joannes* v. *Bennett*, 5 Allen (Mass.), 169.
[1234] *Krebs* v. *Oliver*, 12 Gray, 239.
[1235] *Adcock* v. *Marsh*, 8 Ired. 360.
21

the defendant, the deputy clerk of the peace for the county of
K., to print the register of electors for the county, the expense
of which was defrayed from the county rate, and allowed by
the justices at quarter sessions; afterwards the defendant employed another printer, who agreed to do the work at a lower
rate than that which the plaintiff required, and he wrote a letter to the " finance committee " appointed to superintend such
expenses, in the conclusion of which he imputed improper motives to the plaintiffs in the demand which they made, and
characterized their demand as " an attempt to obtain a considerable sum of money from the county by misrepresentation."
In an action for libel, it was held that the occasion of writing
the letter *primâ facie* rebutted the presumption of malice,
but that it was a question for the jury whether the sentence
complained of as exceeding the privilege was evidence of malice.[1296] The defendant, *bonâ fide* believing that the plaintiff,
who was a clerk to one M., a customer of the defendant's, and
who had been sent to the defendant's shop by M., had, while
there, stolen a box from an inner room, went to M., and, after
telling him of his loss, intimated his suspicion of the plaintiff,
saying, " There was no one else in the room, and he must have
taken it." Held, that the communication was privileged by
the occasion.[1297] A letter written to B., concerning the plaintiff, who was steward of B.'s estate, was held to be privileged.[1298] A communication made by one subscriber to a charity to another subscriber to the same charity, respecting the
conduct of the plaintiff, the medical attendant in the employ
of such charity, held not to be privileged.[1299] Where the alleged libel was contained in a hand-bill offering a reward for
the recovery of bills, and stating that the plaintiff was believed
to have embezzled them ; held, that if done with the view
solely to protect persons liable on the bills, or for the convic-

[1296] *Cooke* v. *Wilkie*, 30 Eng. Law & Eq. R. 284 ; 5 El. & Bl. 328 ; 24 Law
Jour. Rep. N. S. 367, Q. B.; 1 Jur. N. S. 610 ; 3 Com. Law Rep. 1090.

[1297] *Amann* v. *Damm*, 8 C. B. N. S. 597.

[1298] *Cleaver* v. *Senaude*, 1 Camp. 268 n.

[1299] *Martin* v. *Strong*, 5 Adol. & El. 535 ; 1 Nev. & P. 29.

tion of the offender, it was a good defence, and that, in order
to show the *bonâ fides* of the defendant, evidence of his having preferred a charge of the same nature against the plaintiff
was admissible.[1240]   A communication by a landlord to his tenant, respecting the conduct of sub-tenants, or persons in the
employ of the tenant, is conditionally privileged; as where
the defendant complained to E., his tenant, that her lodgers, of
whom the plaintiff was one, behaved improperly at the windows, and he added that no moral person would like to have
such people in his house.[1241]   So communications made by an
employer to his employé, or by an employé to his employer,
are conditionally privileged in certain cases.   Thus, defamatory
words spoken by an employer to his overseer, intended to protect the employer's private interests and property, spoken without malice, were held privileged.[1242]   The communication of an
agent to his principal, touching the business of his agency, and
not going beyond it, is privileged, and is not actionable without proof that the defendant did not act honestly and in good
faith, but intended to do a wanton injury to the plaintiff.[1243]
The defendants, bankers at L., received from C. & Co., of Y.,
for collection, a note drawn by plaintiffs, merchants at L.; the
plaintiffs took up the note at maturity, the 19th of April, by
giving a draft on defendants' bank, in which they kept their
account.   The draft overdrew the plaintiffs' account, but was accepted by a clerk of the defendant, who, in reply to an offer of
one of the plaintiffs to transfer an amount standing to his individual credit sufficient to meet the check, declared that to be unnecessary.   The plaintiffs' account was made good on the 25th of
April, and on 28th of April defendants remitted to C. & Co.
the amount of the note, and added a postscript: " Confidential.   Had to hold over a few days for the accommodation of

---

[1240] *Finden* v. *Westlake*, 1 Mo. & Malk. 461.

[1241] *Knight* v. *Gibbs*, 3 Nev. & M. 467; 1 Adol. & El. 43.   Besides that the
tenant was interested to know the character of her lodgers, the defendant was
interested to maintain the reputation of his house.

[1242] *Easley* v. *Moss*, 9 Ala. 266.

[1243] *Washburn* v. *Cooke*, 3 Denio, 110.

L. & H.."—the plaintiffs. On the trial there was no evidence
as to malice ; the plaintiffs had a verdict on which judgment
was entered, and the case went to the Court of Appeals, where
the judgment was reversed and a new trial ordered ; and the
court said, " Assuming that the defendant made the communication in perfect good faith, as we must on this question of
privilege, his act was not to be deemed officious, as it related to
the very business with which he was intrusted." [1344] The
sheriff levied upon certain cattle of W., and they were wrongfully driven away, whereby he was likely to be damnified ; he
employed C., a law student, to ascertain the facts, and to advise
what course it was best to pursue ; held that C.'s letter to the
sheriff, stating facts implicating W., and advising his arrest for
larceny of the cattle, was privileged. [1345] The communication
of a pastor to his parishioners, relating to matters not spiritual,
is not necessarily privileged ; as where the plaintiff, who had
been for twenty years schoolmaster at the national school of the
adjoining parishes of C. and I., of which the defendant, the
rector of C., and another person, the vicar of I., were trustees,
was requested by the defendant to undertake the Sunday-school
of his parish ; he declining to do so, was removed from the
mastership of the national school ; he afterwards, intending to
gain a livelihood by it, set up a school in the defendant's parish,
in a schoolroom used as a dissenting chapel. In a letter addressed to his parishioners, the defendant told them that the
plaintiff's attempt betrayed a spirit of opposition to authority, and justified the managers of the national school in removing him ; that " no rightly-disposed Christian, who received in
simple faith the teaching of inspiration, ' Obey them who have
the rule over you, and submit yourselves,' could expect God's
blessing to rest upon such an undertaking," and warned them
against countenancing it, either by subscriptions or sending
their children to it for instruction ; that it would be a schismatical school, and those who aided the plaintiff in any way would

[1344] *Lewis* v. *Chapman*, 16 N. Y. 369 ; rev'g 19 Barb. 253.

[1345] *Washburn* v. *Cooke*, 3 Denio, 110.

be partakers with him in his evil deeds; they were to mark
them which cause divisions and offences, and avoid them, &c.
On the trial the presiding judge held the communication a
privileged one, and in the absence of any evidence of malice,
ordered a verdict for the defendant; on motion for a new trial
this direction was held erroneous, and that the jury should
have determined whether the publication was not malicious on
its face.[1246]

§ 242. When once a confidential relation is established between two persons with regard to an inquiry of a private nature, whatever takes place between them relative to the same
subject, though at a time and place different from those at
which the confidential relation began, may be entitled to protection as well as what passed at the original interview; and it
is a question for the jury whether any future communication
on the same subject, though apparently casual and voluntary,
did not take place under the influence of the confidential relation already established between the parties, and therefore entitled to the same protection.[1247]

§ 243. Where a publication would be privileged if made,
and because made to some certain person, the privilege may be
forfeited by the publication being made to some other person;
as where C. was employed, for compensation, by certain merchants in New York, in obtaining information concerning the
business character and standing of their customers, and others
in other States, doing business in New York. He wrote for
their use, from the residence of T. & Co., a letter unfavorably
representing them, and on his return had it and similar letters
printed in a pamphlet, which he gave privately to his employers *and others*, some of whom had dealt with T. & Co. Held,
that although the publication might have been privileged if
made only to such of his employers as were interested in the
pecuniary standing of T. & Co., the privilege was lost by the

[1246] *Gilpin* v. *Fowler*, 26 Eng. Law & Eq. R. 386: 9 Ex. 615; 23 Law Jour.
Rep. N. S. 152, Ex.; 18 Jur. 292.
  [1247] *Beatson* v. *Skene*, 5 Hurl. & N. 838. See *ante*, note 1198.

publication being made to other persons.[1248] And so held of a
circular letter sent by the secretary of a society for the protection of trade to the members of such society.[1249] And with regard to the report by the officers of a corporation to the stockholders, of the result of their investigation into the conduct of
their officers and agents, with their conclusions upon the evidence collected by them, it was held to be a privileged communication, but that the privilege extended only to making the
report, and not to the preservation of it in the form of a book
for distribution among the stockholders and in the community.[1250] And where the defendant published an advertisement
calling a meeting of the creditors of the plaintiff, and in addition defamatory remarks concerning the plaintiff, the publication was held not to be privileged, because the meeting of creditors might have been called in a less public manner.[1251] And
although a bank director may be privileged at a meeting of the
board to speak of the credit of a merchant or customer of his
bank, he is not privileged so to speak, even to a co-director, in
any other place or at any other time than at such meeting during its session.[1252] The publication, by the directors of an incorporated society for promoting female medical education, in
their annual report, of a " caution to the public " against trusting a person who had formerly been employed to obtain and
collect subscriptions in their behalf, but had since been dismissed, was held to be justified so far only as it was made in
good faith, and was required to protect the corporation and the
public against false representations of that person; and that

---

[1248] *Taylor* v. *Church*, 1 E. D. Smith, 279; 4 Selden, 452; and see *Beardsley*
v. *Tappan*, in note 732, *ante* ; *Cook* v. *Hill*, 3 Sandf. 341.

[1249] *Getting* v. *Foss*, 3 Car. & P. 160.

[1250] *Phil. & R. R. Co.* v. *Quigley*, 21 How. U. S. Rep. 202. The plaintiff, a
policy holder in an insurance company, published a pamphlet attacking the directors of the company; the directors published a reply, and charged that plaintiff had sworn in opposition to his own handwriting; held that the reply was
privileged, if published to vindicate the company. (*Koenig* v. *Ritchie*, 3 Fost. &
Fin. 413.)

[1251] *Brown* v. *Croome*, 2 Stark. Cas. 297.

[1252] *Sewell* v. *Catlin*, 8 Wend. 291.

the questions, whether the directors had acted in good faith, and had not exceeded their privilege, were for the jury.[1253] The plaintiff, having the defendant's bond, advertised it for sale; the defendant published a statement of the circumstances under which the bond had been given, with this conclusion: "His [plaintiff's] object is either to extract money from the pockets of an unwary purchaser, or, what is more likely, to extort money from me;" held not privileged.[1254]   A. understanding that B. imputed to C., a relative of A.'s, the passing to him of a piece of forged paper, told B., untruly, that he was authorized by C. to call upon him and investigate the matter, and B. thereupon repeatedly asserted C.'s guilt of the crime; held, that these assertions were unnecessary and useless, and were not privileged, and it seems they would not have been privileged if A. had been C.'s agent to call upon B. for information.[1255]

· § 244. There are, however, some cases where the publication to others than those immediately interested or concerned does not forfeit the privilege; as where the plaintiff, a female, went to the store of the defendant to make a purchase, and after she left, the shopman, missing a roll of ribbon, supposed she had taken it, and so informed his employer, the defendant; the following day the plaintiff was passing the defendant's store; the defendant seeing her, called her in, and taxed her with the theft, which the plaintiff denying, the defendant detained her and sent for her father, and in his presence charged the plaintiff with stealing the ribbon; after some altercation the plaintiff was permitted to depart, and afterwards brought an action for slander, in which action it was held at *nisi prius* that the repetition of the charge to the plaintiff's father was, under the circumstances, a privileged publication.[1256]   And

---

[1253] *Gassett* v. *Gilbert*, 6 Gray (Mass.) 94.

[1254] *Robertson* v. *McDougall*, 4 Bing. 670; 1 Mo. & P. 692; 3 Car. & P. 259.

[1255] *Thorn* v. *Moser*, 1 Denio, 488; and see *Robinet* v. *Ruby*, 13 Md. 95.

[1256] *Fowler* v. *Homer*, 3 Camp. 294, and *ante* note 1203; also *Toogood* v. *Spyring*, 1 Cr. M. & R. 181; 4 Tyrw. 582; *Manby* v. *With*, 18 C. B. 544; 37 Eng. Law & Eq. R. 403; *Taylor* v. *Hawkins*, 5 Eng. Law & Eq. R. 253: 16 Q. B. 308.

where, in an action for slander, it appeared that the defendant,
in the presence of a third person, not an officer of justice,
charged the plaintiff with having stolen his property, and afterward repeated the charge to another person, also not an officer,
who was, with the consent of the plaintiff, called in to search
him, held the charge was privileged if the defendant believed
in its truth, acted *bonâ fide*, and did not make the charge before more persons or in stronger language than was necessary.[1257]

§ 245. There is a well recognized right to what is termed
"give a character to a servant." This right may be thus described: An ex-employer may, without rendering himself liable
in an action for slander or libel, state orally or in writing, and as
well without as with a previous request, all that he may *believe* to
be true concerning his ex-employee. The right must be exercised in good faith, *i. e.* without malice. It appearing that the
publication was made in what is termed "giving a character,"
the presumption is that it is made *bonâ fide*, and the burden is
upon the plaintiff to show malice. The legal excuse for such a
publication is *belief in the truth* of the matter published; if the
publisher does not believe in the truth of what he publishes,
his publication is malicious, because made without legal excuse.
Notwithstanding this legal excuse, if the publication is made
with a design to injure the person whom its language concerns,
the publication is malicious, because not made in good faith. A
publication, malicious in either of these meanings of that term,
is unprivileged. Malice is established when it is shown that
the matter published was false within the knowledge of the publisher; or malice may be established by showing a bad motive
in making the publication; as that it was made more publicly
than was necessary to protect the interests of the parties concerned, or that it contained matter not relevant to the occasion,
or that the publisher entertained ill-will towards the person
whom the publication concerned. Although the right now under
consideration is one exercised in connection with the relation of

---

[1257] *Padmore* v. *Lawrence*, 11 Ad. & El. 380; 3 Per. & D. 209.

master and servant, it does not arise from that relation, at least
in the manner generally supposed, nor is the right restricted within the limits ordinarily assigned to it. The relation of master
and servant, or of employer and employee, is one created by contract; with the determination of the contract the relation expires,
and at the expiration of the relation ceases all the rights and duties which, during its continuance, existed between the parties.
Thenceforth the parties occupy the same relative positions as if
no contract of hiring and serving had ever been made. It cannot be that because A. has been in B.'s employ, B. thereby ac-
quires a right to publish concerning A. anything he would not
have been permitted with impunity to publish had such relation never existed. Hence the right now in question must rest
on some other foundation, or arise in some other way, than
upon the fact that the person spoken or written of has been in
the employ of the publisher.[1238] On examination it will be perceived that this right of an *ex-employer* to give, as it is termed,
a character to his *ex-employee*, is nothing more than a consequence of the right to communicate one's belief, which is referred to and illustrated in a preceding section [§ 241]. An
employer is charged with the duty of exercising due care in
the selection and retention of properly qualified employees or
agents, and is liable for all the acts of his employees done in
his service. In addition, the employer has more or less to trust
the safety of his person and his property to the employee; the
employer, therefore, is peculiarly interested to know the character and capacity of every person who either is already in his
employ, or is desirous of entering his employ. He can obtain
this knowledge only from the employee himself, or from information furnished by those to whom the employee may be known.
To limit the source of this knowledge to the employee himself,

---

[1238] That seems a monstrous proposition of Sir T. Wilde's in the argument of
Coxhead v. Richards [see *ante*, note 1230], that "the servant authorizes the master to libel him," and yet perhaps it is warranted by the reasoning in many decisions, and it is the only assumption for basing a distinction between the case of
an ex-employer speaking of his ex-employee and the case of any other person
(one not an employer) making a communication to a party interested.

would manifestly operate, in the majority of cases, to prevent
the obtaining any information worth the having; but because
the employer is interested to know the character and capacity
of those in his employ, or who are candidates for employment
by him, every one, not a former employer only, who honestly
believes himself possessed of knowledge on the subject which
the employer is interested to know, may, with or without a
previous request, in good faith, communicate such his belief to
the employer. In such cases the communication is made not to
promote the interest of the person making it, but either to
serve the interests of the employer, or to injure the employee.
No one is under any obligation to disclose his belief; he does
not owe it as a duty, either to the employer or the employee, to
make any communication on the subject. Making the communication is the exercise of a right, and is optional [§ 39].
This right is exercised under the double peril that by speaking disparagingly of the employee, the speaker may be sued by
the employee for slander, and by speaking approvingly of the
employee he may be sued by the employer for misrepresentation.[1289] Hence this right is usually exercised with reluctance;
and as, where the communication is made without request, less
evidence of ill-will may be required than in the case of a communication made upon a request, it seldom happens that such
communications are made without request; and because the
character and capacity of an employee will be by no one so well
known as by the one in whose service he has been, it happens
the ex-employer is the person to whom, in the majority of
instances, application will be made for information respecting
the character and capacity of a candidate for employment, not
because the ex-employer is the only one having the right to
give information, but because he is supposed to be best qualified to give information on the subject. The exercise of this
right should be encouraged, not only for the benefit of the employer, but of the employee; if the ex-employer refuses, as he

---

[1289] Defendant's letter of recommendation of the plaintiff, if untrue, would
have rendered him liable to any one injured thereby. (*Fowles* v. *Bowen*, 30 N.
Y. 20; and see *Pasley* v. *Freeman*, 3 Term R. 51.)

lawfully may,[1200] to answer any inquiries respecting his ex-employee, the probable inference is that he can say nothing favorable, and will not incur the risk of saying anything unfavorable. These views have been expressed judicially, as thus: "But the rule is general, and it seems to me to be quite a mistake to suppose that it is the privilege only of persons giving characters. There are two other classes of persons materially interested in the maintenance of the privilege—the persons accepting characters, and those of whom characters are given. It is a most important privilege for the encouragement of all honest servants. They are sufficiently protected against the abuse of it by that limitation of it to which all agree—that if a master, going beyond it, wantonly and maliciously make a false statement as to the character of his servant, the express malice takes away all the privilege."[1261]

§ 246. The subject of the preceding section [§ 245] is illustrated by the decisions to which we proceed to refer. Thus, it is said,[1262] a *bonâ fide* character given of a servant that she was saucy, &c., if there be no malice (which must be directly proved), will not ground an action of slander, though the servant was prevented from getting a place thereby; and, though a letter giving a false character of a servant may be the ground of an action, yet, if written as an answer to a letter sent, not with a view to obtaining a character, but with an intention of obtaining such an answer as should be the ground of an action, no action can be sustained.[1263] A servant cannot maintain an action against his former master, for words spoken, or a letter written by him in giving a character of the servant, unless the latter prove the malice as well as falsehood of the charge, even though the master make specific charges of fraud. As where the plaintiff, who had been in the employ of the defendant,

---

[1260] No action lies for refusing to give information as to the character or capacity of a former employee. (*Carrol* v. *Bird*, 3 Esp. 204.)

[1261] Wightman, J., *Gardner* v. *Slade*, 13 Jurist, 828; 13 Adol. & El. N. S. 796; and see in note 1270, *post*.

[1262] *Edmonson* v. *Stephenson*, Bull. N. P. 8.

[1263] *King* v. *Waring*, 5 Esp. 14.

afterwards applied to one R. for employment. R. inquired of the defendant concerning plaintiff, and in consequence of what was told him by defendant, refused to employ plaintiff. Upon this, C., plaintiff's brother-in-law, called upon the defendant for an explanation, and then the defendant wrote C., " Two days I gave him (plaintiff) money to go into the city and buy books. When he came home I desired him to reckon up his accounts; he did so. But being one day more curious than I sometimes was, I looked over his account, article by article, and in one book I well knew the price of, I found he had charged me one shilling more than it cost, and that shilling he kept in his pocket," with statements of other frauds ; on the trial the plaintiff had a verdict, subject to the opinion of the court on a special case ; upon the argument of the case judgment was ordered for the defendant.[1264] Where, in an action of slander, it appeared that the plaintiff had applied to the under-sheriff to be appointed an officer, the latter applied to the defendant as to the fitness of plaintiff, held that the answer of the defendant was conditionally privileged.[1265] Where A. introduced the plaintiff to defendant, a ship's captain, who employed plaintiff as his mate, defendant afterwards dismissed plaintiff from his service, and wrote A. that he had done so on account of the intemperate habits of the plaintiff, this was held a privileged communication.[1266] The defendant being about to dismiss the plaintiff from his employ, called in a friend to hear what passed, and having dismissed the plaintiff, refused to give him a character, alleging to those who applied for information respecting the plaintiff, that he, defendant, had discharged the plaintiff for dishonesty. The plaintiff's brother afterwards inquired of the defendant why he had treated the plaintiff in such

---

[1264] *Weatherstone* v. *Hawkins*, 1 Term R. 110.

[1265] *Sims* v. *Kinder*, 1 Carr. 279.

[1266] *Tremaine* v. *Parker*, 12 Law Times, 312. A letter addressed to a person on whose recommendation the writer had taken the plaintiff into his service, to the effect that his (plaintiff's) conduct had not justified the character given of him, and that he had left a balance unaccounted for, and that he ought not to be recommended for morality or honesty ; this was held to be privileged. (*Dixon* v. *Parsons*, 1 Fost. & Fin. 24.)

a manner, and that he (defendant) was keeping plaintiff out of employ. The defendant answered, "He has robbed me; and I believe for years past," adding that he concluded so from the circumstances under which he had discharged the plaintiff. Erle, J., said, " The calling in a witness was consistent with a wish to spread defamation; it was consistent also with the wish to do what a prudent man would desire to do. But if the effect of the evidence is equal both ways, the onus of proving malice lies upon the plaintiff. As to the words spoken to the plaintiff.'s brother, no malicious motive appears. The evidence, indeed, related to only one robbery, whereas the defendant spoke of having been robbed for years. But the communication was made in answer to an inquiry by the plaintiff's brother, and there are no circumstances to show that the extent of the statement actually made proceeded from malice, or went beyond what might be said by a person honestly wishing to tell the whole truth." [1267] The plaintiff had been in the employ of the defendant and dismissed on a charge of theft. Plaintiff afterwards went to defendant's house to be paid his wages, and was in conversation with the defendant's servants, when the defendant, addressing his servants, said, " I discharged that man [the plaintiff] for robbing me; do not speak any more to him, in public or private, or·I shall think you as bad as him." Maule, J., said, " The evidence does not raise any probability of malice, and is quite as consistent with its absence as with its presence; and considering that the mere possibility of malice which is found in this case, and in all cases where it is not disproved, would not be sufficient to justify a finding for the plaintiff, and it was right not to leave the question of malice to the jury." [1268] A defendant who had dismissed two servants, told one in the absence of the other, You have both been robbing me; it was held conditionally privileged.[1269] The plaintiff being in the service

<hr>

[1267] *Taylor* v. *Hawkins,* 16 Q. B. 808; 5 Eng. Law & Eq. R. 253; 20 Law Jour. Rep. N. S. 313, Q. B.; 15 Jurist, 706; and *ante,* notes 1256, 1257.

[1268] *Somerville* v. *Hawkins,* 10 C. B. 583; 15 Jurist, 450; 3 Eng. Law & Eq. R. 503.

[1269] *Manby* v. *With,* and *Eastmead* v. *With,* 37 Eng. Law & Eq. R. 408.

of the defendant was discharged without any previous notice, and the plaintiff considering himself entitled to a month's wages, in lieu of the notice, refused to quit the defendant's house until those wages were paid him, whereupon the defendant had the plaintiff removed by a police officer. The defendant called on one Holland, in whose employ the plaintiff had previously been, and complained of plaintiff, requesting Mr. Holland not to give plaintiff another character. Subsequently, the plaintiff applied to Mr. Hand for employment, who inquired of defendant and received from him a letter, the material portion of which was as thus : " Rogers [the plaintiff] did not live with me six months, as he has told you, and I wish I had never taken him into my house, as he is a bad tempered, lazy, impertinent fellow, and has given me a great deal of trouble. I was obliged to send for a police officer to put him and his things out of my house ; as I look upon it he will take any advantage he can." On the trial the court left it to the jury to say if the defendant had acted maliciously ; the verdict was for the plaintiff: leave was reserved to the defendant to move to enter a nonsuit. He moved, but his motion was refused.[1270] Where the defendant, the plaintiff's former mistress,

---

[1270] *Rogers* v. *Clifton*, 3 B. & P. 587, on the motion for a nonsuit, Lord Alvanley, Ch. J., said, " If it were to be understood that whenever a master gives a bad character to a servant who has quitted his service, he may be forced by the servant, in justification, to prove the truth of what he has stated, it would be impossible for any master (so understanding the law, at least with any regard to his own safety) to give any character but the most favorable to a servant, *and consequently impossible for a servant not entitled to the most favorable character to obtain any new place.* Unquestionably the master is not bound to substantiate the truth of what he says in giving a character to his late servant, but it is equally clear that the servant may, if he can prove the character to be false, and the question between the master and servant will always, in such a case, be, whether what the former has spoken concerning the latter be malicious and defamatory ; " and per Rooke, J., " a master may, at any time, *whether asked or not,* speak of the character of his servant, provided that he speak in the honesty of his heart, and an action cannot be maintained against him for so doing ; at the same time, masters are not warranted in speaking ill of their servants from heat and passion." Where the plaintiff charged his servant with robbing him, and the robbery charged consisted in giving away pieces of bread, the court charged the jury that if the pieces of bread given away were such pieces as the servant might reasonably suppose the

had, in a letter inquiring as to her character, stated acts of misconduct during the time of the plaintiff's being in her service,
and also *subsequently* to her having left it, and the defendant
had also stated the same to the persons who originally recommended the plaintiff to her; held, that the latter part of the
letter was a privileged communication, and which the defendant was bound to make, and that the parol statement having
been made to the parties only who recommended her, was not
officious, nor evidence of malice, which in such an action is the
gist, and must be expressly proved.[1271] In an action for slander
of the plaintiff, in her character of a domestic servant, the
plaintiff proved that, having lived some time with the defendant, she changed service upon a character given to her by the
defendant; that, some time afterwards, the defendant's wife, in
a letter to her new mistress, alluded to the plaintiff, and to the
character first given of her as being unmerited; that thereupon
the new mistress requested further information, and was told,
by the defendant's wife, that she had discovered, since the time
of the giving of the first character, that the plaintiff was dishonest. Held, that there was no evidence to be submitted to
the jury of malice in the defendant's wife, and that the communication was privileged. If a servant obtain a place upon the
strength of a character given by his master, and the master
afterwards discover circumstances which induce him to believe
that the character was undeserved, he is morally bound to inform the new master of those circumstances, and the communication made concerning them is a privileged communication.[1272]
The plaintiff had been in the employ of defendant and his
partners; on plaintiff leaving their employ, defendant and his
partners gave him a written recommendation, and plaintiff
afterwards went into the employ of C. Subsequently, defendant saw C., and said he desired to set him right in regard to a

master would not object to his giving away, the master was not justified in the
charge of robbery, and the servant might recover. (*Roberts* v. *Richards*, 3 Fost.
& Fin. 507.)

[1271] *Child* v. *Affleck*, 9 B. & C. 403.

[1272] *Gardner* v. *Slade*, 13 Jurist, 826; 11 Law Jour. Rep. 884, Q. B.; 13 Law
Times, 282.

young man in his employ, the plaintiff, that he was a liar, and he had doubts of his honesty; held a conditionally privileged communication.[273] The letter of recommendation, if untrue, would have rendered him liable to any one injured thereby, and he was privileged to say what he did for his own protection. Plaintiff was in the service of the defendants [husband and wife] as governess for fourteen·months. After she left she sought an engagement elsewhere, and on an inquiry being made to the defendant (the wife) concerning the plaintiff, the defendant answered in writing, "I parted with her (the plaintiff) on account of her incompetency and not being lady-like nor good tempered," adding, "May I trouble you to tell her (the plaintiff) that this being the third time I have been referred to, I beg to decline any further applications." Evidence was given of plaintiff's competency and of her being lady-like and good tempered. It was left to the jury to say whether the letter was written maliciously, and that stating what was untrue was evidence of malice. The plaintiff had a verdict, and the court above refused to disturb it.[274] Where the plaintiff's master (the defendant) had, on his quitting his service, and being about to enter on another, written of his own accord a letter informing the party that he had discharged the plaintiff for misconduct, and on receiving a letter inquiring the particulars, had written the libellous letters for which the action was brought; held, that although *a party might set himself in motion to induce inquiries by a third party*, and the answers, although slanderous, might come within the scope of a privileged communication; yet in such a case it would be a question for the jury to say if the defendant acted *bonâ fide*, or maliciously intending to do the servant an injury.[275]

§ 247. As respects publications concerning candidates for *office*, we take upon ourselves, with due deference to the decisions, to say, that the same rule applies to them as to communications

[273] *Fowles* v. *Bowen*, 30 N. Y. 20.

[274] *Fountain* v. *Boodle*, 3 Ad. & El. N. S. 5; 2 Gale & Dav. 455.

[275] *Pattison* v. *Jones*, 8 B. & C. 587; 3 C. & P. 383; 3 M. & R. 101.

made concerning candidates for employment generally [§ 245]. The rule, as we suppose, must be the same for every *kind* of employment, and *office* is only another name for *employment*. The right which one has to speak concerning a candidate for employment as a mechanic, is neither more extensive nor more limited than the right one has to speak of a candidate for the office of a legislator or a judge. As respects a candidate for employment generally, so with respect to a candidate for office; the publication, to be privileged, must, with certain exceptions [§ 244], be limited to the persons interested. A general publication, as well to those interested as to those not interested, would not be privileged. Again, the matter published must be such as is relevant to the subject-matter, and necessary to be known by the persons in interest for their own protection. Thus the publication in a newspaper of defamatory matter concerning a candidate for appointment, was held not privileged, and that to have been privileged the publication should have been limited to the appointing power [§ 243];[1276] so limited it would have been privileged; as where the defendant, at the request of a senator of the United States, in order to give him information as to the fitness of the plaintiff for the office to which he was nominated, spoke the words charged in the declaration, and referred to the records of a court for their confirmation, it was held that there was nothing from which to imply malice, and that the plaintiff could not sustain his action.[1277] Where a candidate for the representation of a borough circulated an address to the electors, asking for their suffrages, and claiming to be a fit and proper person to represent them in Parliament, and an elector in that borough published *in a newspaper* two letters addressed to the candidate, the first in answer to the circular, and the second in consequence of the treatment he had received from the candidate on the day of nomination at the hustings, and both letters contained imputa-

[1276] *Hunt* v. *Bennett*, 19 N. Y. 173, affirming 4 E. D. Smith, 647.

[1277] *Law* v. *Scott*, 5 Har. & J. 438. A statute in Pennsylvania provides: No person shall be subject to prosecution by indictment for investigating official conduct of public officers, &c.

22

tions on the private character of the candidate; on the trial of
an action for libel the judge charged the jury that the occasion
did not justify the publication, and the plaintiff had a verdict.
On a motion for a new trial it was claimed that it was justifiable for an elector *bonâ fide* to communicate to the constituency any matter respecting a candidate which the elector believed to be true and material to the election. *The principle
was conceded by the court to be correct, but was held inapplicable because the communication had not been confined to the
constituency of the plaintiff, but had been published in a newspaper.*[1278] Where the plaintiff was candidate at a general election for re-election as State Governor, the defendant published
defamatory matter of the plaintiff in " An address to the electors of the State of New York;" in an action of libel for this
publication, it was contended on the part of the defendant that
the plaintiff could not recover unless upon proof of " *express
malice.*" The court denied this position, and held that malice
was to be implied from the falsity of the publication.[1279]

§ 248. Insanity is a complete defence to an action for slan-

[1278] *Duncombe* v. *Daniell*, 8 C. & P. 213; 1 W. W. & H. 101, Denman, C. J.
However large the privilege of electors may be, it is extravagant to suppose that
it can justify the publication to *all the world* of facts injurious to a person who
happens to stand in the situation of a candidate.

[1279] *Lewis* v. *Few*, 5 Johns. 1. In *Harwood* v. *Astley*, 4 Bos. & Pul. 47; 1 N.
R. 47, an action for slander of a candidate for election to Parliament, the plaintiff
succeeded and had judgment, which the court, on writ of error, affirmed principally, if not solely, on the ground that the jury must have found the publication
to be *malicious*, and therefore not privileged. Officers and candidates for offices
may be canvassed, but not calumniated. (*Seely* v. *Blair*, Wright, 358, 683. See
Brewer v. *Weakley*, 2 Overt. 99; *Root* v. *King*, 7 Cow. 613, affirmed 4 Wend. 113,
note to Amer. edit. of Stark. Slan. vol. 1. p. 301.) In *Mayrant* v. *Richardson*, 1
Nott & McC. 327, an action of slander against a candidate for office, it was held
by Nott, J., that when a man becomes a candidate for public honors, he makes
profert of himself for public investigation. No one has the right to impute to
him infamous crimes or misdemeanors, but talents and qualifications are mere
matters of opinion, of which the electors are the only judges, and in that case it
was held that imputing weakness of understanding to a candidate for Congress
was not actionable. In *Com'wealth* v. *Clapp*, 4 Mass. 163, Parsons, C. J., says:
" When a man shall consent to be a candidate for a public office, conferred by the
electors of the people, he must be considered as putting his character in issue, so

der or libel.[1250] Fools and madmen are tacitly excepted out of all laws.[1251] A judgment in an action for slander was perpetually enjoined, upon the ground that at the time of the speaking the words, and of the rendition of the judgment, the defendant was insane in reference to the subject of the slander.[1252]

§ 249. Drunkenness is not a defence to an action for slander or libel,[1253] nor is infancy;[1254] but drunkenness may, perhaps, be a matter of mitigation.[1255]

§ 250. It is a good defence to an action for libel, that after the publication the plaintiff agreed with the defendant to

far as may respect his fitness and qualification for office." But see *Curtis* v. *Mussey*, 6 Gray, 261; *Aldrich* v. *Press Print. Co.*, 9 Miu. 133.

[1250] *Bryant* v. *Jackson*, 6 Humpf. 199; *Yeats* v. *Reed*, 4 Blackf. 163; *Dickinson* v, *Barber*, 9 Mass. 225. Perhaps delirium tremens is a defence; for it is a species of insanity, and like insanity from other causes, affects the responsibility for crime. (*Maconnehey* v. *The State*, 5 Ohio, N. S., 77; *O'Brien* v. *The People*, 48 Barb. 275.) A lunatic is liable for a trespass. (*Weaver* v. *Ward*, Hob. 134; *Krom* v. *Schoonmaker*, 3 Barb. 647; *Bullock* v. *Babcock*, 3 Wend. 391; *Rae's* Medical Juris. 110; *Mason* v. *Keeling*, 12 Mod. 332; 2 Monthly Law Reporter, N. S. 487.) In the chapter in the Roman Law entitled "*Si quis Imperatori Maledixerit*," is a passage, which being interpreted reads: "If the evil speaking proceed from levity, it is to be despised; if from madness, it is to be pitied; if from a sense of wrong, it is to be forgiven."

It is not a defence to an action of slander or libel, that the words were not spoken in earnest, but as a jest, and that the defendant did not expect to be believed. (*Hutch* v. *Potter*, 2 Gilman, 725; Holt on Libel, 290, 291; *Long* v. *Eakle*, 4 Md. 454; *McKee* v. *Ingalls*, 4 Scam. 30; Wood's Civil Law, 247; and see *Pieter Tonneman* v. *Jan De Witt*, Valentine's Corporation Manual for 1849, p. 402; Addison on Contracts, 261.)

[1251] Holt, Ch. J., *City of London* v. *Vanacker*, Carthew, 483.

[1252] *Horner* v. *Marshall*, 5 Munf. 466.

[1253] *McKee* v. *Ingalls*, 4 Scam. 30. As to defence of intoxication in an action on an express contract, see *Gore* v. *Gibson*, 13 M. & W. 623.

[1254] *Defries* v. *Davis*, 1 Bing. N. C. 692; 1 Scott, 594. An infant two years old is not liable *criminaliter* for a nuisance erected on his lands. (*The People* v. *Townsend*, 3 Hill, 479.) And one aged only eleven years, seized of lands in the actual occupation of his guardian, in socage is not indictable for the non-repair of a bridge *ratione tenure*. (*Rex* v. *Sutton*, 5 Nev. & Man. 353.) See cases collected in a note in 5 Monthly Law Reporter, N. S. 364, Boston, Nov. 1852.

[1255] *Howell* v. *Howell*, 10 Ired. 84. And see *Iseley* v. *Lovejoy*, 8 Blackf. 462; *Gates* v. *Meredith*, 7 Ind. 440.

accept the publication of an apology in full for his cause
of action, and that such apology had been published.[1286]
And it seems that an agreement that the slanderer should
write a letter to a third party, exculpating the person slandered from the charge, is satisfaction of the injury, and his
so doing is evidence of an accord and satisfaction.[1287] Formerly a defence of accord and satisfaction did not require to
be specially pleaded.[1288] Now it must be pleaded specially.

§ 251. A former recovery for the *same* cause is a bar to an
action for slander or libel.[1289] A judgment in an action of slan-

[1286] *Boosey* v. *Wood*, 3 Hurl. & Colt. 484. An agreement not to bring any action in consideration of the defendant's destroying certain documents relating to
the charge imputed to the plaintiff, which the defendant accordingly destroyed,
held to be evidence of accord and satisfaction. (*Lane* v. *Applegate*, 1 Stark. 97.)
Where, in an action of slander, an agreement had been made, in consequence of
which the defendant signed a paper stating that "at his request the plaintiff had
consented on his paying the costs of the action as between attorney and client,
and making an apology for his conduct, to stay the proceedings therein," the
court held that it was an absolute and not a conditional agreement, and in default of defendant paying the costs, made a rule absolute for signing the judgment as for want of a plea. (*Yardrew* v. *Brook*, 2 Nev. & M. 835.) As to the
settlement of an action for slander as the consideration for a promise, see *Keson*
v. *Barclay*, 2 Penn. St. R. 531; approved *Morey* v. *Newfane Township*, 8 Barb.
653. By Statute 6 & 7 Vict. ch. 96, it is provided that in any action for defamation, the defendant, after notice, may give in evidence, in mitigation, the making
or offer to make an apology.

[1287] *Smith* v. *Kerr*, 1 Barb. 155. See *Eiffe* v. *Jacob*, 1 Jebb & Symes, 257.
An accord and satisfaction by one or some of several wrong-doers, is a satisfaction as to all. (*Strang* v. *Holmes*, 7 Cow. 224; *Knickerbacker* v. *Colver*, 8 *Id.*
111.) It follows that a partial satisfaction, by one of several wrong-doers, is a
satisfaction *pro tanto* as to all. (*Merchants' B'k* v. *Curtis*, 37 Barb. 320.) As to
a plea of apology and payment into court in England, see Stat. 6 & 7 Vict. ch.
96; 15 & 16 Vict. ch. 76; *Chadwick* v. *Herepath*, 3 C. B. 885; *O'Brien* v. *Clements*, 3 Dowl. & L. 676; *Lafone* v. *Smith*, 3 Hurl. & N. 735; 4 *Id.* 158; *Ingram*
v. *Ferguson*, 1 New Pr. Cas. 486.

[1288] 2 Greenl. Ev. 321; *Lane* v. *Applegate*, 1 Stark. 97; *King* v. *Waring*, 5
Esp. 13; *Eiffe* v. *Jacob*, 1 Jebb & S. 257.

[1289] *Campbell* v. *Butts*, 3 N. Y. 173. The plaintiff having once recovered,
cannot afterwards recover for any subsequent loss by the same words. (Bull. N.
P. 7.) Where the cause of action is the same, a judgment between the same parties is binding on each, and it is immaterial that the form of action is different, if
the cause of action be the same. (*Hitchin* v. *Campbell*, 2 Bl. R. 827.)

der, for a particular charge, bars any other action against the
defendant in that action for the same charge, though made on
a different occasion, if made before suit brought; and, therefore, though there be but one count for particular words, proof
that they were spoken by defendant on distinct occasions before suit commenced is competent.[1290] It is no bar to an action
for slander or libel that in a former action for the publication
of the same words, on an occasion different from that alleged in
the declaration, the defendant obtained a verdict and judgment
in his favor. It was not for *the same* cause of action.[1291] A recovery by the husband for slanderous words spoken of himself
and wife, is not a bar to another action by the wife for the same
slanderous words, in which the husband is joined as a nominal
party plaintiff.[1292] A recovery in an action for malicious prosecution is a bar to a subsequent action for slander, for the accusation uttered for the purpose of having the arrest made, and
on the occasion when it was made.[1293] But where the defendant published the accusation before or after making his complaint to have the plaintiff arrested, an action for that publication is not barred by the recovery in the action for the malicious prosecution.[1294] An application for a criminal information against a party for the publication of a libel, which appli-

[1290] *Root* v. *Lowndes*, 6 Hill, 518.

[1291] *Henson* v. *Veach*, 1 Blackf. 369.

[1292] *Bash* v. *Sommer*, 20 Penn. (8 Harris) 159; and see *ante*, note 120. A recovery against one of several parties to a joint tort frequently precludes the
plaintiff from proceedings against any other party not included in such action.
(Cro. Jac. 74; Yelv. 68.) But where the evidence and the damage in the two actions might be different, as where two persons on different occasions have published the same libel, separate actions may be supported against each. (2 B. &
P. 69.) Where a verdict with nominal damages (40s.) had been obtained against
the publisher of a libel, that was held not to be any justification in an action
against the author of the libel, nor to furnish any reason for not giving substantial
damages, and the plaintiff had a verdict for £450. (*Frescoe* v. *May*, 2 Foster &
Fin. 123.) The pendency of other actions against other publishers of the same
defamatory matter, not a mitigating circumstance. (*Harrison* v. *Pearce*, 1 Foster
& Fin. 567.)

[1293] *Sheldon* v. *Carpenter*, 4 N. Y. 579.

[1294] *Rockwell* v. *Brown*, 36 N. Y. 207.

cation has been refused, is no bar to an action on the case for the same ground of complaint.[1295] At one time the defence of a former recovery might be given in evidence under the general issue;[1296] now, the defence of a former recovery must be pleaded.

§ 252. Whatever else may be intended by the phrase "freedom of the press," or "liberty of the press," it means the freedom or liberty of those who conduct the press. This freedom or liberty, properly understood, means only that for which Milton put forth his eloquent plea: "unlicensed printing." "The liberty of the Press consists in printing without any previous license, subject to the consequences of law. The licentiousness of the Press is Pandora's box, the source of every evil."[1297] "The liberty of the Press is connected with natural liberty. The use and liberty of speech were antecedent to Magna Charta, and printing is only a more extensive and improved kind of speech."[1298] "The liberty of the Press, therefore, properly understood, is the personal liberty of the writer to express his thoughts in the more improved way invented by human ingenuity in the form of the Press."[1299] "The liberty of the Press consists in the right to publish with impunity, truth with good motives and for justifiable ends, whether it respects governments, magistracy, or individuals."[1300] In the

---

[1295] *Wakley* v. *Cooke*, 16 Law Jour. Rep. 225, Ex.; 9 Law Times, 513; 16 M. & W. 822.

[1296] *Campbell* v. *Butts*, 3 Coms. 173.

[1297] Attributed to Lord Mansfield, cited *Root* v. *King*, 7 Cow. 628, and commented on 1 Mence on Libel, 158.

[1298] Essay on the liberty of the Press, chiefly as it respects personal slander, page 6, Bishop Hayter.

[1299] Holt on Libel, B'k 1, ch. iv.

[1300] Hamilton arg. The People v. Croswell, 3 Johns. Cas. 360. And see The Federalist, No. 81; The Fourth Estate; Areopagitica, a speech for the liberty of unlicensed printing (Holt White's edition is the best); Story on the Constitution, §§ 1880 to 1889; 1 Tindal's Continuation of Rapin's History of England, 350; remarks on Pulteney's bill to prohibit the circulation of unlicensed newspapers.

sense of unlicensed, the press has been free since A. D. 1694.[1301]
And except in respect to newspapers, no greater degree of liberty for the press has ever been claimed. But as respects newspapers, it is argued that the exigencies of the business of a
newspaper editor demand a larger amount of freedom. That
circumstances do not permit editors the opportunity to verify the
truth, prior to publication, of all they feel called upon to publish, and that they should not be responsible for the truth of
what they publish. Some concessions have already been made
to these arguments. At present the law takes no judicial cognizance of newspapers, and independently of certain statutory
provisions the law recognizes no distinction in principle between a publication by the proprietor of a newspaper,.and a
publication by any other individual.[1302] A newspaper proprietor is not privileged as such in the dissemination of news, but is
liable for what he publishes in the same manner as any other individual.[1303] This being the case, after referring to the statutory
provisions affecting publications in newspapers, it will be unnecessary separately to consider what a newspaper proprietor may or

---

[1301] On the introduction of the printing press into England, at the expense of
the Government, the press was regarded as a State right, and subject to the co-
ercion of the crown. (See *Hills* v. *University of Oxford*, 1 Vernon, 275; *Basket*
v. *University of Cambridge*, 2 Burr. 661.) It was regulated, therefore, by the
King's proclamations, prohibitions, charters of privileges and licenses, and then
by the decrees of the Court of Star Chamber until the abolition of that court in
1641. The Long Parliament in 1643 assumed the power of licensing, and this was
continued by various statutes till 1694. The printing press was regarded as too
dangerous a contrivance to be suffered to be free. Governor Dongan was instructed
(A. D. 1688) not to allow any printing press in New York, although Massachusetts
had at that time enjoyed a printing press for nearly thirty years. The Constitution
of the United States provides: Congress shall make no law abridging the freedom of speech or of the press. (Am'd'mt of 1789, art. i.) The Constitution of
New York provides: Every citizen may freely speak, write, and publish his sentiments on all subjects, being responsible for the abuse of that right, and no law
shall be passed to restrain or abridge the liberty of speech or of the press.
(Constitution of 1846, art. 7, § 8.) This is repeated in the bill of rights of that
State, and similar provisions are, we believe, to be found in the Constitution of
every State of the Union.

[1302] *Davison* v. *Duncan*, 36 Eng. Law & Eq. R. 218; *Campbell* v. *Spottiswoode*,
8 Law Times Rep. N. S. 201; 3 Fost. & Fin. 421.

[1303] *Scheckell* v. *Jackson*, 10 Cush. 25.

may not publish with impunity; we can review his rights and
duties under the general head of criticism.[1304]

§ 253. To criticise, in its widest signification, means passing an opinion, commenting. In this sense every one is continually criticising, and every one is as continually furnishing an
occasion for criticism. Criticism may mean praise or censure.
The latter is the sense in which it is most frequently employed,
and is the only sense in which it enters into our present inquiry.
We use criticism as a synonym for " fault-finding." Sometimes
the term criticism is limited so as to indicate only " fault-finding" in matters of literature and art, or in respect to persons
engaged in offices of public trust. We do not attempt to define, with any degree of precision, what is the ordinary sense of
the term criticism, because we believe it has no definite conno-
tation, and because we do not recognize any distinct or inde-

---

[1304] Among the statutory provisions relating to libels in newspapers are: 38
Geo. III. ch. 78, entitled, An act to prevent the publication of newspapers by persons not known, &c., among other provisions requires that before any newspaper
is started the proprietor must file an affidavit, by the printer, publisher, and proprietor, stating the place where the paper is to be printed, and its title. This
act was amended 5 Wm. IV. ch. 2. 32 Geo. III. ch. 60, entitled, An act to remove
doubts respecting functions of juries in cases of libel. This is the statute enabling juries to give a general verdict in actions for libel. The 18th section
provides for a discovery in actions of libel. 60 Geo. III. ch. 8, amended 1 Geo.
IV. ch. 73; to prevent and punish blasphemous libels. 60 Geo. III. ch. 9; to
restrain abuses arising from the publication of blasphemous libels. This act requires newspaper proprietors to give security to pay the damages and costs in
actions for libels published in the papers owned by them. 6 & 7 Vict. ch. 96;
an act to amend the law respecting defamatory words and libel. (Amended 8 &
9 Vict.) It provides, among other things, that in actions for libels in newspapers
or periodicals, the defendant may plead that the libel was inserted without actual
malice and without gross negligence, and *before* the action, or at the earliest opportunity afterwards, he published an apology, and gives liberty with the plea of
apology to pay money into court. This act it has been held does not apply to
criminal prosecutions. *Reg.* v. *Duffy*, 2 Cox. Cr. Cas. 45; as to this statute, see
Chadwick v. *Herepath*, 3 C. B. 885; *O'Brien* v. *Clements*, 3 Dowl. & L. 676;
Smith v. *Harrison*, 1 Fost. & Fin. 365; *Jones* v. *Mackie*, 8 Law Rep. 1, Ex. As
to the statutes of Geo. III. see *Re* Chaplin, 2 Hurl. & Colt. 270; *Re* Clements, 12
Law Times, 380; 18 Law Jour. 304. Ex.; *Re* Gregory, 13 Law Times, 142; 8 Eng.
Law and Eq. Rep. 579. See in notes 1122, 1287, *ante ;* and Laws of N. Y. 1852,
ch. 165; *Id.* 1868, ch. 430; *Sanford* v. *Bennett*, 24 N. Y. 20.

pendent right, such as seems generally supposed to be implied
in or to exist under the designation of *criticism*. In our opinion, one cannot, by styling defamatory matter criticism, and
the defamer a critic, escape from those rules which apply to
defamatory matter generally.

§ 254. Criticism admits only of the division into criticism
of persons and criticism of things. What one does, one's actions, are things, and as such have a separate existence, distinct
from the person. *Every action, every thing* one does, is naturally and necessarily the subject of comment. *Every action,
every thing* one does, confers a privilege upon every person to
speak or write *concerning such action or thing.* As to such action or thing every one may, in good faith, speak or write whatever seems to him fit to be spoken or written [§ 204]. Save
good faith, there is no limit to criticism concerning a man's actions, or his creations. "God forbid (exclaimed Baron Alderson)[1305] that you should not be allowed to comment on the
conduct of all mankind, provided you do it justly and honorably."
" No one can doubt the importance in a free government of the
right to canvass the *acts* of public men, and the tendency of
public measures ; to censure boldly the conduct of rulers and
to scrutinize the policy and plans of government. This is the
great security of a free government." [1306] " An editor may comment freely on the *acts* of government, officers or individuals,
and indulge in occasional mirth and wit, and it is only when
the character of the publication is malicious, and its tendency
to degrade and excite to revenge, that it is condemned by the
law and subjects the publisher to prosecution." [1307] " Liberty
of criticism must be allowed, or we should have neither purity
of taste or of morals. Fair discussion is essentially necessary
to the truth of history and the advancement of science. That
publication, therefore, I shall never consider as a libel, which
has for its object, not to injure the reputation of any individ-

---

[1305] *Gathercole* v. *Miall,* 15 M. & W. 319.

[1306] Story on the Constitution, § 1888.

[1307] *Tappan* v. *Wilson,* 7 Ohio, 193.

ual, but to correct misrepresentations of fact, to refute sophistical reasoning, to expose a vicious taste in literature, or to censure what is hostile to morality." [1308]

§ 255. But, *as respects the person*, except in the instances and to the extent heretofore pointed out, *there is no privilege of criticism.* Defamatory language concerning a person, can never be justified on the ground that it was published as a criticism. Whenever defamatory matter concerning a person is justifiable, it is on some other ground than criticism. "No man has a right to render the person or abilities [inseparable incidents to the person] of another ridiculous." [1309] "I think no *personal* ridicule of the author is justifiable." [1310] If an author "has made himself ridiculous by his writings, he may be ridiculed; if his works show him to be vicious, his reviewer may say so. *But the latter has no right to violate the truth in* either respect." [1311] "If the jury can discover anything *personally* slanderous against the plaintiff (an author) unconnected with the works he has given to the public, in that case the plaintiff has a good cause of action." [1312] Without pretending to elicit the

---

[1308] L'd Ellenborough, *Tabart* v. *Tipper*, 1 Camp. 350; and s :e *Cooper* v. *Stone*, 24 Wend. 442. An application for an information was refused against 'one for publishing that Ward's pill and drop had done great mischief in twelve different cases, and that they were a compound of poison and antimony, &c. (*Rex* v. *Roberts*, 3 Bac. Abr. *tit.* Libel, 492.)

[1309] Holt, Ch. J., *Rex* v. *Tutchin*, 2 L'd Raym. 1061.

[1310] Best, Ch. J., *Thompson* v. *Shackell*, 1 Mo. & Malk. 187.

[1311] *Cooper* v. *Stone*, 24 Wend. 442. Does not this mean the reviewer can only justify ridiculing *an author*, or accusing *him* of being vicious, by a defence of truth.

[1312] L'd Ellenborough, *Carr* v. *Hood*, 1 Camp. 358. But in the same case his Lordship is reported to have said: " If the defendant only ridiculed the plaintiff *as an author*, the action could not be maintained."

In the case of *Stuart* v. *Lovell*, 2 Stark. Cas. 73, the plaintiff being one of the proprietors of the Courier newspaper, brought his action for libel against the defendant, the editor of the Statesman newspaper. Lord Ellenborough, in charging the jury, observed: " In the first place, the plaintiff was described as the prostituted Courier, and his full-blown baseness and infamy were represented as holding him fast to his present connections, and preventing him from forming new ónes. It was certainly competent in *one public writer to criticise another*, ex-

true source of the confusion of thought so obvious in all the
dicta and decisions upon the subject of criticism, we venture to
assert that the difficulty is occasioned by, (1) overlooking the distinction between language concerning the person and language
concerning a thing; and (2) in treating certain persons—
authors, artists, &c.—as if a rule applied to them and to their
productions, different from the rules which apply to the manufacturer and the merchant. It seems not to have been kept in
view that an author is but a producer, and the maker of a
watch is *an author* equally with the maker of a book. There
is nothing at this day in the vocations of the author, the actor,
the painter, or the sculptor which makes the rights and duties
of those who follow them less or greater than the rights and
duties of those engaged in any other employment. We *should*
judge language concerning an author, or an artist, by the same
rules as we judge language concerning a lawyer, or a physician,
a merchant, or a mechanic. " There is no doubt that a man
who is an author has a right to have his character protected the
same as if he acted in any other capacity. However, notwithstanding that, whatever is fair and can be reasonably said of
the works of authors, *or of themselves as connected with their
works*, is not actionable, unless it appear that under the pre-
text of criticising *the works*, the defendant takes the opportunity of attacking the character of *the author*, and then it will
be a libel." [1318] " I will not stop to weigh the argument which
would disfranchise him (the plaintiff) because he is an

erting his talents in all the latitude of free communication belonging to a *public*
writer; and so it appeared to Lord Kenyon, in *Heriot* v. *Stuart*, 1 Esp. Cas. 337,
that the *opinions and principles* of a public writer were open to criticism and ridicule, in the same way as those of any other author, but that the privilege did
not extend to calumnious remarks on the *private character* of the individual. In
that respect, the editor of a newspaper enjoyed the rights of protection in common with every other subject. Since, then, the defendant in this case had stigmatized the defendant as the venerable apostle of tyranny and oppression, and as
a man whose full-blown baseness and infamy held him fast to his present connection, because they left him without the power of forming new ones; in all this
he had undoubtedly overstepped the limits which had been drawn and by which
his conduct ought to have been regulated."

[1318] Tenterden, C. J., *Macleod* v. *Wakley*, 3 C. & P. 311.

author." [1314]   The essential questions in every case of criticism
are, (1) Does the matter upon its face concern a thing; (2) and
if it does, was it composed and published in good faith.   Whatever other questions may arise, they are but secondary, and
are, as already noticed [§ 204], material only so far as they
serve to furnish answers to the two essential questions above
mentioned.

§ 256. It was held to be within the limits of criticism to
publish of a newspaper: " It is the most vulgar, ignorant, and
scurrilous journal ever published in Great Britain." [1315]   This
affected only the character of the newspaper, and not (except
remotely) the reputation of any person.   So it is within the
limits of criticism to publish of a painting, that it was a mere
daub, with other strong terms of censure; [1316] or of an architect,
that he acts on absurd principles of art. [1317]   In both of the two
last preceding cases, it was left to the jury as a question of fact,
whether the censure was unfair and intemperate, and intended
to injure the persons of the plaintiffs.   It was held not to be
within the limits of criticism to publish of the plaintiff, a flor-
ticultural exhibitor, " the name of G. is to be rendered famous
in all sorts of dirty work; the tricks by which he, and a few
like him, used to secure prizes, seem to have been broken in
upon by some judges, more honest than usual.   If G. be the
same man who wrote an impudent letter to the Metropolitan
Society, he is too worthless to notice; if he be not the same
man, it is a pity that two such beggarly souls could not be
crammed into the same carcass." [1318]   Nor is it within the lim-

---

[1314] *Cooper* v. *Stone*, 24 Wend. 442. In all cases of criticism, "The question is
one of good faith." (*Id.*) " The only question is, whether there was any excess
in the comments, that was matter entirely for the jury." (Cockburn, C. J., *Kelly*
v. *Tinling*, 1 Law Rep. 701, Q. B.) If it be shown that the comment is unjust,
is malevolent and exceeding the bounds of fair opinion, it is actionable. (*Dibdin* v. *Swan*, 1 Esp. 28.)

[1315] *Heriot* v. *Stuart*, 1 Esp. Cas. 437; but it was in that case held *actionable*
to publish of a newspaper, that it was low in circulation.

[1316] *Thompson* v. *Shackell*, 1 Mo. & Malk. 187.

[1317] *Soane* v. *Knight*, 1 Mo. & Malk. 74.

[1318] *Green* v. *Chapman*, 4 Bing. N. C. 92; 5 Sc. 340.

its of criticism to write of the publisher of a magazine, that he had inserted in his magazine a series of articles, the greater part of which were false and of a gross character;[1319] nor to write of a book publisher, that he had published books of an immoral character, and ascribing to him the authorship of some silly rhymes.[1320] Where the plaintiff, a surgeon, had presented a petition to Parliament against empirics and irregular practitioners, and defendant, in a medical journal, had commented on the petition, reflecting on the plaintiff for ignorance, and particularly in chemical knowledge; and the judge had directed the jury, that if they considered the libel a fair comment on the petition, and not a malicious effusion against the plaintiff, and also if they considered that it imputed to him ignorance in chemistry only, and not in his profession as a surgeon, to find for the defendant, which they did; the Court granted a new trial.[1321] Where the plaintiff, a " marine store dealer," had exhibited a placard in front of his store, offering certain prices for kitchen stuff, candle ends, pewter, plated goods, &c., and proposing to fetch them from private houses. Some observations upon this placard had been made by a magistrate officially, upon which the defendant published in a newspaper an article headed, " Encouraging servants to rob their masters," and imputing that the placard was calculated or intended to encourage servants to rob their masters. The placard was held to be a proper subject of criticism, and as the article did not go be-

---

[1319] *Colburn* v. *Whiting*, cited Cooke on Defam. 58, and see *Cooper* v. *Stone*, 24 Wend. 432. Where it is said not to be within the limits of criticism to impute to an author, falsehood and unworthy motives in the production of a book.

[1320] *Tabart* v. *Tipper*, 1 Camp. 350, the rhymes were:

> There was a little maid,
> And she was afraid
> Her sweetheart would come to her,
> She bound up her head,
> When she went to bed,
> And she fastened her door with a skewer.

and were followed by this line:

> Dixin ego vobis Aulicam quandam inessee elegantiam.

[1321] *Dunne* v. *Anderson*, 3 Bing. 88. The reporter, erroneously as we think, puts this decision on the ground that presenting a petition to Parliament is an act not obnoxious to criticism. The error for which the new trial was granted was the direction to find for the defendant if the imputation was of ignorance in chemistry only.

yond the placard, or attack the plaintiff in any thing not fairly
arising out of that document, it was held privileged.[1322]

[1772] *Paris* v. *Levy*, 9 C. B. N. S. 342; 2 Fos. & Fin. 71 (99 Eng. C. L. & Eq.
Rep.) It was held not to be a libel upon a dealer in coal in L., who had advertised genuine Franklin coal for sale, to publish the following advertisement:
"Caution.—The subscribers, the only shippers of the true and original Franklin
coal, notice that other coal dealers in L. than our agent, J. S., advertise Franklin
coal. We take this method of cautioning the public against buying of other
parties than J. S., if they hope to get the genuine article, as we have neither
sold nor shipped any Franklin coal to any party in L., except our agent, J. S."
(*Boynton* v. *Remington*, 3 Allen, 397.)
    In a previous note (No. 1087) we directed attention to the views of Lord Chief
Justice Cockburn on criticism; we recur to the subject to give some extracts from
his charge in the case of *Seymour* v. *Butterworth*, reported at length in the "Law
Magazine and Law Review" (London), February, 1863, and given in an abridged
form in The Monthly Law Reporter (Boston), May, 1863; also reported 3 Fost.
& Fin. 372. The plaintiff, a barrister, Recorder of Newcastle-upon-Tyne, and
member of Parliament, sued for an alleged libel upon him, published in the Law
Magazine. We find in the charge, (1.) A man's public political conduct is matter for the freest and fullest discussion on the part of a writer in a public journal.
(2.) To animadvert on those who lend themselves to a system of buying and selling votes in Parliament, "is within the legitimate province of a *public writer*,"
but if he goes beyond that, and asserts that one "has bargained to sell his vote,"
it is a charge which no man, whether writing in public or in private, ought to dare
to make. (3.) All men who occupy public positions must submit, now and then, to
be a little roughly handled, and to be uncourteously and even unjustly treated,
and people must not be too thin-skinned in reference to such matters. It has
happened to everybody who has had anything to do with public life, to have, at
one time or other, observations made upon his conduct and motives, which, in all
probability, at the bottom of his heart he has felt to be unfounded and unjust;
but we submit to it, and why? because we know that upon the whole, that bringing, by means of the public press, the conduct and motives of public men to the
bar of public opinion, is the best security for the discharge of public duty.
(4.) It is claimed that although the conduct of a public man is open to public
discussion, his *private conduct* is not, and that it does not lie in the mouth of a
man, who has attacked another with reference to his *private conduct*, to say, I did
it only in the fair discharge of a public duty. But there is this distinction in
this case, that, however true that proposition may be with reference to the *private
conduct* of a *private individual*, the plaintiff does not occupy the position of a
private individual.   *   *   *   It is impossible to say the plaintiff was
not a *public man*, and that his conduct, if it had reference to his fitness to be a
public man and to occupy a public position, was not a matter fit for discussion.
(5.) I must dissent from the proposition, that where a man holds a public position in which integrity, honesty, and honor are essential and indispensable qualifications, if in his private conduct he shows he is destitute and devoid of those

§ 257. As the right of criticism is confined to criticising actions or things, it necessarily follows that as a preliminary to all

essential elements, that it is not a fair subject for public animadversion and hostile criticism, *so long as the writer confines himself within the bounds of truth and within the limits of fair and just observation.* Elsewhere in the charge his Lordship speaks of the rights and duties of a public writer, and generally speaks as if a public writer was a person with peculiar rights and duties, whereas the law recognizes no such office as that of a public writer, and gives him no privileges except as mentioned *ante*, note 1122. We do not consider sound the distinction between public men and private men, and public acts and private acts. To say, as is said in the fifth of the foregoing extracts, that one may criticise "*so long as the writer confines himself within the bounds of truth and within the limits of fair and just observation,*" is merely saying one may publish the truth and criticise where it is fair and *just* to do so. To limit criticism to just criticism, is in effect to toll the right of criticism, as it substitutes the judgment of the jury for the judgment of the critic. In another case, *Strauss v. Francis*, also tried before Lord Cockburn (we quote from a newspaper report), the plaintiff was the author of a novel called "The Old Ledger," and the defendant, the editor of the Athenæum. The defendant published a criticism of this novel, for which the plaintiff brought an action for libel, and on the trial withdrew a juror. The defendant then published an article under the heading "The Rights of Criticism," in which he republished the original criticism, with comments on the trial at which the plaintiff withdrew a juror. The judge charged the jury, "that the action related to two separate matters of complaint, which should be kept distinct—first, the review of the work ; next, the comments on the trial. The republication of the criticism on the work brought it under the notice of the jury, and it would be for them to say whether the criticism was fair and reasonable, or whether the writer of it was actuated by malice. That it was severe there could be no doubt, but the question was, was the severity warranted by the nature of the book. It was conceded that it was of vast importance to literature, and through literature, to the morals, religion, good taste, and good feelings of the public, that works which were laid before them for their perusal should be of such a character that they would improve and not demoralize. It was, therefore, right and wholesome that criticism, so long as it was fair and just, should be allowed the largest latitude. Authors courted criticism, because, if it were favorable, it would secure popularity for, and extend the circulation of, their works; but, as they challenged criticism, they should submit to it when it was adverse, so long as it was not prompted by recklessness or malice. It had been contended on behalf of the plaintiff that it was unfair to select isolated passages from a work and fasten on them, disparaging the spirit and character and object of the entire book; but that observation was open to this remark, that it was not because a work might, as a whole, be good, that a critic, if he found many passages of an obnoxious character, must abstain from commenting on them. That some of the passages read warranted the charge of indelicacy, some the charge of profanity, and many of them the charge of gross vulgarity, was, he thought, a matter as to which

right of criticism, it must appear that the action or thing criti-
cised had an existence; therefore, a justification on the ground

---

they could not fail to give an answer in the affirmative. The fair critic was a prosecutor who brought to the bar of public opinion, offenders against good taste, against
delicacy and propriety. The work in question was denounced as being abomina-
ble. That was no doubt a strong expression. It was for the jury, having the
book before them, and having heard what had been said for and against it, to
say whether the criticism in question was a fair representation of the character
of the work. The jury found for the defendant. See 4 Fost. & Fin. 939, 1107.
In another case, *Campbell* v. *Spottiswoode*, we quote from the London Quarterly
Review of April, 1865, art. Libel. The plaintiff, the editor of the British Standard, had published in that newspaper a series of appeals on behalf of Missions
to China. The alleged libel was an article published in the Saturday Review,
commenting on those appeals, and in which the plaintiff was called an "impos-
tor," and charged "with scandalous and flagitious conduct." On a trial, before
Lord Cockburn, the plaintiff had a verdict, the judge charging the jury that the
defendant had exceeded the limits of criticism, and added, "It cannot be said
that because a man is a public man, a writer is entitled not only to pass judgment
upon his conduct, but to ascribe to him corrupt and dishonest motives." A motion for a new trial was denied; Lord Cockburn, in giving judgment (8 Law
Times Rep. N. S. 201; 3 Fost. & Fin. 421, note), said, "But it seems to me
that a line must be drawn between hostile criticism upon a man's public conduct
and the motives by which that conduct may be supposed to be influenced, and
that you have no right to impute to a man in his conduct as a citizen—even
though it be open to ridicule or disapprobation—base, sordid, dishonest or
wicked motives, unless *there is so much ground for the imputation that a jury shall be
of opinion, not only that you may have honestly maintained some mistaken belief
upon the subject, but that your belief is well founded and not without cause.*" We do
not understand the part in *italics.* In our opinion his Lordship should have said
that you must not impute dishonest or wicked motives, unless you can establish
the truth of the imputation. He came very near to our views in *Turnbull* v.
Bird (we still quote from the London Quarterly), in which he charged the jury,
"if you are of opinion that the defendant, in the comments that he made, was
guilty of any *wilful* mis-statement of fact, either by the exaggeration of what
actually existed, or by the partial suppression of what actually existed,
so as to give it another color, or if he makes his comments with any
mis-statement of fact, *which he must have known to be a mis-statement, by the
exercise of ordinary care,* then he loses his privileges, and the occasion does not
justify the publication." (See 2 Fost. & Fin. 508.) We should indorse this if
the words in *italic* were omitted. See, however, *Cooper* v. *Lawson*, 8 Adol. & El.
746.

Publication, by Reform Commissioners, of a report imputing bribery to
plaintiff, was held not privileged. (*Wilson* v. *Reed*, 2 Fost. & Fin. 149.) The
plaintiff was the publisher of Zadkiel's Almanac, an astrological publication; the
defendant charged that the plaintiff, being the publisher of that silly work, had

of criticism can never prevail, unless the existence of the action or thing, which the criticism is alleged to concern, is either admitted or proved. An alleged criticism consists in the statement or assumption of certain *facts*, and of comments thereon. Where these facts are not admitted, to constitute a justification their existence must be shown. Hence, to justify a criticism, it is sometimes necessary to allege, that the facts which warrant *a* criticism exist, and that the comment on those facts is fair. Where the defamatory matter was that plaintiff, a tradesman in London, became surety for the petitioners in the Berwick election petition, and falsely stated on oath a sufficient property qualification, when, in truth, he was not able to pay his debts. It then asked why the plaintiff, being unconnected with Berwick, should take so much trouble and incur such an exposure of embarrassments, and proceeded: "There can be but one answer to these queries—he is hired for the occasion." The defendant justified as true all the publication, except the charge of being hired, as to which no mention was made, and, as a further defence, that the publication was a correct report of judicial proceedings, with a fair and *bond fide* commentary thereon. Held, it was properly left to the jury to say whether the imputation that the plaintiff was hired was a fair comment.[1338]

§ 258. As criticism is *opinion*, it can never be *primarily* material to inquire into its justness. The right to criticise implies the right to judge for oneself of the *justness of the criticism*. It would be but a delusion to say one has the right to criticise *provided* the criticism be just. The justness or unjustness can never be more than matter of opinion. The test

_____

gulled by means of a magic bull of crystal in which future events could be seen; held that this could be justified by proving that plaintiff, knowing it to be an imposture, took money from the public for the use of said bull. (*Morris* v. *Belcher*, 8 Fost. & Fin. 614.) See *Eastwood* v. *Holmes*, 1 Fost. & Fin. 347. A publication of a report of an inspector of charities under the charitable trust act, containing a letter written several years previously, reflecting on plaintiff, held conditionally privileged. (*Cox* v. *Feeney*, 4 Fost. & Fin. 13.)

[1338] *Cooper* v. *Lawson*, 8 Adol. & El. 746.

always is, was the criticism *bonâ fide*. It is like the case of one writing concerning the sanity of another; the test of the justification is not, was the statement such as a man of sound sense would have made, but was it the honest conviction of the publisher [§ 206]. Although that was a case of comment or giving an opinion, or criticism, was a criticism *concerning the person*, and found its justification, not in its being a criticism, but because the publication was made to protect the interest of another. In like manner, when it is argued that the right to criticise rests upon the interest which the community generally may have in the subject of the criticism, it is a confusion of two different and distinct rights. The community are no more interested in the person or reputation of any one, than in the person or reputation of any other member of society. Nor is there any foundation for the distinction sometimes attempted to be drawn between the *public* and the *private* character or standing of an individual; and although there are isolated *dicta* that appear to favor the idea that a person occupying a public situation is thereby rendered, personally, a subject of criticism, yet, as we conceive, the context of these *dicta* so far explains them as to limit the right of criticism to the *actions*. Thus it has been said: "Every man has a right to discuss matters of public interest. A clergyman with his flock, an admiral with his fleet, a general with his army, and a judge with his jury—we are all of us the subjects for public discussion; and provided a man, whether in a newspaper or not, publishes a comment on a matter of public interest, fair in tone and temperate, although he may express opinions that you may not agree with, that is not a subject for an action for libel; because whoever fills a public position, renders himself open to public discussion; and if any part of his public acts is wrong, he must accept the attack as a necessary though unpleasant circumstance attaching to his position. In this country everything, either by speech or writing, may be discussed for the benefit of the public. No doubt, therefore, the defendant was at liberty to discuss the opinions or proceedings of the plaintiff. If he has done it fairly, temperately and calmly, then he is not a fit subject for an action for libel."[1294] "Every individual has a right to comment on *those acts* of public men which concern him as a subject of the realm, if he do not make his commentary a cloak for malice and slander. There is, indeed, a material distinction between publications relating to public and to private *persons*, as regards the question whether they be libellous. That criticism may reasonably be applied to a public man in a public capacity, which might not be applied to a private individual."[1295] The first sentence in this last quotation refers to acts, and is correct; and although the remarks in the subsequent sentences profess to apply to *persons*, yet they can be regarded as stating the law correctly only by limiting them to the *acts* of public men. Apart from the obsolete statutes of *scandalum magnatum* there is no distinction of persons, nor any division of persons into public and private [§ 181].

§ 259. The *supposed* distinction between matters of fact and matters of opinion, is sometimes referred to as marking the difference between justifiable or unjustifiable comment or criticism. Criticism, it is said, is matter of opinion ; and that while all expression of opinion is justifiable, a statement of fact is not justifiable, unless on the ground of truth.[1296] This view is unsound. In one sense it is merely the expression of an opinion to say of a minister he entered the pulpit in a towering passion ; but such an assertion cannot be justified as criticism.[1297]

§ 260. Stress is sometimes laid upon the fact that the criticism is upon a *public* act, implying that it is the publicity of the act upon which the right of comment depends. We shall not attempt to distinguish between public and private acts, because we are of the opinion that it cannot directly make any difference in the right to criticise, whether the act be done privately or publicly. It was this supposed distinction between

[1294] Bramwell, B., *Kelly* v. *Sherlock*, 1 Law Rep. 689, Q. B.

[1295] *Parmiter* v. *Coupland*, 6 M. & W. 108.

[1296] See *Popham* v. *Pickburn*, 7 Hurl. & Nor. 891 ; *ante*, § 163, and note 398.

[1297] *Walker* v. *Brogden*, 19 J. Scott, N. S. 64.

public and private acts, which occasioned the dubiety on the
question whether a sermon, not otherwise published than by its
delivery from the pulpit, by a minister to his congregation, was
the subject of criticism.[1328]   A churchwarden having written to
the plaintiff, the incumbent, accusing him of having desecrated
the church, by allowing books to be sold in it during the service,
and by turning the vestry-room into a cooking apartment,
the correspondence was published without the permission of
the plaintiff, in the defendant's newspaper, with comments on
the plaintiff's conduct.   Held, that the correspondence involved
a subject of *public* interest, which might be made the subject of
public discussion, and the publication of the correspondence was
not actionable, unless the language used was stronger than the
limits of fair criticism allow.[1329]   Upon principle, private acts
are, equally with public acts, the subjects of criticism.   But
whether the act be a public or a private act, may make a difference in determining whether the criticism was in good faith.

[1328] *Gathercole* v. *Miall*, 15 M. & W. 319 ; 10 Jurist, 337 ; 7 Law Times, 89 ; 15
Law Jour. Rep. 179, Ex.   In the same case it was held that the conduct of the
vicar of a parish, in establishing a parochial institution for charitable purposes, by
the rules of which all persons not members of the Church of England are excluded
from the benefit of the charity, is not a public act or the act of a public func-
tionary, so as to entitle the public press or others to comment on it as such.

[1329] *Kelly* v. *Tinling*, 1 Law Rep. 699, Q. B.

CHAPTER X.

Corporations are legal persons. Their rights and duties assimilated to those of natural persons. Can act only through agents. May carry on business, sue and be sued, and are liable for injuries committed by agents. Corporations may have a reputation. Language concerning corporations. Actions by corporations for libel. Corporations cannot be guilty of slander. May be guilty of libel.

§ 261. Corporations, whether aggregate or sole, are *legal persons.* Hitherto, attention has been directed *exclusively* to language published by or which concerned *natural* persons or their affairs; it will now be in order to consider the rights and duties of *legal* persons or corporations in respect to the publication of language. The topic has been comparatively but little adjudicated, and to the decisions upon it the remarks contained in a former section [§ 15] appear peculiarly applicable. The great and ever increasing number of corporations, assuming all the functions of individuals, has created a tendency in the modern decisions to assimilate, so far as possible, the rights and duties of corporations to the rights and duties of natural persons.[1330] It is the distinctive feature of a corporation that it can *only* act by or through its officers or agents;[1331] for even in the case of a corporation sole, the individual who represents that corporation, and the corporation, are distinct entities. Ordinarily, a corporation may acquire and possess property, and carry on business, and it may sue and be sued in like manner as

---

[1330] *Conro v. Port Henry Iron Co.,* 12 Barb. 28.

[1331] *First Baptist Church v. Brooklyn Fire Ins. Co.,* 18 Barb. 69; Story on Agency, § 16.

an individual, and is liable for an injury committed by its servants or agents, in all cases where, under like circumstances, an individual would be liable.[1882] Accordingly, it has been held that an action lies against a corporation for malicious prosecution or for a trespass.[1883]

§ 262. A corporation, like an individual, may have a reputation, and a good reputation is equally as valuable to a corporation as to a natural person;[1884] and as an individual may sustain injury by language affecting his reputation, so in like manner may a corporation. As in regard to language affecting individuals, we distinguish between language concerning the person as such, and language concerning the person in a trade, and language concerning a thing or the affairs of a person ; so in regard to language affecting corporations, we must distinguish between language concerning a corporation for different objects, as those engaged in manufacturing, trading or banking, and those not so engaged, and language concerning the things of a corporation. Of course language concerning the corporators is not within the limits of our present inquiry. Where the defendant published, with other defamatory matter, that his hat had been stolen by *some* of the members of No. 12 Hose Company. The Hose Company was a volunteer association, and the members of the Association brought a joint action for this publication. Held, that the action could not be maintained.[1885]

[1882] *First Baptist Church in Schen.* v. *Schen. & Troy R. R. Co.*, 5 Barb. 80, and see *Pritchard* v. *Corporation of Georgetown*, 2 Cranch Cir. Ct. 191 ; *Watson* v. *Bennett*, 12 Barb. 196 ; *New Haven R. R. Co.* v. *Schuyler*, 34 N. Y. 30, 208 ; *Hunter* v. *Hudson River R. R. Co.*, 20 Barb. 507 ; *Sharp* v. *Mayor of New York*, 40 Barb. 273 ; *Rochester White Lead Co.* v. *City of Rochester*, 3 Coms. 468 ; *Green* v. *London Omnibus Co.*, 6 Jurist, N. S. 228.

[1883] *Eastern Counties Railway* v. *Brown*, 6 Ex. 314 ; *Roe* v. *Birkenhead Railway Co.*, 7 Ex. 36 ; *Goodspeed* v. *East Haddam Bank*, 22 Conn. 530. In *Owsley* v. *Montgomery &c. R. R. Co.*, 1 Ala. (S. C.) 485, it was held, but as we conceive erroneously, that a corporation, although liable for false imprisonment, was not liable for malicious prosecution ; and in *Childs* v. *State B'k of Mo.*, 2 Ben. 213, it was held that neither an action for malicious prosecution, for slander, nor for false imprisonment, could be maintained against a corporation ; and see *Stevens* v. *Midland Counties R'way*, 10 Ex. 855 ; 26 Eng. Law & Eq. R. 410. .

[1884] *Trenton Ins. Co.* v. *Perrine*, 3 Zab. 402.

[1885] *Giraud* v. *Beach*, 3 E. D. Smith, 337.

§ 263. Language concerning a corporation not engaged in any business, can hardly occasion, and certainly does *not necessarily* occasion it any pecuniary injury; therefore, in regard to language concerning such a corporation, no action can be maintained except upon proof of special damage; but as regards a corporation engaged in manufacturing, trading or banking, or other occupation in which credit may be material to its success, there language concerning such a corporation calculated to injuriously affect its credit, must *necessarily* occasion it pecuniary injury, and in such a case an action may be maintained by the corporation without proof of any special damage. Thus as regards language concerning corporations, some is actionable *per se*, and some is actionable only by reason of special damage.

§ 264. In the case of an action by a corporation, a mutual life insurance company, against the editor of a newspaper, for libel in charging that the affairs of the company were mismanaged, it was alleged that the words were published of and concerning the company in their business, and of and concerning the directors of the company, and of and concerning the president, vice-president and secretary of the company, and of and concerning the property and concerns of the company, and of and concerning the conduct and management of the property and concerns of the company by the aforesaid directors and officers of the company; and special damage was charged to have resulted to the company in a loss of its business, and a diminution of its profits. On demurrer to the complaint, it was held that "a corporation aggregate may maintain an action for a *libel* for words published of them concerning their trade or business, by which they have suffered special damage." And that, "in alleging special damage, it is not always necessary to name the customers whose business has been lost by the defamation; but if the nature of the business is such as to render that impracticable, the loss of the business may be alleged generally."[1836] In another case it was held that a joint stock company, incorpo-

---

[1836] *Trenton Ins. Co. v. Perrine,* 3 Zab. 402.

rated under the statute 19 and 20 Vict., ch. 47, might maintain an action for libel, and that, too, against a shareholder in the company.[1337] And in that case it was said there may be particular kinds of libel which do not affect a corporation, but if injury ensues an action may be maintained. Where the defendant published in a periodical, that the plaintiff, an incorporated bank, " was liable at any time to be closed up by an injunction," the plaintiff brought an action for libel, alleging that since the publication divers persons had refused to receive the notes of the plaintiff, and had refused to deal with it. To this complaint there was a demurrer; the demurrer was overruled, and it was held that a good cause of action was alleged without any allegation of special damages that the law recognized the rights of a corporation to its property as effectually as in the case of an individual. An appeal was taken to the general term, where the decision was affirmed.[1338] Where an act of Parliament, after reciting the difficulties experienced by joint-stock companies in suits for recovering debts and enforcing obligations, and in the prosecution of offenders, enacted that actions commenced by the Hope Company for recovering debts, enforcing claims or demands then due, or which thereafter might become due or arise to the company, might be commenced, and indictments for offences be preferred, in the name of the chairman. Held, that the chairman might sue for a libel on the company, although it was not a corporate body.[1339]

§ 265. As a corporation can act only by or through its officers or agents [§ 261], and as there can be no agency to slander [§ 67],[1340] it follows that a corporation cannot be guilty of slander; it has not the capacity for committing that wrong. If an officer or an agent of a corporation is guilty of slander, he is

---

[1337] *Metropolitan Saloon Omnibus Co.* v. *Hawkins*, 4 Hurl. & Nor. 87.

[1338] *Shoe and Leather B'k* v. *Thompson*, 18 Abb. Pra. R. 413.

[1339] *Williams* v. *Beaumont*, 10 Bing. 260; 3 M. & Sc. 705; and see *Woodward* v. *Cotton*, 1 Cr. M. & R. 44.

[1340] *Moloney* v. *Bartley*, 3 Camp. 210; *Hecker* v. *DeGroot*, 15 How. Pra. R. 314; and note 50, *ante*.

personally liable, and no liability results to the corporation.
But as all concurring in the authorship or publication of a libel
are alike responsible as publishers [§§ 115, 117, and note 113],
there is nothing to prevent a corporation from being, *in law*,
the publisher of a libel, and from being held liable as such publisher. A corporation may sanction the publication of a libel,
and, in such a case, the corporation is the publisher of the libel,
and liable in like manner as an individual ; not because, as is
sometimes said, a corporation may act with malice, but because
it has a capacity for voluntary action, and is responsible for
such action. It is as possible for a corporation as for an individual to act maliciously, *i. e.* with a bad intent. Accordingly it
has been held, that a corporation aggregate may well, in its corporate capacity, cause the publication of a defamatory statement
under such circumstances as would imply malice, in law, sufficient to support the action ; and there may be circumstances by
which express malice in fact might be proved, such as to make
a corporation aggregate liable therefor in its corporate capacity.[1841]

[1841] *Whitfield* v. *South-East R. R. Co.* 1 Ell. B. & E. 115; *Phil. R. R. Co.* v.
Quigley, 21 How. U. S. Rep. 202; *Aldrich* v. *Press Printing Co.,* 9 Min. 183;
Alexander v. *N. East. R. R. Co.,* 34 Law Jour. Rep. N. S. 152; Q. B. 11 Jurist,
N. S. 619.

CHAPTER XI.

§ 266. The preceding chapters of this essay have been devoted to a consideration of *the law* relating to the wrongs called slander and libel. We have now to treat of *the remedy by action* for these wrongs. The diversity of the procedure in the courts of the several States, renders it impossible to compress within any convenient space, or into any convenient form, the practice, pleadings, and proceedings in actions in all the States. To trace in detail the whole proceedings in an action in any one State, would be to exceed the limits of our subject. We purpose, therefore, to exhibit so much of the course of procedure in an action in the courts of the State of New York, as applies either exclusively to the action of slander or libel, or as may have been adjudicated upon. Our remarks, therefore, while they will more particularly refer to the State of New York, will occasionally extend to other States and to the practice in the courts of England. As the Code of Procedure of the State of New York has been the model for the codes of procedure of other States, references to the Code of New York will have a wide field of practical utility.

§ 267. The action for slander or libel is commenced by summons, in the form known as a summons for relief. It must, with certain exceptions, be commenced within two years of the time of the publication, and within the lifetime of the person affected by the defamatory matter ;[1342] it cannot be brought in a court of a justice of the peace.[1343] It may be brought in the Marine Court of the City of New York, if the damages *claimed* do not exceed $500. And in cases which might be brought in the Marine Court, if the action is brought in any other court the plaintiff can recover only Marine Court costs.[1344] The plaintiff in an action for slander or libel cannot issue an attachment against the property of the defendant,[1345] but the defendant, whether male or female, may be arrested and held to bail at the commencement of the action, or at any time before judgment therein ; and after the return unsatisfied of an execution against the property of the defendant, an execution may issue against his person.[1346] A married woman sued with her, husband may be held to bail.[1347] If the plaintiff fails in the action, a judgment against him for the costs may, after an execution against his property has been returned unsatisfied, be enforced by an execution against his person.[1348] The plaintiff may be

[1342] Code of Pro., § 93; see *post*, *Parties*. In some cases in England, the plaintiff must give notice of action. See *Norris* v. *Smith*, 10 A. & E. 190; *Beechey* v. *Sides*, 9 B. & C. 806; *Lidster* v. *Borrow*, 9 A. & E. 654.

[1343] Code of Pro., § 54. Actions for libel and slander are excepted from the jurisdiction of the County Courts in England, 9 and 19 Vict., ch. 95; 12 and 13 Vict., ch. 101; 13 and 14 Vict., ch. 61; 15 and 16 Vict., ch. 54.

[1344] Laws of N. Y. 1853, p. 1165; *Murray* v. *De Gross*, 3 Duer, 668.

[1345] And so in So. Carolina, *Sargent* v. *Helmbold*, Harper, 219.

[1346] Code of Pro., §§ 179, 288; see *Baker* v. *Swackhamer*, 5 How. Pra. Rep. 251; *Straus* v. *Schwarzwaelden*,, 4 Bosw. 627; *Brooks* v. *McLellan*, 1 Barb. 627; *Davis* v. *Scott*, 15 Abb. Pra. Rep. 127; *Pearson* v. *Picket*, 1 McCord, 472; *Newton* v. *Rowe*, 8 Sc N. R. 26; *Defries* v. *Davies*, 3 Dowl. Pra. Cas. 629. A defendant in custody on an execution for damages in slander or libel, is not discharged therefrom by the English Bankrupt law; see 1 Doria & McCreas' Law of Bankruptcy, 349. Query as to the United States Bankrupt Law.

[1347] *Schaus* v. *Putscher*, 25 How. Pra. Rep. 436.

[1348] *Kloppenburg* v. *Neefus*, 4 Sandf. 655.

required to give security for costs, as in other actions.[1349]   The summons may be served by publication.[1350]

§ 268. The actions of slander and libel are of the kind known as *transitory*.[1351]   The place of trial (the venue) should be the county in which the parties, or some of them, reside ; or if none of the parties reside in the State, then in any county the plaintiff may designate,[1352] subject in every case to the power of the court to change the place of trial.[1353]   The parties to the action, the pleadings, and the evidence, will be considered hereafter.

§ 269. In certain cases either party is entitled to the production and inspection of documents in the possession or con-

---

[1349] Court refused to increase amount of security to cover expenses of foreign witnesses. (*Pizani v. Lawson*, 5 Sc. 418.)   Actions for slander or libel may be consolidated; see an instance, *Whiteley v. Adams*, 15 C. B. N. S. 392; 10 Jurist, N. S. 47.   The court refused to consolidate actions for the same libel, one against the publisher and the other against the editor of the newspaper in which the libel was published. (*Cooper v. Weed*, 2 How. Pra. Rep. 40.)   Where A and B having recovered in separate actions against different parties engaged in the publication of the newspaper in which the libel was published, commenced other actions against the same parties, each suing the party against whom the other had recovered, the court, on motion, refused to stay the proceedings in the second actions. (*Martin v. Kennedy ; Bunning v. Perry*, 2 Bos. & Pul. 69.)

[1350] Code of Pro., § 135; see *Waterhouse v. Hatfield*, 9 Irish Law Rep. 38.

[1351] *Hull v. Vreeland*, 42 Barb. 543; *Owen v. McKean*, 14 Ill. 459; *Teagle v. Deboy*, 8 Blackf. 134; and see *Wickham v. Baker*, 4 Blackf. 517.

[1352] Code of Pro., § 125.   Formerly it was a ground for arresting or setting aside the judgment if the *venue* was laid in the wrong county.   This was altered by the statutes 16 and 17 Car. 2, ch. 8; 4 Anne, ch. 16; *Clerk v. James*, Cro. Eliz. 870; *Craft v. Boite*, 1 Saund. 241.

[1353] Code of Pro., § 126.   As to changing *venue*, see *Phillips v. Chapman*, 5 Dowl. Pr. Cas. 250; *Ryder v. Burke*, 10 Ir. Law Rep. 476; *Robson v. Blackman*, 2 Dowl 645; *Clements v. Newcombe*, 1 Cr. M. & R. 776; 3 Dowl. Pr. Cas. 425; *Pybus v. Scudamore*, 7 Sc. 124; *Hobart v. Wilkins*, 1 Dowl. 460; *Wheatcroft v. Mouseley*, 11 C. B. 677; 20 Eng. Law and Eq. R. 296; *Pinckney v. Collins*, 1 T. R. 571; *Clissold v. Clissold*, 1 T. R. 647; *Metcalf v. Markham*, 3 T. R. 652; *Barnes v. Holloway*, 8 T. R. 150; *Hitchon v. Best*, 1 B. & P. 299; *Lucan v. Cavendish*, 10 Ir. Law Rep. 536; *Callagher v. Cavendish*, 3 Ir. Law Rep. 375; *Root v. King*, 4 Cow. 403; *Shaftsbury's case*, 1 Vent. 364; *Greenslade v. Ross*, 3 Dowl. Pra. Cas. 697; *Tallent v. Morton*, 1 M. & P. 188.

trol of his adversary.[1854] Where in an action for a libel the plaintiff moved for an order upon the defendant to deliver to him a copy of a printed book in his, defendant's, possession, in order to enable him, plaintiff, to prepare his complaint in the action, *per curiam:* Without expressing any opinion as to the propriety of compelling a defendant, in an action for a libel, to deliver to the plaintiff a copy of the libel, I am clearly of the opinion that this motion should not be granted, because: 1. The affidavits do not show what is stated in the book of which the plaintiff seeks a discovery, and therefore the court cannot decide whether it is material or not. 2. Because the affidavits do not specify any particular information desired, so that the court could order a sworn copy to be delivered. 3. Because the plaintiff is not entitled to the whole book, but only to the particular article on which his action is founded.[1855] Upon an application in an action for libel, for leave to examine a defendant before service of any complaint, the court much doubted the propriety of exercising the power of the court to enable the plaintiff to obtain facts upon which to frame his complaint.[1856] And in an action against certain individuals named, and certain others not named (except by fictitious names), for a libel in a newspaper of which the defendants named, with the others not named, were alleged to be the proprietors, the plaintiff, alleged that the names of the proprietors were unknown to him, and that it was pretended that the newspaper was the property of a corporation, and asked for an inspection of the books of such corporation to enable him to ascertain the true names of the proprietors of the newspaper. The application was denied.[1857]

§ 270. In England a bill of discovery is allowed in certain cases in an action for libel,[1858] and interrogatories may be exhib-

---

[1854] Code of Pro., § 388 ; 2 Rev. Stat. of N. Y. 199, Court Rule 14.

[1855] *Lynch* v. *Henderson*, 10 Abb. Pra. R. 345, *note.*

[1856] *Keeler* v. *Dusenbury*, 1 Duer, 661.

[1857] *Opdyke* v. *Marble*, 44 Barb. 64.

[1858] As to a bill of discovery in aid of an action for libel, see *Macauley* v. *Shackell*, 1 Bli. N. S. 96; 2 Sim. & St. 79; *Wilmot* v. *McCabe*, 4 Sim. 203; *March*

ited to ascertain the precise words used,[1389] but the court refused to permit a plaintiff to exhibit interrogatories to the defendant, the answers to which, if in the affirmative, would tend to show that he composed or published the libel, and would therefore criminate him.[1390] In an action for imputing to the plaintiff that he was the author of a scandalous letter, which the defendant in his plea justified as true, the court allowed the plaintiff an inspection of the letter by certain witnesses, in order that he might be prepared to negative its being his hand-writing.[1391]

§ 271. In one case,[1392] in an action for libel, the court ordered the defendant to produce certain documents in his possession for the inspection of the plaintiff. This was disapproved of in a subsequent case,[1393] where an application for an order to inspect the manuscript of articles that had been published in a newspaper was denied.

§ 272. On the principle that before a party utters a slander he should be prepared to justify, it has been said that the courts will not give the defendant an inspection of documents in the possession of the plaintiff to enable the defendant to prepare a plea of justification; thus where A charged B with forging an I O U, and B sued A in slander for uttering such charge, the court refused the application of the defendant for an inspection of the I O U, although he alleged that the I O U was in the possession of the plaintiff, that he (defendant) had reason to believe it was in reality a forgery, and that he could not safely

---

v. *Davison*, 9 Paige, 580; Stat. 32 George III, ch. 60; *Stewart* v. *Nugent*, 12 Legal Observer (London), 210.

[1390] *Atkinson* v. *Fosbrook*, 1 Law Rep. 628, Q. B.; 14 Law Times N. S. 553.

[1390] *Tapling* v. *Ward*, 6 Hurl. & Nor. 749; but see *Baker* v. *Lane*, 3 Hurl. & Colt. 544; 34 Law Jour. N. S. 57, Ex.; 10 Jurist, N. S. 117; 11 Law Times, N. S. 38, as explained in *Beckford* v. *D'Arcy*, 1 Law Rep. 354, Ex.; 14 Law Times, N. S. 629.

[1391] *Curtis* v. *Curtis*, 3 M. & Sc. 819.

[1392] *Perrott* v. *Morris*, 8 Irish Jurist, 384.

[1393] *Findlay* v. *Lindsay*, 7 Irish Com. Law Rep. 1.

plead without inspecting it.[1364] Where an order had been made in an action of libel giving the defendant leave, under 14 and 15 Vict. ch. 99, § 6, to inspect the books of the plaintiff, a motion by the defendant to extend the time to make the inspection, was denied on the ground that the order for inspection ought never to have been made, and *per curiam.* A man who publishes a libel should be in a position to prove it, and it would be a monstrous thing if a man could publish a libel, imputing insolvency to a mercantile house, and then to come to this court and ask for an order to inspect the plaintiff's books, in the hope of being able to get up a case. If the defendant is a shareholder, he has other means of obtaining an inspection, and we can only regard him as a defendant in an action for libel.[1365]

§ 273. In Massachusetts and in Maine, by statutes, a bill of particulars of the language which the plaintiff intends to prove may be ordered.[1366] These are cases where the precise words alleged to have been published were not set forth in the complaint. In England an order was made for a statement of the occasions upon which the words were published.[1367]

§ 274. If the defendant does not answer, he admits the allegations of the complaint and the truth of the innuendoes.[1368] The plaintiff must issue a writ of inquiry, and have his damages assessed by a sheriff's jury, not by a referee.[1369] The

---

[1364] *Day* v. *Tuckett,* 1 Ball Court Rep. 203; but see *Browning* v. *Aylwin,* 7 B. & C. 204, where an inspection was allowed.

[1365] *Metro. Saloon Co.* v. *Hawkins,* 4 Hurl. & Nor. 146; 1 F. & F. 413; see, however, *Steadman* v. *Arden,* 15 M. & W. 587.

[1366] *Clark* v. *Munsell,* 6 Metc. 373; *True* v. *Plumbey,* 36 Maine (1 Heath), 466.

[1367] *Slator* v. *Slator,* 8 Law Times, N. S. 856; and see *Wicks* v. *Macnamara,* 36 Law Jour. 419, Ex.; *Early* v. *Smith,* 12 Irish Com. Law Rep., p. xxxv of Appendix.

[1368] Code of Pro., §§ 168, 246; *Tillotson* v. *Cheetham,* 3 Johns. 56. After judgment by default it is too late to object to the *venue.* (*Wickham* v. *Baker,* 4 Blackf. 517.)

[1369] Voorhies' Code, 446 *i,* 9th ed.; and see *Schewer* v. *Klein,* 15 La. Ann. 303.

court may order the writ of inquiry to be executed before a
judge.[1870] On the execution of the writ the plaintiff is not
required to give any evidence of publication.[1871] The defendant,
on the execution of the writ, will not be allowed to read parts
of the publication not set forth in the complaint, in order to
give a meaning to the words set forth in the complaint different
from that alleged by the plaintiff;[1872] and semble, the defendant
will not be allowed to give evidence of the truth of the language complained of.[1873]

§ 275. The trial of the issues in an action for slander or libel
must be by jury, unless a jury trial is waived, or the parties, by
consent, try the issue before the court without a jury, or before
a referee, or submit them to arbitration.[1874] In case of a trial
by jury, the court may order a struck jury, but will not do so

<hr/>

[1870] *Casneau* v. *Bryant*, 6 Duer, 668; and see *Dillaye* v. *Hart*, 8 Abbott Pra.
Rep. 394; *Hays* v. *Berryman*, 6 Bosw. 679.

[1871] *Tripp* v. *Thomas*, 3 B. & Cr. 427; 5 D. & R. 276; 1 Carr. 477. In this
case it was also held, that although the plaintiff gives no evidence, the jury are
not limited to giving nominal damage. It has been held that after assessment of
damages on a writ of inquiry, the plaintiff cannot, without leave of the Court,
enter a *nolle prosequi* as to one count, and take judgment for the others. (*Backus*
v. *Richardson*, 5 Johns. 476.)

[1872] *Tillotson* v. *Cheetham*, 3 Johns. 56.

[1873] *Lewis* v. *Few*, Anthon, 75. Held not sufficient ground for staying a writ of
inquiry that the House of Commons had voted the publication privileged.
(*Stockdale* v. *Hansard*, 8 Dowl. 148.)

[1874] Code of Pro., § 253. Instances of actions for slander and libel being
referred. *Bonner* v. *McPhail*, 31 Barb. 106; *Rockweller* v. *Brown*, 86 N. Y. 207;
Sanford v. *Bennett*, 24 N. Y. 20; arbitration, see *Grosvenor* v. *Hunt*, 11 How.
Pra. Rep. 355; *Grayson* v. *Meredith*, 17 Ind. 357. An award about calling a
butcher a bankrupt was referred to a trial at law because of the excessiveness of
the damages given on the award. (*Cooper* v. *The Butcher of Croydon*, 3 Ch. R, 76.)
In 2 Vern. R. 251, it is said there was another reason besides the excessive
damages for setting aside the award. That reason was the relationship of the
arbitrator to one of the parties. See an award that defendant should make submission and acknowledge himself sorry for all trespasses and *words*. (*Cartwright*
v. *Gilbert*, 2 Browl. 48.) As to amount of costs, where an action of slander was
referred, and plaintiff recovered less than forty shillings damages. (*Fream* v.
Sergeant, 8 Law Times, N. S. 467.)

in trials to be had in the city of New York.[1375] The court may refuse to try the cause if the trial will involve an attack upon the chastity of a third person not a party to the action.[1376] In case of a new trial, the re-trial may be before the judge who presided on the first trial.[1377]

§ 276. It is supposed that in actions for slander or libel, the plaintiff has, in every case, the right to begin.[1378] The right to begin is so far within the discretion of the court, that an erroneous ruling in respect to it will neither entitle to a new trial nor render the judgment voidable by appeal.[1379] But in England it has been held that an erroneous ruling as to the right to begin, entitles the objecting party to a new trial.[1380] And so in Alabama.[1381]

§ 277. Counsel, in opening, should not state facts which they are not prepared to prove; but a disregard of this rule will not entitle the opposite party to disprove a statement of counsel.[1382] Nor is a party limited in his proof to the opening of his counsel.[1383] Counsel, in summing up, should confine

[1375] *Genet* v. *Mitchell*, 4 Johns 186; *Thomas* v. *Rumsey*, 4 Johns. 482; *Thomas* v. *Crosswell*, 4 Johns. 491; *Nesmith* v. *Atlantic Mut. Ins. Co.*, 8 Abb. Pra. Rep. 423.

[1376] *Loughead* v. *Bartholomew*, Wright, 90. As to right of judge to refuse to try a cause, see *De Costa* v. *Jones*, Cowp. 729; *Squires* v. *Whisken*, 3 Camp. 140; *Ditchen* v. *Goldsmith*, 4 Camp. 152; *Brown* v. *Leeson*, 2 H. Black. 43; *Egerton* v. *Furzman*, 1 C. & P. 613; *Henken* v. *Guers*, 2 Camp. 408.

[1377] *Fry* v. *Bennett*, 3 Bosw. 200; 28 N. Y. 329.

[1378] *Littlejohn* v. *Greeley*, 13 Abb. Pra. R. 41. See *Wood* v. *Pringle*, 1 Mo. & Rob. 277; *Sawyer* v. *Hopkins*, 9 Shep. 268; *Huntington* v. *Conkey*, 33 Barb. 218; *Ayrault* v. *Chamberlain*, 33 Barb. 233; *Carter* v. *Jones*, 6 C. & P. 64; 1 M. & Rob. 281; *Mercer* v *Whall*, 5 Q. B. 462.

[1379] *Fry* v. *Bennett*, 3 Bosw. 200; 28 N. Y. 329.

[1380] *Ashley* v. *Bates*, 15 M. & W. 589; *Booth* v. *Milnes*, 15 M. & W. 669; 4 D. & L. 52; 15 Law Jour. 354, Ex.; *Doe* v. *Brayne*, 17 Law Jour. 127, C. P.; *Hinkman* v. *Firnie*, 3 M. & W. 505; but see *Brandford* v. *Freeman*, 5 Ex. 734; *Burrell* v. *Nicholson*, 1 M. & Rob. 304; *Bird* v. *Higginson*, 2 A. & E. 160.

[1381] *Chamberlain* v. *Gaillard*, 26 Ala. 504.

[1382] *Duncombe* v. *Daniell*, 8 C. & P. 223.

[1383] *Nearing* v. *Bell*, 5 Hill, 291.

themselves to the facts proved; but a disregard of this rule is not a ground for a new trial.[1394] The summing up of counsel may, it seems, affect the damages. Thus in an action for libel brought by an attorney, the defendant's counsel having ridiculed the profession and assailed the character of the plaintiff, Lord Chief Justice Cockburn told the jury that if they thought it was a libel, and directed against the plaintiff, "a defence of that description is ten-fold, if not an hundred-fold, an aggravation of any libel which can be brought against a man for any departure from the propriety of his profession, * * * a most grievous aggravation, and one which it is your bounden duty to take into your serious consideration." [1395]

§ 278. Where the publication is denied, the libel should not be read to the jury until after the defendant's counsel has called witnesses to prove the publication, but a disregard of this rule is not a ground for a new trial.[1396] As a general rule the defendant is entitled to have read on the trial the whole publication containing the alleged libellous matter.[1397]

§ 279. Where the defences are a general denial and justification, the plaintiff may, before resting his case, either give all his evidence to defeat the justification,[1398] or content himself by proving the allegations of his complaint only, in which case he will be restricted in his reply to such evidence only as goes exactly to answer the facts proved by the defence.[1399] The evidence is usually closed with the plaintiff's rebutting testimony.[1400]

[1394] *Fry* v. *Bennett*, 3 Bosw. 202; 28 N. Y. 331.

[1395] Note to *Ofroever* v. *Hoffman*, 16 U. C. Q. B. Rep. 445.

[1396] *Taylor* v. *State of Georgia*, 4 Geo. 14.

[1397] *Weaver* v. *Lloyd*, 1 C. & P. 295; *Thornton* v. *Stephen*, 2 M. & Rob. 45; *Cooke* v. *Hughes*, Ry. & M. 112; 2 Greenl. Ev. § 423; *Rex* v. *Lambert*, 2 Camp. 398; *Rutherford* v. *Evans*, 6 Bing. 451; 4 C. & P. 74.

[1398] *Brown* v. *Murray*, Ry. & Mo. 254; *Ayrault* v. *Chamberlain*, 33 Barb. 234; *York* v. *Pease*, 2 Gray, 282.

[1399] *Pierrepoint* v. *Sharpland*, 1 Carr. 448.

[1400] *Teagle* v. *Duboy*, 8 Blackf. 134.

It is discretionary with the court to allow additional testimony on the part of either party, after he has once closed;[1391] and where there is a plea of justification, the plaintiff may, before resting his case, give evidence of express malice.[1392]

§ 280. The plaintiff may, on the trial, abandon one or more of the causes of action he has alleged in his complaint,[1393] or where the alleged defamatory matter is divisible, may withdraw a portion of the matter set forth in the complaint.[1394] A defendant was not allowed to withdraw a plea of justification,[1395] but a refusal to allow such a withdrawal was in one case held error.[1396] Where the defendant had pleaded the general issue and a plea of apology, leave to withdraw the plea of apology was denied, the plaintiff swearing he would be prejudiced.[1397] It was held that a written statement made by the defendant, in which he disclaimed any evil intentions toward plaintiff, could not be given in evidence on the trial, and if allowed by the plaintiff to be given in evidence, could not be sent out with the jury.[1398] Where the plaintiff, on the trial, abandons a part of the defamatory matter, the part abandoned may be referred to, to show the meaning of the part retained.[1399]

§ 281. The jury are to determine, as a question of fact, the customary meaning of a word,[1400] and the meaning of doubtful

---

[1391] *Wilborn* v. *Odell*, 29 Ill. 456.

[1392] *Fry* v. *Bennett*, 3 Bosw. 202; but see *Winter* v. *Donovan*, 8 Gill, 370.

[1393] *Kirkaldy* v. *Paige*, 17 Verm. 256; *Stow* v. *Converse*, 4 Conn. 17; *Gould* v. *Weed*, 12 Wend. 12.

[1394] *Healer* v. *Degant*, 3 Ind. 501; *Genet* v. *Mitchell*, 7 Johns. 120.

[1395] *Clinton* v. *Mitchell*, 3 Johns. 144; *Lent* v. *Butler*, 3 Cow. 370; *Lee* v. *Robertson*, 1 Stew. 136.

[1396] *Fitzgerald* v. *Ferguson*, 25 Ill. 138. In Pennsylvania the withdrawal of the plea is within the discretion of the court. (*Rush* v. *Cavanagh*, 2 Barr, 187.)

[1397] *Sullivan* v. *Lenihan*, 7 Irish Law Rep. 463.

[1398] *Hamilton* v. *Glenn*, 1 Penn. St. Rep. 340.

[1399] *Genet* v. *Mitchell*, 7 Johns. 120.

[1400] *Law* v. *Cross*, 1 Black U. S. Rep. 583. See *Edsall* v. *Brooks*, 3 Robertson, 284 ; *Barnett* v. *Allen*, 1 Fost. & Fin. 125; *Wachter* v. *Quenzer*, 29 N. Y. 547.

words,[1401] and whether the language was or was not ironical.[1402] "Where words are capable of two constructions, in what sense they were meant is a question of fact to be decided by the jury."[1403] Thus if in one sense the language imputes a crime, and in the other sense does not, the jury are to say in which sense the language is to be understood.[1404] And where A. said to B., "You have killed one negro and nearly killed another," held that the jury were to say whether the words were used in a defamatory sense or not;[1405] so where the language was, "You are a thief. You stole hoop-poles and saw-logs from D. and M.'s land," held that it was properly left to the jury to decide if the charge was taking timber or hoop-poles already cut—which was a felony—or with cutting down and carrying away timber to · make hoop-poles, which was a trespass.[1406] Where words apparently charging a crime are published, it is proper to instruct the jury that the words are actionable if uttered with intent to charge the crime.[1407]

§ 282. Where the plaintiff, in an action for libel, had set out in his declaration an article published by the defendant in a newspaper, which the plaintiff claimed to be libellous, and, on the trial, the defendant selected a certain portion of the words of such article, which he claimed were proved to be

---

[1401] *Hays* v. *Brierly*, 4 Watts, 392.

[1402] *Reg.* v. *Browne*, Holt, 425; 11 Mod. 86; *Andrews* v. *Woodmansee*, 15 Wend. 232; *Boydell* v. *Jones*, 4 M. & W. 446; 7 Dowl. Pra. Cas. 210.

[1403] 1 Stark. Slan. 60; *Van Vechten* v. *Hopkins*, 5 Johns. 221; *Dexter* v. *Taber*, 12 Id. 240; *McKinley* v. *Rob*, 20 Id. 356; *Gorham* v. *Ives*, 2 Wend. 534; *Gibson* v. *Williams*, 4 Wend. 320; *Blaisdell* v. *Raymond*,14 How. Pra. Rep. 265; *Bennett* v. *Williamson*, 4 Sandf. 60.

[1404] *Cregier* v. *Bunton*, 2 Rich. 395; 11 Humph. 507; *Ex parte Bailey*, 2 Cow. 479; and see 1 Amer. Lead. Cas. 153; *Davis* v. *Johnston*, 2 Bailey, 579; *Welsh* v. *Eakle*, 7 J. J. Marsh. 424; *Lucas* v. *Nichols*, 7 Jones' Law (N. C.) 82; *Snyder* v. *Andrews*, 6 Barb. 47; *Thompson* v. *Grimes*, 5 Ind. (Porter) 385; *Smith* v. *Miles*, 15 Verm. 245; *Usher* v. *Severance*, 2 App. 9; *Turrill* v. *Dolloway*, 26 Wend. 383; *Jones* v. *Rivers*, 3 Brevard, 95.

[1405] *Hays* v. *Hays*, 1 Humph. 402; *Chalmers* v. *Payne*, 2 C. M. & R. 156.

[1406] *Dexter* v. *Taber*, 12 Johns. 239; and *Stockdale* v. *Tarte*, 4 Adol. & El. 1016; *Tuson* v. *Evans*, 3 Perr. & D. 396.

[1407] *St. Martin* v. *Desnoyer*, 1 Min. 156.

true, and if otherwise, were not libellous, and so he prayed the
court to instruct the jury; the court, after defining a libel, and
pointing out what would constitute one, instructed the jury
that they might consider the whole libellous matter in connection with the circumstances proved or admitted, and say what
was the meaning of the writing—what it imputed to the plaintiff, as to motives, objects, principles, acts, and character; and
if they were such as to make the writing libellous according to
the definition previously given, and it was false and malicious,
they would find the matter libellous, and sufficient to sustain
the action; it was held, that this direction was unexception-
able.[1408] A banker, remitting the proceeds of a note sent to
him for collection, appended to his letter the words "Confidential. Had to hold over for a few days for the accommodation
of L. & H.," who were the makers. Held that these words have
not necessarily an injurious meaning, and that their interpretation was a matter for the jury.[1409] Where the libel was copied
by the defendants from another paper, with the word "fudge"
added thereto, held that it was for the jury to say with what
motive the publication was made, and whether that word was
only to give a color at a future day.[1410]

§ 283. Where, at the time of speaking defamatory words,
the defendant qualifies them by other words, the jury are to
determine from all that took place at the time, whether à crime
was or was not charged; but to justify the application of this
principle the qualification or explanation must not only accom-
pany the words, but must be sufficiently explicit to enable
those who hear the same, and who are presumed to acquire all
their knowledge of the transaction from what was said at the
time, reasonably to understand to what the words refer, and
that the meaning which the words standing alone would convey was not the meaning intended.[1411]

[1408] *Graves* v. *Waller*, 19 Conn. 90.
[1409] *Lewis* v. *Chapman*, 16 N. Y. 369; and see *Simmons* v. *Morse*, 6 Jones' Law (N. C.), 6.
[1410] *Hunt* v. *Algar*, 6 C. & P. 245.
[1411] *Van Akin* v. *Caler*, 48 Barb. 60.

§ 284. It is for the judge to decide whether the language is capable of the meaning ascribed to it by the innuendo, and for the jury to decide whether such meaning is truly ascribed.[1412] Thus where the defamatory matter was concerning K., which it was alleged meant King George the Third, held that the jury were to decide if such was its meaning.[1413] The judge may give his opinion that the publication complained of conveys a certain meaning, and that therefore it is libellous, but still it is for the jury to say whether or not the publication does convey the meaning which the judge ascribes to it.[1414] Where the words were that the plaintiff " will lie, cheat, steal, and swear," it was held that the court might, in answer to a broad request of the defendant's counsel to charge that the evidence did not support the declaration, say to the jury that these words might import that the plaintiff stole.[1415] The plaintiff, D., who had worked for F. in making pill boxes by a machine owned and kept secret by F., left F., and set up a machine for making similar boxes on his own account. F., when speaking of D.'s said machine, said, " D. stole my patterns to get up his castings by." Held, that it was for the jury, and not for the court, to decide whether F. intended, by these words, to charge D. with the crime of larceny.[1416] The alleged libel stated that plaintiff had, under certain specified circumstances, been surety for another, and then asked the question why he had become such surety, and answered by saying: There could be but one answer—he was hired for the occasion. It was left to jury to say if this was a fair comment, and if so to find for defendant. The jury found for defendant; and on motion for a new trial, the court, although of opinion that the

---

[1412] *Blagg* v. *Sturt*, 10 Q. B. 899; 16 Law Jour. 39, Q. B.; 11 Jur. 101; *Cooper* v. *Greeley*, 1 Denio, 361; *Vanderlip* v. *Roe*, 23 Penn. St. R. 82; *Barger* v. *Barger*, 18 Penn. St. R. 489; *Hemmings* v. *Gasson*, 1 Ell. B. & E. 346; *Justice* v. *Kirlin*, 17 Ind. 588.

[1413] *Rex* v. *Woodfall*, 5 Burr. 2661.

[1414] *Empson* v. *Fairford*, W. W. & D. 10; 1 Jurist, 20.

[1415] *Dottarer* v. *Bushey*, 16 Penn. St. R. 204.

[1416] *Dunnell* v. *Fiske*, 11 Metc. 551.

charge of being hired was not a just inference from the facts
stated, held that the question had been correctly submitted to,
the jury, and refused to disturb the verdict.[1417] ·Where the
charge was "I have a suspicion that you have robbed my
house," innuendo that plaintiff had stolen certain goods of the
defendant, held that it was properly left to the jury to say
whether the defendant meant to impute an absolute charge of
felony, or only a suspicion of felony.[1418] In an action of slander, the words laid did not, in express terms, charge the crime,
which, by innuendo, it was stated the defendant meant to impute to the plaintiff, and there was no inducement showing of
what the words were spoken; the circuit judge charged, that
the declaration would suffice if the jury believed that the words
would well carry the meaning that had been ascribed to them.
Held, that such charge was proper, and a verdict for the plaintiff was sustained.[1419]

§ 285. Whether the facts charged in the publication are
true, is a question for the jury.[1420] Where the charge was that
plaintiff had traitorously betrayed the secrets of his government, it was held to be a question for the jury to say if he had
traitorously betrayed the secrets of his government.[1421] And
where the charge was that the plaintiff was a *great* defaulter,
and the proof was that he was a defaulter, held that it was for
the jury to say whether he was a *great* defaulter.[1422] And leaving it to the jury whether or not the defendant had made a
true·statement of a judicial proceeding, was held· to be
proper.[1423]

§ 286. It is the exclusive province of the court to determine the construction of the language published, and to deter-

---

[1417] *Cooper* v. *Lawson*, 8 Adol. & El. 746.
[1418] *Tozer* v. *Mashford*, 4 Eng. Law & Eq. R. 451; 0 Ex. 539; 20 Law Jour.
Rep. N. S. 224, Ex.
[1419] *Marshall* v. *Gunter*, 6 Rich. 419.
[1420] *Thomas* v. *Croswell*, 7 Johns. 264: *Van Vechten* v. *Hopkins*, 5 Johns. 211.
[1421] *Genet* v. *Mitchell*, 7 Johns. 90.
[1422] *Warman* v. *Hine*, 1 Jurist, 820.
[1423] *Huff* v. *Bennett*, 4 Sandf. 120.

mine whether or not upon its face it is actionable *per se*,[1424] and whether or not the language on its face is concerning the plaintiff,[1425] or concerning him in his professional character.[1426] But on not guilty pleaded whether the defamatory matter was published concerning the plaintiff, or whether by the person mentioned the plaintiff was intended, is a question of fact for the jury.[1427] Where the declaration alleged the publication of a certain "libel concerning the plaintiff," but contained no innuendo, colloquium, or inducement to connect the publication with the plaintiff, and no evidence but the publication itself was offered to connect him therewith, it was held to be a question for the court, as a question of construction, to determine whether or not the publication referred to the plaintiff.[1428] Where no extrinsic facts are offered in evidence, or if the language is ambiguous, the question of libel or no libel is in a civil action a question of law,[1429] and as neither the statute of 32 George the Third, enabling the jury to give a general verdict in an action for libel, nor the similar provision in the Revised Statutes of New York, apply to civil actions,[1430] the judge may charge the jury, whether or not, as a question of law, a publication is libellous on its face,[1431] and it is the duty of the jury to follow the instructions of the judge.[1432] It is the practice for the judge

---

[1424] *Reeves* v. *Templar*, 2 Jurist, 187; *Matthews* v. *Beach*, 5 Sandf. 256; *Green* v. *Telfair*, 20 Barb. 11; *Fry* v. *Bennett*, 5 Sandf. 54; *Haight* v. *Cornell*, 15 Conn. 74; *Mix* v. *Woodward*, 12 Conn. 262; *Thompson* v. *Grimes*, 5 Ind. 385; *McKinley* v. *Robb*, 20 Johns. 351; *Archbold* v. *Sweet*, 5 C. & P. 219; 1 Mo. & Rob. 162.

[1425] *Barrows* v. *Bell*, 7 Gray (Mass.) 251.

[1426] *Tomlinson* v. *Brittlebank*, 1 Har. & W. 573.

[1427] *Van Vechten* v. *Hopkins*, 5 Johns. 211; *Green* v. *Telfair*, 20 Barb. 11; *Godson* v. *Home*, 1 Brod. & Bing. 7.

[1428] *Barrows* v. *Bell*, 7 Gray (Mass.) 301.

[1429] *Snyder* v. *Andrews*, 6 Barb. 43.

[1430] *Hunt* v. *Bennett*, 19 N. Y. 173; *Levi* v. *Milne*, 4 Bing. 195; *Snyder* v. *Andrews*, 6 Barb. 55; *Dollaway* v. *Turrell*, 26 Wend. 399.

[1431] *Darby* v. *Ouseley*, 36 Eng. Law. & Eq. R. 518; *Wagaman* v. *Byers*, 17 Md. 183; *Hunt* v. *Bennett*, 19 N. Y. 173.

[1432] *Hakewell* v. *Ingram*, 2 Com. Law Rep. 1397; 28 Eng. Law & Eq. R. 413; *The State* v. *Jeandell*, 32 Penn. St. Rep. 475; and see *Duffy* v. *The People*, 26 N. Y. 588; *Rex* v. *Burdett*, 4 B. & Ald. 131; 2 Bennett & Hurd Lead. Cr. Cas. 388; *The State* v. *Croteau*, 23 Verm. 14; *U. S.* v. *Morris*, 1 Curtis, 58; *Baylis* v. *Law-*

first to give a legal definition of libel, and then to leave it to
the jury to say whether the facts necessary to constitute that offence, have been proved to their satisfaction.[1453] The judge may
state under what circumstances language in itself actionable
may be spoken with impunity, and by way of illustration put
a case differing in some respects from that before the court.[1454]
He is bound, upon a proper motion, to rule whether or not the
declaration sets forth a cause of action.[1455] But in charging
the jury, the judge is not bound to give his opinion as to the
nature of the publication as a matter of law.[1456] And where
the judge charged, "I find a difficulty in saying whether it
[the publication] is a libel or not. Gentlemen, can you assist
me?" a motion for a new trial on the ground of misdirection
was denied.[1457] But it is no misdirection that the judge, in addition to leaving the proper questions to the jury, stated his
own opinion as to the libellous nature of the publication.[1458]
Although the judge is to leave it to the jury whether, under
the circumstances, the publication is a libel, on the general
issue guilty or not guilty, yet if they find a verdict for the defendant on that issue, in a case in which no question is made
as to the fact of publication, nor as to its application to the
plaintiff, the court will set aside the verdict.[1459] And where

rence, 11 Adol. & El. 925; Rex v. Dean of St. Asaph, 21 How. St. Tr. 847; 3 T.
R. 428, note; Sixth Rep. of Crim. Law Comm'rs, A.D. 1841; Forsyth's Hist. of
Trial by Jury, 268; 2 Camp. Ch. Justices, 478; 3 Id. 56; Rex v. Miller, 20 How.
St. Tr. 892; Rex v. Woodfall, 5 Burr. 2661; Shattuck v. Allen, 4 Gray, 541;
Com'wealth v. Anthes, 5 Gray, 185; Com'wealth v. Porter, 10 Metc. 263; Goodrich
v. Davis, 11 Metc. 473; Com'wealth v. Abbott, 13 Metc. 120; Pearce v. The State,
13 N. Hamp. 536; The People v. Croswell, 8 Johns. Cas. 337.

[1453] Parmiter v. Coupland, 6 M. & W. 105.
[1454] Taylor v. Robinson, 29 Maine, 323.
[1455] Shattuck v. Allen, 4 Gray (Mass.) 540; Matthews v. Beach, 5 Sandf. 256.
[1456] Parmiter v. Coupland, 6 M. & W. 105; Snyder v. Andrews, 6 Barb. 43.
[1457] Baylis v. Lawrence, 3 Perr. & D. 526.
[1458] Darby v. Ouseley, 36 Eng. Law & Eq. R. 518; Snyder v. Andrews, 6 Barb.
55; and see Empson v. Fairford, W. W. & D. 10; 1 Jurist, 20.
[1459] Hakewell v. Ingram, 28 Eng. Law & Eq. R. 413; 2 Com. Law Rep. 1397;
and see Levi v. Milne, 4 Bing. 195; Long v. Eakle, 4 Md. 454; Usher v. Severance, 20 Maine, 9; Goodrich v. Davis, 11 Metc. 474.

the action was for calling the plaintiff a thief, and the defence
was that the defendant so explained the words-that the charge
did not amount to an imputation of felony, the court being of
opinion that the defence failed, charged the jury that the plaintiff was entitled to a verdict, and that the only question for
them to determine was the amount of damages. The defendant excepted to this charge, and on appeal it was held to be
proper.[1440]

§ 287. Where the circumstances of the publication are controverted or uncertain, a case is presented in which the court is
to instruct the jury what condition of circumstances would render the publication privileged, and then leave it to the jury to
determine the character of the publication, and give a verdict
accordingly. For the jury cannot decide whether a libel was
published on a justifiable occasion, without being told by the
court what facts would constitute such an 'occasion.[1441] The
uncertainty as to the facts may consist either in the happening
or not happening of certain events, or in the question whether
or not the language exceeded the privileged limits.

§ 288. The facts being uncontroverted, the court is to determine whether or not the publication is privileged.[1442] If the
court decides that the publication is *absolutely* privileged, that of
course determines the action; if the court decides the publication is *conditionally* privileged, then it is a matter of law for
the court to determine whether there is any *intrinsic* or *extrinsic* evidence of malice. If the court decides this question in the
negative, it directs a nonsuit or a verdict for the defendant,
without reference to the jury.[1443] But if the court decides there
is any evidence, either in the language of the publication itself

---

[1440] *Van Akin* v. *Caler*, 48 Barb. 58.

[1441] *Duncan* v. *Brown*, 15 B. Monr. 186.

[1442] *Darby* v. *Ousley*, 36 Eng. Law & Eq. R. 518; *Wenman* v. *Ash*, 13 C. B.
836.

[1443] *Cooke* v. *Wildes*, 5 El. & Bl. 328; *Somerville* v. *Hawkins*, 10 C. B. 583;
Taylor v. *Hawkins*, 16 Q. B. 308; *Harris* v. *Thompson*, 13 C. B. 333; *Wenman* v.
Ash, id. 836; *Fry* v. *Bennett*, 5 Sandf. 54; *Jarvis* v. *Hathaway*, 3 Johns. 180.

[intrinsic evidence], or in the circumstances of its publication, from which a want of good faith or a bad intent [malice] on the part of the publisher may be inferred, it then becomes the duty of the court to submit to the jury, with appropriate in-- structions, and as a question of fact for their determination, whether in making the publication the publisher acted in good faith or otherwise;[1444] for the question of malice in such a case is always a question of fact to be determined by the jury.[1445] Thus where the defendant had charged and caused the plaintiff to be searched for a brooch missing, but afterwards found in the defendant's possession, held to be a question for the jury whether the charge was made *bonâ fide*, and that the circum- stances and occasion of making it should be left to their consid- eration;[1446] and to entitle a plaintiff " to have the question of malice submitted to the jury, it is not necessary that the evi- dence should be such as *necessarily* leads to the conclusion that malice existed, or that it should be inconsistent with the non-existence of malice, but it is necessary that the evidence should raise a probability of malice, and be more consistent with its existence than with its non-existence;[1447] and where the only evidence of malice was claimed to be on the face of the publication, held that it ought to have been left to the jury to determine whether there was any malice.[1448]   But where the libel purported to be the report of a proceeding in the insolvent court, and imputed to the insolvent's landlord (the plaintiff) that he colluded with the insolvent in putting in a fictitious distress; held, that the judge ought not to have left it as a question to the jury whether the defendant *intended* to injure

---

[1444] *Lancey* v. *Bryant*, 30 Maine (17 Shep.), 466; *Powers* v. *Smith*, 5 B. & A. 850; *Abrams* v. *Smith*, 8 Blackf. 95.

[1445] *White* v. *Nicholls*, 3 How. U. S. Rep. 266; *Blackburn* v. *Blackburn*, 4 Bing. 395; *Robinson* v. *May*, 2 J. P. Smith, 3; *Bodwell* v. *Osgood*, 3 Pick. 379; *Too-good* v. *Spyring*, 1 Cr. M. & R. 181; *Bromage* v. *Prosser*, 6 D. & R. 296; *Haight* v. *Cornell*, 15 Conn. 74; *Gardner* v. *Slade*, 13 Ad. & Ell. N. S. 796; *Pattison* v. *Jones*, 8 B. & C. 578.

[1446] *Padmore* v. *Lawrence*, 3 Perr. & D. 209.

[1447] *Somerville* v. *Hawkins*, 10 C. B. 583; and see *Taylor* v. *Hawkins*, 16 Q. B. 308; *Harris* v. *Thompson*, 13 C. B. 333; *Wenman* v. *Ash*, 13 C. B, 836.

[1448] *Gilpin* v. *Fowler*, 26 Eng. Law & Eq. R. 386; 9 Ex. 615; 18 Jur. 292.

the plaintiff, but that if he thought the tendency of the publication injurious to the plaintiff, he ought to have told them it was actionable, and the plaintiff entitled to a verdict.[1449]

§ 289. The amount of damages is to be determined by the jury, but the court should instruct them as to the rules by which they should be governed in fixing the amount.[1450] A general instruction to find such damages as under all the circumstances they thought right, was held to be improper.[1451] It was held no ground for exception that the judge *advised* the jury to give only nominal damages.[1452] A charge that compensatory damages are to be given where the publication is without malice, and that compensatory damages are such as will repay the costs and trouble of the suit and of disproving the defendant's allegations, was held right,[1453] although it has been held erroneous to charge the jury to take into consideration the expense to which the plaintiff has been put by being compelled to come into court to vindicate his character.[1454] It is usual to tell the jury that they are not to consider the effect of the verdict upon the costs; yet it has been held in one case that if the jury ask what amount of damages will carry costs, there is no reason why the judge should not tell them.[1455] In an action of slander for words imputing unchastity to the plaintiff, the jury were instructed that the rule with respect to damages was, to give such as were commensurate with the injury sustained by the acts charged and proved against the defendants; that if the

---

[1449] *Haire* v. *Wilson*, 9 B. & Cr. 643.

[1450] *True* v. *Plumley*, 36 Maine, 466.

[1451] *Duncan* v. *Brown*, 15 B. Monr. 186.

[1452] *Matthews* v. *Beach*, 5 Sandf. 256. Where the judge recommended the jury to give nominal damages, but the jury gave £5 damages, the court refused to set the verdict aside. (*Chilvers* v. *Greaves*, 5 M. & G. 678.) The right of the court to direct a verdict for nominal damages doubted. (*Strong* v. *Kean*, 13 Irish Law Rep. 93.)

[1453] *Armstrong* v. *Pierson*, 8 Clarke (Iowa), 29.

[1454] *Hicks* v. *Foster*, 13 Barb. 663.

[1455] *Kelmore* v. *Abdoolah*, 27 Law Jour. Rep. 307, Ex. Costs cannot be allowed as damages. (*Shay* v. *Tuolumne Water Co.*, 6 Cal. 286.) The effect of the verdict upon the costs is to be laid entirely out of consideration, and with which the jury have nothing to do. (*Mears* v. *Griffin*, 2 Sc. N. S. 15.)

plaintiff was an innocent and virtuous female, and her character had been destroyed by the slanders of the defendant and
others, they might give liberal damages; but if the plaintiff had
so destroyed her character, by her own lewd and dissolute conduct, as to have sustained no injury from the words spoken by
the defendant, they might give only nominal damages. This
was held correct.[1456]

§ 290. In general, prospective damages are not to be allowed, and damages arising after suit brought are not to be
taken into account,[1457] although it has been held that the jury
are to consider the probable future as well as the actual past;[1458]
and. in an action of libel upon copartners, held the jury
might consider the prospective injury to the copartnership;[1459]
and in a case of libel on the plaintiff in connection with a steam
vessel, he was allowed to show diminished earnings of the vessel subsequent to the bringing of the action.[1460] Where in consequence of the defamation the plaintiff lost an office dependent
on the will of his superior, it was held the jury were to consider
both the nature and tenure of the office, and not give the value
of an annuity certain.[1461] Where the damage proved was the
loss of a situation of fifty pounds a year, and the jury gave a
verdict for sixty pounds, the court refused to disturb it.[1462]
Mental suffering and sickness induced by the publication are
not such natural consequences of defamation as to amount to
special damage,[1463] and in a joint action by partners, it was held
that no damages could be given for any injury to the private
feelings of the plaintiffs, but only for such injury as they had

---

[1456] *Flint* v. *Clarke*, 13 Conn. 364.
[1457] *Goslin* v. *Corry*, 7 Mann. & G. 343; *Kcenholts* v. *Becker*, 3 Denio, 346;
Phil. R. R. Co. v. *Quigley*, 21 How. U. S. Rep. 202; Mayne on Damages, 277.
[1458] *True* v. *Plumley*, 36 Maine, 466; *Harrison* v. *Pearce* 1 F. & F. 507.
[1459] *Gregory* v. *Williams*, 1 Carr. & K. 658.
[1460] *Ingram* v. *Lawson*, 6 Bing. N. C. 212.
[1461] *Lever* v. *Torrey*, 1 Murray, 350.
[1462] *Jackson* v. *Hopperton*, 17 C. B. 829.
[1463] *Terwilliger* v. *Wands*, 17 N. Y. 54; *Wilson* v. *Goit*, 17 N. Y. 442; overruling *Brandt* v. *Towsley*, 13 Wend. 253; *Fuller* v. *Fenner*, 16 Barb. 333, and
Swift v. *Dickerman*, 31 Conn. 285.

sustained in their joint trade.[1464]   The jury must give some damages,[1465] and where actual ill-will is shown, they may give exemplary or vindictive damages.[1466]   The damages cannot exceed the amount claimed, and a direction to that effect is proper;[1467] and where the plaintiff had a verdict for more damages than he claimed in his declaration, the court refused him leave to amend the declaration so as to keep the verdict.[1468]

§ 291.   Where there are several counts, and a verdict is entered generally on all the counts, and entire damages are given, if one count is bad, the judgment will be arrested, and a *venire de novo* awarded.   But if the judge who tried the cause certifies that the evidence applied only to the good counts, or it is otherwise apparent that the defective count has not influenced the amount of the verdict, the verdict will be amended by confining it to the good counts.   Where there is any doubt as to any one count, it is prudent to have the damages assessed severally, or to abandon the doubtful count, and take a verdict on the other counts only.[1469]   By a defective count is meant a

---

[1464] *Haythorn* v. *Lawson*, 3 Car. & P. 196.

[1465] *Jewett* v. *Whitney*, 43 Maine, 242; although it may be shown that defendant was benefited by the defamation.   See *post*, Mitigation.

[1466] *Taylor* v. *Church*, 8 N. Y. 452; *Hunt* v. *Bennett*, 4 E. D. Smith, 647; 19 N. Y. 173; *Fry* v. *Bennett*, 4 Duer, 247; *Kinney* v. *Hosea*, 3 Harring. 397; *Gilbreath* v. *Allen*, 10 Ired. 67; *Cramer* v. *Noonan*, 4 Wis. 231; *Hosley* v. *Brooks*, 20 Ill. 115; *Knight* v. *Foster*, 39 N. Hamp. 576.   The right to give vindictive damages has been questioned.   See *Austen* v. *Wilson*, 4 Cush. 273; *Taylor* v. *Carpenter*, 2 Wood. & M. 1; 2 Greenl. Ev. tit. Damages; Sedgwick on Damages, Appendix, 1st edit. and 4th edit. p. 532.   It was held in an action for assault that vindictive damages might be given, although the defendant had previously been indicted for the same assault, and fined $250.   (*Cook* v. *Ellis*, 6 Hill, 467.)

[1467] *Pool* v. *Devers*, 30 Ala. 672.

[1468] *Curtis* v. *Lawrence*, 17 Johns. 111.   The declaration may, it seems, be amended on the terms of submitting to a new trial (*Bowman* v. *Early*, 3 Duer, 691), if the defendant insists on a new trial.   (*Corning* v. *Corning*, 2 Selden, 98.)

[1469] See 2 Stark. Sland. 107; Heard on Libel, §§ 303, 304; *Fry* v. *Bennett*, 28 N. Y. 326; *Holt* v. *Scholefield*, 6 T. R. 694; *Lloyd* v. *Morris*, Willes R. 443; *Bennett* v. *Wells*, 12 Mod. 420; *Grant* v. *Astle*, 2 Doug. 730; *Empson* v. *Griffin*, 11 Adol. & El. 187; *Leach* v. *Thomas*, 2 M. & W. 427; *Gould* v. *Oliver*, 2 Scott N. R. 630; 2 M. & G. 208; *Lewin* v. *Edwards*, 9 M. & W. 720; *Day* v. *Robinson*,

count which shows no cause of action; a count which contains actionable words, together with words not actionable, would not be defective so as to affect a verdict on such count. In such a case it is intended that the verdict applied only to the actionable words.[1470]

§ 292. Where there is a misjoinder of several counts, and general damages are assessed, judgment will be arrested. In cases of misjoinder of counts, the verdict may be taken for the plaintiff on the counts properly joined, and for the defendant on the other count or counts, or the plaintiff may enter a *nolle prosequi* as to the count or counts improperly joined.[1471] Where there were two counts upon the same words, but published at different times, a general verdict for the plaintiff was upheld.[1472] A general verdict on five counts held not responsive to either

1 Ad. & El. 558; 2 N. & M. 884; *Angle* v. *Alexander*, 7 Bing. 119; *Eddowes* v. *Hopkins*, 1 Doug. 377; *Reg.* v. *Verrier*, 12 Adol. & El. 331, overruling *Williams* v. *Breedon*, 1 Bos. & Pul. 329. See also *Union Turnpike Co.* v. *Jenkins*, 1 Caines, 392; *Hopkins* v. *Beadle*, id. 347; *Lyle* v. *Clason*, id. 583; *Livingston* v. *Rogers*, id. 587; *Stafford* v. *Green*, 1 Johns. 565; *Cooper* v. *Bissell*, 15 Johns. 318; *Sayre* v. *Jewett*, 12 Wend. 135; *Addington* v. *Allen*, 11 Wend. 374; *Case* v. *Buckley*, 15 Wend. 327; *Yrisarri* v. *Clements*, 3 Bing. 432; *Neal* v. *Lewis*, 2 Bay, 204; *Hogg* v. *Wilson*, 1 Nott & McC. 216; *Kennedy* v. *Lowry*, 1 Binney, 397; *Shafer* v. *Kintzer;* id. 537; *Paul* v. *Harden*, 9 S. & R. 23; *Smith* v. *Cleveland*, 6 Metc. 332; *Baker* v. *Sanderson*, 3 Pick. 348; *Cornwall* v. *Gould*, 4 Pick. 444; *Patten* v. *Greeley*, 17 Mass. 182; *Barnard* v. *Whiting*, 7 Mass. 358; *Barnes* v. *Hurd*, 11 Mass. 57; *Sullivan* v. *Holker*, 15 Mass. 374; *Clark* v. *Lamb*, 6 Pick. 512; *Kingsley* v. *Bill*, 9 Mass. 198; *Dryden* v. *Dryden*, 9 Pick. 546; *Hayter* v. *Moat*, 2 M. & W. 56; *Gregory* v. *Duke of Brunswick*, 7 Sc. N. R. 972; *Harker* v. *Orr*, 10 Watts, 245; *Ruth* v. *Kutz*, 1 Watts, 489; *Gosling* v. *Morgan*, 32 Penn. St. Rep. 273; *Pemberton* v. *Colls*, 16 Law Jour. Rep. 403, Q. B.; 11 Jurist, 1011; *Cook* v. *Cox*, 3 M. & S. 110; *Clement* v. *Fisher*, 7 B. & Cr. 459; 1 M. & R. 281. A verdict supported by one count held good. *Marshall* v. *Gunter*, 6 Rich. 419; *Graves* v. *Waller*, 19 Conn. 90; *Bloom* v. *Bloom*, 5 S. & R. 391; *Hoag* v. *Hatch*, 8 Monthly Law Rep. N. S. 686.

[1470] Mayne on Damages, 237; *Bridges* v. *Horner*, Carthew, 230; *Nicholls* v. *Reeve*, 1 Freeman, 83; *Cheetham* v. *Tillotson*, 5 Johns. 430; *Griffith* v. *Lewis*, 8 Q. B. 844; *Alfred* v. *Farlow*, 8 Q. B. 853; *Lloyd* v. *Morris*, Willes, 443; *Hughes* v. *Rees*, 4 M. & W. 204; *Campbell* v. *Lewis*, 3 Barn. & Ald. 392; *Edwards* v. *Reynolds*, Hill & Denio, Sup. 53; *Sherry* v. *Frecking*, 4 Duer, 452.

[1471] *Corner* v. *Shew*, 3 M. & W. 350; *Kitchenman* v. *Skeel*, 3 Ex. 49; *Knightley* v. *Birch*, 2 M. & S. 533.

[1472] *Bradley* v. *Kennedy*, 2 Greene, 231.

count.[1473] A verdict that "the defendant spoke and published the words in the complaint specified," was upheld.[1474] And so of a verdict that found "the defendant guilty of wilful. and malicious slander." [1475] In an action for libel there were eight special pleas of justification, and issue thereon; the jury found for the plaintiff on three issues, and for the defendant on the residue of the pleas; the verdict was held void because it did not assess the plaintiff's damages on the issues found for him.[1476] A plea of justification in an action for a libel contained three material allegations, as to one of which the jury expressed themselves of opinion that the proof failed. The judge told them that, to warrant a finding in favor of the defendant, they must be satisfied that all three of the allegations were substantially made out. The jury, after two hours' deliberation, returned a verdict for the defendant upon that plea. The court refused to set it aside.[1477]

§ 293. As the amount of damages in an action for slander or libel is always a subject for the exercise of the sound discretion of the jury, who may give more or less according to their conclusions from the whole case respecting the motives of the publisher,[1478] a verdict in such an action will not be set aside for excessive damages unless there is some suspicion of unfair dealing,[1479] or "unless the case be such as to furnish evidence of prejudice, partiality or corruption on the part of the jury." [1480] The case must be very gross, and the damages enormous, to justify ordering a new trial on a question of damages.[1481] A new

[1473] Cock v. Weatherby, 5 S. & M. 333.

[1474] Carlock v. Spencer, 2 Eng. 12.

[1475] Benaway v. Congre, 3 Chand. 214; and see Harding v. Brooks, 5 Pick. 244; Scott v. Cook, 1 Duvall, 314.

[1476] Clement v. Lewis, 3 B. & B. 297; 3 B. & A. 702.

[1477] Napier v. Daniell, 3 Sc. 417; 2 Hodges, 187; 3 Bing. N. C. 77.

[1478] Davis v. Davis, 2 N. & M. 81; Trabue v. Mayo, 3 Dana, 138.

[1479] Mayson v. Sheppard, 12 Rich. Law, S. C. 254.

[1480] Lawyer v. Smith, 1 Denio, 207; Harlin v. Hopkins, 9 Johns. 36; Jarvis v. Hathaway, 3 Johns. 180; Rundell v. Butler, 10 Wend. 119; Bailey v. Dean, 5 Barb. 297; Spencer v. McMasters, 16 Ill. 405.

[1481] Tillotson v. Cheetham, 2 Johns. 63; Coleman v. Southwick, 9 Johns. 45;

trial was granted on payment of costs, and under peculiar circumstances, where the verdict was £150,[1482] and so where the damages were $5,000.[1483] There is nothing to forbid the granting a new trial, in a proper case, for insufficient damages, but the granting a new trial for insufficient damages is of rare occurrence. Where the plaintiff was a minister of the gospel, and the damages only one farthing, the court refused a new trial.[1484] The court may order a new trial unless the plaintiff consents to reduce the damages. Thus where the damages were $600, the court ordered a new trial, unless the plaintiff would consent to reduce them to $200.[1485]

§ 294. A new trial will not be granted because a verdict for defendant should have been for plaintiff with nominal dam-

Southwick v. Stevens, 10 Johns. 443; Root v. King, 7 Cow. 613; Moody v. Baker, 5 Cow. 351; Cole v. Perry, 8 Cow. 214; Ostrom v. Calkins, 5 Wend. 263; Douglas v. Tousey, 2 Wend. 352; Cook v. Hill, 3 Sand. 341; Riley v. Nugent, 1 A. K. Marsh. 431; Ryckman v. Parkins, 9 Wend. 470. The court refused to grant a new trial for excessive damages where the amount was severally $1,000 (Bell v. Howard, 4 Litt. 117); $300, charge horse stealing (Faulkner v. Wilcox, 2 Litt. 369); $2,736, charge perjury (Sanders v. Johnson, 6 Blackf. 51); $500, charge horse stealing (Teagle v. Deboy, 8 Blackf. 134); £750, charge against a minister of the gospel (Highmore v. Harrington, 3 C. B. N. S. 142); $334 (Ross v. Ross, 5 B. Monroe, 20); $212 (St. Martin v. Desnoyer, 1 Min. 156); $4,000 (Litton v. Young, 2 Met. (Ky.), 558); $15,000 (Trumbull v. Gibbons, N. Y. Judicial Repository, 1); $10,000 (Fry v. Bennett, 4 Duer, 247); £1,000 (Gfroever v. Hoffman, 16 Up. Can. Q. B. R. 441); $707 (Shute v. Barrett, 7 Pick. 82); $591 (Oakes v. Barrett, 7 Pick. 82); $3,500 (McDougall v. Sharp, 1 City Hall Recorder, 154); $1,400 (Bodwell v. Osgood, 3 Pick. 379; and see Baker v. Briggs, 8 Pick. 122; Sargent v. ——, 5 Cow 106; Mayne on Dam. 347; Chambers v. Caulfield, 6 East, 256; Hewlett v. Crunch ley, 5 Taunt. 277; Coffin v. Coffin, 4 Mass. 1; Neal v. Lewis, 2 Bay, 204; Edgar v. Newell, 24 Up. Can. Q. B. Rep. 215; Myers v. Curry, id. 470; Treanor v. Dona hue, 9 Cush. 228; Wood v. Gunston, Style, 463, referred to Clapp v. Hudson River R. R. Co. 19 Barb. 465; Bruton v. Downes, 1 Fost. & F. 668.

[1482] Swan v. Clelland, 13 Up. Can. Q. B. Rep. 335; and the plaintiff having died since the verdict was rendered, defendant was put under terms not to assign death of plaintiff as error, if on new trial the verdict was for the plaintiff.

[1483] Nelle v. Harrison, 2 McCord, 230.

[1484] Kelly v. Sherlock, 1 Law Rep. 686, Q. B. and see Mears v. Griffin, 2 Sc. N. S. 15; Irwin v. Cook, 24 Texas, 244.

[1485] Potter v. Thompson, 22 Barb. 87.

25

ages.[1486] A new trial will be granted to admit newly discovered evidence to support a defence of not guilty, but not to support a justification.[1487] A new trial was refused where since the verdict for the plaintiff he had been convicted, partly on the evidence of the defendant, of the offence charged.[1488] A new trial was refused where a witness for the plaintiff had since the trial been convicted of perjury.[1489] Where plaintiff obtained a verdict for one shilling damages, in consequence, as he supposed, of the admission of improper evidence, it was held that having recovered a verdict, he could not insist on his objections to evidence, and a new trial was refused.[1490]

§ 295. Actions for slander and libel are in the nature of a penal action, and though the jury find for the defendant against the weight of evidence, a new trial is never [seldom] granted.[1491] To warrant a new trial on the ground that the verdict is against evidence, it must be a very clear case.[1492] A new trial was granted because the language published did not warrant the innuendoes;[1493] and so where the innuendo was disproved.[1494]

§ 296. In New York, if the plaintiff recover less than $50 damages, he can recover no more costs or disbursements than damages.[1495] The defendant may, at any time before verdict,

[1486] Patton v. Hamilton, 12 Ind. 256; Rundell v. Butler, 10 Wend. 119. See, however, Levi v. Milne, 4 Bing. 195.

[1487] Beers v. Root, 9 Johns. 64.

[1488] Symnus v. Blake, 2 C. M. & R. 416; 4 Dowl. Pra. Cas. 263; 1 Gale, 182.

[1489] Eakins v. Evans, 8 Up. Can. Q. B. Rep. 383, O. S.

[1490] Rogers v. Munns, 25 Up. Can. Q. B. Rep. 153; and see Smith v. Kerr, 1 Barb. 155; Case v. Marks, 20 Conn. 248.

[1491] Ex parte Bailey, 2 Cow. 479; Hartin v. Hopkins, 9 Johns. 36.

[1492] Root v. King, 7 Cow. 613, affirmed 4 Wend. 113; Paddock v. Salisbury, 2 Cow. 811; Kelly v. Partington, 4 B. & Ad. 700; Fisher v. Clement, 10 B. & Cr. 472; Blackburn v. Blackburn, 4 Bing. 395; 1 M. & P. 33; Broom v. Gosden, 1 C. B. 728; Hunt v. Bennett, 4 E. D. Smith, 657.

[1493] Yrisarri v. Clement, 8 Bing. 432.

[1494] Johnston v. McDonald, 2 Up. Can. Q. B. Rep. 209.

[1495] Code of Pro. § 304.

offer to allow judgment to be taken against him for a certain sum with costs; the non-acceptance by plaintiff of such an offer will subject him to costs subsequent to its service, unless he recover a more favorable judgment.[1496] In England, if the damages in an action for slanderous words are less than forty shillings, the plaintiff, by statute 21 James I, recovers no more costs than damages; the statute was held not to apply to actions where the special damages are the gist of the action, nor to slander of title nor to libel.[1497]

[1496] Code of Pro. § 385.

[1497] As to costs in the courts of England, *Skelton* v. *Seward*, 1 Dowl. 411; *Skinner* v. *Shoppee*, 6 Bing. N. S. 131; *Simpson* v. *Hardie*, 2 M. & W. 84; 5 Dowl. 304; *Foster* v. *Pointer*, 8 M. & W. 395; 1 Dowl. 28; 9 C. & P. 718; *Empson* v. *Fairfax*, 3 Nev. & P. 385; *Dodd* v. *Crease*, 2 Cr. & M. 223; 4 Tyrw. 74; 2 Dowl. 269; *Lafone* v. *Smith*, 4 Hurl. & Nor. 158; *Saville* v. *Jardine*, 2 H. Black. 531; *Halford* v. *Smith*, 4 East, 567; *Richards* v. *Cohen*, 1 Dowl. 533; *Goodall* v. *Ensall*, 3 Dowl. 743; *Grenfel* v. *Pierson*, 1 Dowl. 400; *Turner* v. *Horton*, Willes, 438; *Andrews* v. *Thompson*, 8 Bing. 431; *Forbes* v. *Gregory*, 1 Cr. & M. 435; 1 Dowl. 679; *Harrison* v. *Bush*, 84 Eng. Law & Eq. R. 112; *Biddulph* v. *Chamberluin*, 24 Eng. Law & Eq. R. 204; *Kelly* v. *Partington*, 5 B. & Ad. 645; 2 Ney. & M. 460; *Prynne* v. *Brown*, 1 Dowl. N. S. 680; 2 Stark. Sland. 113; Stat. 58 Geo. III. ch. 30; 3 & 4 Vict. ch. 24. As to costs in Vermont, see *Nichols* v. *Packard*, 16 Verm. 147. In Indiana, see *Skinner* v. *Bronnenburg*, 18 Ind. 363.

CHAPTER XII.

PARTIES.

Question as to parties anticipated. Action by alien. Outlaw. Rebel. Executors or administrators. Married woman. Husband and wife. Partners. General rule as to joinder. Action against husband and wife. Contribution.

§ 297. The questions who may sue and who may be sued, of course generally depend upon the prior questions of rights and liabilities, and therefore, to some extent, the question of parties has been anticipated.[1498] Subject to any exceptions which have been or may be mentioned, the rules as to parties which prevail in actions for torts generally apply to the actions for slander and libel.

§ 298. It was held that an alien friend, although residing in a foreign country, might maintain an action for a libel published in England.[1499] Where the plaintiff in an action for libel was at the commencement of the action an outlaw, of which the defendant was ignorant until after notice of trial, the court after the trial stayed the proceedings, but removed the stay on the outlawry being reversed.[1500] In an unreported case in New York (*Cummings* v. *Bennett*), it being shown that the plaintiff in an action for libel was an unpardoned rebel, the court at special term made an order dismissing the complaint, but the general term reversed the order. In an action for

---

[1498] *Ante,* §§ 115, 119, notes 113, 117, 118, 119, 120. Where there were two actions for the same libel, one against the editor and the other against the publisher of the newspaper in which the publication was made, an application to consolidate was denied. (*Cooper* v. *Weed,* 2 How. Pra. R. 40; and see *post,* note 1517.)

[1499] *Pisani* v. *Lawson,* 6 Bing. N. C. 90; 8 Dowl. 57; 8 Sc. 182.

[1500] *Somers* v. *Holt,* 8 Dowl. Pr. Cas. 506.

words imputing murder, the court allowed the defendant until the next term to plead, upon the ground that the plaintiff was to be tried for the alleged murder on an indictment then pending.[1501]

§ 299. By the common law, actions of tort die with the person, and this rule applies to actions for slander [1502] and libel, except in those States where a different rule is prescribed by statute. In New York, actions of tort, except slander and libel, survive.[1503] But the death of a plaintiff after a judgment in his favor, and pending an appeal from the judgment, does not abate the appeal, and the personal representatives of the deceased may be substituted as respondents.[1504] By statute in Maine, actions for slander and libel survive, and may be maintained in the name of the executor or administrator.[1505] A right of action for slander or libel is not assignable, and does not pass under a general assignment by a judgment creditor to a receiver of his estate.[1506]

§ 300. By statute in New York, a married woman may sue alone and without her husband, for slander or libel; [1507] and so in Pennsylvania.[1508] It has been held that the New York Stat-

---

[1501] *Gibson* v. *Niven*, Barnes' Notes, 224.

[1502] 1 Wm. Saund. 316 *a*, 6th ed.; *Nettleton* v. *Dinehart*, 5 Cush. 543; *Walters* v. *Nettleton*, 5 Cush. 544; Walford on Parties, 1392, 1449.

[1503] 2 Rev. Stat. of N. Y. 447, §§ 1, 2. By statute in Ohio and Maryland, the right of action for slander or libel does not survive. In *Ireland* v. *Champneys*, 4 Taunt. 884, an action for libel, after interlocutory judgment and writ of inquiry executed, the plaintiff died, held that final judgment could not be entered, the suit having abated by the plaintiff's death. See *Kramer* v. *Waymark*, 1 Law Reports, Ex. 243.

[1504] This was done in *Sanford* v. *Bennett*, 24 N. Y. 20.

[1505] *Nutting* v. *Goodridge*, 46 Maine, 82. In Iowa, by statute, an action of libel is not abated by the death of the defendant. (*Carson* v. *McFadden*, 10 Iowa [2 With.], 91.) Death of a defendant after an appeal, held to abate the appeal. (*Long* v. *Hitchcock*, 3 Ham. 274.)

[1506] *Hudson* v. *Plets*, 11 Paige, 180; and see *Dowling* v. *Brown*, 4 Irish Com. Law Rep. 265.

[1507] Laws of N. Y. 1860, ch. 90; *Id.* 1862, ch. 172.

[1508] *Rangler* v. *Hummell*, 37 Penn. St. R. 130.

ute does not authorize a suit for slander by a wife against her husband.[1509] And it was held in Pennsylvania, that a married woman could not maintain an action for slander published at the instance of her husband.[1510]

§ 301. Independently of any statutory provision for language actionable *per se*, published concerning a married woman, or concerning a woman who afterwards marries, the action should be brought in the name of the husband and wife.[1511] In such a case the damage is to both plaintiffs, and the right of action in case of the death of the husband survives to the wife; but if the wife dies before verdict, the action abates.[1512] For language concerning a married woman, but actionable only because of special damage to the husband, the husband must sue alone.[1513] These rules are not affected by the fact that the husband and wife live apart under a deed of separation.[1514] Where an action was brought by a wife living apart from her husband under articles of separation, in the names of her husband and herself, for defamatory words spoken of her, it was held that a release of the cause of action executed by the husband was a bar to the suit, although in the articles of separation the husband had covenanted that suits might be brought in the joint names of himself and his wife, for any injury to

---

[1509] *Freethy* v. *Freethy*, 42 Barb. 641 ; as to the right of a wife to protection against slander by her husband, see Deut. xxii. 13, 22.

[1510] *Tibbs* v. *Brown*, 2 Grant's Cas. (Penn.) 39.

[1511] 1 Stark. Slan. 349; *Ebersol* v. *King*, 3 Binney, 555; *Newton* v. *Rowe*, 8 Sc. N. R. 26; *Dengate* v. *Gardiner*, 4 M. & W. 5; *Grove* v. *Hart*, Sayre, 33; *Baldwin* v. *Flower*, 3 Mod. 120; *Long* v. *Long*, 4 Barr, 29.

[1512] *Stroop* v. *Swartz*, 12 S. & R. 76 ; and see *Smith* v. *Hixon*, Str. 977, and 3 T. R. 627. Case for words by husband and wife against defendants, husband and wife; pending the action the male defendant died, and his widow remarried. The court inclined that the writ abated, but took time to advise. (*White* v. *Harwood*, Style, 138 ; Viner's Abrid. Baron and Feme, *A. a.*)

[1513] *Williams* v. *Holdridge*, 22 Barb. 396; *Gazynski* v. *Colburn*, 11 Cush. 10; *Grove* v. *Hart*, Bull. N. P. 7; *Saville* v. *Sweeney*, 1 Nev. & M. 254 ; 4 B. & Adol. 514; *Horton* v. *Byles*, 1 Sid. 387; *Long* v. *Long*, 4 Barr, 29 ; 1 Stark. Slan. 350; *Bash* v. *Sommer*, 20 Penn. St. R. 159; *Coleman* v. *Harcourt*, 1 Lev. 140; *Klein* v. *Hentz*, 2 Duer, 633.

[1514] *Beach* v. *Ranney*, 2 Hill, 309.

the person or character of the wife.[1515] For a charge of a joint larceny by husband and wife, *semble* the husband should sue alone, because the wife is *primâ facie* not liable criminally for a larceny committed in the presence of her husband.[1516]

§ 302. Where the language published concerns both husband and wife, the husband may sue alone for the injury to him, and the husband and wife may sue jointly for the injury to the wife.[1517] In an action by husband and wife, a plea that the plaintiffs were not man and wife at the time of the commencement of the action is a good plea in bar.[1518] But it is not a defence to an action by husband and wife that the plaintiffs were not married at the time of the publication complained of.[1519] Where the husband and wife are improperly united as plaintiffs, and there is no demurrer, the error is cured by verdict,[1520] or by omitting to demur.[1521]

§ 303. For language published concerning partners in the way of their trade, all the partners may or should join;[1522] but if the language concerns and injuriously affects either partner

---

[1515] *Beach* v. *Beach*, 2 Hill, 260.

[1516] *Bash* v. *Sommer*, 20 Penn. St. R. 159.

[1517] *Gazynski* v. *Colburn*, 11 Cush. 10; *Bash* v. *Sommer*, 20 Penn. St. R. 159; *Emington* v. *Gardiner*, 1 Selw. N. P. 301; *Smith* v. *Hobson*, Style, 112; *Ebersoll* v. *King*, 3 Binney, 555; *Hart* v. *Crow*, 7 Blackf. 351, *ante*, note 118. The court will not order such actions to be consolidated. Anon. Selwyn N. P. 301; *Swithin* v. *Vincent*, 2 Wils. 227; *Subley* v. *Mott*, Bull. N. P. 5.

[1518] *Chantler* v. *Lindsey*, 16 Law Jour. R. 16, Ex.; 16 M. & W. 82; 4 Dowl. & L. 339.

[1519] *Spencer* v. *McMasters*, 16 Ill. 405; and see *Benaway* v. *Congre*, 3 Chand. 214. But in an action by husband and wife, for words imputing adultery to the wife, it was held necessary to aver that they were husband and wife at the time of the publication. (*Ryan* v. *Madden*, 12 Verm. 51.)

[1520] *Russell* v. *Corne*, 1 Salk. 119; 2 L'd Raym. 1081; *Todd* v. *Bedford*, 11 Mod. 264; *Lewis* v. *Babcock*, 18 Johns. 443.

[1521] Code of Pro. N. Y. § 145. This defect cannot be insisted upon under a demurrer that the complaint does not state a cause of action. (*Eldridge* v. *Bell*, 12 How. Pra. R. 547.) No action can be maintained for the price of libellous pictures. (*Fores* v. *Johnes*, 4 Esp. 97.) A printer cannot recover for printing a libel. (*Poplett* v. *Stockdale*, R. & M. 337.) Nor could an action be maintained for breach of a contract to furnish manuscript of defamatory matter. (*Gale* v. *Leckie*, 2 Stark. R. 107.) Or for pirating a libellous book. (*Stockdale* v. *Onwhyn*, 5 B. & C. 173.)

[1522] *Cook* v. *Batchellor*, 3 B. & P. 150; 2 East, 426; *Le Fanu* v. *Malcolmson*, 1

individually, he may sue alone.[1523] The general rule is that where the injury is several, each person injured must sue separately and alone; as if one say, "A. and B. murdered C.," or "Either A. or B. murdered C.," A. and B. cannot maintain a joint action.[1524]

§ 304. For a publication by a married woman of defamatory language, the action must be against her and her husband.[1525]

§ 305. In certain cases the plaintiff is entitled to elect *de melioribus damnis* [§ 119], or as to which of several parties he will sue, but neither in such cases nor in any other case can there be any contribution between the parties, it being a general rule of law that there is no contribution between wrong-doers.[1526]

Ho. of L'ds Cas. 637; 13 Law Times, 61; *Foster* v. *Lawson*, 3 Bing. 452; 11 Moore, 360; Browl. Rediv. 81; *Haythorn* v. *Lawson*, 3 Car. & P. 196; *Pechell* v. *Watson*, 8 M. & W. 691; 2 Wm. Saund. 117, 6th ed.

[1523] *Taylor* v. *Church*, 1 E. D. Smith, 279; *Harrison* v. *Bevington*, 8 Car. & P. 708; *Robinson* v. *Marchant*, 7 Q. B. 918; *Fidler* v. *Delavan*, 20 Wend. 57; *Longman* v. *Pole*, 1 M. & M. 223.

[1524] *Smith* v. *Cooker*, Cro. Car. 513; 10 Mod. 198. As to one action against several for one libel, see *Harris* v. *Huntington*, 2 Tyler, 147; *Watts* v. *Fraser*, 7 C. & P. 369; *Miller* v. *Butler*, 6 Cush. 71; *Glass* v. *Stewart*, 10 S. & R. 222, ante, note 1498.

[1525] *Head* v. *Briscoe*, 5 Car. & P. 484; and see *ante*, note 118; *Swithin* v. *Vincent*, 2 Wils. 227; *Burcher* v. *Orchard*, Style, 349; 2 Wm. Saund. 117 d, 6th ed.

[1526] See *Merryweather* v. *Nixon*, 8 T. R. 186 and notes thereto; 2 Smith's Lead. Cas. and in addition *Moscati* v. *Lawson*, 7 C. & P. 32; *Andrews* v. *Murray*, 33 Barb. 354, citing *Miller* v. *Fenton*, 11 Paige, 18; *Coventry* v. *Barton*, 17 Johns. 142; *Peck* v. *Ellis*, 2 Johns. Ch. 131; *Pearson* v. *Skelton*, 1 M. & W. 504. No contract will be *implied* to indemnify a party against the consequences of an illegal act, *e. g.* the publication of a libel. (*Shackell* v. *Rosier*, 3 Sc. 59; 2 Bing. N. C. 634.) And *semble* the proprietor of a newspaper convicted and fined for the publication of a libel in his paper, which libel was inserted without his knowledge or consent by the editor, has no right of action against the editor for the damages sustained through such conviction. (*Colburn* v. *Patmore*, 1 C. M. & R. 83; 4 Tyr. 677.) One cannot take security to be indemnified against the consequences of an illegal act. (Domat Civil Law, B'k iii. tit. 4, § 1, div. viii; and same book and title, § 5, div. 1; and see *Howe* v. *Buffalo & Erie R. R.* 38 Barb. 124; *St. John* v. *St. John's Church*, 15 Barb. 346.) A promise to indemnify one for publishing a libel, is void. (*Arnold* v. *Clifford*. 2 Sumner, 238.)

CHAPTER XIII.

PLEADING.—THE COMPLAINT.

General requisites of a complaint. Complaint for language concerning a person only to be considered. Inducement. Colloquium. Publication. Matter published. Innuendo. Special damage. Several counts. Supplemental complaint.

§ 306. The complaint corresponds to the declaration in the common law system of pleading. Its general requisites are that it must state (1) the name of the court in which the action is pending; (2) the names of the parties; (3) the county in which it is desired the issues shall be tried; (4) the facts which constitute the cause of action; (5) a demand of relief. It must be subscribed by the plaintiff or his attorney, and may, at the option of the plaintiff, be verified. Of these several requisites we purpose to consider in detail only the fourth—the statement of the facts which constitute a cause of action.

§ 307. The statement of a cause of action must necessarily differ more or less according to the difference in the state of facts of each particular case. But there are certain allegations essential in every case to the sufficiency of such a statement; we will show what are these allegations, and endeavor to explain the rules by which their sufficiency may be tested. We premise by observing that we address ourselves exclusively to the statement of a cause of action for slander or libel *concerning the person.* Such a statement may be conveniently considered under the following heads: (1) The inducement; (2) The colloquium; (3) The act of publication; (4) The statement of the defamatory matter published; (5) The innuendoes; (6) The damages.

§ 308. *The Inducement.* — We attempted in a previous chapter [Ch. VII.] to explain (1) that the actionable quality of language was dependent upon its construction, and (2) how the construction may be affected by a variety of extrinsic circumstances. It is the office of the inducement to narrate the extrinsic circumstances which, coupled with the language published, affects its construction and renders it actionable; where standing alone and not thus explained, the language would appear either not to concern the plaintiff, or if concerning him not to affect him injuriously.[1527] This being the office of the inducement, it follows that if the language published does not naturally and *per se* refer to the plaintiff nor convey the meaning the plaintiff contends for, or if it is ambiguous or equivocal, and requires explanation by some extrinsic matter to show its relation to the plaintiff and make it actionable, the complaint must allege by way of inducement the existence of such extrinsic matter;[1528] but that where the language published is

---

[1527] " Inducement is the statement of the facts out of which the charge arises, or which are necessary or useful to make the charge intelligible." Tindal, Ch. J., *Taverner* v. *Little,* 5 Bing. N. C. 678.

[1528] Inducement is necessary where the language does not naturally and *per se* convey the meaning which the plaintiff would attribute to it, and where a reference to some extrinsic fact is necessary to explain it. (*Dorsey* v. *Whipps,* 8 Gill, 457; *Fry* v. *Bennett,* 5 Sandf. 54; *Hull* v. *Blandy,* 1 Y. & J. 480; *Gosling* v. *Morgan,* 32 Penn. St. R. 273; *Galloway* v. *Courtney,* 10 Rich. Law (S. C.) 414; *The State* v. *Neese,* 2 Tayl. 270; *Cannon* v. *Phillips,* 2 Sneed (Tenn.) 185; *Edgerly* v. *Swain,* 32 N. Hamp. 478; *Smith* v. *Gafford,* 31 Ala. 35; *Lumpkins* v. *Justice,* 1 Smith (Ind.), 322.) Where the language is claimed to be *ironical,* it must be so alleged in the inducement. (*Boydell* v. *Jones,* 4 M. & W. 446; 7 Dowl. Pra. Cas. 210.) In slander the words stated in the declaration were, "Thou set fire to those buildings, and thou wilt never be easy till thou hast told it." There was no introductory averment that the houses had been feloniously burned. A rule for arresting the judgment was made absolute. (*Rigby* v. *Heron,* 1 Jur. 558.) A complaint on a charge that plaintiff had carried away a deposition taken before a justice of the peace, must show that the deposition was taken in a proceeding in which the justice had jurisdiction, otherwise the carrying away the deposition would not be any criminal offence. (*Ayres* v. *Covell,* 18 Barb. 260.) Where, in an action of slander brought by an unmarried female, the plaintiff's petition alleged that the defendant had charged her with having given birth to a child, without any averments showing that the hearers understood that the language used conveyed a charge of bastardy, or imputed a want of chastity to the plaintiff, to which petition the defendant demurred, it was held that the demurrer should be sustained. (*Wilson* v. *Beighler,* 4 Iowa, 427.)

actionable *per se*, where there is no ambiguity, either in respect to the person whom the language concerns or in respect to the actionable quality of the language, that in such cases no inducement is necessary.[1529] Hence it will be perceived that inducement is not essential to the sufficiency of a statement of a cause of action in every case, but in those cases only where, without the facts contained in the inducement, the publication would not naturally and *per se* refer to the plaintiff nor convey the meaning the plaintiff contends for, nor be construed as actionable.

§ 309. In England the Common Law procedure act has abrogated the necessity of any matter of inducement in order to show the defamatory meaning of the language published, and enacts that the plaintiff may aver that the matter complained of was used in a defamatory sense, specifying such defamatory sense, without any prefatory averment to show how such matter was used in that sense, and such averment shall be put in issue by the denial of the alleged libel or slander; and where the matter set forth, with or without the alleged meaning, shows a cause of action, the declaration shall be sufficient.[1530]

§ 310. In New York, the Code of Procedure of that State dispenses with the necessity of any inducement to show that

---

[1529] No inducement is necessary where (1) the language is *prima facie* actionable *per se*. (*Dorsey* v. *Whipps*, 8 Gill, 457; *McGough* v. *Rhodes*, 7 Eng. 625.) (2) Where the language in its ordinary acceptation imports a charge of crime. (*Robinson* v. *Keyser*, 2 Foster (N. H.), 323; *Bricker* v. *Potts*, 12 Penn. St. R. (2 Jones) 200.) And see *Smith* v. *Hamilton*, 10 Rich. Law (S. C.), 44; *Goodrich* v. *Davis*, 11 Metc. 473. As if the words impute a charge that the plaintiff burnt his barn, with intent to defraud the insurers, it is not necessary to aver that the barn was insured, nor to prove that it was insured. (*Case* v. *Buckley*, 15 Wend. 327.) And generally it is not necessary to aver facts implied by the alleged defamatory language. If one say of J. S. " He hath killed his cook," it need not be averred that J. S. had any cook. (*Holt* v. *Taylor*, Sty. 66; and see *Billing* v *Knight*, 2 Bulst. 42.) " Thou hast forged the will of R."—it need not be averred that R. was dead, it is implied. (*Dorrel* v. *Jay*, Vent. 149.) " He hath robbed the Hockly Butcher," need not be averred there is any Hockly Butcher, for if there is not the fault is the greater. (*Smith* v. *Williams*, Comb. 247.) See *post*, § 315, and *ante*, note 140.

[1530] 15 & 16 Vict. ch. 76; Finlason's Com. Law Proc. Act, 137.

the plaintiff is the person referred to, by providing that "In an action for libel or slander it shall not be necessary to state in the complaint any extrinsic facts for the purpose of showing the application to the plaintiff of the defamatory matter out of which the cause of action arose, but it shall be sufficient to state generally that the same was published or spoken concerning the plaintiff, and if such allegation be controverted the plaintiff shall be bound to establish, on trial, that it was so published or spoken."[1531] This statute merely dispenses with the inducement to show the application of the language to the plaintiff; it does not dispense with the necessity of averments of extrinsic facts to show the meaning of ambiguous language. And in New York, where the language published is not defamatory on its face, and becomes so only by reference to extrinsic facts, the existence of those facts must be alleged in the complaint.[1532]

§ 311. The matter of inducement, when necessary, is usually inserted prior to the statement of the matter published; but this, although the more orderly arrangement, is not essential; so that the necessary inducement is to be found in the complaint, its location seems immaterial.[1533]

§ 312. Where there are several counts in the complaint, each count must be prefaced with appropriate matter of inducement; but where the inducement to one count is applicable to a subsequent count, it may be applied to such subsequent count by reference thereto and without repeating it.[1534] In slander, the first count charged a trial, that plaintiff gave evidence, and that the words were spoken of and concerning the trial, &c.; and the third count charged that the words

[1531] Code of Pro. § 164.

[1532] *Pike* v. *Van Wormer*, 5 How. Pra. Rep. 171; 6 *Id.* 99; *Deas* v. *Short*, 16 *Id.* 322; *Fry* v. *Bennett*, 5 Sandf. 54; *Blaisdell* v. *Raymond*, 4 Abb. Pra. Rep. 446; *Hallock* v. *Miller*, 2 Barb. 630; *Carroll* v. *White*, 33 Barb. 615.

[1533] *Brittain* v. *Allen*, 2 Dev. 120; 3 *Id.* 167; but see what is said *Caldwell* v. *Raymond*, 2 Abb. Pra. Rep. 193.

[1534] *Loomis* v. *Lerick*, 8 Wend. 205; and see *Tindall* v. *Moore*, 2 Wilson, 114.

therein set forth, were published of the plaintiff, and of and
concerning the action tried as aforesaid, and of and concerning
the evidence of the plaintiff given on the said trial as aforesaid. Held, that the third count was sufficient.[1535]

§ 312. Where inducement is necessary, it should be stated
in a traversable form.[1536] Thus, where it was alleged, by way of
inducement, that reports were in circulation about the plaintiff,
imputing something disgraceful, to which the publication referred, it was held insufficient, and that the reports themselves
should have been set forth.[1537] And where the alleged libel
was the publication of a notice that the plaintiff had married
E. E., and the inducement relied upon as making the publication actionable was that E. E. was a common prostitute, but
the complaint did not allege this fact otherwise than as follows:
" Married, J. W. C." (plaintiff meaning) " to E. E." (meaning
a public prostitute known by that name), "that E. E. is a public prostitute, and well known to be so," the complaint was, on
demurrer, held insufficient.[1538]

§ 313. Where the inducement is essential to the sufficiency
of the statement of the cause of action, and where, without
the facts stated as inducement, no cause of action would be
shown, there the existence or non-existence of those facts is
material, and of course may be controverted by the defendant;
if not controverted they are admitted, and need not be
proved;[1539] if controverted, they must be proved, as part of
the plaintiff's case. But where the inducement is not essential
to the sufficiency of the statement of the cause of action, and
where, without the facts stated as inducement, a cause of action
can be shown, then the inducement is mere surplusage, redun-

[1535] *Crookshank* v. *Gray*, 20 Johns. 344. See *post*, § 347.
[1536] *Caldwell* v. *Raymond*, 2 Abb. Pra. Rep. 193. And see *Cass* v. *Anderson*,
33 Verm. (4 Shaw) 182; *Carter* v. *Andrews*, 16 Pick. 1.
[1537] *Stone* v. *Cooper*, 2 Denio, 293.
[1538] *Caldwell* v. *Raymond*, 2 Abb. Pra. Rep. 193.
[1539] *Duke* v. *Jostling*, 3 Dowl. 618; *Chalmers* v. *Shackell*, 6 C. & P. 475.

dant matter; no material issue can be raised upon it; it
should not be controverted, and if controverted need not be
proved.[1540] An example of superfluous inducement is the preliminary panegyric upon the plaintiff's character, with which
it is so customary to preface all complaints for slander or libel.
As it is unnecessary to the statement of a cause of action to aver the plaintiff's innocence, either by a general
averment of good character, or a general averment of the
falsity of the matter published, or by any particular averment, no such averment can be made the subject of an
issue.[1541]

§ 314. Where the charge was, " He [plaintiff] is a pitiful fellow and not able to pay his debts, it was held not necessary to
aver, by way of inducement, that the plaintiff was no pitiful fellow and was able to pay his debts;[1542] and where the charge
was that plaintiff had given money to the defendant as a bribe,
it was held, on motion in arrest of judgment, not necessary for
the plaintiff to allege that he did not give the money.[1543]
Where the charge was of forging a note, the plaintiff averred,
by way of inducement, that the note was genuine, this was
held to be immaterial, equivalent only to the customary allegation of innocence, and did not require to be proved;[1544] so,
where the charge was being guilty of treason, and the plaintiff
alleged his innocence, it was held that he did not thereby impose on himself the burden of proving the allegation.[1545]

§ 315. It will be convenient here to refer to the rule of
pleading and of evidence, that where the defamatory matter
states expressly or by necessary implication the existence of
certain facts, the plaintiff may accept the statement and rely

---

[1540] *Cox* v. *Thomason*, 2 Cr. & J. 361.
[1541] Strachey's Case, Sty. 118.
[1542] *Hooker* v. *Tucker*, Holt R. 39.
[1543] *Bendish* v. *Lindsey*, 11 Mod. 194.
[1544] *Harman* v. *Carrington*, 8 Wend. 488.
[1545] *Coleman* v. *Southwick*, 9 Johns. 45.

upon it, without being obliged either to allege it in his pleading or. to establish its truth by evidence;[1546] the defendant is
estopped from *denying* the truth of his own charge. Thus,
where the words of a lawyer were, "He arresteth without
taking out writs," or "He is a knave in his practice," it was held
that these words implied that the plaintiff was an attorney, and
dispensed with any inducement of that fact.[1547] And in slander for charging the plaintiff with the crime of murder, it is
not necessary to allege as inducement the death of the person
said to be murdered;[1548] and generally it is unnecessary to show
that the offence charged could have been committed,[1549] or that
the plaintiff was physically capable of committing the crime
alleged against him.[1550]

§ 316. As the plaintiff's right to redress depends entirely
upon the fact that the defamatory matter concerned him
[§ 131], in order to show a right of action, that fact must appear on the face of the complaint. Where the language published was unequivocal and directly referred to the plaintiff,
the colloquium, of which presently, was alone sufficient to
show this fact. But where the language was ambiguous in
respect to the person to whom it applied, there, formerly, it
was necessary; and where the common law system of pleading
prevails, it still is necessary to state as inducement the circumstances which make it apparent that the language does concern

[1546] *Jones* v. *Stevens*, 11 Price, 235; *ante*, note 1529, and *post*, Evidence. For
the words, "That is the man who killed my husband," no allegation of the death
of the husband is necessary. (*Button* v. *Haywood*, 8 Mod. 24.) "You hired J. S.
to forge a bond;" no allegation that any bond was forged is necessary. (Cro.
Car. 337.)

[1547] *Bell* v. *Thatcher*, Freem. 277. And so, where the language was, "He is a
paltry lawyer, and plays with both hands." (2 Rolle Rep. 85.)

[1548] *Tenney* v. *Clement*, 10 N. Hamp. 52; and see *Carter* v. *Andrews*, 16 Pick.
1; *Stone* v. *Clark*, 21 Pick. 51; *Stallings* v. *Newman*, 26 Ala. 300; *Eckert* v.
Wilson, 10 S. & R. 44; contra, *Chandler* v. *Holloway*, 4 Porter, 17. See *ante*, note
447.

[1549] *Colbert* v. *Caldwell*, 3 Grant (Penn.) 181; but see *Sawyer* v. *Hopkins*, 9
Shep. 268.

[1550] *Chambers* v. *White*, 2 Jones' Law (N. C.) 383.

the plaintiff;[1551] and it was not sufficient to aver generally that
the language was published concerning the plaintiff.[1552] By
statute the rule is otherwise in New York.[1553]

§ 317. We have seen that the actionable quality of language
is sometimes affected by the circumstance that it affects the
plaintiff in some certain capacity [§§ 132, 179]; when therefore
the plaintiff claims that the language is actionable, because it
concerns him in some certain capacity or 'occupation, and it
does not upon its face imply that he is in such capacity or occupation [§ 315], the complaint should properly allege by way of
inducement that he filled such capacity, or was in, or carried
on, or exercised such occupation *at the time of the publication
complained of.* This may be shown by an averment that the
plaintiff is of such a trade, or has carried on or exercised it for
divers years, without adding last part,[1554] because a person once

---

[1551] *Hale* v. *Blandy*, 1 Y. & J. 480; and see *Brown* v. *Lamberton*, 2 Binney, 84;
Van Veehten v. *Hopkins*, 5 Johns. 211; *Harper* v. *Delph*, 3 Ind. 225; *Parker* v.
Raymond, 3 Abb. Pra. R. N. S. 343.

[1552] *The State* v. *Henderson*, 1 Rich. 179.

[1553] *Ante*, § 310. And there is a like provision in the law of Missouri.
(*Strieber* v. *Wensel*, 19 Mis. (4 Bennett) 513; and Wisconsin (*Van Slyke* v. *Carpenter*, 7 Wis. 173). "A distinct averment in regard to the person spoken of, and
a clear reference of the calumnious words to that person, is all that is required."
(*Miller* v. *Parish*, 8 Pick. 383.) See *post*, §§ 340, 341. See 1 Stark. Sland. 390.
Of what is there stated the following is an abridgment: Where the plaintiff's
name is mentioned, though a further description be given, the general averment
is sufficient (Cro. Eliz. 429) without alleging that the further description applied
to the plaintiff; as where the speaking was alleged to be of the plaintiff, and the
words were, "T." (meaning the plaintiff) "is thy brother." And where the
words were, "Captain Nelson is a thief," held not necessary to allege that plaintiff was a captain or known by that name. Where the plaintiff can show he was
intended, he can maintain the action. (*Ante*, note 132.) Thus, for the words, "The
parson of Dale is a thief," he who was parson of Dale at the time may sue. (3
Bulst. 326) And where the defendant spoke of that murderous knave Stoughton, held that one Thomas Stoughton might sue. (Sheppard, Action of Slander,
59.)

[1554] *Tuthill* v. *Milton*, Yelv. 159; Cro. Jac. 222; and see 2 Rolle R. 84; *Dodd*
v. *Robinson*, All. 63; *Collis* v. *Malin*, Cro. Car. 282; *Beaumond* v. *Hastings*, Cro.
Jac. 240.

in any certain occupation is presumed to continue therein. [§ 189.] But where the language affects the plaintiff in an office he holds during pleasure, a different rule, it is said, prevails, and the plaintiff's continuance in office must be alleged.[1555] The complaint need not allege that the plaintiff gains his livelihood by his occupation [§ 182], nor that the plaintiff has qualified himself for the office or employment in which he is defamed. Thus, where the alleged libel concerned a candidate to serve in Parliament, it was held that the declaration need not set out the writ to show the plaintiff was such candidate.[1556] But the occupation of the plaintiff should be described in apt terms. Thus, in an action by a barrister, it was held that he should allege he was *homo consiliarius et in jure peritus,* and that it was not sufficient to allege he was *eruditus in lege.*[1557] "The declaration ought not merely to state that such scandalous conduct was imputed to the plaintiff in his profession, but also to set forth in what manner it was connected by the speaker with that profession."[1558]

§ 318. Where the language is actionable of the plaintiff as an individual, then, although it may also affect him in some occupation, it is not necessary to allege as inducement that the plaintiff exercised such occupation; and even if alleged, it need not be proved, because there is a cause of action without it. [§ 179.][1559] Thus, in an action for setting up near plaintiff's house an inscription insinuating that it was a house of ill-fame, &c., the declaration alleged that the plaintiff carried on the business of a retailer of wines; but the court held, that as the inscription was not alleged to have been published concern-

---

[1555] *Tuthill* v. *Milton,* Yelv. 159; Cro. Jac. 222.

[1556] *Harwood* v. *Astley,* 1 New R. 47; and *post,* § 320.

[1557] 1 Stark. Slan. 402. A complaint setting forth that the plaintiff was "engaged in the wooden-ware business," sufficiently describes his employment as that of a buyer and seller of wooden-ware. (*Carpenter* v. *Dennis,* 3 Sandf. 305.)

[1558] Denman, C. J., *Ayre* v. *Craven,* 2 Adol. & El. 2; 4 Nev. & M. 220 and see *Alexander* v. *Angle,* 1 Cromp. & J. 143.

[1559] *Gage* v. *Robinson* 12 Ohio 250

26

ing the plaintiff as a retailer of wine, it might be struck out of
the declaration, and need not be proved.[1560] And in like manner, if the plaintiff has two trades and both are alleged as inducement, and the language is actionable as affecting the plaintiff in one of them, proof of his exercising that one trade will
suffice.[1561]

§ 319. Too great minuteness in matter of inducement is to
be avoided, because in general the proof must be co-extensive
with the allegation; as where the plaintiff alleged that he was
an attorney, that he conducted a particular suit, and afterwards
alleged that the defamatory matter was concerning his conduct
in that suit, it was held that he must prove the existence of that
suit.[1562] And in an action for a libel on a constable, respecting
his conduct in the apprehension of persons stealing a dead
body, and part of the conduct stated in the first count was that
of carrying the dead body to Surgeon's Hall, and the second
count spoke of "his conduct respecting the said dead body,"
the court held that it was necessary in both counts to prove the
introductory allegation that the body was carried to Surgeons'
Hall; for the words, "the said body," in the second count, incorporated all the descriptive circumstances introduced in the
first; the plaintiff need not have burthened himself with the
proof of such a fact; but the libel being stated of and concerning his conduct as to the dead body, it became most important
to prove that part of his conduct.[1563] But it said,[1564] "The omission to prove facts unnecessarily alleged will not be fatal unless
by the form and mode of pleading they have been made descriptive of that which is material."

§ 320. It need not be alleged that the plaintiff was *legally*

[1560] *Spall* v. *Massey*, 2 Stark. R. 559.

[1561] *Figgins* v. *Cogswell*, cited *Chalmers* v. *Shackell*, 3 C. & P. 477; 8 M. & S.
369. See *post*, n. 1674. But where the plaintiff alleged that he was proprietor
and editor of a newspaper, it was held insufficient for him to prove himself proprietor only. (*Heriot* v. *Stewart*, 4 Esp. 437.)

[1562] *Parry* v. *Collis*, 5 Esp. 339.

[1563] *Teesdale* v. *Clement*, 1 Chit. 603.

[1564] 1 Stark. Sland. 407.

qualified or *licensed* to exercise the calling in which the language affects him ; if he was not so qualified or licensed, it is matter of defence to come from the defendant. In an action for slander the plaintiff alleged that he was *in medicinis doctor*, and it was moved in arrest of judgment that he did not show he was licensed, but adjudged for the plaintiff.[1565] And so in an action by a physician for words of him in his profession, it is sufficient for him to aver that he had used and exercised the profession of a physician ; but where a plaintiff in such a case went further, and averred that he was a physician, and had duly taken the degree of a doctor of physic, it was held that he must prove his degree as stated.[1566]

§ 321. In a complaint founded upon a charge of *false swearing* as a witness, such a charge not being actionable *per se* [§ 171], to show a cause of action there should be an *inducement* of the pendency of a suit or judicial proceeding, in which the plaintiff was examined as a witness, and a *colloquium* that the charge was concerning the plaintiff as such witness.[1567] If there were several suits between the same parties, tried on the same day, it is not necessary, it seems, to distinguish in which suit the false swearing occurred.[1568] And where the suit or proceeding was before a court or officer of limited jurisdiction, it must be further shown that such court or officer

---

[1565] Dr. Brownlow's Case, Mar. 116, pl. 3 ; and *ante*, §§ 182, 183.

[1566] *Moises* v. *Thornton*, 8 T. R. 303.

[1567] *Stone* v. *Clark*, 21 Pick. 51 ; *Gale* v. *Hays*, 3 Strobh. 452 ; *Sharp* v. *Wilkie*, 2 Humph. 434 ; *Williams* v. *Spears*, 11 Ala. 138 ; and *semble* it should be alleged that defendant intended to impute a charge of perjury. (*Wood* v. *Scott*, 13 Verm. 42 ; *Sanderson* v. *Hubbard*, 14 *Id.* 462.) It is not necessary to state what the witness testified. (*Whitaker* v. *Carter*, 4 Ired. 461.) A complaint for slander set out that in a suit before a justice, P. W. was a witness to material matter ; that defendant, in a conversation concerning said trial and concerning the plaintiff, being guilty of subornation of perjury, published, &c., the words, " P. F. swore to a lie, and you (plaintiff) hired him." It was objected to the complaint, that it did not allege that the conversation was of and concerning the testimony of P. F. on the trial. Held, after verdict, the complaint was good. (*Shimer* v. *Bronnenbury*, 18 Ind. 863.)

[1568] *Harris* v. *Purdy*, 1 Stew. 231.

had jurisdiction of the suit or proceeding; an averment that the justice then and there had jurisdiction of the action, was held sufficient without setting forth the facts which gave the jurisdiction.[1569] The plaintiff need not show that the justice was duly commissioned.[1570] A declaration which alleged that the words were spoken "whilst the plaintiff was giving testimony as a witness under the solemnities of an oath, before an acting justice of the peace,"[1571] and a declaration which alleged that the plaintiff was, at the instance of the defendant, examined on oath administered by a justice, according to law, as a witness for the defendant, were held sufficiently to allege jurisdiction.[1572] "Squire H." was held a sufficient description of P. H., esquire, a justice of the peace.[1573]

§ 322. It should be alleged that the testimony was material to the point in issue, but it is not necessary to show to what particular degree the point, in respect to which a party is charged with false swearing, was material to the issue. If it goes to prove a material circumstance or link in the chain of evidence, it is sufficient.[1574] And it has been said that an aver-

---

[1569] *Sanford* v. *Gaddis*, 13 Ill. 329.

[1570] *Pugh* v. *Neal*, 4 Jones' Law (N. C.), 367. It was held not necessary to allege either that the justice had jurisdiction or that the testimony was material. (*Dalrymple* v. *Lofton*, 2 M'Mullan, 112.) But as to the necessity of alleging jurisdiction, see *Shellenbarger* v. *Norris*, 2 Carter (Ind.), 285; *Jones* v. *Marrs*, 11 Humph. 214; *Chapman* v. *Smith*, 13 Johns. 78; *Bonner* v. *McPhail*, 31 Barb. 106; *Cannon* v. *Phillips*, 2 Sneed (Tenn.) 185.

Where the charge is that the plaintiff committed *perjury*, that implies a false swearing before a competent tribunal, and jurisdiction need not be alleged. (*Green* v. *Long*, 2 Cai. 91.) Where the charge is perjury committed in a foreign state, it must be averred that by the laws of such state perjury is an offence to which is annexed an infamous punishment. (*Sparrow* v. *Maynard*, 8 Jones' Law (N. C.), 195; and see *ante*, note 350.)

[1571] *Lewis* v. *Black*, 27 Miss. (5 Cush.) 425.

[1572] *Shellenbarger* v. *Norris*, 2 Carter (Ind.), 285.

[1573] *Call* v. *Foreman*, 5 Watts, 331; and see *ante*, note 220; "N. T., esquire, aforesaid," held sufficient description of a justice of the peace. (*Canterbury* v. *Hill*, 4 Stew. & Port. 224.)

[1574] *Hutchins* v. *Blood*, 25 Wend. 413; and see *Witcher* v. *Richmond*, 8 Humph. 473.

ment of the materiality of the evidence may be altogether omitted ;[1575] at least the absence of such an allegation will be cured by verdict.[1576] It is not necessary to allege that the justice had authority to administer the oath.[1577] But it should be alleged that the plaintiff was legally sworn.[1578] The defendant cannot show as a defence that the plaintiff was not a competent witness.[1579] The absence of allegations of jurisdiction in the justice, or materiality of the testimony, may be cured by a plea of justification,[1580] or by a verdict.[1581]

§ 323. *The Colloquium.*—Properly the colloquium or allegation of *a discourse* is the allegation that the language published was concerning the plaintiff, or concerning the plaintiff and his affairs, or concerning the plaintiff and the facts alleged as inducement. But the term colloquium is frequently employed as synonymous with inducement, or to signify the inducement and the colloquium properly so called. As heretofore stated [§ 316], it must be shown on the face of the complaint that the language was published concerning the plaintiff, and the proper mode of doing this is by a direct averment that the publication was "of and concerning the plaintiff." This

[1575] *Wetsel* v. *Lennen*, 13 Ind. 535; *Cannon* v. *Phillips*, 2 Sneed, 185.

[1576] *Niven* v. *Munn*, 13 Johns. 48. In slander for the charge of perjury, the materiality of the alleged false testimony is for the court to determine, and if left to the jury it is error. (*Steinman* v. *McWilliams*, 6. Barr, 170; *Power* v. *Price*, 12 Wend. 500; affirmed 16 Wend. 450.) Or ground for a new trial. (*Dalrymple* v. *Lofton*, 2 M'Mullan, 112.)

[1577] *Sanford* v. *Gaddis*, 13 Ill. 329; but see *Jones* v. *Marrs*, 11 Humph. 214.

[1578] *Sanderson* v. *Hubbard*, 14 Verm. 462.

[1579] *Harris* v. *Purdy*, 1 Stew. 231. A declaration in slander, charging the words spoken as follows: "He (meaning plaintiff) has sworn falsely," &c., "against me (meaning defendant), and *he* (meaning defendant) could prove it," was held bad after verdict; by "he" in the latter clause, as pleaded, the defendant could not have meant himself. (*Bowdish* v. *Peckham*, 1 Chip. 146.) But see post, note 1705.

[1580] *Witcher* v. *Richmond*, 8 Humph. 473; *Attebury* v. *Powell*, 29 Miss. (8 Jones) 429; *Saunderson* v. *Hubbard*, 14 Verm. 462.

[1581] *Palmer* v. *Hunter*, 8 Mis. 512; *Morgan* v. *Livingston*, 2 Rich. 573; *Niven* v. *Munn*, 13 Johns. 48; but see *Wood* v. *Scott*, 13 Verm. 42.

averment may, however, be supplied by any equivalent allegation, and may be altogether dispensed with where it appears
otherwise with sufficient certainty on the face of the complaint,
that the publication was in fact concerning the plaintiff.[1522]
And although, in actions for slander and libel, inducement may
be necessary to explain the matter alleged to be libellous, it is
enough to state in the declaration that the publication was " of
and concerning " the plaintiff, without also stating that it was

[1522] It is sufficient to aver substantially that the words were spoken of plaintiff; an express averment of the fact is not necessary. (*Brown* v. *Lamberton*, 2
Binn. 34; *Brashen* v. *Shepherd*, Ky. Dec. 294; *Nestle* v. *Van Slyke*, 2 Hill, 282;
but see *Titus* v. *Follett*, 2 Hill, 318; *Tyler* v. *Tillottson*, 2 Hill, 508; *Cave* v.
Shelor, 2 Munf. 193; *Harper* v. *Delp*, 3 Ind. 225; *Rex* v. *Marsden*, 4 M. & S.
164; *Bakhein* v. *Hildreth*, 14 Gray (Mass.) 221.) On demurrer, where the words
did not name the plaintiff, the omission of a colloquium of and concerning the
plaintiff was held fatal, and not aided by the innuendoes. (*Milligan* v. *Thorn*, 6
Wend. 412; and see *Church* v. *Bridgman*, 6 Miss. 190.) Nor by the verdict, the
language being in the third person. (*Sayre* v. *Jewett*, 12 Wend. 135.) If there
be a colloquium sufficient to point the application of the words to the plaintiff, if
spoken maliciously, he must have judgment. (*Lindsey* v. *Smith*, 7 Johns. 359.)
Where actionable words are spoken to a plaintiff, it is sufficient to allege a discourse with him, without an averment that the words were concerning the plaintiff; but where the words are in the third person, as, " He is a thief," there, although a discourse of the plaintiff is alleged, it must also be alleged that the
words were concerning the plaintiff. And it is not sufficient in such a case to
connect the words with the plaintiff by an innuendo. (1 Stark. Sland. 364.)
But where a discourse of the plaintiff is laid, and there is an innuendo of the
plaintiff, it seems that the want of a direct averment that the words were concerning the plaintiff must be pointed out by special demurrer [motion to make
certain]; but if no discourse concerning the plaintiff is alleged, then the want of
an allegation that the words concerned him would be a defect in substance. (*Id.*;
Skutt v. *Hawkins*, 1 Rolle R. 241.) If a plaintiff has omitted, in his declaration,
to state that the libel was spoken of himself, he may supply the same by parol
evidence. (*Newbraugh* v. *Curry*, Wright, 511.) Where A. says of B. & C., " you
have committed such an offence," though B. & C. may have separate actions, the
words must be alleged to have been spoken of both. (Cro. Car. 512.) Where
the declaration states a colloquium with G., of and concerning the children of G.,
and of and concerning C., one of the children of G., and the plaintiff in the suit,
in particular, and that the defendant said, " Your children are thieves, and I can
prove it," the colloquium conclusively points the words, and designates the plaintiff as one of the children intended. And a colloquium is sufficient to give application to words still more indefinite. (*Gidney* v. *Blake*, 11 Johns. 54; but see
what is said 1 Stark. Sland. 385.)

" of and concerning " such matter,[1583] or of and concerning the plaintiff in the occupation alleged in the inducement.[1584] Where the declaration alleged that the defendant published a libel of and concerning the plaintiff, containing, &c., the false libellous matters following (without saying of and concerning the plaintiff); held, in error, that for want of an averment that the particular matter was of and concerning the plaintiff, and there being no innuendo that such matter related to him, the declaration was bad, and a *venire de novo* was awarded.[1585] A declaration which alleged that the plaintiffs were traders under the firm of T. & Co., and averring that, in a discourse of and concerning them, their circumstances and business, the defendant said, " T. & Co. are down," &c., without repeating that this was said of and concerning the plaintiffs, was held bad on special demurrer, although good in substance.[1586]

§ 324. A publication by the defendant must be alleged. The publication need not be set forth in any technical form of words.[1587] But it must be alleged positively, and not by way of recital ;[1588] and, therefore, a declaration which commenced, " For that *whereas* " the defendant intending, &c., spoke, &c., was held bad on special demurrer.[1589] In slander for English words it should be alleged that the defendant spoke the words in the presence and hearing of *divers* persons,[1590] or of certain

[1583] *O'Brien* v. *Clement*, 4 D. & L. 563; *Gutsole* v. *Mathers*, 1 M. & W. 495; *Shimer* v. *Bronnenburg*, 18 Ind. 363.
[1584] *Wakley* v. *Healey*, 18 Law Jour. Rep. 241, C. P.; *contra*, see *Barnes* v. *Trundy*, 31 Maine (1 Red.), 321.
[1585] *Clement* v. *Fisher*, 7 B. & Cr. 459; 1 M. & Ry. 281.
[1586] *Titus* v. *Follett*, 2 Hill, 318; and see *Taylor* v. *The State*, 4 Geo, 14.
[1587] *Baldwin* v. *Elphinstone*, 2 W. Black. 1037, note 104, *ante*. It was held sufficient to allege that the defendant was the proprietor of the newspaper in which the alleged libel was published. (*Hunt* v. *Bennett*, 19 N. Y. 173.)
[1588] *Donage* v. *Rankin*, 4 Munf. 261.
[1589] *Brown* v. *Thurlow*, 4 D. & L. 301; 16 M. & W. 36; *Coffin* v. *Coffin*, 3 Mass. 358; *Houghton* v. *Davenport*, 23 Pick. 235.
[1590] To allege a speaking merely, is not sufficient. (Style, 70; 1 Stark. Sland. 360.) In Indiana, by statute it is sufficient merely to allege the speaking. (*Girard* v. *Risk*, 11 Ind. 156.)

persons, naming them,[1591] or of certain persons named and
divers others, not naming the others.[1592] Published *ex vi termini*, imports a speaking in the presence and hearing of a
third party;[1593] and, therefore, to allege that the defendant
published the words, is sufficient without averring specially
the presence of others.[1594] And an allegation that the words
were spoken would be sufficient, without stating the presence
of any third person, if accompanied by any averment which
necessarily implies a publication to a third person,—as that the
defendant *palim et publicé promulgant de querente*.[1595] In the
case of English words, it is not necessary to allege that the
persons present either heard or understood what was said; for
until the contrary is made to appear, it will be intended that
those present both heard and understood the words; but in the
case of a publication of foreign words, it must be alleged that
the persons present understood them.[1596]

§ 325. Where the publication was made in writing, *published* is the proper and technical term by which to allege the
publication, and this without reference to the precise degree in which the defendant was instrumental to the publication.[1597] But any equivalent allegation will suffice. Where it
was alleged that the defendant printed and caused to be printed
in the St. James' Chronicle, that was held sufficient,[1598] and so
was the allegation that the defendant "did publish *and* cause and
procure to be published," a certain libel addressed to the plaintiff,[1599] but where the allegation was that the defendant *scripsit*,

[1591] *Burbank* v. *Horn*, 39 Maine (4 Heath), 233; *ante*, note 106.
[1592] *Bradshaw* v. *Perdue*, 12 Geo. 510; *Ware* v. *Cartledge*, 24 Ala. 622.
[1593] *Duel* v. *Agan*, 1 Code Rep. 134; note 106, *ante*.
[1594] *Barton* v. *Barton*, 3 Iowa, 316.
[1595] *Taylor* v. *How*, Cro. Eliz. 861. Prior to the statute 2d Geo. II. ch. 14,
pleadings in the courts of England were in Latin, which will explain why the
quotations from the pleadings in the early decisions are in Latin.
[1596] *Wormuth* v. *Cramer*, 3 Wend. 394; 1 Stark. Slan. 360; Cro. Eliz. 396, 480,
865; Cro. Jac. 39; Cro. Car. 199; Noy, 67; Golds. 119; *Zerg* v. *Ort*, 3 Chandler,
26; and see *ante*, notes 97, 98.
[1597] *Lamb's Case*, 9 Rep.; 1 Stark. Sland. 359.
[1598] *Baldwin* v. *Elphinstone*, 2 W. Black. 1037.
[1599] *Waisted* v. *Holman*, 2 Hall, 172. But to allege that defendant composed

fecit, et publicavit seu scribi fecit et publicari causavit, it was
held to be insufficient, and judgment was arrested on account
of the uncertainty of the disjunctive charge.[1600] To allege that
the defendant is proprietor of a certain newspaper named, and
that the libel was published in such paper, was held a sufficient
averment of a publication by the defendant.[1601] But to allege
that defendant sent a letter to plaintiff which was received and
read by him, does not show a sufficient publication.[1602] If a defamatory writing is shown to have been put in a situation in
which it might have been read, it is unnecessary to allege that
it was in fact seen or read.[1603]

§ 326. The place of publication may be alleged with a *videl-
icet.*[1604] It is not material and need not be proved as laid.[1605]

§ 327. The time of speaking the words is not material.[1606]
In one case, it was held that the words might be laid with a
continuando,[1607] but this was denied on the ground that words
spoken at one time constitute one cause of action, and words
spoken at another time constitute another cause of action.[1608]
The *continuando,* however, was held to be surplusage, and not
ground for special demurrer.[1609] An allegation, "and further,
that defendant, on divers days and times, between that day and
the commencement of this action, spoke the same words,"
was struck out as redundant.[1610]

---

wrote, and delivered a certain libel addressed to the plaintiff, was held insufficient. (*Id.*)

[1600] *Rex* v. *Brereton,* 8 Mod. 328.

[1601] *Hunt* v. *Bennett,* 4 E. D. Smith, 647, affirmed 19 N. Y. 193.

[1602] *Lyle* v. *Clason,* 1 Cai. 581.

[1603] *Giles* v. *The State,* 6 Geo. 276 ; note 103, *ante.*

[1604] *Burbank* v. *Horn,* 39 Maine (4 Heath), 233.

[1605] *Jeffries* v. *Duncombe,* 11 East, 226 ; *ante,* § 110.

[1606] *Potter* v. *Thompson,* 22 Barb. 87; *Hosley* v. *Brooks,* 20 Ill. 115; but
see *ante,* § 109.

[1607] *Burbank* v. *Horn,* 39 Maine (4 Heath), 233.

[1608] *Swinney* v. *Nave,* 22 Ind. 178; *ante,* § 113.

[1609] *Cummins* v. *Butler,* 3 Blackf. 190.

[1610] *Gray* v. *Nellis,* 6 How. Pra. Rep. 290.

§ 328. It should appear on the face of the complaint by some appropriate averment, that the publication was made *without legal excuse.* *Ex malitia* in its legal sense, imports a publication that is false, and made without legal excuse;[1611] an averment that the publication was made with malice or maliciously has ever been and is still the customary averment; but any form of words from which malice [absence of excuse] can be inferred, as that the publication was made falsely or wrongfully, will suffice.[1612] Neither the term malice,[1613] nor falsely, nor wrongfully, is essential,[1614] at least after verdict.[1615] A declaration which charged the publication to be "malicious, injurious, and unlawful," was held sufficient.[1616] Where it appeared on the face of the declaration that the defamatory matter was published in an affidavit in a proceeding in an action, and was pertinent to the matter in hand, held that the declaration was demurrable, because, notwithstanding the allegation that the publication was false and malicious, it appeared on the face of the declaration that the publication was a privileged one.[1617]

§ 329. The complaint should set out, and purport to set out, the very words published.[1618] The proper term by which

---

[1611] *Johnson* v. *Sutton,* 1 T. R. 489 ; Cro. Car. 271.

[1612] Moor, 459; Owen, 451 ; Noy, 35 ; *ante,* note 71.

[1613] *Opdyke* v. *Weed,* 18 Abb. Pra. Rep. 223 ; *Viele* v. *Gray,* 10 Id. 6; *ante,* note 86.

[1614] Style, 392. An allegation that the publication was a libel, held equivalent to an allegation that it was false and malicious. (*Hunt* v. *Bennett,* 19 N. Y. 176.)

[1615] 2 Saund. 242; *White* v. *Nichols,* 3 How. U. S. Rep. 266, 284.

[1616] *Rowe* v. *Roach,* 1 Man. & Sel. 304.

[1617] *Garr* v. *Selden,* 4 N. Y. 91.

[1618] *Finnerty* v. *Barker,* 7 N. Y. Legal Observer, 317; *Sullivan* v. *White,* 6 Irish Law Rep. 40; *Whitaker* v. *Freeman,* 1 Dev. 271; *Lee* v. *Kane,* 6 Gray (Mass.), 495; *Taylor* v. *Moran,* 4 Met. (Ky.) 127; *Commonwealth* v. *Wright,* 1 Cush. 46. A new trial was granted because the words published were not set forth in the complaint literally. (*Walsh* v. *The State,* 2 McCord, 248.) Certain States provide by statute what words shall be actionable. (§ 153.) It is held that acts declaring what words are actionable are public laws, of which courts are bound to take notice, and the complaint or declaration need not recite or refer to the stat-

to indicate that the very words are set forth is *tenor*.[1619] "Tenor and effect" is now held to be sufficient, but there is a decision to the contrary.[1620] It is not sufficient to allege that words were published to the effect following,[1621] or in substance as follows,[1622] or purporting,[1623] or that the words were in substance as follows, or according to the purport and effect following, or in manner and form following,[1624] or that the words were of a certain tenor,

---

ute (*Sanford* v. *Gaddis*, 13 Ill. 329; *Elam* v. *Badger*, 23 Ill. 498), except by alleging that the words were published against the form of the statute in such case provided (*Terry* v. *Bright*, 4 Md. 430); but the absence of this allegation will be cured by verdict. (*Wilcox* v. *Webb*, 1 Blackf. 258.) As to declaring upon the statutes of Virginia and Georgia, see *Moseley* v. *Moss*, 6 Gratt. 534; *Holcombe* v. *Roberts*, 19 Geo. 588; *Hanks* v. *Patton*, 18 Geo. 52.

[1619] *Commonwealth* v. *Wright*, 1 Cush. 46; *Wright* v. *Clements*, 3 B. & Ald. 503. To allege "a certain receipt for money, as follows, that is to say," was held equivalent to an allegation "according to the tenor following, or in the words and figures following, that is to say." (*Rex* v. *Powell*, 1 Leach C. C. 77, 4th ed.; 2 East P. C. 976; 2 Wm. Black. R. 787.) In a declaration for slander of plaintiff in his trade, a count alleging that the defendant, in a certain discourse in the presence and hearing of divers subjects, falsely and maliciously charged the plaintiff of being in insolvent circumstances, and stating special damage, but without setting out the words, was held ill. (*Cook* v. *Cox*, 3 M. & S. 110.)

[1620] *Newton* v. *Stubbs*, 3 Mod. 71; 2 Show. 435.

[1621] *Ford* v. *Bennett*, 1 Ld. Raym. 415; *Rex* v. *Bear*, 2 Salk. 417.

[1622] *Wright* v. *Clements*, 3 B. & Ald. 503. Where a declaration for a libel sets out a publication which refers to a previous publication, but, unless by reference to the language of the previous publication, contains no libel, such previous publication must be considered as incorporated in the publication complained of, and must appear in the declaration to be set out *verbatim*, and not merely in substance. Therefore judgment was arrested as to the second count of a declaration, which, after reciting that defendant published a statement "*in substance* as follows," setting out the publication charged in the first count, charged that defendant afterwards published, of and concerning plaintiff, and of and concerning the first publication, a statement that the copper tank was fitted up in a schooner belonging to plaintiff. (*Solomon* v. *Lawson*, 8 Q. B. 823.)

[1623] *Wood* v. *Brown*, 6 Taunt. 169; and see *Cook* v. *Cox*, 1 M. & S. 110, alleging the speaking of certain words, or words of the same import, was held good after verdict. (*Bell* v. *Bugg*, 4 Mumf. 260.)

[1624] *Bagley* v. *Johnston*, 4 Rich. 22; *Watson* v. *Music*, 2 Mis. 29; *Zeig* v. *Ort*, 3 Chand. (Wis.) 26; *Bassett* v. *Spofford*, 11 N. Hamp. 127; *Churchill* v. *Kimball*, 3 Ham. 409; *Rex* v. *May*, 1 Doug. 193. A count in slander stating that defendant charged plaintiff with the crime of forgery, held bad (*Fundt* v. *Yundt*, 12 S. & R.

import, and effect.[1625] Nor are quotation marks sufficient to indicate that the exact words are set forth.[1626] Where the defamation consists in the adoption of words spoken by another, the declaration must set forth the words with the same particularity as though the action were against that other.[1627]

§ 330. Where the words were published in a foreign language, the foreign words must be set forth,[1628] together with a translation into English. To set forth the foreign words alone, or the translation alone would not be sufficient.[1629] The omission to set forth a translation may be rectified by an amendment.[1630] On a general denial, the plaintiff must prove the correctness of the translation, but its correctness is admitted by a demurrer.[1631] To allege a publication of English words and prove a publica-

---

427); and so of perjury (*Ward* v. *Clark*, 2 Johns. 10); and where a count alleged that defendant charged plaintiff with the crime of theft, without setting out the exact words, it was held bad after verdict. · (*Parsons* v. *Bellows*, 6 N. Hamp. 289.) In Massachusetts, even before the statute of 1852, it was held sufficient to allege that defendant accused plaintiff of a certain crime, as stealing, without setting out the words spoken (*Pond* v. *Hartwell*, 17 Pick. 269; *Allen* v. *Perkins*, Id. 309; *Gardner* v. *Dyer*, 5 Gray, 22; *Nye* v. *Otis*, 8 Mass. 122; *Whiting* v. *Smith*, 13 Pick. 364; *Gay* v. *Homer*, 13 Pick. 535: and see *Kennedy* v. *Lowry*, 1 Binn. 393; *Grubs* v. *Keyser*, 2 McCord, 305); but in that State the defendant is entitled to a bill of particulars setting forth the exact words. (See *Payson* v. *Macomber*, 3 Allen, 71.) A count in slander alleging that defendant wrongfully and without reasonable cause "imposed the crime of felony" upon the plaintiff, was held good after verdict. (*Davis* v. *Noakes*, 1 Stark. 377; *Hill* v. *Miles*, 9 N. Hamp. 9.) In actions for malicious prosecution, it is sufficient to declare *quod crimen felonice imposuit*, without stating the words. (*Pippet* v. *Hearn*, 5 B. & Ald. 634; *Blizard* v. *Kelly*, 2 B. & C. 283; *Davis* v. *Noake*, 6 M. & S. 33.)

[1625] *Forsyth* v. *Edmiston*, 5 Duer, 653.
[1626] *Commonwealth* v. *Wright*, 1 Cush. 46.
[1627] *Blessing* v. *Davis*, 24 Wend. 100.
[1628] *Zenobia* v. *Axtell*, 6 T. R. 162.
[1629] *Wormouth* v. *Cramer*, 3 Wend. 394; *Setterman* v. *Ritz*, 3 Sandf. 734; *Zeig* v. *Ort*, 3 Chand. 26; *Kerschbaugher* v. *Slusser*, 12 Ind. 453; *Hickley* v. *Grosjean*, 6 Blackf. 351; *Rehauser* v. *Schwerger*, 3 Watts, 28.
[1630] *Zenobia* v. *Axtell*, 6 T. R. 162; *Rehauser* v. *Schwerger*, 3 Watts, 28; *Jenkins* v. *Phillips*, 9 C. & P. 766. An amendment was allowed by inserting the foreign words. (*Debouz* v. *Lehind*, 1 Code Rep. N. S. 235.) See *Variance*.
[1631] *Hickley* v. *Grosjean*, 6 Blackf. 351.

tion of words in another tongue is a variance,[1632] and cause for a nonsuit.[1633]

§ 331. The object, or one of the objects, of obliging a plaintiff to set forth in his complaint the very words complained against, is, that the defendant may, if he desires it, by demurring, have the benefit of taking the opinion of the court upon the actionable quality of the words.[1634]

§ 332. One exception to the rule now under consideration is said to be, when the words published are so obscene as to render it improper that they should appear upon the record, and in such case the statement of the words may be omitted altogether, and a description substituted; but the reason for not setting forth the exact words must appear by proper averments on the face of the complaint.[1635]

§ 333. The omission to set forth in the declaration the very words published is a variance, and in the practice at common law the omission was not cured by verdict, and might be taken advantage of by motion in arrest of judgment.[1636] The degree of certainty with which the defamation must be set forth depends upon the subject-matter. Where the defamation consists mainly in postures and movements, the use of language somewhat general is unavoidable; and where a declaration alleged, that the defendant published of and concerning a certain court-martial, and of and concerning the plaintiff as a member thereof, a defamatory libel and caricature, consisting of a picture representing and pointing out the court-martial, and the plaintiff as a member thereof, by their position and certain gro-

---

[1632] *Keenholts* v. *Becker*, 3 Denio, 346; *Kerschbaugher* v. *Slusser*, 12 Ind. 453.

[1633] *Zenobia* v *Axtell*, 6 T. R. 162; *Zeig* v *Ort*, 3 Chand. 26.

[1634] *Wood* v. *Brown*, 6 Taunt. 169.

[1635] *Commonwealth* v. *Tarbox*, 1 Cush. 46; *Commonwealth* v. *Holmes*, 17 Mass. 336. Indecent words tending only to aggravate the damages need not be repeated in the declaration. (*Stevens* v. *Handley*, Wright, 121.)

[1636] *Gutsole* v. *Mathers*, 1 M. & W. 495; *Wright* v. *Clements*, 3 B. & A. 508. And see *Variance*.

tesque resemblances, &c., it was held, after verdict, to be averred with sufficient certainty that the plaintiff was specifically and individually libelled.[1637]

§ 334. The rule now under consideration does not render it necessary to set forth the whole of the matter published : it is sufficient to set forth the particular passages complained of, provided they are divisible from and their meaning is not affected by the other and omitted passages.[1638] It is sufficient to set out the words which are material, and additional words, which do not diminish nor alter the sense of the words truly alleged, may be omitted.[1639] But enough must be set forth to show the sense and connection in which words set forth were used; otherwise there will be a variance, even if the precise words laid are proved to have been spoken.[1640] Where several passages are extracted from the same publication, care should be taken to show that such is the case, as by prefacing the first extract with the allegation, in a certain part of which said libel there was and is contained, &c., and by prefacing the subsequent extracts with the allegation, and in a certain other part of which said libel there was and is contained, &c.[1641] But unless the insertion of the whole matter published would be oppressive and embarrassing, there is no objection to setting forth the whole of the matter published. Thus, where in slander the words set

---

[1637] *Ellis* v. *Kimball*, 16 Pick. 132. Judgment was arrested in an action for slander respecting a bribe, because the charge did not specify to whom the money was given. (*Purdy* v. *Stacey*, 5 Burr. 2698.) A declaration in slander for charging the plaintiff with larceny, held good after verdict, although it did not set forth the name of the owner of the property alleged to have been stolen by plaintiff. (*Thompson* v. *Barkley*, 27 Penn. St. R. 263.) It is not necessary to set forth the imputation of an offence with the same particularity as in an indictment. (Id.; *Niven* v. *Munn*, 13 Johns. 48.)

[1638] *Culver* v. *Van Anden*, 4 Abb. Pra. Rep. 375; *Rex* v. *Brereton*, 8 Mod. 329; *Sidman* v. *Mayo*, 1 Rolle R. 429.

[1639] *Spencer* v. *McMasters*, 16 Ill. 405; *Weir* v. *Hoss*, 6 Ala. 881; *Buckingham* v. *Murray*, 2 Car. & P. 46.

[1640] *Edgerly* v. *Swain*, 32 N. Hamp. 478.

[1641] *Tabert* v. *Tipper*, 1 Camp. 350; *Cooke* v. *Hughes*, 1 Ry. & M. 112.

out were, "*Your wife is a damned Irish woman, and has got the palsy, and your son is insane*, and you are a damned thief," the court, on motion, refused to strike out as redundant the words in *italic*.[162] In an unreported case in New York, in which the plaintiff set out, without innuendoes, the whole of the publication [nearly an entire column in a newspaper], on defendant's motion an order was made requiring the plaintiff to specify the particular passages on which he relied as defamatory.

§ 335. It is an elementary rule of pleading that whatever is alleged must be alleged with certainty; and one of the means of ensuring certainty in a complaint for slander or libel is an *innuendo*.[163] Among the attempts to define an innuendo and explain its function are the following: The office of an innuendo is to aver the meaning of the language published.[164] An innuendo means nothing more than the words "*id est*," "scilicet," or "*meaning*" or "*aforesaid*," as explanatory of a matter sufficiently expressed before.[165] It is in the nature of a *prædict*. It may serve for an explanation, to point a meaning where

[162] *Deyo* v. *Brundage*, 18 How. Pra. Rep. 221.

[163] *Rodeburgh* v. *Hollingsworth*, 6 Ind. 339.

[164] *Watson* v. *Nicholas*, 6 Humph. 174. The office of the innuendo is to explain doubtful words or phrases, and annex to them their proper meaning. It cannot extend their sense beyond their usual and natural import, unless something is put upon the record by way of introductory matter with which they can be connected. In such case, words which are equivocal or ambiguous, or fall short, in their natural sense, of importing any libellous charge, may have fixed to them a meaning, certain and defamatory, extending beyond their ordinary import. (*Beardsley* v. *Tappan*, 1 Blatch. C. C. 588.) And to the like effect, see *Dorsey* v. *Whipps*, 8 Gill, 457; *Nichols* v. *Packard*, 16 Verm. 83; *Patterson* v. *Edwards*, 2 Gilman, 720; *Andrews* v. *Woodmansee*, 15 Wend. 232; *Taylor* v. *Kneeland*, 1 Douglass, 67; *Gosling* v. *Morgan*, 32 Penn. St. R. 273; *The State* v. *Henderson*, 1 Richardson, 179; *Caverley* v. *Caverley*, 3 Up. Can. Rep. 338, O. S.; *Van Vechten* v. *Hopkins*, 5 Johns. 211; *Caldwell* v. *Abbey*, Hardin, 529; *McCuen* v. *Ludlam*, 2 Harr. 12; *Beswick* v. *Chappel*, 8 B. Mon. 486; *Benaway* v. *Coyne*, 8 Chand. (Wis.) 214; *Vaughan* v. *Havens*, 8 Johns. 109; *Gomperts* v. *Levy*, 1 Perr. & Dav. 214; *Dodge* v. *Lacy*, 2 Carter (Ind.), 212; *Cramer* v. *Noonan*, 4 Wis. 231.

[165] *Rex* v. *Horne*, 2 Cowper, 688; approved *Reg.* v. *Virrier*, 4 Per. & D. 161.

there is precedent matter, expressed or necessarily understood or known, but never to establish a new charge. It may apply what is already expressed, but cannot add to nor enlarge nor change the sense of the previous words.[1646] If the words before the innuendo do not sound in slander, no meaning produced by the innuendo will make the action maintainable, for it is not the nature of an innuendo to beget an action.[1647] An innuendo helps nothing unless the words precedent have a violent presumption of the innuendo." [1648] The business of an innuendo is by a reference to preceding matter to fix more precisely the meaning.[1649] " The office of an innuendo is to explain not to extend what has gone before, and it cannot enlarge the meaning of words, unless it be connected with some matter of fact expressly averred." [1650] The innuendo " is only a link to attach together facts already known to the court." [1651]

§ 336. An innuendo cannot perform the office of a colloquium;[1652] in other words, the want of a colloquium cannot be supplied by an innuendo.[1653] The absence of a *colloquium*, showing by extrinsic matter that the words charged are actionable, is not supplied by an innuendo attributing to those words

[1646] 1 Stark. Sland. 418; *Rex* v. *Greepe*, 2 Salk. 513; 1 L'd Raym. 256; 12 Mod. 189; 1 Saund. 243; *Van Vechten* v. *Hopkins*, 5 Johns. 220; *McClaughry* v. *Wetmore*, 6 Johns. 83; *Thomas* v. *Croswell*, 7 Johns. 271; *Weed* v. *Bibbins*, 32 Barb. 315.

[1647] *Barham* v. *Nethersole*, Yelv. 21.

[1648] *Castleman* v. *Hobbs*, Cro. Eliz. 428.

[1649] *Rex* v. *Aylett*, 1 T. R. 63.

[1650] *Patterson* v. *Edwards*, 2 Gilman, 720; *Van Vechten* v. *Hopkins*, 5 Johns. 211. The innuendo cannot introduce new matter. (*Taft* v. *Howard*, 1 Chip. 275; *Nichols* v. *Packard*, 16 Verm. 83; *Wier* v. *Hoss*, 6 Ala. 881.) Or change the ordinary meaning of language. (*Hays* v. *Mitchell*, 7 Blackf. 117.)

[1651] Cooke on Defamation, 94.

[1652] *Fitzsimmons* v. *Cutler*, 1 Aik. 33; *The State* v. *Henderson*, 1 Richardson, 179; *Lindsey* v. *Smith*, 7 Johns. 359.

[1653] *Church* v. *Bridgman*, 6 Mis. 190; *Milligan* v. *Thorn*, 6 Wend. 412; *Sayre* v. *Jewett*, 12 Wend. 135; *Hawkes* v. *Hawkey*, 8 E. R. 427; *Joralemon* v. *Pomeroy*, 2 New Jersey, 271. The words, " Thereby accusing the plaintiff of stealing," in a declaration immediately following words, alleged to have been spoken, which

a meaning which renders them actionable.[1654] Words not in themselves actionable, cannot be rendered so by an innuendo, without a prefatory averment of extrinsic facts, which makes them slanderous.[1655] If the words charged do not imply a criminal charge, subject to infamous punishment, an innuendo will

---

do not of themselves amount to a charge of larceny, without any precise *collo-quium* or averment showing such to have been the intention, are not sufficient to make the declaration good. (*Brown* v. *Brown*, 2 Shep. 317.) Where, in an action for slander, the declaration alleged that the defendant had said of the plaintiff that he had set fire to his own premises, innuendo that plaintiff had been guilty of wilfully setting fire to the premises which, whilst in his occupation, had been destroyed by fire, it was held, on motion in arrest of judgment, that the court could not after verdict presume that the jury had found that defendant meant to impute to plaintiff that he had done it unlawfully or feloniously, as well as wilfully. (*Sweetapple* v. *Jesse*, 2 Nev. & M. 36; 5 B. & Adol. 27.) In slander, the declaration stated that the plaintiff was a justice of the peace, and that the defendant, meaning to injure and expose him to prosecution for corruption, &c., in a certain discourse, &c., said of the plaintiff, in his office of justice: "L. (meaning the plaintiff) had been feed by A. W. (meaning A. W., who lately had a cause pending and determined before the plaintiff), and that he (the defendant meaning) could do nothing when the magistrate was in that way against him (the defendant meaning). After verdict, the declaration was held sufficient. (*Burtch* v. *Nickerson*, 17 Johns. 217.) Where the words in themselves were such as were usually applied to the keeper of a gambling house, and obviously imputed to the plaintiff fraudulent and dishonorable conduct; held, that the declaration might be supported, although the words might not be capable, by innuendo, of being referred to any particular malpractices. (*Digby* v. *Thomson*, 1 Nev. & M. 485.) An averment in a declaration that the defendant had spoken of and concerning the plaintiff these words: "N. [meaning the plaintiff] burnt it [meaning the store], and he [meaning the plaintiff] knew it, and I [meaning the defendant] can prove it," preceded by a *colloquium* that the words were spoken of and concerning the burning of a store owned by the defendant, and followed by an averment that the words were intended to charge the plaintiff with a felonious burning, &c.,' was held sufficient. (*Nichols* v. *Packard*, 16 Verm. 83.)

[1654] *Holton* v. *Muzzy*, 30 Verm. (1 Shaw), 365.

[1655] *Watts* v. *Greenleaf*, 2 Dev. 115. See *Brown* v. *Brown*, 2 Shep. 317; *Harris* v. *Burley*, 8 N. Hamp. 256; *Beswick* v. *Chappel*, 8 B. Monr. 486; *Dottarer* v. *Bushey*, 16 Penn. State Rep. (4 Harris), 204; *Moseley* v. *Moss*, 6 Gratt. 534; *Watson* v. *Hampton*, 2 Bibb, 319; *Hale* v. *Blandy*, 1 You. & Jar. 480. A declaration containing words which, in common understanding, would import the crime against nature, preceding them with an averment that they were intended to charge the plaintiff with that crime, and following them with an averment that they were so understood, is good. (*Goodrich* v. *Woolcot*, 3 Cow. 231; affirmed, 5 Cow. 714.)

27

not help them; but when they are used in a double sense, the plaintiff may, by an innuendo, aver the meaning with which he thinks they were spoken, and the jury may find whether they were spoken with that meaning or not.[1656] Thus, where the charge was that the plaintiff lived by swindling and robbing the public, here the language might mean either fraud or felony. The plaintiff, in his declaration, alleged that it meant to charge him with being guilty of felony and robbery. On the trial it was held to impute only a charge of fraud, and as a charge of fraud is not actionable *per se* the plaintiff failed in his action.[1657]

§ 337. An innuendo cannot *extend* the meaning of defamatory matter, unless by reference to matter of inducement. The innuendo must be supported by the inducement.[1658] Where there was no inducement, and the allegation was, " T. Barham (the plaintiff) hath burnt my barn " (meaning my barn at that time full of corn); after verdict for the plaintiff judgment was arrested, because to burn the barn was only a trespass, and the innuendo meaning a barn full of corn, extended the signification of the word *burn*, and was unwarranted.[1659] It should have been averred that the plaintiff had a barn full of corn, and that in a conversation about that barn, the defendant had spoken the words charged; then the innuendo that barn meant " my barn full of corn," would have been good. In libel, an innuendo imputing to the plaintiff larceny of plants and flowers of the defendant, and motion in arrest of judgment, on the ground that larceny could not be committed of flowers, and so

---

[1656] *Dottarer* v. *Bushey*, 16 Penn. St. Rep. (4 Harris), 204.

[1657] *Smith* v. *Carey*, 3 Camp. 461.

[1658] *Taylor* v. *Kneeland*, 1 Doug. 67; *The State* v. *Henderson*, 1 Rich. 179; *Stucker* v. *Davis*, 8 Blackf. 414. A judgment in slander will not be arrested because an innuendo enlarges the natural meaning of the words spoken. (*Shults* v. *Chambers*, 8 Watts, 300; *Solomon* v. *Lawson*, 8 Q. B. 823.) But if rejecting the innuendo as surplusage, the words are not actionable *per se*, judgment must be arrested. (*Barham* v. *Nethersole*, Yelv. 21; *Gainsford* v. *Blatchford*, 7 Price, 544; 6 Price, 36.)

[1659] *Barham* v. *Nethersole*, Yelv. 21.

the innuendo was too large; it was held sufficient after verdict, as the term *flowers* must be taken to have meant such flowers as were capable of being the subject of larceny, by being detached, or otherwise.[1660] · And where the language of the plaintiff, as clerk of a company, was, " You have done many things with the company for which you ought to be hanged, and I will have you hanged before," &c.; and there was an *innuendo* that the plaintiff had been guilty of felonies punishable by law with death by hanging, it was held sufficient, on motion in arrest of judgment.[1661] The word forsworn cannot by an innuendo alone be interpreted perjury. Thus where the allegation was, " John Holt (meaning the plaintiff) hath forsworn himself (meaning that the plaintiff had committed wilful and corrupt perjury); after verdict for the plaintiff judgment was arrested, because the innuendo was unwarranted by any inducement.[1662] In slander, the plaintiff averred that he had in due manner put in his answer on oath to a bill filed against him by the defendant in the Court of Exchequer, but did not proceed to aver any colloquium respecting that answer, with reference to which the words were spoken; and then alleged that the defendant said of him that he was forsworn, · innuendo that the plaintiff had perjured himself in what he had sworn, in his aforesaid answer to the said bill; held, that this innuendo could not, without the aid of such a colloquium, enlarge the sense of the words by referring them to the answer averred in the prefatory part of the

---

[1660] *Gardiner* v. *Williams,* 2 Cr. M. & R. 78; 3 Dowl. Pra. Cas. 796. In this case, one of the counts set forth the following passage of a letter from the defendant to one P.: " I have reason to suppose that many of the flowers of which I have been robbed are growing upon your premises " [thereby meaning that the plaintiff had been guilty of larceny, and had stolen from the defendant certain plants, roots, and flowers of the defendant, and had unlawfully disposed of them to P., and unlawfully placed them in P.'s garden]. The previous part of the letter stated that the plaintiff, whom P. had taken into his employ as a gardener, had been in the defendant's employ in the same capacity, and had been discharged for dishonesty; held, on error, that the innuendo was not too large. (1 M. & W. 245.)

[1661] *Francis* v. *Roose,* 3 M. & W. 191.

[1662] *Holt* v. *Scholefield,* 6 Term R. 691.

declaration to have been put in.[1663]   Where the declaration only
alleged the intention to impute misconduct, and that the defendant maliciously published a notice, "That any person giving information where property belonging to the plaintiff, a prisoner
in the King's Bench prison, might be found, should receive five
per cent. on the goods recovered," an innuendo that thereby the
plaintiff had been guilty of concealing his property, with a
fraudulent and unlawful intention, was held bad, on demurrer,
as enlarging the meaning of the terms used.[1664]   In an action for
a libel, the first count, after the usual prefatory averments, proceeded thus: "What possessed Lord H. (meaning thereby the
said Lord Lieutenant of Ireland), if he knew anything about
the country, or was not under the spell of vile and treacherous
influence, to make his first visit, and that carefully puffed, to
Long's, the coachmaker (meaning thereby the said plaintiff),
the other day? If mere trade was his (meaning thereby the
said Lord Lieutenant's) object, he had several respectable houses
open to him" (meaning thereby that the house and place of business of the said plaintiff were not respectable, and that the said
visit was paid thereto for political objects). *Held*, that the
innuendo did not enlarge the sense of these words, which were
fully capable of the meaning given to them.[1665]   And where the
declaration stated that the plaintiff was a trader, and employed
by the board of ordnance to relay the entrance of their office
with new asphalte, and that the defendant falsely said of him
in his said trade, and in reference to the work: "The old materials have been relaid by you in the asphalte work executed in
front of the ordnance office, and I have seen the work done."
Innuendo that the plaintiff had been guilty of dishonesty in
the conduct of his said trade, by laying down again the old
asphalte which had been before used at the entrance of the
ordnance office, instead of new asphalte, according to his contract. *Held*, on motion to arrest the judgment, that the decla-

---

[1663] *Hawkes* v. *Hawkey*, 8 East, 427.

[1664] *Gompertz* v. *Levy*, 1 Perr. & Dav. 214.

[1665] *Barrett* v. *Long*, 16 Eng. Law & Eq. R. 1; 3 Ho. of Lords Cas. 395.

ration was sufficient, and the innuendo was not too large, as it
put no new sense on the words, but only imputed intention to the
speaker.[1066] Where the words set forth were, that A was murdered, and the plaintiff was concerned in it and had a hand in
it, innuendo meaning that the plaintiff aided and assisted in
the commission of the murder, it was held to be sufficient.[1067]
The first count of a declaration charged the speaking these
words of and concerning the plaintiff: "You are a bloody
thundering thief, and all your family. I can prove you and
them to be thieves. I can prove you (meaning plaintiff) to go
down the river (meaning the river Thames) with ships of eight
feet water (meaning ships drawing eight feet water), charging
the owners for ten feet, &c.; and you (meaning plaintiff) are
obliged to move from one parish to another" (meaning thereby
that the plaintiff was guilty of dishonesty, and of charging
more for the pilotage of certain ships than he was by law entitled to do). *Held*, that the words were actionable without
any innuendo, but that those put were proper.[1068] "I have
heard that a maid of Sir J. K.'s should report, that he being
sick and she looking through a hole of the door, saw a *priest*
(innuendo *a popish priest*) give the eucharist and extreme unction;" * * * and "saw a popish priest *anoint* (innuendo
extreme unction) him." *Held*, after verdict, that *priest* was
rightly construed *popish priest*, and *anoint* was rightly construed extreme unction.[1069] Where the words charged as libellous were, "Who was deprived of a two-penny justiceship, for
malpractice in packing a jury," and they were explained, by an
innuendo, as meaning "that the plaintiff had packed a jury,
and had been guilty of malpractice in packing a jury," it was
held that the innuendo was warranted by the words charged.[1070]

[1066] *Baboneau* v. *Farrell*, 28 Eng. Law & Eq. R. 339; 15 C. B. 360; 24 Law J.
Rep. (N. S.) C. P. 9; 1 Jur. N. S. 114.
[1067] *Tenney* v. *Clements*, 10 N. Hamp. 52.
[1068] *Sempsey* v. *Levy*, 2 Jurist, 776.
[1069] *Knightly* v. *Marrow*, 3 Lev. 68.
[1070] *Mix* v. *Woodward*, 12 Conn. 262. In an action for slander, the innuendoes
"meaning to insinuate and falsely represent," "meaning to insinuate and be un-

§ 338. Where language is ambiguous, and is as susceptible of a harmless as of an injurious meaning, it is the function of an innuendo to point out *the meaning* which the plaintiff claims to be the true meaning, and the meaning upon which he relies to sustain his action. This applies whether the ambiguity be patent or latent [§ 128],[1671] and whether or not there are any facts alleged as inducement.[1672] By this means the defendant is informed of the precise charge he has to meet, and to deny or justify; but the plaintiff is subjected to the risk that if he claims for the language a meaning which is not the true one, or one which he is unable to make out satisfactorily, he may be defeated on the ground of *variance* or *failure of proof*. For when the plaintiff, by his innuendo, puts a meaning on the language published, he is bound by it, although that course may destroy his right to maintain the action; as where the alleged slander was that "Mrs. B.'s time has come around (innuendo that the usual period of parturition had arrived), and he (plaintiff) is down there getting a child away from her. He is procuring an abortion upon her." It was held that but for the interpretation the plaintiff had, by the innuendo, put on the words "her time has come around," the words were actionable, but with that meaning they were not actionable, and plaintiff was bound by the interpretation he had himself supplied.[1673] And so where the plaintiff alleged that he was treasurer and collector of certain tolls, and that defendant published of him (plaintiff), as such treasurer and collector, "You are gathering the toll for your own pocket," innuendo that

---

derstood," or "meaning and intending to represent," "that the plaintiff had stolen the money aforesaid," indicate that the defendant's charge against the plaintiff was that he had stolen the money, and therefore were sufficient. (*Hoyt* v. *Smith*, 32 Vt. (3 Shaw), 304.)

[1671] *Griffith* v. *Lewis*, 8 Q. B. 841; *Joralemon* v. *Pomeroy*, 2 New Jer. 271; *Watson* v. *Nicholas*, 6 Humph. 174. But "it is not allowable to interpret what has no need of interpretation." (*McCluskey* v. *Cromwell*, 1 Kernan, 601; and *ante*, note 129.)

[1672] *Clegg* v. *Laffer*, 3 Moo. & Sc. 727; 10 Bing. 850; *Williams* v. *Stott*, 1 C. & M. 675; *Smith* v. *Carey*, 3 Camp. 461.

[1673] *Butler* v. *Wood*, 10 How. Pra. R. 222.

plaintiff, being such treasurer and collector, was guilty of collecting tolls to improperly apply them to his own use; on the trial, the plaintiff having proved that he was treasurer only, and not collector, the variance was considered fatal, and the plaintiff was nonsuited; for the words were applicable to the plaintiff rather in his character of collector than treasurer, and the plaintiff was bound to prove the words applicable to the plaintiff in the manner which he himself had pointed out by innuendo.[1674]

§ 339. If the innuendo consists of two distinct allegations, which can be separated without destroying the sense of either of them, and one of them is and the other is not warranted by the alleged libellous matter, the latter may be rejected and the count will be valid.[1675] Therefore, in an action of slander, where the words alleged to have been spoken clearly charged the killing of a horse, and the innuendo was that the defendant intended to charge the plaintiff with arson, it was held that the innuendo might be stricken out, and the declaration sustained upon the charge of killing the horse.[1676]

§ 340. The following innuendoes were held to be proper, without any inducement to support them: Bishops, innuendo Bishops of England;[1677] Ministers, innuendo the Ministers of the King of England;[1678] The Navy, innuendo the Royal Navy of this kingdom;[1679] Chevalier, innuendo the Pretender;[1680] Little Gentleman on the other side of the water, innuendo the Prince of Wales;[1681] Door, innuendo The Outer

[1674] *Sellars* v. *Tell*, 3 B. & C. 655; see *ante*, note 1561.
[1675] *Barrett* v. *Long*, 8 Irish Law Rep. 331.
[1676] *Gage* v. *Shelton*, 3 Rich. 242.
[1677] Baxter's Case, 3 Mod. 69.
[1678] Anon. 11 Mod. 99.
[1679] Tutchin's Case, 5 State Trials, 590.
[1680] *Rex* v. *Matthews*, 9 State Trials, 682.
[1681] Anon. 11 Mod. 99.

Door ;[1682] Death, innuendo Murder ;[1683] His, innuendo the defendant ;[1684] mere man of straw, innuendo he was insolvent.[1685].

§ 341. The following innuendoes were held to be unwarranted, there being no inducement to support them : Thomaston, innuendo the State Prison situate in the town of Thomaston ;[1686] He fired his house, innuendo he voluntarily fired his house ;[1687] She is sick, innuendo she has had a child ;[1688] Tanmoney, innuendo money the produce of the sale of Tan ;[1689] She is a bad girl, innuendo a prostitute ;[1690] Public house, innuendo bawdy house ;[1691] Thou hast stolen half an acre of my corn, innuendo the corn growing upon half an acre of ground reaped and put into shocks by the defendant ;[1692] You are a regular prover under bankruptcies, innuendo that plaintiff was accustomed to prove fictitious debts under commissions of bankruptcy ;[1693] He had corn from B.'s barn, innuendo that he had stolen corn from B. ;[1694] my landlord, innuendo the plaintiff ;[1695] Your father, innuendo the plaintiff ;[1696] Thy son, innuendo the plaintiff.[1697]

[1682] *Rex* v. *Aylett*, 1 T. R. 63.

[1683] *Oldham* v. *Peake*, 2 W. Black. 959.

[1684] Muck's Case, 8 Mod. 30. Filly horse, innuendo the plaintiff's wife, his name being Hoss. (*Weir* v. *Hoss*, 6 Ala. 881 ; and see *ante*, note 132.)

[1685] *Eaton* v. *Johns*, 1 Dowl. Pra. Cas. N. S. 602.

[1686] *Emery* v. *Prescott*, 54 Maine, 389.

[1687] Anon. 11 Mod. 220.

[1688] *Smith* v. *Gafford*, 33 Ala. 108.

[1689] *Day* v. *Robinson*, 1 Ad. & Ell. 554.

[1690] *Snell* v. *Snow*, 13 Metc. 278.

[1691] *Dodge* v. *Lacey*, 2 Cart. 212; *ante*, note 184.

[1692] *Castleman* v. *Hobbs*, Cro. Eliz. 428.

[1693] *Alexander* v. *Angle*, 1 Tyrw. 9; 1 C. & J. 143; 7 Bing. 119; 4 M. & P. 870.

[1694] *Wheeler* v. *Haines*, 1 Perr. & Dav. 55; 9 Adol. & Ell. 286 n; *Harvey* v. *French*, 2 Moo. & S. 591.

[1695] Cro. Car. 40; 1 Stark. Sland. 386.

[1696] Golds. 187; Cro. Eliz. 416, 439; Cro. Car. 92, 173; Mo. 365.

[1697] *Shalmer* v. *Foster*, Cro. Car. 177; but see *Wiseman* v. *Wiseman*, Cro. Jac. 107, where it was alleged the defendant spoke the words *de præfato querente ex-*

§ 342. Evidence cannot be introduced to support or explain an innuendo.[1608] "I never knew an innuendo offered to be proved."[1609] Its truth must always appear from precedent averments.[1700] An issue cannot be raised upon the truth of an innuendo.[1701] Where an averment or colloquium introduces extrinsic matter into a complaint, that is proper subject of proof.[1702] Whether the language is *capable* of bearing the meaning assigned by the innuendo, is for the court; whether the meaning is *truly* assigned to the language, is for the jury.[1703]

§ 343. Where the language is not in itself applicable to the plaintiff, no innuendo can make it so.[1704] But where the matter published on its face appears to apply to a class of individuals, the plaintiff may by an innuendo show that the publication applied to him; that is, not extending the sense of the matter. Therefore, where the declaration alleged that the plaintiff was owner of a factory in Ireland, and charged that the defendant published of him and of the said factory a libel, imputing that, "in some of the Irish factories " (meaning thereby the plaintiff's) "cruelties were practised," though there was no allegation otherwise connecting the libel with the

---

istente fratre suo naturali, and adjudged for plaintiff. Where the description may apply to one of a class, as brothers or sons, it is unnecessary for the plaintiff to aver that he is the only brother or only son. (1 Stark. Sland. 388.) See *ante,* note 1582.

[1608] *The State* v. *Henderson,* 1 Richardson, 179; *Van Vechten* v. *Hopkins,* 5 Johns. 211; *Gidney* v. *Blake,* 11 Johns. 54; see *Johnston* v. *McDonald,* 2 Up. Can. Q. B. Rep. 209.

[1609] Pollexfen arg. Rosewell's Case, 8 State Trials, 1058, admitted by court and opposite counsel, cited and approved *Van Vechten* v. *Hopkins.* 5 Johns. 226.

[1700] *Taylor* v. *Kneeland,* 1 Douglass, 67.

[1701] *Fry* v. *Bennett,* 5 Sandf. 54; *Commonwealth* v. *Snelling,* 15 Pick. 335.

[1702] *Van Vechten* v. *Hopkins,* 5 Johns. 24.

[1703] *Blagg* v. *Sturt,* 10 Q. B. 899; *Broome* v. *Gosden,* 1 C. B. 728; *Barrett* v. *Long,* 3 Ho. of Lords Cas. 395; *Babonneau* v. *Farrell,* 15 C. B. 360; *Hemmings* v. *Gason,* 5 Irish Law Rep. 498.

[1704] See in note 182, *ante.*

plaintiff, was, after verdict, held good.[1705] . If the plaintiff is
designated by another name in the libel, his real name may be
designated by an *innuendo*.[1706]   In libel the plaintiff averred
that she was the mother of one Edward J. Barker, and that
defendant, knowing this, to defame her published "of the Bar-
kers—that was the name of his reputed father, what was his
mother's I either never knew or have forgot, but I know it
was not Barker," innuendo that plaintiff was the mother of an
illegitimate child, on demurrer held that the declaration was
good.[1707]   A count in libel, after averring that a sum of money
was standing in the Bank of England, at the time of the
death of one W. T., in his name, alleged that the defendant
published concerning the plaintiff, and concerning such money,
the following libel : " There is strong reason for believing that
a considerable sum of money was transferred from Mr. T.'s
[meaning the said W. T.'s] name in the books of the Bank of
England, by power of attorney obtained from him by undue
influence, after he became mentally incompetent to perform
any act requiring reason and understanding " [thereby meaning
that the plaintiff had transferred, or caused to be transferred,
the said money from the said W. T.'s name in the said books

[1705] *Le Fanu* v. *Malcomson*, 1 House of Lords Cas. 637 ; 13 Law Times, 61 ;
Parker v. *Raymond*, 8 Abb Pra. Rep. 843 ; *Marsden* v. *Henderson*, 22 Up. Can.
Q. B. Rep. 585.   There needs no innuendo when the words are spoken to the
plaintiff himself. (2 Rolle Rep. 243.)   "You have bewitched my mare," innuen-
do the mare of the *plaintiff* instead of the *defendant*, held good after verdict.
(*Smith* v. *Cooker*, Cro. Car. 512), but see *ante*, note 1579.

[1706] *Hays* v. *Brierley*, 4 Watts, 392.   "Mr. Deceiver" (meaning the plaintiff),
held good on writ of error. (*Fleetwood* v. *Curle*, Cro. Jac. 557.)   The following
was held sufficient to point out the plaintiff "This diabolical character, like
Polyphemus, the man-eater, has but one eye, and is well known to all persons
acquainted with the name of a certain circumnavigator," meaning to allude to the
plaintiff's name. (*J'Anson* v. *Stuart*, 1 T. R. 748.)   A declaration in slander,
which, averring a colloquium concerning the plaintiff and A., charged the defendant with saying that A. thinks it a hard matter to commit fornication with
"his niece" (meaning the plaintiff), was held sufficient, without an averment
that the plaintiff was A.'s niece. (*Miller* v. *Parish*, 8 Pick. 384.)

[1707] *Anderson* v. *Stewart*, 8 Up. Can. Q. B. Rep. 243 ; and see *ante*, note 1697.

of the said bank, by means of a power of attorney obtained by him from the said W. T., by undue influence exercised by him over the said W. T., at a time when the said W. T. had become and was mentally incompetent to give a power of attorney, and to perform any act requiring reason and understanding]. Held, after verdict for plaintiff, on motion in arrest of judgment, that the libel was sufficiently shown to point to the plaintiff.[1708] Averments were introduced into the declaration, of words spoken by the defendant imputing dishonesty to L., the name of L. being followed by the innuendo, " meaning the plaintiff's agent and clerk," but there was nothing else in the declaration showing any connection between L. and the plaintiffs. Held, that in the absence of a direct averment connecting L. with the plaintiffs or their business, the words alleged to have been spoken concerning him were not actionable in favor of the plaintiffs.[1709] Where the alleged libel consisted of a passage in a newspaper warning certain persons to avoid the traps laid for them by desperate adventurers, innuendo the plaintiff amongst others, was *after verdict* held sufficiently to point out the plaintiff.[1710] Where there was no colloquium that the defamatory matter was concerning the justices of Suffolk, and it did not appear on the face of the alleged libel that it applied to such justices, it was held that the defamatory matter could not be connected with or applied to such justices by means of an innuendo.[1711]

§ 344. If a complaint is sufficient without the innuendo, the innuendo may be rejected as surplusage;[1712] the innuendo may

---

[1708] *Turner* v. *Merryweather*, 13 Jur. 683; 18 Law Jour. C. P. 155; 12 Law Times, 474.

[1709] *Smith* v. *Hollister*, 32 Verm. (3 Shaw) 695.

[1710] *Wakley* v. *Healey*, 18 Law Jour. 241, C. P.

[1711] *Rex* v. *Alderton*, Sayre, 280; and, to the like effect, *Hawkes* v. *Hawkey*, 8 East, 427; *Savage* v. *Robery*, Cowper, 680.

[1712] *Commonwealth* v. *Snelling*, 15 Pick. 335; *Mosely* v. *Moss*, 6 Grattan, 534; *Cooper* v. *Greeley*, 1 Denio, 360; *Harvey* v, *French*, 1 Cr. & M. 1, affirmed 2 Mo. & Sc. 591; *Gage* v. *Shelton*, 2 Rich. 242; *Giles* v. *The State*, 6 Geo. 276.

always be rejected when it merely introduces matter not necessary to support the action,[1713] or when it is incongruous,[1714] or
too broad;[1715] an innuendo that the attorney-general spoken of
meant the attorney-general for the County Palatine of Chester
was so rejected.[1716]

§ 345. Special damages or those damages which are not
the necessary consequence of the language complained of
[§§ 197 to 202], must be specially alleged in the complaint, or
the plaintiff will not be allowed on the trial to go into evidence
to prove such damages.[1717] Where the language is actionable
per se, special damage need not be alleged;[1718] but if the language is not actionable *per se*, special damage must be alleged.
Allegations of special damages are not traversable. They are
inserted in the complaint to apprise the defendant of what he
must be prepared to rebut on the trial.[1719] Where the declaration set forth that the plaintiff was a ship-master, the words defaming him as such, and that, by reason of the same, "certain

---

[1713] *Thomas* v. *Croswell*, 7 Johns. 264; *Croswell* v. *Weed*, 25 Wend. 621; *Carter* v. *Andrews*, 16 Pick. 1; *Carroll* v. *White*, 33 Barb. 621; *Hudson* v. *Garner*, 22
Miss. (1 Jones) 423; *Rodebaugh* v. *Hollingsworth*, 6 Ind. 839.

[1714] *Gardiner* v. *Williams*, 2 Cr. M. & R. 78; 3 Dowl. Pra. Cas. 796.

[1715] *Benaway* v. *Coyne*, 3 Chand. (Wis.) 214; *Barrett* v. *Long*, 16 Eng. Law &
Eq. R. 1; 3 Ho. of Lords Cas. 395.

[1716] *Roberts* v. *Camden*, 9 East, 93; and see *Day* v. *Robinson*, 4 Nev. & M. 841;
West v. *Smith*, 4 Dowl. 703.

[1717] *Squier* v. *Gould*, 14 Wend. 159; *Strang* v. *Whitehead*, 12 *Id.* 64; *Birch* v.
Benton, 26 Miss. (5 Jones) 155; *Johnson* v. *Robertson*, 8 Porter, 486; *Barnes* v.
Trundy, 31 Maine, (1 Red.) 321; *Bostwick* v. *Nicholson*, Kirby, 65; *Bostwick* v.
Hawley, *Ib.* 290; *Shipman* v. *Burrows*, 1 Hall, 399; *Harcourt* v. *Harrison*, *Ib.*
474; *Geare* v. *Britton*, Bull. N. P. 7; *Wilson* v. *Runyon*, Wright, 651. Nor to give
evidence of a general loss of reputation. (*Herrick* v. *Lapham*, 10 Johns. 281.) A
complaint for words in writing charging insanity need not allege special damage.
(*Perkins* v. *Mitchell*, 31 Barb. 461.) So in an action by one of several partners.
(*Robinson* v. *Marchant*, 7 Q. B. 918.)

[1718] *Hicks* v. *Walker*, 2 Greene (Iowa) 440.

[1719] *Malony* v. *Dows*, 15 How. Pra. R. 265.

insurance companies in the city of New York refused to insure any vessel commanded by him, or any goods laden on board any vessel by him commanded;" *Held*, that the allegation was too general, and that proof could not be given under it of the refusal of a particular company to insure the plaintiff's vessel.[1720] Where the allegation was, that certain persons, naming them, who would otherwise have employed plaintiff, refused so to do; *Held*, that the allegation was not supported by evidence that certain other persons would have recommended plaintiff to the persons named in the declaration, and that if the plaintiff had been so recommended, the persons named in the declaration would have employed him; the not employing being not on account of the slander, but of the non-recommendation.[1721] In an action of slander imputing incontinence to the plaintiff, it was held enough to state, that the plaintiff was occasionally employed to preach to a dissenting congregation at a certain licensed chapel, from which he derived considerable profit, and that, by reason of the scandal, " persons frequenting the chapel had refused to permit him to preach there, and had discontinued the emoluments which they would otherwise have given him," without saying who those persons were, or by what authority they had excluded him, or that he was a preacher duly qualified according to statute (10 Anne, c. 2);[1722] and in an action for slander for words spoken of the plaintiff in his trade or business, with a general allegation of loss of business, it is competent to the plaintiff to prove, and the jury to assess damages for a general loss or decrease of trade, although the declaration alleges the loss of particular customers as special damage, which is not proved.[1723] As a general rule the customers should be

---

[1720] *Shipman* v, *Burrows*, 1 Hall, 399.

[1721] *Strong* v. *Foreman*, 2 C. & P. 592.

[1722] *Hartley* v. *Herring*, 8 T. R. 130.

[1723] *Evans* v. *Harries*, 38 Eng. Law & Eq. R. 347; 1 Hurl. & Nor. 251. The plaintiff may aver a general diminution of business, or particular instances of damage; in the latter case the names of the customers lost should be given. (*Hamilton* v. *Walters*, 4 Up. Can. Rep. 24, O. S.)

named,[1724] but this is not always necessary.[1725]   The omission of
the names of the customers lost, amounts only to a want of defi-
niteness, and in New York is to be taken advantage of by a
motion to make definite and certain; not by demurrer.[1726]

§ 346. Where loss of certain customers, naming them, is alleged, the best evidence in support of such allegation is the testimony of the persons named ; [1727] and so where it is alleged that
certain persons, naming them, refused to employ the plaintiff,
the best evidence of such refusal is the testimony of the persons
named.[1728]   In an action for words not actionable *per se*, the declaration alleged for special damage, that, in consequence of the
speaking of the words, four of plaintiff's customers ceased to deal
with him.   Three of those persons proved only that they ceased
to deal with plaintiff in consequence of reports they had heard
in the neighborhood ; but the fourth proved the speaking by
the defendant of words substantially as charged, and stated that
he did not deal with plaintiff afterwards.   *Held*, some evidence
of special damage.[1729]

§ 347. A plaintiff may unite in one complaint a cause of
action for slander with a cause of action for libel, or for malicious prosecution,[1730] or slander of title.[1731]   A cause of action in

---

[1724] Mayne on Damages, 278, 817; *Feise* v. *Linder*, 3 B. & P. 372. In New
York it was held that a general averment of loss of customers is not a sufficient
allegation of special damages, and that no proof of loss of customers can be given
under such an allegation. (*Tobias* v. *Harland*, 4 Wend. 537 ; and see *Hallck* v.
Miller, 2 Barb. 630.) The loss of a customer is special damage, although if the
dealing had taken place the plaintiff would have lost by it. (*Storey* v. *Challands*, 8
C. & P. 234.)

[1725] *Trenton Ins. Co.* v. *Perrine*, 3 Zab. 402.

[1726] *Hewitt* v. *Mason*, 24 How. Pra. R. 366.

[1727] *Tilk* v. *Parsons*, 2 Car. & P. 201.

[1728] *Johnson* v. *Robertson*, 8 Porter, 486.

[1729] *Bateman* v. *Lyall*, 7 C. B. (N. S.) 638.

[1730] *Martin* v. *Mattison*, 8 Abb. Pra. Rep. 3; *Shore* v. *Smith*, 15 Ohio, 173; *King*
v. *Waring*, 5 Esp. 13 ; *Manning* v. *Fitzherbert*, Cro. Car. 271 ; *Hull* v. *Vreeland*,
42 Barb. 543 ; *Delegal* v. *Highley*, 3 Bing. N. C. 950.

[1731] *Cousins* v. *Merrill*, 16 Up. Can. C. P. Rep. 114. By statute in Ireland, in
an action for slander or libel, counts may be added for false representation of
plaintiff's goods. (*McNally* v. *Oldham*, 8 Law Times Rep. N. S. 604.)

a plaintiff singly for slander of him in his partnership business, cannot be joined with a cause of action in him and his partners jointly.[1732] Several sets of words, imputing the same charge, and laid as of the same time, may be included in one count.[1733] You may put into one count all the words published at one time, but not words published at different times.[1734] A complaint which sets out an entire conversation in which the slander was spoken, contains only one cause of action although the conversation consists of several parts, each of which is actionable.[1735] The second count of a declaration in slander charged that in another discourse of and concerning plaintiff, &c., the defendant spoke these words : " You, Mrs. G. (the plaintiff), have used them for years," (innuendo that plaintiff had used fraudulent weights, and cheated in her trade) ; and also in the last-mentioned discourse, in answer to a question put by the plaintiff, as to whether the defendant had said to one J. G. that the plaintiff's son had used two balls to the plaintiff's steelyard, these other words : " to be sure I did," &c. ; and also these other words, &c. ; *Held*, that as there was but one continued discourse at the same time, this was but one count, although the words set out were divided into several sentences.[1736] In New York, where the complaint contains several causes of action, each cause of action must be separately stated and numbered,[1737] and be perfect in itself.[1738]

[1732] *Robinson* v. *Marchant*, 7 Q. B. 918.

[1733] *Rathbun* v. *Emigh*, 6 Wend. 407 ; *Miligan* v. *Thorn*, 6 Wend. 412 ; *Dioyt* v. *Tanner*, 20 Wend. 190 ; *Churchill* v. *Kimball*, 3 Ohio, (Ham.) 409 ; *Hoyt* v. *Smith*, 32 Verm. (3 Shaw) 304.

[1734] *Hughes* v. *Rees*, 4 M. & W. 204. It is allowable to include in the same declaration divers distinct words of slander of different import. (*Hall* v. *Nees*, 27 Ill. 411.) It is sometimes a question whether a declaration consisted of one or more counts. See *Cheatham* v. *Tillotson*, 5 Johns. 430 ; *Griffith* v. *Lewis*, 8 Q. B. 841.

[1735] *Cracraft* v. *Cochran*, 16 Iowa, 301.

[1736] *Griffiths* v. *Lewis*, 8 Q. B. 841 ; 7 Law Times, 177.

[1737] Court Rules, 19 ; *Pike* v. *Van Wormer*, 5 How. Pra. Rep. 171.

[1738] *Holt* v. *Muzzy*, 30 Verm. (1 Shaw) 365 ; *Sinclair* v. *Fitch*, 3 E. D. Smith, 689.

§ 348. In New York a supplemental complaint is permitted. A plaintiff in an action for libel may be allowed to serve a supplemental complaint setting out matter material to the action, occurring after the commencement of the action. And in that case a supplemental complaint was allowed, setting up alleged special damage occasioned by the publication of the libel, and occurring after the service of the original complaint.[1799]

[1799] *Scott* v. *Hallock*, MS. Gen. Term Superior Court New York, 19 Dec. 1857.

CHAPTER XIV.

The answer corresponds to plea. What it must contain. Plea to part of a count. Answer of justification must give color, show a lawful occasion, and deny malice. Several answers. Defence of truth must be pleaded. How pleaded. Where the charge is general. Where the charge is specific. Certainty in statement of facts. Answer of justification bad in part, bad altogether. Mitigating circumstances.

§ 349. The *answer* corresponds to the *plea* in the common law system of pleading. In New York it is provided as to an answer generally, that it "must contain (1) a general or specific denial of each material allegation of the complaint controverted by the defendant, or of any knowledge or information thereof sufficient to form a belief; (2) a statement of any new matter constituting a defence or counter-claim, in ordinary and concise language, without repetition." And with regard to answers in the actions for slander and libel, it is provided "the defendant may, in his answer, allege both the truth of the matter charged as defamatory, and any mitigating circumstances to reduce the amount of damages; and whether he prove the justification or not, he may give in evidence the mitigating circumstances." [1140]

[1140] Code of Pro. § 149, 165. An answer which merely states that the defendant did not utter the words alleged at the place and time alleged, may be good as a general denial. (*Sulenger* v. *Lusk,* 7 How. Pra. Rep. 430.) As to a general denial in Maryland. (*Hagan* v. *Hendry,* 18 Md. 177.) A plea that the letter containing the defamatory matter was intended for the plaintiff himself, but by mistake was handed to his employer, was held bad. (*Fox* v. *Broderick,* 14 Irish

28

§ 350. The general issue in an action for slander or libel was " not guilty; " and this had probably a larger effect than has a "general denial" under the New York Code, by which we intend that under the "general issue" matters of defence were admitted which would not be admitted under the "general denial." (See *post, Evidence under general issue*.) Under the New York system of pleading, every defence not consisting of a mere denial must be specially pleaded. Much relating to the subject of the plea or answer has been anticipated [§ 211 to 216], and much more on the subject will be found under the head of Evidence.

§ 351. It was held in New York that a plea in bar must answer the whole count, but that one plea might state several defences, *i. e.* different defences to different parts.[1741] Perhaps the rule is, that, if the matter is divisible, although contained in one count, a defendant may plead to part of the matter of one count.[1742]

§ 352. An answer of justification must give color to the extent of admitting, for the purposes of the answer only, the publication complained of.[1743] But this admission cannot be

---

Law Rep. 453.) In an action for libel the defendant at first pleaded not guilty, but afterwards pleaded, to the further maintenance of the action, that the plaintiff had recovered damages against another person for the same grievances. New assignment, that the present action was brought for other and different grievances. Plea to new assignment, not guilty. Held, that this did not admit the innuendoes, and that, by pleading not guilty to the new assignment, the defendant had raised precisely the same issue as if the libel had been set out in the declaration, and the defendant had pleaded not guilty to it. (*Brunswick [Duke of]* v. *Pepper*, 2 Car. & K. 683.)

[1741] *Cooper* v. *Greeley*, 1 Denio, 365; and see *Ames* v. *Hazard*, 6 R. I. 335. That plea may apply to part of libel, see *Spencer* v. *Southwick*, 11 Johns. 573.

[1742] See *Edwards* v. *Bell*, 1 Bing. 403; *Cooper* v. *Lawson*, 1 Perr. & D. 15; *O'Connell* v. *Mansfield*, 9 Ir. Law Rep. 179; and see *ante*, note 292, and *Torrey* v. *Fields*, 10 Verm. 353.

[1743] *Fidler* v. *Delavan*, 20 Wend. 57; *Wilson* v. *Beighler*, 4 Iowa, 427; *Vanderveer* v. *Sutphin*, 5 Ohio, N. S. 293; *Edsall* v. *Russell*, 2 Dowl N. S. 641; 5 Sc. N. S. 801; *Davis* v. *Matthews*, 2 Ham. 257; *Folsom* v. *Brown*, 5 Foster, N. Hamp. 114; *Samuel* v. *Bond*, Litt. Sel. Cas. 158; *Buddington* v. *Davis*, 6 How.

used to defeat a denial by a separate answer. Because "one plea cannot be taken in to help or destroy another, but every plea must stand or fall by itself." [1744] A plea of privileged publication must show a lawful occasion, and a denial of malice; a plea which only alleged that the defendant spoke the words on such occasion, firmly believing them to be true, was held bad for want of an express or implied denial of malice. [1745]

§ 353. The defendant may in one answer set up a general denial, or not guilty, and a justification on the ground of truth. [1746] But he cannot, with not guilty as to the whole declaration, plead a special plea of apology and payment into court under the statute 6 & 7 Vict. ch. 96, as to part of the declaration. [1747] Although a defendant may be allowed with not guilty to plead the mere fact that the words were a fair comment without malice, he cannot with not guilty interpose a plea alleging the existence of certain facts, and that the alleged

Pra. R. 402; *Porter* v. *McCreedy*, 1 Code Rep. N. S. 88. A plea of justification held bad unless accompanied with a traverse of the publication in a manner to insult. (*Crawford* v. *Millton*, 12 S. & M. 328.) See *Carlock* v. *Spencer*, 2 Eng. 12.

[1744] *Grills* v. *Marcella*, Willis, 380; *Kirk* v. *Nowell*, 1 T. R. 125; *Montgomery* v. *Richardson*, 5 C. & P. 247; and see cases collected Voorhies' Code, 296 c, 8th edit.; contra, see *Jackson* v. *Stetson*, 15 Mass. 48; *Alderman* v. *French*, 1 Pick. 1; *Cilley* v. *Jenness*, 2 N. Hamp. 89; *Whittaker* v. *Freeman*, 1 Dev. 280; *Wheeler* v. *Robb*, 1 Blackf. 330; *Wright* v. *Lindsay*, 20 Ala. 428; *Doss* v. *Jones*, 5 Howard (Miss.), 158; Rev. Stat. of Mass. ch. 100, § 18; *Hix* v. *Drury*, 5 Pick. 260.

[1745] *Smith* v. *Thomas*, 2 Bing. N. S. 372; 2 Sc. 543; 4 Dowl. Pra. Cas. 333. Except in defences of privileged publication, the denial of malice forms an immaterial issue. (*Fry* v. *Bennett*, 5 Sandf. 54.)

[1746] *Buhler* v. *Wentworth*, 17 Barb. 649; *Hollenbeck* v. *Clow*, 9 How. Pra. Rep. 289; *Ormsby* v. *Brown*, 5 Duer, 665; *Payson* v. *McComber*, 3 Allen (Mass.) 69; *Miller* v. *Graham*, 1 Brevard, 283; *Smith* v. *Smith*, 39 Penn. St. Rep. 441; and see *Kelly* v. *Craig*, 9 Humph. 215; contra, *Attebury* v. *Powell*, 29 Miss. (8 Jones) 429. To a declaration containing three counts for three distinct libels, the court refused to allow the defendant to plead one general plea of justification. (*Honess* v. *Stubbs*, 7 C. B. N. S. 555.)

[1747] *O'Brien* v. *Clement*, 15 M. & W. 435; 3 D. & L. 676; 15 Law Jour. Rep. 285, Ex.

libel was a fair comment on transactions of public notoriety. The fact of fair comment is involved in not guilty.[1748]

§ 354. A defendant, to avail himself of the defence of truth, must set it up as a defence by plea or answer.[1749] The defence of truth may be interposed, although the power to punish for the offence has been tolled by lapse of time,[1750] or although the plaintiff has been tried upon the charge and acquitted[1751] or pardoned.[1752]

§ 355. That the justification on the ground of truth must be as broad as the charge, and must justify the precise charge, has already been considered. [§ 212.] We have now but to point out some other requisites of a plea or answer on the ground of truth. These depend upon whether the charge is general or specific. Where the charge is in general terms, the answer must state the facts which show the charge to be true. It is not sufficient merely to allege that the charge is true.[1753] As if the charge be that the plaintiff is a swindler,[1754] or a thief, or a perju-

---

[1748] *Lucan* v. *Smith*, 38 Eng. Law & Eq. R. 395. The fact that the same matter which is specially pleaded might be given in evidence under the general issue, is not always a sufficient ground for rejecting the special plea. (*Parker* v. *McQueen*, 8 B. Monroe, 16.) In an action for a libel contained in two letters published in a newspaper, the defendant pleaded that the second letter (itself actionable) was a fair comment upon the facts in the first letter; held bad. (*Walker* v. *Brogden*, 19 J. Scott, N. S. 64.)

[1749] *Ante*, § 211 to 216, note 1031; *Manning* v. *Clement*, 7 Bing. 367; 2 Greenl. Ev. 424; *Hagan* v. *Hendy*, 6 R. I. 335; *Frederitze* v. *Odenwalder*, 2 Yeates, 243. The plea of truth is an issuable plea. (*Woodward* v. *Andrews*, 1 Brev. 310.)

[1750] *Ankin* v. *Westfall*, 14 Johns. 234. Where the words were actionable *per se*, a plea of not guilty within two years, held good. (*Quinn* v. *Wilson*, 13 Irish Law Rep. 381.)

[1751] *Cooke* v. *Field*, 3 Esp. 133; *England* v. *Burke*, Id. 80.

[1752] *Ante*, note 1031 and § 158.

[1753] *Fry* v. *Bennett*, 5 Sandf. 69; *Lawton* v. *Hunt*, 4 Rich. 458; *Atteberry* v. *Powell*, 29 Mis. (8 Jones), 429. *Billings* v. *Waller*, 28 How. Pra. Rep. 97. Where a particular meaning is alleged, it is not sufficient to say the charge is true, with the addition of time, place, and circumstance. (*Fidler* v. *Delavan*, 20 Wend. 57.)

[1754] *J'Anson* v. *Stuart*, 1 T. R. 748. It is not a justification of a charge of plaintiff being a swindler to allege that defendant delivered to plaintiff goods to

rer, or a murderer,[1755] or that he stole a watch,[1756] or certified a
lie,[1757] or was of intemperate habits,[1758] or received a bribe,[1759] or
perverted the law.[1760]. The distinction seems to be that where
the charge is a conclusion or inference from certain facts, there
the plea must set up the facts which warrant such an inference;
but where the charge is of some specific act or acts, there it is
sufficient if the plea allege that the charge is true. Thus if it
be said of a man that he is a swindler, this is an inference from
his actions, and which can be proved only by showing acts of
fraud on the part of the plaintiff amounting to swindling; and,
therefore, as we have seen, to justify a charge of being a swindler, the plea must allege the facts upon which the defendant
relies to make out the charge. When the charge is general,
and the answer merely an averment that the charge is true, the
plaintiff *may* under the New York Code apply to have the
answer made "definite and certain;" but he is not obliged to do
this, he *may* lie by and on the trial object to the reception of

---

sell on commission, that he failed to return them or to account for them, and that
he made an assignment for the benefit of his creditors. (*Herr* v. *Bamberg*, 10 How.
Pra. Rep. 128.)

[1755] Anon. 3 How. Pra. Rep. 406; 4 *Id.* 98, 347; *Sayles* v. *Wooden*, 6 *Id.* 84;
Johnson v. *Stebbins*, 5 Ind. 364. Where the words complained of were, "'She is a
thief, and has stolen my gold pen and pencil," held that the answer might properly allege a variety of thefts by the plaintiff of different articles, as going to justify the words "She is a thief." (*Jaycocks* v. *Ayres*, 7 How. Pra. Rep. 215.) A
charge of forgery against a whole community was held to be justified by alleging
a falsification of poll books. (*Fellows* v. *Hunter*, 20 Up. Can. Q. B. Rep. 382.)

[1756] *Anibal* v. *Hunter*, 6 How. Pra. Rep. 255,

[1757] *Jones* v. *Cecil*, 5 Eng. 593.

[1758] *Buddington* v. *Davis*, 6 How. Pra. Rep. 401.

[1759] *Van Ness* v. *Hamilton*, 19 Johns. 349.

[1760] *Riggs* v. *Denniston*, 3 Johns. Cas. 198. In an action of slander, when the
charge is made directly, the plea of justification should aver the truth of the
charge, as laid in the declaration; but when the charge is made by insinuation and circumlocution, so as to render it necessary to use introductory matter
to show the meaning of the words, the plea should aver the truth of the charge
which the declaration alleges was meant to be made. (*Snow* v. *Witcher*, 9 Ired.
346.)

any evidence in support of such a plea, either in bar or in mitigation.[1761]

§ 356. As to specific charges. Where the charge is specific, there the answer need only to allege that the charge is true. Thus in an action for calling the plaintiff thief, and saying he stole two sheep of J. S., the defendant pleaded that the plaintiff stole the same sheep, by reason of which he (defendant) called plaintiff thief, as well he might, and the plea was held good.[1762] And so where the charges were of theft of certain articles specified, and of practicing prostitution, specifying instances;[1763] and where the charge was that the plaintiff, as inspector of drugs, had improperly passed an adulterated article, an answer merely alleging the charge to be true was held to be sufficient.[1764] A plea that the defamatory matter " is true in substance and effect " means that it is true in every material particular.[1765] To

---

[1761] *Wachter* v. *Quenzer,* 29 N. Y. 553; *Tilson* v. *Clark,* 45 Barb. 181; and see *Brickett* v. *Davis,* 21 Pick. 404. Generally, upon the trial the plaintiff cannot object to the insufficiency of a plea of justification (*Evans* v. *Franklin,* 26 Mis. 5 Jones, 252), as he might have demurred; but if the justification be proved, the defendant is entitled to a verdict on that plea (*Edmonds* v. *Walter,* 3 Stark. R. 7); and see *Churchill* v. *Hunt,* 2 B. & A. 685; 1 Ch. 480; *contra* as to a notice of justification. (*Thompson* v. *Bowers,* 1 Doug. 321.) Held to be error for the court to charge of its own motion that the plea is so defective as not to be available to the defendant. (*Bryan* v. *Gurr,* 27 Geo. 378.)

[1762] 1 Rolle Abr. 87. Where the original charge is in itself specific, the defendant need not further particularize it in his plea. (1 Stark. Slan. 478.)

[1763] *Steinman* v. *Clark,* 10 Abb. Pra. R. 132.

[1764] *Van Wyck* v. *Guthrie,* 4 Duer, 268. A general plea averring the plaintiff's residence in O. county, his being known to divers citizens there, and having a bad reputation among them, is good. (*Cooper* v. *Greely,* 1 Den. 347.)

[1765] *Weaver* v. *Lloyd,* 4 D. & R. 230. A plea to an action for libel purporting to be the report of a trial " that the alleged libel was in substance a true report of the trial," was held bad on demurrer. (*Flint* v. *Pike,* 6 D. & R. 528; 4 B. & C. 473.) To a declaration for an alleged libel published in a newspaper, purporting to be an account of the trial of an action, the plea stated that at the trial the counsel made the speech set out in the alleged libel, and that certain witnesses proved all that had been so stated; held bad, on demurrer, for that the plea ought to have detailed such evidence, and shown the truth of the facts so stated, and not merely have stated the conclusion which the party himself drew from the evidence. (*Lewis* v. *Walter,* 4 B. & A. 605.)

a charge of being a liar, a plea that "sundry honest men,
to wit, A. B.," &c., naming them, "and others, believed and
considered the plaintiff not to be a man of truth, but addicted
to falsehood," would not be sufficient justification.[1766]

§ 357. The facts which show the charge to be true must be
stated with certainty,[1767] so that the court may see whether the
defendant was justified in what he published;[1768] and (when a
reply was necessary) so that the plaintiff might have an opportunity of denying and taking issue upon the facts alleged; and
it was no excuse for general pleading that the subject comprehended a multiplicity of facts tending to prolixity, nor that the
plea was not more general than the charge.[1769] Where a declaration stated that plaintiff was lawfully possessed of mines and
of ore gotten from them, and was in treaty for the sale of the
ore, and that the defendant published a malicious, injurious,
and unlawful advertisement, cautioning persons against purchasing the ore, &c., *per quod* he was prevented from selling;
to which the defendant pleaded in justification, that the shareholders in the mines thought it their duty to caution persons
against purchasing the ore, &c. (pursuing the words of the advertisement); this plea was held ill on special demurrer; first,

---

[1766] *Brooks* v. *Bemiss*, 8 Johns. 455. Under a plea of justification on the ground
of truth, the defendant cannot show that he believed the charge true. (*Hix* v.
Drury, 5 Pick. 296.) Justification of a libel, that there was a reason for thinking
the imputation was true for what had been said; held bad on demurrer, unless it
is stated what had been said, and by whom. (*Lane* v. *Howman*, 1 Price, 76.) To
constitute a justification, the answer should aver the truth of the defamatory
matter charged. It is not sufficient to set up the facts which only tend to establish the truth of such matter. (*Thrall* v. *Smiley*, 9 Cal. 529.) Where it was
alleged that the defendant spoke of the plaintiff, "I am told M. (plaintiff) was the
man who killed the pedler, and I believe it," a plea which averred that defendant was told plaintiff was the man who murdered the pedler, and that the defendant did believe it, was held bad. (*Muma* v. *Harmer*, 17 Up. Can. Q. B. Rep.
293.)

[1767] *Van Ness* v. *Hamilton*, 19 Johns. 349; *Riggs* v. *Denniston*, 3 Johns. Cas.
198.

[1768] *Torrey* v. *Field*, 10 Verm. 353; *Johnson* v. *Stebbins*, 5 Ind. 364.

[1769] *Van Ness* v. *Hamilton*, 19 Johns. 349.

because it did not disclose the names of the adventurers, or who they were; and secondly, because it did not show that the defendant made the publication under the direction of the shareholders.[1770] And where the plaintiff, a justice of the peace, brought an action against the defendant for charging him with pocketing all the fines and penalties forfeited by delinquents whom he had convicted, without distributing them to the poor, or in any manner accounting for a sum of £50 then on hand, the defendant pleaded that the plaintiff was a justice of the peace, and that during the time he acted as such he convicted sundry persons in sundry sums of money, for divers offences against divers statutes, which sum, amounting together to £50, he received of the persons so convicted, and had not paid over the same as required by law. On special demurrer, the plea was held bad [not sufficiently certain] for not stating the names of the persons who paid said sums of money, and the amount which each person paid.[1771] Where the libel stated that the plaintiff, as manager of the opera, employed his critics in attacking, in corrupt and purchased newspapers, the females of his company, it was held that the justification of such a charge must state the names of the critics, of the females, and of the corrupted newspapers, and the substance of the articles, and the time and place of their publication.[1772] But where the libel charged that certain exhibitions of opera by the plaintiff were an unfit resort for respectable people, and that they were attended by persons of certain specified immoral and illegal occupations or pursuits—held that an answer justifying such charge need do no more than reaffirm the statement contained therein, and need not specify the names of the persons who attended such exhibitions; and certainly this will be the case where the defendant alleges that the names of such persons are unknown to him.[1773] Where the charge was that the plaintiff made himself invisible on account of too much borrowing and

---

[1770] *Rowe* v. *Roach,* 1 M. & S. 304.

[1771] *Newman* v. *Bailey,* 2 Ch. C. T. M. 665.

[1772] *Fry* v. *Bennett,* 5 Sandf. 54.

[1773] *Maretzek* v. *Cauldwell,* 2 Robertson, 715.

not paying, innuendo that plaintiff ran away, held that an
answer which stated "it is true the plaintiff made himself invisible on account of too much borrowing and not paying, that is,
ran away," was insufficient.[1174] And in an action of slander in
charging the plaintiff, a pawnbroker, with the practice of duffing,
i. e. of doing up damaged goods and pledging them again, a
plea alleging that the plaintiff did do up *divers* damaged goods
and repledge to divers persons, &c., was held bad on special
demurrer, for not stating specific instances and persons.[1175] And
where the libel charged an attorney with general misconduct,
viz. gross negligence, falsehood, prevarication, and excessive
bills of costs in the business he had conducted for the defendant, a plea in justification repeating the same general charges,
without specifying the particular acts of misconduct, was, upon
demurrer, held insufficient.[1176] A declaration alleged that plaintiff was cashier to Q., and that defendant, in a letter addressed
to Q., wrote, "I conceive there is nothing too base for him
(plaintiff) to be guilty of." Plea, in justification, alleged that
plaintiff signed and delivered to defendant an I. O. U., and
afterwards, on having sight thereof, falsely and fraudulently
asserted that the signature was not his; and the plea averred
that the libel was written and published solely in reference to
this transaction. Held a sufficient justification, as the libel
must be understood with reference to the subject-matter.[1177]

§ 358. It is said that to justify a charge of crime, the plea or
answer must specify the crime with certainty,[1178] and show the

---

[1174] *Wachter* v. *Quenzer*, 29 N. Y. 552.

[1175] *Hickinbotham* v. *Leach*, 2 Dowl. Pra. Cas. N. S. 270; 10 M. & W. 361.
To an action for slander in charging the plaintiff with stealing corn and fodder
from various persons, a plea of justification leaving blanks for the dates and
amounts would be bad on special exception, but cannot be attacked on a general
exception. (*George* v. *Lemon*, 19 Texas, 150.)

[1176] *Holmes* v. *Catesby*, 1 Taunt. 543.

[1177] *Tighe* v. *Cooper*, 7 El. & B. 639. A plea of justification need not meet the
exact words of the libel, but may adopt the sense put by the innuendo, and justify
that. (*O'Connor* v. *Wallen*, 6 Irish Com. Law Rep. 378.)

[1178] *Nall* v. *Hill*, Pick. 325. When any circumstance is stated which describes

commission of the crime with as much certainty as in an indictment for such crime.[1779] In an action of slander for charging
the plaintiff with having stolen the defendant's shingles, a justification stating that the plaintiff had sold the defendant shingles
without authority, and afterward denied that he knew anything
respecting them, without alleging that the plaintiff took them
privately or feloniously, was held not to amount to a charge of
larceny, and bad as a justification.[1780] To a charge of procuring an abortion it was held not a sufficient plea that the plaintiff assisted in procuring an abortion, without allegations showing the assistance criminal.[1781] Where the charge was that
plaintiff " swore falsely," without reference to any judicial or
other proceeding in which an oath could have been lawfully
administered, a plea of justification pointing the plaintiff to
the time, place, and occasion of his false swearing, and alleging
the truth of the words spoken, was held to be good.[1782] Where
the charge is perjury, the plea must allege not only that the
defendant testified to what was untrue, but that he did so
knowingly,[1783] and that the matter testified to was material.[1784]
If the charge be of having sworn falsely in a judicial proceeding, without the necessary averments to make the slander
amount to an imputation of perjury, then a plea of justification, that the plaintiff did swear falsely in the particular pro-

---

or identifies the offence, it must be averred for the purpose of showing that it is
the same offence. (*Sharpe* v. *Stephenson*, 12 Ired. 348.)

[1779] *Snyder* v. *Andrews*, 6 Barb. 43; *Steele* v. *Phillips*, 10 Humph. 461.

[1780] *Shepard* v. *Merrill*, 13 Johns. 475.

[1781] *Bissell* v. *Cornell*, 24 Wend. 354.

[1782] *Sanford* v. *Gaddis*, 13 Ill. 329. To an action of slander for charging the
plaintiff with having forged a certain instrument of writing, the truth was pleaded
in justification. Held, that such a plea could not be objected to because it avers
the forged instrument to be in the plaintiff's possession or destroyed. Held, also,
that in a plea with such an averment, the instrument need not be so particularly
described as would be otherwise required. (*Kent* v. *David*, 3 Blackf. 801.)

[1783] *Chandler* v. *Robison*, 7 Ired. 480.

[1784] *McGough* v. *Rhodes*, 7 Eng. 625; *Harris* v. *Woody*, 9 Mis. 113. It is no
justification to an insinuation of perjury against the plaintiff (who had sworn to

ceeding, would be sufficient.[1785] Where the charge is that the plaintiff perjured himself on a particular occasion, the justification must be confined to that.[1786] Thus in slander for charging the plaintiff with committing perjury in making a certain statement, set out in the declaration, as a witness in a certain case, the defendant pleaded that the plaintiff did commit perjury by making that statement, and that on the same trial he committed perjury by another statement made by him on the same trial, and not set out in the declaration. On demurrer to both pleas, the first was held good, and the second bad.[1787] In an action for slander in charging the plaintiff with perjury, a plea was that the words were spoken in reference to the testimony of the plaintiff on the trial of a cause, and after setting out the parties, the nature of the action, and the questions litigated, it stated the evidence given on such trial, and averred that *the words were spoken in reference to certain parts of the testimony (specifying them) which were not material to the issue, and that the defendant was so understood by the hearers;* it was held that the words in *italic* were irrelevant.[1788] A plea in an action of slander for charging the plaintiff with committing a felony, which admits the speaking of the words charged, but avers other facts in order to show that the words were not actionable, must show either that it appeared by the whole of defendant's statements, in the same conversation and company, that no fel-

---

an assault by A. B. on him), that it did appear (which was the suggestion in the libel) from the testimony of every person in the room, &c., except the plaintiff, that no violence had been used by A. B., &c.; for *non constat* thereby that what the plaintiff swore was false. Neither is it sufficient in a justification to such a libel, where the extraneous matter was so mingled with the judicial account as to make it uncertain whether it could be separated, to justify the publication by general reference to such parts of the supposed libel as purport to contain an account of the trial, &c., and that the said parts contain a just and faithful account of the trial, &c. (*Stiles* v. *Nokes*, 7 E. R. 493.)

[1786] *Sanford* v. *Gaddis*, 13 Ill. 329. "The answer should set forth the evidence and what was actually sworn to by the plaintiff at the time alleged " (3 Ch. Pl. 1089; Yates' Plead. 430; *Woodbeck* v. *Keller*, 6 Cow. 122), and the Code of New York has not altered the rule in this respect. (*Tilson* v. *Clark*, 45 Barb. 180; *Wachter* v. *Quenzer*, 29 N. Y. 553.)

[1787] *Palmer* v. *Haight*, 2 Barb. 210.

[1788] *Starr* v. *Harrington*, 1 Smith, 350.

[1788] *Allen* v. *Crofoot*, 7 Cow. 46.

ony had been committed, and therefore that there was no charge of felony, or that the charge was made known to the defendant by a third person, named in the plea, before he uttered the words.[1788]

§ 359. If a material part of a plea of justification fails, the plea fails altogether. Thus, in an action for libel, the declaration set out the whole of a long letter, in which the defendant imputed to the plaintiff improper conduct in various transactions which had taken place in reference to a ditch of the plaintiff's, alleged by the defendant to be a nuisance. The defendant pleaded " as to so much of the libel as related to, and charged the plaintiff with, the keeping of the nuisance," a plea which attempted to justify every sentence in the letter. The jury found that the plaintiff kept the ditch as a nuisance, but negatived the improper conduct imputed to the plaintiff in the letter. Held that, upon this finding, the plaintiff was entitled to a verdict.[1790]

§ 360. In some States, by statute, a notice or specification of the defence is substituted for a plea in answer. Such a notice must, it seems, contain all the material allegations of a plea or answer.[1791]

§ 361. In New York, and in some other States, by statute the defendant may, *in connection with a general denial*, and with or without a defence of justification, set up in his answer mitigating circumstances to reduce the amount of damages.[1792]

[1788] *Parker* v. *McQueen*, 8 B. Monr. 16.

[1790] *Biddulph* v. *Chamberlayne*, 6 Eng. Law & Eq. R. 347; 17 Q. B. 351. Where in an action for a libel, in reference to an advertisement by the plaintiff tending to injure the defendants, his former partners, in their trade, the defendant justified, and relied on the construction of such advertisement, as set out in the introductory part of the declaration; held, that that not supporting the inferences in the libel, the plaintiff was entitled to recover. (*Chubb* v. *Flannagan*, 6 C. & P. 431.)

[1791] *Van Derveer* v. *Sutphin*, 5 Ohio, N. S. 293; *Brickett* v. *Davis*, 21 Pick. 404; *Shepard* v. *Merrill*, 13 Johns. 475; *Mitchell* v. *Borden*, 8 Wend. 570; *Bissell* v. *Cornell*, 24 Wend. 354.

[1792] Code of Pro. § 165; *Bush* v. *Prosser*, 11 N. Y. 347; *Bisby* v. *Shaw*, 12 N. Y. 67; *Dolevin* v. *Wilder*, 34 How. Pra. R. 488; *Van Benschoten* v. *Yaple*, 13 Id. 97; *Heaton* v. *Wright*, 10 Id. 79; *Ayres* v. *Covill*, 18 Barb. 260.

But it would seem that a defendant cannot set up mitigating circumstances alone, without any other answer constituting a defence, because an answer merely setting up mitigating circumstances would not raise an issue.[1792] Mitigating circumstances are such circumstances as the well-established rules of law allow to be given in evidence in mitigation of damages,[1793] and what those circumstances are will be considered under the head of Evidence. The question whether the facts set up are or are not such as should be permitted to be given in evidence in mitigation, is properly to be decided by the judge on the trial of the issue of fact.[1794] And, therefore, although a plaintiff may move, prior to the trial, to strike out as irrelevant or redundant allegations of facts which the defendant avers he will prove on the trial in mitigation,[1795] yet where there is any doubt as to whether or not the facts alleged in the answer would be received in evidence on the trial, the motion, prior to the trial, should be denied. Where a defendant seeks to mitigate damages by pleading facts and circumstances which induced him, at the time of making the charge, to believe it true, (1) the facts and circumstances must be such as would reasonably induce, in the mind of a person possessed of ordinary intelligence and knowledge, a belief of the truth of such charge; (2) it must also appear that the defendant, before and at the time of making the charge, knew such facts and circumstances, and (3) that he was, by reason of the facts and circumstances so set forth, induced to believe in the truth of the charge. Unless it contain all those allegations, it may be stricken out on motion. Upon a motion to strike out, as redundant or irrelevant, matter set up in mitigation, the court is to see whether such matter can, by any possibility, be received in evidence; if it can, it should not be stricken out. It should not be stricken out if the court has the slight-

---

[1792] *Newman* v. *Otto*, 4 Sandf. 669; *Maretzek* v. *Cauldwell*, 19 Abb. Pra. R. 40; but see *Van Benschoten* v. *Yaple*, 13 How. Pra. Rep. 97.

[1793] *Graham* v. *Jones*, 1 Code Rep. N. S. 181.

[1794] *Newman* v. *Harrison*, 1 Code Rep. N. S. 184; *Fry* v. *Bennett*, 5 Sandf. 54.

[1795] *Van Benschoten* v. *Yaple*, 13 How. Pra. Rep. 97.

est doubt as to its inadmissibility.[1797] It is supposed that, in
New York, the defendant on the trial can give in evidence
only such matter of mitigation as he has set up in his answer,
and that if the answer does not contain any matter of mitigation, no evidence in mitigation can be admitted on the trial.
On an assessment of damages, where there is no answer, matter
in mitigation may be received. Although matter in mitigation of damages is not a subject of demurrer, yet if set up in
the answer, without its being stated that they are set up in
mitigation merely, the plaintiff may infer they are set up in
bar, and may demur to them.[1798]

§ 362. As in other actions, the defendant may demur to the
complaint; but Lord Coke said it was "an excellent point of
learning in actions for slander" not to demur, but to take advantage of the declaration not disclosing a cause of action, either
on the trial or by motion in arrest of judgment.[1799] It has been
held that, though a count in slander contain some words which
are actionable and others which are not, the defendant cannot
plead as to the former and demur as to the residue, but must either
plead or demur to the whole count.[1800] But again it has been held,

---

[1797] *Dolevin* v. *Wilder*, 34 How. Pra. Rep. 488.

[1798] *Newman* v. *Otto*, 4 Sandf. 668; *Fry* v. *Bennett*, 5 *Id.* 54; *Matthews* v.
Beach, *Id.* 256; *Meyer* v. *Schultz*, 4 *Id.* 664; *Stanley* v. *Webb*, *Id.* 21.

[1799] If the words laid in the declaration are not actionable, the defendant must
demur, or move in arrest of judgment. (*Dorsey* v. *Whipps*, 8 Gill, 457.) He cannot avail himself of the defect at the trial (*Blunt* v. *Zuntz*, Anthon, 180; *Boyd*
v. *Brent*, 3 Brevard, 241) to nonsuit the plaintiff. (*Lumby* v. *Allday*, 1 Cr. & J.
301; 1 Tyrw. 217.) It seems to be otherwise in New York, where, on the trial,
the defendant may insist that the complaint does not disclose a cause of action.
It must be remembered that in New York the demurrer is general only, and that
the special demurrer has been superseded by a motion to make definite and
certain.

[1800] Bronson, J., *Root* v. *Woodruff*, 6 Hill, 420, citing as to libel, *Sterling* v.
Sherwood, 20 Johns. 204; *Riggs* v. *Denniston*, 3 Johns. Cas. 198, and saying the
same rule had been applied in actions for slander, though not reported; and see
Taylor v. *Carr*, 3 Up. Can. Q. B. Rep. 306. It is conceded that the rule is otherwise in Eng'and, and *Clarkson* v. *Lawson*, 6 Bing. 587, is cited. Held that a defendant may demur to a part of the words laid in a count for slander. *Abrams* v.
Smith, 8 Blackf. 95; *Wyant* v. *Smith*, 5 *Id.* 294.

that where a libel contains *distinct* charges, the defendant may
plead or demur to particular parts of it; yet where several
statements tend to one conclusion or imputation, it is not permissible to select and deal separately with one, either by plea
or demurrer.[1801] A defendant cannot single out some of the
words in a declaration and demur to them.[1802] If a count by
husband and wife contains words actionable *per se*, as well as
others spoken of the wife, the defendant cannot demur, and
may, on the trial, object that the action for the latter words
cannot be maintained by both.[1803] In an action for libel where
the answer contained (1) a denial of the publication, (2) a justification, the plaintiff demurring to the answer, specifying only
objections to the matter of justification, judgment was given
for the plaintiff on the demurrer; held that the denial remained
on the record, and raised an issue of fact.[1804]

[1801] *Eaton* v. *Johns*, 1 Dowl. Pra. Cas. N. S. 602; and see *McGregor* v. *Gregory*, 2 *Id.* 769; 11 M. & W. 289.

[1802] *Taylor* v. *Carr*, 3 Up. Can. Q. B. Rep. 306.

[1803] *Beach* v. *Ranney*, 2 Hill, 309.

[1804] *Matthews* v. *Beach*, 4 Selden, 173; but see *Parrett Nav. Co.* v. *Stower*, 8 Dowl. Prn. Cas. 405.

CHAPTER XV.

Allegation of pleadings and proof should correspond. Variance in New York. General rules as to variance. Immaterial variance. ·Material variance. Amendment.

§ 363. The general rule as to variance is that the allegations of the pleading and the proof must correspond, otherwise there is a variance, and the plaintiff fails;[1805] but now in New York it is enacted by statute that "no variance between the allegation in a pleading and the proof shall be deemed *material* unless it have actually misled the adverse party to his prejudice," and when the variance is shown to be material, the court may order an amendment.[1806] The following decisions upon variance are in cases not within the Code of New York.

§ 364. Ordinarily it is sufficient if the words proved correspond substantially with those alleged.[1807] But although any mere variation of the form of expression is not material, the words alleged cannot be proved by showing that the defendant published the same meaning in different words,[1808] even if equivalent and of similar import.[1809] A count for slanderous words

---

[1805] In actions of slander and libel the language charged must be proved as laid. (*Birch* v. *Benton*, 26 Mis. (5 Jones), 153; *Horton* v. *Reavis*, 2 Murph. 380.) A variance is fatal. (*Stanfield* v. *Boyer*, 6 Har. & J. 248; *Winter* v. *Donovan*, 8 Gill, 370; *Harris* v. *Lawrence*, 1 Tyler, 156.)

[1806] Code of Proc. § 169. As to amendment of variance in Indiana (*Proctor* v. *Owens*, 18 Ind. 21).

[1807] *Coghill* v. *Chandler*, 83 Mis. 115; *Smith* v. *Hollister*, 3 Shaw (Verm.) 695; *Taylor* v. *Moran*, 4 Metc. (Ky.) 127; *Williams* v. *Minor*, 18 Conn. 464.

[1808] *Smith* v. *Hollister*, 3 Shaw (Verm.) 695.

[1809] *Wilborn* v. *Odell*, 29 Ill. 456; *Taylor* v. *Moran*, 4 Metc. (Ky.) 127; *Norton* v. *Gordon*, 16 Ill. 38. It is not sufficient to prove words equivalent to those al-

spoken affirmatively is not supported by proof that they were
spoken by way of interrogation.[1810]   Proof of words spoken in
the second person will not support counts for words spoken in
the third person, and *vice versa*.[1811]

§ 365. The plaintiff need not prove all the words laid, but
he must prove enough of them to sustain the action.[1812]   It is
sufficient if the gravamen of the charge as laid is proved,[1813]
and unless the additional words qualify the meaning of those
proved so as to render the words proved not actionable, the
proof is sufficient.[1814]   It is necessary for the plaintiff to prove

leged. (*Moore* v. *Bond*, 4 Blackf. 458; *Slocum* v. *Kuykendall*, 1 Scam. 187; *Olmstead* v. *Miller*, 1 Wend. 506; *Watson* v. *Musie*, 2 Mis. 29; *Fox* v. *Vanderbeck*, 5
Cow. 513; *Armitage* v. *Dunster*, 4 Doug. 291.)

[1810] *Barnes* v. *Holloway*, 8 T. R. 150; *Sanford* v. *Gaddis*, 15 Ill. 228; *King* v.
Whitley, 7 Jones Law (N. C.) 529.   If in an action of slander the words be proved
to be spoken affirmatively as they are laid, the charge is supported, though it appear that they were spoken in answer to a question put by a third person. (*Jones*
v. *Chapman*, 5 Blackf. 88.)

[1811] *Cock* v. *Weatherby*, 5 Smedes & Marsh. 333; *Miller* v. *Miller*, 8 Johns. 74;
Stannard v. *Harper*, 5 M. & Ry. 295; *M'Connell* v. *M'Coy*, 7 S. & R. 223; *Cul-
bertson* v. *Stanley*, 6 Blackf. 67; *Williams* v. *Harrison*, 8 Mis. 411; *Wolf* v. *Rodi-
fer*, Har. & J. 409; *Avarillo* v. *Rogers*, Bull. N. P. 5; *Rex* v. *Berry*, 4 T. R. 217;
Phillips v. *Odell*, 5 Up. Can. Q. B. Rep. O. S. 483; *Sanford* v. *Gaddis*, 15 Ill. 228.
Evidence of the words, " You are a broken down justice," does not support an indictment for speaking of the magistrate the words, " He is a broken down justice."
(4 T. R. 217; but see Cro. Eliz. 503.)   Words proved to have been spoken in the
second person, sustain a count for slander in which the words are in the third
person. (*Daily* v. *Gaines*, 1 Dana, 529; *Huffman* v. *Shumate*, 4 Bibb, 515.)

[1812] *Fox* v. *Vanderbeck*, 5 Cow. 513; *Purple* v. *Horton*, 13 Wend. 9; *Nestle* v.
Van Slyck, 2 Hill, 282; *Skinner* v. *Grant*, 12 Verm. 456; *Scott* v. *McKinnish*, 15
Ala. 662; *Hancock* v. *Stephens*, 11 Humph. 507; *Inaley* v. *Lovejoy*, 8 Blackf. 462;
Sanford v. *Gaddis*, 15 Ill. 228; *Whiting* v. *Smith*, 13 Pick. 364; *Loomis* v. *Swick*,
3 Wend. 205; *Wheeler* v. *Robb*, 1 Blackf. 330; *Chandler* v. *Holloway*, 4 Port. 17;
Berry v. *Dryden*, 7 Mis. 324; *Coghill* v. *Chandler*, 33 Mis. 115; *Geary* v. *Connop*,
Skin. 333.

[1813] *Hersh* v. *Ringwalt*, 3 Yeates, 508; *Wilson* v. *Natrous*, 5 Yerg. 211; *Cheadle*
v. *Buell*, 6 Ham. 67; *Pursell* v. *Archer*, Peck, 317; *Miller* v. *Miller*, 8 Johns. 74;
Cooper v. *Marlow*, 3 Mis. 188; *Barr* v. *Gaines*, 3 Dana, 258; *McClintock* v. *Crick*,
4 Iowa, 453; *Baldwin* v. *Soule*, 6 Gray, 321; *Scott* v. *McKinnish*, 15 Ala. 662;
Bassett v. *Spofford*, 11 N. Hamp. 127; *Merrill* v. *Peaslee*, 17 N. Hamp. 540.

[1814] *Sanford* v. *Gaddis*, 15 Ill. 228; *Merrill* v. *Peaslee*, 17 N. Hamp. 540;
Smart v. *Blanchard*, 42 N. Hamp. 137.   The plaintiff need not prove all the

some of the words precisely as charged, but not all of them, if
those proved are in themselves slanderous; but he will not be
permitted to prove the substance of them in lieu of the precise
words.[1815] Where the whole of the words laid in any one count
constitute the slanderous charge, the whole must be proved.
But, where there are distinct slanderous allegations in any
count, proof of any of them is sufficient.[1816] The plaintiff may
prove more words than are set forth in the complaint, provided
the additional words do not change the meaning of those set
forth.[1817]

§ 366. An action for slanderous words imputing to the
plaintiff misconduct as a constable, is not sustained by proving
words imputing misconduct to him, as an agent of the executive of one State, for the arrest, in another State, of a fugitive
from justice.[1818] Where the words were alleged to have been
spoken of and concerning the plaintiff as treasurer and collector of certain tolls, and the innuendo corresponding thereto,
and the proof was only of his being treasurer, and he failed in
making out his appointment to be collector; held, that for
want of such proof he was properly nonsuited.[1819] For words
spoken of a physician, alleging that he was not entitled to prac-

---

words set forth in the declaration, provided he proves enough to sustain his cause
of action, and the words proved do not differ in sense from those alleged. (*Nichols*
v. *Hayes*, 13 Conn. 155; *Nestle* v. *Van Slyck*, 2 Hill, 282; *McKee* v. *Ingalls*, 4
Scam. 30; *Scott* v. *Renforth*, Wright, 55.)

[1815] *Easley* v. *Moss*, 9 Ala. 266; *Morgan* v. *Livingston*, 2 Rich. 573; *Creelman*
v. *Marks*, 7 Blackf. 281; *Patterson* v. *Edwards*, 2 Gilman, 720. Although the
libel read in evidence contained matter in addition to that set out in the declaration, there is no variance, if the additional part do not alter the sense of that
which is set out. (*M'Coombs* v. *Tuttle*, 5 Blackf. 431; *Cooper* v. *Marlow*, 3 Mis.
186; *Rutherford* v. *Evans*, 6 Bing. 451; 4 Car. & P. 74.) Thus, in *Tabart* v. *Tipper*, 1 Camp. 350, the rhymes (see *ante*, note 1320) were set out in the declaration
without the line in Latin which followed them; it was held the omission was immaterial.

[1816] *Flower* v. *Pedley*, 2 Esp. 491.

[1817] *Wilborn* v. *Odell*, 29 Ill. 456.

[1818] *Kinney* v. *Nash*, 3 Coms. 177.

[1819] *Sellers* v. *Killen*, 4 B. & Cr. 655; 7 D. & Ry. 121.

tice as such; held, first, that the plaintiff was bound to prove not only that he practised as a physician, but that he practised *lawfully.*[1820] In an action for these words spoken by defendant of the plaintiff in his profession of a physician: "Dr. S. has upset all we have done, and die he [the patient] must." It was proved that the plaintiff had practised several years as a physician, and having been called in during the absence of a physician, who with the defendant attended the patient, the defendant, as apothecary, made up the medicines prescribed by the plaintiff for the patient in question. *Quaere,* whether, on this declaration, it was necessary for the plaintiff to produce a diploma, or other direct evidence that he had taken a degree in physic, in order to maintain the action.[1821] Where the declaration alleged the plaintiff to be an attorney, and that the words were spoken of him in his professional character, the words being actionable without any reference to such character; held, that mere proof of his having been admitted, without showing that he had practised or had taken out his certificate, was not a fatal variance.[1822]

§ 367. The following have been held to be immaterial variances : the date of publication ;[1823] a difference in the tense of the words, as *had* for *has* ;[1824] the transposition of the names of the parties to the suit, as a witness in which the plaintiff was charged with having sworn falsely ;[1825] alleging that the offence

[1820] *Collins* v. *Carnegie,* 3 Nev. & M. 703; 1 Ad. & El. 695.

[1821] *Smith* v. *Taylor,* 1 N. R. 196. In an action by an apothecary, what is sufficient proof of his qualification as such. (*Wogan* v. *Somerville,* 1 Moore, 102; 7 Taunt. 401.)

[1822] *Lewis* v. *Walter,* 3 B. & Cr. 138; 4 D. & R. 810.

[1823] *Thrall* v. *Smiley,* 9 Cal. 529; *Gates* v. *Bowker,* 18 Verm. (3 Washb.) 23 ; *Commonwealth* v. *Varney,* 10 Cush. 402; *Potter* v. *Thompson,* 22 Barb. 89.

[1824] *Wilborn* v. *Odell,* 29 Ill. 456.

[1825] *Teague* v. *Williams,* 7 Ala. 844. In an action of slander, the plaintiff alleged that the slanderous words were spoken relative to testimony of the plaintiff in a suit in which S. was plaintiff and H. defendant. Held, that evidence aliunde was admissible to show that the record of an action by S. and W. against H. was the action referred to in the declaration, and that there was no variance. (*Hibler* v. *Servoss,* 6 Mis. 24.)

was committed on Saturday instead of Sunday;[1826] a discrep-
ancy in the title of a paper;[1827] where it was alleged that the
publication was in the presence of B. held not necessary to
prove such allegation.[1828]   On an allegation that the defendant
charged the plaintiff with perjury in a suit of A. and B., *v.* C.
and D., the variance is not fatal if it be shown that the charge
was made in reference to the case of a cross-bill, by one of the
defendants in such case, against the complainant and co-defend-
ants.[1829]   And where the declaration on a libel stated that certain prosecutions had been preferred against M., and that, " in
furtherance of such proceedings," certain sums of the parish
funds had been appropriated to discharge the expenses ; but
the libel charged the money to have been so applied after the
proceedings had terminated : held, that it being immaterial to
the defamatory character of the libel when the money was so
applied, the variance was immaterial.[1830]   So a slight variance
in the names of the defendants in the indictment, as set forth
in the declaration and contained in the record, may be cured
by parol proof of the identity of the persons.[1831]   Where the
words charged in one count were, " He is a thief," and in another, " He is a thief, and stole the hay and hay-seed from D.'s
barn," and the proof was that the defendant said, at one time,
that he was " a thief, and stole the hay-seed out of the barn,"
and at another that he had " stolen hay and hay-seed that had

---

[1826] *Sharpe* v. *Stephenson*, 12 Ired. 348.

[1827] *The State* v. *Jeandell*, 5 Harring. 475.

[1828] *Goodrich* v. *Warner*, 21 Conn. 432.

[1829] *Wiley* v. *Campbell*, 5 Monr. 560. A charge of false swearing, in a proceeding between A. and B., held sustained by proof of a proceeding between A.
and B. and wife. (*Dowd* v. *Winters*, 20 Mis. (5 Bennett) 361.

[1830] *May* v. *Brown*, 3 B. & Cr. 113 ; 4 D. & R. 670. It is a general rule, that
the variance between the allegation and the proof will not defeat a party, unless
it be in respect of matter which, if pleaded, would be material. (*Id.*) Where
the words are actionable without the inducement, the insertion of what is not
material and not proved, does not occasion a variance of which advantage can be
taken. (*Cox* v. *Thomason*, 2 Cr. & J. 361; 2 Tyrw. 411.) And see *Bourke* v.
Warren, 2 C. & P. 307.

[1831] *Hamilton* v. *Langley*, 1 M'Mullan, 498.

belonged to D," it was held that the words charged were sufficiently proved.[1832]

§ 368. The following are additional instances of immaterial variance :

ALLEGATION.	PROOF.
He stole hogs.	He stole a hog.[1833]
The girl that *hired* with us.	The girl that lived with us.[1834]
A. committed forgery.	A. and B. committed forgery.[1835]
We supposed that they had become aware of the fact.	We supposed that they had by this time become aware of the fact.[1836]
He stole my staves and nails.	He is a damned rogue, for he stole my staves and nails, and I can prove it.[1837]
She has had a bastard child.	If I have not been misinformed, she had a bastard child.[1838]
You are perjured.	Are you not afraid, as you have perjured yourself ?[1839]
Mr. K.'s wife is a whore.	She (Mr. K.'s wife) is a whorish bitch.[1840]

[1832] *Williams* v. *Miner*, 18 Conn. 464.
[1833] *Barr* v. *Gains*, 3 Dana, 258.
[1834] *Robinett* v. *Ruby*, 13 Md. 95.
[1835] *Nichols* v. *Hayes*, 13 Conn. 155.
[1836] *Smiley* v. *McDougal*, 10 Up. Can. Q. B. Rep. 113.
[1837] *Pasley* v. *Kemp*, 22 Miss. (1 Jones) 409.
[1838] *Treat* v. *Browning*, 4 Conn. 408.
[1839] *Commons* v. *Walters*, 1 Port. 377.
[1840] *Scott* v. *McKinniah*, 15 Ala. 662.

ALLEGATION.	PROOF.
You stole *one* of my sheep.	You stole my sheep and killed *it*.[1841]
Riot.	Riot and assault.[1842]
Poppenheim is a very bad man; he is a calf-thief, and the records of the court will prove it.	Poppenheim is a very bad man; he is a calf-thief; he has been indicted for calf-stealing, and the records of the court will prove it.[1843]
Your (plaintiff's) house is a bawdy house, and no respectable person will live in it.	You (plaintiff's wife) are a nuisance to live beside of. You are a bawd, and your house no better than a bawdy house.[1844]
Ware Hawk, you must take care of yourself there, *mind what you are about.*	Ware Hawk, you must take care of yourself there.[1845]

§ 369. It was held a material variance where the declaration alleged that the defendant charged the plaintiff with a crime, and the proof disclosed merely that defendant said he supposed the plaintiff to be guilty of such crime.[1846] Where the declaration charged the defendant with speaking slanderous words, and the proof was that he procured another to speak them;[1847] where the declaration charged the defendant with

---

[1841] *Robinson* v. *Wallis*, 2 Stark. Rep. 194. The word *it* showing that only one sheep was meant.

[1842] *Hamilton* v. *Langley*, 1 M'Mullan, 498.

[1843] *Poppenheim* v. *Wilkes*, 1 Strob. 275.

[1844] *Huckle* v. *Reynolds*, 7 C. B. N. S. 114.

[1845] *Orpwood* v. *Barkes*, 4 Bing. 261.

[1846] *Dickey* v. *Andros*, 32 Verm. (3 Shaw), 55. Where, in case for a malicious prosecution, the declaration alleged that an express charge of felony was made against plaintiff, but it appeared that the defendant had only deposed to a suspicion that he had committed it, held no variance, it being the only meaning which could be imputed to the accusation. (*Davis* v. *Noake*, 6 M. & S. 29.)

[1847] *Watts* v. *Greenlee*, 1 Dev. 210.

speaking defamatory words, and the proof was that defendant
signed a written complaint charging the plaintiff with larceny ;[1848] where the declaration charged the defendant with saying that plaintiff, a single woman, had had a child, and the
proof was that defendant, said, in his opinion plaintiff was
pregnant with child.[1849] An allegation of slander as to the
cleanliness of the plaintiff's person (a cook), as of the defendant's actual knowledge, held, not supported by proof of the
words as to the defendant's belief or understanding only.[1850] An
allegation that words were spoken concerning three plaintiffs
(partners) in their joint trade, is not supported by proof that
the words were addressed to one of the plaintiffs personally.[1851] Where the words set forth, in their ordinary sense,
import a charge of crime, if they are proved to have been so
spoken in connection with other words as to rebut the idea of
criminality, there is a fatal variance ;[1852] and where an innuendo
gives a specific meaning to the language published, that meaning must be proved, or there will be a variance.[1853] Where the
declaration in an action of slander alleges that the words spoken
were in reference to an oath taken by the plaintiff before the
register and receiver of a land office, touching the entry of land,
proof of an oath taken before a notary public concerning the
same subject-matter, does not support the allegation ;[1854] and
where the declaration for maliciously charging the plaintiff with
felony stated that the defendant went before R.. C. Baron
Waterpark, of *Waterfork*, in the county of, &c., and the proof
was that his title was Baron Waterpark, of *Waterpark*, &c. ;

[1848] *Hill* v. *Miles*, 9 N. Hamp. 9.

[1849] *Payson* v. *Macomber*, 3 Allen (Mass.), 69. A count in slander, alleging that
the defendant charged upon the plaintiff an act of fornication, witnessed by a particular person, is not sustained by proof of words charging an act of fornication
witnessed by another person, or by proof of words implying a charge of habitual
fornication and lewdness with the person named in the declaration. (*Id.*)

[1850] *Cook* v. *Stokes*, 1 M. & Rob. 237.

[1851] *Solomons* v. *Medex*, 1 Stark. Cas. 191.

[1852] *Edgerly* v. *Swain*, 32 N. Hamp. 478.

[1853] *Williams* v. *Stott*, 1 Cr. & M. 675; 3 Tyrw. 688.

[1854] *Phillips* v. *Beene*, 16 Ala. 720.

held a fatal variance.[1855] Where the libel given in evidence contained two references (showing it to be the language of a third person respecting the plaintiff), and which were omitted in the libel set forth in the declaration; held, that the meaning of the paragraphs being different, the variance was fatal.[1856] An action upon a libel charging in one count that the defendant published it as purporting to be a letter from A. to B., and in another charging generally that the defendant published the libellous matter; held not to be sustained by proof of a publication wherein the defendant stated that in a debate in the Irish House of Commons several years before, the attorney-general of Ireland had read such a letter, and then stating the libellous matter as said by him in commenting upon that letter; for it was said the characters of the several libels were essentially different, though the slander imputed might be the same.[1857]

§ 370. An indictment for a libel charged that the defendant set up, in public, a board on which a painting or picture of a human head, with a nail driven through the ear, and a pair of shears hung on a nail, and the proof was that a human head, showing a side face, with an ear, a nail driven through the ear, and a pair of shears hung on the nail, was inscribed or cut in the board by means of some instrument, but was not painted. Held, that there was a fatal variance between the allegation and the proof, and that the defendant must be acquitted.[1858] In an action of slander, one of the counts charged the defendant with having made a voluntary affidavit, and caused certain false statements to be written therein, to wit: "that there was a certain quantity of American soap, which to his certain knowledge was sold at Curaçoa (by the plaintiff) at six dollars, current money." The affidavit, as offered in evidence by the plaintiff, stated the same words, except that the words "per box" were added after the words "six dollars." Held, that

---

[1855] *Walters* v. *Mace,* 2 B. & A. 756: 1 Ch. 507.
[1856] *Tabart* v. *Tipper,* 1 Camp. 353.
[1857] *Bell* v. *Byrne,* 13 East, 554.
[1858] *The State* v. *Powers,* 12 Ired. 5.

the variance was fatal.[1859] The averment was that A., before a magistrate, maliciously charged B. with felony ; the information contained a mere charge of tortious conversion, upon which a warrant for felony was improperly founded. The variance was held fatal.[1860] If a declaration count upon a charge of perjury upon a particular occasion, proof of a general charge of perjury is inadmissible to sustain it.[1861]

§ 37.1. The following are additional instances of material variance :

ALLEGATION.	PROOF.
Whore.	Strumpet.[1862]
That the plaintiff, who was postmaster at F., embezzled certain papers.	Defendant had no doubt the papers were embezzled at F., or he thought the papers were embezzled at F.[1863]
L. is pregnant and gone with child seven months.	Have you heard anything about L.'s being pregnant by Dr. P.[1864]

[1859] *Wilson* v. *Mitchell*, 3 Har. & J. 91.

[1860] *Tempest* v. *Chambers*, 1 Stark. Rep. 67. In slander the allegation was, He burnt Knox's barn. The proof was that defendant added, Because one of the girls would not marry him. It was doubted if a variance. Where the inducement was of a conversation of Mr. Knox's barn which had been burnt, and that defendant said of plaintiff and of said barn, He burnt Knox's barn ; proof that defendant spoke the words, He burnt Knox's barn, without proof of the colloquium respecting the burning of Mr. Knox's barn, was held insufficient. (*Manly* v. *Cory*, 3 U. C. Q. B. R. 380.)

[1861] *Emery* v. *Miller*, 1 Denio, 208.

[1862] *Williams* v. *Bryant*, 4 Ala. 44; *contra*, see *Cook* v. *Wingfield*, 1 Stra. 555; *ante*, notes 641, 1071. A charge of being "a whore and a common prostitute" is not supported by proof of words amounting to a general charge of unchastity. (*Doherty* v. *Brown*, 10 Gray (Mass.) 250.)

[1863] *Taylor* v. *Kneeland*, 1 Doug. 67.

[1864] *Long* v. *Fleming*, 2 Miles, 104.

ALLEGATION.	PROOF.
Dr. F. is not a physician, but a twopenny bleeder.	If Dr. F. is a twopenny physician, I am none. I am a regular graduate and no quack.[1865]
He burnt my barn, innuendo feloniously burnt.	There is the man that burnt my barn; if he was not guilty of it he would not carry pistols.[1866]
He stole wheat last winter.	He, defendant, said he, plaintiff, stole away the wheat in the night, and I was well aware of it, and would have put him in jail for doing it.[1867]
That persons who would otherwise have retained and employed the plaintiff, wholly declined and refused so to do.	That other persons would have recommended the plaintiff, and that the persons named in the declaration would have employed plaintiff on such recommendation.[1868]
You swore false.	You have sworn false.[1869]
She is a great thief.	She is a bad one.[1870]
That plaintiff then had three or four vessels in the river.	That plaintiff had given out that there were three or four vessels in the river.[1871]

[1865] *Foster* v. *Small*, 3 Whart. 138.
[1866] *Van Keurin* v. *Griffis*, 2 Up. Can. Q. B. Rep. 423.
[1867] *McNaught* v. *Allen*, 8 Up. Can. Q. B. Rep. 304.
[1868] *Sterry* v. *Foreman*, 2 Car. & P. 592.
[1869] *Sanford* v. *Gaddis*, 15 Ill. 228.
[1870] *Hancock* v. *Winter*, 2 Marsh. 502.
[1871] *Wood* v. *Adams*, 6 Bing. 481; 4 C. & P. 268.

ALLEGATION.	PROOF.
This is my umbrella. He stole it from my back-door.	It is my umbrella. He stole it from my back-door.[1872]
Stolen.	*Taken* out of my yard.[1873]
You robbed the mail.	I am not like you, running about the country with forged deeds and robbing the mail, as you did.[1874]
Plaintiff had sworn a lie, and it is in him, for he had sworn what he, defendant, could prove to be a point-blank lie.	Plaintiff had sworn off a just account, and that he, defendant, could or would prove it.[1875]
You would steal, and you will steal.	A man that would do that would steal.[1876]
I, defendant, was summoned as a grand juror at last court, but I got the court to excuse me from serving, for if I had served I would have been bound to have indicted W. for theft.	If I, defendant, had served on the grand jury, I would have been bound to have indicted Mr. Street, the plaintiff.[1877]
Mismanagement or ignorance.	Ignorance or inattention.[1878]
There was a collusion between A., B., and C.	There was a collusion between A. and B.[1879]

[1872] *Walters* v. *Mace*, 2 B. & A. 756; 1 Ch. 607. The allegation concerned a thing present, and the proof a thing not present.

[1873] *Shepherd* v. *Bliss*, 2 Stark. Rep. 510.

[1874] *McBean* v. *Williams*, 5 Up. Can. Q. B. Rep. O. S. 689.

[1875] *Berry* v. *Dryden*, 7 Mis. 324.

[1876] *Sties* v. *Kemble*, 27 Penn. St. Rep. 112.

[1877] *Street* v. *Bushnell*, 24 Miss. (3 Jones) 328.

[1878] *Brooks* v. *Blanshard*, 1 Cr. & M. 779; 3 Tyrw. 844.

[1879] *Johnson* v. *Tait*, 6 Binn. 121.

ALLEGATION.	PROOF.
You stole a dollar from A.	You stole a dollar from B.[1880]
Venereal disease.	Disgraceful disease.[1881]

§ 372. In New York, under the Code of Procedure, great latitude of amendment is allowed ; besides the right to amend once of course, the court may order an amendment before or upon the trial, or at any time thereafter.[1882] Prior to the Code of Procedure, plaintiff allowed to amend inducement after issue, where otherwise the right of action would have been barred by the statute of limitations.[1883] Plaintiff allowed to insert additional words, but not a new cause of action.[1885] Plaintiff allowed to insert a newly discovered cause of action.[1886] Defendant permitted to add an additional justification.[1887] Amendments too, seem to be allowed with great liberality in the courts in

---

[1880] *Self* v. *Gardner*, 15 Mis. 480.

[1881] *Wagaman* v. *Byers*, 17 Md. 183. These following are adjudged material variances: If the declaration be for these words, "Thou *procuredst* eight or ten of thy neighbors to perjure themselves," and the jury find that he said, Thou *hast caused* eight or ten, &c., for it might be a remote cause, scilicit, without procurement. Nar. (the declaration), He *is* a bankrupt. Verdict, He will be a bankrupt within two days. Nar. He is a thief. Verdict, He stole a horse. Nar. Thou art a murderer. Verdict, He is, &c. Nar. *I know* him to be a thief. Verdict, *I think* him to be a thief. And at p. 330: Nar. Strong thief. Verdict, Thief. Nar. I say, &c. Verdict, I affirm or I doubt not. Nar. The plaintiff will do such a thing. Verdict, I think in my conscience he will do such a thing. (1 Trials per Pais, 329.)

[1882] Code of Procedure, §§ 169, 172, 173.

[1883] *Tobias* v. *Harland*, 1 Wend. 93. Leave to add a new count granted (*Conroe* v. *Conroe*, 47 Penn. St. R. 198), but denied after right of action had been barred by statute of limitations. (*Smith* v. *Smith*, 45 Penn. St. Rep. 403.)

[1885] *Weston* v. *Worden*, 19 Wend. 648. Plaintiff permitted on the trial to add a new cause of action. (*Miles* v. *Van Horn*, 17 Ind. 245.)

[1886] *Williams* v. *Cooper*, 1 Hill, 637. Leave to add a justification refused. (*Waters* v. *Guthrie*, 2 Bailey, 106).

[1887] *Graham* v. *Woodhull*, 1 Car. 497. Defendant on trial allowed to strike out general issue and plead a justification. Anon. 1 Hill (So. Car.) 251.

England ; thus another count was allowed to be added after a rule for a new trial.[1888] On the trial the words charged were allowed to be amended, the substance of the allegation remaining the same.[1889] Plaintiff allowed to amend by alleging that the words were spoken of him in his character of auctioneer.[1890] Amendment by striking out innuendoes refused.[1891] Leave to plead a justification, after verdict, denied.[1892]

[1888] *Wyatt* v. *Cocks*, 10 Moore, 504. And see *Clarke* v. *Albert*, 1 Gale, 358. The statutes as to amendments to be liberally construed. (*Smith* v. *Knowelden*, 9 Dowl. 40.)

[1889] *Pater* v. *Baker*, 3 C. B. 831; *Foster* v. *Pointer*, 9 Car. & P. 718; *Saunders* v. *Bate*, 38 Eng. Law & Eq. R. 409; and see *Lister* v. *McNeal*, 12 Ind. 302.

[1890] *Ramsdale* v. *Greenacre*, 1 F. & F. 61.

[1891] *Prudhomme* v. *Fraser*, 1 M. & Rob. 435; 2 Adol. & El. 645.

[1892] *Kirby* v. *Simpson*, 3 Dowl. Pra. Cas. 791. Leave to add a plea of the statute of limitations refused. (*Allensworth* v. *Coleman*, 5 Dana, 315.) But granted. (*Brickett* v. *Davis*, 21 Pick. 404.)

CHAPTER XVI.

EVIDENCE FOR PLAINTIFF.

Proof—of publication—of oral publication—of publication in writing—of defendant's liability. Opinion of witnesses as to meaning. Proof of inducement—of plaintiff's good reputation—of malice—to aggravate damages. Falsehood not evidence of malice. Other publications by defendant—subsequent publications—publication after commencement of action. Defendant's ill-will to plaintiff. Ill-will to plaintiff of persons other than the defendant. The publication itself evidence of malice. Attempted justification an aggravation. Evidence in reply.

§ 373. If the publication is denied, a publication must be proved, and the publication proved must be one for which the defendant is responsible. On this subject much has already been said in a previous chapter [Ch. VI. 3]. Whether there has been any publication by the defendant is a question of fact for the jury, but what amounts to a publication for which the defendant is responsible as publisher is a question of law for the court. If the facts were, that the defendant has posted up a libel in a public place, but had taken it down again before any one had read it, there would in point of law be no publication, but if it were doubtful whether before it was taken down some one had not read it, that would be a question of fact for the jury.[1909]

§ 374. The post-mark on a letter has been held *prima facie*

[1909] Stark. Ev. tit. *Law and Fact.*

evidence of the publication of the letter.[1894] The production
by the plaintiff on the trial of a letter addressed to a third person held evidence of the publication of the letter, without the
oath of the person to whom the letter is addressed.[1895] Where
the letter produced was addressed to a person in Scotland, with
the seal broken and a post-mark of a place in England, where
it was proved to have been received and forwarded, held *primâ
facie* evidence that the letter was received by the party to
whom it was addressed, and of its publication.[1896] Where the
defamatory matter was contained in a letter addressed by the
defendant to the plaintiff, and there was no evidence of its publication, other than the production of the letter by the plaintiff,
it was held not sufficient;[1897] but where in addition it was
shown that the letter was in the handwriting of the defendant,
and that he had read it aloud in the presence of several persons, it was held that the letter might be read to the jury.[1898]
The defendant had been chairman of a public meeting, at
which the libel in question had been signed by him, and ordered by the meeting to be published: on a demurrer to
evidence, an affidavit of the defendant, and one of A, which
the defendant in his own affidavit referred to as correct, stating
that the address was ordered to be published, and admitting
and justifying the publication, together with a copy of the
address annexed to the affidavits, and referred to in them, were
held sufficient evidence of publication.[1899]

[1894] *Shipley* v. *Todhunter*, 7 C. & P. 680; *Hitchon* v. *Best*, 1 B. & B. 299; *Rex*
v. *Watson*, 1 Camp. 215; *Rex v. Johnson*, 7 East, 65; *Fletcher* v. *Braddyll*, 3 Stark.
Cas. 64; *Rex* v. *Williams*, 2 Camp. 505; *Rex* v. *Girdwood*, East P. C. 1116.

[1895] *Callan* v. *Gaylord*, 3 Watts, 321.

[1896] *Warren* v. *Warren*, 1 Cr. M. & R. 250; 4 Tyrw. 850; *Stocken* v. *Collen*, 7
M. & W. 515.

[1897] *McIntosh* v. *Matherly*, 9 B. Monr. 119.

[1898] *McCombs* v. *Tuttle*, 5 Blackf. 431. See note 102, *ante*. Evidence of the
reading the libel in a public place, and of comments upon it in defendant's hearing, and that it was put up on handbills by persons unknown, was permitted to
be proved. (*Rice* v. *Withers*, 9 Wend. 138.)

[1899] *Lewis* v. *Few*, 5 Johns. 1.

§ 375. Where a witness who heard the words spoken immediately committed them to writing, he may, on swearing that
he wrote down the exact words, read what he wrote in evidence. But if the words were not written down until some
time after the witness heard them, although he may not
read his memorandum in evidence, he may refer to it to refresh
his memory.[1900] In actions of slander, witnesses cannot be
allowed to state the impression the words used made upon their
minds, but they must state positively, or as near as memory will
allow, the exact words.[1901]

§ 376. In an action of libel against the proprietor of a
newspaper, a copy of the paper bought at the office, if alleging
on its face that it was the property of the defendant, is sufficiently connected with the defendant by proof, and a paragraph
in it is relevant to read to the jury to show the circulation of
the paper.[1902] On a declaration in slander, consisting of a single count, in which the slanderous words were alleged to have
been uttered by the defendant "on the 1st day of November,
1856, and on divers other days and times before the purchase
of the plaintiff's writ," it was held, that the plaintiff might, in
support of his action, prove a single uttering of the slander by
the defendant on any day prior to the date of the writ.[1903]   A
declaration alleged that the defendants published, or caused to
be published, in a certain pamphlet, a libel concerning the
plaintiff. From the evidence, it appeared that the defendants
were instrumental in procuring the vote of a medical society
expelling the plaintiff therefrom for gross immorality. The

[1900] *Sandwell* v. *Sandwell*, Holt R. 295 ; and see *Huff* v. *Bennett*, 6 N. Y. 337.

[1901] *Teague* v. *Williams*, 7 Ala. 844 ; *Alley* v. *Neely*, 5 Blackf. 200; *contra*,
Hawks v. *Patton*, 18 Geo. 52.   Where, in an action for slander, it is important to
show that the charge proved by a witness for the plaintiff had reference to a
trial, it is not indispensable for the witness to give the exact words of the defendant showing such reference; but, if this is desired, they should be elicited
on cross-examination. (*Douge* v. *Pearce*, 13 Ala. 127.)

[1902] *Fay* v. *Bennett*, 4 Duer, 247.

[1903] *Rice* v. *Cottrell*, 5 Rhode Island, 340; and as to proving time of publication,
see *Richardson* v. *Roberts*, 23 Geo. 215; *Wright* v. *Britton*, 1 Morris, 286.

vote was published among the transactions of the society, by the regular committee of publication, of which the defendants were not members. Held, that the allegation in the declaration was not supported.[1904] That one had heard of a slanderous report with regard to the plaintiff, is evidence to prove the circulation of the report, but not to prove that the defendant circulated the report.[1905]

Where a declaration for publishing a libel does not purport to set it forth in *haec verba*, and a libel corresponding with the declaration is produced on the trial, if the jury believe that the defendant published any part of the libellous matter, they must find for the plaintiff.[1906] It is calculated to mislead the jury to refer it to them to determine whether the defendant "in substance" spoke or published the words charged, without explaining the meaning that the law would attach to that expression in connection with the proof of the slander charged.[1907]

§ 377. The words of a defamatory writing cannot be proved by parol, until it has been shown that the writing itself cannot be produced.[1908] But if after the publication the defendant obtains possession of the writing and refuses to produce it, in that case secondary evidence of its contents may be given.[1909] Where, to prove the defendant the *author* of a libel which the defendant had notice to produce, A. was called, who swore he received the manuscript of the libel from the defendant and returned it to him. But on cross-examination the witness stated that he had not delivered the manuscript to the defendant himself, but had delivered it to his [the witness'] own servant to deliver to the defendant. A.'s servant was called, who testified that he

---

[1904] *Barrows* v. *Carpenter*, 11 Cush. 456.

[1905] *Schwartz* v. *Thomas*, 2 Wash. 167.

[1906] *Metcalf* v. *Williams*, 3 Litt. 387.

[1907] *Attebury* v. *Powell*, 29 Mis. (8 Jones) 429.

[1908] *Simpson* v. *Wiley*, 4 Porter, 215; *Aspinwall* v. *Whitmore*, 1 Root, 408; and see *McGrath* v. *Cox*, 3 Up. Can. Q. B. Rep. 332.

[1909] *Winter* v. *Donovan*, 8 Gill, 370; *Le Merchant's case*, 2 T. R. 201; *Layer's case*, 6 State Tr. 229.

delivered the manuscript to the defendant's servant; held, not sufficient to enable the prosecutor to give parol evidence of the existence of the paper, nor for considering the defendant as the *author* of the libel.[1910] There are instances of the courts having refused to compel the production of the writing, and at the same time have excluded secondary evidence of its contents; as, where the communication was addressed to the governor of a State respecting a State officer, the court held that the governor to whom it was addressed might exercise his own discretion as to its production, and excluded parol evidence of its contents.[1911]

§ 378. Where the defamatory writing has been lost, secondary evidence of its contents may be given.[1912] Where the libel [a song] from which the publication took place was lost, a

---

[1910] *Rex* v. *Pearce*, Peake's Cases, 75.

[1911] *Gray* v. *Pentland*, 2 S. & R. 23; 4 S. & R. 420; and see *Wyatt* v. *Gore*, Holt's Cases, 299; *Oliver* v. *Bentick*, 3 Taunt. 456. In an action for libel, pending in the Circuit Court of the District of Columbia, the Hon. Edwin M. Stanton, Secretary of War, was summoned as a witness to produce an original letter addressed to the former Assistant Secretary of War, Dana, which letter contains the matter alleged to be libellous. Mr. Stanton put in an affidavit respectfully submitting his objections to the production of the paper in question, and asking to be discharged from further attendance. The affidavit bore the following indorsement: "Sir: Letters on file with the Heads of Departments are privileged communications. Unless their publication has been authorized, no copies should be taken at private request, and the production of the original cannot be compelled in a suit between individuals. It has been ruled that such communications cannot be made the foundation of an action for libel. Then I think the head of a department is bound not to produce a paper on file in his office. Such a letter as you describe is a privileged communication. (Signed.) J. Speed, Attorney-General." And in an action for libel, it was held that a member of Parliament could not be examined as to what was said by the plaintiff in the course of a debate in Parliament. (*Plunkett* v. *Cobbett*, 5 Esp. 136.) The plaintiff having failed in his application to the Senate for the removal of the injunction of secrecy, the testimony of a Senator was admitted to prove that plaintiff's nomination had been rejected by the Senate. (*Law* v. *Scott*, 5 Har. & J. 438.) It has been held to be optional on the part of counsel whether he will disclose what passed in court on his making a motion. (*Curry* v. *Walter*, 1 Esp. 456.)

[1912] *Gates* v. *Bowker*, 18 Verm. (3 Washb.) 23; *Weir* v. *Hoss*, 6 Ala. 881.

printer was allowed to produce a similar one printed at the
same time and which he proved corresponded with the one
lost.[1913] Where, to sustain an action of libel, the proof sought
to be made was, that the publication was by an affidavit, made
by the defendant before a magistrate, imputing to the plaintiff
the offence of hog stealing, and the only evidence of the existence of the affidavit was an imperfect memorandum of it, in
the handwriting of the magistrate, who was alive and out of
the State, and there was no sufficient proof of its being, in
whole or in part, a copy; it was held, that the evidence was
not sufficient to sustain the action.[1914]

§ 379. In an action against the proprietor of a newspaper
for a libel contained in it, proof that the paper came from the
defendant's office, and was one copy of an edition of the same
date, and alleging on its face that he is the proprietor, is proof
of a publication by him;[1915] and so in such an action testimony
by a subscriber for the paper, upon being shown the number of
the paper containing the article in question, that it was in all
respects similar to the paper left at his office, and that he had
read the article contained in the paper produced in the one left
at his office, is sufficient proof of publication, without producing
the paper left at his office.[1916] And where a witness swore that
he was a printer, and had been in the office of the defendant
when a certain paper was printed, and he saw it printed there,
and the paper produced by the plaintiff was, he believed,
printed with the types used in the defendant's office; held, that
this was *primâ facie* evidence of the publication by the defendant.[1917] The witness in this case might have refused to testify
on the ground that he inculpated himself,[1918] but as he did not

---

[1913] *Johnson* v. *Hudson*, 7 Ad. & Ell. 233, n.

[1914] *Sanders* v. *Rollinson*, 2 Strobh. 447.

[1915] *The State* v. *Jeandell*, 5 Harring. 475; *Fry* v. *Bennett*, 4 Duer, 247.

[1916] *Huff* v. *Bennett*, 4 Sandf. 120; and see *Commonwealth* v. *Blanding*, 3 Pick.
304.

[1917] *Southwick* v. *Stevens*, 10 Johns. 442; *McCorkle* v. *Burns*, 5 Binney, 340.

[1918] *Moloney* v. *Bartley*, 3 Camp. 210.

claim his privilege his testimony was properly received; and so 'it was held in the case of a witness who had written the defamatory matter at the request of the defendant.[1919]

. § 380. Proof that the defendant gave a bond to the stamp-office for the duties on the advertisements in a newspaper under the statute 29 George III., ch. 50, and that he had occasionally applied at the stamp-office respecting the duties, was held to be sufficient evidence of his being the publisher of such newspaper.[1920] And the production of a certified copy of the affidavit required by the statute 38 George III., ch. 78, with a newspaper containing the libel, corresponding with the paper described in the affidavit; held, to be sufficient evidence of publication by the defendant.[1921] Where, in an action for libel in a newspaper, the one put in had the place of publication " at the corner of Charles street and Hadfield street, in the parish of M.," the certificate of the stamp-office declaration was at " No. 23, Charles street," in the parish, &c.; held, sufficiently to identify the newspaper as published by the declarant, within the 6th and 7th William IV., ch. 76.[1922]

§ 381. The publication of a libel in a newspaper may be proved by producing the copy of the newspaper filed in the office of the commissioner of stamps,[1923] or by producing a copy filed in the office of publication of such newspaper.[1924] On the trial of an action for a libel in a newspaper, a witness stated that he was president of a literary institution having eighty members; that about the date of the paper proved, one was

---

[1919] *Schenck* v. *Schenck*, 1 Spencer, 208.

[1920] *Rex* v. *Topham*, 4 T. R. 126. Distributing newspapers containing defamatory matter and receiving pay for them through an agent, is sufficient evidence of publication by defendant. *The State* v. *Davis*, 8 Yeates, 128.

[1921] *Mayne* v. *Fletcher*, 9 B. & Cr. 382; *Rex* v. *Hunt*, 9 B. & Cr. 382, n.; *Rex* v. *Hart*, 10 East, 94.

[1922] *Baker* v. *Wilkinson*, 1 Carr. & M. 399; *Rex* v. *Donnison*, 4 B. & Ad. 698.

[1923] *Cook* v. *Ward*, 6 Bing. 409.

[1924] *Rex* v. *Pearce*, Peake's Cas. 75.

brought (he could not say by whom) to the reading-room of the institution, and left there gratuitously; that, a fortnight after, it was taken away without his authority, and never returned; that he had searched for it and could not find it, and believed it to be lost or destroyed; that the title of it was the same as that proved, and, as far as he could judge from a glance at it, it contained the libel in question, and he believed it was a copy of that paper. He was not cross-examined. Held, first, that secondary evidence of the contents of the copy was properly admitted; secondly, that there was evidence for the jury that the paper so sent to the institution was a copy of that which contained the libel; thirdly, that, though sent by a person unknown, it was evidence against the defendant, not to show malice, but to affect the damages, by showing the extent of circulation.[1825] But where a defendant alleged, in mitigation, that a libellous book was published against him by plaintiff, and in support of such allegation a bookseller produced, from his own possession, a printed book, stating his belief that it is one of a number of copies published at his shop; held, that this was not evidence for the jury that another book with the same contents was actually published.[1826]

§ 382. Where a person has admitted that he was the author of a libel in a certain newspaper, any other newspaper of the same impression may be read to the jury, and is not secondary evidence.[1827] A newspaper may be read in evidence although not stamped.[1828] To prove the publication of a libellous pamphlet, a witness testified that she received from the defendant a copy of a pamphlet, of which she read some portions, and lent it to several persons in succession, who returned it to her, and although there was no mark by which she could identify it, she

---

[1825] *Gathercole* v. *Miall*, 15 M. & W. 319; 15 Law Jour. Rep. 179, Ex.; 10 Jurist, 337; 7 Law Times, 89.

[1826] *Watts* v. *Fraser*, 7 Ad. & E. 223; 1 Mo. & Rob. 451; *Moore* v. *Oastler*, 1 Mo. & Rob. 451.

[1827] *McLaughlin* v. *Russell*, 17 Ohio, 475; *Woodburn* v. *Miller*, Cheves, 194.

[1828] *Rex* v. *Pearce*, Peake's Cas. 75; 1 Esp. 456.

believed the copy produced to be the same, but could not swear that it was; held, that this was evidence of publication proper to be left to the jury.[1929] Where a number of placards is printed, and a party adopts and uses some of them, all the rest are duplicate originals, and one of them may be read against such party, without notice to produce.[1930] But placards in the windows of third persons, setting forth the forthcoming contents of the newspaper in which the libel was contained; held, inadmissible against the author, unless he were connected with the publication of them.[1931] If the manuscript of a libel be proved to be in the handwriting of the defendant, and it be also proved to have been printed and published, this is evidence to go to the jury that it was published by the defendant, although there be no evidence given to show that the printing and publication were by his direction.[1932] And as handwritings may be compared, in an action for libel, if the testimony is corroborated from other sources,[1933] papers in the handwriting of the defendant, found in the house of the editor of the newspaper in which the libel was published, were held admissible to prove the publication by the defendant.[1934]

§ 383. The defendant's liability as publisher may be proved by showing: a copy of the alleged libel in the defendant's handwriting,[1935] addressed to the editor of a newspaper;[1936] or

---

[1929] *Fryer* v. *Gathercole*, 18 Law Jour. Rep. 887, Ex.; 13 Jurist, 542; 13 Law Times, 285.

[1930] *Rex* v. *Watson*, 2 Stark. Rep. 190.

[1931] *Raikes* v. *Richards*, 2 Car. & P. 562.

[1932] *Reg.* v. *Lovett*, 9 Car. & P, 462.

[1933] *Cullan* v. *Gaylord*, 3 Watts, 321; *Waddington* v. *Cousins*, 7 Car. & P. 595; see *Rex* v. *Cator*, 4 Esp. 117; *Case of the Seven Bishops*, 4 State Tr. 388.

[1934] *Tarpley* v. *Blabey*, 2 Bing. N. S. 437; 2 Sc. 642; 7 Car. & P. 395; *May* v. *Brown*, 3 B. & Cr. 113; *Finnerty* v. *Tipper*, 2 Camp. 72; *Wakley* v. *Johnson*, 1 Ry. & M. 422. In an action for services in preparing reports for a newspaper, the authorship being in question, it is not competent to ask the opinion of a witness (founded merely on his having read the articles and professing a knowledge of the plaintiff's style of writing) as to whether the reports were written by the plaintiff. (*Lee* v. *Bennett*, How. Ct. of App. Cas. 202.)

[1935] *McCombs* v. *Tuttle*, 5 Blackf. 431.

by showing that defendant paid the printer or publisher of a newspaper for the insertion of the defamatory matter in the newspaper of such printer or publisher; [1987] or by showing the defendant's admission of authorship.[1988] Where the defendant admitted that he was the author of the alleged libel, *errors excepted*, held that the burden was on him to show that the errors were material.[1989] The fact that the defendant made the publication to the witness under an injunction of secrecy, is no objection to the proof of the publication by such witness.[1940] •

§ 384. The court and jury, and not the witnesses, are to construe the words.[1941] And the opinions of witnesses as to the meaning of the language published is not admissible,[1942] and, therefore, a witness cannot be asked how he understood the words published,[1943] nor be permitted to state what meaning he understood the defendant to convey by the words.[1944] The words being unambiguous, it is not competent for a witness to say that he understood the publisher to mean differently from the common import of the words.[1945] The plaintiff and de-

---

[1986] *Bond* v. *Douglass*, 7 C. & P. 626.

[1987] *Schenck* v. *Schenck*, 1 Spencer, 208.

[1938] *Commonwealth* v. *Guild*, Thacher's Crim. Cas. 329; *Rex* v. *Burdett*, 4 B. & A. 717; *The Seven Bishops' Case*, 4 State Trials, 304.

[1939] *Rex* v. *Hall*, Str. 416.

[1940] *McGovern* v. *Manifee*, 7 Monr. 314.

[1941] *Olmsted* v. *Miller*, 1 Wend. 510. In *Weed* v. *Bibbins*, 32 Barb. 315, held that evidence of what was generally understood by "the Cunningham affair" was improperly admitted. And see *Justice* v. *Kirlin*, 17 Ind. 588; *Wachter* v. *Quenzer*, 29 N. Y. 552; and *ante*, ch. vii. and §§ 281, 286.

[1942] *Smart* v. *Blanchard*, 42 N. Hamp. 137. Unless the words are ambiguous, and their application doubtful, in which case the testimony of hearers as to how they understood the words is admissible. (*Id.*; and see *Barton* v. *Holmes*, 16 Iowa, 252; *Smith* v. *Miles*, 15 Verm. 245.) In *Leonard* v. *Allen*, 11 Cush. 241, an action for slander, not by direct words, but by expressions, gestures, and intonations of voice, it was held competent for witnesses who heard the expressions to state what they understood the defendant to mean by them, and to whom he intended to apply them.

[1943] *Wright* v. *Paige*, 36 Barb. 438.

[1944] *Snell* v. *Snow*, 13 Metc. 278.

[1945] *Potts* v. *Pacs*, 7 Jones' Law N. C. 558.

fendant being present at a tavern where there had been a raffle, defendant said, "I am surprised at ·R. allowing a blackleg in this room." On the trial, a witness being asked what he understood by "blackleg," answered, "A person in the habit of cheating at cards." Held, by Pollock, C. B., and Watson, B., that the evidence was proper; and by Martin and Bramwell, BB., that it was not proper.[1946] Nor can a witness be asked to whom he understood the defamatory matter to apply.[1947]

§ 385. Matter of inducement, if put in issue, must be proved.[1948] If not put in issue, no proof of it is necessary, and no evidence respecting it is admissible. Matter of inducement is not put in issue by a plea of not guilty.[1949] Matter of inducement may be proved by parol.[1950] When the words are actionable only by reason of their relation to extrinsic facts, such facts must be proved; as where the words were charged as spoken of a constable, imputing misconduct in the execution of a bench warrant, the words not being actionable in themselves, it was held that the warrant must be proven.[1951] In an action against the editor of a newspaper for a libellous publication, it is admissible for the plaintiff to show articles in subsequent numbers of the same paper, for the purpose of proving that the plaintiff was the person intended to be defamed.[1952]

§ 386. Pursuant to a rule already referred to [§ 315], the defamatory matter, so far as it goes, is evidence of the intro-

---

[1946] *Barnett* v. *Allen*, 3 Hurl. & Nor. 376; 1 Fost. & Fin. 285. Jury told to consider if words had conveyed meaning of a person who had gambled so as to be liable to a criminal prosecution. (*Id.*)

[1947] *Rangler* v. *Himmel*, 37 Penn. St. R. 130. Held that a witness may say who is meant by the libel. (*Smalley* v. *Stark*, 9 Ind. 386.) See *ante*, § 97, notes 99, 132, 150.

[1948] "It is still necessary under the plea of not guilty to prove the colloquium." Cooke on Defam. 145.

[1949] *Gwynne* v. *Sharpe*, 1 Carr. & M. 532.

[1950] *Southwick* v. *Stevens*, 10 Johns. 443.

[1951] *Kinney* v. *Nash*, 3 N. Y. 177.

[1952] *White* v. *Sayward*, 33 Maine, 322.

ductory averments.[1962] Thus for words spoken respecting the plaintiff's trade; if the words assume that, at the time they were spoken, the plaintiff was engaged in such trade, there is no need of proving that fact.[1964] Where it was to be plainly inferred, from the general tenor of the libel, that it was the object of the writer to represent the plaintiff as holding a situation of trust and confidence, and that he had abused it, held that it was sufficient to sustain the allegation in the declaration of plaintiff's holding such situation.[1965] A declaration in libel stated as inducement that the plaintiff was a surgeon and member of the College of Surgeons, which said college had the power of expelling persons guilty of unprofessional conduct, and of unprofessionally advertising themselves and their cures. The libel was alleged to be published of and concerning the plaintiff as such surgeon, and of and concern-

---

[1962] *Rutherford* v. *Evans,* 6 Bing. 451. In this case the plaintiff declared in respect of a libel upon him as " Surveyor of the New England Company;" held sufficient for him to prove employment by a company generally known by that name.

[1964] *Healer* v. *Degant,* 8 Ind. 501; *Rodebaugh* v. *Hollingsworth,* 6 Ind. 339; *Berryman* v. *Wise,* 4 T. R. 366. Where, in an action for a libel against the plaintiff, a medical practitioner, of and concerning him in his said practice, no evidence was offered of the plaintiff being of any regular degree, the libel stating him to be a quack, and that certain persons had the misfortune to come within his doctrinal prescriptions; held, that if the jury considered that the libel spoke of him as a medical practitioner, the case was not withdrawn from their consideration, although they might not give the same damages as to a person proved to be a regular practitioner. (*Long* v. *Chubb,* 5 C. & P. 55.) Where the declaration alleged that there were such states as C. and B., that the plaintiff and one H. had been appointed minister plenipotentiary and consul-general respectively from those states to this country, the libel on the face of it admitted that there were such states; and it being proved at the trial that the plaintiff had been appointed such officer for the one state, and H. for the other, held that the allegations were sufficiently made out. (*Yrissari* v. *Clements,* 3 Bing. 432.)

[1965] *Bagnall* v. *Underwood,* 11 Price, 621. In an action for a libel the defendant pleaded justification, and in his plea introduced certain passages from a pamphlet written by plaintiff, upon which plea issue was joined. Held, that this was not so far an adoption of the whole pamphlet as true, as to enable the plaintiff to read other passages from it, to show that the defendant was the aggressor in the controversy which led to its publication. (*Kearney* v. *Gough,* 5 Gill & Johns. 457.)

ing the said college and its said power. One of the libels complained of contained a statement that the college had the power of expelling its members. The second plea* was that the plaintiff was not a surgeon and member of the College of Surgeons having the power of expelling persons guilty of unprofessional conduct, and of unprofessionally advertising themselves and their cures. Held, that the traverse put in issue the power of the college to expel, and that the statement in the libel itself was not sufficient evidence of such power.[1056]

§ 387. It is a vexed question whether in an action for slander or libel the plaintiff may, in aggravation of the damage he has sustained, introduce evidence of his good reputation prior to the publication complained of; on this point, as upon all the others relating to the proceedings in an action, we can do no more than call attention to the decisions upon the subject. Although it may be true that in an action for slander or libel the reputation of the plaintiff is in issue, it is nevertheless true that, as a general rule, the reputation of the plaintiff is assumed to be good until the contrary is shown [§§ 313, 314]; and that, unless some blot upon the plaintiff's reputation is set up as a mitigating circumstance, or his reputation is otherwise assailed, he is not permitted for any purpose to introduce any evidence on the subject; thus it has been held that evidence cannot be given of the fairness of the plaintiff's character [reputation], even where a justification is pleaded, unless attacked by the defendant.[1057] But held, also, that where the general

---

[1056] *Wakley* v. *Healey*, 18 Law Jour. Rep. 426, Ex.; 13 Law Times, 259.

[1057] *Shipman* v. *Burrows*, 1 Hall, 399; *Harcourt* v. *Harrison*, 1 Hall, 474; *Cornwall* v. *Richardson*, 1 Ry. & M. 305; 1 C. & Y. 106; *Severance* v. *Hilton*, 4 Foster, 147; *McGee* v. *Sodusky*, 5 J. J. Marsh. 185; *Inman* v. *Foster*, 8 Wend. 602; *Dame* v. *Kenney*, 5 Fost. 818; *Petrie* v. *Rose*, 5 Watts & Serg. 364; *Holley* v. *Burgess*, 9 Ala. 728; *Chubb* v. *Gsell*, 34 Penn. St. R. 114; *Miles* v. *Van Horn*, 17 Ind. 245; and see *Rhodes* v. *James*, 7 Ala. 574; *Rector* v. *Smith*, 11 Iowa, 302; *Tibbs* v. *Brown*, 2 Grant's Cases (Penn.) 39; *Fleetcraft* v. *Jenks*, 3 Whart. 158; *McCabe* v. *Platter*, 6 Blackf. 405; contra, *Scott* v. *Peebles*, 2 Sm. & M. 546; *Byrket* v. *Monohon*, 7 Blackf. 88. It is not competent for the plaintiff to make proof of his good character, in reply to evidence of the truth of the charge. (*Houghtaling* v. *Kilderhouse*, 1 Coms. 530; affirming 2 Barb. 149; *Matthews* v. *Huntley*, 9 N. Hamp. 146; *Springstein* v.

issue only is pleaded, the plaintiff may give evidence of his good character.[1968] In slander for the charge of perjury, where the plaintiff is permitted to give evidence of his character to protect himself, it is error to confine him to evidence of his general character for truth and veracity.[1959] A witness called by the plaintiff in an action of slander, in support of the plaintiff's general character, stated that some persons spoke very ill and some very well of it. Held, that the plaintiff might ask the witness in what particulars some people spoke against him.[1960]

§ 388. Where the language is actionable and the publication does not appear to be on any occasion which renders it privileged, there the language is presumed to be false and malicious, i. e., published without lawful excuse.[1961] But where the publication is *primâ facie* privileged, the onus of proving malice in fact, i. e., that the defendant was actuated by motives of personal spite or ill-will, is upon the plaintiff. The

Field, Anthon, 185; *Her* v. *Cromer*, Wright, 441; *Stow* v. *Converse*, 3 Conn. 325.) Where the charge is such that the defendant's evidence in justification, though insufficient to prove it, has a tendency to affect the general character of plaintiff, on the subject of the charge, he may reply by evidence of general good character in that particular. (*Wright* v. *Schroeder*, 2 Curtis, C. C. 548.)

[1958] *Williams* v. *Greenwade*, 3 Dana, 432; *King* v. *Waring*, 5 Esp. Cas. 14; *Bennett* v. *Hyde*, 6 Conn. 24; *Romayne* v. *Duanes*, 3 Wash. C. C. 246; *Sample* v. *Wynn*, Busbee Law (N. C.) 319; *Howell* v. *Howell*, 10 Ired. 82; *Burton* v. *March*, 6 Jones' Law N. C. 409.

[1959] *Steinman* v. *McWilliams*, 6 Barr, 170.

[1960] *Leonard* v. *Allen*, 11 Cush. 241.

[1961] *Fry* v. *Bennett*, 5 Sandf. 54; *Estes* v. *Antrobus*, 1 Miss. 197; *McKee* v. *Ingalls*, 4 Scam. 30; *Parke* v. *Blackiston*, 3 Harring. 373; *Kinney* v. *Hosea*, Id. 397; *Farley* v. *Ranck*, 3 Watts & Serg. 554; *Erwin* v. *Sumrow*, 1 Hawks, 472; *Dexter* v. *Spear*, 4 Mason, 115; *Bodwell* v. *Osgood*, 3 Pick. 379; *Weaver* v. *Hendrick*, 30 Miss. (9 Jones) 502; *Roberts* v. *Camden*, 9 East, 93; *Usher* v. *Severance*, 2 App. 9; *Yeates* v. *Reed*, 4 Blackf. 463; *Gilmer* v. *Enbank*, 13 Ill. 271; *Root* v. *King*, 7 Cow. 613; affirmed, 4 Wend. 113; *Trabue* v. *Mayo*, 3 Dana, 188; *Byrket* v. *Monohon*, 7 Blackf. 83; *Hudson* v. *Garner*, 22 Miss. (1 Jones) 423; *Curtis* v. *Massey*, 6 Gray, 261. The jury cannot infer the want of malice from the fact that the words were spoken only once, and stated as a common report. (*Mason* v. *Mason*, 4 N. Hamp. 110.)

existence or non-existence of this intent is a question for the
jury.[1002] "The want of proof on the part of the defendant
that the slander was true is not enough [to prove malice], and
the plaintiff, to maintain his action, must show that the charge
was false, before he can ask the jury to find the slander to be
malicious." [1003]

§ 389. It is said that falsehood *may* be evidence of malice.[1004] But the mere falsity of a publication without its being
shown that the publisher knew it to be false, is not *per se* evidence of malice. Thus, where the alleged libel was a complaint made by the defendant of the incompetency of the plaintiff, a surveyor, who had been sent to him for employment, and
the *innuendo* charged that the defendant meant that the plaintiff was not a competent and skilful surveyor, held, that evidence of the general competency and abilities of the plaintiff
was inadmissible to show malice.[1005] Making a statement which
is untrue to the knowledge of the party making it, is evi-

[1002] *Pattison* v. *Jones*, 8 B. & C. 578; 3 M. & R. 101; *Bromage* v. *Prosser*, 4 B.
& C. 247; 6 Dow. & R. 296; *Child* v. ' *Affleck*, 9 B. & C. 403; *Kelly* v. *Partington*, 4 B. & Ad. 700; 3 N. & M. 116; *Toogood* v. *Spyring*, 4 Tyrw. 582; 1 C. M.
& R. 573; *Kine* v. *Sewell*, 3 M. & W. 297; *Wright* v. *Woodgate*, 2 C. M. & R.
573; Tyrw. & G. 12; *Liddle* v. *Hodges*, 2 Bosw. 537; *Somerville* v. *Hawkins*,
10 C. B. 583; 15 Jurist, 450. The question of malice is for the jury to determine, upon all the facts and conversations in connection with which the words
were spoken. (*McKee* v. *Ingalls*, 4 Scam. 30; *Erwin* v. *Sumrow*, 1 Hawks, 472;
Smith v. *Youmans*, Riley, 88; *Robinson* v. *May*, 2 Smith, 3; *Roberts* v. *Camden*,
9 East, 93; *Coleman* v. *Playsted*, 36 Barb. 26.) In judging of the malicious
character of an alleged libel, the jury may take into consideration the whole
publication; and if it contains statements concerning other persons, which are
malicious, the jury may infer therefrom, that what is said of the plaintiff is also
malicious. (*Miller* v. *Butler*, 6 Cush. 71, and see *Caddy* v. *Barlow*, 1 M. & R.
275.)

[1003] *Fowler* v. *Bowen*, 30 N. Y. 26; and see *Edwards* v. *Chandler*, 14 Mich. 471;
Rogers v. *Clifton*, 3 B. & P. 587.

[1004] *Fairman* v. *Ives*, 5 B. & Ald. 645. Where part of a defamatory publication is shown to be true, the falsehood of the other part may be left to the jury
as evidence of malice. (*Blagg* v. *Sturt*, 10 Q. B. 897; 8 Law Times, 135.)

[1005] *Brine* v. *Bazalgette*, 18 Law Jour. Rep. 348, Ex.

dence of malice.[1966] On the trial of an action for slander, the plaintiff's witnesses proved that the slanderous statements were untrue in fact, but also that they were the natural and reasonable inferences from what took place, and which they professed to describe, and that the defendant was present at the occurrence which the slanderous statements referred to. The judge ruled that the occasion was privileged, but that the plaintiff must have a verdict unless the defendant proved that the statements were made without malice. Held, a right direction; the presence of the defendant being some evidence that the statements were made with a knowledge that they were untrue.[1967] To show that the defendant knew of the falsity of a charge of theft published by him the plaintiff was permitted to prove that after the time when the theft was alleged to have been committed by plaintiff, the defendant continued upon friendly terms with plaintiff.[1968]

§ 390. The plaintiff may prove in aggravation of the damages, his rank and condition in society,[1969] malice [ill-will] in defendant [§ 392, *post*], that defendant knew the charge to be false,[1970] other publications of words *not actionable*,[1971] or which are actionable,[1972] if, as is said, the right of action on such

---

[1966] *Fountain* v. *Boodle*, 2 Galo & D. 455; 5 Q. B. 5; *Harris* v. *Thompson*, 18 C. P. 338; *Sexton* v. *Brock*, 15 Ark. 345; *Farley* v. *Ranck*, 3 Watts & Serg. 554.

[1967] *Hartwell* v. *Vesey*, 9 C. B., N. S. 882. In slander, with general issue only pleaded, the plaintiff cannot in the first instance, give evidence tending to prove the defendant's knowledge of the falsity of the words spoken. (*Hartrauft* v. *Hesser*, 34 Penn. St. R. 117.)

[1968] *Burton* v. *March*, 6 Jones Law (N. C.) 409.

[1969] *Tillotson* v. *Cheetham*, 3 Johns. 56; *Hosley* v. *Brooks*, 20 Ill. 115; *Larned* v. *Buffington*, 3 Mass. 546; *Bodwell* v. *Swan*, 3 Pick. 376; *Howe* v. *Perry*, 15 Pick. 506; *Smith* v. *Lovelace*, 1 Duvall (Ky.), 215; *Justice* v. *Kerlin*, 17 Ind. 588; contra, see *Gandy* v. *Humphries*, 35 Ala. 617.

[1970] *Bullock* v. *Cloyes*, 4 Verm. 304; *Stow* v. *Converse*, 3 Conn. 325.

[1971] *Allensworth* v. *Coleman*, 5 Dana, 315. Slanderous words, not laid in the declaration, cannot be proved in aggravation of damages. (*Vincent* v. *Dixon*, 5 Ind. (Porter) 270; *Schenck* v. *Schenck*, 1 Spencer, 208; *Botelar* v. *Bell*, 1 Md. 173.)

[1972] *Lee* v. *Huson*, Peake, 166; *Bond* v. *Douglass*, 7 C. & P. 626; but see *Cook* v. *Field*, 3 Esp. 133.

word is barred by the statute of limitations.[1973] Subsequent
defamatory remarks upon the plaintiff[1974] and after the commencement of the action.[1975] In slander of a physician in his
profession, the currency of the slanderous report in the place
of his practice, following the utterance of the same by the defendant, may be given in evidence, as well as the effect of such
report upon the professional gains of the plaintiff, in aggravation of damages, without strict proof connecting the current
report with the slander of the defendant; the fact of such connection being for the jury, and not for the court to pass upon.[1976]
A libel charged M. with kidnapping a free colored man, and
referred to two numbers of a newspaper which showed the
transaction *in full; Held*, an aggravation of the libel.[1977] If

---

[1973] *Breckett* v. *Davis*, 21 Pick. 404; *Throgmorton* v. *Davis*, 4 Black. 174. But
words not laid in the declaration cannot be proved to make the words laid actionable. (*Jones* v. *Jones*, 1 Jones Law (N. C.), 495.) And where words actionable in
themselves, and not set out in the declaration are admitted in evidence to prove
malice, the court must caution the jury that they are not to increase the damages
on account of such words. (*Latton* v. *Young*, 2 Met. (Ky.) 558; *Barrett* v. *Long*,
8 Ir. Law Rep. 331; *Scott* v. *McKinnish*, 15 Ala. 662; *Burson* v. *Edwards*, 1 Carter, (Ind.) 164.)

[1974] *Chubb* v. *Westley*, 6 C. & P. 436. Where the words complained of are unambiguous, held, that proof of the publication subsequently of other words of the
same import, is inadmissible. (*Pearce* v. *Ormsby*, 1 M. & Rob. 455; *Symmons* v.
Blake, Id. 447.)

[1975] *Barwell* v. *Adkins*, 2 Sc. N. S. 11; *Healer* v. *Degant*, 3 Ind. 501; *Williams*
v. *Harrison*, 3 Miss. 411; *Hutch* v. *Potter*, 2 Gilman, 75; *Kean* v. *M'Laughlin*, 2
S. & R. 469; *contra, McGlenery* v. *Keller*, 3 Blackf. 488.
    In an action for a libel in a weekly periodical publication, a witness was
allowed to prove a purchase of a copy after the action brought. (*Plunkett* v.
Cobbett, 2 Selw. N. P. 1042; 2 Esp. 136.) If a defendant, after action brought,
issues a new publication, mingling the matter for which he has been sued with
new libellous matter, he cannot call upon the court to analyze the publication,
and separate what refers to the former libel, from the new slanderous matters it
may contain; but the whole may be read in evidence. (*Schenck* v. *Schenck*, 1
Spencer, 208.) As to proof of repetition of the slander not being admissible to
aggravate the damages, see *Burson* v. *Edwards*, 1 Carter, (Ind.) 164; *Shortley* v.
Miller, 1 Smith, 395; *Lanter* v. *McEwen*, 8 Blackf. 495; *Forbes* v. *Myers, Id.* 74.

[1976] *Rice* v. *Cottrell*, 5 R. I. 340. In *Hotchkiss* v. *Lothrop*, 1 Johns. 286; *Dole* v.
Lyon, 10 Johns. 447, doubted if defendant being indemnified was not admissible
in aggravation. *Semble* not, as indemnity void. *Ante*, note 1526.

[1977] *Nash* v. *Benedict*, 25 Wend. 645.

the publication was in a newspaper, the plaintiff may, to aggravate the damages, prove the extent of the circulation of that paper at the time of the publication of the alleged libellous matter, and to prove this, may give a copy of the defendant's paper in evidence containing a statement of the amount of circulation.[1978]

§ 391. The plaintiff, to aggravate damages, cannot prove the defendant's wealth,[1979] nor that it was currently reported that defendant had charged the plaintiff with the crime mentioned in the declaration,[1980] nor that the plaintiff had suffered distress of mind.[1981]

§ 392. The plaintiff may prove express malice—i. e., ill-will or hostility on the part of the defendant towards the plaintiff, either to aggravate the damages[1982] or to defeat a defence of privileged publication.[1983] To establish such malice, the

[1978] *Fry* v. *Bennett*, 28 N. Y. 330.

[1979] *Myers* v. *Malcolm*, 6 Hill, 292; *Ware* v. *Curtledge*, 24 Ala. 622; *Palmer* v. *Haskins*, 28 Barb. 90; *Morris* v. *Barker*, 4 Harring. 520; but see *Fry* v. *Bennett*, 4 Duer, 247; *Bennett* v. *Hyde*, 6 Conn. 24; *Case* v. *Marks*, 20 Conn. 248; *Adcock* v. *Marsh*, 8 Ired. 360; *Karney* v. *Paisley*, 13 Iowa, (5 With.) 89; *Humphries* v. *Parker*, 52 Maine, 502; *Hosley* v. *Brooks*, 20 Ill. 115; *Lewis* v. *Chapman*, 19 Barb. 252.

[1980] *Leonard* v. *Allen*, 11 Cush. (Mass.) 241.

[1981] *Terwilliger* v. *Wands*, 17 N. Y. 54; *Wilson* v. *Goit*, Id. 442; contra, *Swift* v. *Dickerman*, 31 Conn. 285.

[1982] *Fry* v. *Bennett*, 28 N. Y. 330; *True* v. *Plumley*, 36 Maine (1 Heath), 466; *Sawyer* v. *Hopkins*, 9 Shep. 268; *Jellison* v. *Goodwin*, 43 Maine, 287; 2 Greenl. Ev. § 418. Proof of malice in Connecticut. (*Moore* v. *Stevenson*, 27 Conn. 14.) Until some of the actionable words laid have been proved, evidence of the *quo animo* of the defendant is inadmissible. (*Abrams* v. *Smith*, 8 Blackf. 95.)

[1983] *Baboneau* v. *Farrell*, 28 Eng. Law & Eq. R. 339; 15 C. B. 360; 24 Law Jour. Rep. N. S. 9, C. P.; 1 Jur. N. S. 14; *Littlejohn* v. *Greeley*, 13 Abb. Pra. Rep. 41; *Suydam* v. *Moffat*, 1 Sandf. 459; *Root* v. *King*, 4 Wend. 113; *Garrett* v. *Dickerson*, 19 Md. 418; see *Holt* v. *Parsons*, 23 Texas, 9. It is no objection to a recovery for the slanderous words charged, that the publication of the same words has been proved against the defendant in a former action between the same parties, for the purpose of proving malice. (*Swift* v. *Dickerman*, 31 Conn. 285; *Campbell* v. *Butts*, 3 N. Y. 173.)

plaintiff may, it is held, in some cases, give in evidence other
publications by the defendant of defamatory language concerning the plaintiff, whether it be the same as or other than the
language declared upon, if of the like import.[1984] But the better opinion appears to be, that evidence of a charge of a *different nature* and at a different time from that alleged in the declaration, is inadmissible to prove malice or for any purpose.[1985]
This is in effect only another form of the rule that actionable
words not counted upon cannot be given in evidence,[1986] unless
a suit upon them is barred by the statute of limitations,[1987] and

---

[1984] *Burson* v. *Edwards*, 1 Carter (Ind.) 164; *Pearson* v. *Lemaitre*, 6 Sc. N. S.
607; 5 Man. & G. 700; *Delegal* v. *Highley*, 8 C. & P. 444; *Elliott* v. *Boyles*, 31
Penn. St. R. 65; *The State* v. *Jeandell*, 5 Harring. 475; *Price* v. *Wall*, 2 Quart.
Law Jour. 63.   Proof may be given of the publication of other words of like import. (*Thompson* v. *Bowers*, 1 Doug. 321; *Stearns* v. *Cox*, 17 Ohio, 590; *Taylor*
v. *Moran*, 4 Metc. (Ky.) 127.)   Extracts from a newspaper, being separate and
independent libels not declared on, may be offered in evidence to prove express
malice or as showing the *quo animo ;* such words cannot be made the foundation
of a recovery of damages for an injury the plaintiff may have suffered from them,
but can only affect the damages by showing the degree of the malice. (*Van
Derveer* v. *Sutphin*, 5 Ohio (N. S.) 293.)

[1985] *Howard* v. *Sexton*, 4 Coms. 157.   Although in slander, the plaintiff, to prove
the *animus*, may show a repetition of the words, or of such as show the same
train of thought, yet he cannot give in evidence other words which may be subject of another action; held, also, that it appearing that the plaintiff had recovered in another action against the defendant's son, what passed after the verdict, by way of proposal to compromise the second one, was admissible to show
that it was not vexatiously prosecuted. (*Deffries* v. *Davies*, 7 C. & P. 112.)

[1986] *Rundell* v. *Butler*, 7 Barb. 260; *Mead* v. *Daubigny*, Peake, 125; and see
Campbell v. *Butts*, 3 Coms. 173; *Keenholts* v. *Becker*, 3 Denio, 346; *Thomas* v.
Croswell, 7 Johns. 264; contra, *Duvall* v. *Griffith*, 2 Har. & Gil. 30; *Scott* v. *Mc-
Kinnish*, 15 Ala. 662; *Long* v. *Chubb*, 5 C. & P. 55; *Burton* v. *Brand*, 3 Green,
248; *Brittain* v. *Allen*, 2 Dev. 120; 3 Dev. 167.

[1987] *Inman* v. *Foster*, 8 Wend. 602; *Throgmorton* v. *Davis*, 4 Blackf. 174;
Flamingham v. *Boucher*, Wright, 746; see, also, *Lincoln* v. *Chrisman*, 10 Leigh,
338.   In an action of slander for words imputing perjury, an affidavit of the defendant, on which an indictment had been preferred, and which had been made
so long before as to be barred by the statute of limitations, charging the plaintiff
with the same perjury set out in the declaration, is admissible in evidence, as
proof of the repetition of the same words in a different form, and with more deliberation, and to show the *quo animo*. (*Randall* v. *Holsenbake*, 3 Hill (S. C.)
176.

their admission, where the statute has run, is opposed to principle, as it in effect restores a cause of action which has been taken away by the law.[1988] It seems clear that a repetition by the defendant of the defamatory matter complained of, is admissible to prove malice in fact; and it is said that within this rule any act or language of the defendant tending to show malice beyond that implied by the original publication, the subject of the action, may be proved.[1989]

§ 393. In an action for libel, the defendant pleaded the general issue, and also a plea under the 6th and 7th Vict., c. 96, denying actual malice, and stating an apology. On the trial, the plaintiff, in order to prove malice, tendered in evidence other publications of the defendant, going back above six years before the publication complained of, held, that these publications were admissible in evidence;[1990] but the court should, in such a case, call attention to the distance of time elapsed before the subsequent statements, and that those statements might have referred to some other and subsequent matter, so as not to show malice at the time of the publication complained of.[1991]

§ 394. A plaintiff may, to prove malice, give evidence of a publication by the defendant made subsequently to the publication declared upon, when the subsequent publication is of a like import with that declared upon or relating thereto, or is not actionable of itself, or explains any ambiguity in the matter declared upon.[1992] And in an action for words imputing per-

---

[1988] *Root* v. *Lowndes*, 6 Hill, 518.

[1989] *Fry* v. *Bennett*, 28 N. Y. 328. Damages recovered for previous slander may be given in evidence to show malice. (*Symmons* v. *Blake*, 1 M. & Rob. 477.)

[1990] *Barrett* v. *Long*, 16 Eng. Law & Eq. Rep. 1; 3 Ho. of Lords Cas. 395; 8 Ir. Law Rep. 331.

[1991] *Hemmings* v. *Gasson*, 36 Law Jour. Rep. 252, Q. B.; 1 El. B. & E. 346.

[1992] *Pearce* v. *Ormsby*, 1 M. & Rob. 455; *Mix* v. *Woodward*, 12 Conn. 262; *Williams* v. *Miner*, 18 Id. 464; *Symmons* v. *Blake*, 1 M. & Rob. 477; *Baldwin* v. *Soule*, 6 Gray, 321; *Shock* v. *McChesney*, 2 Yeates, 473; *Smith* v. *Wyman*, 4 Shep. 13; *Howard* v. *Sexton*, 4 Cons. 157; *Kendall* v. *Stone*, 2 Sandf. 269; *Kennedy* v. *Gifford*, 19 Wend. 296; *Miller* v. *Kerr*, 2 McCord, 285; *Pearson* v. *Le Maitre*, 6 Sc. N. S. 607; 5 Man. & G. 700.

31

jury, the plaintiff was allowed, for the purpose of showing the
quo animo, to give in evidence an indictment subsequently preferred by the defendant against him, and which was ignored.[1903]
But in an action of slander, for charging the plaintiff with
stealing two beds, it was held not competent for the plaintiff,
for the purpose of showing malice, to prove that the defendant
subsequently entered a complaint against him, before a magistrate, for stealing a lot of wood and old iron; first, because the
words used in the complaint did not relate to the charge which
was the subject of the action; and secondly, because such using
of the words was a proceeding in a course of justice, before a
magistrate having jurisdiction of the supposed offence.[1904]

§ 395. The plaintiff may, it seems, to prove malice, give
evidence of defamatory publications by the defendant concerning him, *after* the commencement of the action; but the authorities are conflicting.[1905] In general, what occurs after the commencement of the action is inadmissible; but where the words
published led to the arrest of the plaintiff after the commencement of his action, it was held that the defendant might have
excluded all evidence of what took place after the commencement of the action, but having consented to its admission, the
jury were at liberty to take it into consideration.[1906]

§ 396. Where evidence of another or other publications than
that declared upon is or are admitted for the purpose of showing malice only, the jury should be instructed that it is admitted for that purpose alone, and that they are not to give damages for other than the words charged in the declaration.[1907] An

---

[1903] *Tate* v. *Humphrey,* 2 Camp. 73, *n.*

[1904] *Watson* v. *Moore,* 2 Cush. 133.

[1905] *Howell* v. *Cheatem,* Cooke, 247; *Scott* v. *Montainger,* 2 Blackf. 454; *Teagle*
v. *Deboy,* 8 Blackf. 134; *Warne* v. *Chadwell,* 2 Stark. 457. Slanderous words,
spoken since the suit was commenced, are admissible in evidence to show the
sense in which the words laid were spoken. (*Carter* v. *M'Dowell,* Wright, 100;
and *M'Donald* v. *Murchison,* 1 Dev. 7.)

[1906] *Goslin* v. *Corry,* 8 Sc. N. S. 21; 7 Man. & G. 343.

[1907] *Scott* v. *McKinnish,* 15 Ala. 662; *Barrett* v. *Long,* 8 Ir. Law Rep. 331.

instruction was given to the jury to the effect that a letter
written by defendant and given in evidence by the plaintiff,
was admissible only to show malice, and for no other purpose,
and that they had a right to award such damages to plaintiffs
as they thought them entitled to under all the circumstances
proved in the case; held, that the caution to the jury in respect
to the effect of the letter was not sufficient.[1998]

§ 397. Evidence tending to make out an admission by the
defendant, subsequently to the speaking of the words, of a dispute existing between him and the plaintiff before the speaking
of the words, about a sum of money claimed to be due from
the defendant to the plaintiff, is admissible to show express malice.[1999] So to prove malice plaintiff may give evidence tending
to show that defendant coveted the possession of plaintiff's
land, and hoped by defaming him to compel him to remove;[2000]
but he cannot show that defendant had, by promises of reward
and threats of vengeance, endeavored to prevent the attendance
of witnesses for plaintiff.[2001]

§ 398. In an action of slander for charging an infant with
larceny, evidence of a previous quarrel between the defendant
and the plaintiff's father and next friend, is inadmissible to
prove malice in the defendant towards the plaintiff.[2002] In an
action against the *publisher* of the magazine in which the libel
was published, evidence of personal malice of the editor against
the plaintiff was held inadmissible.[2003] So the refusal of the
editor of a newspaper to publish a retraction of the libel was
held not to be evidence of malice against the publisher of such
newspaper.[2004] On the trial of an action for a libel in a news-

[1998] *Letton* v. *Young*, 2 Metc. (Ky.) 558.
[1999] *Simpson* v. *Robinson*, 18 Law Jour. Rep. 73, Q. B.; 13 Jur. 187.
[2000] *Morgan* v. *Livingston*, 2 Rich. 573.
[2001] *Kirkaldie* v. *Paige*, 17 Verm. 256.
[2002] *York* v. *Pease*, 2 Gray, 282.
[2003] *Robertson* v. *Wylde*, 2 M. & Rob. 101.
[2004] *Edsall* v. *Brooks*, 2 Robertson, 414; 33 How. Pra. Rep. 191.

paper, it appeared that the defendant employed F. to print the newspaper in question, and that S., one of F.'s workmen, had *set up* the article in the absence of the defendant and of the editor of the paper, held that the plaintiff could not ask a witness if he heard S. express any ill-will towards the plaintiff.[2005] In the same case, it was held that the plaintiff might give in evidence an article published in a subsequent number of the same newspaper, with the defendant's knowledge and consent, justifying the publication of the article complained of as libellous, though such article was not published until after the action was commenced.

§ 399. The language itself may be evidence of malice, and where the occasion renders the publication *primâ facie* privileged, the jury may take the language into consideration to determine the intent with which the publication was made.[2006]

§ 400. Interposing a justification which the defendant either abandons or fails to prove, may be regarded as an aggravation of the original wrong, and may be taken into consideration by the jury in estimating damages.[2007]   It is evidence of mal-

---

[2005] *Goodrich* v. *Stone*, 11 Metc. 486.

[2006] *Wright* v. *Woodgate*, 2 C. M. & R. 573; *Tyrw. & G.* 12; *Gilpin* v. *Fowler*, 9 Ex. 615; *Cooke* v. *Wildes*, 5 El. & Bl. 328; *Liddle* v. *Hodges*, 3 Bosw. 537; 18 N. Y. 48; *Howard* v. *Sexton*, 4 N. Y. 161; *Fero* v. *Ruscoe*, *Id.* 162; *Garrett* v. *Dickerson*, 19 Md. 418; *Hotchkiss* v. *Porter*, 30 Conn. 414; *White* v. *Nicholls*, 3 How. U. S. Rep. 266; *Tuson* v. *Evans*, 12 Adol. & El. 733, said to be overruled.

[2007] *Fero* v. *Ruscoe*, 4 N. Y. 162; *Wilson 'v. Robinson*, 14 Law Jour. Rep. 196, Q. B.; 9 Jurist, 726; *Lee* v. *Robertson*, 1 Stew. 138; *Richardson* v. *Roberts*, 23 Geo. 215; *Pool* v. *Devers*, 30 Ala. 672; *Updegrove* v. *Zimmerman*, 13 Penn. St. R. (1 Harris), 619; *Gorman* v. *Sutton*, 32 *Id.* 247; *Doss* v. *Jones*, 5 How. (Miss.), 158; *Robinson* v. *Drummond*, 24 Ala. 74; *Beasley* v. *Meigs*, 16 Ill. 139; *Spencer* v. *McMasters*, *Id.* 405; *Smith* v. *Wyman*, 4 Shep. 13; *contra*, *Murphy* v. *Stout*, 1 Smith, 256; *Shortley* v. *Miller*, *Id.* 395; *Shank* v. *Case*, 1 Carter (Ind.), 170; *Millison* v. *Sutton*, *Id.* 508; *Starr* v. *Harrington*, *Id.* 515; and see *Swails* v. *Butcher*, 2 Carter. 84; *Sloan* v. *Petrie*, 15 Ill. 425; *Thomas* v. *Dunaway*, 30 Ill. 373; *Rayner* v. *Kinney*, 14 Ohio, N. S. 283; *Pallet* v. *Sargent*, 36 N. Hamp. 496.

The judge, in addressing the jury, commented upon the fact that the defendant had refused, at the trial, to make an apology and withdraw his justification,

ice,[2008] and of continued malice.[2009] A justification on the ground of truth was held not to be an aggravation of the charge, where the defendant had reason to believe the charge to be true,[2010] or where the plea of truth was so defective that no judgment could have been entered upon it,[2011] or where the plea was withdrawn before the trial.[2012] Where in an action for a libel defendant pleaded not guilty and a justification; he offered no proof of the justification, but gave evidence to show that the publication was made under circumstances rendering it a privileged communication. Held, that the jury, in forming their opinion (upon the first issue, whether or not the communication was privileged), ought not to take into consideration the fact that the justification had been pleaded and abandoned.[2013]

§ 401. In an action for a libel, the defendant, to justify a charge made by him against the plaintiff of unfairness and partiality as collector of the United States taxes, proved that the plaintiff had refused to receive bills of a certain bank in payment of a tax. To rebut this evidence, the plaintiff offered a letter of instructions to him from the commissioner of the revenue, designating the description of the bills which the plaintiff should receive. It was held that such evidence was admissible as negativing the charge of unfairness and partiality in the plaintiff's conduct.[2014] It was in the same case held· that the

---

though he gave no evidence in support of it, as evidence of malice. Held no misdirection. (*Simpson* v. *Robinson*, 11 Law Times, 266; 18 Law Jour. Rep. 73, Q. B.; 13 Jur. 187.) That the defendant procured evidence to prove the truth of his charges, and then declined to plead in justification, may be properly referred to the jury on the question of malice, though not on that of damages. (*Bodwell* v. *Osgood*, 3 Pick. 879.)

[2008] *Jackson* v. *Stetson*, 15 Mass. 48; *Alderman* v. *French*, 1 Pick. 1.

[2009] *Wilson* v. *Nations*, 5 Yerg. 211.

[2010] *Byrket* v. *Monohon*, 7 Blackf. 83; and see *Shortley* v. *Miller*, 1 Smith, 895.

[2011] *Braden* v. *Walker*, 8 Humph. 34.

[2012] *Gilmore* v. *Borders*, 2 How. (Miss.), 824.

[2013] *Wilson* v. *Robinson*, 7 Q. B. 68; 9 Jurist, 726; 14 Law Jour. N. S. 196, Q. B.

[2014] *Slow* v. *Converse*, 8 Conn. 325.

plaintiff could not repel a charge of partial and unjust conduct, in the exaction of commissions not authorized by law, by showing that such commissions were taken honestly, through a mistaken construction of the law.

CHAPTER XVII.

*What evidence is admissible depends upon what plea or an-
swer is interposed. What may be proved under the general
issue. Evidence to support a justification. Plaintiff's reputation in issue. Inquiry limited to plaintiff's general reputation—and to his reputation prior to the publication complained of. Truth in mitigation. Conduct of plaintiff
leading to belief in truth. Report or suspicion of plaintiff's
guilt in mitigation. Plaintiff's standing and condition
in society. Prior or subsequent declarations of defendant.
Heat and passion. Previous publications by the plaintiff.
Controversies between plaintiff and defendant prior to the
publication. Circumstances not admissible in mitigation.*

§ 402. What evidence the defendant may give depends upon
what plea or answer he has interposed. His proof must correspond with his plea. Under the common law system of pleading
and procedure, many matters of defence might be given in evidence under the general issue which now require to be specially
pleaded. So, too, under the common law system, mitigating
circumstances could not be pleaded, but were admitted in evidence under the general issue ; and this is still the rule where
there is not any statutory provision on the subject. In New
York and some other States provision is made by statute allowing the defendant, in actions for slander and libel, to set forth in
his answer the mitigating circumstances he will prove upon the
trial. Some of the effects of these statutory provisions have
already been referred to under the head of Pleading ; other effects will he noticed hereafter.

§ 403. Under the general issue the defendant was at liberty to prove anything which destroyed the plaintiff's cause of action ;[2015] he might disprove the fact of publication, or show that the matter published was not of an injurious character, or that the publication was privileged ;[2016] as being a fair comment on a matter of public concern ;[2017] any circumstance which tended to disprove malice ;[2018] or that plaintiff procured the publication with a view to an action ;[2019] and where the libel consisted of a

---

[2015] *Barber* v. *Dixon*, 1 Wils. 45; and see *O'Donoghue* v. *M'Govern*, 23 Wend. 26. Where the words clearly impute a felony, if the defendant do not justify, he cannot show that the words related to an act which might have been innocent. (*Laine* v. *Wells*, 7 Wend. 175.)

[2016] *O'Brien* v. *Clements*, 15 Law Jour. Rep. 285, Ex.; 3 D. & L. 676. Where the defence is privileged communication, it need not be specially pleaded. (*Lillia* v. *Price*, 1 Nev. & P. 16; 5 Dowl. 432; *Richards* v. *Boulton*, 4 Up. Can. Q. B. Rep. O. S. 95; *Abrams* v. *Smith*, 8 Blackf. 95.) But it may be specially pleaded, (*Dunn* v. *Winters*, 2 Humph. 512) and it seems it must be pleaded in Massachusetts. (*Goodwin* v. *Daniels*, 7 Allen (Mass.), 61.) In New York it must be pleaded. In England, in actions of slander of the plaintiff in his office, profession, or trade, the plea of not guilty will operate to the same extent precisely as at present in denial of speaking the words, of speaking them maliciously and in the sense imputed, and with reference to the plaintiff's office, profession, or trade; but it will not operate as a denial of the fact of the plaintiff holding the office, or being in the profession or trade alleged. (Reg. Gen. H. T., 4 Will. 4; 2 C. & M. 23; 10 Bing. 477; 3 Nev. & M. 9; 5 B. & Adol. ix.) All matters in confession and avoidance shall be specially pleaded. (*Ib.*)

[2017] *Lucan* v. *Smith*, 38 Eng. Law & Eq. R. 395.

[2018] *Weaver* v. *Hendrick*, 30 Mis. (9 Jones) 502; *Smith* v. *Smith*, 39 Penn. St. R. 441; *Sims* v. *Kinder*, 1 Carr. 279; *Van Deusen* v. *Sutphin*, 5 Ohio N. S. 293; *Swift* v. *Dickerman*, 31 Conn. 285; *Williams* v. *Miner*, 18 Conn. 464; *Thomas* v. *Dunaway*, 30 Ill. 373; *Brunswick* v. *Pepper*, 2 C. & K. 683; *Remington* v. *Congdon*, 2 Pick. 310; *Gilman* v. *Lowell*, 8 Wend. 573. And in New York, under a general denial and a proper statement in the answer, any circumstance to disprove malice may be shown, although it tended to prove the truth of the charge. (*Bush* v. *Prosser*, 11 N. Y. 347; *Bisby* v *Shaw*, 12 N. Y. 67; *Dolevin* v. *Wilder*, 34 How. Pra. Rep. 488.) Where there is any the slightest doubt in the mind of the judge as to whether the facts set up in mitigation tend to disprove malice, he should permit them to be proved, and submit the question of malice to the jury. (*Id.*)

[2019] *Sutton* v. *Smith*, 13 Miss. 120. Plaintiff's motive in bringing the action is immaterial to the issue on a plea of justification. (*Bradley* v. *Kennedy*, 2 Greene, (Iowa) 231.)

report of proceedings the publication of which was not privileged, it was held that it might be shown under the general issue and in mitigation that the report, although not correct, was an honest one, and intended to be a fair account of the transaction referred to.[2020] The general issue amounted to a denial of the special damage,[2021] and the general good reputation of the plaintiff [§ 406], but it admitted the inducement [2022] and the falsity of the charge.[2023] The defences of accord and satisfaction, former recovery, truth and illegality of plaintiff's occupation, must be specially pleaded [§§ 250, 251, 354, 183.]

§ 404. As to the proof of a justification, it is held that, in an action for slander or libel, the charge complained of being the commission of a criminal offence, the same degree of evidence is necessary to sustain a plea of justification as would be necessary to convict the plaintiff in a criminal prosecution for the same offence.[2024] At least the defendant must prove the crime charged to the satisfaction of the jury,[2025] and beyond a reasonable doubt.[2026] The plea must be substantially proved,[2027] or the plaintiff is entitled to recover.[2028] Where the charge is crime, a conviction of the plaintiff of the crime is, in general, admissible to sustain a justification, but it is only *prima facie* evi-

---

[2020] *Smith* v. *Scott*, 2 Car. & K. 580; and see *East* v. *Chapman*, 1 Mo. & Malk. 46; *Charlton* v. *Watson*, 6 C. & P. 385.

[2021] *Wilby* v. *Elston*, 8 C. B. 142.

[2022] *Fradley* v. *Fradley*, 8 C. & P. 572; *Power* v. *Heming*, 10 M. & W. 564.

[2023] *Sheahan* v. *Collins*, 20 Ill. 325.

[2024] *Landis* v. *Shanklin*, 1 Carter, (Ind.) 92; *Shoulty* v. *Miller, Ib.* 554; *Gants* v. *Vinard, Ib.* 476; *Newbit* v. *Statuck*, 35 Maine, (5 Red.) 315; *Dwinell* v. *Aiken*, 2 Tyler, 75; *Seely* v. *Blair*, Wright, 683; *Steinman* v. *McWilliams*, 6 Barr, 170; *Willmet* v. *Harmer*, 8 C. & P. 695; *Swails* v. *Butcher*, 2 Carter, (Ind.) 84; *Woodbeck* v. *Keller*, 6 Cowen, 118; *contra, Folsom* v. *Brown*, 5 Foster, (N. Hamp.) 114; *Kincade* v. *Bradshaw*, 3 Hawks, 63.

[2025] *Offutt* v. *Earlywine*, 4 Blackf. 460. Evidence of plaintiffs being suspected is not sufficient. (*Commons* v. *Walters*, 1 Porter, 323.)

[2026] *Shortly* v. *Miller*, 1 Smith, 395.

[2027] *Napier* v. *Daniell*, 3 Sc. 417; 2 Hodges, 187; 3 Bing. N. C. 77.

[2028] *Kincade* v. *Bradshaw*, 3 Hawks, 63.

dence, and must be excluded if the defendant was a witness in the criminal prosecution.[2029] A plea of justification of libel, that the plaintiff had been guilty of bigamy, requires as strong proof as on an indictment for that offence; but a plea justifying a charge of polygamy, held sustained by proof of actual marriage in two instances, and of cohabitation and reputation as to a third.[2030] To sustain a plea of justification of a charge of perjury, the testimony of two witnesses at least, or of one witness and strong corroborating circumstances, are necessary.[2031] And the defendant must prove not only that the plaintiff's testimony was false, but that it was wilfully and corruptly false.[2032] The corrupt intent, however, is inferable from the falsity of the testimony.[2033] To establish the justification, the testimony which the plaintiff gave on the trial when the alleged perjury was committed, may be received as evidence to be considered by the jury.[2034] Under an allegation in the libel that the defendant had crushed the Hygeist system of wholesale poisoning, and that several vendors had been convicted of manslaughter, held, that it was not necessary for the defendant to prove that the system had been entirely crushed, and that proof of the

[2029] *Maybee* v. *Avery*, 18 Johns. 352. This was at the time when parties could not be witnesses in their own behalf in civil actions. Where they can be such witnesses, probably the exception stated in the text does not apply.

[2030] *Wilmet* v. *Harmer*, 8 C. & P. 695.

[2031] *Bradley* v. *Kennedy*, 2 Greene (Iowa) 231; *Steinman* v. *McWilliams*, 6 Barr, 170; *Byrket* v. *Monohon*, 7 Blackf. 83; *Woodbeck* v. *Keller*, 6 Cowen, 118; *Newbit* v. *Statuck*, 35 Maine, (5 Red.) 31; *Dwinelle* v. *Aiken*, 2 Tyler, 75. This rule was somewhat qualified in *Kincade* v. *Bradshaw*, 3 Hawks, 63; *Spruil* v. *Cooper*, 16 Ala. 791. See 3 Phillips' Ev., Cowen & Hill's, and Edwards' notes, tit. in index Slander.

[2032] *McKinly* v. *Robb*, 20 Johns. 351. That is to say he must prove technical perjury. (*Hicks* v. *Rising*, 24 Ill. 566.)

[2033] *Hopkins* v. *Smith*, 3 Barb. 599.

[2034] *Newbit* v. *Statuck*, 35 Maine, (5 Red.) 315; *Arrington* v. *Jones*, 9 Port. 139. It must be shown that the false swearing was in regard to a material point. (*McGlenary* v. *Keller*, 3 Blackf. 488.) In an action of slander, for charging the plaintiff with perjury in a judicial proceeding, the defendant on the plea of "not guilty," may prove what the words sworn by the plaintiff were, in mitigation of damages. (*Grant* v. *Hover*, 6 Munf. 13.)

conviction of two vendors for manslaughter sufficiently proved the plea, although the evidence as to the death being occasioned by not complying with the printed regulations in some respects varied from the allegation, there being evidence for the jury as to the cause of death.[2085]

§ 405. Where the words laid charge the plaintiff with having committed a certain offence, evidence will not be received that he committed a different offence, neither with the same or with other persons.[2086] As where the plaintiff was charged with adultery with J. S., it was held that proof of adultery with others than J. S. could not be received.[2087] Where the plaintiff was charged with keeping a house of ill-fame, it was held that evidence of unchaste and lascivious conduct of the plaintiff's family, not establishing the offence was inadmissible for any purpose.[2088] And where the charge was of perjury on a certain occasion, held that defendant could not justify by proof of perjury on any other occasion than that alleged.[2089] To a charge that defendant had had connexion with a mare, innuendo been guilty of the crime against nature with a beast, defendant gave notice that he would prove on the trial that plaintiff had had connexion with a *cow*, and on the trial offered

[2085] *Morrison* v. *Harmer*, 3 Bing. N. C. 755.

[2086] *Pallet* v. *Sargeant*, 36 N. H. 496; *Sharpe* v. *Stephenson*, 12 Ired. 348; *Barthelemy* v. *The People*, 2 Hill, 257. Under a plea of justification for charging plaintiff with fornication with a certain man, evidence that her child is a bastard is not sufficient. (*Richardson* v. *Roberts*, 23 Geo. 215.) Where the words charged the stealing of D.'s hay, and the defendant offered evidence to prove that the hay, the subject of the theft so charged, was the joint property of the plaintiff and D., so that in legal effect no such crime was or could have been committed, it was held, that as the charge was unequivocally a charge of theft, so intended and so received, the evidence offered by the defendant was inadmissible. (*Williams* v. *Miner*, 18 Conn. 464.)

[2087] *Matthews* v. *Davis*, 4 Bibb, 173; and see *Walters* v. *Smoot*, 11 Ired. 315.

[2088] *Bush* v. *Prosser*, 13 Barb. 221.

[2089] *Aldrich* v. *Brown*, 11 Wend. 596; *Whitaker* v. *Carter*, 4 Ired. 461. But where the charge was larceny, held that defendant might offer evidence to prove a particular larceny of the same description as that charged. (*Adams* v. *Ward*, 1 Stew. 42.)

to prove the allegation in his notice, the court refused to receive
it, either in bar or in mitigation, on the ground that it was not
a justification of the specific charge laid, but of another charge
distinct as to the subject-matter.[3040] A libel charging hardness towards the poor, dissoluteness of morals, and habits
of vice and calumny, as conclusions deducible from particular
instances enumerated and arranged in it, cannot be supported
by proof of other instances of conduct, not detailed or alluded
to in it.[3041]

§ 406. The plea of not guilty put in issue the general character [reputation] of the plaintiff, and therefore upon a plea of
not guilty only, the defendant might give in evidence in mitigation the general bad character [reputation] of the plaintiff,
before and at the time of the publication complained of. This
" principle so much discussed at an early day and for a time left
unsettled, has since been so well established by authority as not
now to be open for discussion;[3042] and such evidence was also

---

[3040] *Andrews* v. *Vanduzer*, 11 Johns. 88.

[3041] *Barthelemy* v. *The People*, 2 Hill, 248.

[3042] Jewett, J., *Hamer* v. *McFarlin*, 4 Denio, 509, citing *Foot* v. *Tracy*, 1 Johns.
46; *Springstein* v. *Field*, Anthon's N. P. 185; *Paddock* v. *Salisbury*, 2 Cow. 811;
Douglass v. *Tousey*, 2 Wend. 352; *Root* v. *King*, 7 Cow. 613; S. C. in error, 4
Wend. 113; and see *Gilman* v. *Lowell*, 8 Wend. 573; *Scott* v. *McKinnish*, 15 Ala.
662; *Pope* v. *Welsh*, 18 Ala. 631; *Fuller* v. *Dean*, 31 Ala. 654; *Anthony* v. *Stephens*, 1 Miss. 254; *Bryan* v. *Gurr*, 27 Geo. 378; *Eastland* v. *Caldwell*, 2 Bibb,
21; *Bowditch* v. *Peckham*, 1 Chip. 145; *Bridgman* v. *Hopkins*, 34 Verm. 532;
Lamos v. *Snull*, 6 N. Hamp. 413; *Sawyer* v. *Eifert*, 2 N. & M. 511; *Seymour* v.
Morrill, 1 Root, 459; *Vick* v. *Whitfield*, 2 Ham. 222; *De Witt* v. *Greenfield*, 5 Ham.
225; *Brunson* v. *Lynde*, 1 Root, 354; *Wolcott* v. *Hull*, 6 Mass. 514; *Alderman* v.
French, 1 Pick. 1; *Parkhurst* v. *Ketchum*, 6 Allen, 406; *Buford* v. *McLuniff*, 1 N.
& M. 268; *Henry* v. *Norwood*, 4 Watts, 347; *Young* v. *Bennett*, 4 Scam. 43; *Sanders* v. *Johnson*, 6 Blackf. 50; *McCabe* v. *Platter*, 6 Blackf. 405; *Burke* v. *Miller*,
6 Blackf. 155; *Steinman* v. *McWilliams*, 6 Barr, 170; *McNutt* v. *Young*, 8 Leigh,
542; *Stone* v. *Varney*, 7 Metc. 86; *Bowen* v. *Hall*, 12 Metc. 232. *Sheahan* v. *Collins*, 20 Ill. 325; *Bell* v. *Parke*, 11 Irish Law Rep. 485. As to the rule in England, see *Jones* v. *Stevens*, 11 Price, 235, where it is said, it is not competent to a
defendant to plead a justification, as of plaintiff's general bad character, in general and indefinite terms, but he is bound to state facts specially to give the plaintiff an opportunity of denying them; such pleas are demurrable; and it is an

admissible where the defendant, in addition to not guilty, put in a plea of justification, and gave evidence to support it, but failed to establish it.[2043] Whether in New York such evidence would be admissible under a general denial and without any circumstances in mitigation set up in the answer, does not appear to have been decided in any reported case. In our opinion, to entitle a defendant in the courts of New York to question the general character of the plaintiff, he should state in his answer his intention to give such evidence on the trial.[2044]

§ 407. When an inquiry into the reputation of the plaintiff is permissible, it is his general reputation taken as a whole, and not his reputation as to any particular act or in any particular transaction, that is to be inquired of;[2045] and, therefore, evidence cannot be given of his guilt of any specific act of misconduct;[2046] as that he had been guilty of false-swearing.[2047]

---

abuse of the court to put them on record; neither can he any more be permitted to give particular or general evidence of that nature in mitigation of damages, than to plead it in bar of the action. See *Morris* v. *Langdale*, 2 B. & P. 284. Evidence of general bad reputation of plaintiff was rejected, there being no plea of justification. (*Edgar* v. *Newell*, 24 Up. Can. Q. B. Rep. 215; *Myers* v. *Curry*, 22 *Id.* 470.) In an action for slander for charging the plaintiff, a female, with want of chastity, the judge directed the jury "that if they should find that plaintiff had so destroyed her character by her own lewd and dissolute conduct as to have sustained no injury from the words spoken, they might give only nominal damages." (*Flint* v. *Clark*, 13 Conn. 361; and see *Conroe* v. *Conroe*, 47 Penn. St. R. 198.)

[2043] *Hamer* v. *McFarlin*, 4 Denio, 509. It was held otherwise in *Jackson* v. *Stetson*, 15 Mass. 48, and that case was followed in *Alderman* v. *French*, 1 Pick. 1. But *Jackson* v. *Stetson* was questioned. *Cilley* v. *Jenness*, 2 N. Hamp. 89; *Whitaker* v. *Freeman*, 1 Dev. 280; and see *Stone* v. *Varney*, 7 Metc. 86; 2 Stark. Ev. 878; and the cases cited in the last preceding note. There being no plea of justification, evidence of plaintiff's bad character in mitigation rejected. (*Bracegirdle* v. *Bailey*, 1 F. & F. 536.)

[2044] *Anon.*, 8 How. Pra. Rep. 434; and see *Stiles* v. *Comstock*, 9 *Id.* 48.

[2045] *Steinman* v. *McWilliams*, 6 Barr, 170.

[2046] *Andrews* v. *Van Deuser*, 11 Johns. 38; *Vick* v. *Whitfield*, 2 Ham. 222; *Dewitt* v. *Greenfield*, 5 Ham. 225; *Lamos* v. *Snell*, 6 N. Hamp. 413; *Sawyer* v. *Eifert*, 2 N. & M. 511; *Burke* v. *Miller*, 6 Blackf. 155; *Freeman* v. *Price*, 2 Bailey, 115; *Ridley* v. *Perry*, 4 Shep. 21; *Matthews* v. *Davis*, 4 Bibb, 173; *Bowen* v. *Hall*, 12 Met. 232; *Parkhurst* v. *Ketchum*, 6 Allen, 406.

[2047] *Luther* v. *Skeen*, 8 Jones' Law (N. C.), 356.

Where the charge was that the plaintiff, a physician, had no
professional knowledge or skill, and lost almost all his patients,
it was held that proof of particular instances in which the
plaintiff had shown want of knowledge and skill, for the purpose of mitigating damages, was inadmissible.[2048] And although it has been said that when a defendant may give evidence of the general bad reputation of the plaintiff, he is not
confined to the subject-matter of the defamation complained
of,[2049] yet in an action for charging the plaintiff with perjury,
it was held erroneous to admit evidence of his general bad
character for truth.[2050] And where the charge as proven was
of burning a jail and murdering a man in it, but there was
some evidence that it was only of aiding an escape from the
jail, held, that the evidence that the defendant was reputed
guilty of the latter offence, was inadmissible for any purpose.[2051] The defendant imputed to the plaintiff, who was a
clergyman, these words: "Mr. S. said the blood of Christ had
nothing to do with our salvation, more than the blood of a
hog." Held, that testimony tending to prove that the plaintiff
denied the divinity of Christ and the doctrine of his atone-

[2048] *Swift* v. *Dickerman*, 31 Conn. 285. And such evidence would not be admissible for the purpose of showing the professional reputation of the plaintiff,
as reputation can only be proved by the direct testimony of those who are acquainted with it, and not by particular facts. (*Id.*)

[2049] *Sayre* v. *Sayre*, 1 Dutcher, 235; *Lamos* v. *Snell*, 6 N. Hamp. 413; *Sawyer*
v. *Eifert*, 2 N. & M. 511; see, however, *Wright* v. *Schroeder*, 2 Curtis, C. C. 548.
The inquiry should be confined to the plaintiff's general character for integrity
and moral worth, or to conduct similar in character to that with which he was
charged by the defendant. (*Leonard* v. *Allen*, 11 Cush. 241.)

[2050] *Steinman* v. *McWilliams*, 6 Barr, 170. In an action for charging the
plaintiff with perjury, the plaintiff proved the speaking of the words charged,
and then asked the witness what was the plaintiff's general character when on
oath and when not on oath, as a man of truth. The witness answered the question
favorably to the plaintiff. The defendant's counsel then, in cross-examining the
witness, asked him what was the plaintiff's general moral character, and the
plaintiff objected to the question. Held, that the question ought to be answered,
because it was on cross-examination, and because the answer might furnish evidence in mitigation of damages. (*Lincoln* v. *Chrisman*, 10 Leigh, 338.)

[2051] *Cole* v. *Perry*, 8 Cow. 214.

ment, and said he was a created being, a good man and perfect, his death that of a martyr, but that there was no more
virtue in his blood than that of any creature, was not admissible, either in justification or mitigation.[2052] In an action of
slander for having called the plaintiff a thief, and saying that
" he had stolen his [defendant's] spar," the defendant, in mitigation of damages, offered in evidence the record of a verdict
and judgment in his favor against A., for having taken maliciously, and converted to his own use, the spar in question, it
was held that such evidence was inadmissible.[2053] And where
the charge was that the plaintiff was a thief, and had stolen
the defendant's corn, and the defendant justified, held that
evidence that the parties were tenants in common of some
corn, and that the defendant had taken secretly, unfairly, and
dishonestly, more than his share, was not admissible either in
justification or mitigation. Mistake, to mitigate, must be mistake of facts and not of law.[2054]

§ 408. The rule in relation to proof of the character of the
plaintiff is, that the inquiry must be made as to his general reputation where he is best known, and the witness ought ordinarily to come from his neighborhood. But what the extent
of such neighborhood is, and what credit is to be given to witnesses near and remote, are questions for the jury in determining
the general character of the person in question.[2055] One who went
to the place of the plaintiff's former residence to learn her char-

---

[2052] *Skinner* v. *Grant,* 12 Verm. 456.

[2053] *Watson* v. *Churchill,* 5 Day, 256.

[2054] *Bisbey* v. *Shaw,* 15 Barb. 578.

[2055] *Powers* v. *Presgroves,* 38 Miss. 227. The reputation of the plaintiff,
among the minority of his neighbors, is inadmissible. (*Id.*; and see *Swift* v.
Dickerman, 31 Conn. 285.) In an action for accusing the plaintiff of unchaste-
ness, where a witness deposes that the plaintiff's character for chastity is bad,
it is not necessary that the witness should first have been asked whether he
knows the plaintiff's general character for chastity. (*Senter* v. *Carr,* 15 N.
Hamp. 351.) A witness who has stated that the plaintiff's character for moral
worth is bad, may be asked, on cross-examination, what immorality is imputed
to him. (*Leonard* v. *Allen,* 11 Cush. 241.)

acter while there, is not competent to prove it; nor if plaintiff
kept boarders at the time of the slander, is evidence of their opinion admissible; nor can one testify who knows nothing about
the plaintiff's reputation but what he heard from witnesses at a
prior circuit.[2056] A jury, in estimating character, are to take
the testimony of witnesses who are supposed to be able or capable of reflecting, in general terms, the judgment of the public.[2057] Proof of the bad reputation of the plaintiff, although
of a kind that could not have been caused by the slander, must
be of his reputation prior to or at the time of the publication
complained of.[2058] His bad reputation subsequent to the publication complained of, may have been the effect of such publication.

§ 409. The defence of truth must be specially pleaded.
The defendant cannot, under the general issue, prove the truth
of the publication complained of.[2059] But if the plaintiff give
in evidence parts of the publication not set forth in the declaration, the defendant may, under the general issue, justify such
parts.[2060] The proof of the repetition by the defendant of the
words complained of, after the commencement of the action, will
not confer upon the defendant the right under the general issue
to give evidence of the truth of the matter published.[2061] And
under the general issue the defendant cannot, even *in mitigation*,
give evidence of any facts which conduce to prove the truth, or
which form a link of evidence to that end.[2062] The rule was

---

[2056] *Douglass* v. *Tousey*, 2 Wend. 352.

[2057] *Luther* v. *Skeen*, 8 Jones' Law (N. C.), 356.

[2058] *Douglass* v. *Tousey*, 2 Wend. 352. Where the charge was of general unchastity, it was held that under the general issue the general bad reputation of
the plaintiff might be shown in mitigation. (*Conroe* v. *Conroe*, 47 Penn. St. R.
198.)

[2059] *Beardsley* v. *Bridgeman*, 17 Iowa, 290. See § 251, *ante*.

[2060] *Henry* v. *Norwood*, 4 Watts, 347; and see *Woodburn* v. *Miller*, Cheves,
194; *Burke* v. *Miller*, 6 Blackf. 155; *Stow* v. *Converse*, 4 Conn. 18; *Wagner* v.
Holbrunner, 7 Gill, 296.

[2061] *Teagle* v. *Deboy*, 8 Black. 134.

[2062] *Purple* v. *Horton*, 13 Wend. 9; *Scott* v. *McKinnish*, 15 Ala. 662; *Teagle*

that evidence in mitigation must be such as admitted the
charge to be false.[2063] And if a defendant failed to establish a
plea of justification, he was not entitled to any benefit from
the evidence given in support of such plea, and which *tended*
to prove the truth of the charge.[2064] Nor was a defendant allowed to prove in mitigation any circumstance which tended
to prove the truth of the charge, although he expressly dis-
avowed a justification, and admitted the falsity of the charge.[2065]
But he might prove in mitigation circumstances which induced
him erroneously to make the charge complained of, and thereby
rebut malice, *provided* the evidence did not necessarily imply
the truth of the charge or tend to prove it true.[2066] The Code
of New York has so far modified these rules as to admit in
mitigation, circumstances which *tend* to prove the truth of the
charge, and to give a defendant [who has claimed the right
by his answer] the benefit of evidence in support of a plea or
answer of justification, when such evidence falls short of proof
but nevertheless *tends* to prove the truth of the charge;[2067] and
to admit in mitigation anything which occasioned the defendant, at the time of making the publication, to believe it to be
true.[2068]

v. *Deboy*, 8 Blackf. 134; *Thompson* v. *Bowers*, 1 Doug. 321; *Swift* v. *Dickerman*,
31 Conn. 285; *Wagstaff* v. *Ashton*, 1 Harring. 503; *Grant* v. *Hover*, 6 Munf. 18;
Henson v. *Veatch*, 1 Blackf. 369; *Else* v. *Ferris*, Anthon, 23; *Gilman* v. *Lowell*,
8 Wend. 573; and see *Owen* v. *McKean*, 14 Ill. 459; *Williams* v. *Miner*, 18 Conn.
464; *McAlister* v. *Sibley*, 25 Maine (12 Shep.), 474. Particular facts, which
might form links in the chain of circumstantial evidence against the plaintiff,
cannot be received under the general issue in mitigation of damages. (*Wormouth* v. *Cramer*, 3 Wend. 395.)

[2063] *Cooper* v. *Barber*, 24 Wend. 105.

[2064] *Fero* v. *Ruscoe*, 4 N. Y. 162.

[2065] *Petrie* v. *Rose*, 5 Watts & Serg. 364; *Watson* v. *Moore*, 2 Cush. 133; *Regnier* v. *Cabot*, 2 Gilman, 34; *Vesey* v. *Pike*, 3 C. & P. 512.

[2066] *Minesinger* v. *Kerr*, 9 Barr, 312.

[2067] *Bush* v. *Prosser*, 11 N. Y. 347; *Bisby* v. *Shaw*, 12 N. Y. 67.

[2068] *Dolevin* v. *Wilder*, 34 How. Prs. Rep. 488; *Stanley* v. *Webb*, 21 Barb. 148.
As to the rule that the defendant might show in mitigation belief in the truth
not amounting to the actual truth, see *Williams* v. *Miner*, 18 Conn. 464; *Stees* v.
Kemble, 27 Penn. St. R. 112; *Hutchinson* v. *Wheeler*, 35 Verm. (6 Shaw) 330;

§ 410. Whether or not the defendant may, in mitigation of damages, give evidence of improper conduct of the plaintiff calculated to invite the language complained against, and affording just ground to believe them true, seems doubtful. In one case, for words impugning the chastity of the plaintiff's wife, the defendant was permitted to prove, in mitigation of damages, that the plaintiff's wife and an unmarried man had lived together alone in one house.[2069]

§ 411. It has·been held in some cases that the defendant may, in mitigation of damages, prove that *prior* to the publication complained of, a general report or suspicion existed that the plaintiff had committed the act charged.[2070]

[2069] *Gilman* v. *Lowell*, 8 Wend. 573; *Byrket* v. *Monohon*, 7 Blackf. 83. Testimony offered by the defendant to show that the words charged were spoken with reference to a bill in chancery which he supposed was sworn to by the plaintiff, and did contain false allegations, but which he afterwards ascertained was sworn to by another, is inadmissible in mitigation of damages. (*Owen* v. *McKean*, 14 Ill. 459; but see *Purple* v. *Horton*, 13 Wend. 9; *Van Derveer* v. *Sutphin*, 5 Ohio, N. S. 293.) For the purpose of proving that the owner of a building which has been set on fire has reason to believe that a particular person was the incendiary, and used good faith in making statements charging him with the crime, evidence that he was informed of declarations and acts of the suspected person, tending to show his guilt, is competent. (*Lawler* v. *Earle*, 5 Allen (Mass.), 22.)

[2069] *Reynolds* v. *Tucker*, 6 Ohio, N. S. 516; and see *Bradley* v. *Heath*, 12 Pick. 163; *Haywood* v. *Foster*, 16 Ohio, 88; *Minesinger* v. *Kerr*, 9 Barr, 312; *Shoulty* v. *Miller*, 1 Carter (Ind.), 544; but such evidence was rejected, although the defendant also proposed to show that at the time the words were uttered a public investigation was going on, involving an inquiry into the plaintiff's conduct, and was a subject of public remark. (*Knight* v. *Foster*, 39 N. H. 576; and see *Regnier* v. *Cabot*, 2 Gilman, 34.) Evidence of the defendant's suspicions on the subject is inadmissible. (*Henson* v. *Veatch*, 1 Blackf. 369.)

[2070] *Wetherbee* v. *Marsh*, 20 N. Hamp. 561; *Case* v. *Marks*, 20 Conn. 248; *Bridgman* v. *Hopkins*, 34 Verm. (5 Shaw) 532; *Van Derveer* v. *Sutphin*, 5 Ohio, N. S. 293; *Young* v. *Slemons*, Wright, 124; *Knobel* v. *Fuller*, Peake Ad. Cas. 139; *Cooke* v. *Barkley*, 1 Penn. N. J. Rep. 169; *Smith* v. *Richardson*, Bull. N. P. 9; *Fuller* v. *Dean*, 31 Ala. 654; *Morris* v. *Barker*, 4 Harring. 520; *Springstein* v. *Field*, Anthon, 185; *Foot* v. *Tracy*, 1 Johns. 45; *Henson* v. *Veatch*, 1 Blackf. 369; *Commons* v. *Walters*, 1 Port. 323; *Fletcher* v. *Burroughs*, 10 Iowa (2 With.), 557; and see *Moyer* v. *Pine*, 4 Mich. 409; *Bradley* v. *Gibson*, 9 Ala. 406; *Sheahan* v. *Collins*, 20 Ill. 325.

The decisions to the contrary are quite numerous.[2071] What two or three persons had said in relation to plaintiff's character, was held inadmissible.[2072] In case for slander, imputing gross ill-treatment by the plaintiff of a female; under the plea not guilty, the evidence of the plaintiff showing that the words were spoken in answer to an inquiry whether he had not imputed, &c., and inquiry by the plaintiff who was the author of the slander, the defendant replying that he had heard of the imputation, and that the report was current, and that he had reason to believe it true, but refused to give up the reporter, held that the defendant might show, by cross-examination, that such report had in fact prevailed, and was a topic of conversation before the uttering of the words by the defendant.[2073] In an action for a libel, the defendant, to support a charge against the plaintiff of having set up and supported an infidel club, offered evidence that a club to which the plaintiff belonged had the general character of an infidel club. It was held that such evidence was not admissible, either to justify or mitigate the charge.[2074]

§ 412. The defendant may, in mitigation of damages, show the plaintiff's standing and condition in society.[2075]

[2071] *Young* v. *Bennett*, 4 Scam. 43; *Sanders* v. *Johnson*, 6 Blackf. 50; *Fisher* v. *Pattison*, 14 Ohio, 418; *Scott* v. *M'Kinnish*, 15 Ala. 662; *Anthony* v. *Stephens*, 10 Mis. 254; *Haskins* v. *Lumsden*, 10 Wis. 359; *Beardsley* v. *Bridgman*, 17 Iowa, 290; *Alderman* v. *French*, 1 Pick. 1; *Bowen* v. *Hall*, 12 Met. 232; *Hancock* v. *Stephens*, 11 Humph. 507; *Skinner* v. *Powers*, 1 Wend. 451. In —— v. *Moor*, 1 M. & S. 284; the defendant was permitted, on cross-examination of a witness for the plaintiff, to ask whether he had not heard reports of plaintiff being guilty of offences similar to the offence charged. See Taylor on Evidence, 315, 2d edit., where the English authorities are collected, and are by the author said to preponderate in favor of the reception of the evidence of general suspicion in mitigation. And see *Wolmer* v. *Latimer*, 1 Jurist, 19.

[2072] *Regnier* v. *Cabot*, 2 Gilman, 34.

[2073] *Richards* v. *Richards*, 2 Mo. & Rob. 567.

[2074] *Stow* v. *Converse*, 4 Conn. 17.

[2075] *Larned* v. *Buffington*, 3 Mass. 546; *Bodwell* v. *Swan*, 3 Pick. 376; *Howe* v. *Perry*, 15 Pick. 506.

§ 413. The declaration of a defendant, made *prior* to the publication complained of, may be given in evidence to mitigate the damages; as where the defendant had employed a printer to print the libel complained of, it was held that he might, to show the absence of ill-will, and to mitigate damages, prove that at the time of the employment he instructed the printer to keep the matter as private as possible.[2076] But declarations or acts of a defendant, made *subsequently* to the publication complained of, cannot be received in mitigation.[2077] A full and unqualified retraction of the libel complained of, is admissible in mitigation.[2078]

§ 414. The defendant may set up, in mitigation of damages, that he made the publication in a moment of heat and passion, induced by the immediately preceding acts of the

---

[2076] *Taylor* v. *Church*, 8 N. Y. 452; and see *Stallings* v. *Newman*, 26 Ala. 300; *Hagan* v. *Hendry*, 18 Md. 177; *Bond* v. *Douglass*, 7 C. & P. 629; *Viners* v. *Serrell*, Id. 163; *Inman* v. *Foster*, 8 Wend. 602. It was held proper, on the trial of an indictment against the editor of a newspaper for libel, to ask a witness if at the time of the publication the defendant was not absent and knew nothing of the transaction. (*Commonwealth* v. *Buckingham*, Thacher's Crim. Cas. 29.)

[2077] *Scott* v. *McKinniah*, 15 Ala. 662; *Bradford* v. *Edwards*, 32 Ala. 628. In *Yeates* v. *Reed*, 4 Blackf. 463, it was held that defendant's efforts to prevent the circulation of the libel complained of, was not receivable in mitigation. The defendant cannot, to support his plea of justification, give evidence of transactions or conversations between himself and others, to which the plaintiff was not privy. (*Jenkins* v. *Cockerham*, 1 Iredell, 309; and see *Barfield* v. *Britt*, 2 Jones' Law (N. C.) 41.)

[2078] *Hotchkiss* v. *Oliphant*, 2 Hill, 510. But hesitation, lurking insinuation, an attempted perversion of the import of the language of the first libel, or a substitution of one calumny for another, only aggravate the offence; and if the publisher, when advised of his error, hesitate to correct it, the case rises into a case of premeditated wrong, and he becomes a fit subject for exemplary punishment. (Id.) A subsequent explanation and qualification of the slander is not competent evidence under a plea of justification. (*Luthan* v. *Berry*, 1 Port. 110; and see *Alexander* v. *Harris*, 6 Mumf. 465.) Defendant's subsequent assertions of the truth of the slander is not evidence of its truth. (*Rice* v. *Withers*, 9 Wend. 138.) As to the effect of a withdrawal, or recantation, see *Larned* v. *Buffington*, 3 Mass. 546; *Brown* v. *Brown*, 3 Ind. 518; *Alderman* v. *French*, 1 Pick. 19; *Kent* v. *Bonzey*, 38 Maine (3 Heath), 435; *Mapes* v. *Weeks*, 4 Wend. 663; 6 & 7 Vict. ch. 96; 8 & 9 Vict. ch. 95. In *Linney* v. *Matton*, 13 Texas, 449, it was held that an

plaintiff.[2079] The defendant may, therefore, in mitigation, prove prior publications by the plaintiff of a provoking character.[2080] Acts or publications of persons other than the plaintiff are not receivable in mitigation; as where the plaintiff's father, shortly before the uttering of the slander, used irritating language to the defendant, held that that fact was inadmissible in mitigation.[2081] Where, in an action for libel, the defendant sought to give in evidence libellous publications by the plaintiff of the defendant in newspapers and periodical works; held, that to make such admissible, it must be shown that they came to the knowledge of the party supposed to be provoked thereby, and that the court could not infer from the mere depositing news-

immediate retraction of a charge made orally, and in the presence of all who heard the charge, was a defence to an action founded on such charge. Where one called another a rogue, in the hearing of bystanders, in a moment of irritation, and in reference to his unwillingness to settle a debt due him, and no injury resulted from the words, it was held not actionable. (*Articta* v. *Articta*, 15 La. An. 48.) In Alabama, retraction before suit, is, by statute, made mitigation; see *Bradford* v. *Edwards*, 32 Ala. 628.

[2079] *Dolevin* v. *Wilder*, 34 How. Pra. Rep. 488. A defendant who would rely upon heat of passion in mitigation of damages, must set forth the acts and language of the plaintiff which he claims caused his passion. It is not sufficient to allege simply that he uttered the words in heat of passion caused by plaintiff. In slander, if the words were spoken through the heat of passion, or under excitement produced by the immediate provocation of the plaintiff, such excitement or passion may be shown in mitigation of damages; and in Iowa, without alleging them specifically in the answer. (*McClintock* v. *Crick*, 4 Iowa, 453); and see *Steever* v. *Beekler*, 1 Miles, 146; *Brown* v. *Brooks*, 3 Ind. 518; *Larned* v. *Buffington*, 3 Mass. 546.

The fact that the slanderous words were spoken in a sudden heat of passion, or under great provocation, should be considered by the jury in mitigation of damages. (*Powers* v. *Presgroves*, 38 Miss. 227; *Ranger* v. *Goodrich*, 17 Wis. 78; *Duncan* v. *Brown*, 5 B. Monr. 186; *Traphagen* v. *Carpenter*, 1 City Hall Reporter, 55; *Else* v. *Ferris*, Anthon, 23.)

[2080] *Thomas* v. *Dunaway*, 80 Ill. 373; *Wakley* v. *Johnson*, 1 Ry. & Mo. 422. The defendant may, in mitigation, give evidence that the plaintiff has been in the practice of villifying him, and that he was influenced to use the language with which he is charged by the abuse of the plaintiff, and that may be shown by the defendant's declaration. The jury is to determine whether the language which the defendant used was used because of such provocation received from the plaintiff. (*Botelar* v. *Bell*, 1 Md. 173.) But see cases in note 2084.

[2081] *Underhill* v. *Taylor*, 2 Barb. 348.

papers in the defendant's name, as editor, at the stamp-office, under 38 Geo. III., c. 78, § 17, that they were published by, or came to the knowledge of, the defendant.[2082]

§ 415. All the circumstances connected with the publication complained of should go to the jury;[2083] and therefore, in an action for a libel, the defendant may give in evidence a former publication by the plaintiff, to which the libel was an answer, to explain the subject-matter, occasion, and intent of the defendant's publication, and in mitigation of damages.[2084] And a previous publication by the plaintiff, to which the alleged libel is an answer, is admissible. The judge, before admitting or excluding it, may peruse it, in order to decide upon its character.[2085] And all papers referred to in a libel may be admitted for the purpose of explanation and interpretation.[2086] A postscript is admissible.[2087] Prefixing a previous publication as a text to the libel complained of, does not *per se* make such previous publication admissible in evidence.[2088]

[2082] *Watts* v. *Fraser*, 2 Nev. & P. 157. Always, where mitigating circumstances are offered in evidence for the purpose of repelling the presumption of malice, it should be shown that the defendant knew of them at the time he made the charge. (*Swift* v. *Dickerman*, 31 Conn. 285; *Dolevin* v. *Wilder*, 34 How. Pra. Rep. 488; *Reynolds* v. *Tucker*, 6 Ohio, N. S. 516.)

[2083] *Cook* v. *Barkley*, 1 Penn. 169.

[2084] *Hotchkiss* v. *Lathrop*, 1 Johns. 286. A prior publication by plaintiff not admissible in justification. (Id.; *Southwick* v. *Stevens*, 10 Johns. 443.) Other libels alleged to have been published by the plaintiff of the defendant, not relating to the same subject, are not admissible in evidence, either in bar of the action or in mitigation of damages, both on the ground that the plaintiff had no notice of such defence, as well as of the inconvenience, by leading to a multiplicity of inquiries. (*May* v. *Brown*, 3 B. & Cr. 113; 4 D. & R. 670.) See *Watts* v. *Fraser*, 7 C. & P. 369.

[2085] *Maynard* v. *Beardsley*, 7 Wend. 560; 4 Wend. 336.

[2086] *Nash* v. *Benedict*, 25 Wend. 645; *Mullett* v. *Hulton*, 4 Esp. 248.

[2087] *Coleman's Case*, 2 City Hall Recorder, 49.

[2088] *Gould* v. *Weed*, 12 Wend. 12. A subsequent publication cannot be given in evidence to determine the character of a publication, whether it is libellous or not. Two articles, to be so used, must appear simultaneously in the same paper or book. (*Usher* v. *Severance*, 2 App. 9.)

§ 416. Controversies between the plaintiff and defendant prior to the publication complained of, and having no connection with the subject-matter of the publication, cannot be shown to mitigate the damages.[2089] Nor are previous publications by the plaintiff concerning the defendant admissible in mitigation, unless so immediately preceding the publication by the defendant as fairly to raise the presumption that the defendant made the publication under the impulse of the provocation.[2090] The defendant may show, in mitigation, that he was provoked to the publication complained of by some contemporaneous or nearly contemporaneous act or declaration of the plaintiff. Simply to show provoking acts or declarations by the plaintiff *prior* to the publication by the defendant, is not sufficient.[2091] In an action for a libel, in which the plaintiff was charged with being "a degraded scoundrel, liar and blackguard," it was held that the defendant might be allowed to prove, under the general issue, in mitigation of damages, that the plaintiff, shortly prior to the publication of said libel, charged the defendant with false swearing in a cause in which he was a witness.[2092] In an action of slander against husband and wife, for words spoken by the wife, it is not competent for the defendants to prove that circumstances relating to the plaintiff's conduct were communicated to the husband before the slanderous words were uttered.[2093]

[2089] *Lester* v. *Wright*, 2 Hill, 320. In an action of slander for words actionable in themselves, claiming general damages only; held, that, under the plea of the general issue, evidence that, during the six years prior to the trial, inveterate feelings of hostility had existed between the plaintiff and defendant, and that the plaintiff had taken every opportunity to irritate the defendant, was inadmissible. (*Porter* v. *Henderson*, 11 Mich. 20.)

[2090] *Maynard* v. *Beardsley*, 7 Wend. 560; 4 Id. 336; *Gould* v. *Weed*, 12 Id. 12; *Child* v. *Homer*, 13 Pick. 503 ; *Walker* v. *Winn*, 8 Mass. 248. A question to a witness, as to the state of feeling between the parties, must refer to the time of the slanderous speaking. (*Justice* v. *Kirlin*, 17 Ind. 588.)

[2091] *Moore* v. *Clay*, 24 Ala. 235; *Watts* v. *Fraser*, 2 Nev. & P. 157; W. W. & D. 451; 7 Ad. & El. 223; 1 Jurist, 671; 1 M. & Rob. 491; *Moore* v. *Oastler*, 1 M. & Rob. 451; *Bourland* v. *Eidson*, 8 Gratt. 27.

[2092] *Davis* v. *Griffith*, 4 Gill & Johns. 342.

[2093] *Petrie* v. *Rose*, 5 Watts & Serg. 364.

§ 417. The defendant cannot, to mitigate damages, give evidence of his poverty;[2094] of his apparent good humor at the time of speaking the words;[2095] that no one believed anything he said;[2096] that the defendant was not the author of the slander, and that he named the author at the time of the publication;[2097] that the publication did not injure, or that it benefit-

---

[2094] *Myers* v. *Malcolm*, 6 Hill, 292; *Palmer* v. *Haskins*, 28 Barb. 90; and see cases cited, note 1979, *ante*.

[2095] *Weaver* v. *Hindreck*, 30 Mis. (9 Jones), 502. Defendant being intoxicated at the time of publication, said to be a matter of mitigation. (*Howell* v. *Howell*, 10 Ired. 84.)

[2096] *Howe* v. *Perry*, 15 Pick. 506; *contra*, *Gates* v. *Meredith*, 7 Ind. 440. An imputation of theft, made in the presence of one witness only, who stated that he did not believe the charge, held no reason for restricting the damages to a nominal amount. (*Markham* v. *Russell*, 12 Allen, 573.) The fact that the words were spoken in the presence of one witness only, was held to be receivable in mitigation in *Traphagen* v. *Carpenter*, 1 City Hall Reporter, 55.

[2097] *Treat* v. *Browning*, 4 Conn. 408; *contra*, *Bennett* v. *Bennett*, 6 O. & P. 588; *Easterwood* v. *Quinn*, 2 Brev. 64. But see *ante*, § 210. Under some circumstances, the defendant may prove, in mitigation, that he derived his information from others. (*Kennedy* v. *Gregory*, 1 Binn. 85; *Galloway* v. *Courtney*, 10 Rich. Law, S. C. 414; but see *Thompson* v. *Bowers*, 1 Doug. 321; *Anthony* v. *Stephens*, 1 Mis. 254.) And from whom or how he derived his information (*Leister* v. *Smith*, 2 Root, 24); as that the charge was taken from the journals of Congress (*Romayne* v. *Duane*, 3 Wash. C. C. 246); or copied from another paper. (*Davis* v. *Cutbush*, 1 Fost. & Fin. 487.) That the defendant published the libel on the communication of a correspondent, held not admissible in mitigation. (*Talbutt* v. *Clarke*, 2 M. & Rob. 312.) Where A. published a libel taken from a paper published by B., as an extract from a paper published by C., it was *held*, in an action brought by C. against A., that the testimony of D. that he had heard A., before he published the libel, ask E. whether he had not seen it in the paper of C., and that E. answered that "he had," was inadmissible in mitigation of damages; but that E. himself should be produced, if his declaration were proper evidence. (*Coleman* v. *Southwick*, 9 Johns. 45.) In an action for the publication of a libel, the defendant asked a news collector, who wrote a part of the article complained of, "What inquiries and examinations he made, and what sources of information he applied to, before making the communication" which tended to charge the plaintiff with dishonesty and bad faith? Held, that the question was incompetent, and that the defendant, as a foundation for such question, could not prove that there was a general anxiety in the community in regard to the facts stated in the publication. (*Sheckell* v. *Jackson*, 10 Cush. (Mass.) 25.) And see *Bond* v. *Kendall*, 36 Verm. 741, where it was held that the defendant could not show the libel was a letter to B. containing the result of inquiries made concerning the plaintiff at request of B.

ed the plaintiff;[2098] or that others had previously published the
same words;[2099] a declaration of the plaintiff that the publication did him no injury;[2100] or that he believed the defendant
was not the author but only the repeater of the slander;[2101] that
plaintiff was an enemy of his [defendant's];[2102] that plaintiff
is a quarrelsome person;[2103] or a malicious person;[2104] that
plaintiff had boasted of committing offences of a like character
with that charged;[2105] that plaintiff was in the habit of abusing
the defendant;[2106] that plaintiff was a common libeller;[2107] that
plaintiff has sometimes published slander of other persons not
the defendant;[2108] or has threatened so to do;[2109] a former recovery;[2110] that defendant declared he could prove the truth of

---

[2098] *Calhoun* v. *M'Means*, 1 N. & M. 422; *Rex* v. *Woodfall*, Lofft, 776. No man
shall set up his own iniquity as a defence any more than as a cause of action.
(Mansfield, Ch. J., *Montifiore* v. *Montifiore*, W. Black. 363; see *Stewart* v. *Wilkinson*, 7 Law Times, 81; *Fry* v. *Bennett*, 28 N. Y. 328.

[2099] *Saunders* v. *Mills*, 6 Bing. 213.

[2100] *Porter* v. *Henderson*, 11 Mich. 20. In *Quigley* v. *Phila. &c. R. R. Co.* (21
How. U. S. Rep. 209), the defendants gave evidence of declarations by the plain-
tiff that the matters out of which the libel arose had improved his business. See
Ostrom v. *Calkins*, 5 Wend. 263; and *ante*, note 1465.

[2101] *Evans* v. *Smith*, 5 Monr. 363.

[2102] *Craig* v. *Catlet*, 5 Dana, 325.

[2103] *Hosley* v. *Brooks*, 20 Ill. 115; *M'Alexander* v. *Harris*, 6 Mumf. 465.

[2104] *Forshee* v. *Abrams*, 2 Clarke (Iowa), 572.

[2105] *Pallet* v. *Sargent*, 36 N. Hamp. 496.

[2106] *Goodbread* v. *Leathitter*, 1 Dev. & Bat. 12; *Wakley* v. *Johnson*, 1 Ry. & M.
422; *May* v. *Brown*, 3 B. & Cr. 113; *M'Alexander* v. *Harris*, 6 Mumf. 465; *contra*, see *Botelar* v. *Bell*, 1 Md. 173. In a suit for slander, for charging the plaintiff with perjury, the defendant cannot show that, upon a wholly different occasion, the plaintiff called him a liar and a perjured wretch. (*Porter* v. *Henderson*,
11 Mich. 20.)

[2107] *Maynard* v. *Beardsley*, 7 Wend. 560; 4 Id. 336; *Gould* v. *Weed*, 12 Id. 12.

[2108] *Forshee* v. *Abrams*, 2 Clarke (Iowa) 571.

[2109] *Cochran* v. *Butterfield*, 18 N. Hamp. 115.

[2110] The defendant is not allowed to give in evidence, in mitigation of damages, a former recovery of damages against him, in favor of the same plaintiff, in
another action for a libel, which formed one of a series of numbers published in
the same gazette, and containing the libellous words charged in the declaration in
the second suit. (*Tillotson* v. *Cheetham*, 3 Johns. 56.)

the words;[2111] or in an action for slander of husband and wife, that they lived unhappily together;[2112] or kept a disorderly house.[2113]

[2111] *James* v. *Clarke*, 1 Iredell, 397.

[2112] *Anon.*, 1 Hill (S. C.) 251.

[2113] *Watson* v. *Moore*, 2 Cush. 133.

APPENDIX.

ADDITIONS AND CORRECTIONS.

Add to note 26—

A person, whose name was on the register of persons whose notes had been protested, applied to the Court of Session, in Scotland, for an interim interdict to prevent, so far as his own name was concerned, the publication of a copy of the register. The court decreed for the application. Held, by the Lords, reversing that decree, that the interdict ought not to have been granted. (*Fleming* v. *Newton*, 1 Ho. of Lords' Cas. 363.) "The king has no authority to restrain the press." (Mansfield, Ch. J., *Stationers' Co.* v. *Partridge.*)

Page 30, note 17, line 3, for "Brougham" read "Lyndhurst."

INDEX.

———•••———

ACTRESS, charge of intermarriage with, is actionable, § 177.
　　　　　libel upon, § 201.
ADJECTIVE WORDS, may confer a right of action, § 105.
ADMINISTRATOR, words concerning, § 196.
　　　　　See EXECUTOR.
ADMISSION, by defendant, effect of, § 383.
ADULTERER, charge of being, not actionable, § 174.
ADULTERY, what words import, § 144 (a).
　　　　　charge of, actionable in certain States, §§ 153–173.
　　　　　charge of, not actionable, § 160, 172, 190.
ADVERTISEMENT in newspaper, when privileged, §§ 240, 243.
ADVICE, when privileged, § 241.
ADVOCATE, privilege of, § 225.
AFFIDAVIT, made in the course of a legal proceeding, cannot give a right
　　　　　of action for libel, § 222, n. 1091.
AGENCY. See COMMERCIAL AGENCY.
AGENT, cannot do a wrong as such, n. 50.
　　　　　liability of principal for acts of, § 122, n. 124, 125.
　　　　　See PRINCIPAL AND AGENT.
AGGRAVATION OF DAMAGES, by mode of conducting cause, § 277.
　　　　　　　　　　evidence for the purpose of, §§ 387, et seq.
ALABAMA, to call a woman whore is actionable in, n. 516.
ALDERMAN, words concerning, § 196.
ALIEN, action by, § 298.
ALLEGATION, positive, what amounts to, § 144 (ii, jj).
　　　　　divisible, what is, § 145.
AMENDMENT, to retain verdict, § 290.
　　　　　of complaint, n. 1630.
　　　　　when allowed, § 372.
AMBO DEXTER, meaning of, n. 140.
AMBIGUOUS LANGUAGE, how construed, § 140, n. 160.
AND AND FOR, distinction between, § 144 (b).
ANGLO-SAXON, the term objected to, n. 87.
ANSWER, corresponds to plea, § 349.
　　　　　effect of not making, § 274.
　　　　　what amounts to a general denial, n. 1740.
　　　　　of justification must give color, § 352.
　　　　　several defences in, § 353.
　　　　　of truth, requisites of, § 355.
　　　　　of mitigating circumstances, § 361.
　　　　　demurrer to, § 362.
　　　　　　　　　See PLEA, MITIGATING CIRCUMSTANCES.
　　　　　to inquiry, when privileged, § 241.
APOLOGY, defence of, § 250.
　　　　　withdrawal of plea of, § 280.

EVIDENCE—*continued.*

of other publications by defendant to prove malice, §§ 393–396.

of admissions by defendant, § 397.

of personal ill-will, § 398.

of malice on the face of the libel, § 399.

of malice, from interposing a justification which is not proved, § 400.

by plaintiff to rebut defendant's evidence, § 401.

for defendant, § 402.

under general issue, § 403.

to sustain a plea of justification, §§ 404, 405.

of plaintiff's reputation in mitigation, § 406.

of plaintiff's general reputation, §§ 407, 408.

of truth under general issue, § 409.

of truth, or tending to prove the truth of the matter published, in mitigation, § 409.

of acts of plaintiff, inducing a belief of the truth of the charge complained of, § 410.

of general reports or suspicion of plaintiff's guilt, § 410.

of plaintiff's standing and condition in society in mitigation, § 412.

of defendant's declarations in mitigation, § 413.

of heat and passion in mitigation, § 414.

of prior publications of plaintiff in mitigation, § 415.

of controversies between plaintiff and defendant in mitigation § 416.

of defendant's poverty not admissible in mitigation, § 417.

what not receivable in mitigation, § 417.

of loss of customers, § 346. See VARIANCE.

EXCISE. See BOARD OF EXCISE.

EXCOMMUNICATED, charge of having been, is actionable, §§ 173, 177.

EXECUTOR, actions of slander or libel by, § 299.

EXEMPLARY DAMAGES, when allowed, § 290.

EX PARTE AFFIDAVITS, publication of, not privileged, n. 1156.

EX PARTE PROCEEDINGS, report of, how far privileged, § 231.

FACT *and opinion,* supposed distinction between, § 259.

FALLING SICKNESS, charge of having, doubtful if actionable, § 175.

FALSE HEIR, charge of producing, held actionable, § 173.

FALSEHOOD, charge of, is actionable, § 177.

FALSE SWEARING, charge of, actionable in Arkansas and Illinois, § 158, n. 482.

not actionable, n. 354.

actionable, § 171.

charge of, is actionable if in writing, § 177. See FORSWORN.

KEY, charge of stealing, § 170.
KIDNAPPING, charge of, is actionable, § 177.
KILL, KILLED, KILLING, meaning of the terms, § 144 (*m*).
KILLING, charge of, actionable, § 168.
KNAVE, import of the term, § 144 (*n*), *n*. 537.
　　　charge of being, is actionable, § 173, *n*. 665, 703.
KNOWLEDGE of plaintiff, how it affects the meaning of language, § 141.
KNOWN, import of the term, § 144 (*o*).

LACEMAN, words concerning, *n.* 795.
LAMPOONER, *n.* 5.
LANDLORD *and tenant*, communications between, how far privileged,
　　　§ 241 (p. 323).
LAND-MARKS, charge of removal, involves moral turpitude, § 155.
　　　charge of removing, is actionable, § 173.
LAND SURVEYOR, words concerning, § 192.
LANGUAGE, formerly no action for, unless the words if true would endan-
　　　ger life, *n.* 40.
　　　joint publication of, §§ 118, 119.
　　　construction of, § 125.
　　　ambiguous or unambiguous, § 126.
　　　kinds of ambiguity of, § 127, 128.
　　　ambiguous, as to whether it concerns a person or a thing, § 131.
　　　　　how construed, *n.* 149, 160.
　　　may give a right of action when it concerns one in trade,
　　　　　although not actionable as applied to an individual as
　　　　　such, § 132.
　　　a means of effecting injury, §§ 1–7.
　　　oral or written, § 1.
　　　construction of, § 125.
　　　effect of, § 2.
　　　coarseness of, in former times, *n.* 33.
　　　is not a trespass, *n.* 2.
　　　when it amounts to a breach of the peace, *n.* 26.
　　　can have no effect until published, § 23.
　　　must assume the form of propositions, § 24.
　　　must concern a person or a thing, §§ 25, 130.
　　　effect of its publication must be direct or indirect, or both, § 26.
　　　direct effects of, § 27.
　　　effect of, the same whether oral or written, § 29.
　　　must produce some effect, § 30.
　　　impossible to anticipate all the indirect effects of, § 31.
　　　affects the reputation, § 32.

LANGUAGE—*continued.*
>actionable *per se*, and language actionable by reason of special damage, distinction between, § 147.
>supposed origin of such distinction, § 56.
>effect of time on meaning of, *n.* 142.
>effect of extraneous circumstances upon meaning of, § 135.
>ambiguous, how construed, § 140, *n.* 160.
>what is actionable, § 146.
>actionable *per se*, § 147.
>jury to determine meaning of, § 281.
>to be set forth in complaint, § 329.
>presumed to be false and malicious, § 388.
>evidence of facts alleged, § 386.
>evidence of malice, § 399.

LARCENY, what will amount to a charge of, § 144 (*p r*), *n.* 216, 261.
>in Illinois, child under ten years cannot be guilty of, *n.* 854.
>charge of, actionable, § 170. See ROBBERY, STEALING, THIEF.

LAW *of libel*, what understood by, § 18.
>denounced as vague, § 15, *n.* 12.
>*ecclesiastical*, part of English common law, *n.* 11.
>no status in New York, *n.* 11.

LAWSUIT, implies a judicial proceeding, *n.* 499.

LEGAL EXCUSE, what is, § 64.
>distinction between, and defence, § 65.

LEGISLATIVE PROCEEDINGS are privileged, § 217.
>supposed to be secret, § 217.
>when to be with open doors, *n.* 1081.
>publication of, how far privileged, § 219.

LEGISLATOR, privilege of, § 217.

LEGISLATURE, petition to, is privileged, § 237.

LEPROSY, charge of having, is actionable, § 175.

LEPROUS KNAVE, actionable, § 175.

LETTER CARRIER, words of, § 182.

LETTERS, confidential, not privileged, *n.* 1200.
>See BREAKING OPEN, PRIVATE LETTERS.

LIABILITY, extent of, §§ 67, 68, *n.* 49, 50.
>of defendant, how proved, § 382.

LIAR, what imports a charge of being, § 144 (*q*).
>charge of being, not actionable, § 174.
>charge of being, actionable if in writing, § 177.
>charge of being, against a merchant's clerk, actionable, § 192.

LIBEL, what it is, §§ 4, 9, *n.* 132, § 17.
>action not maintainable for cost of printing, *n.* 1521.
>remedy for, § 9.

34

PLAINTIFF—*continued.*

effect of death of, § 299.

evidence of good reputation of, to aggravate damages, § 386.

evidence of his rank and condition to aggravate damages, § 390.

evidence of occupation of, § 883.

distress of mind not damage to, § 391.

ill-will of defendant towards, to aggravate damages, § 392.

evidence for, § 873 *et seq.* See Evidence.

general reputation of, is put in issue, § 406.

inquiry into reputation of, § 407.

evidence of standing and condition in society to mitigate damages, § 412.

evidence of acts of, in mitigation, § 414, *et seq.*

benefits to, by libel, cannot be shown, *n.* 2098, 2000.

PLEA, formerly only one, allowed, § 211.

to whole or part of complaint, § 212.

effect of, not interposing, § 274.

withdrawal of, on trial, § 280.

answer corresponds to, § 349.

that publication by mistake, *n.* 1740.

of general issue, § 350.

in bar must answer the whole count, § 351.

of truth, requisite of, § 355.

justifying a charge of crime, § 358.

of justification failing in part fails altogether, § 359.

notice in lieu of, § 360. See Answer.

PLEADING, how construed, *n.* 161.

defamatory matter in, will not give a right of action for libel. § 221.

certainty in, § 335.

formerly in Latin, *n.* 1595.

and proof to correspond, § 363. See Answer. Complaint.

PLUNDERED, does not mean a felonious taking, § 144 (*w*).

not actionable, § 174.

POCKY RASCAL, query if actionable, *n.* 410.

POCKY WHORE, not actionable, § 165.

POISON, meaning of the term, § 144 (*z*).

charge of administering, *n.* 352, 446, 529, 551, § 168, 173, 190, 193.

POLICE OFFICER, words concerning, § 196.

words published to, *n.* 1183. See Constable.

POLTROON, charge of being, when actionable in Tennessee, § 153.

PORK BUTCHER, words concerning, § 190. See Butcher.

POSTMASTER, words concerning, § 196.

complaint to, held privileged, *n.* 1192.

www.ingramcontent.com/pod-product-compliance
Lightning Source LLC
Chambersburg PA
CBHW022126020426
42334CB00015B/772